DO
WHAT
THOU
WILT

DO WHAT THOU WILT

A LIFE OF ALEISTER CROWLEY

Lawrence Sutin

ST. MARTIN'S PRESS
NEW YORK

www.stmartins.com

Design by Nancy Resnick

ISBN 0-312-25243-9

First Edition: September 2000

10 9 8 7 6 5 4 3 2 1

CONTENTS

ACKNOWLEDGMENTS

The researching and writing of this biography has occupied a goodly portion of my time over the decade 1989–99. It would be impossible to thank everyone who assisted me with information and moral support over that period. But the following persons and institutions deserve mention here.

The initial inspiration to write a life of Aleister Crowley came from my good friend Greg Overlid, a resolute explorer of conceptual frameworks. Another dear friend and fellow writer, Marshall Fine, commiserated with me throughout the winding emotional road from initial proposal to final publication.

The staffs of the Warburg Institute, University of London; the Harry Ransom Humanities Research Center, University of Texas at Austin; the Liddell Hart Center for Military Archives, King's College, University of London; the British Museum, London; and the Wren Library, Trinity College, Cambridge University, were helpful during my researches at those institutions. While in Great Britain from January to April 1990, I enjoyed the hospitality of several persons knowledgeable as to Crowley, notably Geraldine Beskin, Richard Cavendish, Nicolas Culpepper, Clive Harper, Francis X. King, Anthony Naylor, Keith Richmond, Timothy d'Arch Smith, Stephen Skinner, Michael Staley and Isabel Sutherland. Upon my return to the United States, I drew upon the Crowley expertise and archives of Gerald and Marlene Cornelius and William E. Heidrick.

Throughout the entire decade of work, the support and friendship of Hymenaeus Beta, *Frater Superior*, O.T.O., has been of enormous value. It was he who was the sole reader of my initial draft—in excess of 1,800 pages—and it was he who kindly and thoroughly scrutinized the final version that is now before the reader. No other person outside of St. Martin's Press has so served as reader and querent, and no other person could have done so fine a job. While Hymenaeus Beta is a religionist and I am an outsider and skeptic with respect to the Thelemic creed, his criticisms of my writing were always respectful and made in the service of factual truth. Nonetheless, he and I disagree on numerous points as to the interpretation of Crowley's life, and my views as set forth in this book should not be mistaken as representing his own. Naturally, any errors that remain in the text are solely my responsibility.

As for my wife, Mab, who bore with me through years of labor that did little to support our family, and that are likely to receive little thanks from the world at large, words fail me.

INTRODUCTION An Overview of the Magical Tradition, in Which It Is Suggested that the Raging Battle Between Jesus and Satan Be (For the Moment) Set Aside in Order that the True Nature of the Magus Be Understood

Biographers are fond of observing that their subjects have been much misunderstood.

Among other reasons, this view serves nicely to justify their labors. Why trouble the reader with a fresh portrait when clarity reigns?

In the case of Aleister Crowley (1875–1947), one is compelled to conclude that he has been as greatly misunderstood as any biographer could wish. In truth, "misunderstanding" hardly serves to convey the degree of hatred and fear which the name of Crowley—aka "The Great Beast" and "The Wickedest Man on Earth"—continues to inspire to the present day. The popular image endures of Crowley as a vicious Satanist who employed illicit drugs and perverted sex to enliven the weary charade of his blasphemous "magick" (Crowley's own distinctive spelling for his development of traditional magic).

Virtually every current handbook on the "cult crisis" in America features a purple-prose paragraph on the sinister Crowley who has inspired numberless depravities culminating in ritual rape and murder. Amongst scholars, it is common to dismiss Crowley as "notorious" and his theories as "mercifully obscure" without having scrupled to read his books. To question this blackest of black assessment of Crowley— merely to suggest a touch of gray—is to inspire suspicion that you are in cahoots with the Satanists.

Crowley is, admittedly, a complicated case. One can hardly blame people for feeling hatred and fear toward Crowley when Crowley himself so often exulted in provoking just such emotions. Indeed, he tended to view those emotions as inevitable, given what he regarded as the revolutionary nature and power of his teachings and the prevailing hypocrisy of society—and not merely that of his native Britain, mind you, but of the whole of the Christianized West and, for good measure, of the entire unawakened world. Antagonism toward the religious powers that be was the essence of Crowley's vision of his life and of his mission—Crowley who brandished and popularized his role as the "Beast" of Revelations come to life, the selfsame 666 proclaimed in the Biblical text as "the number of a man." Small wonder that the evils of Satanism are laid at his feet. As one disciple of the Beast has observed, "There is no sense in trying to whitewash Crowley's reputation. Aleister spent most of his life systematically blackening it."

Clearly, this Crowley fellow was an egregious sort—a shameless scoffer at Christian virtue, a spoiled scion of a wealthy Victorian family who embodied many of the worst John Bull racial and social prejudices of his upper-class contemporaries, a blisteringly arrogant opportunist who took financial and psychological advantage of his admirers, an unadmiring and even vicious judge of most of his contemporaries, a sensualist who relished sex in all forms, a hubristic experimenter in drugs who was addicted to heroin for the last twenty-five years of his life. No question that the sheer egotistical bombast of the man could be stupefying. For the Beast regarded himself as no less than the Prophet of a New Aeon that would supplant the Christian Era and bring on the reign of the Crowned and Conquering Child, embodiment of a guiltless, liberated humanity that had, at last, chosen to *become* the gods it had merely worshiped in the past.

But as for any alleged sympathy with the Christian Devil, Crowley viewed Satanism as a tawdry sport unworthy of his time and skills. Satanism depends, for its demonic fervor, on the dialectical existence of a vibrant Christianity that it can revile. The archetypal Satanic rite, the Black Mass, is structured closely upon the Catholic Mass. The catharsis of the Black Mass stems from the impassioned belief that ritual desecration—compelling Christ to appear in the Host at the command and under the power of Satan—is a sizzling blasphemy. Satanism forms a syzygy with Christianity—an intertwined, oppositional heresy asserting the power of the Adversary as against the reign of the Son, a reign which alone gives the Black Mass its meaning. Crowley, the Beast, the Prophet, wanted far more. Revile Christianity (but not Christ, mind you) as he might, seek its downfall as he did, Crowley desired nothing less than the creation of a full-fledged successor religion—complete with a guiding Logos that would endure for millennia, as had the teachings of Jesus. "Thelema" was the Logos Crowley proclaimed, Greek for "Will." "Do what thou wilt shall be the whole of the law" was its central credo. Let us concede that this credo—so redolent, seemingly, of license and anarchy, dark deeds and darker dreams—terrifies on first impact, as does Crowley the man.

Crowley makes for a grippingly vile Gothic protagonist. He has been a popular model for fiction writers in search of villains with the requisite chill. W. Somerset Maugham devoted a novel, *The Magician* (1906), to Crowley's malevolent charms; other fiction writers who have modeled villains on the Beast include James Branch Cabell, Dion Fortune, Christopher Isherwood, M. R. James, Anthony Powell, H. R. Wakefield, Dennis Wheatley, Colin Wilson, and Robert Anton Wilson. The British playwright Snoo Wilson scored a London stage hit in the 1970s with his play *The Beast*. Crowley's exotic appeal has not been limited to literature. Since his appearance on the cover of The Beatles' album *Sgt. Pepper's Lonely Hearts Club Band* (1967)—a photo of Crowley with shaven head and piercing eyes, his most enduring iconographic image—the Beast has endured in the world of rock music in various guises, influencing the lyrics of the Rolling Stones, Led Zeppelin, David Bowie, Darryl Hall, Sting, Ozzy Osbourne, The Clash, and The Cure, not to mention scores of less familiar hardcore, punk, and industrial bands. It would seem that Crowley is as irresistible a fantasy for the counterculture (which typically casts him as a defiant rebel who stood for individual freedom first and foremost, this despite Crowley's lifelong aristocratic—and even, at times, fascistic—bent in politics) as he is for Christian fundamentalists (who have, paradoxically, succeeded in perpetuating Crowley's fame by casting him as the Evil Exemplar best suited to sustain a healthy fear of the Devil in the faithful).

But beneath the greasepaint of these popular images, does there remain a Crowley worthy of the serious attention of the intelligent reader?

It is the claim of this biography that such a Crowley does exist. Indeed, as the twentieth century has come to a close, it is clear that Crowley stands out as one of its more remarkable figures. A "minor" figure he may be, if one measures him on a scale of ultimate deeds. But such calipers will nullify all but a handful of those who shaped our times. Crowley is most emphatically a part of the spiritual history of this century, and as such it behooves us to reckon with him both sensibly and sensitively. Say what you will of Crowley, judge his failings as you will, there remains a man as protean, brilliant, courageous, and flabbergasting as ever you could imagine. There endure achievements that no reasoned account of his life may ignore.

Consider, briefly for now, the foremost of these:

(1). Crowley was an inveterate and adventurous traveler as well as an accomplished mountain climber who tested his skills on two of the most difficult Himalayan peaks—K2 and Kanchenjunga.

(2). Crowley was one of the first Western students of Buddhism and yoga to approach these teachings not as primitive or exotic theories, but rather as modes of spiritual development that had to be gauged experientially. In this, Crowley anticipated the spread of Eastern spiritual practice in the West.

(3). Crowley was a prolific poet who displayed, intermittently, a pure and genuine talent. This was acknowledged by otherwise unadmiring contemporaries such as G. K. Chesterton and William Butler Yeats (for whose famous poem "The Second Coming" with its "rough beast, its hour come round at last," Crowley may have been a source of influence). Further, Crowley wrote (usually under pseudonymous guises) some of the most daringly original—and unrecognized—homoerotic poems of this century. Crowley consciously utilized poetry to explore his forbidden bisexuality and to defy cultural taboos. The standard surveys of twentieth-century gay literature will someday be revised to take in Crowley's contributions.

(4). Crowley was a gifted fiction writer whose occult narratives, in particular, place him in the supernatural tale tradition of Algernon Blackwood, Arthur Machen, and H. P. Lovecraft—a tradition that exercises an ongoing influence on the popular modern-day horror and science-fiction genres.

(5). Crowley was a scholar of depth and breadth whose researches bore such creative fruit as, for example, a radically new design for the traditional Tarot deck. The "Crowley deck," as it is popularly termed, remains in wide use today.

(6). As a prose stylist, Crowley was a master Modernist whose fierce impatience with restrictions on form and thought link him to fellow iconoclasts of his era such as D. H. Lawrence, Wyndham Lewis, and Ezra Pound.

(7). Crowley was—again, like D. H. Lawrence—a technically unsophisticated but viscerally compelling painter in what might loosely be called the Expressionist mode. Crowley's canvases, which are today avidly sought out by collectors, create a jarring impact by virtue of their swirling color sense—hot, bright yellows, etched wounds of reds, blues from the dead of night.

(8). Crowley was a mystical writer of rare sophistication and originality, one who brilliantly reformulated, into twentieth-century terms, the vital insights of the Western esoteric tradition—a tradition that extends across recorded history, from the legends of King Solomon and the Egyptian Hermes Trismegistus through the writings of the Gnostics and Neo-platonists to the alchemists, Rosicrucians, and Freemasons. Crowley thus may fairly (or unfairly, depending upon one's point of view) be regarded as the primary fount of that diverse, fertile, and occasionally ridiculous range of movements loosely termed "New Age."

(9). Crowley was one of the rare human beings of this or any age to dare to prophesy a distinctive new creed and to devote himself—with some success—to the promulgation of that creed. Adherents of Crowley the Prophet of Thelema (we are not speaking here of self-styled Satanists who shave their heads and parrot random phrases from Crowley's writings) number in the low thousands worldwide—a less than imposing figure, but one that fails to take into account a high level of organization, ongoing publishing efforts, and ardent devotion to the cause.

Whether or not one agrees with any or all of the teachings of Thelema can remain, for present purposes, a secondary concern for the reader, who may rest assured that this biography seeks neither to encourage nor to dissuade potential "converts." As Edward Gibbon observed: "For the man who can raise himself above the prejudices of party and sect, the history of religion is the most interesting part of the history of the human spirit." Crowley's heights and depths are no mere heresies and phantasms, but rather the possibilities—and, at times, distant foreshadowings, for Crowley dared greatly and roamed wildly—of that human spirit.

But for all Crowley's accomplishments, a gulf in sympathy with our protagonist is likely to have persisted in the reader. The figure of Aleister Crowley remains strangely alien, particularly when one attempts to assimilate him into the standard frameworks of cultural achievement.

The reason for this has to do—in large measure—with the perplexing nature of the Western esoteric tradition from which Crowley springs. More particularly, it has to do with the scorn and befuddlement which flood the thoughts of most persons today when the subject of magic is broached.

For Crowley was first and foremost a magus: a devoted adept of the art of high magic.

Hearing the word "magic," too many are likely to think of a discomfited rabbit being yanked by the ears from a trick top hat. Or perhaps there arises the vision of a Faust-like spiritual miscreant who enters into the legendary pact with the Devil: giddying forbidden powers that grant a mere spree of earthly delight in exchange for one's eternal soul.

If Crowley is to be understood, it is essential also to understand—at least in basic terms—the history of magical thought and practice in the West. In so doing, one must bear in mind the dilemma posed by Isaac Bashevis Singer with regard to the occult tradition—that "we are living in an era of amnesia. We have forgotten those vital truths that man once knew and by whose strength he lived."

Crowley recognized the dilemma full well. The era of amnesia had induced not merely forgetfulness but also outright contempt for the tradition he revered and equated with the highest forms of mysticism. In his masterwork, *Magick in Theory and Practice* (1930), Crowley explained that his own term, "Magick," was to be distinguished from the "Magic" that had attracted "dilettanti and eccentrics" who sought "an escape from reality." Crowley quite honorably confessed that "I myself was first consciously drawn to the subject in this way." But this early infatuation with the sheer mystery of the occult was soon supplanted by something far stronger, as Crowley underscored through the use of a typographical emphasis—akin, in its effect, to concrete poetry—that transforms the plain prose page into a kind of magical invocation:

> Let me explain in a few words how it came about that I blazoned the word
> **MAGICK**
> upon the Banner that I have borne before me all my life.
>
> Before I touched my teens, I was already aware that I was The Beast whose number is 666. I did not understand in the least what that implied; it was a passionately ecstatic sense of identity.
>
> In my third year at Cambridge [University, 1897–98], I devoted myself consciously to the Great Work, understanding

thereby the Work of becoming a Spiritual Being free from the constraints, accidents, and deceptions of material existence.

I found myself at a loss to designate my work, just as H. P. Blavatsky [the founder, in 1875, of the Theosophical Society] some years earlier. "Theosophy", "Spiritualism", "Occultism", "Mysticism", all involved undesirable connotations.

I chose therefore the name

"MAGICK"

as essentially the most sublime, and actually the most discredited, of all the available terms.

I swore to rehabilitate

MAGICK,

to identify it with my own career; and to compel mankind to respect, love, and trust that which they scorned, hated and feared. I have kept my Word.

But the time is now come for me to carry my banner into the thick of the press of human life.

I must make

MAGICK

the essential factor in the life of

ALL.

To comprehend Crowley, one must comprehend what he meant by "Magick"—the "discredited" tradition he swore to "rehabilitate."

Magick, for Crowley, is a way of life that takes in every facet of life. The keys to attainment within the magical tradition lie in the proper training of the human psyche itself—more specifically, in the development of the powers of will and imagination. The training of the will—which Crowley so stressed, thus placing himself squarely within that tradition—is the focusing of one's energy, one's essential being. The imagination provides, as it were, the target for this focus, by its capacity to ardently envision—and hence bring into magical being—possibilities and states beyond those of consensual reality. The will and the imagination must work synergistically. For the will, unilluminated by imagination, becomes a barren tool of earthly pursuits. And the imagination, ungoverned by a striving will, lapses into idle dreams and stupor.

If one considers will and imagination alone, the precepts of magic and of everyday common sense seem in accord. The gulf arises with the question of how magic impacts upon the universe *beyond* the psyche of the adept. Magic claims that such impact is accomplished through dimensions variously termed as "etheric" or "astral" realms or the "divine light." The unifying idea behind these terms is that these are media through which the magus may project his willed imagination. Such a view, anathema to common sense, is corroborated by the most revered mystics of every creed. The difference between magic and more ascetic lines of mysticism is that the mystic does not tarry in these realms, which are deemed dangerous as they distract from the ultimate goal of merging with the One. The magus, by contrast, explores each such realm and attains to a knowledge that shows the multifarious Self to be none other than the One. In this way, the mystic and the magus come at last (if they are worthy) to the same end.

Magical practice is guided by a conviction as to the fundamental unity of macrocosm and microcosm. The famous injunction of the Hermetic *Emerald Tablet*—ascribed to Hermes Trismegistus, and dating from roughly the first century C.E.—proclaims: "In truth certainly and without doubt, whatever is below is like that which is above, and whatever is above is like that which is below, to accomplish the miracles of one thing." From this insight derives the metaphor of the "magical mirror" favored by Crowley—the universe reflects the self and the self the universe, an infinite chain of myriad changes that the magus alone can encompass. As Crowley put it, with respect to the task of the human magus: "The Microcosm is an exact image of the Macrocosm; the Great Work is the raising of the whole man in perfect balance to the power of Infinity." Such an aim can seem decidedly hubristic, and Crowley was vain enough, often enough, in its pursuit. But Crowley did also recognize the hubris of the swollen self, and his genuine revulsion against it spurred him to singular efforts at escaping its domain.

There is a strict distinction between low (or "black") and high (or "white") magical aspirations—a distinction which Crowley regarded as of utmost importance. The difficulty of drawing a manageable line is explained by occult historian Richard Cavendish: "High magic is an attempt to gain so consummate an understanding and mastery of oneself and the environment as to transcend all human limitations and become superhuman or divine.[. . .] Low magic is comparatively minor and mechanical, undertaken for immediate worldly advantage, to make money or take revenge on an enemy or make a conquest in love. It tails off into the peddling of spells and lucky charms. The distinction between the two types is blurred in practice and many magicians have engaged in both."

Among these latter was Crowley. For one who devotes his life to magic, it becomes all but inevitable to blur the distinction between "high" and "low," for one is readily seduced into seeing the distinction as meaningless. As above, so below. Who but the magus, who has *experienced* "above" and "below"—and not merely read of them—may judge what actions bring about their true harmony? Why heed the criticisms of the visionless ones, bound by a morality that merely serves their own base, practical ends?

As Emile Durkheim noted, "Magic takes a sort of professional pleasure in profaning holy things." If so, then Crowley was a consummate magical professional. But there have been professionals on the religious side as well—persons who were adept at linking all magical practice with nefarious powers. These accusers play a role in what scholar Elaine Pagels has termed "the social history of Satan"—"because Christians as they read the gospels have characteristically identified themselves with the disciples for some two thousand years they have also identified their opponents, whether Jews, pagans, or heretics, with forces of evil, and so with Satan." In the course of human history, the dividing line between "respectable" religion and "disrespectable" magic has depended less upon careful analysis than upon the fiat of the governing belief system of society.

Make no mistake. Magic is, at its highest levels of theory and practice, a most articulate challenge to the ways of the dominant religions. And why not? Its lineages are as rich and varied as theirs.

The magus is the figure who stands before the gates of religion and issues the most powerful challenge of all—equality of knowledge of, and access to, the divine realm. The magus dares to reach out toward the gods by way of theurgy—high magic capable of influencing, and even merging with, Godhead itself. Such a challenge cannot be ignored by those who preach in the name of any one true faith.

No civilization lacks its efflorescence of magical beliefs. The Babylonians, Egyptians, and Hebrews all fertilized the growth of a body of magical lore that spawned myriad fulsome visions of the universe—each with its teachings and legends. Hermes Trismegistus, Zoroaster, King Solomon, Apollonius of Tyre, Pythagoras—these were the names of magi to which legends attached most vividly.

With these visions, with these claims to power, the newly founded Christian religion waged combat. Nowhere is the battle more clearly described than in the accounts—in the Book of Acts, and in various apocryphal works and patristic writings—of the downfall of the Gnostic leader Simon, dubbed Simon Magus. Simon was born in Samaria and was said to have early on learned the arts of magic by traveling to Egypt. During the early Apostolic era, Simon gained control of a Gnostic group after besting its former leader, one Dositheus, in a magical contest. The sole female member of the group, Helen (alleged by Christians to have been a prostitute), became the consort of Simon and the embodiment of *Ennoia*, the First Thought of the Father and the Mother of All. As Mircea Eliade has noted, "The union of the 'magician' and the prostitute insured universal salvation because their union is, in reality, the reunion of God and divine Wisdom."

Simon and Helen were worshipped as gods in Samaria and even in Rome; statues of Zeus and Athena were at times adapted to the worship of the new Gnostic couple. Christian opponents of Simon alleged that he and his followers practiced magic and free love—a coupling of vices which would recur in attacks against magi (such as Aleister Crowley, who, as the Great Beast, coupled with a series of Scarlet Women) down through the centuries.

The inevitable magical contest for supremacy—one which parallels that of Moses and the Egyptian priests before Pharaoh—took place in Rome. Peter accuses Simon before Emperor Nero. The irony of the mad Nero acting as judge between two such adversaries emphasizes that the stakes here had to do with practical concerns of political prestige. Peter allows that Simon is a powerful magus; but he insists that Simon's power is as nought before his own. The reply of Simon, according to one account (that of a Christian apologist of roughly the third century A.D.), set the prevailing tone for the battle between Church and magus for centuries to come:

> But you [Peter] will, as it were bewildered with astonishment, constantly stop your ears that they should not be defiled by blasphemies, and you will turn to flight, for you will find nothing to reply; but the foolish people will agree with you, indeed will come to love you, for you teach what is customary with them, but they will curse me, for I proclaim something new and unheard of . . .

Just such a gauntlet, in just such a tone—earnest in its fervor, enticing in its promise of "new and unheard of" wisdom, hubristic in its scorn for the beliefs and loves of the "foolish people"—was thrown by Crowley to the preachers of Christendom.

Sexuality, in both its active and its chaste forms, has played a pervasive role in the Western magical tradition. There have undoubtedly been numerous sexual abuses committed by occult pretenders and rapacious Satanists. Nonetheless, the consistent approach of the Church and of Christian writers has been to link *all* magic with moral licentiousness—a licentiousness which, in the case of genuine adepts, disappears when the difference in spiritual frameworks is recognized.

The practice of sexual magic—which forms one of the primary bases for Crowley's notoriety—will be examined in greater detail as the events of his life unfold. For now, be it noted that sexuality played a persistent role in magico-mystical practices of the West in the centuries prior to Christ—and has continued to do so, albeit in a surreptitious manner, in the centuries since. Eliade compared Indian Tantric and Shivaite sexual practices with those of certain Gnostic sects. For the reader who experiences visceral disgust at the thought of sexual emissions as sacred components of worship, Eliade's scholarly conclusion may serve as a palliative: "All of these systems seem to have in common the hope that the primordial spiritual unity can be reconstituted through erotic bliss and the consumption of semen and the menses. In all three systems the genital secretions represent the two divine modes of being, the god and the goddess; consequently, their ritual consumption augments and accelerates the sanctification of the celebrants."

What is described here is sexuality as sacramental ritual, with semen and menses serving the same efficacious role—for those who believe—as the wine and wafer. If the reader can give no credence to sexuality in this sense, a goodly portion of the life and writings of Aleister Crowley is instantaneously transformed into the worst sort of libertine shamming.

Whatever one thinks of Crowley's sexual morés—and Crowley could be lustful and crude and, at times, even vicious toward his partners—sexuality as a means to gnosis became, from the middle decades of his life, a guiding reality for him. As such, purely personal attachments could seem as nothing to him: a personal love between sexual partners is unnecessary for the religious sexual practices cited by Eliade. Indeed, the cruelty that shows itself in too many of Crowley's relationships was clearly fostered by the impersonality that sex took on for him. But Crowley was no hypocrite and his magick was no mere ruse for obtaining sex; when sex was all Crowley wanted, he was hardly ashamed to say so.

The once proud standing of the magus was utterly shattered for those who accepted the Christian teaching that all magical powers and supplications (aside from those practiced by the Church) stemmed from the demonic realm. The Inquisition, formally established in 1233, had as its task to root out the heresies, including magic, that beset the Church despite the best efforts of its scholastic Doctors to establish doctrinal unity. Recall that "heretic" derives from the Greek *hairetikos*, meaning "able to choose."

The heretical choice was viewed unequivocally as wrong. Raymond Lull, Paracelsus, and Cornelius Agrippa—three of the foremost magi of the late Medieval and Renaissance eras—were among the large number of authors whose works were banned under the *Index Librorum Prohibitorum* (*Index of Forbidden Books*) established by the Church; this *Index* was not discontinued until 1966, nineteen years after Crowley's death. The burning at the stake in 1600 of Giordano Bruno, the most gifted of Renaissance magi, was a stern reminder of the consequences of heresy. Crowley, some three centuries later, paid a price—ostracism—that fell short of execution, but still reflected the old warfare.

Magic, by the time Crowley came to it, was a fragmented body of knowledge that had been periodically taken apart and assembled again by its more—and less—illuminated theorists. Perceptive critics such as Idries Shah have pointed to "deteriorated psychological procedures" that were thus incorporated into the magical literature. A sign of this deterioration, according to Shah, is excessive reliance upon induced peaks of emotion that do not complete the work of spiritual transformation:

> Magic is worked through the heightening of emotion. No magical phenomena take place in the cool emotion of the laboratory. When the emotion is heightened to a certain extent, a spark (as it were) jumps the gap, and what appears to be supernormal happenings are experienced.{ . . . } Because certain emotions are more easily roused than others, magic tends to center around personal power, love and hatred. It is these sensations, in the undeveloped individual, which provide the easiest fuel, emotion, "electicity" for the spark to jump the gap which will leap to join a more continuous current.

The root motives that spurred Crowley's magical explorations were based—we have his testimony as to this, in his *Confessions*—upon emotional forces that had dominated him from childhood. While it would be extreme to characterize a man of Crowley's brilliance as an "undeveloped individual," power, love, and hatred are indeed vital fuels—and temptations—in his life.

Crowley, a gifted dialectician, made the task of measurement as difficult as possible for his biographers. Esoteric traditions universally acknowledge that the black-and-white distinctions of ordinary consciousness may be merely shallow delusions. Crowley, secure in having transcended such delusions, insisted that any deviation from the sacred "Great Work"—the forging of a link between the human soul and the divine presence, or, as Crowley often phrased it, the "Knowledge and Conversation of the Holy Guardian Angel"—is "black magic." In *Magick in Theory and Practice,* he reminded readers of their lack of competence to judge a Master of the Temple—that is, an adept such as Crowley believed himself to have become. The boldfacing is Crowley's own:

> There are, however, many shades of grey. It is not every magician who is well armed with theory.[. . .] **Until the Great Work has been performed, it is presumptuous for the magician to pretend to understand the universe, and dictate its policy. Only a Master of the Temple can say whether any given act is a crime.** "Slay that innocent child?" (I hear the ignorant say) "What a horror!" "Ah!" replies the Knower, with foresight of history, "but that child will become Nero. Hasten to strangle him!"
>
> There is a third, above these, who understands that Nero was as necessary as Julius Caesar.

And there may be a fourth who recognizes the limitations of the "foreknowledge" of even the wisest Knowers, as well as the absence of proof that any murder or other act of cruelty is so "necessary" as to justify suffering.

Magic, it may be, lends itself all too readily to base temptations. Crowley was sorely tempted, and too often the temptations prevailed. Surely it is not too much to say on his behalf that there were times, as well, where he prevailed and cast useful light. If a general rule for assessment of Crowley's work may be offered: He was at his best when pointing the way to diligent individual effort, and at his worst when purporting to govern his fellows and to forecast the course of history. Alike at his best and at his worst, he may be seen as instructive.

We now conclude what is, of necessity, a mere sketch of the Western magical tradition. But without such a sketch, the life of Crowley might seem as no more—to a reader accustomed to standard categories of cultural attainment—than a series of puzzling delusions and barbarities.

But always, underlying the whole of that life, there is the promise of spiritual transformation—of Crowley himself, and of the world in which he lived—through magic. That promise has retained its allure through the ages, not least in our "modern" era.

Indeed, as Crowley argued in "modern" terms, magical phenomena are as real—or questionable—as any other phenomena. That is, their "reality" depends on sense perceptions acting upon our brain; these sense perceptions cannot be equated with noumenal or ultimate reality. But they are all we have, whether we speak of the existence of a chair or of an angelic or demonic spirit. Their creative employment in magical ritual—by means of sight and touch (the special setting, wardrobe, and implements), sound (invocations), smell (incense and perfume), taste (sacramental wine and bread), and mind (the experience itself, and reflection thereon)—cannot be dismissed as unreal. For the human brain responds to magical ritual as it does to a stirring sunset or a beautiful painting.

Magic *works* in some manner—that much history confirms beyond question. Gifted men and women have happily devoted their lives to perfecting its practice. Ruling powers—religious and secular—have persistently held its practitioners suspect. What greater testimony can there be to the power of magic than the enduring love and fear it inspires?

To gauge *how* magic works, one can do no better than to turn to the strange, wondrous, and saddening career of Aleister Crowley—the magus and Beast par excellence for our times.

CHAPTER ONE

The Strange Transformation of One Edward Alexander ("Alick") Crowley, a Pious Christian Boy of the Late Victorian Upper Class, Into Aleister Crowley, Poet, Gent., and Magical Adept in Waiting (1875–98)

I t was in the heart of a peaceful and prosperous England, in the town of Leamington in the county of Warwickshire, at the genteel address of 30 Clarendon Square, between eleven and twelve P.M. on the night of October 12, 1875, with the astrological sign of Leo in the ascendant, that Emily Crowley bore a baby son, the firstborn heir to the fortune of her husband, Edward.

The son was given the name of his father and grandfather: Edward Crowley. The newborn's middle name of Alexander was taken from a pious friend of the father, and in very early childhood it was explained to the boy that "Alexander" meant "helper of men," a meaning that left an enduring impress.

In his autobiographical *Confessions,* Crowley sought to establish his place in the lineage of magi. One standard feature of the myth is the appearance of special physical features at birth. In the third person, Crowley describes his newborn self:

> He bore on his body the three most distinguishing marks of a Buddha. He was tongue-tied, and on the second day of his incarnation a surgeon cut the fraenum linguae [a membrane attaching the underside of the tongue to the bottom of the mouth]. He had also the characteristic membrane, which necessitated an operation for phimosis [abnormal tightness of the foreskin which necessitated a late circumcision] some three lus-

tres [fifteen years] later. Lastly, he had upon the center of his heart four hairs curling left to right in the exact form of a Swastika.

This self-portrait reveals both Crowley's absorption with his lineage and, as well, the sort of shameless bluff that often lies concealed beneath his assured tone. Of his birth in the county of Warwickshire he wrote: "It has been remarked a strange coincidence that one small county should have given England her two greatest poets—for one must not forget Shakespeare (1550–1616)." In making the jibe (a tacit and wry acknowledgment of his own frustrated yearning for fame as a poet), Crowley casually ascribes the wrong birth year to the Bard, who was born in 1564.

In the *Confessions*, Crowley declares that he will tell the truth, but insists upon limitations: "The truth must be falsehood unless it be the whole truth; and the whole truth is partly inaccessible, partly unintelligible, partly incredible and partly unpublishable—that is, in any country where truth in itself is recognized as a dangerous explosive."

With these caveats—which allow the memoirist an ample creative freedom—we may turn to the *Confessions* with both interest and caution. As to his birth characteristics, for example, it is untrue that being "tongue-tied" is one of the primary distinguishing marks of a Buddha. Indeed, Gautama, the Indian prince who became the Buddha, is described in the *Buddha-Karita* of Asvaghosha (whose first-century work remains the most revered biography within Buddhism), as having declared his mission eloquently at the very moment of his emergence from his mother's womb: " 'I am born for supreme knowledge, for the welfare of the world,—thus this is my last birth,'—thus did he of lion birth, gazing at the four quarters, utter a voice full of auspicious meaning." Not even Crowley dared to give himself so fine a speech at his own nativity.

If Crowley was imaginative in terms of his spiritual lineage, he was utterly sincere as to its significance to him. The same is true of his paternal lineage. The Crowleys, he asserted, were of Celtic origin, with branches in Ireland and Brittany. Family tradition had it that the Crowleys were strong supporters of fellow Welshman Henry Tudor, the Earl of Richmond who became Henry VII; the Welsh Crowleys fought for him at the Battle of Bosworth in 1485, and established themselves in England in the wake of his triumph.

The adult Crowley would draw from this Celtic ancestry as it suited him: for example, during World War I, he preferred to be Irish rather than English, for reasons to be examined in due course. But the more prosaic facts as to family finances and religion would exercise the most enduring influence.

Crowley was heir to the luxurious life that the British Empire could offer to its fortunate upper class. Father Edward came from a wealthy Quaker family. His own father Edward, Crowley's grandfather, made his fortune as a brewer, establishing a number of public houses that sold Crowley Ale and sandwiches. Edward, who had no necessity to make a living, became a self-appointed preacher of the word of God—and a formative role model.

Wealth affected the spirituality of both father and son. It is a truism that class affects character. But in Victorian England class distinctions were severe enough—even for the white domestic population—to create what would now be called a "third world" level of poverty and despair amongst the lower classes. As historian E. J. Hobsbawm observed, "In the 1870s eleven- to twelve-year–old boys from the upper-class public schools were on average five inches taller than boys from industrial schools, and at all teen-ages three inches taller than the sons of artisans." Fellow historian Barbara Tuchman described the ruling class of the 1890s (the decade in which Crowley came into manhood and family fortune): "Fed upon privilege, the patricians flourished. Five at least of the leading ministers in [Conservative Prime Minister] Lord Salisbury's Government were over six feet tall, far above the normal stature of the time. Of the nineteen members of the Cabinet, all but two lived to be over seventy, seven exceeded eighty, and two exceeded ninety at a time when the average life expectancy of a male at birth was forty-four and of a man who had reached twenty-one was sixty-two. On their diet of privilege they acquired a certain quality which Lady Warwick could define only in the words, 'They have an air!'" These stark realities enable one to appreciate the extreme importance to Crowley—through all the magical transformations of his psyche—of his status as an English gentleman.

Religion was the second great influence that flowed through his family. His parents were devoted to an intensely sectarian creed, that of the Plymouth Brethren. Plainly, Crowley grew to despise the Brethren as he came of age. Yet his new religion of Thelema recapitulates the Brethren worldview in several vital respects. The paradoxical truth is that Crowley was an astonishing emulator of the creed he professed to hate.

The Brethren sect was founded in the late 1820s by John Nelson Darby, an Irish-born Anglican priest who became vehemently disenchanted with the Church of England. Darby had come to see all churchly institutions as unjustified by Scripture and hence as false custodians of the teachings of Christ. The name Plymouth Brethren emerged from the early influence of the meetings at Providence Chapel in Plymouth. By 1848, there were roughly six thousand Brethren adherents in Britain. From the first, the movement attracted primarily educated members of the upper classes, such as Edward Crowley. Its lure consisted, in large measure, in the pared-down simplicity of its three central precepts: (1) An insistence on the literal truth of Scripture (as embodied strictly in the King James Translation); (2) Elimination of all priestly authority—all worshippers were equal at Brethren meetings, and free to speak as the Holy Spirit moved them; and (3) An imminentist belief in the Second Coming so strong that, as Crowley later observed, "preparations for a distant future—such as signing a lease or insuring one's life— might be held to imply lack of confidence in the promise, " 'Behold, I come quickly.' "

It was in this highly charged atmosphere—set between the fervid expectation of Christ's coming and the vigilant shunning of Satan—that Crowley the boy was raised. When one compares the structure of Brethren beliefs with those of the new religion of Thelema established by Crowley, the parallels are fundamental and unmistakable. Such was the impress that the earnest and dedicated Edward, and the fond but fearful Emily, made upon their son.

It was on behalf of the Brethren cause that Edward Crowley became a lay preacher. But it was Emily who enforced the ways of the Brethren at home, and it is to her that we shall turn first.

Emily Crowley, who first bestowed upon her son the epithet of "Beast," was born Emily Bertha Bishop. Little is known of her early years. Crowley tells us that she was raised in a Devon and Somerset family, had an oriental appearance that won her the nickname of "the little Chinese girl" during her school days, and had a talent for watercolor painting. Beyond this, his judgments upon her were uniformly severe. Crowley wrote of how, in his late teen-age, he saved his mother (whom he heard crying out from a distance, by way of what he termed inexplicable "psychic phenomena") from slipping down a precipice. This action he described as a "regrettable incident of impulsive humanitarianism." At the heart of Crowley's complaints was his conviction that Emily had been ruined by her religious beliefs. Upon marrying Edward Crowley in 1874, Emily had converted to the Plymouth Brethren creed. Crowley felt keenly the barriers she posed to his childhood reading:

My intellectual avidity was enormous, yet I was absolutely cut off from literature.[. . .] David Copperfield was barred because of Little Em'ly, for she was a naughty girl; besides, Emily was my mother's name, and to read the book might diminish my respect for her. One of my tutors brought down *The Bab Ballads* [by W. S. Gilbert], one of which begins:

Emily Jane was a nursery maid.

My mother threw the book out of the house and very nearly threw him after it.

With a trace of sympathy, Crowley allowed that "her powerful natural instincts were destroyed by religion [. . .] Yet there was always a struggle; she was really distressed, almost daily, at finding herself obliged by her religion to perform acts on the most senseless atrocity."

This element of reluctant understanding bespeaks a more subtle degree of feeling for his mother than Crowley ever expressed directly in his writings. The *Confessions* contain one scene that testifies particularly strongly to this. At roughly age sixteen, Crowley explained, the repressive atmosphere of his home made him "prepared to go out of my way to perform any act which might serve as a magical affirmation of my revolt." This "magical affirmation" proved to be sexual intercourse with the family parlor maid. "And I had her on my mother's very bed!" Crowley was an admirer of Freud and aware of the theory of the Oedipal complex. One need not insist on the truth of that complex to find it odd that Crowley failed to consider—at least in his writings—how it might apply to exultant sex on his mother's bed.

For all of Crowley's bluster against her in the *Confessions*, there remained a difficult love and even spiritual kinship between them. Emily, it would seem, was not quite so hidebound a bigot as Crowley would have us believe, nor was he quite so thankless a son. We are compelled to go abruptly forward in time to find testimony in support of these assertions. The English poet Ethel Archer, who was a close friend of Crowley's in the years prior to World War One, wrote a novel, *The Hieroglyph* (1932), in which the main protagonist, occultist Vladimir Svaroff, is (by Archer's own testimony) modeled entirely upon her memories of Crowley in that period. Here is an account of a meeting between mother and son circa 1910: "To hear Vladimir being chided by his mother like a very small and naughty boy, and to see him calmly accepting the situation, was both humorous and quaint.[...] That Madame Svaroff adored her son there could be no question; that she equally believed him to be entirely given over to the Evil One was beyond question likewise. She prayed for him without ceasing, but she refused to have in her rooms a single article of his personal belongings—even his pipe and a few books being banished to the attics." Archer's narrator goes on to insist, surprisingly, that Madame Svaroff possessed, along with her piety, an admirable sense of humor, "and in this trait one could see the unmistakable likeness of mother to son."

Beyond the humor, there was tenderness outright. There survives a letter by Emily dated December 12, 1912—the same period as the fictionalized events of *The Hieroglyph*. Referring to Crowley as "Alec" (Crowley himself spelled his childhood nickname "Alick"), Emily writes, with more pathos than asperity: "I very much wish that he would treat his mother better & give her a little more of his company." She goes on to note with approval that her son is following the advice of her lawyer with respect to investments—hardly a sign of intransigent filial rebellion.

And yet, there is the stark fact that it was Emily Crowley who bestowed upon her son the sobriquet that would dominate his own inner identity: that of the Beast. How could a mother love her son and yet see him as the Adversary? Crowley offers his own explanation. "In a way, my mother was insane, in the sense that all people are who have watertight compartments to the brain, and hold with equal passion incompatible ideas, and hold them apart lest their meeting should destroy both.[...] But my mother believed that I was actually Anti-christ of the Apocalypse and also her poor lost erring son who might yet repent and be redeemed by the Precious Blood." Crowley never tells us if there was a specific incident in his childhood that inspired this maternal belief, but he does confide that, at a very early age, he himself was drawn to the figure of the Beast. Crowley (again writing of himself in the third person) takes pains to argue that this identification was nothing out of the ordinary for a child whose only allowable reading was the Holy Scripture. Its most bloodcurdling prophecies served as his fairy tales—deliciously forbidden fantasies:

> The Elders and the harps seemed tame. He preferred the Dragon, the False Prophet, the Beast and the Scarlet Woman, as being more exciting. He reveled in the descriptions of torment. One may suspect, moreover, a strain of congenital masochism. He liked to imagine himself in agony; in particular, he liked to

identify himself with the Beast whose number is the number of a man, six hundred and three score six. One can only conjecture that it was the mystery of the number which determined this childish choice.

Perhaps it was this fascination shown by her son that inspired Emily to dub him the Beast. But however this originated, it was no minor tease, coming as it did from a woman who believed in the literal truth of the Bible. To a remarkable extent, Emily foresaw and believed in the destiny of her son, however much she fought against it. If the bond between mother and son seems intact, even after the studied vitriol of the *Confessions* (written after her death), the secret of its strength lies in the mother's knowing recognition of what her son might become.

There is a sharp dichotomy in Crowley's feelings for his parents, stated with fervor in the *Confessions*: "His father was his hero and his friend, though, for some reason or other, there was no real conscious intimacy or understanding. He always disliked and despised his mother. There was a physical repulsion, and an intellectual and social scorn. He treated her almost as a servant." As vehement as is Crowley's contempt for Emily, the tribute to his father reads, in its hesitant way, as more troubling still. Hero worship can thrive as a distant emotion, but friendship without "intimacy or understanding" is a difficult friendship indeed. Nonetheless, the parallels between Crowley and his father are as striking as one could wish. The one key distinction—that the son reviled the faith his father devoted his life to preaching—seems, in retrospect, relatively unimportant when compared to the cognitive patterns that endured.

Edward Crowley was born in 1834 and, as previously mentioned, came into a fortune by way of his Quaker father's brewery. Edward not only failed to enter the family business, he also rejected the family's pietist faith, devoting himself instead to writing and preaching on behalf of the Brethren. Edward did not omit to teach the faith at home: by age four, young Crowley was a fluent reader of the Bible, which was studied daily in the home, just after breakfast. The theme of *momento mori* was an obsession for Edward. Crowley recalled accompanying his father on evangelizing tours in which they would go from village to village on foot:

He would notice somebody cheerfully engaged in some task and ask sympathetically its object. The victim would expand and say that he hoped for such and such a result. He was now in a trap. My father would say, 'And then?' By repeating this question, he would ferret out the ambition of his prey to be mayor of his town or what not, and still came the inexorable 'And then?' till the wretched individual thought to cut it short by saying as little as uncomfortably as possible. 'Oh well, by that time I shall be ready to die.' More solemnly than ever came the question, 'And *then?*' In this way my father would break down the entire chain of causes and bring his interlocutor to realize the entire vanity of human effort. The moral was, of course, 'Get right with God.'

The reason for Crowley's choice of magic as a lifework was to escape the mortal coil and to achieve something undying—like unto the Christian heaven of his father. He once wrote of the magical quest for divine union: "The adventure of the Great Work is the only one worth while; for all others are but interludes in the sinister farce of Life and Death, which limits all merely human endeavor."

As befitted the notion of his father as hero, Crowley sought—in his *Confessions*—to make of him as great a paragon as possible, given his repugnant Brethren beliefs. How else could the Prophet of the New Aeon exonerate a father who so embodied the Old? Crowley stressed that Edward was, for all his misguided religion, a gentleman and a "natural" aristocrat. In Crowley's view, this was evidenced by Edward's pronounced leadership qualities, which shone forth amongst the Brethren. But Crowley inflated his father's deeds in the way adoring sons do. Neither Brethren chroniclers nor outside scholarly researchers have adjudged Edward Crowley as a principal figure in the Brethren movement. Indeed, his name does not appear in the standard volumes on the sect. In Crowley's eyes, however, Edward towered over his peers and "swayed thousands by his eloquence." Given the small number of Brethren in Great Britain, and the cramped meeting room settings in which Edward typically preached, the claim of "thousands" lacks any credibility. In a further telling passage, Crowley describes his frustration in watching Edward "ostentatiously" avoid the assumption of authority with his fellow Brethren. Not even their puritanical shunning of the flesh galled Crowley so much as their failure to grant Edward his due. And Crowley was determined not to fall victim to his father's fate:

The boy seems to have despised from the first the absence of hierarchy among the Brethren, though at the same time they formed the most exclusive body on earth, being the only people

that were going to heaven.[. . .] The Plymouth Brethren refused to take any part in politics. Among them, the peer and the
peasant met theoretically as equals, so that the social system of
England was simply ignored. The boy could not aspire to become prime minister or even king; he was already apart from
and beyond all that. It will be seen that as soon as he arrived at
an age where ambitions are compelled to assume concrete form,
his position became extremely difficult. The earth was not big
enough to hold him.

The fervor of his convictions drove Edward—as it would his son—to
self-publish spiritual tracts that could edify the "common man." These
tracts were issued in pamphlet from throughout the 1860s and were
distributed by Edward himself. There is no resemblance in prose style
between father and son; Edward was a staunchly pedestrian explicator
of his creed. But there are surprising parallels between the father's
Brethren beliefs and Crowley's magical creed of Thelema.

Crowley was, for example, much reviled for his belief in the efficacy
of blood sacrifice (there is a furious trail of legends that have the Beast
taking human lives in pursuit of magical power). But in father Edward's
tract *The Plymouth Brethren (So Called)/Who They Are—Their
Creed—Mode of Worship, &c./Explained in A Letter to his Friends and
Relations* (1865), the concrete saving power of Christ's sacrificial blood
is stressed repeatedly. Those who would be saved must recognize that
"there can be no remission of sins without the shedding of blood (Heb.
ix. 22).[. . .] You may be hoping and doing, but if you are not trusting
wholly and only to the blood of Jesus, all your efforts and hopes are
worthless." (Crowley cited this very same Biblical passage with approval
in his *Magick in Theory and Practice* (1930.) As for those Christians still
ensnared in the doctrinal delusions of the established churches, Edward
saw that their fate would be to stray ever farther from the truth of Jesus, "waxing bolder and bolder against God until Antichrist himself
shall be revealed, who shall oppose and exalt himself above all that is
called God." Note that the fury of father and son alike was directed at
the Christian establishment of England; in this, Crowley was no rebel,
but rather a faithful son.

Always recalcitrant in a secondary role (even that of a son), Crowley did
try, now and then, to put his father in his place. Edward is dubbed "the
younger" in the *Confessions*, though Crowley himself, named after his

father (and hence the third in a line of Edwards), rightly deserves that epithet. The fact that Edward preached the Brethren ways while living off inherited shares of the family brewery was also a source of satire for Crowley. In the autobiographical preface to his poetic drama *The World's Tragedy* (1910), Crowley parodies the typical Christian as an abstemious fop and hypocrite: "Wine? The great curse of our day, my dear sir.[. . .] Beer? Well, perhaps a little beer—for he has shares in a brewery." But by the time he came to write the *Confessions* (in the early 1920s), even this inconsistency was forgiven, with Edward looking all the more kindly and enlightened for embracing it:

> He [Edward] said that abstainers were likely to rely on good works to get to heaven and thus fail to realize their need of Jesus. He preached one Sunday in the town hall [of Redhill], saying 'I would rather preach to a thousand drunkards than a thousand T-totallers.' They retorted by accusing him of being connected with 'Crowley's Ales'. He replied that he had been an abstainer for nineteen years, during which he had shares in a brewery. He had now ceased to abstain for some time, but all his money was in a waterworks.

The contempt for good works unaccompanied by genuine faith was fiercely held by Edward Crowley the preacher. Indeed, Edward embraced, quite unawares, a paradoxical tenet first emphasized by the Gnostics—that a fulsome indulgence in sin could lead to the highest spiritual realizations. Crowley described his father's stance this way: "In the case of the sinner, it was almost a hopeful sign that he should sin thoroughly. He was more likely to reach that conviction of sin which would show him his need for salvation.[. . .] It was the devil's favourite trick to induce people to rely on their good character." Edward could not have foreseen that within this doctrine lay the seed of a new faith that would, as promulgated by his son, abrogate sin altogether.

The untimely death of Edward Crowley from cancer of the tongue on March 5, 1887, when he was forty-three and his son only eleven, shattered the boy and transformed his psyche and outlook. So great was his fear of losing his father that the change commenced with the very first diagnosis of his father's disease in May 1886. "It is as if the event which occurred at the time created a new faculty in his mind. A new factor had arisen and its name was death." By contrast, consider his chilled reaction to the death of his infant sister (Crowley's only sibling who lived a mere five hours) in 1880, when Crowley was five: "The incident made a curious impression on him. He did not see why he should be disturbed so uselessly. He couldn't do any good; the child was dead; it was none of his business." Crowley summed up this difference in response through sanguine bravado: "This attitude continued through his life. He has never attended any funeral but that of his father, which he did not mind doing, as he felt himself to be the real centre of interest."

The boy's attitude toward his schooling and religion was perceived to decline. In 1885, the year prior to the diagnosis, Crowley had been transferred by his father from the St. Leonard's school to the Brethren-run Ebor School in Cambridge. It was in a spirit of adoration for his father that Crowley accepted this transfer: "Accordingly, he aimed at being the most devoted follower of Jesus in the school. He was not hypocritical in any sense." Upon Edward's death, however, there was a change so pervasive that even Crowley sounds a puzzled note: "It is impossible to suppose that the character of the school had completely changed between my father's death and my return from the funeral. Yet before that I was completely happy and in sympathy with my surroundings. Not three weeks later, Ishmael was my middle name." Three weeks after Edward's death, Crowley committed a school offense for the first time. In classroom lessons, he probed at the inconsistencies of Biblical texts. An example recalled by Crowley: how could Christ have been in the grave for three days and three nights if he was crucified on Friday and rose again on Sunday? One might translate the query here more bluntly: How could death truly be evaded?

Edward's death proved that it could not. The tension became extreme. Trapped within the Brethren belief system and shattered within himself, Crowley was compelled (logically, as it were) to undergo an enantiodromia: to move to the opposite pole from Christ (his former ideal, by way of Edward) and to ally himself with the Adversary by mocking the transparent falsehoods of the Christian faith, such as the triumph over death:

> The apparent discrepancy [as to the three days] in the gospel narrative aroused no doubt in my mind as to the literal truth of either of the texts. Indeed, my falling away from grace was not occasioned by any intellectual qualms; I accepted the theology of the Plymouth Brethren. In fact, I could hardly conceive of the existence of people who might doubt it. I simply went over to Satan's side; and to this hour I cannot tell why.

For those who would use this passage to brand Crowley as a Satanist, any attempt at clarification will read as untoward apology. Simply stated, however, Crowley's going over "to Satan's side" is a description not of his enduring life viewpoint but rather of an adolescent grief that expressed itself in the most extreme form of rebellion open to him— impiety. But the defiant schoolboy saw himself as the paradoxical pre-server of the faith. As Crowley later explained: "It seems as if I possessed a theology of my own which was, to all intents and purposes, Chris-tianity. My satanism did not interfere with it at all; I was trying to take the view that the Christianity of hypocrisy and cruelty was not true Christianity. I did not hate God or Christ, but merely the God and Christ of the people whom I hated."

The rebellion against the Brethren—which included the tacit rejec-tion of father Edward, who failed his son and the faith by dying—was the first emergence of Crowley the man. Note how the pain is expressed with impeccable logic and calm, even as it transfigures the voice of the *Confessions* and the life itself:

> Previous to the death of Edward Crowley, the recollections of his son, however vivid or detailed, appear to him strangely im-personal. In throwing back his mind to that period, he feels, al-though attention constantly elicits new facts, that he is investigating the behaviour of somebody else. It is only from this point that he begins to think of himself in the first person. From this point, however, he does so; and is able to continue this autohagiography in a more conventional style by speaking of himself as I.

Following the death of Edward in 1887, Emily Crowley moved with her son from Redhill, Surrey, to the then Thistle Grove (now Drayton Gardens) section of London, where her brother, Tom Bond Bishop, resided. Edward's estate was sufficient to provide financially for his fam-ily. But the Victorian ethos required a *paterfamilias*; Bishop thus came to act in Emily's stead as Crowley's guardian as to matters of schooling and preparation for manhood. This state of affairs could not have been less to the boy's liking. Crowley deemed Bishop "a ruthless, petty tyrant; and it was into this den of bitter slavery that I was suddenly hurled from my position of fresh air, freedom and heirship."

But it was not at home, but rather at the Ebor School in Cambridge, that Crowley underwent an agony of the soul that would set him apart—

once and for all, one may conclude in retrospect—from his English peers. Upon no institution or person did Crowley pile the coals of hatred with more vehemence than upon the Ebor School and its headmaster, the Reverend H. d'Arcy Champney, a former Anglican priest who had converted to the Brethren. Consider a mere portion of Crowley's paean of rage (entitled "A Boyhood in Hell") against the Ebor School:

> May God bite into the bones of men the pain of that hell on earth (I have prayed often) that by them, it may be sowed with salt, accursed for ever! May the maiden that passes it be barren and the pregnant woman that beholdeth it abort! May the birds of the air refuse to fly over it! May it stand as a curse, as a fear, as an hate, among men! May the wicked dwell therein!

The style is that of the Biblical prophets. The King James cadence is a constant in Crowley's rhetorical flights, whether fiery or magisterially calm.

But this rage toward Champney and his school arose only *after* Edward's passing. It is tempting to conclude that the boy's grief transformed a perfectly ordinary public school (a private school in American usage) into a horrific psychic crucible. But the charges made by Crowley against the Ebor School and Champney parallel, in all fundamental details, criticisms raised against English public schools by respected historians of the era.

Champney, like other British schoolmasters of the era, was extremely concerned over two potential actions: homosexual contact and solitary masturbation. To Victorian educators and physicians, the latter was every bit as disgraceful as the former. An understanding of the governing sexual beliefs of the era is essential, as it illuminates the surprising linkage between Victorian theory on the physical and spiritual primacy of semen and the sexual magick of Crowley's mature works. Just as in matters of religion, so too in his stress upon sex, Crowley was as much of his age as he was in opposition to it.

Consider certain fundamentals of Victorian sexology. The emission of semen, in and of itself, was viewed as a serious threat to the health of males of all ages. William Acton, a Member of the Royal College of Surgeons and a prolific writer on sexual issues, was unwavering as to the absence of any appropriate role for sex within childhood or adolescence: "In a state of health no sexual impression should ever affect a child's mind or body. All its vital energy should be employed in building up the growing frame, in storing up external impressions, and educating the brain to receive them." Even fully mature males were warned of the dangers of excessive intercourse within the bonds of marriage; sex outside of marriage was, of course, unthinkable. As a delicate adjunct to these warnings, it was stressed that women little desired sex aside from its necessary role in procreation. As an inevitable side effect, prostitution was rife within Victorian society, formally condemned but tacitly condoned as a necessary measure for proper gentlemen, albeit an unseemly influence on the morals of young women of the lower classes.

These viewpoints most certainly left their mark on the young Crowley, who imbibed from the public school atmosphere of sexual watchfulness and suspicion a lingering puritanism. To a certain degree, sex never lost its sense of naughtiness for him. Further, Crowley largely accepted the notion, implicitly embodied in Victorian sexology, of women as secondary social beings in terms of intellect and sensibility. And finally, Crowley acquiesced in the Victorian notions of sperm as the "vital energy" of life and virility as the hallmark of manly well-being; his later borrowings from Indian Tantrism only reinforced these emphases. Where Crowley ultimately differed was in his willingness to spend that "vital energy" liberally.

Champney and the Ebor School employed fearsome punitive measures against those who transgressed—or who were believed, through malicious talebearing, to have transgressed—against the bounds of propriety. Here is Crowley's central tale of injustice at the hands of Champney:

> [A] boy named Glascott, with insane taint, told Mr. Champney that he had visited me (twelve years old) at my mother's house during the holidays—true so far, he had—and found me lying drunk at the bottom of the stairs. My mother was never asked about this; nor was I told of it. I was put into "Coventry", i.e. no master nor boy might speak to me, or I to them. I was fed on bread and water; during play hours I worked solitary round and round the playground. I was expected to 'confess' the crime of which I was not only innocent, but unaccused.
>
> The punishment, which I believe criminal authorities would consider severe on a poisoner, went on for a term and a half. I was, at last, threatened with expulsion for my refusal to 'confess', and so dreadful a picture of the horrors of expulsion did they paint me—the guilty wretch, shunned by his fellows, slinks on through life to a dishonoured grave, etc.—that I actually chose to endure my tortures and to thank my oppressor.

Physically, I broke down. The strain and the misery affected
my kidneys; and I had to leave school altogether for two years.

Corporal punishment was a frequently employed means of discipline
at the Ebor School, as it was in public schools throughout England. J. R.
de S. Honey, an authority on Victorian public schools, explains the psychological framework of the repeated and severe canings of the backs
and buttocks of errant young boys: "Victorian prep schools and public
schools must have been a paradise for sadistically-inclined masters and
boys.[. . .] So regularly was recourse had to corporal punishment in
Victorian schools, and so great the zeal which was expected of the performer, that its exercise must have accommodated a wide spectrum of
motives and feelings.[. . .] It was presumably the predilections of such
products of English schools which helped to fasten upon sado-masochis-
tic practices, at least across the Channel, the nickname *le vice anglais*."
    Crowley acknowledged, in the *Confessions*, that as a child he had a
streak of "congenital masochism" that revealed itself in fantasies of
physical agony; a particular favorite was to imagine himself, while in
such agony, as the Beast of the Book of Revelation. It is with this background of brutality in mind that one can approach, with a modicum of
comprehension—if not sympathy—one of the most appalling incidents
in the *Confessions*. At roughly age fourteen, shortly after he left the
Ebor School, Crowley committed the cold-blooded murder of a cat:

> I had been told 'A cat has nine lives.' I deduced that it must be
> practically impossible to kill a cat. As usual, I became full of am-
> bition to perform the feat.[. . .] I therefore caught a cat, and
> having administered a large dose of arsenic I chloroformed it,
> hanged it above the gas jet, stabbed it, cut his throat, smashed its
> skull and, when it had been pretty thoroughly burnt, drowned it
> and threw it out of the window that the fall might remove the
> ninth life. In fact, the operation was successful; I had killed
> the cat. I remember that all the time I was genuinely sorry for
> the animal; I simply forced myself to carry out the experiment
> in the interest of pure science.

One of the strangest aspects of this ghastly passage is the absence of
any acknowledgment that the violence was satisfying to the boy. Many
children have tormented animals; those readers who have their own experiences to recall may judge for themselves the plausibility of Crowley's account.

The ultimate withdrawal of Crowley from the Ebor School, at age thirteen, came about through the intervention of his hated *paterfamilias*, Bishop, who decided that the accusations made against his young ward were preposterous. Bishop also recognized the physical deterioration of the boy, who was suffering from albuminuria (a urinary disorder), as well as from flaring asthma attacks. The diagnosing physician feared that Crowley would not live to manhood. Bishop brought the boy home. For the next two years, Crowley had private tutors.

As a final parting shot at the Ebor headmaster, Crowley alleges in the *Confessions* that, shortly after his departure, the "insanity" of Champney "became patent" and his school was terminated. Neither of these jibes are correct. Champney remained as headmaster until 1900 (some twelve years after Crowley's departure), with the school thereafter continuing its existence for some years in the new location of Bexhill. The retrospective fury which Crowley levels at Champney was due, in part, to his adolescent failure to have bested his nemesis. As Crowley conceded, with a note of grudging respect: "The battle between myself and the school was conducted on the magical plane, so to speak. It was as if I had made wax figures of the most inoffensive sort, that yet were recognized by the spiritual instinct of Champney as idols or instruments of witchcraft. I was punished with absolute injustice and stupidity, yet at the same time the mystical apprehension of Champney made no mistake."

Bishop now resolved that the boy's full recovery required plentiful open-air exercise, including fishing and mountain climbing jaunts in Wales and Scotland. These delighted Crowley. As for academics, Bishop made an experiment of blending private tutors with a day school in nearby Streatham. The day school regimen resulted in two signal experiences. The first was the boy's tardy discovery of the masturbatory vice that had so obsessed Champney. As Crowley observed, "Here was certainly a sin worth sinning and I applied myself with characteristic vigour to its practice." The second was Crowley's creation of an inadvertent but highly effective explosive device. The same astonishing tunnel-vision science that led to the nine-time killing of the cat was at work, only in this case the victim was Crowley himself. It began with his budding interest in chemistry, in which subject he was a star pupil in the school. In the autumn of 1890, the young Crowley packed a large jar with ingredients including a full two pounds of gunpowder. The site was the Streatham school playground. The intent was to launch a schoolboy rocket. The impact was literally shattering—windows on the nearby buildings were left in shards. As for Crowley, he was forced to have dozens of bits of gravel surgically removed from his face and was blindfolded until Christmas Day out of fear that he would lose his sight by using his traumatized eyes. Crowley's summation: "Strangely enough, I was the only person injured. Throughout I enjoyed the episode; I was the hero, I had made my mark!"

Bishop resolved to find suitable role models for the impressionable adolescent—pious young tutors who would instill not merely knowledge but the eternal principles of the Evangelical spirit. If Crowley is to be believed, Bishop's efforts at screening tutors were an abject failure. With one of these tutors, a Reverend Fothergill, Crowley engaged in a pitched argument while the two were off on a fishing expedition at a loch near Forsinard, Scotland. Crowley threw first Fothergill's rod and then Fothergill himself into the loch. The reverend retaliated by capsizing the rowboat in which Crowley sought to make his escape and then attempting to drown the lad. That night, hostilities were further intensified when Crowley flagrantly wooed and won a local girl. Fothergill, a broken tutor, returned with the boy to London; there was, as Crowley tells it, a further sexual dalliance en route in Carlisle, as a way of repeating his "victory." A subsequent tutor joined in sexual battle with the boy in an altogether different mode by making homosexual advances. "I did not allow him to succeed," Crowley wrote, "not because I could see no sin in it [conscious sin, be it remembered, was at this time the keynote of Crowley's adolescent rebellion] but because I thought it was a trap to betray me to my family."

The tutors did succeed in helping Crowley to progress rapidly in mathematics, literature, Greek, and Latin. Equally important, however, was the freedom to read what he wished, which had previously been denied him. At Forsinard, Crowley discovered certain old folios of Shakespeare and pored over them night after night, convinced now that "poetry was of paramount importance." Crowley went on to make a survey of English verse. Of the Victorian poets, he embraced Swinburne, the sweep and sonority of whose lyrics had a lasting influence. The yearning to achieve greatness as a poet took hold in the boy.

From amongst the unavailing tutors there emerged, in Crowley's eyes, one shining figure who befriended the boy at a time when friendship must have been badly needed. Archibald Douglas was a young Oxford graduate whom Bishop hired in 1891. Douglas and Crowley traveled together to the English town of Torquay on what was to have been a bicycle outing:

> Though Douglas called himself a Christian, he proved to be both
> a man and a gentleman. I presume that poverty had compelled

the camouflage. From the moment that we were alone together he produced a complete revolution in my outlook upon life, by showing me for the first time a sane, clear, jolly world worth living in. Smoking and drinking were natural. He warned me of the dangers of excess from the athletic standpoint. He introduced me to racing, billiards, betting, cards and women. He told me how these things might be enjoyed without damaging oneself or wronging others. He put me up to all the tricks. He showed me the meaning of honour. I immediately accepted his standpoint and began to behave like a normal, healthy human being. The nightmare world of Christianity vanished at the dawn. I fell in with a girl of the theatre in the first ten days at Torquay, and at that touch of human love the detestable mysteries of sex were transformed into joy and beauty. The obsession of sin fell from my shoulders into the sea of oblivion.[. . .] It was a period of boundless happiness for me.

Crowley's pointed insistence on the immediacy of his transformation from a sin-ridden soul to a pagan embracer of life is typical of his approach to psychological issues. The evidence of his later life resoundingly contradicts this claim. But there is no reason to doubt that Crowley did indeed experience a rapturous psychic release. Bishop soon thereafter dismissed Douglas; but, as Crowley later wrote, "it was too late; my eyes were opened and I had become as a god, knowing good and evil." Crowley returned to a public school room-and-board setting in the second or middle term of 1891. The choice of Malvern College, an esteemed school, was based in part upon the perceived need of a bracing climate to bolster the boy's still delicate health.

But Malvern, at which Crowley remained for three terms concluding in 1892, left no great impression upon Crowley, and Crowley reciprocated in kind, failing to win any academic prizes or to place on the Honors list. When, after three terms, he had come to dislike the regimen at Malvern, he invented "abominations" concerning conditions at the school such that mother Emily gladly withdrew him. Crowley looked forward to the greater freedom of private tutors. But Emily thwarted him here, promptly enrolling him in the Tonbridge School, where he remained for the Lent, Summer, and Christmas terms of 1892.

Crowley, who turned seventeen while at Tonbridge, now at last—through holidays filled with vigorous fishing and climbing—recovered his physical health. As a result, he was exultantly feeling his oats. "By the time I reached Tonbridge I had developed a kind of natural aristocracy. People were already beginning to be afraid of me and there was no question any longer of bullying."

Again, Crowley failed to win academic honors. The problem was lack of application. Crowley, who had no doubts as to his intelligence, could not bring himself to work to please his masters. But if the masters of Malvern and Tonbridge failed to inspire Crowley, at least they did not terrify him as Champney had. This eased the need to lash out at all things Christian. As Crowley explained it: "The problem of life was not how to satanize [. . .] it was simply to escape from the oppressors and to enjoy the world without interference of spiritual life of any sort." The boy who had always lived in an atmosphere of acute spiritual tension— whether under his mother, his uncle, or a strict schoolmaster—was now resolved upon exploring the sexual realm.

But not even sex—one might better say, sex least of all—could remain outside of the spiritual domain for Crowley. As Crowley himself put it: "Pleasure as such has never attracted me. It must be spiced by moral satisfaction." The most delectable moral satisfaction came from defying authority. But his inexperience led to a sexual mishap that necessitated withdrawal from Tonbridge at the end of 1892. Crowley contracted gonorrhea from a liaison with a Glasgow prostitute. There was nothing unusual in young male members of the British upper class seeking out prostitutes. Yet Crowley felt a lasting embarrassment over the incident, as evidenced by the fact that he never directly spoke of it in his published writings. In one account, he blames the "vile system"— Victorian Evangelicalism and its refusal to educate young men as to the facts of life—for handing him over "bound and blindfold to the outraged majesty of nature."

Crowley may have been compelled ignobly to depart Tonbridge, but his family maintained its resolve to keep him in a school setting. A compromise of a kind was reached. He would live with a Brethren tutor in Eastbourne, but he would also attend day classes at Eastbourne College. Predictably, Crowley found the tutor restrictive and once engaged in an all-out fistfight with him. His studies at Eastbourne were more productive, especially in chemistry and in French language and literature. He also joined the chess team. Crowley had learned the game at age six, but Eastbourne was his first competitive setting and he shined, beating the adult town champion and writing a chess column for the local paper.

Also at this time, Crowley blossomed as an athlete. The sport of rock climbing now became both an escape and an ecstatic employment of physical and strategic skills. In 1892, at age sixteen, during a visit with his mother to Skye, he devoted himself in earnest to mastering technique. By the following summer, he had progressed sufficiently to scale the four highest fells in the vicinity of Langdale in a marathon single-day climb. But Crowley's favorite site for climbing was Beachy Head, a chalk cliff face near Eastbourne. As he later explained: "Chalk is probably the most dangerous and difficult of all kinds of rock. Its condition varies at every step. Often one has to clear away an immense amount of debris in order to get any hold at all. Yet indiscretion in this operation might pull down a few hundred tons on one's head." It was on Beachy Head that Crowley perfected a style of climbing that would set him apart from his contemporaries. As sudden movements could lead to disaster on chalk, Crowley—who as a young man was lithe of build, but without exceptional strength—was forced to adopt a sinuous approach, with his body in continuous movement. As he wrote: "One does not climb the cliffs. One hardly even crawls. Trickles or oozes would perhaps be the ideal verbs." Crowley enjoyed the Beachy Head setting so greatly that he resided there for some weeks in a small tent. "It was," he enthused, "my first experience of camp life which is, one thing with another, the best life I know. The mere feeling of being in the fresh air under the stars when one goes to sleep, and of waking at dawn because it is dawn, raises one's animal life ipso facto to the level of poetry." It would be one of Crowley's later marks, as a magician, to test his capacities in rigorous outdoor settings.

Crowley joined the Scottish Mountaineering Club in 1894 and made his first trip to the Alps that same year. The Alps would become Crowley's favorite vacation site during his years at Cambridge University (from 1895 to 1898), and it was on the Alpine slopes that Crowley formed influential friendships—and animosities—within the climbing community that would shape considerably the course of his early manhood. His impressive list of Alpine climbs included the first guideless traverse of the Monch, the first descent of the west face of the Trifthorn, and a challenging ascent of the north-northeast ridge of Mont Collon. Amongst the prominent British climbers who would testify as to Crowley's skills during this period were T. S. Blakeney, Norman Collie, Sir Martin Conway and Tom Longstaff, who deemed Crowley "a fine climber, if an unconventional one." Collie, with Conway as a second, proposed Crowley for membership in the prestigious English Alpine Club in 1898. But Crowley was rejected—a snub he never forgave.

In October 1895, Crowley turned twenty. He now cut a distinguished figure as a young man of means. It was to Cambridge that Crowley was sent for his final polishing as a gentleman. His subsequent three years at Trinity College, Cambridge, were among the happiest of his life, and constituted the seal of his emancipation from family authority and the Brethren creed. Crowley never took a degree at Cambridge, declining to take the final formal steps to receive his diploma on the grounds that it was unbefitting of and unnecessary to a gentleman: "I had no intention of becoming a parson or a schoolmaster, to write B.A. after my name would have been a decided waste of ink." Nonetheless, his identification with Trinity College was intense. His first rooms were at 16 St. John's Street, overlooking St. John's Chapel. During his opening term, Crowley resolved to devote himself to English literature. His reading during these years is striking both for its breadth and for the persistence of its influence. The greatest of his passions at this time was the poet Shelley, whose exaltation of individual freedom thrilled him. Sir Richard Burton, the late Victorian scholar, poet, and travel writer who had, in midcentury, journeyed in disguise to Mecca, emerged as a model against whom Crowley could measure his own future course. Burton wrote enthralling accounts of his adventures, both physical and spiritual. He also composed *The Kasidah*, an English poem in which Burton, under the pseudonym Haji Abdu el-Yezdi, successfully took on the style and outlook of classical Sufi poets such as Hafiz and Omar Khayyam. Crowley would adopt, in certain later works (particularly those dealing with his bisexual range of desire), this same pseudonymous approach to the framing of controversial ideas, playing with the preconceptions of the reader as Burton had done by adopting a romantic name from the East.

With ample funds at his disposal, Crowley the student purchased books (often in fine printings, such as the Kelmscott Press edition of Chaucer) in great quantity and lined his rooms with them from floor to ceiling, further filling four revolving walnut bookcases. Having perfected his sanctum, Crowley nonetheless shied away from the role of a bookish intellectual:

> I spent the whole of my time in reading. It was very rare that I got to bed before daylight. But I had a horror of being thought a 'smug'; and what I was doing was a secret from my nearest friends. Whenever they were about I was playing chess and cards. In the daytime I went canoeing or cycling. I had no occupations which brought me into close touch with any great body of undergraduates. I even gave up the habit of going round to see people, though I was always at home to anyone who chose to call.

It was in his private quarters (he remained at 16 St. John's Street his first two years, then divided his time between 35 Sidney Street and 14 Trinity Street in the final year of 1897–98)—and not in the lecture halls—that Crowley carried on the bulk of his studies at Trinity. In his general examinations, which focused primarily on mathematics and the classics, he always earned a respectable "second class," but for one "first class" showing in the Easter Term of 1897.

Crowley cut an impressive enough figure when he did go forth from his rooms, adopting the fashionable Decadent style. His wardrobe was replete with pure silk shirts and outsized floppy bow ties; he favored gaudy rings set with semiprecious mineral stones. While Crowley later described himself as largely indifferent to his classmates, this seems to have been a retrospective romantic pose. Crowley was, in fact, active in the Magpie and Stump, a Trinity debating society that met weekly in the lecture rooms of the Old Court. The Magpie and Stump had the ambiance of a gentleman's private club. Crowley wrote in his *Confessions* that he could not take the Magpie and Stump seriously: "It seemed to me absurd for these young asses to emit their callow opinions on important subjects." But the weekly records disclose that Crowley was an active member with an all-but-perfect attendance record over the period 1895–97; only in his final year at Cambridge did his devotion begin to wane. As members could choose their sides on debate, the record of Crowley's stances is of some interest in determining his views as a young man. He defended the proposition "That genius is only a manifestation of insanity"; this was a commonplace theory in the nineties, fostered by the then-influential writings of the German thinker Max Nordau, and it was one that long continued to intrigue Crowley. He opposed the proposition "That black is white", though he would soon enough come to regard the union of contradictions as the keystone to spiritual progress. Regrettably, there is no record of Crowley's participation on the night of February 19, 1897, when the members of the Magpie and Stump voted—by an 11–8 margin—in favor of the proposition that "This House sympathizes with Satan in his sorrows." This vote by his peers casts light on the tendency, common within Crowley's generation, to regard Satan as more a romantic than an evil figure. Crowley was far from alone in his rebellion against Christian morals, though he distinguished himself in the lengths to which he would carry it.

Crowley was also active in the university Chess Club. In his freshman year, he promptly triumphed over its president. It was then arranged for him to play H. E. Atkins, who would go on to become the seven-time

amateur champion of England. Atkins trounced him, and Crowley had
for the first time encountered his decisive better at chess. Undeterred,
Crowley went on to devote two hours a day to the game by his second
year at Cambridge. His frank ambition was to become a world champion. But during the long vacation of 1897, Crowley visited Berlin while
a major chess conference was underway. The sight of his ultimate ambition promptly cured him of it:

> I had hardly entered the room where the masters were playing
> when I was seized with what may justly be described as a mys-
> tical experience. I seemed to be looking on at the tournament
> from outside myself. I saw the masters—one, shabby and blear-
> eyed; another, in badly fitting would-be respectable shoddy; a
> third, a mere parody of humanity, and so on for the rest. These
> were the people to whose ranks I was seeking admission. 'There,
> but for the grace of God, goes Aleister Crowley,' I exclaimed to
> myself with disgust, and then and there I registered a vow never
> to play another serious game of chess.

The sermons of father Edward as to the limits of worldly ambition
had once again shown their power. A similar realization deflected Crowley from the only practical career choice that he entertained during his
Cambridge days: that of entering the British Diplomatic Service. Crowley could afford to ignore the problem of earning a living once he left
Cambridge—he was due to come into an inherited fortune of some
£40,000. But politics, dressed in the conservative forms of courtly intrigue and romantic ritual, held a sufficient allure for Crowley to consider a diplomatic career. While at Cambridge, he took up the study of
Russian in order to qualify himself for service at what he regarded as
the most brilliant of European courts, that of the Czar at St. Petersburg.
Indeed, Crowley journeyed to St. Petersburg to study Russian on its native soil during the long vacation of 1897, though he seems never to
have progressed in the language. The special lure of diplomacy for
Crowley—as he wrote in the *Confessions*—was that it afforded "the
greatest opportunities for worldly enjoyment, while at the same time
demanding the highest qualities of mind. The subtlety of intrigue has
always fascinated me."

The urge for intrigue remained, but the pursuit of a diplomatic career
ended abruptly in October 1897, when Crowley fell ill. His condition
was not life-threatening, but he nonetheless felt himself drawn to consider seriously his own mortality for the first time:

There was no fear of death or of a possible 'hereafter'; but I was appalled by the idea of the futility of all human endeavor. Suppose, I said to myself, that I make a great success in diplomacy and become ambassador to Paris. There was no good in that—I could not so much as remember the name of the ambassador a hundred years ago.[. . .]

I did not go into a definite trance in this meditation; but a spiritual consciousness was born in me corresponding to that which characterizes the Vision of the Universal Sorrow, as I learnt to call it later on. In Buddhist phraseology, I perceived the First Noble Truth—*Sabbe Pi Dukkham*—everything is sorrow.

Following upon his renunciation of chess by only a few short months, this October 1897 experience confirmed for Crowley that no worldly career could satisfy his personal longings. The key was to find that which was "immune from the forces of change"—a paradoxical goal when one considers that Crowley would come to define the essence of the art and science of magick as that of "causing Change to occur in conformity with Will."

What course lay open to him? "Spiritual facts" were alone worthy of his attention. As it happened, Crowley had recently encountered just such a "fact." Nine months earlier, on New Year's Eve 1897, Crowley was spending his holiday vacation from Cambridge in Stockholm. At midnight, there occurred an upheaval that Crowley only elusively delineates in the *Confessions:* "I was awakened to the knowledge that I possessed a magical means of becoming conscious of and satisfying a part of my nature which had up to that moment concealed itself from me. It was an experience of horror and pain, combined with a certain ghostly terror, yet at the same time, it was the key to the purest and holiest spiritual ecstasy that exists." In *The Equinox of the Gods,* however, Crowley provided a further telling clue when he described himself, on this night, as having been "Admitted to the Military Order of the Temple." The part of Crowley's "nature" that had until now been concealed from him was his bisexuality, revealed through his first homoerotic experience.

What Crowley claimed to have experienced here, by way of his sexual awakenings, was the goal of magical invocation—an encounter with an immanent deity. This is confirmed by an admittedly florid and veiled account of this same New Year's Eve in *The Temple of Solomon the King* (1909), authored by J. F. C. Fuller but editorially supervised by Crowley. This account does plainly indicate, however, that the Christian view of redemption and grace was still predominant in Crowley's psyche, for all his claims of having left it behind, in adolescence, with his lost virginity:

> Then came the great awakening. Curious to say, it was toward the hour of midnight on the last day of the year when the old slinks away from the new, that he happened to be riding alone, wrapped in the dark cloak of unutterable thoughts.[. . .] Freedom had he sought, but not the freedom that he had gained. Blood seemed to ooze from his eyelids and trickle down, drop by drop, upon the white snow, writing on its pure surface the name of Christ. Great bats flitted by him and vultures whose bald heads were clotted with rotten blood. "Ah! the world, the world . . . the failure of the world." And then an amber light surged round him, the fearful tapestry of torturing thought was rent asunder the voices of many angels sang to him. "Master! Master!" he cried, "I have found thee . . . O silver Christ. . . . "
>
> Then all was Nothingness . . . nothing . . . nothing . . . nothing, and madly his horse carried him into the night.
>
> Thus he set out on his mystic quest toward that goal which he had seen, and which seemed so near, and yet, as we shall learn, proved to be so far away.

The experience stirred Crowley, but he was rather more bewildered than enlightened. For all that, it would be a mistake to doubt his sincerity. During the following year of 1897—the same year that chess and diplomacy fell by the wayside—there arose in Crowley a passion for esoteric knowledge into the very basis of existence. This passion would never abate. The path had been chosen.

As a young man of means, intellect, and romantic inclinations, Crowley carried on his "mystic quest" with a flourish. His first field of study was alchemy, the rigorously experimental blending of the physical and spiritual realms. Crowley drew sustenance from some of the basic alchemical terms and principles. "Vitriol," one of the suggested primary materials for creation of the Philosopher's Stone, was an acronym for this Hermetic clue, *Visita Interiora Terrae Rectificando Invenies Occultam Lapiderm:* Visit the Interior of the Earth and by Purifying you will Find the Secret Stone. Further, the Renaissance physician and magus Paracelsus pointed out that the alchemical elements sulfur (fiery, male, soul) and salt (passive, female, body) can form a transcendent union with "philosophical mercury" (flux, bisexual, spirit). Reconciling these three elements led one to the Philosopher's Stone, the medicine of souls.

All this was suggestive for Crowley. There was a possibility of spiritual ascent, even adventure, through active knowledge of the world and oneself.

But alchemy, for Crowley, did not possess the allure of ritual magic. Alchemy was an all too gradual purification. Magic was the direct and empowering contact with the divine. As he wrote in *Magick* of the systole and diastole of invocation and evocation: "In invocation, the macrocosm floods the consciousness. In evocation, the magician, having become the macrocosm, creates a microcosm." Evocation by way of traditional magical ceremony—the rituals of the medieval grimoires, or magical textbooks—enabled one to pay "special attention to the desired part of yourself[. . .] It is the potting-out and watering of a particular flower in the garden, and the exposure of it to the sun."

This special focus on desired qualities within oneself was irresistible to the young Crowley. But the process of evocation invited indulgence of the worst sorts of personal obsession. And for Crowley, release from the thrall of Christian dualism and sin was an obsession par excellence. Small wonder that his first stumbling steps toward magical practice involved a fascination with heresy. Later, in the *Confessions*, he wrote with arrogant ablomb: "The forces of good were those which had constantly oppressed me. I saw them daily destroying the happiness of my fellow-men. Since, therefore, it was my business to explore the spiritual world, my first step must be to get into personal communication with the devil." But in a contemporaneous account—a prologue to his first book of verse, *Aceldama* (1898)—Crowley told of the anguish he felt at this time in pitting his own spiritual explorations against the accepted Christian God. In December 1897, he sought the advice of C. G. Lamb, a demonstrator in the Cambridge engineering department:

> It was a windy night, that memorable seventh night of December, when this philosophy was born in me. How the grave old Professor wondered at my ravings! I had called at his house, for he was a valued friend of mine, and I felt strange thoughts and emotions shake within me. Ah! how I raved! I called to him to trample me, he would not. We passed together into the stormy nigh. I was on horseback, how I galloped around him in my phrenzy, till he became the prey of a real physical fear! How I shrieked out I know not what strange words! And the poor good old man tried all he could to calm me; he thought I was mad! The fool! I was in the death struggle with self: God and Satan fought for my soul those three long hours. God conquered—

now I have only one doubt left—which of the twain was God? Howbeit, I aspire!

The "death struggle" may have been "with self," but Crowley staged the struggle in terms of the dramatic dichotomy of God and Satan. Given such protagonists, the potentially pivotal role of ceremonial magic was obvious. A chance recommendation by a Cambridge bookseller led Crowley to a collection of medieval grimoire extracts edited with extensive commentary by A. E. Waite and luridly titled (by its London publisher) *The Book of Black Magic and Pacts* (1898). Waite was a mystically inclined man of letters and a scholar of esoteric lore against whom Crowley would direct—in the decades to come—a persistent and largely unjust stream of critical abuse. But he would never deny that it was Waite who served as his first influential guide into the world of magic. Waite had intimated in his text that there was an organization that had preserved the true rites of initiation—as to which black magic was but a defiled reflection. Crowley promptly wrote to the elder Waite an admiring letter in which he earnestly requested aid in contacting this organization. Waite replied with a missive suggesting that Crowley read *The Cloud Upon the Sanctuary* by the German Councillor Karl von Eckartshausen (1752-1813). This Crowley proceeded to do at Watsdale Head during Easter vacation in 1898.

The Cloud Upon the Sanctuary was the single most influential text—after the Bible and *The Book of the Law*—in the whole of Crowley's life. Eckartshausen presented, in an ornate style, the mystical thesis that there exists an "invisible and interior Church" or "society of the Elect" that exists quite apart from any established church. The text of *Cloud* is dominated by pious Christian imagery, which only served to further its impact upon Crowley. As he later summarized it: "The incarnation was a mystical or magical operation which took place in every man. Each was himself the Son of God who had assumed a body of flesh and blood in order to perform the work of redemption."

At the time that Crowley was reading *Cloud* at Watsdale Head, he was on vacation with the one person with whom, during his years at Cambridge, he had fallen deeply in love. This was Herbert Charles Pollitt (who preferred to go by the first name of Jerome), four years Crowley's senior, who had already earned a bachelor's and master's degree from Cambridge but remained in residence in the town as a widely admired entertainer. The source of Pollitt's renown was his performances as a dancer and female impersonator for the university Footlights Dramatic Club, of which Pollitt had served as president in 1896. Female impersonations were a staple of the male-dominated club, and Pollitt was well within Footlights tradition in creating his own female character, the elegant "Diane de Rougy" (modeled after the flamboyant Parisian dancer Liane de Pougy). Amongst Pollitt's most popular acts was a convincingly sensuous performance of a "Serpentine Dance." Indeed, *The Cambridge A.B.C.*, a satirical magazine, described Pollitt as an *"androgyne troublant . . . ou troublante gynandre,"* charges that Crowley may have been recalling when he stressed, in the *Confessions,* that Pollitt showed not the "slightest symptoms" of androgyny. But Pollitt's performance in *The Mixture Remixed*—a music hall farce—drew raves from a local reviewer who declared that Diane de Rougy, in a dark wig and successive silk outfits of white, black, and silver, danced "in a manner which would make many women green with envy.[. . .] he reminded me forcibly of one of Rosetti's women brought to life."

According to Crowley, this stage allure sadly did not carry over to Pollitt's day-to-day male existence. "Pollitt was rather plain than otherwise. His face was made tragic by the terrible hunger of the eyes and the bitter sadness of the mouth." Crowley and Pollitt met in the lodgings of the president of the Footlights Club in October 1897. Relations between them soon grew impassioned and consciously exalted. Consider Pollitt's customary line of farewell at each parting between them: "To the reseeing I kiss your hands and feet." But in the *Confessions,* Crowley cannot speak of their relationship without indignant—and false—denial of its physical erotic component:

> The relation between us was that ideal intimacy which the Greeks considered the greatest glory of manhood and the most precious prize of life. It says much for the moral state of England that such ideas are connected in the minds of practically every one with physical passion.[. . .]
>
> To him I was a mind—no more.[. . .]
>
> It was the purest and noblest relation which I had ever had with anybody. I had not imagined the possibility of so divine a development. It was, in a sense, passionate, because it partook of the white heat of creative energy and because its intensity absorbed all other emotions. But for this very reason it was impossible to conceive of it as liable to contamination by any grosser qualities. Indeed, the universe of sense was entirely subordinated to its sanctity.

It is startling—this uneasy, self-righteous protestation by a man who is known to the world as a shameless sensualist. As a matter of societal perception, Crowley was deeply ashamed of his homosexual aspect, as it conflicted with his status as a manly gentleman coming of age. Crowley was willing to be iconoclastic when it came to Christianity, but he felt compelled to take a virulent stance against the effeminate decadence— as perceived by late Victorian society—of homosexuals. The famous libel action that brought down Oscar Wilde took place in 1895—Crowley's first year at Cambridge—and feelings ran high in the academic milieu as to the justness of Wilde's imprisonment. The young Crowley, who might have been expected to admire so articulate a rebel, took precisely the opposite approach. In his *Mysteries: Lyrical and Dramatic* (1898), Crowley included a scathing verse attack—written in December 1897, two months *after* meeting Pollitt—against a Cambridge homosexual (possibly Pollitt himself) who had championed Wilde's cause.

As Crowley took care to stress in the *Confessions*, he was heterosexually active throughout his college days, the bulk of his affairs being brief and unemotional liaisons either with prostitutes or young women who resided in the town. He insisted that forty-eight hours of abstinence were "sufficient to dull the fine edge of my mind." As a result, he was compelled to devote otherwise valuable time to finding partners: "The stupidity of having had to waste priceless hours in chasing what ought to have been brought to the back door every evening with the milk!" There was more than inconvenience to contend with; in 1897, Crowley contracted a case of syphilis and had to undergo mercurializing treatments. The misogynist bluster in the *Confessions* underscores just how outraged, during his Cambridge days, Crowley was by his heterosexual relations. They were openly permitted, and yet he could find in them no worth to equal that of Pollitt: "They had no true moral ideals. They were bound up with their necessary preoccupation, which was the function of reproduction.[. . .] Intellectually, of course, they did not exist."

In January 1898, Crowley took rooms at 14 Trinity Street, in which he and Pollitt spent much time together. The decor, as described by Crowley in a later unpublished short story, "The Sage," reflected his growing commitment to magic, a commitment that Pollitt could not embrace:

In this room of contradiction there was one corner more curious even than any. Elsewhere the floor was covered with a carpet;

rich sombre peacock blue with an uncertain snaky pattern of deep purple; but here was laid a circular Venetian mosaic. Around its edge ran a band of white marble stones, with what was apparently an inscription. The characters were those of an unfamiliar language; they were inlaid in vivid red. Within this band the circle was yellow of a tint suggesting jaundice; the repellent effect was emphasized by the devices, crabbed and crooked, wrought in it of some sickly green eloquent of all unwholesomeness from mal-de-mer and arsenic to carrion in corruption, and even by the formidably severe lines of the great black star of six points in the unicursal drawing of which sensitive spirits might divine an intention of brutal perversity and blasphemous diabolism.

Until his affair with Pollitt, Crowley had consciously avoided the literary coteries of his own generation. But Pollitt offered Crowley an easy entree into the Decadent world, and he took advantage of it. Amongst the personages he met was the Decadent artist *par excellence*, Aubrey Beardsley, who was to die later that year. At root, however, the Decadents failed to appeal to Crowley; the gist of his complaint against them was similar to that which he leveled against Pollitt: a pessimism that failed to take into account the rich spiritual possibilities of life. As Crowley later wrote:

The intense refinement of its thought and the blazing brilliance of its technique helped me to key myself up to a pitch of artistry entirely beyond my original scope; but I never allowed myself to fall under its dominion. I was determined to triumph, to find my way out on the other side. To me it is a question of virility.[. . .] No matter to what depths I plumb, I always end with my wings beating steadily upwards toward the sun.

Due in part to Pollitt's influence, the year 1898 became a watershed for Crowley's poetic ambitions, which he fostered by publishing himself. The practice of an author himself bearing printing costs and then being distributed by a publisher (who, bearing no financial risk, was generally willing to consign titles regardless of sales potential) did not then bear the "vanity press" stigma that it does today. The publisher whom Crowley chose was another member of Pollitt's milieu, Leonard Smithers, who is best remembered as the only British publisher to have had the courage to publish works by Oscar Wilde—most notably *The*

Ballad of Reading Gaol (1898) and *The Importance of Being Earnest* (1899)—in the aftermath of Wilde's trial. Smithers also produced fine editions of late Victorian erotica, and sold Crowley at least one title in this genre. To evade prosecution for pornography, Smithers employed such tactics as the use of blatantly pseudonymous author names and places of publication. Crowley relished the satiric possibilities here, as well as the practical benefits, and wasted little time in employing them himself.

Smithers served as the designer and publisher of Crowley's first two books of poems—*Aceldama,* and the notorious erotic collection *White Stains*—both published in 1898. These are the two most important works of Crowley's prolix Cambridge years. Consider the sheer output Crowley achieved as a young poet—it underscores his ambition here, which survived even after chess and diplomacy had been decisively rejected. His subsequent books of this period were printed by a man recommended to Crowley by Smithers (who went bankrupt in 1899): Charles Thomas Jacobi, manager of the Chiswick Press. These include *The Tale of Archais* (1898), *Songs of the Spirit* (1898), *The Poem* (1898), *Mysteries: Lyrical and Dramatic* (1898); and *Jephthah and Other Mysteries* (1899). In general, it may be said that Crowley's early poetry is rich in ideas—drawing especially upon the Bible and Christian theology, esoteric lore, classical mythology, and philosophy—but woefully short on original imagery and organic musicality. But there were two contexts in which Crowley's verse could take life: spiritual perplexity and erotic obsession. These two contexts are exemplified by *Aceldama* and *White Stains*, respectively. They are each remarkable in terms of psychology, and especially so given the age of their author. For quite different reasons, Crowley published each pseudonymously.

The full title of Crowley's first book is *Aceldama, a Place to Bury Strangers In. A Philosophical Poem.* On its title page, the author is indicated only as "a gentleman of the University of Cambridge"—an homage to Shelley, whose *The Necessity of Atheism* (1811) had been published by the young poet—just before his expulsion from Oxford—as the work of a "Gentleman of the University of Oxford." Crowley paid for one hundred copies to be printed, two on pure vellum, ten on a kind of paper known as Japanese vellum, and eighty-eight in an "ordinary" edition on handmade paper. Although few copies were sold, and the one review the book received deprecated its morals, Crowley was delighted by the publication. "My scheme *from the first,*" he would later confide, with respect to the design and issuance of his books, "was to create complexity and rarity."

Aceldama consists solely of the title poem, which runs some thirty-two stanzas. "Aceldama" means "Bloody Field" in ancient Hebrew and is the name of the field Judas purchased with the pieces of silver earned for betraying Jesus. On that field, the Book of Acts tells us, Judas fell headlong and burst asunder, his entrails pouring out. The "silver Christ" whom Crowley encountered in Stockholm on New Year's Eve 1897 returns in the penultimate stanza of *Aceldama* as a final hope after an arid and difficult spiritual quest:

> Master! I think that I have found thee now:
>> Deceive me not, I trust thee, I am sure
>> Thy love will stand while ocean winds endure.
> Our quest shall be our quest till either brow
>> Radiate light, till death himself allure
>>> Our love to him
>> When life's desires are filled beyond the silver brim.

If *Aceldama* was the outpouring of Crowley's "unconscious self," *White Stains* was—if you accept Crowley's account—a conscious strategy by his artistic self to explore the roots of sexual and spiritual decay. The young Crowley invented—as the persona for the "magical affirmations" of *White Stains*—a young English poet named George Archibald Bishop (a snipe at Uncle Tom Bond Bishop), a contemporary of Swinburne and a forerunner of the Decadents; Bishop is identified on the title page as a "Neuropath of the Second Empire." As if one authorial veil were not enough, Crowley coined another: An anonymous, sanctimonious editor who provides a scholarly "Preface" which warns that the book is for the eyes of "Mental Pathologists" alone. The poems that follow run the gamut of the prominent perversions in the judgment of the late Victorian era: lesbianism, homosexuality, bisexuality, bestiality, sadism, masochism, priapic lust worshipped as the life force, necrophilia.

It would have been legally imprudent for Crowley to adopt a less rigorous rationale for *White Stains*. Even in 1898, it was a necessary caution for publisher Smithers to have the typesetting done abroad by a Dutch firm. Crowley would not, or could not, publicly acknowledge that *White Stains* reflected his own sexual fears and desires. There is, for example, a joyous poem in praise of homosexual love in the bottom position, "A Ballad of Passive Paederasty," which deserves a place in any wide-ranging anthology of gay poetry. Crowley's own delight—and "shame"—with Pollitt as a lover is manifest:

Of man's delight and man's desire
   In one thing is now weariness—
To feel the fury of the fire,
   And writhe within the close caress
Of fierce embrace, and wanton kiss,
And final nuptial done aright,
   How sweet a passion, shame, is this,
A strong man's love is my delight!

There was, in addition to the "shame," a further barrier between the two men. Pollitt had no enthusiasm for Crowley's magic, no optimism to match Crowley's own sense of possible attainments. As Crowley later wrote, "I felt in my subconscious self that I must choose between my devotion to him and to the Secret Assembly of the Saints." The farewell scene between them is one of the very rare instances in the *Confessions* in which Crowley displays remorse and regret:

> I told him frankly and firmly that I had given by life to religion and that he did not fit into the scheme. I see now how imbecile I was, how hideously wrong and weak it is to reject any part of one's personality. Yet these mistakes are not mistakes at the time: one has to pass through such periods; one must be ruthless in analysis and complete it, before one can proceed to synthesis. He understood that I was not to be turned from my purpose and we parted, never to meet again. [. . .]
>
> It has been my lifelong regret, for a nobler and purer comradeship never existed on this earth, and his influence might have done much to temper my subsequent trials.

The "part" of his "personality" that Crowley here tacitly acknowledged having rejected was his homosexual aspect. Pollitt went on to serve in the Royal Army Medical Corps during World War One. He died in London in 1942.

As Crowley's Cambridge years came to an end in May 1898, he had reached a life resolution. He would find the Hidden Church, the Secret Assembly of Chiefs, alluded to by Eckartshausen. He had no career ambitions; the inheritance from father Edward had made them unnecessary, at least for the time being. Meanwhile, he spent as he wished. His youthful profligacy would come to haunt Crowley in the final decades of his life, when—having exhausted the fortune that, carefully husbanded, could have sustained him for life—he would live for extended periods on the bitter edge of poverty. Crowley blamed Bishop and mother Emily for his lack of thrift: "I was taught to expect every possible luxury. Nothing was too good for me; and I had no idea of what anything cost. It was all paid for behind my back[. . .] I doubt whether any one in history was ever furnished with such a completely rotten preparation for the management of practical affairs."

One can only wonder as to the result had Bishop seriously attempted to restrict Crowley's spending; as it was, Crowley strongly resented his uncle's restraints on allowable pocket money (as opposed to credit)—in the vain hope that limits on cash would discourage splurges on books, theater, tobacco, and women. Crowley's later magical philosophy forbade both the earning of money through magic and any haggling over the price of books and materials necessary to one's magical work.

If Crowley had no practical career in mind, he nonetheless was fired by at least one worldly aspiration. Fame, above all, was the laurel he wished for. So intent was Crowley that, in its pursuit, he had chosen a new first name for himself while at Cambridge. A book he had read suggested that the ideal measure for a famous name was a dactyl followed by a trochee. Crowley had long loathed his common first name of Alick, particularly because "it was the name by which my mother called me."

And so Crowley chose Aleister, a variant Gaelic form of his middle name Alexander, and an homage to the contemplative hero of Shelley's poem, "Alastor of The Spirit of Solitude." Aleister Crowley was thus born, a name Crowley described tellingly in the *Confessions* as a *"nom de guerre."* He added sanguinely that "I can't say that I feel sure that I facilitated the process of becoming famous. I should doubtless have done so, whatever name I had chosen."

CHAPTER TWO

In Which Aleister Crowley Takes the Magical Name Perdurabo ("I Shall Endure to the End") But Appears to Lose His Way Amidst the Schisms of the Golden Dawn and the Temptations of this Vale of Tears (1898–1900)

In three spheres—poetry, mountain climbing, and spiritual truth—Crowley yearned for ultimate achievement, while possessing but a callow understanding of the world outside the manicured lawns of Trinity. The loftiness of his goals, and the persistent onset of unforeseen difficulties, combined to produce in him a fervor and a tension that set him apart from his contemporaries. For good or ill, the Crowley of young manhood was a figure whom none, it would seem, could encounter without vehement reaction.

In each of these three spheres, Crowley retained—for all his ambition—a realistic sense of himself as a mere aspirant. As a result, he was open to influence from friends and mentors to an extent that had not showed itself since the death of his father eleven years before, and would not recur in his maturity. Thus, in the year following his May 1898 departure from Cambridge, Crowley formed a series of remarkably fateful friendships.

The first of these—which one could assign to the sphere of artistic ambition—was begun in a Cambridge bookshop in May 1898, just as Crowley was about to leave academia behind. Crowley's debut volume of verse, *Aceldama*, drew the interest of an undergraduate, four years Crowley's junior, named Gerald Festus Kelly. Soon thereafter, Kelly met Crowley who, with his large, dark eyes and lank of brown hair falling over his brow, fit the part of the soulful poet. Kelly had more the look of a bantam, with a thrusting chin and a patrician nose and brow.

Kelly would go on to enjoy a career as one of the foremost British portrait painters of the twentieth century. By the time of his death in 1972, he was Sir Gerald Kelly, the onetime president of the august British Royal Academy. His youthful friendship with the notorious Aleister Crowley had become, in retrospect, an embarrassment. But it was a vital friendship in its time, fostered by shared artistic ambitions and by certain formative parallels in their backgrounds.

For Kelly was also the son of a clergyman, the Reverend Frederick Festus Kelly, the Anglican vicar of St. Giles. The reverend did his utmost to instill religion in his son, but failed. So it was that both Kelly and Crowley looked upon Cambridge as a sanctuary from the restraints of family and religion. Both, of course, continued to draw financially upon their well-heeled families. Kelly, in his later years, offered a simple explanation of what drew them together. "I liked him; we made each other laugh; but he was a *poseur*, a great pretender to scholarship and languages." The sense of Crowley as a *poseur* came much later for Kelly. In his youth, he regarded Crowley as the most religious man he had ever met—including his own pious father. Crowley succeeded, in the first years of their friendship, in enticing Kelly to dabble in magical ritual. Dabbling was as far as Kelly went. Their strongest bond was their support of one another as emerging artists. From 1898 to 1905, Crowley submitted virtually all of his poetry to Kelly for initial comment. When Kelly was, on rare occasion, disapproving, Crowley was genuinely anguished.

In the summer of 1898, Crowley formed his second great friendship of this year. Oscar Eckenstein, sixteen years Crowley's senior, was a mountain climber who embodied the physical and mental discipline that Crowley saw as the essential values of athleticism. As Crowley later put it with admirable candor. "Eckenstein recognized from the first the value of my natural instincts for mountaineering, and also that I was one of the silliest young asses alive." It was to Eckenstein that Crowley would owe his considerable progress as a climber.

Eckenstein was born in London in 1859, the son of a German socialist father and an English mother. Iconoclasm was a family trademark, and Eckenstein manifested it by growing a massive brown beard, dressing with absolute disregard for his appearance, and walking about London—in good weather and bad—in straw sandals. For all this vigorous activity, Eckenstein suffered from the same chronic asthma as did Crowley.

Eccentricities aside, Eckenstein was a markedly practical man. He took degrees in chemistry at London and Bonn, and early on secured a position as a railway engineer that afforded him financial security and the flexibility to travel abroad for long periods, so as to pursue his passion for mountaineering. In 1892, Eckenstein was a key member of the expedition led by Sir William Martin Conway to the Karakoam range of the Himalayas; Eckenstein later wrote an acerbic account, *The Karakoams and Kashmir: an account of a journey* (1896), in which the patronizing use of "journey" made it clear that Eckenstein viewed the famed Conway as a timid leader and a spoiled favorite of the Alpine Club—a British institution that Eckenstein, remarkably, managed to despise even more than did Crowley. (Unlike Crowley, however, Eckenstein never applied for admission.)

Eckenstein shared with Crowley a passion for the writings of Sir Richard Burton, the Victorian explorer and man of letters. Eckenstein amassed a rare collection of books and documents by or relating to Burton that he later bequeathed to the Royal Asiatic Society. There is this testimony from a friend of Eckenstein's, a fellow railroad man: "O.E. often spoke of him [Burton] to me, in our talks about the philosophies of India and the East, and I do know that it was O.E.'s and Burton's intense interest in Eastern philosophies, especially mental telepathy, which brought them together at one time." Telepathy is a technique utilized by advanced Sufis, with whom Burton had studied firsthand during his travels. Whether Eckenstein possessed knowledge of Sufi techniques is unknown. Oddly, Eckenstein seems never to have confided his meeting with Burton to Crowley, for Crowley surely would have mentioned it in the *Confessions,* which included this paean to the two men: "Sir Richard Burton was my hero and Eckenstein his modern representative, so far as my external life was concerned." Eckenstein would come to take a role in the development of Crowley's inner as well as "external" life, and perhaps the connection with Burton explains why he was capable of doing so.

How distinguished a climber was Eckenstein? The question is important, because Crowley claimed so very much for his friend—and, tangentially, for himself—as a tactician and mountaineer. The world records (at the time) asserted by Crowley for Eckenstein and himself included "the greatest pace uphill over 16,000 feet—4,000 feet in 1 hour 23 minutes on Iztaccihuatl in 1900." This was a peak in Mexico on which Crowley and Eckenstein trained together in preparation for their 1902 Himalayan expedition to Chogo Ri or K2 (the world's second highest mountain), an adventure to be described in Chapter Three, which produced a putative world record of its own—"the greatest number of days spent on a glacier—65 days on the Baltoro." The Alpine Club never recognized these achievements, but then it is doubtful that Crowley or Eckenstein ever informed the Club of them.

As for athleticism and technique, Crowley recalled that "Eckenstein, provided he could get three fingers on something that could be described by a man far advanced in hashish as a ledge, would be smoking his pipe on that ledge a few seconds later, and none of us could tell how he had done it; whereas I, totally incapable of the mildest gymnastic feats, used to be able to get up all sorts of places that Eckenstein could not attempt." There is testimony from other climbers of the era on Eckenstein, and their judgment does not fall altogether short of Crowley's lavish praise. Tom Longstaff, a future Alpine Club president, regarded Eckenstein as "a rough diamond, but a diamond nonetheless." But the verdict of the *Alpine Journal* (a publication of the Alpine Club) was that "Eckenstein, though a competent climber, and ever ready to discuss his theories, generally left the lead on a climb to someone else." As will be seen, Eckenstein *did* take the lead in his Himalayan expedition with Crowley—with decidedly mixed results.

There were, however, two achievements in mountaineering as to which praise for Eckenstein is unanimous. The first is the development of the "Eckenstein crampon," a metal clawlike device that enabled climbers to traverse icy slopes without constantly cutting steps. The second was in climbing theory. Eckenstein was the first major proponent of what has come to be called "balance climbing"—a careful control and use of the body that was, in the judgment of one climbing historian, "ultimately to revolutionize the standards of rock work" by applying "the problems of climbing difficult rocks the principles of stress and strain which he [Eckenstein] used in his [engineering] work."

During their first summer of climbing together, in 1898, Crowley and Eckenstein, with a small number of fellow climbers, were encamped in the Alps on the Schonbuhl glacier below the Dent Blanche. Even in this difficult setting, Crowley kept up with his esoteric studies. The book that most occupied him was a tome—ponderous in style, perplexing in content—entitled *The Kabbalah Revealed*, which consisted of English translations of certain sections of the Jewish *Zohar (Book of Splendor)*, based on the sixteenth-century Latin versions of the Christian kabbalist Knorr von Rosenroth. The English translator was one Samuel Liddell Mathers, an impoverished, English-born autodidact and occultist who had taken on a second middle name, MacGregor, based on his alleged noble descent from that Scottish clan. The name MacGregor Mathers was unfamiliar to Crowley. It would not remain so for long.

Crowley's health began to suffer during the lengthy encampment on the glacier, and he decided to come down to the town of Zermatt for some relaxation. One evening, in a beer hall, Crowley began carrying on about alchemy in hopes of impressing his drinking companion. Much to Crowley's chagrin, his companion knew a great deal more about the subject than he did. This was Julian Baker, a man some ten years Crowley's senior, who made a living in London as an analytical chemist and had conducted some practical work in alchemy. The knowledge displayed by Baker sparked a desperate determination in Crowley. The next morning, Baker checked out of the hotel in which he and Crowley were both guests. When Crowley learned of this sudden departure, he chased down Baker—who was hiking—after a pursuit on foot of some ten miles. At that point, Crowley shared with Baker his yearnings for spiritual brotherhood. Baker hinted that he knew of just such a brotherhood, and that, once back in London, he could introduce Crowley to a man who was, by Baker's assessment, "much more of a Magician than I am."

For Crowley, the prospect could not have been more enticing. In late summer, he left off his Alpine pursuits and returned to establish himself in the imperial capital of his homeland. In the previous year of 1897, London had been the site of the Diamond Jubilee—a glorious celebration of the stability of Victoria's reign and of the Empire, which now extended over one-quarter of the land surface of the planet. In the late 1890s, for those with the requisite fortune, it was London, not Paris, that prevailed as the center of elegance. Small wonder that the young Crowley would soon yield to a goodly number of its temptations.

But Crowley persevered in searching out the secret brotherhood. Baker, in September, fulfilled his promise to introduce Crowley to a greater magician. This was George Cecil Jones—the third great friend to emerge in 1898—a gaunt and bearded Welshman five years Crowley's senior who, in Crowley's view, "bore a striking resemblance to many conventional representations of Jesus Christ." Like Baker, Jones earned a living as an analytical chemist, and Crowley admired the "scientific spirit" that Jones brought to his magical studies. Jones lived to the south of London in Basingstoke; Crowley became an ongoing houseguest and promptly began his first guided lessons in magical practice.

Jones would remain a trusted ally of Crowley's for the next decade. He was a thoroughly decent man devoted to the magical development of his will and imagination, who recognized the same ambitions in Crowley and gave the young man a grounding in the rudiments, including the art of astral travel and the meditational practices outlined in a text entitled *The Book of the Sacred Magic of Abra-Melin the Mage*. While there is a claim in the *Abra-Melin* manuscript that it was translated into French from Hebrew in 1458, the original Hebrew manuscript has never been found and scholarly opinion now places *Abra-Melin* as an eighteenth-century pseudonymous work. Details of provenance aside, its quietist approach to magical attainment offered precisely that which Crowley found lacking in traditional grimoires, or magical textbooks, which were "better adapted to the ambitions of love-sick agricultural labourers than to those of educated people with a serious purpose." By contrast, the aim of *Abra-Melin* is to produce—after six months of seclusion devoted to an ever-heightening discipline of meditation, prayer, and study—the combined mystical and magical result of "attainment of the Knowledge and Conversation of the Holy Guardian Angel." The successful completion of the course of practice set forth in *Abra-Melin* became an obsession with Crowley over the next eight years of his life; we shall review his attempts in due course.

Meanwhile, Jones and Baker were agreed that the time was right to introduce Crowley to the magical society of which they were members. Indeed, both men had contravened their oaths to that society by instructing Crowley in its secret techniques. But further progress now necessitated formal contact. So it was that Jones proposed Crowley for membership in the Hermetic Order of the Golden Dawn, which had been in existence for some eleven years, since 1887.

With gratifying rapidity, the initiation of Aleister Crowley as a Neophyte of the Hermetic Order of the Golden Dawn was scheduled for the evening of November 18, 1898. The setting was Mark Masons' Hall in London—a less than grand edifice despite the imposing name. But Crowley approached the ritual at a high pitch of tension and expectation. He inquired of Baker if it was common for people to die during the ceremony. As Crowley later allowed: "I had no idea that it was a flat formality and that the members were for the most part muddled middle-class mediocrities. I saw myself entering the Hidden Church of the Holy Grail. This state of my soul served me well. My initiation was in fact a sacrament."

The task of the Neophyte ritual is to transform the consciousness of the "Candidate" by severing the continuity of his life and directing him upon the hitherto invisible spiritual path. Entry into the Golden Dawn meant, as its name implied, an awakening to the light. The yearning for light, and the blindness and material bondage of the Candidate seeking it, were hallmarks of the Neophyte ritual. Crowley would have been led robed and hoodwinked into the consecrated Temple. About his robe would have been three cords symbolizing the restricting powers of Nature, and more subtly, the potential spiritual purity of the human mind as symbolized by the three highest kabbalistic sephiroth, known as the Three Supernals. At the East of the Temple sat the representative figures of the Three Chiefs of the Outer Order. Behind them was a kabbalistic Veil of Paroketh that separated this Outer Order Neophyte ceremony from the higher wisdom of the Second Order, yet intimated that such higher wisdom was to come. For those Candidates receptive to the drama of ritual—and Crowley was such a one—the Neophyte ceremony was an experience never to be forgotten.

The layout of the Temple, including obelisks and a central altar, were suggestive of the lower sephiroth of the kabbalistic Tree of Life. At this point the Candidate was entering the lowest and most earthly of the sephiroth, Malkuth, and hence he would be designated, as the ritual proceeded, as "child of Earth." Early on, the Candidate is "sealed" with a motto; that chosen by Crowley was *Perdurabo* (I shall endure to the end). It was a statement of concentrated will as to his magical ambitions that Crowley would live by unflinchingly. Shortly thereafter there came an oath "to keep inviolate the secrets and mysteries of our Order." Crowley would breach this oath fulsomely some eleven years later, in the aftermath of his break from Mathers.

After three "Mystic Circumambulations," much solemn instruction and warnings as to the difficulties of the path ahead, the candidate is made to kneel and then to rise again. The hoodwink and bandages are removed. The Hierophant—symbolic of the Candidate's Higher Self—addresses him thusly: "Child of Earth, long hast thou dwelt in Darkness! Quit the Night, and seek the day." Then would come the proclamation: "Frater Perdurabo, we receive thee into the Order of the Golden Dawn!" And then the mystic words *"Khabs Am Pekht"* (in Egyptian) and *"Konx Om Pax"* (in Greek) meaning "Light in Extension"—the extending of the supernal light to the highest faculties of the Candidate, no longer a mere "Child of Earth."

Crowley would seldom fail, in his future diaries, to note November 18, 1898, as the anniversary of his first initiation.

What was the nature of the Golden Dawn, such that it could offer to an intelligence as demanding as that of Crowley a ritual that transformed him? The mysterious circumstances surrounding the formation of the Golden Dawn have received extensive attention from scholars and will be only briefly told here. The story of its rise and fall serves as a parable of the astonishing range and potential—and the appalling pretentions—of those on the magical path. Crowley would come to play his own part in the history of the Golden Dawn, and he too would mirror these extremes. Most importantly, he would take away from his brief active period in that society—from November 1898 to April 1900—the framework of scholarship, symbolism and ritual that would permeate his writings throughout his life.

One must bear in mind that to be a member of an occult secret society in Crowley's time was a far different affair than in the "cult"-conscious atmosphere of present times. There was then a sense of participating in a grand but hidden tradition that was intertwined with the history of Europe—and was now carried on by a daring and enlightened *avant-garde*. In the 1890s, interest in the occult had reached a peak not only in Britain but also on the Continent. Paris had become a center of esoteric activity, with a number of self-styled Rosicrucian groups. The inspiration for much of the magic in Paris was Eliphas Levi, the *nom de plume* of Alphonse Louis Constant, a onetime candidate for the Catholic priesthood who, after a struggle of conscience, found truths better suited to his tastes in the hermetic tradition. Levi died in May 1875, some four months before Crowley was born. Crowley would, nonetheless, later claim Levi as one of his previous incarnations, Levi's soul having passed into the fetus Crowley *in utero*.

The London success of the Theosophical Society sprang full blown from the inventions of its principal founder, the famed and flamboyant Helena Petrovna Blavatsky, a Russian-born self-proclaimed medium and seer. In her massive works, *Isis Unveiled* (1877) and *The Secret Doctrine* (1888), Blavatsky offered an imaginative and rhetorically powerful syncretist blending of Western esotericism and Eastern mysticism, and attempted as well to heal the rift between science and religion in the West by pointing to their common ultimate aims. Blavatsky specified, as the source of the wisdom offered in her writings, perfected "Mahatmas" who dwelled in Tibet and were called upon to watch over the evolution of humankind and lead it into a new age of Universal Brotherhood.

Among those stirred by Blavatsky was the poet William Butler Yeats. Yeats would go on to play a critical role in the history of the Golden Dawn and in Crowley's own magical development, as we shall see. In an 1892 letter, the poet declared:

> If I had not made magic my constant study I could not have written a word of my Blake book, nor would *The Countess Kathleen* have ever come to exist. The mystical life is the centre of all that I do and all that I think and all that I write. It holds to my work the same relation that the philosophy of Godwin held to the work of Shelley and I have always considered myself a

voice of what I believe to be a greater renaissance—the revolt of the soul against the intellect—now beginning in the world.

Yeats credited to his Golden Dawn years a magical teaching—the training of the astral vision—"that has been perhaps the intellectual chief influence on my life up to perhaps my fortieth year." In its beginning stages, this method employs intensely colored "Tattwa" symbols representing the four primary elements and the fifth element of akasha, or spirit, as well as their subdivisions and combinations. As Yeats progressed, he found that rituals of evocation, as well as intensive prayer, could induce still more intense visions. In his memoirs, Yeats was scrupulous in acknowledging both the lasting influence of these visions upon his art and the limited nature of their import upon his spiritual development: "I allowed my mind to drift from image to image, and these images began to affect my writing, making it more sensuous and more vivid. I believed that with the images would come at last more profound states of the soul, and so lived in vain hope."

A key difference between Yeats and Crowley—as fellow initiates into the Golden Dawn—emerges here. For Crowley, the hope would not, by his own judgment, prove vain. Crowley lacked the humility of Yeats, but Crowley's ardor and capacity for magical practice were the greater. But Yeats did not doubt the efficacy of magic. The poet performed a magical healing on his uncle, George Pollexfen (also a Golden Dawn initiate) in the period 1894–95. Pollexfen had fallen ill from polluted smallpox vaccine. Yeats came to his bedside: "He was in delirium and with a high temperature, and when I asked what he saw said 'red dancing figures.' Without saying what I was doing I used the symbol of water and the divine names connected in the kabalistic system with the moon. Presently he said that he saw a river flowing through the room and sweeping all the red figures away."

Amidst the welter of secret societies during this period, two characters now step to center stage as the principal founders of the Golden Dawn: William Wynn Westcott and the aforementioned Samuel Liddell MacGregor Mathers. To Westcott goes the honor of setting the marvelous apparatus of the Golden Dawn into motion. Westcott had earned a medical degree at University College, London, but his primary interests were in esoteric learning. In 1887, he took the first decisive steps to create the Golden Dawn. There continues to be controversy, in both esoteric and scholarly circles, as to the circumstances of its founding, but the traditional account, in basic terms, is as follows: In August 1887, the

Reverend A. F. A. Woodford, who was active in Masonic circles, gave to Westcott some sixty pages (found in a secondhand bookstall) of what has come to be known as the "Cypher MS." Woodford died four months later, thus depriving the curious of his testimony. The cipher or artificial alphabet of the manuscript derived from a work of Renaissance occult scholarship with which Westcott was familiar, the *Polygraphia* of Abbot Johann Trithemius. Upon deciphering it, Westcott saw that he had come upon an extended skeletal outline for a series of five initiatory rituals. There were certain Masonic influences, but the rituals allowed for both "Fratres" and "Sorores"—men and women. The rituals also drew from alchemy, astrology, kabbalah, and the teachings of Eliphas Levi on the intertwined relationship between the twenty-two paths of the kabbalistic Tree of Life and the twenty-two Trumps of the Tarot deck. Enclosed with them was a cover letter of sorts—written in the same cipher—which gave the name and forwarding address of one Fräulein Anna Sprengel, an exalted Rosicrucian who lived in Stuttgart, Germany, and who was a Chief Adept in a secret society called *"die Goldene Dämmerung."* In Westcott's translation this became "the Golden Dawn."

Between 1887 and 1890, there was an alleged correspondence between Westcott and Sprengel, whose magical motto was *Sapiens dominabitur astris* (the wise person will be ruled by the stars) or "S.D.A.", as her secretary signed her letters. In 1890, a Frater of S.D.A. wrote to Westcott with the news of her sudden death and the unequivocal statement that no further communications would be forthcoming from Germany. But the intervening years had accomplished their purpose: the establishment, in Britain, of the Golden Dawn, an occult secret society with links to a purported continental esoteric tradition. In just over a decade, the question of the authenticity of the Cypher MS. and of Fräulein Sprengel and her Goldene Dämmerung would rage with sufficient fury to rend the Golden Dawn asunder.

The wiser Golden Dawn members came, soon enough, to see Fräulein Sprengel and her revelations as a kind of fable, bitter or sweet or irrelevant, depending upon one's temperament. Arthur Machen, whose tales of the supernatural remain classics of the genre, was initiated into the Golden Dawn in 1899 but remained only briefly active. Machen later observed of the society's founding that "so ingeniously was this occult fraud 'put upon the market' that, to the best of my belief, the flotation remains a mystery to this day. But what an entertaining mystery; and, after all, it did nobody any harm." Crowley—who refrained from passing final judgment on the existence of Fräulein Sprengel—termed the traditional account of the Golden Dawn's founding as "probably fiction" but insisted that it was irrelevant in terms of the value of its magical teachings: "You will readily understand that the genuineness of the claim matters no whit, such literature being judged by itself, not by its reputed sources."

Crowley's own judgment of the Golden Dawn "literature" was that, amidst much prosaic ore, there was genuine gold in two of the rituals: those of the Neophyte and the Adeptus Minor grades. The chief author of these rituals, and the man who would supplant Jones as Crowley's magical teacher, was Mathers. The parallels between Mathers and Crowley are such that one can see, in the figure of the future Beast of the New Aeon, an enduring palimpsest presence that is Mathers, the creator of that which was distinctly *magical* in the Golden Dawn. Unlike Westcott, who made no public claims of magical power, Mathers would hold himself forth to the members of the Golden Dawn as one who possessed a living connection to the more-than-human "Secret Chiefs"—the ultimate source of all occult wisdom. It was this latter claim by Mathers, perhaps, that would compel Crowley, the future prophet, not only to renounce his former teacher, but to revile his name. The connection to the Chiefs would be Crowley's own.

As the foremost leader of what is, beyond doubt, the most famous magical society of modern times, Mathers stands forth in the dual and contrasting roles of inspired teacher and egomaniacal autocrat. The dozens of essays and lectures, as well as the Golden Dawn rituals themselves, testify to Mather's ability to produce original writings of value. Yeats would delineate the change in Mathers over the years of his rule of the Golden Dawn: "I believe that his mind in those early days did not belie his face and body—though in later years it became unhinged, as Don Quixote's was unhinged—for he kept a proud head amid great poverty."

Little is known of the early life of Mathers. He was born the son of a commercial clerk in 1854. His father died when Mathers was young, intensifying the bond between mother and son. Mathers lived with his mother in Bournemouth until her death in 1885, when he was thirty-one. Due in part to limited family resources, he received no university training and left school altogether at the age of sixteen after four years at Bedford Grammar, where he was grounded in classical studies. Westcott, six years Mathers's senior but greatly his superior in wealth and formal education, became a patron for Mather's studies, providing guidance as to suitable texts as well as financial assistance that enabled Mathers to move to London. Just as Crowley would later bristle at Mathers's claims to power, Mathers chafed at the looming presence of Westcott.

Yeats acknowledged Mathers as an inspiration in his own spiritual development as a poet: "It was through him mainly that I began certain studies and experiences, that were to convince me that images well up before the mind's eye from a deeper source than conscious or subconscious memory." According to Yeats, Mathers bore the scar of a saber wound "got in some student riot that he had mistaken for the beginning of war." In their discussion of the Jacobite battle for the crown of Britain, Yeats found that, for Mathers, "the eighteenth century controversy still raged. At night he would dress himself in Highland dress, and dance the sword dance, and his mind brooded upon the ramifications of clans and tartans." Mathers's devotion to physical training and competition led him to boxing. Yeats's account is poignant: "One that boxed with him nightly has told me that for many weeks he could knock him down, though Mathers was the stronger man, and only knew long after that during those weeks Mathers starved." The poet summarized the impact made by Mathers on so many Golden Dawn members:

> Mathers had much learning but little scholarship, much imagination and imperfect taste, but if he made some absurd statement, some incredible claim, some hackneyed joke, we would half consciously change claim, statement or joke, as though he were a figure in a play of our composition. [. . .] in body and in voice at least he was perfect; so might Faust have looked in his changeless aged youth. [. . .] Once when I met him in the street in his Highland clothes, with several knives in his stocking, he said, "When I am dressed like this I feel like a walking flame," and I think that everything he did was but an attempt to feel like a walking flame. Yet at heart he was, I think, gentle, and perhaps even a little timid.

According to Yeats, Mathers would sometimes spit blood during his magical practices, "lived under some great strain" and was prone to drinking, on occasion, excessive quantities of brandy, "though not to drunkenness." Crowley, once he broke with Mathers, would term him a drunk outright.

For all his extravagances, Mathers had retained the trust of his patron, Westcott, who appointed him one of the Three Secret Chiefs who would oversee the Golden Dawn. Mathers was to draw up, on the basis of the Cypher MS., suitable rituals for the five grades of the Outer Order: Neophyte, Zelator, Practicus, Theoricus, Philosophus. Each grade was based upon one of the sephiroth of the kabbalistic Tree of Life, with attributions extending on to astrology, alchemy, Tarot, Hebrew god names and angelic realms, and the symbolism of the Egyptian divine panoply. Passage through these grades, as authorized by the Secret Chiefs, would ready the aspirant for a further initiation into the Second Order, that of the *Ordo Rosae Rubeae et Aureae Crucis* (Ruby Rose and Golden Cross; commonly abbreviated to R.R. et A.C.), the domain of practical magic, divination, and directed astral travel. Beyond was the Third Order, the three grades that reflected the Three Supernal Sephiroth of the Tree of Life, the realms of the Secret Chiefs as to whom Westcott, Mathers, and Woodman were mere reflections, as it were. Never in the course of the Golden Dawn were these three latter grades—Magister Templi, Magus, and Ipsissimus—bestowed. These were the grades that Crowley, in the decades to come, would claim by way of initiatory rituals of his own devising.

In 1888, the initial year of recruitment, fifty-one members were enrolled in the Golden Dawn. Within three years, the ranks of Golden Dawn initiates had swelled to 126, 48 of whom were women. Yeats was initiated in March 1890, taking as his magical motto—emblematic of the new self of the initiate—*Demon Est Deus Inversus* (The Devil is the converse of God), which embodied the Gnostic teaching that the alleged Devil of the Bible was in fact the source of true godly wisdom in this occluded would; in all likelihood, Yeats had first encountered this motto in Blavatsky's *The Secret Doctrine*, in which it served as a chapter heading. (It was just such a viewpoint that would contribute to Crowley's later branding as a Satanist.)

The clamor for more magic led to the creation by Mathers, in 1891, of rituals for the Second Order which had thus far existed in name only. Mathers would claim, as his source of inspiration, a mysterious adept named Frater Lux e Tenebris (Light and Darkness), whose real-life identity (if he indeed existed) has never been ascertained. Mathers was thus asserting a link—beyond the ken of even Westcott—to the ultimate Secret Chiefs. Indeed, Mathers now flourished in many respects. In 1890, he married Mina (who later called herself, in good Celtic fashion, Moina) Bergson, the sister of the renowned French philosopher Henri Bergson. Mina—as to whose ethereal beauty Yeats attested—was devoted to her husband and applied her considerable artistic gifts to the creation of ritual decor. Through the financial support of Annie Horniman, the first Golden Dawn member to be initiated into the Second Order, in December 1891—the couple moved to Paris in 1892, where Mathers established his own temple. London operations were left to Westcott to oversee.

At first, selected members of the Outer Order were invited by the Secret Chiefs to enter the Second Order. But the selectivity declined over the years. By the end of 1897—the year prior to Crowley's arrival— there had been a total of 323 Outer Order initiations, with 97 subsequent initiations into the Second Order. This impressive growth entailed severe growing pains. In 1896, due to what Mathers perceived to be a growing insubordination within the Second Order (in particular, the withdrawal of financial support by Horniman), Mathers sent to all Second Order members a manifesto demanding that they each send him "a written statement of voluntary submission." Mathers insisted that he was entitled to such obedience, given his unique link to the Secret Chiefs. He cited the enormous strain that this link had cost him, including the loss of blood Yeats had observed. Mathers was a martyr to the cause of the Second Order, yet would insist upon a price for his sacrifice: "But unless the Chiefs are willing to give me the Knowledge, I cannot obtain it for you:—neither will I give it to you unless I know that the Order is being worked conformably with their wishes and instructions."

The manifesto succeeded. Virtually all Second Order members complied with its terms; Horniman alone was formally expelled. Mathers carried on through the contributions of other members. But there were many who, while compliant, remained skeptical. Once, Yeats wrote, he confronted Mathers: "I said, 'How do you know you are not hallucinated?' He said, 'The other night I followed one of these strangers [Chiefs] down that passage', pointing to a narrow passage from the garden to the street, 'and fell over the milk boy. The boy said, 'It is too bad to be fallen over by two of you.'" Yeats concluded that the "break-up" of Mathers "had begun."

There was one further barrier to Mathers's unquestioned leadership status, and that was the presence of Westcott. That presence was removed in March 1897, when the London officials who administered Westcott's work as a coroner were somehow informed of his extensive connections with a secret occult society. Westcott, to keep his position, resigned. It was the suspicion of many, including—later—Crowley, that Mathers had engineered this dilemma. The result, at any rate, was clear: Mathers was now the undisputed head of the Golden Dawn.

By December 1898, Crowley had passed the requisite written examination for initiation into the Zelator $1°=10°$ grade, the kabbalistic symbolism of which revolved around the spiritual element of Earth. He took the grades of Theoricus $2°=9°$ (Air) and Practicus $3°=7°$ (Water) in January and February of 1899, became a Philosophus in May 1899, and later boasted of his "rapid" progress through the Outer Order. In truth, given the relative ease of passage through the lower grades, his progress was merely punctual. But the abundance of rote learning began to grate on Crowley. In retrospect, he conceded that "my intellectual snobbery was shallow and stupid. It is vitally necessary to drill the aspirant in the groundwork." The Second Order now became the vital capstone to be attained with all possible speed. But there was a required interval of seven months between the Philosophus grade and Second Order initiation, which further required a special invitation from Mathers.

During this period, Jones and Baker had been teaching their young pupil astral vision techniques. Crowley kept a diary record of eighteen astral visions conducted from November 1898 to New Year's Day 1899. (This diary confirms that, even as he practiced his astral technique, the newly initiated Neophyte was still attending Christian family prayer sessions.) A decade later, Crowley would offer (through the words of his acolyte, Fuller) this defense for his early visions—and for visionary reality as a whole: "A true vision is to awakenment as awakenment is to a dream; and a perfectly clear co-ordinate vision is so nearly perfect a Reality that words cannot be found in which to translate it, yet it must not be forgotten that its truth ceases on the return of the seer to the Material plane."

But the perfection of these visions could not quell troubling memories of the past. Thoughts of his Cambridge lover Pollitt were haunting Crowley. Significantly, he chose the hours between ten and eleven P.M. on New Year's Eve 1899 as the time for an "Operation" in which, as his private diary discloses, he sought "to destroy a shell, i.e. to exorcise my Qliphoth [base emotions] about P——[Pollitt] and so either to cure or kill, as alive or dead respectively." The need for a vision that could "cure or kill" was based upon the guilty sense that Crowley's own "evil persona" had caused Pollitt to sin. Crowley's discomfort with his homosexual nature was at the root of this guilt, hence the perplexed ambivalence in his description of his feelings for Pollitt as either "alive or dead."

Crowley did not record his success or failure in curing or killing these feelings, and it is unclear whether he had any other male lovers during this period. With women, however, Crowley was highly active. Despite the urging by the Chiefs that sexuality be kept out of relations between Golden Dawn members, Crowley had a particularly impassioned affair with Elaine Simpson, who had been initiated into the Second Order. There has been speculation by scholars that the resistance within the R.R. et A.C. membership to Crowley's being granted an invitation to join the Second Order was due to his "sexual peculiarities" or to an "impending homosexual scandal." The specifics behind these charges will be explored shortly. It is, however, certain that Crowley had created a disagreeable reputation for himself. Blessed with a fortune, little practical acumen, and still less tact, he had wasted little time in establishing himself as a daunting, even frightening figure within the occult milieu of *fin de siècle* London.

In late 1898, Crowley moved from his rooms at the posh Hotel Cecil to the luxurious flat procured for him by his lawyer at 67 and 69 Chancery Lane. It was here that Crowley would undertake the intensive private studies in magic that accompanied his formal progress through the Outer Order grades. Crowley designed and fitted two rooms as temples for the practice of white and black magic, respectively. The dominant decor of the white temple was six large mirrors, six by eight feet, that covered the walls; the black temple, a smaller, cupboard-sized room, featured an altar in the shape of an agile young black man in Eastern garb—a coolie figure to the eyes of the British Empire—standing on his hands and balancing a flat table surface on his feet. Within this black temple stood a human skeleton which, Crowley tells us in his *Confessions,* he "fed from time to time with blood, small birds and the like. The idea was to give it life, but I never got further than causing the bones to become covered with a viscous slime." Crowley is here enjoying the frisson of revulsion he knew would be created in readers, while also mocking his own youthful follies. But there was indeed a genuine conflict within him at this time between the paths of white and black magic. This shows itself in Crowley's account of his first meeting with a man who would supplant Jones and Mathers alike as a magical influence upon Crowley: Allan Bennett.

Bennett, four years older than Crowley, had entered the Golden Dawn in 1894 and was initiated into the Second Order in 1895. He was utterly devoted to Mathers, whom, Bennett declared, "I reverence more than any man." Bennett took on the use of the MacGregor clan surname favored by Mathers and was even "adopted" by Mathers during this period, though this would seem to refer to a magical rather than a legal relationship. Bennett was one of the most luminous minds to be trained in the Golden Dawn framework. Amongst his other studies, he helped Mathers with the work of compiling the *Book of Correspondences*, a tabular grouping of esoteric symbols from around the world which Crowley later expanded into *Liber 777*.

Bennett made a precarious living as an analytical chemist (by remarkable coincidence, the same profession as Jones and Baker); but his career was hampered by spasmodic asthma. The drugs Bennett took for this condition were drawn from the standard legal pharmacopoeia of the time. Crowley described the treatment: "His cycle of life was to take opium for about a month, when the effect wore off, so that he had to inject morphine. After a month of this he switched to cocaine, which he took until he began to 'see things' and was then reduced to chloroform." Bennett thus developed remarkable tolerance levels. One friend recalled that Bennett "went on to experiment with poisons until once he took a tremendous overdose which would have instantly killed another man but which left him quite unharmed."

The setting for the first meeting between Crowley and Bennett was a Golden Dawn ritual ceremony. Crowley had heard of Bennett—whose magical name was Iehi Aour (Hebrew: Let there be light)—by way of his formidable reputation as a magician. Now, during the disrobing that followed the ceremony, Crowley was startled by an immediate challenge from the man himself:

> To my amazement he came straight to me, looked into my eyes, and said in penetrating and, as it seemed, even menacing tones: 'Little brother, you have been meddling with the Goetia!' (Goetia means 'howling'; but is the technical word employed to cover all the operations of that Magick which deals with gross, malignant or unenlightened forces.) I told him, rather timidly, that I had not been doing anything of the sort. 'In that case,' he returned, 'the Goetia has been meddling with you.' The conversation went no further. I returned home in a somewhat chastened spirit; and, having found out where Iehi Aour lived, I determined to call on him the following day.

Bennett's intimation here is confirmed by Crowley's own testimony as to the black magic temple in his Chancery Lane flat. But he was careful to specify that "Iehi Aour never had anything to do with this; and I but little: the object of establishing it was probably to satisfy my instinct about equilibrium."

Crowley found in Bennett an inspiration to work in white magic. The purpose of calling upon Bennett the next day was to invite him to take up lodgings in Crowley's own Chancery Lane flat, to which Bennett— who had been living in a grubby shared tenement—consented. Finances were a matter as to which both men were acutely sensitive. Two years earlier, when Bennett had been badly strapped for funds, a friend had suggested that he approach Mathers for a loan; Bennett refused out of his conviction that relations with his teacher "should be connected wholly with matters occult." Crowley, in like manner, sought to establish a relationship without financial taint. Thus he offered Bennett hospitality but was careful "never to go beyond the strict letter of the word." That is, Crowley wished to avoid giving cash directly to Bennett, as it would have violated the "point of honour" that one ought not to be paid for the teaching of occult wisdom. This point of honor, taken to the extreme that Crowley did, would soon cost him dearly.

There was, from the outset, more than a shared interest in the occult to draw them together. Their backgrounds were strikingly similar: Both had endured unhappy childhoods that included the early death of a father. Both had rejected the intensive Christian piety (Bennett's mother was a devout Catholic) in which they had been raised. And both suffered from asthma, although Bennett's was the far worse case. Crowley's portrait of Bennett is haunting: "Allan Bennett was tall, but his sickness had already produced a stoop. His head, crowned with a shock of wild black hair, was intensely noble; the brows, both wide and lofty, overhung indomitable piercing eyes." Crowley believed that, due to his illness, Bennett "regarded the pleasures of living (and, above all, those of physical love) as diabolical illusions devised by the enemy of mankind in order to trick souls into accepting the curse of existence." This had led Bennett into extensive readings of Buddhist texts. Sexual asceticism was not a viewpoint that Crowley could share, but coming as it did from a Buddhist as opposed to a Christian perspective, Crowley could more easily respect it in Bennett. In this regard, speculation that Bennett and Crowley became lovers must be rejected; it would have been vastly out of character for Bennett, and a confidant of Crowley's later years, Gerald Yorke, denied flatly that such was the case.

Together in the Chancery Lane flat, they devoted themselves to intensive studies in ceremonial magic. Crowley records this instance of Bennett's magical powers—and impatience with scoffers: Bennett had constructed a magic wand out of a long "lustre" or glass prism. "One day, a party of theosophists were chatting skeptically about the power of the 'blasting rod' [wand]. Allan promptly produced his and blasted one of them. It took fourteen hours to restore the incredulous individual to the use of his mind and his muscles." Bennett, like Baker and Jones before him, introduced Crowley to teachings beyond his formal Golden Dawn grade. During 1899, Crowley copied out Second Order rituals that were almost certainly provided to him by Bennett, who would, by the end of the year, see fit to bequeath all of his magical notebooks to Crowley. Bennett's respect for his pupil must have been considerable for him to have breached the rule set by Mathers.

The explorations undertaken by Bennett and Crowley went beyond the confines of Second Order magic to take in the possibilities of alternative consciousness by means of drugs. It must be understood that the social atmosphere and legal consequences of drug experimentation in that period were entirely different from our own. There was already a strong nineteenth-century tradition of using drugs as a means to explore the human mind; Baudelaire, in his *Les Paradis Artificiel,* is the most remarkable writer in a lineage that extends from Samuel Taylor Coleridge and Thomas DeQuincey through the nineties to British poet James Thompson, author of *The City of Dreadful Night,* who was addicted to opium in the form of laudanum, as had been Coleridge and DeQuincey. Laudanum was one of the most frequently taken drugs in England throughout the nineteenth century, readily available in a variety of patent-name preparations as a cure for stomach ailments, a pacifier of the child labor force that worked the factories, and a means to increase the productivity of adult laborers by controlling the diarrhea that stemmed from the appalling sanitation conditions of the slums. Cocaine, cannabis and other consciousness-altering drugs were not as frequently used as laudanum, but they were perfectly legal at this time (the first Dangerous Drugs Act was passed in England in 1920) and obtainable by anyone interested, as Bennett and Crowley certainly were. They experimented avidly in hopes of attaining the Elixir Vitae of the Alchemists: Crowley's rueful summation: "Like Huckleberry Finn's prayer, nuffin' come of it."

The friendship of Bennett and Crowley surely contributed to Crowley's prompt success in forging a relationship with Mathers. In May 1899, Crowley paid a visit to Paris and met his Chief for the first time. Each man had something to gain from the other: Mathers required obedient Golden Dawn members in London; Crowley needed assurance that the Second Order was his to attain, despite his bad relations with the London hierarchy. These were exemplified by Crowley's unfortunate encounters with William Butler Yeats. Yeats was thirty, six years Crowley's senior. But the disparities went far deeper. Yeats was not only Crowley's superior within the Golden Dawn, but also a lionized poet, as Crowley yearned to be.

Crowley requested a meeting with the older poet in the spring of 1899. He presented to Yeats, at this first meeting, the printed proofs of his verse tragedy *Jephthah* and a group of poems entitled *Mysteries:*

Lyrical and Dramatic; these were published together in one volume, at Crowley's expense, that same year. The poem entitled "Perdurabo" (Crowley's magical name) is a naked spiritual autobiography:

> I am not lower than all men—I feel
> Too keenly. Yet my place is not above,
> Though I have this—unalterable Love
> In every fibre. I am crucified
> Apart on a lone burning crag of steel,
> Tortured, cast out; and yet—I shall abide.

The final three words refer, of course, to the literal meaning of Perdurabo.

The earnestness of the young Crowley apparently could not compensate, in Yeats's mind, for the technical deficiencies and rhetorical excesses of his verse. Some two decades later, Yeats would concede that Crowley had written a very few lines of genuine verse. The poet and critic Katherine Raine has suggested that Yeats remained uneasily aware of Crowley's writings well into the new century, and that Crowley the Great Beast and his creed of Thelema, "with its deliberate desecrations and reversals of sacred values," may have echoed in Yeats's poem "The Second Coming," with its "rough beast, its hour come round at last" that "Slouches toward Bethlehem to be born." Raine pointed to a surprising blending of antagonism and unity between the two men: "Yeats and Crowley drew upon a common fund of esoteric tradition and shared a belief that a Second Coming is at hand. Both write of the ending of one Great Year, and of the advent of an antithetical phase; but whereas Crowley placed himself in the services of Antichrist, 'the savage God' of the new cycle, Yeats's fidelity was to 'the old king', to 'that unfashionable gyre', the values about to be obscured to the 'workman, noble and saint' of Christian civilization."

At the time of their 1899 meeting, the differences between the two men prevailed. Yeats attempted to be tactful, but something of his true opinion was conveyed after he glanced through the apprentice page proofs. This infuriated Crowley, who later tried to discount the importance of the rebuff: "I had never thought much of his work; it seemed to me to lack virility.[. . .] However, at that time I should have been glad to have a kindly word from an elder man." When Yeats could offer only "a few polite conventionalities," Crowley, through his powers of "clairvoyance, clairaudience and clairsentience," recognized within Yeats a "black, bilious rage." The root of this rage was obvious enough to Crowley the poet: "What hurt him was the knowledge of his own incomparable inferiority." This insight, which as a matter of aesthetic judgment makes Crowley appear ridiculous, applies far more convincingly to Crowley himself.

A far more severe attack on Yeats was leveled by Crowley in a short story, "At the Fork of the Roads," written a decade after their first meeting and published in Crowley's journal, *The Equinox*. Here Crowley offers what is, by his own testimony, a veiled factual account of the magical warfare that took place between Yeats and himself during this period. In the story, Crowley is Count Swanoff, a poet who has "concealed his royal Celtic descent beneath the pseudonym of Swanoff." Crowley himself took on, in 1899, the pseudonym Count Svareff for reasons that shall be discussed shortly; the reference to a royal Celtic line bespeaks the influence of Mathers, whose Scots-Gaelic Second Order motto *'S Rioghail Mo Dhream* (Royal is my tribe) had at this point been taken up by Crowley, who had it printed on his personal stationery. Houseguest Allan Bennett is the anonymous "master" who serves as Swanoff's ally in fending off the magical attacks being mounted by Will Bute (a contraction of Yeats's first two names), a "poetaster" and "dabbler in magic" who harbored a "black jealousy" against Swanoff. The Gnostic magical name of Yeats—Demon Est Deus Inversus (The Devil is the inverse of God)—is derided in the narrative as "blasphemy."

Crowley and Yeats would soon be pitted as antagonists in the struggle for control of the Golden Dawn, with Yeats abandoning his old friend Mathers while the younger Crowley emerged as his strongest ally. Indeed, Yeats and others in London would cite Crowley as evidence of the pattern of poor judgment that had overtaken Mathers. But Crowley, through Mathers, felt his entry into the Second Order assured and could afford to be indifferent to their claims.

Ensconced in his Chancery Lane flat with Bennett as residing guest, Crowley commenced preparations for an intensive magical working— the Abra-Melin Operation—based on the *Abra-Melin* text (translated by Mathers) to which George Cecil Jones had introduced him just over a year earlier. Crowley planned to commence the Operation on Easter 1900; necessary preliminaries included the consecration of robes, oils, and implements, as well as the ongoing search for a secluded country locale. During these preliminary months, Crowley took on the public pseudonym of Count Vladimir Svareff, a Russian aristocrat new to London. The reason proffered in the *Confessions* was that *"Abra-Melin* warns us that our families will object strenuously to our undertaking the Operation."

If Crowley hoped to evade his mother by the Count Svareff ruse, he failed miserably. Ethel Archer, a later friend of Crowley, recorded this anecdote: Emily, hearing of the preposterous noble pseudonym of her son, paid a visit to his flat and sent in her card announcing herself as "The Countess of Cosmos." Archer noted that this was "a characteristic move of the old lady, that showed both originality and wit" and, further, that in this shared sense of humor "one could see the unmistakable likeness of mother to son." Crowley himself later mocked the pretension of his pseudonym, agreeing with his magical mentor Jones that "a wiser man would have called himself Smith." Given Crowley's limited knowledge of Russian, it is doubtful, in any event, that many Londoners were deceived.

But it is equally doubtful that Crowley spent much of his time playing that outrageous role. The options available to a young man from Cambridge held at least an equal allure. In May 1899, during his visit to Mathers in Paris, Crowley took in Mathers's original stage production (at the Bodinière Theatre) of the *Rites of Isis* and there met an American operatic *prima donna*, Susan Strong, who took him "by storm." According to Crowley, Strong was married to a Texan who had unwisely remained in that state while Strong was performing the role of Venus in the Covent Garden production of Wagner's *Tannhäuser* and mingling with the occult *avant-garde* of London and Paris. She and Crowley had an affair and, by Crowley's account, they became engaged and were resolved to marry immediately, but for the need of Strong to obtain a divorce in Texas. But her return to Texas signaled, instead, an end to the romance.

Strong and Elaine Simpson were Crowley's two great heterosexual loves of this period. But other, more casual affairs made their impacts as well. One of these was with Evelyn Hall, in connection with whom, in his diary, Crowley refers to a mysterious "Great Trouble" that arose in November 1899 and after. As another lover of this period, one Laura, also plays a significant part in the "Great Trouble," the tangled stories behind these affairs conjoin naturally.

The central thread stems from Crowley's genuine concern for his friend, Bennett. The cold, damp climate of London had aggravated his asthma. By 1899, it seemed to Crowley that a move to a tropical climate was essential. This dovetailed with Bennett's desire to study yoga with indigenous teachers in Ceylon. We have already seen that Crowley believed himself precluded from funding Bennett directly. The indirect aid that Crowley would seek involved his aforementioned lover Laura, the wife of a British Army colonel stationed in India. After a torrid beginning, Crowley's passion had cooled, but to his dismay Laura retained her ardor. In response to her plea, Crowley paid a visit to her London hotel and, by his account, played out the following scene:

> She begged me to come back to her and offered to do anything I wanted. I said to her, 'You're making a mess of your life by your selfishness. I will give you a chance to do an absolutely unfettered act. Give me a hundred pounds, I won't tell you whom it's for, except that it's not for myself. I have private reasons for not using my own money in this matter. If you give me this, it must be without hoping or expecting anything in return.' She gave me the money—paid Allan's passage to Ceylon and saved to humanity one of the most valuable lives of our generation.

Her gesture on behalf of Bennett led Crowley to consent to carrying on the affair so long as she promised to leave him to the Abra-Melin Operation (during which nonmaritial sexual relations are strictly forbidden), which he intended to commence at Eastertime of the following year.

This arrangement must have seemed simple and pleasurable enough—it included a fortnight together in Paris—but it came to grief for two reasons. First, Laura sent importuning letters to Crowley even during his Abra-Melin retreat in 1900. Second, the matter of the £100 was reported to the police as theft—most likely by her husband—though Laura refused to prosecute. Matters were further entangled by the attentions paid Laura by another Golden Dawn member, W. E. H. Humphrys, of whom Crowley observed in his diary: "He seems nearly as big a blackguard as myself. I misbehave as usual. O Lord, how long?"

Was the £100 the cause of the "Great Trouble?" There are other, equally likely possibilities. Here enters Crowley's other lover, Evelyn Hall, who in January 1900 warned Crowley by letter that he and his friends at Chancery Lane were being watched by the police. In his diary, Crowley wrote of Hall's warning to him: "This is concerned with 'the brother of a college chum' but no doubt can be entertained of the meaning of her hints. She [Hall] naively assumes the charge to be true!" Given this hint, it seems likely that alleged homosexual activity at Chancery Lane was the cause of the police surveillance. This is bolstered by the fact that Crowley had obtained an unsavory sexual reputation. Elaine Simpson, another of Crowley's heterosexual loves, had informed him that London Second Order members believed him guilty of "sex intemperance" with both sexes.

In late 1899, Crowley learned that his request for initiation into the Second Order had been turned down by the R.R. et A.C. London membership, including Yeats, who now viewed Crowley as "a person of unspeakable life." Yeats offered this justification for refusing Crowley: "[W]e did not think a mystical society was intended to be a reformatory." Crowley himself, as his diary confirms, was aware of behavior that rendered him a "blackguard." He later cited, as one of the causes of this behavior, the strain of magical initiation. Borrowing from Freud and tacitly assigning to magical ritual a function similar to psychoanalytic therapy, Crowley wrote that an "aspirant on the threshold of Initiation finds himself assailed by the 'complexes' which have corrupted him, their externalisation excruciating him, and his agonised reluctance to their elimination plunging him into such ordeals that he seems (both to himself and others) to have turned from a noble and upright man into an unutterable scoundrel." Even his onetime friend Julian Baker would conclude, by 1900, that his onetime protégé was "a man without principles."

But in Jones and Mathers, Crowley had his own powerful allies. He was resolved to continue his preparations for the Abra-Melin ritual. The most challenging step was to find a suitably secluded location in which to conduct the intensive six-month Operation. On this score, as in all matters of ritual conduct, the *Abra-Melin* text is precise and demanding. If the Operator intends to live in a house—as opposed to the stark simplicity of an isolated wood—there must be a room set aside exclusively as an oratory for prayer and magical ritual. A door must issue from this room facing north. Outside this door there must be constructed a terrace covered to the depth of two fingers with fine sand from a riverbed. At the north end of this terrace a lodge is to be constructed wherein spirits both good and evil may be conjured, the evil spirits to be pressed into the service of the good by the worthy Operator if, through ardent effort, the Operation was a success. Crowley hunted for months for a suitable location, until, in August 1899, he came upon the manor of Boleskine and Abertarff, on a southeast rise overlooking Loch Ness, home to the legendary monster. In his *Confessions*, Crowley insisted that he paid twice as much as the manor was worth, which may well be believed; but Boleskine would come to serve as Crowley's home base for over a decade.

He moved there in November 1899. Even prior to the move, the intense course of preparations had served, according to Crowley, to attract to him the Abra-Melin "demons"—the conquest of which is the culminating power conferred by the Operation. It is the prospect of defeating the Operator at the outset that lures the demons. Thus it was that, one night, Crowley and Jones returned to the Chancery Lane flat to find that the white temple was in disarray and that "semi-materialized beings were marching around the main room in almost unending procession." After the move to Boleskine, hired workmen were "put out of action for several hours" by the demons.

But no difficulties could be allowed to stand in the way. The Operation was to be the culminating event of Crowley's life. It is all the more perplexing, then, to trace the repeated ambivalence that led him, in its opening month, to put it aside. The *Abra-Melin* text specifies that the Operator must consider "whether ye be capable, not only of *commencing* but also of *carrying through the Operation unto its end.*" Serious illness alone constitutes an adequate excuse for termination: "Ponder the matter then well before commencing, and only begin the Operation with the firm intention of carrying it out unto the end, for no man can make a mock of the Lord with impunity."

Crowley had been earnest in his preparations for the Operation, but single-mindedness eluded him. In truth, the greatest distractions to Crowley's progress were not Boleskine-based demons, but rather battles for power within the Golden Dawn. Tensions between Mathers and the Second Order members in London—the selfsame members who had refused Crowley's request for initiation—had reached a high point. When Mathers learned of Crowley's rejection by the London Second Order, he resolved to initiate Crowley in his own Ahathoor Temple in Paris.

On January 15, 1900, Crowley interrupted both his *Abra-Melin* preparations and his liaisons with Laura to journey to Paris. The following day, he was admitted to the Second Order. The rituals which Crowley underwent that day must have been *sui generis* as compared to the standard Second Order framework. For Crowley became both a "Lord of the Paths in the Portal of the Vault of the Adepts" and a "5°6□ of the Order of the Golden Dawn." The former title stems from passage through the Portal ritual—a ceremony designed by Mathers to signify the transition from the First (Outer) to the Second (Inner) Order. So transformative was the power of the Portal Ritual that Golden Dawn practice called for a nine-month gestation period prior to full initiation into the Second Order by means of the subsequent Adeptus Minor ritual. Crowley, in receiving both initiations in a single day at Mathers's hand, was being accorded remarkable treatment.

He had become an adept, one deemed to have mastered the knowledge necessary to integrate the fundamental elements of the soul. The Adeptus Minor ritual was—with Mathers as playwright and lead actor—an affair of high drama, drawing upon the central mythos of the Rosicrucian movement: the discovery, 120 years after his death, of the body of Christian Rosenkreutz undecayed in a seven-sided *pastos* (tomb), the seven sides representing the seven traditional planets, the seven days of creation, and the seven lower sephiroth of the kabbalistic Tree of Life. Within the *pastos* lay—as the symbolic presence of Rosenkreutz—the Chief Adept, Mathers himself. At this point the Aspirant—Crowley—is instructed to say: "Out of the darkness let the light arise." Without moving, the Chief Adept replies with one of the most beautiful passages of the ritual—an identification of the new initiate and the master magus Rosenkreutz:

> Buried with that LIGHT in a mystical Death, rising again in a mystical resurrection, Cleansed and Purified through him our MASTER, O Brother of the Cross and the Rose! Like him, O Adepts of all ages, have ye toiled; like him have ye suffered Tribulation. Poverty, Torture, and Death have ye passed through. They have been but the purification of the Gold.
> In the Alembic of thine Heart,
> Through the Athanor of Affliction,
> Seek thou the true stone of the Wise.

The vision of the *pastos* bestowed in Paris on January 16, 1900, would never die within him. In a will executed some three decades later, Crowley requested that his body be "embalmed in the ancient Egyptian fashion and then treated as nearly as possible like that of Christian Rosencreutz" in the Adeptus Minor ritual.

Crowley returned to Boleskine on February 7, still intending to commence the Abra-Melin Operation in March. Disturbances seemed at an end. Elsewhere, however, events were taking on their own momentum. A fierce correspondence now arose between Mathers and the London Second Order. A new allegation by Mathers—in a February 16 letter to the Second Order in London—held that the correspondence alleged to have taken place between Westcott and the mysterious Fräulein Sprengel in Germany, upon which the Golden Dawn had based its foundation and teachings, was a mere forgery. As Mathers put it: "I again reiterate that *every atom* of the knowledge of the Order has come *through me alone* from 0°0□ to 5°6□ inclusive, and that it is I alone who have been and am in communication with the Secret Chiefs of the Order."

These revelations placed Second Order members, including Yeats, in the quandary described in a subsequent written statement by those members: "If his [Mathers's] accusation of forgery be true, he has knowingly, and on his own showing for many years made use of that forgery for his authority as Chief; if this statement be false, he has been guilty of a slander on one to whom he was bound by the most solemn pledges of fraternity and fidelity, both as a member of this Order and as a Freemason." As for Westcott, he refrained, on the advice of counsel, from making any statement unless legally compelled to do so. Privately, to Second Order member Percy Bullock, Westcott asserted that he had received "bona fide posted letters" from Sprengel. But a private avowal would not do when the dignity of the Order was at stake. The Second Order was left, in sum, to sort matters out for itself.

There was a further claim made by Mathers in his February 16 letter that added wonder upon wonder: Fräulein Sprengel herself—who was alleged by both Westcott and Mathers to have died in 1890—was now alive and living in Paris and promising to aid Mathers in putting on his public *Rites of Isis*. The woman whom Mathers believed, at this point, to be Fräulein Sprengel went primarily by the name of Madame Laura Horos, with other aliases including Swami Vive Ananda and Marie Louise of the Commune. She was roughly sixty years of age and obese, though Mathers believed her to possess "the power of changing her appearance from age to youth and *vice versa*." Madame Horos was accompanied, on her visits to Mathers, by her husband Theo, an unprepossessing man thirty years younger. She succeeded in gaining the confidence of Mathers by revealing a knowledge of the Outer Order grades, by reciting the secret motto of Fräulein Sprengel—*Sapiens Dominabitur Astris*—and by relating to Mathers details of a private conversation he had had with the late Madame Blavatsky over a decade ago. Indeed, Madame Horos attributed her weight to having swelled up as a result of absorbing the spirit of Madame Blavatsky (herself very stout) upon the latter's death. Within weeks, Mathers realized that they were frauds. But the realization was a tardy one, for he had by then loaned them copies of Golden Dawn rituals that would come to light in a highly negative fashion late the following year of 1901, when the Horos couple—who had by then used the rituals in an attempt to establish their own Golden Dawn initiations in England—were arrested on charges of rape by Theo, and of aiding and abetting in the rape by Madame Horos. Their December 1901 trial and conviction, with its lurid mix of sex and the occult, generated intense tabloid press coverage. Mathers and the Golden Dawn were held up to excruciating public ridicule.

While all this controversy was brewing Crowley was, for a rare change, on the sidelines up at Boleskine manor. But Crowley had written two letters to the London Second Order respectfully requesting the study materials to which Second Order members were entitled. On March 25, Crowley finally received a definitive no. This response, just two weeks before Easter and the Abra-Melin Operation, galled and galvanized him. There is a terse diary entry in which Crowley deemed the Second Order "apparently mad" and resolved to write to Mathers "offering myself." He affirmed this resolve by a typical Crowley device—a parallel to the life of Jesus Christ: "His Face was fixed as a Flint to go unto Jerusalem." The die was cast. There would be no Operation come Eastertime.

Given that Crowley would himself soon break with Mathers, the justification of leaving off Abra-Melin for Mathers's sake is perplexing. In *The Equinox of the Gods* (1936), Crowley—speaking in the voice of a realized prophet—offered this verdict on Mathers, the Order, and the Abra-Melin Operation: "That the Master proved to be no Master, and the order no Order, but the incarnation of Disorder, had no effect upon the good Karma created by this renunciation of a project on which he had set his heart for so long." By couching the decision as a renunciation rather than a breach of the Abra-Melin oath, it was possible to evade the stern words that Crowley himself had once written: "The Oath is the foundation of all Work in Magick, as it is an affirmation of the Will. An Oath binds the Magician forever."

Crowley did not learn of Mathers's formal acceptance of his services until April 6, when Crowley was confirmed as Mathers's representative and plenipotentiary in England. That day, Crowley went to 36 Blythe Road in London, the address of the Second Order Vault of the Adepts, and asked to be admitted. He was politely put off. That same day he met with Elaine Simpson, his lover and fellow Golden Dawn member, and enlisted her support for the coming struggle.

Having done what he could in London, Crowley traveled to Paris on April 9. Mathers had not been idle in the interval. The epistolary cannonading had reached new intensity with a Mathers letter of April 2 which threatened the use of the "Punitive Current": A "deadly and hostile Current of Will" that could be unleashed by the Chiefs against members who breached their oaths to the Order. Crowley later wrote that he had persuaded Mathers to utilize this Current, but could not resist mocking Mathers for his failure to wield it with effect—"as in the case of the Jackdaw of Rheims, nobody seemed a penny the worse." Crowley further described a Sunday afternoon during which Mathers waged—in the ritual style of the old grimoires—a magical attack against the rebellious Order by "rattling a lot of dried peas in a sieve under the impression that they were the revolted members: as subsequent events proved, they were only the ideas in his head." It seems to have eluded Crowley that these railleries made himself look foolish for his loyalty.

Nonetheless, Mathers and Crowley agreed upon a battle strategy for the capture of the Vault—the symbolic first step in regaining control of the Golden Dawn. According to Crowley, he himself formulated these plans while Mathers passively assented. In essence, they consisted of Crowley going to London, taking control of the Vault in the name and by the authority of Mathers, and then summoning all Second Order members, over the course of several days, to answer a series of questions in the course of an interview as to which they would be pledged to secrecy. Crowley, as the questioner, would wear a mask of Osiris to emphasize the impersonality of his role as Mathers's emissary and judge. These questions would serve as a loyalty test culminating in the signing of a statement avowing Mathers as leader. If the member refused to sign, he or she would be expelled from the Order. These plans formulated, Crowley departed from Paris on April 13.

The battle itself raged for the three days of April 17–19. On Tuesday the seventeenth, Crowley, accompanied by Elaine Simpson, broke into the Second Order rooms at Blythe Road, placed new locks on the door and, most satisfyingly, inscribed "Perdurabo" on the official parchment roll of Second Order initiates (the Second Order would later order this entry removed). Three Second Order members arrived on the scene to object to the forced occupation on the basis that Mathers's authority had been suspended by vote of the London members. A constable was summoned, but as the landlord was absent the question of legal right to possession could not then be resolved. Crowley's new locks remained in place at day's end. On Wednesday the eighteenth, Crowley sent off letters—signed in the name of Mathers—to the Second Order members demanding their presence at the Blythe Road headquarters on April 20. This letter would be utterly ignored.

The stage was set for the *battle royal* on April 19. Crowley was costumed (in accordance with Mathers's instructions as to how to ward off potential magical attacks by Madame Horos) with a mask of Osiris, a dirk of "cold steel," and a MacGregor tartan. But when Crowley arrived at Blythe Road, inimical forces of a different order were barring the way: Yeats and a fellow Second Order member, as well as the landlord—a member of the Trades Protection Association which had blacklisted Crowley for bad debts—and a constable. Crowley left promptly, without threats or altercation, stating that he would consult a lawyer. Later that day, the Second Order formally suspended Mathers and his few supporters and specially declared, with Crowley in mind, that only London initiates were proper members. The Vault—and the Order itself—had been retaken by the rebels.

There were scattered shots in the days that followed, but they hardly mattered. On April 23, Crowley (under the name "Edward Aleister") filed a legal action against Second Order member Florence Farr, claiming that she had detained certain of his papers and other property worth some £15. The Second Order hired its own eminent attorney and counterclaimed that Crowley had stolen certain property on April 19. Further, the Trades Protection Association planned to join the action to press its claims against Crowley. It promised to be a messy battle. Crowley's lawyer promptly filed a voluntary dismissal, including an agreement that Crowley would pay £5 in costs. It was an ignominious end.

One sad aftermath of the "Battle of Blythe Road" was a lingering fear on Yeats's part as regarded Crowley. While undertaking the reform of the Golden Dawn as its new leader, Yeats wearily complained, in a June 6, 1900, letter, of Crowley's ongoing magical threats: "Even the fact that MacGregor's masked man Crowley has been making wax images of us all, and putting pins in them, has not made life interesting." In his memoir *Things Near and Far* (1923), Arthur Machen recalled an anxious meeting with the poet:

> He described the doings of a fiend in human form, a man who was well known to be an expert in Black Magic, a man who hung up naked women in cupboards by hooks which pierced the flesh of their arms. This monster—I may say that there is such a person, though I can by no means go bail for the actuality of any of the misdeeds charged against him—had, for some reason which I do not recollect, taken a dislike to my dark young friend. In consequence, so I was assured, he had hired a gang in Lambeth, who were grievously to maim or preferably to slaughter the dark young man; each member of the gang receiving a retaining fee of eight shillings and sixpence a day—a sum, by the way, that sounds as if it were the face value of a mediaeval coin long obsolete.

The reference by Machen to a "cupboard" is striking, for Crowley used the exact same word in his *Confessions* to describe the Chancery Lane room in which he created his black temple.

While the Second Order regrouped in London, Crowley found himself strangely at odds. Easter had passed and with it the lure of Boleskine and the Abra-Melin opportunity. Crowley returned to Paris to report to Mathers. For the time being, Crowley remained loyal to his defeated Chief, though inwardly he harbored doubts. But the primary problem now confronting him was more basic: What to do with his time? Guests of Mathers in Paris had just returned from Mexico and spoke highly of the locale. There were volcanoes in the central ranges that could offer a climbing challenge. His Chief had neither a practical use for him, nor further teachings to offer. These are the reasons that Crowley sets forth in the *Confessions* for his spur-of-the-moment decision to go on a voyage. It may be that the mysterious "Great Trouble," the pressing claims of creditors, and the unwanted attention of the police during the Chancery Lane period played roles as well.

In any event, travel plans were laid *post haste*. Leaving Boleskine to the care of his servants, and the battered Golden Dawn to the rebels, Crowley sailed in June 1900 for New York, the first stop in a journey that would lead first to Mexico and then extend around the world.

CHAPTER THREE

Years of Wandering in Which Crowley Pursues the Heights of Magic and Mountains, Embraces Buddhism, Then Abandons All for the Love of a Woman and the Life of a Country Laird (1900–04)

E dward Alexander Crowley had become, in turn, Aleister Crowley, Perdurabo, and, most recently, Lord of the Paths in the Portal of the Vault of the Adepts and an Adeptus Minor of the Second Order Rosae Rubeae et Aureae Crucis. For these latter titles, Crowley had Mathers to thank.

And yet, as he set out on his voyage to the New World, Crowley's loyalty to his Chief was marred by inward doubt. However much Crowley might scoff at the attainments of the Second Order rebels, it was plain that they had wrested control of the London Golden Dawn from Mathers, who had put up a poor enough fight on both the magical and the material planes. Whether or not Mathers possessed a genuine link to the Secret Chiefs had become a vexing question for which, as of yet, Crowley had no clear means of obtaining an answer.

Upon graduating from Cambridge, Crowley had yearned to make contact with the Great White Brotherhood. Upon initiation into the Golden Dawn, he had felt certain that such contact had been achieved. But by the time Crowley completed the wanderings to be recounted in this chapter, he would decide for himself that—on the human plane— there were no further teachers for him. The experiences and training gained during these years—from the practice of magic, the pursuit of yogic concentration of mind, and the climbing of mountains—would make him his own master forevermore.

Crowley landed in New York harbor on July 6, 1900. In the *Confes-*

sions, Crowley could not resist a jibe at the Statue of Liberty—"a rejected statue of commerce intended for the Suez Canal." The New York skyscape was merely "a series of disconnected accidents." A severe heat wave kept him largely confined to his hotel room, where he immersed himself in cold baths during his short stay.

It was with a sense of relief that he boarded the train to Mexico City. Once arrived, he found the spirit of the Mexican people immediately to his liking. The absence of a sense of puritanism prompted Crowley to heights of praise:

> Indoors and out nature and art combine to invite Cupid to pay every sort of visit, passionate, permanent, transitory, trivial. The caprice of the moment is the sole arbiter of the event.[. . .] There is no humbug about purity, uplift, idealism, or any such nonsense. I cannot hope to express the exquisite pleasure of freedom.[. . .] The problem of sex, which has reduced Anglo-Saxon nations to hysteria and anxiety, has been solved in Mexico by the co-operation of climate and cordiality.

A hallmark of the *Confessions* is Crowley's resolve to paint an idealized portrait of a fully liberated life. But by the evidence of the poetry written during his stay in Mexico, it is clear that Crowley's "Anglo-Saxon" anxieties had accompanied him. In "The Growth of God," there is the despairing voice of one for whom existence and all its seeming pleasures and consolations (including the idea of God) are but tawdry deceptions:

> I see all Nature claw and tear and bite,
>   All hateful love and hideous: and the brood
> Misshapen, misbegotten out of spite;
>   Lust after death; love in decrepitude.
> Thus, till the monster birth of serpent-man
>   Linked in corruption with the serpent-woman,
> Slavering in lust and pain—creation's ban,
>   The horrible beginning of the human.

The end of the poem affirms that the "seeker" must continue on his path, but the reward shall be, not luminous enlightenment, but rather the discovery of the "word" that "At last shall dissolve thee into rest." In this sentiment, Crowley was approaching the viewpoint of Theravada Buddhism, the path now being pursued by his friend Allen Bennett in

Ceylon. Within a year, Crowley would join Bennett in Ceylon, where this similarity of outlook would be intensified.

In Mexico City, Crowley rented a portion of a house overlooking the Alameda, a park in which prostitution was rife. The year before, in Paris, Crowley had fallen in love with Susan Strong, who had portrayed Venus in Wagner's *Tannhäuser*. Now the erotic lure of the Tannhäuser legend again arose. As Crowley wrote: "One afternoon, in Mexico, I picked up a woman who attracted me by the insatiable intensity of passion that blazed from her evil inscrutable eyes and tortured her worn face into a whirlpool of seductive sin." He returned with her to a slum dwelling where they had sex for some hours and then parted. Afterwards, he found himself quite unsatiated—even to the point of "delirium." Upon returning to his rooms, Crowley promptly devoted himself for sixty-seven consecutive hours—without so much as taking a meal—to the composition of *Tannhäuser*, a "poetical and magical" drama which Crowley adjudged "the climax of the first period of my poetry." Such was the capacity of sex laced exquisitely with sin to exhilarate Crowley. The torment of Tannhäuser is temptation of the flesh. Venus is a "serpent-woman." Her sexuality is the purging fire through which Tannhäuser must pass to attain spiritual resurrection. In Act IV, there is a scene in which Tannhäuser seems to merge with Crowley pursuing sex in the slums of Mexico:

> Mine was, by weariness of blood and brain,
> More bitter fruit of pain
> Sought in the darkness of a harlot's bed,
> To make me as one dead:
> To loose the girders of the soul, and gain
> Breathing and life for the Intelligible;
> Find death, yet find it living. Deep as Hell
> I plunged the soul; by all blind Heaven unbound
> The spirit, freed, pierced through the maze profound,
> And knew Itself, an eagle for a dove.

Crowley privately published *Tannhäuser* in 1902 with a "Preface" that stressed the element of self-portraiture. He dreamed it a study in "the morbid psychology of the Adept" and avowed that it had "been written in the blood of slain faith and hope."

Alone in Mexico, Crowley continued his magical studies. The latter months of 1900 were the first time that Crowley explored *in isolation* the realms of magical ritual. Isolation of at least a relative order would henceforth be a requisite condition for Crowley to do his best magical work. It heightened both his sense of freedom and his level of concentration; when the isolation took place in a distant foreign land, there was the further enhancement of the removal of the Anglo-Saxon world and its unfortunate associations. Most important, isolation served to confirm Crowley as the master of his own magical universe, himself capable of adjudging the degree of attainment his efforts had won him. Thus he accorded himself, on the basis of his work in Mexico and utterly upon his own authority, the exalted 6°=5° magical grade of Adeptus Major—no mean step for one who had been a mere Neophyte rescued from the darkness two years previously. The Adeptus Major grade was just below the 7°=4° Adeptus Exemptus grade habited by Mathers himself.

His growing sense of independence showed itself also in the founding of a new magical society. According to Crowley, Mathers had bestowed upon him a "certain amount of latitude" to initiate into the Golden Dawn suitable new candidates whom he might encounter on his travels. This "latitude" was expanded by Crowley into the creation of the Lamp of the Invisible Light (L.I.L.), which appears to have had at most two members. The first was Crowley himself. The second was an elder personage, possibly apocryphal, named Don Jesus Medina, whom Crowley grandly described as "a descendant of the great duke of Armada fame, and one of the highest chiefs of Scottish rite free-masonry." Having initiated this elder into the L.I.L., Crowley in turn received from the good Don Jesus accelerated Masonic initiation to the 33°, the highest degree of the Scottish Rite. It is noteworthy that Crowley's claim was to the teachings of the loosely defined Scottish Rite and not those of the accepted body of "regular" Freemasonry in England—the United Grand Lodge, with its dominant presence in the aristocratic circles of London. Given his sorry reputation, it is doubtful that Crowley could have persuaded any "regular" lodge in his native land to initiate him into even the first degree.

Don Jesus Medina vanished shortly thereafter, and the L.I.L. was abandoned by Crowley. But his researches continued apace. Himself both the subject and object of his experimentations, Crowley pursued two distinctly practical capabilities: the power of rendering oneself invisible, and the power of transforming at will the tendencies of one's mundane consciousness. As to the former, Crowley attested that: "I reached a point where my physical reflection in a mirror became faint and flickering. It gave very much the effect of the interrupted images of the cinematograph in its early days." This much represents Crowley's own perceptions of himself. But he went on to claim an effect of invisibility upon others, based upon the psychological—*not* magical—theory that "the real secret of invisibility is not concerned with the laws of optics at all; the trick is to prevent people noticing you when they would normally do so. In this I was quite successful. For example, I was able to take a walk in the street in a golden crown and a scarlet robe without attracting attention." We have only Crowley's dubious account of this regal walk. In any event, he would retain a belief in his power of invisibility.

Crowley's experiments in the transformation of mundane or day-to-day consciousness constitute a more original contribution to the magical repertoire. These experiments were refined in a later essay, *Liber Jugorum* (1910), which may be translated as the *Book of the Yoke*. (Note that *Liber Jugorum* is only three pages long; Crowley would come to utilize *Liber* as a formal designation for his magical and mystical—as opposed to literary and personal—writings. These *Libri* are, without exception, written in the adjuring style of the King James Bible prophets.) Crowley credited the initial idea behind *Liber Jugorum* to Robert Louis Stevenson, whose famous novella *The Strange Case of Doctor Jekyll and Mister Hyde* had posed the possibility of two watertight personae within a single human psyche. Crowley drew from this a design for a magical experiment to demonstrate that one's daily persona is altogether secondary and arbitrary—an assemblage of tastes and opinions that one could alter at will, without affecting the essential consciousness within. His procedure in Mexico was as follows: When he wore a certain jeweled ornament over his heart (symbolic of his status as a member of the Second Order of the Golden Dawn), he would attempt to think no thought that did not pertain to his magical progress; when, on the contrary, he removed the ornament, he would seek to become "utterly uninitiate." The mind was thus trained to control speech, action, and thought, so that the dictates of one's higher will could govern daily life. *Liber Jugorum* was destined to contribute to Crowley's ill-repute because of the discipline it recommended. On each occasion when one's speech, action, or thought strayed from the vowed course, one was to "cut thyself sharply upon the wrist or forearm with a razor; even as though shouldst beat a disobedient dog.[. . .] Thine arm then serveth thee both for a warning and for a record." For those unsympathetic to Crowley's magical philosophy, the sight of such willful scarification on the arms of future students (a small number, in practice) was repellant in the extreme.

Wonders and mysteries were plentiful in his practice of this time. But magic had failed to uproot his sense of sin, with its encumbent distance from godhead. As Crowley later explained, "My results were satisfactory so far as they went; but they did not aid my personal progress very much, since I had not formulated an intellectual link between the divine and human consciousness." This failure induced in Crowley a sense of despair. The critical turning point—one that would permanently change the focus and emphasis of Crowley's magical practice—was a visit, in January 1901, by his climbing mentor, Oscar Eckenstein.

The ostensible purpose of Eckenstein's journey was to join with Crowley to climb the high volcanic peaks of central Mexico. But now, at their reunion in Mexico City, a new Eckenstein stepped forward—a mentor on spiritual matters who told Crowley frankly that his magical efforts were flawed because he had not yet undergone a fundamental training in the control of the powers of his mind. In the previous chapter, it was argued that Eckenstein may have achieved some knowledge and training in Sufi techniques. His instructions and advice to Crowley at this time further bear out this hypothesis. Here is Crowley's diary account—in ornate Biblical style, so as to signify its spiritual importance:

> Now, the year being yet young, one Oscar Eckenstein came unto me, & spake.
>
> And he spake not any more (as had been his wont) in guise of a skeptick and indifferent man: but indeed with the very voice & power of a Great Guru or of one definitely sent from such a Brother of the Great White Lodge.[. . .]
>
> Under his direction, therefore, I began to apply myself unto the practice of Raj-yoga[,] at the same time avoiding all, even the smallest, consideration of things occult, as also he bade me.

"Raj-yoga"—or raja yoga, as it is more commonly transliterated—is the most ancient known form of yogic practice, focusing upon control of the mind as a means to bring about spiritual transformation in the practitioner. The exercises suggested by Eckenstein began with the inner visualization of relatively simple objects and figures. Then came exercises for the envisioning of particular persons by means of superimposing a larger image of the person over a smaller version; this exercise offered the further benefit of heightened insights into the character of the person in question. Crowley's progress heartened him. On February 22, 1901, in Guadalajara, he inscribed a fervent prayer in his diary asking that the "Peace of God" and "Christ Jesus our Lord" guide him to the "Higher" and the "Light."

During March 1901, Crowley also traveled with Eckenstein to various Mexican mountain ranges. The two men were intent on preparing themselves for an expedition to the Himalayas. Eckenstein, a veteran of Himalayan treks, was convinced that the setting of Mexico could offer to the younger Crowley two critical elements beyond his Alpine experiences: higher peaks, and the practical challenges of obtaining equipment and other necessities in a non-European, impoverished culture. This same spring of 1901, the two men formulated concrete goals for their proposed Himalayan expedition. Crowley's diary confirms that their intent was to climb a "mountain higher than any climbed previously." Their specific choice of Chogo Ri (designated K2 on the India Survey map) was, at 28,250 feet, the second highest peak in the world, and one which had defied the few European expeditions mounted against it in the late nineteenth century. The two men worked out a long and detailed agreement that established Eckenstein as leader and set stringent conditions for the conduct of the proposed expedition. For example, not a single supply item was to be purchased without Eckenstein's express consent; there would be no interference with the prejudices and beliefs of "native" persons who might be encountered either as indigenous residents or hired as guides and porters; and there was to be nothing to do with women if possibly avoidable.

In March and April, Crowley and Eckenstein completed a series of impressive Mexican climbs. Their first conquest was the beautiful peak of Iztaccihuatl in central Mexico. On the sides of Iztaccihuatl, the two friends made camp at 14,000 feet for some three weeks and climbed the mountain from all sides. Other peaks scaled by the pair included Colima, Nevado, Toluca, and Popocatapetl. Only the Volcan, in the same Colima district as Nevado and Toluca, frustrated the climbers, due to the fact that the Volcan was indeed a still active volcano capable of spewing ash that burned holes in their clothes and heated the rock surface so as to threaten to burn their boot soles as well.

Shortly after the assault on Popocatapetl, Crowley and Eckenstein parted company. Their Himalayan plans were still provisional. For now, Eckenstein would return to England while Crowley continued what would amount to a Grand Tour—a circumnavigation of the globe, which would include as its keynote a visit to his magical mentor, Allan Bennett, now studying yoga in Ceylon. On April 20, Crowley set out on a northward course for San Francisco, where he planned to embark by ship for the Orient. His first stop in America was El Paso, which struck him as embodying the "coarse and brutal barbarism of Texas." Crowley pressed on to San Francisco, where he found the Chinatown district to his liking, spending most of the week of his stay burning joss sticks in the Buddhist temple and observing the Chinese community with fascination. It was to the East that Crowley's thoughts were turned, and on May 3 he embarked on the *Nippon Maru* for Hawaii, where he planned to indulge himself in the pleasures of beach life before pushing on to the Orient. He arrived on the main island on May 9 and promptly suffered a jolt to his well-laid plans by falling passionately in love. The married woman's name was Mary Beaton, an American in her mid-thirties, traveling with her teenage son; her lawyer husband had remained at work on the mainland. She and Crowley met at their hotel in Honolulu and Crowley was at once fascinated by her "imperial" beauty. Crowley's early courtship of her was chaste, though their passion simmered; he convinced Mary—whom he took to calling Alice, as she preferred that name—to accompany him (with son in tow) on the *America Maru* to Japan.

On shipboard, the passion between them kindled into a full-blown affair. At the time, Crowley regarded it as the greatest love of his life. To his friend Gerald Kelly in England, Crowley wrote: "On the boat we fell to fucking of course, but—here's the miracle—we won through and fought our way back to chastity in far deeper truer love." In this letter, Crowley avowed that Alice's sweet influence had saved his soul—his lust had been transmuted into the ecstasy of composing fifty sonnets, one for each day of their brief affair (for they had parted after their arrival at Yokohama, with Alice resolved to return to her husband). Love and poetry had now taken up his mind, as opposed to occultism. Crowley stressed to his friend: "You will not recognize my mind when I come back."

The difference in tone between this contemporary letter and the Crowley of the *Confessions* is telling—typical of the gloss that the Beast laid over his younger, less fearsome self. Some twenty years later, Alice is reduced to a kind of nonentity who served well for poetic inspiration precisely because she was "herself worthless from the point of view of the poet." The later Crowley expressed contempt for Alice for failing to give all for love and instead returning to her husband. At the same time, he insisted that his own nature precluded his ever reciprocating in kind:

> I had intoxicated myself utterly with Alice; I had invested her with all the insignia that my imagination could invent. Yet, loving her with all my heart and soul, she had not seduced me from my service.[. . .] I have loved many women and been loved. But I have never wavered from my Work; and always a moment has come when the woman had to choose between comradeship and

catastrophe. For in truth there was no Aleister Crowley to love; there was only a Word for the utterance of which a human form had been fashioned.

Alice: An Adultery—published by Crowley in 1903—stresses neither chastity nor passion but rather the sinful context of the affair. The thematic progress of the sonnets is predictable and tedious, akin to a gothic romance novel. The dichotomy of lust ("the stain") and pure love shows the lingering Christian outlook. There are, however, occasional moments of original wit, as in the account of the parting on the fiftieth day:

> So the last kiss passed like a poison-pain,
>   Knowing we might not ever kiss again.
>   Mad tears fell fast: "Next year!" in cruel distress
> We sobbed, and stretched our arms out, and despaired,
>   And—parted. Out the brute-side of truth flared;
> "Thank God I've finished with that foolishness!"

Just at this time, back in England, Crowley began to receive favorable reviews for a verse collection entitled *The Soul of Osiris* (1901). No less a critic than G. K. Chesterton, the most gifted Christian apologist of his age, offered measured praise in the *Daily News*. But Chesterton as well took issue with mystical elements in Crowley's verse, declaring that "the poets of Mr. Crowley's school"—by whom Chesterton presumably meant those Decadents for whom alternative forms of spirituality held an allure—"have, among all their merits, some genuine intellectual dangers from this tendency to import religions, this free trade in gods.[. . .] If Mr. Crowley and the new mystics think for one moment that [. . .] a broken temple of Osiris is more supernatural than a Baptist chapel in Brixton, then they are sectarians, and only sectarians of no more value to humanity than those who think that the English soil is the only soil worth defending [. . .] But Mr. Crowley is a strong and genuine poet, and we have little doubt that he will work up from his appreciation of the Temple of Osiris to that loftier and wider work of the human imagination, the appreciation of the Brixton chapel." Crowley, when he later read and replied in print to this review, mocked Chesterton's defense of the prosaic Brixton district of London. But there is evidence that Chesterton's argument stuck in Crowley. Nearly two decades later, in the *Confessions*, Crowley conceded that he had, in this period, wandered in search of a truth he could not place: "I had got to learn that all roads lead to Rome [. . .] and that the Himalayan Brotherhood is to be found in Brixton."

After Mary Beaton deserted him in Japan, Crowley found himself suddenly alone, freed alike from love and from foolishness, but subject still to sudden and vehement impulse. His admiration for the Buddhist outlook, fostered through his friendship with Bennett, was now intensified by a sublime spirit of place. He even sought admission to certain of the local Buddhist monasteries, but was turned away. At the time, this must have been a severe blow to his confidence. But the elder Crowley claimed to find an ultimate triumph in this seeming rejection:

> The Inmost knew that my destiny lay elsewhere. The Lords of Initiation cared nothing for my poetic fancies and my romantic ideals. They had ordained that I should pass through every kind of hardship at the hands of nature, suffer all sorrow and shame that life can inflict. Their messenger [Crowley the future prophet] must be tested by every ordeal—not by those that he himself might choose.[. . .] I turned then sadly from Daibatsu, as I had turned from love, ambition and ease, my spirit silently acquiescing in the arcane arbitrament of the mysterious daimon who drove me darkly onward; how I knew not, whither I knew not, but only this, that he was irresistable as inscrutable, yet no less trustworthy than titanic.

Crowley's stay in Japan was relatively short. He found the Japanese people little to his liking, for the reason—it would seem—that their alleged character reminded him unpleasantly of defects in his own: "Their aristocracy was somehow at odds with mine. I resented their racial arrogance."

As he again took ship—this time to sail on to Bennett in Ceylon—Crowley was in a mental state he seldom admitted to: "not only contrite but confused." In an August 1 diary entry, Crowley recorded the bleak skepticism that beset him: "I exist not: there is no God: no place: no time: wherefore I exactly particularize and specify these things." En route to Ceylon, Crowley made a brief stop in Hong Kong to meet with Elaine Simpson, his fellow Golden Dawn initiate, to whom, by his account, he had paid astral visits while in Mexico. Their reunion in the flesh was far less satisfactory. Simpson was now tepidly married to a wealthy English colonial and having affairs on the side. Worst of all, she had abandoned magic for social ambition and committed the desecration of wearing her Golden Dawn robes and regalia to a fancy dress ball—and winning first prize! The affair was not renewed. Crowley pushed on in his voyage, little savoring the intervening ports of call.

At last, on August 6, he disembarked in the Ceylonese port of Colombo. The following day came the reunion with Bennett, whose health had improved away from the British climate, though he was far from robust. He was serving as tutor to the younger sons of P. Ramanathan, a high-caste Tamil who was the Solicitor-General of Ceylon. Ramanathan was a Shaivite Hindu, that is, one who worshiped the god Shiva, the embodiment of the great cyclical powers of procreation and destruction. As part of his Shaivite beliefs, Ramanathan practiced yoga and served as Bennett's teacher in this area. Ramanathan wrote a book during this period, published under his Shaivite holy name of Sri Parananda and titled *An Eastern Exposition of the Gospel of Jesus according to St. John* (1902), in which he argued that the teachings of Christ could be understood as instructions in yoga. Crowley found Ramanathan a man of "profound religious knowledge" and joined Bennett as Ramanathan's pupil for a short time.

But before Crowley could focus on yoga in earnest, there was the question of Mathers to address. Was he indeed a credible spiritual teacher? Crowley put the following tale by Mathers (as filtered through Crowley) to Bennett and asked that it be verified: Some years before, there had been an argument over metaphysics between Mathers and Bennett. The magical result of their disagreement was to create, in the room in which they sat, the spirit of the Dyad, or the illusion that the universe was ultimately other than One. This troubled state enabled Abra-Melin demons, who had vexed Mathers during his translation of the *Abra-Melin* text, to take the material forms of Mathers and Bennett respectively. Each of these demons found its way to a pistol (which Mathers, a military buff, had on hand) and threatened to shoot the other. Catastrophe was averted when Mathers's wife, Moina, came into the room and thus transformed the Dyad into a harmonious Trinity.

Crowley had found Mathers's story difficult to believe, given his knowledge of Bennett as one inclined neither to possession by demons nor to violence. According to Bennett (again, as filtered through Crowley), the facts were indeed quite different. The argument had been over the god Shiva, to whose worship Bennett had been drawn even prior to departing from England. The Hindu belief which appealed to the austere Bennett, for whom existence was marked by pain and suffering, was that Shiva would someday open his eye and wreak destruction on the universe. Mathers found this belief appalling. When Bennett sought to resolve the argument by assuming the yogic position of Padmasana and chanting, as mantra, the name "Shiva" again and again, Mathers became distraught. First he left the room to take to drink, then he returned and drew a pistol and threatened to kill Bennett if he would not be silent. Bennett, rapt in yogic concentration, continued his chant, and Mathers never pulled the trigger.

The differences between the two accounts led Crowley to conclude that Mathers had lied and was "thus disposed of" in terms of his claims to linkage with the Secret Chiefs. But the choice of this one episode as a litmus test of Mathers's integrity suffers from a sense of arbitrariness. Beyond this, there are two more concrete objections. The first stems from Crowley's retelling of the dispute: If the chanting Bennett was oblivious to Mathers, how did he recall, for Crowley's benefit some years later, Mathers's having left the room for drink and then returning with a pistol? The second is that Bennett, unlike Crowley, was unlikely to have told a story that emphasized Mathers's fondness for liquor and his tawdry fear of death. Crowley's implication, in the *Confessions*, that he and Bennett were now in agreement on Mathers's fallen state, is almost certainly false. Bennett continued to regard himself as a kind of son to Mathers; in a 1902 publication, he listed himself as "Allan Bennett MacGregor," still employing the surname of Mathers's chosen clan.

Mathers, the human link to the Secret Chiefs, occupied precisely the lofty spiritual position that Crowley himself had yearned to hold since adolescence, when he had rued the lack of hierarchy within the Plymouth Brethren that had held back (in the boy's eyes) his father. But his break with Mathers was, in 1901, not yet complete. Not until Crowley felt confident that he had forged his own links with the Secret Chiefs would he formally forsake Mathers.

After roughly a week of studying with Ramanathan, Crowley suggested that he and Bennett rent living quarters in Kandy, in the center of Ceylon, where the two of them could renew the intensive and independent modes of research that had served them in London two years before. Bennett assented, willing to give up his tutorial post due to his resolve to leave behind his Shaivite studies and become a Buddhist monk. By early 1902, Bennett would move to Burma to study Theravada Buddhism in a monastic *sangha* (community), a remarkable step for an Englishman of that time. Bennett's willingness to postpone that step for some months so as to tutor Crowley in yoga may properly be seen as a testimony to their friendship.

The furnished bungalow they rented in Kandy, nestled in the hills with a view of a lake and temple below, was a fitting setting for the study of yoga. Native servants, whom Crowley described as "sleepy and sinister," attended to the practical needs of the two men. Crowley's diaries detail a rigorous meditational practice for some six weeks. There are two surviving notebooks from the period. One, entitled in Hebrew *Sefer HaAin* (*The Book of Nothing*), features an invocation to Shiva on its opening page and is, in essence, a student notebook in which Crowley transcribed the fundamental terms of Hindu yogic philosophy and practice. The second diary, entitled *The Writings of Truth*, appears in different form (edited and enlarged upon) in *The Temple of Solomon the King*, published in *The Equinox* roughly a decade later. In his introductory invocation, Crowley termed himself, amongst other lowly epithets, "the Insect that crawls on Terra" and beseeched the aid of the goddess Bhavani, protectress of worthy students, to guide him in his yogic practice. There is a tone of regret as to past lowly magical pursuits:

> He taketh up the Pen of the Ready Writer, to record those Mysterious Happenings which came unto Him in His search for Himself.
>
> And the Beginning is of Spells & of Conjurations and of Evocations of the Evil Ones: Things Unlawful to write of, dangerous even to think of: wherefore they are not here written. But he beginneth with his Sojourning in the Isle of Lanka [Ceylon, now Sri Lanka]: the time of his dwelling with Maitrananda Swami [Bennett]. Wherefore, O Bhavani, bring Thou all unto the Proper End! To Thee be Glory.

In *The Writings of Truth* notebook, there is a gap between September 13 and 19. In the later *Temple of Solomon the King*, it is recorded that during this period Crowley was "called away for a few days on business (or in disgust?) to Colombo." He returned to Kandy on September 20 resolved to work on *pranayama* (control of the *prana* life force by breathing techniques) and to forsake "these follies of poetry and Vamacharya ('debauchery,' *i.e.* normal life) and health and vain things." The reference to *vamacharya* is most important, as it documents his first known foray into ritual sexual magic. This Sanskrit term refers to a Hindu tantric practice of sexual intercourse that could—if the spiritual aspirations of the participants were untainted by lust—reenact the cosmic coupling and union of Shiva and Sakti (Bhavani). In tantric tradition, *vamachara* is the "left-hand path" that involves physical intercourse with a woman (*vama*) as partner, while the "right-hand path" of *dakshinachara* enacts a symbolic intercourse. There is, in this tradition, no moral judgment attached to the use of "left" and "right," although Western interpreters have frequently interposed a negative connotation to "left" that is native to their own, but not Hindu, cultures. As scholars Ajit Mookerjee and Madhu Khanna have observed of *vamachara:* "According to tantra, those who are unable to cut the three knots of 'shame, hate and fear' are not worthy of being initiated into the path. The fundamental principle of the left-hand path is that spiritual progress cannot be achieved by falsely shunning our desires and passions but by sublimating those very aspects which make one fall, as a means of liberation." In September 1901, Crowley had not yet cut the three knots. Whatever he had done under the name of *vamachara* had induced a sense of "disgust" and "debauchery"—a decline into "normal life." He returned with relief to the isolated practice of yoga.

Yet the question of sex remained a vexing one for Crowley. Note that in the quotation from *Temple* above, "health" is included as one of the follies Crowley had pursued in Colombo. It was Crowley's belief that sexual release was essential to good health. One of the eight basic "limbs" (teachings) of the yogic philosophy is *yama* (control), which includes five basic vows of abstinence that are intended to free the consciousness of the aspirant toward a full dedication to yoga alone. One of these five vows is sexual continence. Crowley could not accept this as an inherently necessary condition for yogic attainment. As he later put it: "One of my principal inhibitions during this period was due to the apparent antinomy between the normal satisfaction of bodily appetites and the obvious conditions of success. I did not solve this completely until my attainment of the Grade of Master of the Temple in 1909, when at last I realized that every thought, word and act might be pressed into the service of the soul, more, that it must be if the soul were ever to be free."

Crowley would come, in his later writings on yoga—*Book 4 (Part 1)* (1912–13) and *Eight Lectures on Yoga* (1939)—to make distinctly original contributions to the study and interpretation of yoga in the West. His joustings with the vows required by *yama* are amongst these. As he wrote in *Book 4* (the boldfacing is Crowley's own), **"let the student decide for himself what form of life, what moral code, will least tend to excite his mind;** but once he has formulated it, let him stick to it, avoiding opportunism; and let him be careful to take no credit for what he does or refrains from doing—it is a purely practical code, of no value in itself." In *Eight Lectures on Yoga,* Crowley insisted that the vows of *yama* were necessarily linked to the culture of one's own native land:

[O]ne's real country—that is, the conditions—in which one happens to be born is the only one in which *yama* and *niyama* [virtue] can be practiced. You cannot dodge your *karma*. You have got to earn the right to devote yourself to Yoga proper by arranging for that devotion to be a necessary step in the fulfillment of your True Will. [. . .] Woe to that seven months' abortion who thinks to take advantage of the accidents of [Western] birth and, mocking the call of duty, sneaks off to stare at a blank wall in China!

Crowley himself, of course, went to Ceylon to learn his yoga. But his later warnings to students often contained tacit acknowledgments of his own past illusions.

There were, in these training days, peaks of realization as well. *The Writings of Truth* tells of two days—October 1 and 2, 1901—in which Crowley claimed to have reached the high yogic state of *dhyana*. Definitions of this state are inadequate and provisional. Crowley, in *Book 4*, quotes the great Hindu philosopher Patanjali, who classified the three highest states of yogic consciousness (*dhyana* being the penultimate): "*Dharana* is holding the mind on to some particular object. An unbroken flow of knowledge in that subject is *Dhyana*. When that, giving up all forms, reflects only the meaning, it is *Samadhi*." On October 1, after reciting *mantras* and practicing *pranayama* for much of the day, Crowley experienced a vision in which the central metaphor of his magical training emerged, ever so briefly, as an overwhelming fact of consciousness:

After some eight hours of this discipline arose The Golden Dawn.

While meditating, suddenly I became conscious of a shoreless space of darkness and a glow of crimson athwart. Deepening and brightening scarred by dull bars of slate-blue cloud arose the Dawn of Dawns, In splendour not of earth & its mean sun, blood-red, rayless, adamant, it rose, it rose! Carried out of myself, I asked not "Who is the witness?" absorbed utterly in contemplation of so stupendous and so marvellous a fact. For here was no doubt, no change, no wavering: infinitely more real than ought "physical" is the Golden Dawn of this Internal Sun!

The surprising aftermath of these two days was an immediate decline in Crowley's desire to practice yoga. It was as though *dhyana* was a mountain peak that he had scaled; once the peak was conquered, the desire to explore other mountains in the range—including the higher summit of *samadhi*—abruptly abated. It would be two years before Crowley again practiced yoga with any degree of seriousness; and that briefly renewed enthusiasm of 1903 would prove to be an aberration. Fundamentally, most of what Crowley knew firsthand of yoga came from his six weeks with Bennett in Ceylon. Yet it cannot be gainsaid that Crowley was a remarkably gifted student and that he made the most of his limited training. If he failed to continue a rigorous yogic training, he certainly did succeed in forging an original theoretical synthesis between yoga and magic, arguing cogently that both aimed, ultimately, at the identical goal of *samadhi*—the obliteration of self through union ("yoga" means "union" in Sanskrit) with the universe.

Having tested himself, to his satisfaction, in yoga, Crowley now turned to an analogous challenge on the physical plane—the assault on K2 or Chogo Ri. It was an odd sidenote to his yogic training that Crowley had decided, in August, not to go on with the expedition, but had been encouraged to do so by Bennett. As a result, Crowley wired Eckenstein on August 23 confirming his commitment to a spring 1902 expedition. According to Crowley, he entrusted £500 to Eckenstein on this date for expedition expenses, and another £500 some weeks later in case of emergency. This would have been a considerable financial outlay; but, as we shall see, Crowley's claims to have bankrolled the Chogo Ri expedition would later be challenged by other members of the expedition.

Nonetheless, the seriousness of his commitment is beyond question. Crowley was to arrive in India first, in early 1902, to make basic supply arrangements. In early November, he and Bennett parted ways. Bennett embarked by boat to Burma to the east, where, in the coastal city of Akyab, he would take residence in a Buddhist monastery, the Lamma Sayadaw Kyoung. Crowley voyaged west to India, there to begin travels that would eventually dovetail with the Chogo Ri expedition. Once arrived, he spent some weeks journeying through the southern Indian provinces. In Madura, Crowley donned a loincloth and took up a posture—with begging bowl—outside a nearby village. By his account, the locals were aware that he was an Englishman, but were impressed nonetheless by his knowledge of yoga. One Indian in particular befriended Crowley and put in a good word for him with the local temple authorities, who allowed him access to secret shrines at which he sacrificed a goat to Bhavani. This adventure delighted Crowley.

While in Madura, Crowley wrote—on November 16 and 17, 1901—the first drafts of two lengthy poems that would be included in the verse and essay volume *The Sword of Song* (1904). Subtitled *The Book of the Beast*, it was dedicated to Bennett under his new Buddhist name, taken on upon admission as a *bhikkhu* (monk) to the monastery at Akyab, of Ananda Metteyya (Metteyya, or Maitreya, is the title of the future-coming Buddha). The poems "Ascension Day" and "Pentecost" constitute an assault upon the intellectual and spiritual integrity of Christian teachings. The poet's Christian mother loves him, yet regards him as the Beast or False Prophet—"And by all sorts of monkey tricks/ Adds up my name to Six Six Six." But he takes on the title of Beast of *Revelation* with pride—"I will deserve it if I can;/ It is the number of a Man."—for it connotes a liberated existence that goes beyond dead ritual, faith mongering and sin consciousness. But Crowley takes care to specify that it is the husk of exoteric dogma in Christianity (and in all organized religions) that earns his hatred, and not the mystical teachings of Christ:

> "But why revile"
> (You urge me) "in that vicious style
> The very faith whose truths you seem
> (Elsewhere) to hold, to hymn supreme
> In your own soul?" Perhaps you know
> How mystic doctrines melt the snow
> Of any faith: redeem it to
> A fountain of reviving dew.
> So I with Christ: but few receive
> The Qabalistic Balm, believe
> Nothing—and choose to know instead.
> But, to that terror vague and dread,
> External worship; all my life—
> War to the knife! War to the knife!

Still resolved to visit Bennett in Burma, Crowley found a new companion to accompany him on the trip—a fellow Englishman named Edward Thornton. On January 21, 1902, they embarked by ship for Rangoon, the first step of the journey to Akyab. En route, a new perplexity arose. This time the issue was not sex, but rather the irreducible fact of earthly suffering—the first of the Four Noble Truths of Buddhism. Shortly after their arrival in Burma, Crowley saw, outside a pagoda, the anguishing sight of a boy aged roughly fourteen who suffered from hydrocephalus: "An enormous head, horrifyingly inane, surmounted a shrivelled body, too feeble even to support it." The impact of this drew Crowley more closely than ever before to the vision of universe offered by the Buddha.

After a brief hunting expedition in the Arakan Hills, Crowley and Thornton returned to Rangoon along the Irrawaddy River by way of a hired boat. This slow southern descent proved a respite from the sense of suffering—indeed, it was one of the joyous interludes of Crowley's life, one which he would remember on into old age. As the boat plowed ahead at a leisurely pace, he potted freely at game birds and fauna with his rifle, viewed the beauties of the tropical countryside and the Burmese villages, and experienced—during a night on which the dugout was moored to a teak tree—a most vivid sexual encounter, while still fully awake, with the Burmese elemental spirit (*Nat*) of that tree. As he avowed in the *Confessions:* "It was a woman vigorous and intense, of passion and purity so marvellous that she abides with me after these many years as few indeed of her human colleagues. I passed a sleepless night in a continuous sublimity of love."

Shortly thereafter, he and Thornton parted. By February 14 Crowley reached Akyab and reunited with Bennett, who, as Bhikkhu Ananda Sasanajotika Metteyya, had won a worshipful devotion on the part of certain Burmese locals who would visit the monastery and bow before him. During Crowley's roughly week-long visit, they discussed the possibilities for the greater dissemination of Buddhist teachings in Europe. For both men—who three years before had studied together as Perdurabo and Iehi Aour—the appeal and importance of magic had faded. For Metteyya, this drift from magic would be a permanent one. In 1903, he founded, in Burma, the International Buddhist Society, from which he issued the influential journal *Buddhism*. In 1908, he led the first Buddhist mission to England. As for Crowley, this attraction to Buddhism—sincere as it was—would scarcely outlast the year.

While visiting Bennett, Crowley plunged again into his poetry, composing the dramatic monologue "Ahab," in the voice of the Biblical king who had flagrantly abandoned the religion of Jahveh (published in *Ahab and Other Poems* (1903)). While Crowley wrote, his old friend Bennett meditated in a nearby hut. When the visit came to an end, the two men parted warmly. There is a diary entry for March 2—some two weeks later—in which Crowley records a dream in which he and Bennett were reunited, fulfilling Crowley's presentiment that this would occur—"and so making my death in N. India possible." Such was the respect and love Crowley felt for Bennett both as friend and teacher. As for "N. India," that was the site of Chogo Ri, or K2. If Crowley was afraid of what he would face there, he had good reason to be. K2 remains one of the most formidable mountaineering challenges in the world. The Eckenstein-Crowley expedition of 1902 was the first attempt upon it; not until 1954 would it finally be scaled.

Even as he awaited Chogo Ri, Crowley continued his philosophical self-examinations. In India, on March 20 and 21, Crowley composed "*Berashith*" (Hebrew for 'in the beginning'; the first word of *Genesis*), an essay he would publish privately in Paris in 1903. In the Paris edition, the author is given as "Abhavananda"—Crowley's chosen Hindu name during his yogic tutelage under Bennett—and its intended audience is "the Sangha [Buddhist community] of the West." Included is a discussion of ceremonial magic in which—in sharp contrast to his later writings—magic is viewed as a mere preparatory training for yoga—that is, "a magnificent gymnasium for those who are not already finished mental athletes.[. . .] When a man has evoked and mastered such forces as Taphtatharath, Belial, Amaimon, and the great powers of the elements, then he may safely be permitted to begin to try to stop thinking."

It had been a year since Eckenstein had introduced him to the techniques of raja yoga in Mexico. It must have been with a sense both of pride and affection that Crowley again greeted his friend in Delhi on March 23, 1902. Eckenstein, as leader, had assembled a core team of four climbers in addition to Crowley and himself. This team Crowley would now meet. He came to dislike most of them intensely, and with none—including Eckenstein—would his relations remain smooth. But together, they would mount an expedition that contemporary historians of Himalayan mountaineering have come to see as remarkable in achievement.

At the time of the Eckenstein-Crowley expedition, the very existence of K2 had been known to Europeans for less than sixty years. It was in 1856 that the British Captain T. G. Montgomerie sighted—from a survey point 137 miles removed—a cluster of peaks in the Karakoram Range that lies just to the east of the Hindu Kush. The sequential numerical entry of peaks in Montgomerie's logbook accounts for the drab name "K2." Amongst the native Baltis, K2 was known as "Chogo Ri" ("giant peak"). It is vital to understand, when considering the difficulties of the Eckenstein-Crowley expedition, that K2 is a far more isolated mountain than most, even in the Himalayas. Everest, by contrast, has relatively neighboring villages. But the closest village to K2, Askole, is a ten-day march away over rugged glacial terrain. Supplying a full-scale expedition to K2 was, and remains, a logistical nightmare.

Small-minded personality disputes can wreak havoc on grand Himalayan explorations, and it was just such a dispute that nearly brought the Eckenstein-Crowley expedition to an end before it had fairly begun. The two hostile parties were Eckenstein and Sir Martin Conway, who in this same year of 1902 had just been named the president of the British Alpine Club. Eckenstein and Conway had a history of ill will that was intimately connected with K2. Ten years earlier, in 1892, Eckenstein had been a member of an expedition, headed by Conway, that would be the first to explore the Upper Baltoro Glacier, which extends southeast of K2. But Eckenstein did not accompany Conway as far as the Upper Baltoro. According to Eckenstein, it was friction between himself and Conway that led him to withdraw; according to Conway, his decision to ask Eckenstein to leave was based on the latter's having become physically unwell. In private, Conway accused Eckenstein—the specifics are unknown—of having attempted to poison him. Eckenstein returned to England after having served six months under Conway in the Karakoram Range, and without ever having obtained Conway's necessary permission to undertake a major climb. Shortly thereafter, on the Upper Baltoro, Conway made the ascents that were to win him knighthood. Amongst these was Pioneer Peak, at 22,600 feet, then a world record. Conway returned to England, published a book on the expedition in which his exploits were humbly but firmly set forth, and became a national hero.

Eckenstein had waited ten years for his return to the Baltoro Glacier. In Crowley's view, there were behind-the-scenes machinations by Conway intended to frustrate Eckenstein at every step. Definite proof here is lacking, but Crowley's charge becomes plausible as one sifts through the evidence. First, Eckenstein found it difficult to convince experienced English climbers—most of whom were Alpine Club members—to join him. Only one Englishman did so—Guy Knowles, twenty-two, just out of Trinity College, Cambridge. Knowles would later agree with Crowley's claim that Conway opposed the expedition, an agreement all the more significant in that Knowles—for reasons we shall soon come to—fairly detested Crowley. The three remaining members of the core team were all continental Europeans with Alpine climbing backgrounds. There were two Austrians, both age thirty-one: H. Pfannl and V. Wesseley. From Switzerland came the physician for the expedition, J. Jacot Guillarmod, age thirty-three. It was a disunified group, with only Eckenstein possessing first-hand experience of the Himalayas.

All the more devastating then, was the seizure of Eckenstein by the Indian authorities. On March 30, in Tret, the deputy commissioner of Rawalpindi arrived to inform Eckenstein that, though not under arrest for any formal charge, he would be detained and compelled to return to Rawalpindi, there to attempt to take up the matter with higher authorities. The timing here was critical. For only in the spring, before the onset of the monsoon season, and in the fall, before the onset of the icelocked winters, are Himalayan climbs practicable. Eckenstein's detainment would mean insupportable months of delay. Eckenstein placed Crowley in command with instructions to lead the team into Kashmir, where Eckenstein would rejoin it when he could. He did so after some two weeks of delay that ended when, after "waylaying one great man" (the phrase is that of the *Friend of India,* which reported on Eckenstein's plight) "in the mail train on his way from Calcutta to Simla," Eckenstein gained the requisite visa to proceed. The "great man" was Lord Curzon, Viceroy of India. In the view of both Crowley and Knowles, Conway had prevailed on Curzon to block Eckenstein, whose threats to tell all to the press at last caused Curzon to relent.

During Eckenstein's detention, Crowley had led the expedition on to Srinigar, the capital of Kashmir. Trouble had arisen with the horse-drawn *ekka* cart drivers, and Crowley was called on to quell the dispute. By his account, the drivers had begun to lag unnecessarily, so as to collect more days of pay—under ten cents a day, a not unusual wage for the region. It was for the sake of dignity, not money, that Crowley felt forced to act: "Had I failed to understand the psychology of the ekka driver, we should have been nagged to death by pin-pricks.[. . .] [The traveler] has to be uniformly calm, cheerful, just, perspicacious, indulgent and inexorable. He must decline to be swindled out of a farthing. If he once gives way, he is done for." There is present here a colonialist bias that at times verged into outright racism. Crowley was, at least, more frank than most Englishmen of his age. As he later wrote: "England is losing India by consenting to admit the existence of the conquered races; by consenting to argue; by trying to find a value for incommesurables. Indian civilization is far superior to our own and to enter into open competition is to invoke defeat. We won India by matching our irrational, bigoted, brutal manhood against their etiolated culture." (Crowley's own "brutal manhood" included a vehement distaste for the notion of Indian men making love with English women.) In the case of the leader of the drivers, Crowley's strategy was to remain impassive through the day, and then—once arrived in camp—to grab him suddenly by the beard (a blood insult by Muslim custom) and beat him with a belt: "The result was that I never had the slightest difficulties with natives in India ever afterwards and was able to practice perfect tolerance of genuine accidents. I had forced them to respect us, which, with an Indian, is the first step to acquiring his love."

Eckenstein rejoined the expedition on April 22. By late May, they had reached Askole, the last village before K2. Here they spent ten days gathering final supplies. So efficient had been their progress that they were two weeks ahead of their own schedule. In Askole, Eckenstein and Crowley had their first serious quarrel. As the expedition was about to cross the Baltoro Glacier, Eckenstein decreed that the baggage of individual team members not exceed forty pounds. But Crowley surpassed this limit due to his insistence on taking along editions of his favorite English poets, including Milton and Shelley, which had been specially bound in vellum so as to better withstand the elements. Eckenstein railed, but Crowley refused to give way, threatening to leave the expedition if his books were disallowed. It was Crowley's belief that this reading matter aided him in maintaining "perfect mental balance" during the difficult weeks to come.

En route to the Baltoro, Crowley once more intervened decisively in the affairs of his porters. This time there came a more sanguine judgment, one that reveals the best of the man. One of the Pathan overseers had been bullying one of the Kashmiri porters and went so far as to make a claim to have somehow won the Kashmiri's old torn coat. What made this claim egregious was that the expedition had provided the Pathans with fine new coats for the journey. Crowley was called on to judge the claim, and in Solomonic fashion ruled that while the Kashmiri's old coat had been fairly won by the Pathan, the Pathan's coat belonged to Crowley himself, who would now take it and—to the delight of the assembled crowd—give it to the Kashmiri.

From this point, the physical conditions became more challenging. Several days of difficult marches over the Baltoro led to the establishment of numerically designated base camps. On June 16, Crowley—leading an advance group of Balti porters—created Camp 8 (16,592 feet) within view of K2. He moved on to establish Camp 9 (17,332 feet) directly beneath the south face of K2, and then ascended to Camp 10 (18,733 feet)—but only after carefully training the Balti porters in the use of climbing ropes and scraped-out ice steps. At this point, Crowley decided that the final ascent could be made along what is now called the Abruzzi Ridge.

Crowley had paid a price for progressing so far, as would all members of the expedition. An extreme alteration of temperature between night and day—and even between sun and shade—made it possible, as one marched along in one's winter dress and gear, to burn from the extreme (in high altitudes) sun on one side of one's face and body and to suffer from extreme cold on the other. On June 29, due to prolonged exposure to the glaring whiteness, Crowley went snow-blind, a temporary but terribly painful condition—like "having red hot sand at the back of one's eyes."

Crowley's choice of the Camp 10 site was not seconded by his team members upon their arrival. A snowstorm that endured for five days— from July 2 to July 6—made the Camp 10 exposure seem ill-advised. But there was a further challenge to Crowley's judgment which he resented still more. Pfannl and Wesseley had gone on to establish a Camp 11 (roughly 20,000 feet) and argued that an ascent up the northeast ridge of K2 from that camp would be preferable to Crowley's proposed route from Camp 10. By vote on July 7, Crowley was overruled. It is impossible, in retrospect, to properly judge the respective merits of the two routes. The eminent mountaineer and author Galen Rowell did note— in his generally admiring account of the Eckenstein-Crowley expedition—that Crowley had fallen victim to a mistaken sense of scale, in the face of the Himalayan vastness, by imagining that a mere two days would suffice for a K2 ascent from Camp 10. But Crowley's firm belief that the alternate route was folly, coupled with the terrible weather, led to his conviction, as July wore on, that "the expedition had failed in its main objective, and I was not in the least interested in killing myself gradually against my judgment."

The worn nerves of the team members, each of whom faced a similar dawning sense of failure, began to show. The sheer physical strain made this all but inevitable. They suffered from cold, lack of exercise (due to cramped tent life during the repeated snowstorms), a limited diet, and the practical difficulties of maintaining a cooking fire, or even smoking pipes, at such high altitudes. Crowley, along with the others, suffered from severe indigestion and weight loss, as well as bouts of malarial fever. At one point, Crowley—while feverish—came for some reason to feel threatened by Knowles and pulled his Colt revolver on him. Knowles, who was well at the time, forcibly disarmed Crowley. This inglorious episode, to which Knowles subsequently attested—indeed, he displayed the captured Colt in his home to the end of his life—does not appear in the *Confessions*, in which the breakdowns of other team members are carefully accounted.

In the case of an illness that afflicted Pfannl, Crowley showed himself to be—despite his contempt for his patient—a remarkable amateur diagnostician. Pfannl and Wesseley had gone off by themselves to establish a Camp 12 (roughly 21,000 feet). At this height, in mid-July, Pfannl's health broke down, with fluid beginning to fill his lungs. He was brought back down to Camp 11, where Crowley concluded that he suffered not from a pathogen-related pneumonia—the usual diagnosis for lung fluids—but from pulmonary edema. This latter condition—it is now known—occurs spontaneously at high altitudes. Pfannl was treated for his pain with morphine and then, with Wesseley, sent back down the mountain by sledge. He lived. As Roswell later observed: "Many climbers died because the drugs used against pneumonia did absolutely nothing for pulmonary edema. By chance, Crowley's group did exactly the right thing by removing Pfannl immediately to lower elevation. The isolation of edema from pneumonia in Crowley's account was long before its time and one of the earliest ever recorded."

The brutal wear and tear of extended encampment at high altitudes led Crowley to another medical realization that—while disputed in his day—has since become accepted. Physiologists are now in agreement that, in altitudes over 17,000–19,000 feet, and varying to some extent with the individual, the human body is subject to constant deterioration. But the common wisdom at the time of the Eckenstein-Crowley expedition—and for some decades after—was that climbers could, with time and practice, "acclimate" to the very highest mountain altitudes. For Crowley, this notion was absurd. "The only thing you can do is to lay in a stock of energy, get rid of all your fat at the exact moment when you have a chance to climb a mountain, and jump back out of its reach, so to speak, before it can take its revenge. To talk of acclimatization is to adopt the psychology of the man who trained his horse gradually to live on a single straw a day, and would have revolutionized our system of nutrition, if the balky brute had not been aggravating enough to die on his hands." Crowley would wrest for himself a dour world record from the hardships of the Baltoro—sixty-eight straight days of glacial life, two more than any other member of the party due to his having served as an advance scout. "I hope I may be allowed to die in peace with it. It would be a sorry ambition in anyone to grasp my laurels and I can assure him that to refrain will bring its own reward."

Eckenstein was one of those who believed in the possibility of acclimatization, but even he had to recognize that the team could hold out only so long. A July 27 letter by Eckenstein to a climbing friend in England—which came, ironically, to be published as a news note in the *Alpine Club Journal*—sounded the surrender: "Never anywhere in the world have I experienced such bad weather.[. . .] Our prospects of ascending a high mountain, or any mountain, are consequently practically nil on this occasion. We expect quite difficulty enough—unless material improvement in the weather ensues—in forcing our way down." As it happened, the descent, begun in early August, was not a particularly difficult one, though the mood of the team members was sullen. At the village of Skardu came the joy of abundant food. Crowley rhapsodized: "There we found fresh ripe grapes, potatoes and green corn. Our joy was unconfined; youth at the prow and pleasure at the helm!" The remainder of the journey was an anticlimax. On September 6 they arrived once more in Srinigar.

A lassitude overcame Crowley at this point. Magic and yoga had palled and Buddhism now seemed a mere philosophical puzzle. As for his status as a climber, the expedition had made its mark as a first attempt, even if it had not conquered K2. But the disregard for Eckenstein and Crowley within Alpine Club circles led to minimal recognition in England. When, for example, Sir Francis Younghusband wrote a history of attempts on Himalayan peaks, he devoted one sentence to the Eckenstein-Crowley expedition, in which he pointedly avoided mention of either: "The Swiss, Dr. Jacot Guillarmod, explored in the same region."

Crowley's travels in the next two months were guided only by the goal of eventual arrival in Paris, where Gerald Kelly now lived and where Mathers could be faced anew. On October 4, he voyaged from India on the S.S. *Egypt*—first to Aden and then, on October 4, to Cairo, where he disembarked and for some weeks led a life of luxury coupled with a careful observation of native Islamic ways. But a meeting with Mathers remained the signal event on the horizon. In a letter to Kelly, there was a dark conspiratorial tone: "I have business also with the chiefs of the Order of which I have recently heard so much and seen so little. But I do not wish my presence in Paris known until the Hour of Triumph[. . .]" Once arrived in Paris, November 1902, Crowley wasted little time in seeing Mathers, but their face-to-face meetings—as to which Crowley remained uncharacteristically reticent—must have been uneasy. Crowley came away with the conviction that Mathers had stolen certain expensive luggage that Crowley claimed to have entrusted to Mathers before leaving for Mexico in June 1900. For a genuine adept to engage in such theft would, of course, have been unthinkable. Adopting Mathers's view that the scheming Madame Horos and her husband—who had deceived Mathers three years earlier—were black magic adepts, Crowley now saw Mathers and his wife Mina as having come under their spell.

Small wonder, then, that in early 1903 magical warfare was launched by Mathers against Crowley, and that the means employed—as testified to by Crowley—should be one favored by Madame Horos: The transformation of a woman from aged crone to youthful, vampiric succubus. In *The Temple of Solomon the King*, the story of Crowley's successful resistance is told. It begins with a plea from Gerald Kelly (who would later dismiss this entire episode as an invention on Crowley's part) to rescue a friend of his—Miss Premble, an American painter—who had fallen into the evil clutches of a much older woman, Mrs. Longworth. Crowley paid a visit to the flat of Mrs. Longworth, who transformed herself, as they spoke, from a "middle-aged woman, worn with strange lusts" into "a young woman of bewitching beauty." It took all of Crowley's magical powers to ward off the attempted seduction, which would have drained him of his blood, or true spiritual life.

The pleasures of the Parisian boulevard were far more amenable. Crowley was a guest, through the winter of 1903, at Kelly's studio in the Montparnasse quarter on the Rue Campagne Premier. Crowley wasted little time in making the rounds and striking up a liaison with Nina Oliver, an artist's model. Crowley would later claim that his "adoration of Nina made her the most famous girl in the quarter for a dozen years and more." According to the later testimony of Kelly, "Crowley was widely unknown in the Montparnasse quarter. His French was poor. He was, for the most part, I fancy, disliked by the few whom he met." Still, there was a rather eminent circle in which Crowley certainly made an impression. It was made up primarily of expatriate Englishmen soaking up the ambience of Paris. These included the British novelists Arnold Bennett and W. Somerset Maugham, the Bloomsbury art critic Clive Bell, the American sculptor Paul Wayland Bartlett, and the Canadian painter James Wilson Morrice. Crowley sought to become one of them, but could not: "It had already been branded on my forehead that I was the Spirit of Solitude, the Wanderer of the Waste, Alastor; for while I entered with absolute spontaneous enthusiasm into the artistic atmosphere of Paris, I was always subconsciously aware that here I had no continuing city."

The response to Crowley bears out his sense of having been branded. He won into their circle by his audaciousness and exotic tales of magic and the remote Himalayas. But their fascination was mingled with great unease. It was Maugham who left the most vivid portrait of Crowley (now age twenty-seven) in this period. Indeed, Maugham devoted an entire novel to him. *The Magician* (1908) had its genesis in meetings between Crowley and Maugham—one year Crowley's senior and already a known writer—at Le Chat Blanc, a cafe on the Rue d'Odessa favored by the circle. In an introduction to *The Magician* written late in his life, Maugham recalled his impressions of Crowley, the model for the nefarious villain, Oliver Haddo:

> I took an immediate dislike to him [Crowley], but he interested and amused me. He was a great talker and he talked uncommonly well. In early youth, I was told, he was extremely handsome, but when I knew him he had put on weight, and his hair was thinning.[. . .] He was a fake, but not entirely a fake.[. . .] He was a liar and unbecomingly boastful, but the odd thing was that he had actually done some of the things he boasted of.

Maugham did not write *The Magician* until 1907, and the novel draws from events in Crowley's life not only from this time in Paris, but also from the intervening years. In his later introduction, Maugham was careful to note that he drew the evil Haddo in a manner "more striking in appearance, more sinister and more ruthless than Crowley ever was." For his part, Crowley would acknowledge the accuracy of the "shirt cuff" method of characterization employed by Maugham: "The hero's witty remarks were, many of them, my own.[. . .] Maugham had taken some of the most private and personal incidents of my life [. . .] He had added a number of the many absurd legends of which I was the central figure." *The Magician*—for all its weakness (acknowledged by Maugham himself) as a work of fiction—exemplified the gothic treatment of Crowley subsequently followed by a host of fiction writers, from M. R. James to Christopher Isherwood to Dennis Wheatley: sensualist, satanist, possessed of a hypnotic gaze and a riveting power over women, driven by the purest of evil hearts. Here is Haddo upon his first entrance into the "Chien Noir" (Maugham's fictionalized name for the Chat Blanc):

> He was clearly not old, though his corpulence added to his apparent age. His features were good, his ears small, and his nose delicately shaped. He had big teeth, but they were white and even. His mouth was large, with heavy moist lips. He had the neck of a bullock. His dark, curling hair had retreated from the forehead and temples in such a way as to give his clean-shaven face a disconcerting nudity. The baldness of his crown was vaguely like a tonsure. He had the look of a very wicked, sensual priest. Margaret [the heroine whom Haddo seduces, marries and

destroys], stealing a glance at him as he ate, on a sudden violently shuddered; he affected her with an uncontrollable dislike.

The story of the clash between Maugham and Crowley upon the novel's publication in 1908 must be reserved for Chapter Five. But it may be noted that Crowley left a vivid corroborating portrait in his pseudonymous novel *Snowdrops from a Curate's Garden* (written in 1904 and published in a private limited edition in France, probably in that same year). *Snowdrops* may best be described as a satire—and wildly lewd celebration—of Victorian pornography. In an ironic foreshadowing of Maugham's novel, Crowley also changed the feline Chat Blanc into a canine "Chien Rouge." It is further ironic that the character of "L . . . "—whom Crowley based on himself (with Gerald Kelly as "D . . .")—so closely paralleled that of Oliver Haddo. Both characters were cutting cafe wits who relished humiliating their adversaries: "D . . .'s cold acumen and L . . .'s superb indignation, expressed in fiery swords of speech, would drive some luckless driveller from the room. Or at times they would hold down their victim, a bird fascinated by a snake, while they pitilessly exposed his follies to the delighted crowd.[. . .] They were feared, these two!"

But Crowley was far more deferential, this same winter, in his relations with the great sculptor Auguste Rodin. While Crowley liked to give the impression of a friendship between them, the truth was that, as a devotee of Rodin's work, Crowley was permitted a brief visit to his studio at Meudon and a chance to talk with the master about his art. The underlying circumstances were as follows: When Crowley first arrived in Paris, he learned of the acrimonious debate surrounding Rodin's recently completed *Balzac*, a sculpture which expressed the spirit of the novelist, but strayed from the realistic poses of the man already familiar to the French public. Crowley rushed to the defense of Rodin by composing a sonnet, "Balzac," which was (along with another Crowley sonnet, "Rodin") subsequently translated into French verse by Marcel Schwob, a Parisian writer of Crowley's acquaintance. Rodin's admiration for Crowley's verse, in translation, included high praise for "its unexpected flower of violence, its good sense and its irony." Some have argued that it was Schwob's excellence as a translator, not Crowley's as a poet, that elicited this praise. But to be fair to Crowley, Rodin's comments pertain to matters of content and stance innate to the English originals. Further, *Rodin in Rime* does contain examples of Crowley the poet at his best, briskly rhythmic and enraptured, as in his sonnet in honor of Rodin's *La Femme Accroupie* (*The Crouching Woman*), which begins:

Swift and subtle and thin are the arrows of Art:
I strike through the gold of the skin to the gold of the heart.
As you sit there mighty in bronze I adore the twist
Of the miracle ankle gripped by the miracle wrist.

Rodin in Rime was ultimately published privately by Crowley in 1907, in a volume that included lithographs by Rodin.

In other writings, of this period, by contrast, Crowley displayed a darkly skeptical outlook. For example, in a poem sent as a New Year's 1903 greeting card to friends, he held out the prospect of Nirvana as the only escape "from the fatal mischief of the world"—a world Crowley deemed equivalent with "Hell." But in "Science and Buddhism," an essay finished during this same winter, Crowley argued, in a more hopeful tone, that an empirical approach to Buddhist teachings could lead to expanded scientific knowledge of human consciousness. The alternative—to conduct science within narrow materialist confines—would lead only to intolerance and a futile split between science and the spirit: "If Science is never to go beyond its present limits; if the barriers which metaphysical speculation shows to exist are never to be transcended, then indeed we are thrown back on faith, and all the rest of the nauseous mess of mediaeval superstition." In recent decades, the view urged by Crowley—quite ahead of its time—for the application of scientific method to the study of the nature of consciousness has earned broad interest.

In April 1903, Crowley left Paris to return to Boleskine—the site, three years earlier, of his proposed Abra-Melin Operation. But now, Crowley found himself at a loss. As he later wrote, "It is strange to look back on myself at twenty-seven, completely persuaded of the truth of the most extravagant claims of mysticism and magick, yet completely disillusioned with regard to the universe." That May, Crowley wrote a summary memorandum of his spiritual progress over the prior four years. In his world travels, he had passed through a stage first of Hinduism and then of nominalist philosophy, in which all deities were viewed as unimportant. His present stage was that of "orthodox" Buddhism and the "Path of Research" into consciousness—the viewpoint expressed in "Science and Buddhism." In that essay, the disparagement of magic was thorough—his prior devotion to that path "has now no particular meaning."

But a philosophical escape hatch, as it were, was provided for in the memorandum. Crowley posited two "reservations" to "orthodox" Buddhism. The first, an affirmation of the value of Hindu meditational techniques, was a minor matter. But his second accorded to magic a unique reality. As Crowley put it: "I cannot deny that certain phenomena do accompany the use of certain rituals; I only deny the usefulness of such methods to the White Adept." Magic was, in short, useful only for black—that is, ego-ridden—purposes. Nonetheless, this latter reservation shows that Crowley could not quite forget the heights and raptures of magic. As an all-but-convinced Buddhist, Crowley was finding himself, despite himself, desperately bored. Magic—with its eloquence, ritual drama, and deliberate intensification of emotion—had been precisely suited to his predilections. He could not, even now, place it in the same dull box of appearances as the rest of the phenomenal universe.

Magic remained on Crowley's mind, however, as evidenced by his completion, in July 1903, of an essay grandly entitled "The Initiated Interpretation of Ceremonial Magic." This would serve as the introduction to an edition, published by Crowley in 1904, of the Goetia, a famed sixteenth-century grimoire attributed to King Solomon. Crowley claimed to have "employed" Mathers (no financial terms are mentioned) to translate the Goetia from various extant Hebrew, Latin, French and vernacular English manuscripts. But in his edition of the Goetia, Crowley accorded credit for the translation not to Mathers but to a "dead hand." To add injury to this insult, it is doubtful that Crowley ever "employed" Mathers. According to J. F. C. Fuller, who would become an intimate friend of Crowley in the years ahead, Crowley had simply helped himself to a copy of the translation in April 1900, during the time of the London revolt, when he had enjoyed brief but unrestricted access to the Golden Dawn files stored in the headquarters of the rebels, the Isis-Urania Temple. If so, then Crowley published the work with neither proper credit nor payment to Mathers—a rank and grievous theft.

But returning the focus to July 1903, the central question becomes: Why bother with the Goetia at this point, when Crowley had already stated in his May 1903 memorandum that magic was of no use to a "White Adept"? In "The Initiated Interpretation of Ceremonial Magic," Crowley allowed that the Goetia could afford satisfactions on the human plane, but claimed higher aspirations for himself: "For me these practices are useless; but for the benefit of others less fortunate I give them to the world, together with this explanation of, and apology for, them." And yet, for all this insistence on the uselessness of magic, Crowley was careful, in his edition of the Goetia, to claim preeminence (specifically, over Mathers) as "ye Wise Perdurabo, that Myghte Chiefe of ye Rosy-Cross Fraternitye, now sepulchred in ye Vault of ye Collegium S.S." Magic may have been a toy to Crowley, but it was a cherished toy.

His "apology" for magic in the essay was a brilliant extension of the spiritual-minded empiricism championed in "Science and Buddhism." There, Crowley insisted that: "The spirits of the *Goetia* are portions of the human brain.[. . .] Our Ceremonial Magic fines down, then, to a series of minute, though of course empirical, physiological experiments, and whoso will carry them through intelligently need not fear the result." The experiment consists, fundamentally, of an intensified focus on a particular desire. As for the literal-minded, who ask if one ever obtains such fantastic results as, for example, to "understand the voices of nature" or "obtain treasure"—Crowley responded by way of analogy and allegory. Analogy: A naturalist learns the significance of many animal sounds that a layperson cannot even distinguish; so may a magical practitioner, through careful observation, develop enhanced understanding of "the voices of nature." Allegory: One's business capacity (ability to "obtain treasure") can be enhanced through the rigorous training of one's mind. In sum, then, in "The Initiated Interpretation of Ceremonial Magic," Crowley had leveled magic to the usefulness—for others—of a psychological self-help tome. As he later commented in the *Confessions*, "My interpretation conformed with the mechanical theory of Victorian physics.[. . .] It was long before I understood that all explanations of the universe are ultimately interchangeable like the geometries of Euclid, Riemann and Lobatchewsky."

One mere earthly desire that Crowley still did possess was for sex. During this summer, he wrote—as Laird of Boleskine Manor—a terse letter to the Vigilance Society in London complaining "that the prostitution in this neighborhood [the small nearby town of Foyers] is most unpleasantly conspicuous." A representative from London was sent up to investigate and found nothing. This finding was communicated to the Laird, who then fired off this postcard as a final salvo of mockery: "Conspicuous by its absence, you fools!" In mid-July, Crowley took matters into his own hands by going to Edinburgh and picking up a woman whom he referred to only as the "red-headed Arabella." It was arranged that she would come to take residence at Boleskine in August.

But then, in early August, Crowley received an invitation from Kelly to join him, along with his sister Rose, his mother, and a few other acquaintances at Strathpeffer, a Scottish locale not far from Boleskine at which they were vacationing. The red-headed Arabella had not yet arrived, and Crowley was bored. He accepted the invitation, though it seemed to promise little. He had met Kelly's sister Rose before. She was a highly attractive woman, three years younger than Crowley, with thick, tumbling auburn hair and a passionate nature. He regarded her as "a charming woman but hardly an intellectual companion." And so, when they conversed together at lunch on August 11, and Rose explained her plight—that she had conducted an unwise but passionate affair with a married man, and that now her family was pressuring her, so as to avoid any further embarrassment, to enter into a marriage with a man she did not love—Crowley felt that he could offer an utterly dispassionate solution.

He himself would marry Rose. It would be a marriage of form only. He would return to Boleskine, and she could return untrammeled to her affair.

If Crowley's offer lacked seriousness, it was sincere enough in terms of a disdain for the Anglican piety personified by Rose's father, the Reverend F. F. Kelly. More fundamentally, as Crowley allowed in the *Confessions*, his suggestion showed an astonishing ignorance of "the elements of psychology" and "the mysterious force of human nature," in that he failed to foresee that the sheer drama of the gesture could induce—as it did in Rose and himself—a genuine love and passion. But his real naïveté was in failing to plumb his own motives for making the suggestion in the first place. For example, Crowley gave no thought to linking his proposal to Rose with his brief engagement to an unnamed English woman eight months earlier, in January 1903, or his engagement to the American opera singer, Susan Strong, in 1899. Marriage was something he both wanted and yet shied away from—a common enough pattern for a man in his twenties. But could not a spur-of-the-moment proposal to Rose—dispassionate in context—be viewed as a subconscious means of evading the fear while reaching the desired state of marriage?

To accomplish the elopement while forestalling interference by her family, the two traveled at once by train to the nearby Scottish town of Dingwall, where the next day—August 12, 1903—a simple declaration of vows before the town lawyer sufficed, under Scottish law, to render the marriage legally binding. Crowley retained sufficient aplomb to dress the part of a Scottish Laird—complete with a dirk which he kissed during the ceremony so as to pledge his faith. As for the bride, Crowley wryly admitted: "I never thought of kissing *her!*"

The two had informed Gerald Kelly of their plans the previous day, before setting off to Dingwall. According to Crowley, Kelly had taken it as a joke and gone on with his game of golf. Their extended absence had sufficed to persuade him otherwise, for, as Crowley tells it with obvious relish, an outraged Gerald Kelly burst into the lawyer's office just after the ceremony was completed and, upon learning that Crowley had married his sister, aimed a futile blow at his new brother-in-law: "I am ashamed to say that I could not suppress a quiet smile."

This later patronizing tone is in marked contrast to a letter written by Crowley to Kelly on the very day of the wedding. As the letter alludes to accusations made by Kelly the previous day, Crowley's later account of Kelly jocularly going on with his golf may be taken as a fabrication. Crowley was fiercely determined to justify himself; he included in this letter a veiled threat of a libel action, perhaps against Kelly himself, to defend his good name. But there was an element of frank sincerity as well. Crowley acknowledged a wanton element in his past. But he insisted upon his essential purity of intention, both as to Rose and as to Buddhist attainment. The letter is, at root, a frank admission of Crowley's shame over his sexual nature—in particular, his bisexuality:

> I may have been a pig-fancier in my youth; but for that very reason I should not attempt to make a sow's ear out of a silk purse [Rose]. It is the ignorant that make such mistakes. I have been trying since I joined the GD in '98 steadily and well to repress my nature in all ways. I have suffered much, but I have won, and you know it. Coffin-worms and their like are as much chips (as opposed to coins) to me as to you. I wanted to seal my victory with a very mighty blow. If I failed, it is of over-generosity, over-trust in your real friendship for me, which you have after all.[. . .]
>
> Why must nine-tenths of my life i.e. the march to Buddhism, go for nothing; the atrophied one hundred thousandth always spring up and choke me, and that in the house of my friends?

The "victory" referred to here is, it would seem, the final conquest of the "atrophied" homosexual element in his "nature" by means of the ultimate heterosexual ratification—marriage. This letter makes it plain that the decision to marry involved issues, for Crowley, that went far beyond Kelly family pressures on Rose. His own identity—and refuge—was being forged as well.

Crowley later described the months following his marriage to Rose as "an uninterrupted sexual debauch." Who, then, was the woman who had stirred in him such a deep and genuine passion, and how had the flames arisen of a sudden?

Rose Edith Kelly was born in 1878, three years after Crowley. Her family was financially comfortable, and she was raised in the fashion of a Victorian gentlewoman—that is, trained in the social graces and excluded from academic or other achievement—the whole overlaid with

Anglican propriety. In 1895, she married a Major Skerritt, R.A.M.C.; until he died two years later, they lived together in South Africa. Through the remainder of her twenties, until she met Crowley, she had affairs and lived, apparently, by means of the support of her dead husband's estate and her own family. Crowley viewed Rose's mother as the source of her daughter's failings: "From her mother she [Rose] inherited dipsomania [alcoholism], and as bad a case for stealth, cunning, falsehood, treachery, and hypocrisy as the specialist I consulted had ever known. This was, however, latent during the satisfaction of sexuality, which ousted all else in her life, as it did in mine."

Whether her symptoms were entirely "latent" early on, or whether Crowley simply paid them no mind, by the end of their wedding day, the two were well on the way to being swept off their feet by each other. That evening, in their hotel in Dingwall, the newlyweds enjoyed a dinner of grouse during which a great deal of champagne was consumed. Thereafter, the bride retired to their room alone. Crowley was now taken with anxiety, wondering if even a marriage of convenience was suitable for an aspiring Buddhist. But he resolved to rise to the occasion as a poet and, seated in the hotel lobby, penned a passionate rondel to his bride that began: "Rose on the breast of the world of spring,/ I press my breast against thy bloom;/ My subtle life drawn out to thee; to thee/ its mood and meanings cling." These latter two lines would prove to be precisely accurate.

The newlyweds promptly became lovers. In his ever-present Oxford edition of Shelley, which had accompanied him to K2, there is a marginal entry dated August 19, 1903, one week after the wedding, alongside a verse in "Epipsychidion" (Greek for soul-union). Shelley argued, in that verse, that "True Love" is an expansive spiritual force, like "Imagination," that develops best by "Gazing on many truths." Shelley warned that:

> Narrow
> The heart that loves, the brain that contemplates,
> The life that wears, the spirit that creates
> One object, and one form, and builds thereby
> A sepulchre for its eternity.

This warning Crowley would not accept. His terse marginal correction to Shelley: "The error here is in supposing that one woman is only one: the right one is many million." Directly beneath, there is a more humble entry dated August 10, 1907, almost exactly five years later: "Hats off to Shelley—he was right." Such, in microcosm, was the course of the marriage.

But what a glorious beginning! For all his subsequent disillusionment, Crowley never lost sight of what had enraptured him in those first years of marriage. Rose possessed a buoyant, adaptive, and adventurous personality, one capable of appreciating, as Crowley did, the dichotomous joys of aristocratic pleasure and rugged travel. She was a muse par excellence, inspiring the best love poems that Crowley would write. His summation of her in the *Confessions* sounds a rare note in Crowley's writing on women—praise not only for her charms, but for her character: "Physically and morally, Rose exercised on every man she met a fascination which I have never seen anywhere else, not a fraction of it. She was like a character in a romantic novel, a Helen of Troy or a Cleopatra; yet, while more passionate, unhurtful. She was essentially a good woman. Her love sounded every abyss of lust, soared to every splendour of the empyrean."

From Dingwall, the newlyweds went on to Boleskine House to carry on a three-week honeymoon. The imminent arrival of the "red-headed Arabella," whom Crowley had picked up in Edinburgh in July, was canceled. The request of the Reverend Kelly for a £10,000 dowry payment by Crowley (the reversal of the tradition by which a dowry was paid by the father of the bride) was not only refused, but countered by Crowley with the insistence (conveyed by way of letters to Gerald, with whom relations had again warmed) that correspondence to Crowley by the Kelly family be addressed to Lord Boleskine, a noble title embossed in gold on his envelopes. Meanwhile, at Boleskine, relations between Crowley and Rose blossomed. Crowley reported only one difficulty: "Once, in the first three weeks or so, Rose took some trifling liberty; I recognized the symptoms, and turned her up and spanked her. She henceforth added the qualities of perfect wife to those of perfect mistress. Women, like all moral inferiors, behave well only when treated with firmness, kindness and justice." Crowley's views here on proper manly behavior were anything but unique for his time.

The two were so happy that they resolved to extend their honeymoon indefinitely. With the vague intention of ultimately paying a visit to Allan Bennett—who, as the monk Ananda Metteyya, was now residing in Rangoon, Burma—they set forth on a world tour of sorts. Their first stop was Paris. Crowley offered a sordid and almost certainly falsified vignette in the *Confessions,* in which he and Rose accidently met with Mina Mathers near the Pont Alexandre III. In Crowley's account,

Mina's face was plastered with make-up, due to Mathers having forced her to pose naked in a prurient Montmartre show; Crowley further implied that Mina had become a prostitute with Mathers as her pimp. All others who knew the couple testified that their sexual fastidiousness was extreme. Crowley's account, published after both their deaths, is the man at his worst.

From Paris, the honeymoon continued through Marseilles and Naples. In November 1903, they arrived in Cairo, where Crowley resolved not only to visit the pyramids—a tourist stop he had omitted the year before—but to use the Great Pyramid itself as a site in which to impress his new wife with his magical powers. The plan was that they would spend the night in the King's Chamber of the Great Pyramid. Crowley employed the "Bornless Ritual," based on a Greco-Egyptian magical papyrus, and probably obtained from Bennett. The ritual—which invokes a multifaceted Godhead—would remain a favorite of Crowley's. He read it on this night by candlelight. But the candle, according to Crowley, soon became unnecessary, as it was supplanted by "astral light":

> The King's Chamber was aglow as if with the brightest tropical moonlight. The pitiful dirty yellow flame of the candle was like a blasphemy, and I put it out. The astral light remained during the whole of the invocation and for some time afterwards, though it lessened in intensity as we composed ourselves to sleep.[. . .] In the morning, the astral light had completely disappeared and the only sound was the flitting of the bats.

Crowley never wavered in his insistence that the light was "no subjective illusion," but he did later deprecate this evening as an "exhibition game of magick."

From Cairo, they continued on to Ceylon. Shortly after their arrival there in December, Rose announced to Crowley that she was pregnant. Their intention had been to continue on to China for a hunting expedition, but this changed with Rose's news. Instead, they transferred the site of the expedition to Hambantota, in southeast Ceylon, and planned to return to Boleskine in time for the delivery of their child. December and early January were spent largely in camping and hunting. On January 7, 1904, while Rose was suffering from an attack of fever, Crowley sat at a camp table and composed "Rosa Mundi," the highwater mark of his achievements as a lyric love poet. The title, which translates as Rose of the World, is a play upon a Rosicrucian symbol. Through his Golden Dawn training, the blossoming Rose on the Cross had become, for Crowley, a preeminent symbol of spiritual awakening from the elemental world unto eternity. But in this poem, the esoteric is blended with the erotic. The first of the nineteen stanzas is the most rhythmically admirable:

> Rose of the World!
> Red glory of the secret heart of Love:
> Red flame, rose-red, most subtly curled
> Into its own infinite flower, all flowers above!
> Its flower in its own perfumed passion,
> Its faint sweet passion, folded and furled
> In flower fashion;
> And my deep spirit taking its pure part
> Of that voluptuous heart
> Of hidden happiness!

The poem appeared in *Rosa Mundi and Other Love Songs* (1905), published privately by Crowley under the pseudonym H. D. Carr.

The hunting expedition ended, Rose and Crowley returned to Kandy, the site of the yoga training with Bennett some two years before. This time, Crowley's stay was brief, and marked by the writing of a bitingly cynical verse play, *Why Jesus Wept* (1904), that portrays the downfall of an innocent young couple—just betrothed—through a series of calculated seductions. Rose's pregnancy led the couple to cancel their proposed visit to Bennett in Rangoon. But they were in no hurry to return to England. When, on January 28, 1904, they took ship from the port of Colombo, their first principal destination was Cairo, where they landed on February 8. Having already displayed the Great Pyramid to his wife by means of astral light, Crowley resolved on an even grander gesture now. They would playact the part of Oriental royalty, as a denouement to their world-spanning honeymoon. Crowley would don the garb of an "Oriental despot" and take the name "Chioa Khan"—the former a transliteration of the Hebrew for "beast," the latter an honorific title. "Chioa Khan" may thus be translated as "Great Beast."

Rose—now dubbed, by Crowley, Ouarda, the Arabic for "Rose"—accepted her role. But soon the play would take on far-different dimensions, and the course of the life of Aleister Crowley would be utterly transformed. Through the unforeseen aid of Ouarda the Seer he would return to magic, skeptical no longer, but seized, rather, by the commanding gods. That April, as the honeymoon came to an end, the seed of the fearsome New Aeon was sown.

CHAPTER FOUR

The Birth of the New Aeon (1904–05)

I n this chapter, the story is told of the episode that shaped the remainder of Crowley's days—the contact he believed to have occurred on April 8, 9, and 10, 1904, with a being whom he sometimes described as a "praeternatural" intelligence, alternately spelled "Aiwass" and "Aiwaz," who dictated to Crowley, as scribe and prophet, the Word of the New Aeon in the form of a gnomic and evocative three-chapter declamation (alternating freely between poetry and prose, and taking on the voices of three divinities) entitled, again alternately, *The Book of the Law* and *Liber Legis* (to name but two variations).

The most famous sentence in this book, familiar to persons who know nothing else of Crowley, is: "Do what thou wilt shall be the whole of the Law." This dictum evokes immediate unease, even fear. With its insistent staccato monosyllables, it testifies to the visceral impact of *The Book of the Law*. Make of that book what you will, it has had a fitful but persistent life from the time it was first written to the close of the twentieth century. And there is every indication that it will continue to exercise an influence on the century to come.

Crowley emphasized that, for *The Book of the Law* to be assessed intelligently, the context in which it was revealed to him had to be understood. Yet so perplexed was Crowley himself by this context that he attempted in three different works, widely separated in time—*The Temple of Solomon the King* (1910), *The Confessions* (1929), and *The Equinox of the Gods* (1936)—to clarify what had happened. There were further such accounts in letters and essays composed throughout the rest of his life. Crowley was literally obsessed with setting the record straight.

But for all his efforts, there remain questions, controversy, and wonderment. This chapter will seek not so much to dispel these—an impossibility, in any event—as to intensify them. A detailed investigation of the facts was anticipated—even invited—by Crowley. In *The Equinox of the Gods* he declared that "at the outset" one should study "the whole of the external circumstances connected with the Writing of the Book, whether they are of biographical or other importance. He should thus be able to approach the Book with his mind prepared to apprehend the unique character of their [sic] contents in respect of Its true Authorship, the peculiarities of Its methods of communicating Thought, and the nature of Its claim to be the Canon of Truth, the Key of Progress, and the Arbiter of Conduct." Crowley asked to be believed on the basis of the facts of his life as *he* presented them. Indeed, he was ardent to be believed—so ardent that his pleading could, at times, become a cry of desperation at a world that would not grant the truth of his contact "with a Being of intelligence and power immensely subtler and greater than aught we can call human," nor recognize his vocation as prophet. And yet, in fulfillment of his first magical name, Perdurabo, he would persist unto the end: "I, Aleister Crowley, declare upon my honour as a gentleman that I hold this revelation a million times more important than the discovery of the Wheel, or even of the Laws of Physics or Mathematics. Fire and Tools made Man master of his planet; Writing developed his mind; but his Soul was a guess until the Book of the Law proved this."

Bearing in mind both the intensity of Crowley's desire to persuade (for all that the *Book* disparaged reasoned persuasion) and the earnestness of his efforts to set the record straight, let us proceed to examine his accounts. It was an extended honeymoon that would lead Crowley to the New Aeon. And it is with the return of the married couple to Cairo that we now begin.

Crowley and Rose, "Chioa Khan" and "Ouarda," arrived in Cairo on February 9, 1904. Crowley was frank as to the motives behind his title and costume:

> I was not for a moment deceived by my own pretext that I wanted to study Mohammedanism, and in particular the mysticism of the fakir, the Darwesh and the Sufi, from within, when I proposed to pass myself in Egypt for a Persian prince with a

beautiful English wife. I wanted to swagger about in a turban with a diamond aigrette and sweeping silken robes or a coat of cloth of gold, with a jewelled talwar by my side, and two gorgeous runners to clear the way for my carriage through the streets of Cairo.

There was no doubt a certain brooding of the Holy Spirit of Magick upon the still waters of my soul; but there is little evidence of its operation.

This stress upon "little evidence" was Crowley's way of insisting that the revelation of the New Aeon—now only three weeks away—was neither anticipated nor desired.

Crowley did study, while in Cairo, with an unnamed "sheikh" who taught him the rudiments of Arabic and of Islamic prayer ritual. Crowley claimed that this sheikh was "profoundly versed in the mysticism and magic of Islam" and that, because he recognized Crowley as an "initiate," provided him with writings on the "Arabic Cabbala" that Crowley would subsequently incorporate into his occult reference compendium 777 (1909). Further, he taught Crowley "many of the secrets of the Sidi Aissawa [a Sufi order]; how to run a stiletto through one's cheek without drawing blood, lick red-hot swords, eat live scorpions, etc." Some of these Crowley allowed were mere "conjuror's tricks," but others were "genuine Magick; that is, the scientific explanation is not generally known." The list of seeming wonders that Crowley sets forth here should not be dismissed; such performances have been witnessed by many observers, not only in Egypt but throughout the Near East and India. There is, however, no record of Crowley himself having performed them.

During this period of study, Crowley also devoted a good deal of time to his golf game. He kept a diary, albeit a sketchy one (Crowley would later rue its "incomplete and fragmentary" nature) that revealed a marked ambivalence about himself and his doings. For Crowley was sporadically inserting deliberately misleading or outright false entries— "blinds," as he termed them—so as to make the full decipherment of this diary impossible for any outside reader. In the Western esoteric tradition, a "blind" refers to a deliberate stylistic technique by which the true spiritual meaning of a writing is concealed from the untrained or profane reader. The question thus arises: Why use blinds for diary entries which, as Crowley himself insisted, reflected a life without spiritual focus?

There is a second, shorter diary from this time, entitled *The Book of Results,* that covers the week from March 16 to March 23. As to this diary, Crowley mentions no blinds, and his later memory proved of substantially greater assistance in elucidating its cryptic entries. The central character in this diary is not Crowley but his wife, Rose, or "Ouarda," indicated by the phonetic initial "W." A few fragmented quotes transcribed by Crowley in *The Book of Results* constitute the sole record of what Rose had to say about the events of this period. Crowley portrayed her as a suddenly arisen seeress—spellbound and insistent. On March 16, in an avowedly frivolous attempt to impress his wife, he recited the same "Bornless One" invocation employed, the previous November, in the King's Chamber of the Great Pyramid. This time his aim was to enable his wife to see "sylphs"—lower astral beings, or elementals, who inhabit the spiritual element of air. But Rose could see no sylphs, and this vexed her husband. He was vexed even further by her claim to have become "inspired" and her repeated insistence that "They're waiting for you!" The next day, March 17, Crowley invoked Thoth, the Egyptian god of wisdom and magic. In his diary, he termed the invocation a "great success"; a later comment offers this motive for the invocation—"presumably to clear up the muddle." The muddle was Rose, who was continuing on this day to make odd, fragmentary statements—"all about the child" and "all Osiris."

The stakes intensified on March 18. For Rose—who had by now become the empowered Ouarda the Seer—was able to reveal to Crowley that the voice seeking, through herself, to address him was that of Horus. Crowley was taken aback, for his wife had, by his testimony, no knowledge of or interest in Egyptology and could scarcely have had a reason to speak the name of that particular god. Crowley now crossexamined Ouarda in detail as to attributes of Horus. Ouarda answered each query correctly. Further, she gave correct responses even when Crowley calculated, on the spot, an arbitrary, nontraditional symbol for Horus and asked Ouarda to choose it from a list of five. Due to his inexact memory, Crowley offered two different possible times for this rigorous cross-examination: March 18, or between March 20 and March 23. If the latter range is correct, then the accuracy of Ouarda's answers becomes far less mysterious. For on March 18 and 19, the seeress had transmitted to Crowley a ritual for the invocation of Horus which was performed with "great success" on March 20. This ritual contained detailed recitations of the nature and forms of Horus that could have given Ouarda the answers to subsequent questions posed by Crowley.

The invocation of Horus afforded the remarkable information, recorded by Crowley in his *Book of Results*, that a new Equinox of the Gods had arrived—that is, a new spiritual aeon had begun—and that "I am to formulate a new link of an Order with the Solar Force." This latter title referred to Horus, who had been invoked in his form as the Sun. As for the precise meaning of "new link," this was not yet clear. But one point was plain: The formulation of this link would necessarily mean the end of Mathers's old Order, the Golden Dawn; the invocation had confirmed, for Crowley, that "the Secret Chiefs of the Third Order [beyond the First and Second Orders of the Golden Dawn] [. . .] had sent a messenger to confer upon me the position which Mathers had forfeited." Crowley had wrestled with the question of a final break with Mathers for nearly four years. Now, at last, he felt certainty: "G.D. to be destroyed, *i.e.* publish its history & its papers. Nothing needs buying. I make it an absolute condition that I should attain *samadhi*, in the God's own interest. My rituals work out well, but I need the transliteration."

This encapsulated battle plan was carried out—Crowley would, five years later, publish the history and rituals of the Golden Dawn in *The Equinox*. The statement "Nothing needs buying" seems to refer to Crowley's conviction that Mathers was entitled to no rights to or payment for those rituals—the same position he took with respect to Mathers's work on *The Goetia*. As for the "absolute condition that I should attain *samadhi* in the God's own interest," the tone conveys a bargain struck between Horus and Crowley: If the latter was to serve properly as a "new link," his spiritual attainments would have to include *Samadhi*, the ultimate yogic state that had eluded him in Ceylon. As for the need for a "transliteration" of his rituals, this likely refers to Crowley's work, at this time, in developing new magical formulae that would form the basis for the rituals and ordeals created by Crowley some two years later for his new magical order—the A∴A∴ (commonly termed the *Argenteum Astrum* or Silver Star).

But even with the "great success" of March 20, Crowley remained suspicious of Ouarda. How could his wife have suddenly become a medium? He decided upon a further test of her powers. Together, on March 21, they went to the Boulak Museum, which neither of them had visited before. Here, with two floors of exhibits to wander through, Crowley instructed Ouarda to find the god Horus without any sort of assistance. Again, her involvement with the March 20 invocation could have been of assistance here, but this possibility is not discussed by Crowley. Ouarda passed by several representations of Horus, a fact he "noted with silent glee." But then they went upstairs:

A glass case stood in the distance, too far off for its contents to be recognized. But W. recognized it! "There," she cried. "There he is!"

Fra. P. [Crowley] advanced to the case. There was the image of Horus in the form of Ra Hoor Khuit painted upon a wooden stele of the 26th dynasty—and the exhibit bore the number 666!

In this account, in *The Temple of Solomon the King,* Crowley portrayed Ouarda's finding of the stele (an upright, inscribed and illustrated slab) as a stunning confirmation of her mediumship. By contrast, in the *Confessions,* Crowley described himself as unmoved at the time. The stele was "quite obscure and undistinguished" and the catalogue number 666 merely an "obvious coincidence."

From March 23 to April 7, Crowley endured a fallow period, uncertain of what was to come of the promised "new link." He did arrange for an assistant curator of the Boulak Museum to translate the hieroglyphic text inscribed on the two sides of stele number 666. This text was, shortly thereafter, versified by Crowley; excerpts from this versification would be included in *The Book of the Law.* The text elaborates upon the central image of the stele, portraying what would become the divine triumvirate of Thelema: Nuit, Hadit, and Ra-Hoor-Khuit. Framing the scene is the sky goddess Nuit, her arching body forming the heavens while her hands and feet touch the earth. Below her is a Winged Globe—the solar Horus, or Horbehutet; Crowley called this god form Hadit. Beneath these two is an Egyptian priest, Ankh-af-na-khonsu, addressing an enthroned Horus in the form of Ra-Hoor-Khuit—a hawk-headed king surmounted by a cobra headband and a solar disk.

It was during this period that Ouarda revealed to her husband that the source of the knowledge she had been transmitting was an emissary of Horus with the mysterious name of "Aiwass." Ouarda could provide no further details as to Aiwass, who gave her information only as he (Crowley imagined Aiwass as male in essence) saw fit. As Crowley described the situation: "Any questions that I asked her were either unanswered, or answered by a Being whose mind was so different from mine that we failed to converse. All my wife obtained from Him was to command me to do things magically absurd. He would not play my game: I must play His." On or about April 7, certain definite orders were issued by Aiwass through Rose. The drawing room of the honeymoon flat they had leased in Cairo was to serve as a "temple." Crowley was ordered "to enter the 'temple' exactly at noon on the three days following, and write down what I heard during one hour, nor more nor less."

Thus it was that, on April 8, 9, and 10, 1904, the three chapters of the *Book of the Law* were written down by Crowley. The method was as follows: Crowley would enter the temple a minute early, so as to seat himself—with a Swan fountain pen and an ample supply of typewriter paper—so as to be ready precisely at noontime. He was alone; Ouarda no longer served as a mediumistic intermediary. Now it was Crowley who would hear the voice of Aiwass. He described this voice as "a rich tenor or baritone" of "deep timbre, musical and expressive, its tones solemn, voluptuous, tender, fierce, or aught else as suited the moods of the message." Aiwass spoke without accent—it sounded to Crowley like a pure "English-in-itself."

Crowley, seated at a writing table which faced a southern wall, never spoke aloud during the sessions and never actually saw Aiwass. He heard the voice coming from behind him, seemingly from a corner of the room. And yet Crowley experienced, during the three days, a vivid "visualization" of Aiwass within his own "imagination." In this visualization, Aiwass possessed "a body of 'fine matter,' or astral matter, transparent as a veil of gauze or a cloud of incense-smoke. He seemed to be a tall, dark man in his thirties, well-knit, active and strong, with the face of a savage king, and eyes veiled lest their gaze should destroy what they saw." The clothing of Aiwass vaguely suggested Assyrian or Persian, as opposed to Arab, dress. In sum, Crowley—at this time—took Aiwass to be an "astral" being or "angel" of an order such as he had encountered before in his magical practice.

He would, in the decades to come, frequently weigh and revise this assessment. Aiwass would become, during these ruminations, "a God or Demon or Devil"; and/or a "praeterhuman" intelligence; and/or a minister or messenger of other Gods; and/or "mine own Guardian Angel"; and/or perhaps (this speculation he fought off with might and main) his own subconscious self. At times, Aiwass inhabited a human body and thus became "a man as I am," as Crowley put it in *The Equinox of the Gods*; Crowley had "been permitted to see Him in recent years in a variety of physical appearances, all equally 'material' in the sense in which my own body is so." Yet, despite these sightings, of certainty there was none. The very first sentence of *The Equinox of the Gods* tellingly refers to Aiwass as "a Being whose nature he [Crowley] does not fully understand."

According to *The Book of the Law* itself: Aiwass was "the minister of Hoor-Paar-Kraat"—the Lord of Silence, another of the forms of Horus, equivalent to the Greek Harpocrates. Crowley would later comment that from Aiwass came "the Speech in the Silence." This "Speech" came intensely at Crowley through each of the three hours of the three days. He filled sixty-five handwritten pages and "pushed hard to keep the pace" by Aiwass, who seemed "alert about the time-limit." Throughout, Crowley felt himself a mere scribe. At times, what he wrote perplexed and disturbed him—indeed, these feelings would persist, as to certain of the passages, for the rest of his life. Crowley later described the "compulsion" that drove on his pen:

> I remember clearly enough the impulse to refuse to go on, and the fierce resentment at the refusal of my muscles to obey me. Reflect that I was being compelled to make an abject recantation of practically every article of my creed [. . .] I was proud of my personal prowess as a poet, hunter, and mountaineer of admittedly dauntless virility; yet I was being treated like a hypnotized imbecile, only worse, for I was perfectly aware of what I was doing.

Much as Crowley emphasized his struggle, he also allowed that there was a fundamental unity of spirit between Aiwass and himself that was *essential* if the dictation was to proceed: "As is well known, there is a limit to the power of the hypnotist; he cannot overcome the resistance of the unconscious of his patient. My own unconscious was thus in alliance with Aiwaz; taken between two fires, my conscious self was paralyzed so long as the pressure lasted."

Leaving aside, for now, the question of who or what Aiwass was, we shall turn instead to what he had to say and how he said it. Immediately, one confronts Crowley's own vehement adjurations against interpretation of the *Book* by anyone but himself. It is an odd contrast: Crowley invites outside scrutiny of his life as a means of assessing the validity of the *Book;* but once the reader commences a study of the text, it is the command of the *Book* that Crowley, and Crowley alone, is capable of resolving its ambiguities. The reader, if perplexed, must alone consult Crowley's own commentaries—and there are a number of these, pursued in various forms over the next two decades. They are by no means consistent in their interpretations, and Crowley himself disparaged their quality and acumen on more than one occasion. Nonetheless, his stance on his own authority was firm: "I lay claim to be the sole authority competent to decide disputed points with regard to *The Book of the Law,* seeing that its Author, Aiwaz, is none other than mine own Holy Guardian Angel, to Whose Knowledge and Conversation I have attained, so that I have exclusive access to Him. I have duly referred every difficulty to Him directly, and received His answer; my award is therefore absolute without appeal."

The *Book* hardly admits of easy summary, much less analytical proof.

It is composed of three chapters of roughly equal lengths, each of which contains a sequence of numbered passages—66, 75, and 79 respectively, a total of 220 in all—that Crowley referred to, in Biblical fashion, as "verses," even though most of the passages are in prose (albeit a highly emotional charged or "poetic" prose). The spelling and grammar are still more idiosyncratic; in Chapter III of the *Book* it is declared that "Spelling is defunct." For Crowley, the awkward spellings and style served two functions—as fertile material for intricate kabbalistic interpretations, and as evidence that he himself, as a "Master of English," could not have authored such a text.

While all of the chapters were dictated by Aiwass, each is in the voice of a different god or goddess depicted on the Boulak Stele. In Chapter I, the speaker is Nuit, the goddess of the heavens. In Chapter II, it is Hadit, a solar form of Horus. In Chapter III comes Ra-Hoor-Kuit ("Horus of the Two Horizons")—that is, Horus the son of Isis and Osiris who, as avenger of the latter's murder, becomes the warrior-slayer of Set or Typhon, the serpent of the Nile. It is Horus, in his many forms, whom Crowley affirms as the archetypal and governing god of his New Aeon. Horus is the spiritual "son" of the previous "mother" and "father" Aeons of Isis and Osiris; one of his epithets in *The Book of the Law* is the "Crowned and Conquering Child." Crowley offered this summary of the aeonic progressions: "The first period is simple, quiet, easy, and pleasant; the material ignores the spiritual; the second is of suffering and death: the spiritual strives to ignore the material. Christianity and all cognate religions worship death, glorify suffering, deify corpses. The new Aeon is the worship of the spiritual made one with the material, of Horus, of the Child, of the Future."

In Chapter I, Nuit informs Crowley that he is to be her "prophet" and to serve as "my heart & my tongue!" Crowley (whom Nuit terms "the Beast," just as Crowley's mother had) and his "Scarlet Woman" (a figure, as is "the Beast," from the *Revelation* of St. John) will bestow *The Book of the Law* to humankind, for whom they will represent, on the earthly plane, the cosmic union of Nuit (the infinite) and her male consort Hadit (the point or center). Nuit is a passionate goddess and demands no less of her worshippers:

Come forth, o children, under the stars, & take your fill of love!
    I am above you and in you. My ecstasy is in yours.
My joy is to see your joy. [I, 12–13]

The "glory of the stars" [I, 15] is the ultimate fulfillment that is potentially available to all of humankind: "Every man and every woman is a star" [I, 3]. But to force a star to contract is to hasten the process of its extinction. Nuit warns: "The word of Sin is Restriction[. . .] There is no bond that can unite the divided but love: all else is a curse." [I, 41] With this verse, ironically, the concept of Sin—from which Crowley yearned to escape—is transported whole cloth into *The Book of the Law*.

But however seductive and enthralling stardom might seem, this is not a call to anarchy. There is a Law that Nuit is bestowing, and she is firm on that point that "the Law is for all." [I, 34] The "word of the Law" [I, 39] is given in Greek; transcribed into English it is *thelema*, meaning will. The worshipers of the New Aeon may be termed "Thelemites" [I, 40]. Nuit offers this tersely monosyllabic summation of the Thelemic teaching: "Do what thou wilt shall be the whole of the Law." [I, 40] As previously mentioned, this is the most famous—and notorious—verse in the *Book*, and is also readily misunderstood.

There is an obvious literary precursor here. Rabelais, in the concluding chapters of his *Gargantua* (1534), described an ideal community—one drawn in distinct contrast to what Rabelais saw as the corruption rife within the Christian monastic orders—named "Theleme." The governing maxim of this community was "Do what you will." In his later essay "The Antecedents of Thelema" (1926), Crowley claimed that Rabelais had, in his *Gargantua*, foreseen the future coming of Crowley, the Great Beast. Questions of prophecy aside, Rabelais was no precursor of Thelema. Joyous and unsystematic, Rabelais blended in his heterodox creed elements of Stoic self-mastery and spontaneous Christian faith and kindness. The Thelema of Crowley is, by contrast, a break rather than an embrace with the past, particularly the Christian past. Crowley also found similarities in the *Book* to the thinking of Nietzsche, whom he had not read prior to April 1904. Nietzsche wrote of a conscious will to power that could be embraced by the *Ubermensch* (superior human; *mensch* includes both sexes) who harmonizes the chaotic emotions within us. Embrace of the will to power rids us of *Ressentiment*, the incessant inner pain borne by those of a "slave" morality who naturally resent the *Ubermensch*. For Nietzsche, a fierce critic of Christianity, *Ressentiment* is fatally embedded in the pieties of the Church. But again, there are vital differences between Nietzsche and the *Book*. Nietzsche frankly affirmed the desire for power, while Crowley sublimated it within the quest for self-transcendence. Nietzsche accepted no gods, while Crowley put forward a new pantheon. Finally, Nietzsche denied that his truths were binding on others, while Crowley proselytized a New Aeon.

Justice to the conception of true will put forward in *The Book of the Law* demands that its persistent linkage—by uninformed critics—with unbridled anarchy and wayward licentiousness be refuted. To an extent, Crowley has himself to blame for the misunderstanding. In the subsequent decades of his life, there were few indulgences, no matter how egregious, that he failed to attribute to his true will, as opposed to an all-too-human set of conflicting and limited desires. But the Thelemic true will of *The Book of the Law*, and of Crowley's commentaries thereon, is a purified state that emerges only after the secondary personality and its emotional ties are left behind utterly: "For pure will, unassuaged of purpose, delivered from the lust of result, is in every way perfect." [I, 42] The governing bulwark that Crowley did impose—or that was imposed upon him by the *Book*—was that true will must be balanced by love, by which he meant neither sentimentality nor romantic love nor even the idealized love of all humankind, but rather the energized focus of one's entire being—including one's sexual energies: "Love is the law, love under will. Nor let the fools mistake love; for there are love and love. There is the dove, and there is the serpent. Choose ye well!" [I, 57] The law of "the dove" was viewed by Crowley as repressed and hypocritical Christian love—a false choice. There is a surprising dictum of St. Augustine, a formative shaper of the Christian tradition: "Love, and do what thou wilt." But the love alluded to by St. Augustine, as Crowley noted, is unguided by will: "St. Augustine's thesis is that if the heart be full of love, one cannot go wrong." The willed serpent love ("the awakening of the Kundalini," as Crowley described it) is true Thelemic love:

> But to love me is better than all things.[. . .] Ye shall gather goods and store of women and spices; ye shall wear rich jewels; ye shall exceed the nations of the earth in splendour & pride; but always in the love of me, and so shall ye come to my joy. I charge you earnestly to come before me in a single robe, and covered with a rich headdress. I love you! I yearn to you! Pale or purple, veiled or voluptuous, I who am all pleasure and purple, and drunkenness of the innermost sense, desire you. Put on the wings, and arouse the coiled splendour within you: come unto me! [I, 61]

The tone of lustful urgency here is remarkable. There are parallels in the invocations of Śiva and Sakti in the Hindu *Tantras*, as well as in the Biblical *Song of Solomon*. Even so, the ravenous passion of Nuit is unique in tone. For Crowley, in his later commentary on the *Book*, this passion stood as a mark of its spiritual superiority to the Christian gospels: "Nuit cries: '*I love you*,' like a lover; when even John reached only to the cold impersonal proposition 'God is love.' She woos like a mistress; whispers '*To me!*' in every ear; Jesus, with needless verb, appeals vehemently to them "that labour and are heavy laden.'"

Given Crowley's own bisexuality, it is striking that the erotic imagery of the *Book* is pronouncedly heterosexual. The explicit instructions on ecstatic union all pertain to the coupling of male and female, as, for example, this maxim on marriage and sexual freedom: "O man! refuse not thy wife, if she will! O lover, if thou wilt, depart!" There is, however, a general clause in which Nuit assents to all manner of sexual preference and conduct, so long as they are in worship of her: "Also, take your fill and will of love as ye will, when, where and with whom ye will! But always unto me." [I, 51] In his commentary on this verse, Crowley was forthright in defending the equality of homosexual practice: "Every one should discover, by experience of every kind, the extent and intention of his own sexual universe.[. . .] He must not be ashamed or afraid of being homosexual if he happens to be so at heart; he must not attempt to violate his own true nature because of public opinion, or medieval morality, or religious prejudice would wish he were otherwise." Yet Crowley went on to complain of the vehemence of those who insisted on the unique "spiritual, social, moral and intellectual advantages" of love between men.

Crowley expressed his disagreement by way of a Biblical metaphor— that of Peter, who denied Christ, after his seizure by the Romans, in fulfillment of the prophecy made to him by Jesus that "before the cock crows you will have disowned me three times." (*John* 14:38) Crowley wrote of public advocates of homosexuality: "Why can't they let one alone? I only stipulate to be allowed to be inconsistent. I will confess their creed, so long as I may play the part of Peter until the cock crow thrice." Crowley here misremembered the Bible, for the cock crowed but once for Peter, whose name here may be serving as a blasphemous pun. This passage underscores Crowley's reluctance to devote himself openly to the cause of homosexual freedom. Thelema would admit the natural propriety of homosexual relations—a signal step in itself, for the time. But Thelema would not—under Crowley's leadership—publicly champion them.

Judged purely on style, Chapter I is the finest portion of *The Book of the Law.* Chapter II—in the male voice of Hadit—is far more shrill. The promised ecstasy is not so much seductive as insistent. Hadit offers elaborations—and a warning: The New Aeon of love and will will be a time of force, blasphemy, and thorough transformation. The contrast in tone between the two chapters is in keeping with the distinctive characters of these two divinities. Nuit, the sky goddess, is "manifestation"—sensual and expansive. Hadit, whose lineage in Egyptian religion is far more obscure, is in "hiding"—contracted male energy, the Kundalini to be awakened in the New Aeon: "I am the flame that burns in every heart of man, and in the core of every star. I am Life, and the giver of Life, yet therefore is the knowledge of me the knowledge of death." [II, 6] Just as do Jehovah and Jesus, Hadit offers the promise of an eternal blessing to those who will believe:

> There is a veil: that veil is black. It is the veil of the modest woman; it is the veil of sorrow, & the pall of death: this is none of me. Tear down that lying spectre of the centuries: veil not your vices in virtuous words: these vices are my service; ye do well, & I will reward you here and hereafter. [II, 52]

Intertwined with this call to freedom—the freedom to love one's true will or fate—is the fierce scorn of Hadit for the weak. Crowley had never been a democrat, nor even a particularly empathetic human being. At times, in his commentaries on this chapter, his sense of justice seemed to prevail, and the disdain of Hadit was interpreted symbolically. For example, Hadit declares: "We have nothing with the outcast and the unfit: let them die in their misery." [II, 21] Crowley argued, in 1909, that " 'the poor and the outcast' are the petty thoughts and the Qlipothic [evil] thoughts and the sad thoughts. These must be rooted out, or the ecstasy of Hadit is not in us. They are the weeds in the garden that starve the flower." But in the early 1920s, Crowley the Social Darwinist and amateur eugenicist drew literal and practical conclusions from the very same verses. The Self weeding out its petty thoughts becomes Nature weeding out the unfit:

> Nature's way is to weed out the weak. This is the most merciful way, too. At present all the strong are being damaged, and their progress hindered by the dead weight of the weak limbs and the missing limbs, the diseased limbs and the atrophied limbs. The Christians to the lions!
>
> Our humanitarianism, which is the syphilis of the mind, acts on the basis of the lie that the king must die. The king is beyond death; it is merely a pool where he dips for refreshment. We must therefore go back to Spartan ideas of education; and the

worst enemies of humanity are those who wish, under pretext of compassion, to continue its ills through the generations. The Christians to the lions!

In Chapter III, the presiding god of the New Aeon, Horus—in his form as the warrior god Ra-Hoor-Khuit—speaks directly for the first time. Crowley may be taken at his word when he declared, in the *Confessions*, that "The third chapter seemed to me gratuitously atrocious." We have the testimony of Gerald Yorke, one of Crowley's closest friends in the last decades of his life, that the warning to "Sacrifice cattle, little and big: after a child" [III, 12] caused Crowley particular disquiet. Yorke noted that Crowley "could never bring himself" to sacrifice cattle or a child, and thus rejected a literal interpretation. (One alternative interpretation, posed in *Magick* (1930), employed "child" as a cipher for the semen used in sexual magic.)

The message of Ra-Hoor-Khuit is one of fearful cataclysms and of radical spiritual transformation. Crowley wrote that Ra-Hoor-Khuit manifested an "inhuman cruelty and wantonly senseless destructiveness as he avenged Isis our mother the Earth and the Heaven for the murder and mutilation of Osiris, Man, her son." In short, the Old Aeon of the dying god—of man preoccupied by his sins and mortality—must be avenged by the New Aeon, in which humanity recognizes its own innate divine spirit. The transformation from Old Aeon to New must be total. Fire, blood, and blasphemy are prominent amongst the birth pangs. There will be ecstatic realizations for the worthy Thelemite. It is by the teachings of Horus that readers of the *Book* must expect to live—and die.

If there is a singular surprise in the message of Ra-Hoor-Khuit as interpreted by Crowley, it is in the role of woman in the New Aeon. Crowley, the Beast 666, desperately required his Scarlet Woman, whose spiritual essence was whoredom. But to understand the significance of this seemingly horrific coupling, one must turn to the Biblical *Book of Revelation*, wherein the enemy of Christianity is named Babylon (a term that many Biblical scholars believe to have served as a cipher to express the author's politically dangerous hatred for Rome). The "famous prostitute" cited in *Revelation*—she who is named, in Crowley's *Book*, the "Scarlet Woman"—is explicitly identified with Babylon, while her "scarlet beast" is identified with devilish powers. When Crowley, in his Thelemic writings, revels in his Scarlet Woman and her whoredom, he is thus spitting in the eye of the Christian vision. But *Revelation* had been, in turn, an equally vehement rejection of the pagan mystery creeds, in Greece and the Middle East, that had honored the sacred prostitutes of temple worship. *The Book of the Law* may thus be seen as an attempt at redress.

Ra-Hoor-Khuit, in Chapter III, addresses the Scarlet Woman in the tone of a stern father god who will punish or reward her according to the degree of her proper worship. She is to defy the Christian *ethos*—"If pity and compassion and tenderness visit her heart" then "vengeance" will follow. [III, 43] She is further to exult in her sexuality and her true will—to live out the role of the prostitute as execrated in *Revelation*. For this, the rewards shall be great:

> But let her raise herself in pride! Let her follow me in my way! Let her work the work of wickedness! Let her kill her heart! Let her be loud and adulterous! Let her be covered with jewels, and rich garments, and let her be shameless before all men!
>
> Then will I lift her to pinnacles of power: then will I breed from her a child mightier than all the kings of the earth. I will fill her with joy: with my force shall she see & strike at the worship of Nu: she shall achieve Hadit.
>
> [III, 44–45]

In one commentary, Crowley described the symbiosis of the Beast and his Scarlet Woman: "I, the Beast 666, am called to shew this worship & to send it forth into the world: By my Woman called the Scarlet Woman, who is any Woman that receives and transmits my Solar Word and Being, is this my Work achieved: for without Woman man has no power. By Us let all men learn that all that may be is their Way of Joy for them to go, and that all souls are of the Soul of True Light." Crowley also adjured that the roles of Beast and Scarlet Woman were not open to individual assumption: "I and my woman alone are chosen for this Work; all others are best and truest as they seek Nuit in their own Way."

His wife, Rose, he took to be the first Scarlet Woman, and he further believed—by the year 1909, when their marriage was in disarray—that the prophesied punishment of Ra-Hoor-Khuit had overtaken her for her disobedience. There would be many more Scarlet Women in his life, and romantic love of the type that had drawn him to Rose was, he insisted, not a necessary element. Rather, it was essential that "the attraction should be spontaneous and irresistable" and that "the machinery should be constructed on similar principals. The psychology of the one should be intelligible to the other." Such, in brief terms, were the conscious principles that Crowley would employ in seeking out his future Scarlet Woman. As for the "child" that the Scarlet Woman might bear, Crowley did not apply this verse to any of his own future biological children, but rather to the creation of "magical" or spiritual children through the sacramental sexual act. This aspect of his interpretation of the *Book* will be discussed at greater length in Chapter Seven.

As we have seen, Crowley was typical of his time in his reductive attitudes toward women. For example, he argued that "women are nearly always conscious of an important part of their True Will, the bearing of children. To them nothing else is serious in comparison.[...]" The assignment of a governing true will to an entire gender seems to contradict the sense of self-discovery that lies at the heart of Thelema. Nonetheless, if Crowley the prophet did not become a feminist by modern standards, he did emerge somewhat from the pervasive chauvinism of his day, going so far as to decry sexual harassment in the workplace (though the harassment he addressed pertained to the frank enjoyment of sex by women workers, rather than to unwelcome advances): "The best women have always been sexually free, like the best men; it is only necessary to remove the penalties for being found out. Let women's labor organizations support any individual who is economically harried on sexual grounds." He also made a pertinent comment as to public health that bears upon the present controversy over public identification of AIDS cases, though Crowley was here addressing heterosexual female—as opposed to gay and lesbian—social freedom: "Sexual disease will be easier to track and to combat, when it is no longer a disgrace to admit it."

As for prostitution, it would be the paradoxical triumph of the Scarlet Woman, the Whore of Babalon, to preside over the extinction of that societal ignominy. Where sexual freedom prevails, payment for gratification declines: "Prostitution (with its attendant crimes) will tend to disappear, as it will cease to offer exorbitant profits to those who exploit it." To those who would seek to defile Thelema by pointing to its celebration of whoredom, Crowley cited the fact that prostitution was socially tolerated, and even tacitly encouraged, in England and throughout the Christian West. Nearly two thousand years after *Revelation*, Crowley sought to redeem the sacred whore and to overthrow the Christian malaise; as in *Revelation*, the imagery is of girding oneself for apocalyptic battle:

It is we of Thelema who truly love and respect woman, who hold her sinless and shameless even as we are; and those who say that

we despise her are those who shrink from the flash of our fal-
chion as we strike from her limbs their foul fetters.

Do we call woman whore? Ay, verily and amen, she is that;
the air shudders and burns as we shout it, exulting and eager.

O ye! Was not this your sneer, your vile whisper that scorned
her and shamed her? Was not "whore" the truth of her, the title
of terror that you gave her in your fear of her, coward comfort-
ing coward with furtive glance and gesture?

But we fear her not; we cry whore, as her armies approach us.
We beat on our shields with our swords. Earth echoes the clamor!

The closing of the third chapter, and of the *Book* itself, asserts, "The
Book of the Law is Written and Concealed. Aum. Ha." Written, because
it is revealed; concealed, because the ignorant will fail to understand it.
Just prior to this, Ra-Hoor-Khuit issues a singular boast as to the impact
of the *Book*. Fools may deride its meaning. "Yet to all it shall seem beautiful. Its enemies who say not so, are mere liars." [III, 68] If it be allowed
(as Crowley did allow) that the *Book* is by no means a uniform stylistic
triumph, there is an element of truth to this claim. There have been, and
will be, readers aplenty who are appalled by the *Book*. But a fair assessment would allow that, intermingled with crudities of content and style,
there may be found verses that attain to a rhythmic, compelling beauty.
Consider, by way of a final example, this piercing exhortation of Hadit:
"A feast for fire and a feast for water; a feast for life and a greater feast
for death!"

The question of style returns one to the vexing issue of authorship.
Crowley's insistence on the "praeterhuman" or—sometimes more emphatically—"divine" origin of the text has given pause even to some of
Crowley's most ardent supporters. A frequent approach has been to
make the question seem irrelevant. For example, Israel Regardie (a student, and later a biographer, of the Beast) insisted that "It really makes
little difference in the long run whether *The Book of the Law* was dictated to him by a preterhuman intelligence named Aiwass or whether it
stemmed from the creative deeps of Aleister Crowley. The book was
written. And he became the mouthpiece for the Zeitgeist, accurately expressing the intrinsic nature of our time as no one else has done to
date." At root, such arguments boil down to this assertion: Take the
Book on its own merits as a remarkable text. But there is—from the biographical perspective—a serious flaw here, which is that Aleister
Crowley, Beast and Prophet, would have none of it. He did not wish to
be let off the hook, as it were, of divine inspiration. True, there were

times when Crowley wrestled with the theory that the *Book* was the product of his own subconscious. But his combative response to this theory was twofold. First, he challenged its proponents to provide "a reason for this explosive yet ceremonially controlled manifestation [the dictation of the *Book*], and furnish an explanation of the dovetailing of Events in subsequent years with His word written and published." Further, Crowley argued that "the law of Parsimony of Thought" served as a rebuttal, as the assumption that "I am, unknown to myself, possessed of all sorts of praeternatural knowledge and power" was an unnecessary elaboration upon a simpler explanation—divine revelation. Neither of these objections is weighty; indeed, they are so weak as to cast doubt on Crowley's ability to perceive the merits of his own case. In this present era of therapeutic glibness, there are numerous psychological explanations to offer as to the *Book* and its lingering impact upon Crowley: wish fulfillment; obsessive identification and oedipal competition with his dead father, who preached the word of God but attained little power or recognition; megalomania coupled with denial; cognitive dissonance that wove even contradictory phenomena into the web of a controlling belief. The list could go on. As for the law of parsimony, most persons would find it more—not less—parsimonious to look to unconscious influences than to accept that the god Horus had declared, to Crowley the chosen one, a New Aeon for humankind.

But to challenge Crowley's arguments here is not to deny that the *Book* can possess—for readers who pursue its teachings earnestly—a weight and import that parallels that of other scriptural texts in other religions. One cannot conclusively establish—except by fiat—the respective spiritual merit of, say, the *Bible*, the *Koran*, the *Science and Health* of Mary Baker Eddy and *The Book of the Law*. The *Book* can and does serve as a scripture for a few thousand modern-day Thelemites. There are those who have warped certain verses of the *Book* to justify the worst of themselves; but this can be done with the *Bible* as well.

But what of the circumstances of the composition of the *Book*? For many, the bizarre trappings of the dictation will foster ineradicable skepticism, if not outright amusement and contempt. Especially given the current spate of "New Age" channelers-for-profit, it is justifiable to take claims of direct access to divine truth with a sizable grain of salt. At the same time, it must be conceded that the experience of receiving a text from what seems to be a source outside of oneself—whether the process be labeled "prophecy," "dictation," "automatic writing," "channeling," or something other—is one that recurs persistently throughout history, and that those who claim to have gone through this experience cannot uniformly be dismissed as mere charlatans. Two twentieth-century examples, roughly contemporary with Crowley, are C. G. Jung's *Septem Sermones ad Mortuos* (1916) and William Butler Yeats's *A Vision* (1925). A brief consideration of these two examples casts a useful comparative light upon Crowley and his *Book*.

Jung left a careful record, in his autobiography, *Memories, Dreams, Reflections* (1963), of the genesis of *Septem Sermones ad Mortuos* (*Seven Sermons to the Dead*), which he put to paper in 1916. According to his friend and editor, Aniella Jaffe, Jung came to see *Septum Sermones* as "a sin of his youth and regretted it." He hesitantly consented to its inclusion as an appendix to his autobiography only (as Jaffe quotes him) "for the sake of honesty." Plainly, Jung attached nothing like the importance to *Septem Sermones* that Crowley did to the *Book*. Nonetheless, Jung believed that the *Septum Sermones* were the product of a decisive encounter with forms of intelligence rooted in the unconscious, yet separate from himself and capable of distinct manifestations in the external world.

Briefly, during the period 1913–17, which included the onset of World War One, Jung was beset by inner doubts and upheavals both as to his role as a psychiatrist and as to the nature of his spiritual convictions. He began to experience both waking visions and dreams in which vivid animal and human figures—archetypal in nature, in Jung's assessment—confronted him in so powerful a manner that he feared the onset of psychosis. In his journals, Jung privately recorded these fantasies, which constituted the preliminary writings leading to the *Septum Sermones*. Although his writing efforts here were conscious, Jung felt that the style of his entries was being imposed upon him. "Archetypes speak the language of high rhetoric, even of bombast. It is a style I find embarrassing; it grates on my nerves, as when someone draws his nails down a plaster wall, or scrapes his knife against a plate. But since I did not know what was going on, I had no choice but to write everything down in the style selected by the unconscious itself."

Amongst the figures who appeared in his dreams, one began to achieve an especial prominence. "I called him Philemon. Philemon was a pagan and brought with him an Egypto-Hellenistic atmosphere with a Gnostic coloration." Through repeated encounters with Philemon and other dream figures, Jung came to "the crucial insight that there are things in the psyche which I do not produce, but which produce themselves and have their own life. Philemon represented a force which was not myself." Nor was Philemon entirely a sympathetic figure. But Jung found himself compelled to recognize this intelligence as higher than his own, even in his own field of specialization: "Psychologically, Philemon represented superior insight. He was a mysterious figure to me. At times he seemed to me quite real, as if he were a living personality. I went walking up and down the garden with him, and to me he was what the Indians call a guru." By 1916, the need to come to terms with this guru-figure had become pressing. "I was compelled from within, as it were, to formulate and express what might have been said by Philemon. This was how the *Septem Sermones ad Mortuos* with its peculiar language came into being."

Let us turn now to our second example, William Butler Yeats and *A Vision*. In Chapter Two, the hostile relations between Crowley and Yeats during their time in the Golden Dawn were discussed, as well as their essential unity in the importance they placed upon magic. The circumstances surrounding the composition of *A Vision*, which reflect this latter viewpoint, have caused marked discomfiture amongst certain Yeats scholars. Yeats gave a brief but striking account in his introduction to the work. In October 1917, just days after his marriage to Georgie Hyde-Lees, Yeats was surprised to find that his wife was "attempting automatic writing. What came in disjointed sentences, in almost illegible writing, was so exciting, sometimes so profound, that I persuaded her to give an hour or two day after day to the unknown writer, and after some half-dozen such hours offered to spend what remained of life explaining and piecing together those scattered sentences. 'No,' was the answer, 'we have come to give you metaphors for poetry.'" The ultimate result of the process, in Yeats's own assessment, was that his poetry had "gained in self-possession and power."

The "we" speaking to Yeats were several unknown teachers—whom he termed "communicators"—as to whose origin, nature or abode he never came to a fixed opinion. Yeats did draw an analogy to the legendary function of the Muses in poetic composition. For those who decried the spiritualist tone of *A Vision*, Yeats offered this elliptic, yet defiant, defense of the full exploration of consciousness: "But Muses resemble women who creep out at night and give themselves to unknown sailors and return to talk of Chinese porcelain—porcelain is best made, a Japanese critic has said, where the conditions of life are hard—or of the Ninth Symphony—virginity renews itself like the moon—except that the Muses sometimes form in those low haunts their most lasting attachments." The role of the Muse outlined here by Yeats bears a limited symbolic resemblance to the Scarlet Woman of Crowley. Yeats was no advocate of sexual magic. But he did see the interplay of masculine and feminine as a key to imaginative realization, and he did recognize that the alleged purity of Christian society masked the realities of that interplay.

Unlike Crowley, who deemed Rose (Ouarda the Seer) the first of his Scarlet Women, Yeats did not identify his Muse with his wife. On the contrary, he frankly characterized her as "bored and fatigued" by the frequent communications, which came ultimately to be conveyed as she slept; as Yeats described it, "My teachers did not seem to speak out of her sleep but as if from above it, as though it were a tide upon which they floated." The end result was the four years of transcriptions by Yeats (from 1917 to 1920), followed by the writing of a *A Vision*. The communicators insisted, during these four years of dictation, that Yeats not speak of the material to others or undertake an independent study of philosophy; there is a rough analogy here to the insistence of Aiwass that Crowley not change a letter of the *Book*. When the dictation finally ended in 1920, Yeats possessed over fifty notebooks' worth of automatic script. The first version of *A Vision* was published in 1925, but it dissatisfied Yeats, who renewed his studies in philosophy—as well as his contacts with the communicators—and later issued a revised edition.

A Vision is an exceptionally challenging work, and an adequate summary of its full contents is beyond the scope of the present discussion. But there are parallels to *The Book of the Law* that are suggestive and instructive. Like Crowley, Yeats was a believer in a sequential progression of spiritual eras or aeons that governed human consciousness. Unlikely Crowley, whose sense of this progression was forward and ultimately indeterminate, Yeats conceived of a cyclical vision of the universe—"the Great Year," as he called it—that had its historical roots in ancient Near Eastern and Greek thought. For Yeats, the Great Year included oscillating shorter eras of roughly two thousand years in length—Yeats's designations for these eras were "primary" and "antithetical." The most recent "primary dispensation" was that of Jesus Christ. The "antithetical influx" that Yeats felt to be arising in his own lifetime was that of the "Rough Beast," a "supernatural incarnation" that Yeats believed would make its presence felt through an upheaval of the Christian epoch. What is most remarkable, for present purposes, is the extent to which Yeats and Crowley—for all their personal and magical differences—concurred in their descriptions of the respective epochs. Here is Yeats in *A Vision:*

> A *primary* dispensation [Christianity] looking beyond itself towards a transcendent power is dogmatic, levelling, unifying,

feminine, humane, peace its means and end; an *antithetical* dispensation [that of the Rough Beast] obeys imminent power, is expressive, hierarchical, multiple, masculine, harsh, surgical.[. . .]

> Somewhere in the sands of the desert
> A shape with lion body and the head of a man,
> A gaze blank and pitiless as the sun,
> Is moving its slow thighs, while all about it
> Reel shadows of the indignant desert birds.

The closing quotation, of course, is from Yeats's poem, "The Second Coming." The possible relationship of the fearsome beast of this poem to Crowley (as speculated upon by critic Kathleen Raine) was discussed in Chapter Two. But there is no definite evidence that Yeats had Crowley in mind, and it is noteworthy that Yeats saw the "complete systematization" of the era of the Rough Beast as a phenomenon yet to come, rather than as the *fait accompli* of Crowley's *Book*.

Yeats made no claims to be a prophet. But there was a shared insight between Crowley and Yeats that a hallmark of the modern age was the pitched yearning for a new revelation. As Yeats argued: "Why should we believe that religion can never bring around its antithesis? Is it true that our air is disturbed, as Mallarme said, by 'the trembling of the veil of the Temple', or 'that our whole age is seeking to bring forth a sacred book'?"

Crowley was convinced that he had brought forth just such a book.

It is not the intention here to strain for flawless and overarching parallels between the received books of Jung, Yeats, and Crowley. Indeed, important distinctions between the three have already been noted. But the similarities are significant as well. *The Book of the Law* may readily be dismissed as the ravings of a self-deluded occultist who wished—despite his protestations—first and foremost to exalt himself. And there may well be some truth in that viewpoint. But it is not the entire truth. The experience that Crowley went through in Cairo in March and April of 1904 bears marked resemblances to those of Jung and Yeats. Human minds of great stature can sense themselves confronted by something other, remarkable, numinous—Yeats did not scruple to count his own experience a "miracle." If the character of Crowley does not seem as savory as that of Jung or Yeats, he was no less sincere than they in his commitment to his life's work. It strains credulity to dismiss him as a mere fraud. And if he was deluded, it was by an experience of great and subtle power that also baffled some of the most profound of his contemporaries.

Crowley was well aware that many would see him as mad or worse. Indeed, he demanded that his *Book* be taken as the purest truth or the purest delusion—thus abandoning the middle ground of 'interesting but inconclusive' taken by Jung and Yeats. In *The Equinox of the Gods*, his final major attempt at an *apologia*, Crowley was adamant that his future readers take a definite stance:

> The reader must face the problem squarely; half-measures will not avail. If there be aught he recognize as transcendental Truth, he cannot admit the possibility that the Speaker, taking such pains to prove Himself and His Word, should yet incorporate Falsehood in the same body, and fence it about with the same elaborate engines. If the Book be but a monument of a mortal's madness, he must tremble that such power and cunning may be the accomplices of insane and criminal arch-anarchs.

Of course, the reader need not assent to this. The examples of Jung and Yeats indicate that Crowley's experience was not quite so unique as he wished to believe. And the examples of literally scores of odd tracts throughout history confirm that shards of what might be seen as "transcendental Truth" may be imbedded in otherwise infirm, absurd, or pernicious viewpoints. Crowley often observed that Truth and Falsehood were mere apparent opposites within a higher Reality that included and superseded both. But in his arguments for the *Book*, this insight strangely fled him. No admixture of Falsehood might be permitted within its prophetic domain.

Yet, try as he might to exclude it, Crowley may have sensed that it was there. The striking paradox of the man is that, for all his lifelong devotion to the cause of Thelema, he often allowed that he himself could not quite overcome an internal resistance to its teachings. He deemed it vicious, amoral, lamentable in its unremitting contempt for pity, crudely styled, disdainful toward his own Buddhistic leanings—these complaints continued throughout the remaining decades of his life. In *The Equinox of the Gods*, for example, Crowley confessed that "my own 'conversion' to my own 'religion' " had not yet taken place, and further protested that he was no "fanatic partisan" of his *Book*. Crowley held passive skepticism of the *Book* in disdain; but he brandished his own tortured ambivalence:

My sincerity and seriousness are proved by my life. I have fought this Book and fled it; I have defiled it and I have suffered for its sake. Present or absent to my mind, it has been my Invisible Ruler. It has overcome me; year after year extends its invasion of my being. I am the captive of the Crowned and Conquering Child.

If ever Crowley uttered the truth of his relation to his *Book*, his teaching of Thelema, and his sense of the purpose and mission of his life, it is here.

Henceforward, as we continue this narrative, Crowley may be taken at his word and seen as a "captive" of the *Book* and of Horus, the Crowned and Conquering Child, the god of Force and Fire who had declared the imminent overthrow of the Old Aeon. But Crowley the aristocrat, Christian born and bred, was very much a child of that old Aeon. Small wonder that he felt himself a captive, that he watched so avidly for the birth signs of the New. Who has not wished for the full and final vanquishing of the past?

The remainder of 1904 was, necessarily, an anticlimax. Crowley and his bride, growing in her pregnancy, departed from Egypt shortly after the dictations of April. Crowley did take care, prior to leaving, to have a replica (or, as the *Book* put it, "abstraction") of the Boulak stele—henceforth termed by Crowley the Stele of Revealing—made for him by a resident artist at the museum. He also had the *Book* manuscript typed and sent off a circular letter to fifteen of his friends—including Bennett, Eckenstein, and George Cecil Jones—declaring that a new Equinox of the Gods had come; pointedly, Mathers was also on the mailing list. Crowley's friends may have been astonished or bemused; there is no record of responses on their part.

Upon arrival in Paris, Crowley socialized with two members of the Chat Blanc circle of 1902–03, Clive Bell and Arnold Bennett. He seems not to have paid Mathers a personal visit to announce the New Aeon. Crowley did, however, send a "formal letter" to Mathers "informing him that the Secret Chiefs had appointed me visible head of the Order, and declared a new Magical Formula. I did not expect or receive an answer. I declared war on Mathers accordingly, but it was a *brutum fulmen* [unwieldy thunderbolt]." The commencement of the rather pathetic magical warfare would await Crowley's return to Boleskine. The portrayals of Mathers's fearsome powers offered in the *Confessions* and in

Crowley's novel, *Moonchild* (written 1917, published 1929) drew from events of this period. In the *Confessions*, Crowley claimed that Mathers had, by his magical attacks from Paris, killed most of the Boleskine hunting dogs and beset the servants with various illnesses. There was also an attack on the pregnant Rose by way of a workman who, by magical means, was driven "suddenly maniacal"; Crowley repulsed him with a salmon gaff.

Together, Crowley and Rose—the Beast and his Scarlet Woman—succeeded in defeating these attacks launched from Paris. Their ironic secret weapon, as it were, was the *Abra-Melin* text which Mathers had translated. According to this text, the only persons capable of gaining the service of the Abra-Melin spirits are those who have persevered to the end of the six-month ritual period and won the knowledge of their Holy Guardian Angel—thereby sanctifying the employment of the spirits for proper spiritual purposes. Crowley, of course, had not completed the Abra-Melin Operation. Nonetheless, at Boleskine, he consecrated the appropriate talismans and gained the service of Beelzebub, one of the Eight Sub-Princes of the Abra-Melin spirits; Beelzebub, in turn, could wield forty-nine servitor spirits. Beelzebub and those servitors were promptly constrained to serve Crowley in the magical battle. As for Rose, she fought beside her husband, participating in the evocations of spirits—how she was entitled to do so, under the terms of the *Abra-Melin* text, is unclear—and also, through her "powers of clairvoyance," envisioning the servitors of Beelzebub, such as Nominon: "A large red spongy jellyfish with one greenish luminous spot. Like a nasty mess." Small wonder Mathers's attacks fell by the wayside.

Crowley could now turn his magical energies to a variety of studies related to the *Book*. These included the creation of secret rites, evidently of a sexual nature (and related to tantric practices, such as the emulation of the prone and passive Shiva in cosmic coupling with the mounted and energetic Shakti) as to which the following diary entry pertains: "But for private work the Beast is Hadit, the Scarlet Woman Nuit, and she is above him ever. Let him never assume power! Let him ever look to her! Amen." This was the first time that Crowley recorded an act of sexual magic with a sense of fulfillment; the repulsion that had overcome him in 1901, when he had first practiced *vamacharya* in Ceylon, was no more.

If the summer of 1904 was a time of private magical labors, it was also a time of social and literary pleasures and familial joy. There were houseguests aplenty, including an aunt of Crowley, Anne Bishop, whom he prevailed upon to look after household affairs while Rose went into her final weeks of the then traditional 'confinement.' Gerald Kelly came for a visit, accompanied by his mother—sufficient evidence that the Kelly family's hostility toward the marriage had been quelled. Also on hand was Ivor Back, an old friend of Crowley who was both a practicing surgeon and an enthusiast of literature; Back would serve as editor for the three volumes of Crowley's *Collected Works* published by their author in 1905 (and containing nearly all of the poetry, plays and essays written up to that time, with the exclusion of the pseudonymous and erotic *White Stains*).

It was during this summer that Crowley resolved, at last, to take greater control over the distribution of his literary works. In truth, he was left with no practical option but to do so. Since 1898, Kegan Paul had published—or more precisely, had distributed, after Crowley paid his own printing costs out of pocket—several volumes of Crowley's verse. Crowley's liking for the firm may have been based, at least in part, on its steadfastly *laissez-faire* attitude toward authors who paid their own way. As bibliographer Timothy d'Arch Smith has noted, "the printing bill footed, Kegan Paul did not much care what their authors wrote about. (The most notorious Kegan Paul author, the Revd Edwin Emmanuel Bradford, between 1908 and 1930, paid for twelve volumes of cheery but flagrantly paedophilic poetry without anyone at Kegan Paul's turning a hair.)"

But if Kegan Paul dwelled little over content, it did keep careful track of sales. The ledgers on Crowley's books were uninspiring. A typical case in point was *Jephthah and Other Mysteries,* for which Crowley had provided eighty-two review copies to the press: Total sales to the public were a mere ten copies. Even this figure exceeded the abject zero sales for *An Appeal to the American Republic* (1899) and *The Mother's Tragedy* (1901). Crowley must have seen that he could hardly do a worse job of marketing on his own. Such was the impetus for the founding of his own publishing imprint—the Society for the Propagation of Religious Truth, which, as d'Arch Smith points out, is "a deliberate mimicry of the two-hundred-year-old Church of England publishing firm, the Society for Promoting Christian Knowledge." Several volumes, including the aforementioned *Collected Works,* would follow in the next few years. Crowley would show great style and wit in his marketing broadsides for the S.P.R.T. volumes. Sales, however, remained nominal.

But the signal event of the summer was not a literary one. On July 28, Rose gave birth to their first child, a daughter, whom Crowley grandly and weightily named Nuit Ma Ahathoor Hecate Sappho Jezebel

Lilith. As Crowley explained: "Nuit was given in honor to our Lady of the Stars; Ma, goddess of Justice, because the sign of Libra was rising; Ahathoor, goddess of Love and Beauty, because Venus rules Libra; I'm not sure about the name Hecate, but it may have been a compliment to the infernal gods; a poet could hardly do less than commemorate the only lady who ever wrote poetry, Sappho; Jezebel still held her place as my favorite character in Scripture; and Lilith, of course, holds undisputed possession of my affections in the realm of demons." Three significant points emerge from all this badinage. First, the very first name of Crowley's first daughter—Nuit—is in direct homage to the goddess of the New Aeon. Second, the second name of his daughter—Ma (or Maat), the Egyptian goddess of justice—is the goddess whom Crowley saw, pursuant to verse III, 34 of the *Book*, as presiding over the future Aeon that would supersede that of Nuit, Hadit, and Ra-Hoor-Khuit. And third, the themes of sexuality and sacred whoredom—central to the *Book*—are pronouncedly present through the names of Ahathoor, Jezebel, and Lilith. In sum, the names given to his daughter are not merely whimsical or outlandish, but a plain testimony to the impact of the *Book* upon him. Again, one finds that, for all Crowley's emphasis on his initial resistance to it, his acceptance of its teachings was equally in evidence.

After the delivery, Rose went through the then traditional extended period of convalescence. Despite the presence of amiable house guests, as well as a live-in nanny to assist with the care of the baby, Rose—by Crowley's testimony—found herself in a profound lassitude, unable to muster even the energy to play a hand of cards. Rose needed entertainment; Crowley resolved to entertain her. As none of the three thousand titles in his personal library interested his wife, Crowley resolved to write a book that would suit her tastes—"the only kind of literature she understood," as he put it. This was pornography. The result, produced with some minor editing assistance from Back and Gerald Kelly, was the pseudonymous volume *Snowdrops from a Curate's Garden*, which included the graphic—and satiric—erotic prose narrative, "The Nameless Novel," the eleven chapters of which were produced by Crowley in eleven days.

There is wit, but seldom light, in "The Nameless Novel," and its recitation of myriad couplings—in which all manner of humans and beasts participate—grows rather quickly tiresome. Crowley, in assessing his own motives, confessed that the pornographic style served to "arouse every instinct of my puritanism with almost insane intensity. I suppose I was really furious at the fact that the wife whom I loved so passionately and honoured so profoundly should be intellectually circumscribed in this way. My only remedy was a *reductio ad absurdum*."

The mention of his own "puritanism" is significant, because the supposed central motive of amusing his wife seems quite plainly a smokescreen—whether intended for himself, or for his future readers, or both, is less clear. Crowley enjoyed creating erotic writings; *White Stains* speaks for itself, as does *The Scented Garden of Abdullah* (composed the very next year, 1905; published 1910). Furthermore, Crowley viewed the writings in *Snowdrops* first and foremost as an attempt to cleanse his puritanism by direct confrontation—"to clean all germs out of the sexual wound," as he expressed it in a letter some two decades later, adding, "My object is not merely to disgust but to root out ruthlessly the sense of sin." But the human personality is not quite so simply transformed, and Crowley himself was no proof of his theory. *White Stains, Snowdrops, The Scented Garden*—none of these forays into forbidden imaginings sufficed to root out the sense of sin within him.

But if amusing Rose was not, in truth, the primary motivation of Crowley in writing *Snowdrops*, she nonetheless figures prominently within it. In certain of the erotic poems included in the volume, the name Rose is used expressly. Crowley later averred that he wrote poems in this vein strictly for the sake of perfecting his craft—"I used to experiment with new forms by choosing a ridiculous or obscene subject, lest I should be tempted to publish a poem whose technique showed inexperience." But are we really to believe that Crowley was seeking primarily to practice the technique of the limerick when he wrote:

> There was a young lady named Rose
> Who filled not one pom but twelve poes
> With piss, sweat, and come,
> Thick slime from her bumb,
> And snot from her bloody old nose.

"Rosa Mystica," also included in *Snowdrops*, is an obscene play upon the doctrine of immaculate conception; the conceit is that the Holy Ghost would have been repulsed by the scent of a woman's genitalia. The opening two lines give a sense of the whole: "Rose, that you are a little sod/ Your shapely pouting asshole shows."

While the tone of the poems are playful, and Rose may well be believed to have enjoyed them (the participation of her own brother in the editing process lends credence to Crowley's testimony here), there is here a radical shift in tone from "*Rosa Mundi*," the ecstatic love poem written on the first night of their marriage. If it be objected that a tone shift is hardly surprising when the goal is to write blatantly obscene verse, there is further evidence that the marriage of Crowley and Rose—just over a year after their elopement—was showing serious strain.

In October 1904, Crowley went off to St. Moritz in Switzerland, so as to make arrangements for Rose and the baby to join him there for the winter. They arrived in November, but in the interim, Crowley had composed a new poem in his serious lyrical vein, entitled *Rose Inferni* (ultimately published in book form in 1907). The title—which translates as Rose of Hell—is indicative. There is a return here to the poetic figuring (so prominent in Crowley's poems from 1898 to 1903) of woman as damned and degrading vampiress, exercising her charms so as to destroy the man of true spirit:

> I see below the beautiful low brow
> (Low too for cunning, like enough!) your lips,
> A scarlet splash of murder. From them drips
> This heart's blood; you have fed your fill on me.
> [. . .] Thirteen centuries ago
> They would have said, "Alas! the youth! We know
> The devil hath from him plucked the immortal soul."
> *I* say: you have dulled my centres of control.

The final line is a warning against erotic bondage to woman: "The love of knowledge is the hate of life."

With the close of winter, the Crowley family returned to Boleskine. There ensued an episode which Crowley cited in his *Confessions* "as a warning to the world of the utter idiocy of women as a class and the criminal idiocy of trained nurses in particular." Rose had not relished her previous pregnancy, and was now experiencing some irregularity in the timing of her periods—or, in Crowley's language, "had not settled down to the normal course of her physiological life." In the spring of 1905, she feared (falsely, as would shortly come clear) that she was again pregnant, and sought an abortion through the aid of her live-in nurse, who dosed Rose repeatedly with ergot (this while Crowley was away on business), which ultimately reached poisonous levels that threatened Rose's life.

In relating this episode, Crowley stressed that abortion is—in a phrase that startles, coming from Crowley's pen—a "sin against the Holy Ghost." He fulminates that he should have prosecuted the nurse.

And, finally, in a kind of blind rage, he lashes out at Rose as an inadequate mother and a nascent demoness:

> My marriage taught me many lessons, and this not the least: when women are not devoted to children—a few rare individuals are capable of other interests—they take a morbid pleasure in conspiring against a husband, especially if he be a father. They take advantage of his preoccupation with his work in the world to conceive and execute every kind of criminally cunning abomination. The belief in witchcraft was not all superstition; its psychological roots were sound. Women who are thwarted in their natural instincts turn inevitably to all kinds of malignant mischief, from slander to domestic destruction.

Crowley gives no specifics of how he was conspired against as a father; indeed, once past the naming of his daughter, there is no further description of her in the prolix *Confessions*. In his later interpretation of the *Book*, he viewed the aborted life as the prophesied slain child of the Scarlet Woman. [III, 43] Yet his still-living daughter Nuit seems to have been left, despite Crowley's vehement trepidations, as women's work to the care of Rose and her nurse. This was hardly atypical for the time. But Crowley's own day-to-day disinterest, coupled with his conviction that motherhood must satisfy any woman, made it impossible for him to regard with empathy the difficulties that Rose—a woman accustomed to social pleasures—faced in adapting to domestic routines.

With his marriage in disarray, Crowley welcomed the first opportunity to flee Boleskine and resume his world travels. This opportunity arose in April 1905, when Dr. J. Jacot Guillarmod—one of the members of the K2 expedition of 1902—visited Crowley at Boleskine. Guillarmod had just published an account of that previous expedition, entitled *Six mois dans l'Himalaya*. (Crowley, too, had contemplated writing on K2; unsurprisingly, he had but faint praise for *Six mois*.) The few mentions of Crowley in Guillarmod's book were innocuous, indicating, in context, an easy respect for Crowley's mountaineering ability. During his visit, Guillarmod proposed a new Himalayan expedition—to Kanchenjunga, a towering peak of some 28,207 feet, the third highest mountain in the world, upon which no Western climbers had ever ventured.

Crowley, for his part, seems to have had little regard for Guillarmod. In the *Confessions*, he dubbed him with the nickname "Tartarin"—after a comically inept Alpinist created by the French fiction writer Alphonse Daudet. During Guillarmod's stay at Boleskine, Crowley played an elaborate prank by convincing him that the "haggis" (in reality, a Scottish meat dish cooked in the stomach of a sheep) was a rare and uniquely ferocious beast of the Scottish highlands, and then sending the trepidatious Guillarmod off to hunt a harmless domestic ram—subsequently served to him at a mock-triumphant banquet.

By his own account, Crowley did not think Guillarmod a particularly gifted climber. Why, then, accept his offer to scale a peak that is still regarded—by Himalayan experts—as posing a more severe mountaineering challenge than even Everest? Crowley did insist upon a position of sole leadership. Guillarmod assented. Within weeks, preparations for the ill-fated expedition were under way.

The debacle that was the 1905 assault upon Kanchenjunga would haunt Crowley for the rest of his days.

CHAPTER FIVE

The Assault on Kanchenjunga, the Establishment of a New Magical Order, and the Wanderlusts of a Magus (1905–08)

To understand the magnitude of achievement, and of failure, achieved by the 1905 Kanchenjunga expedition led by Crowley, two fundamental facts must be kept in mind. The first is that this was the first attempt upon the summit peak of five-peaked Kanchenjunga ("the five treasure houses of the snow" in Nepalese). Not until fifty years later would that uttermost peak be scaled—by a British expedition led by Charles Evans in 1955. The second is that Kanchenjunga is judged by climbers themselves as posing the greatest challenge in all the Himalayas. Sir John Hunt, a member of the 1953 expedition that first conquered Everest, wrote shortly after that triumph: "There is no doubt, that those who first climb Kanchenjunga, will achieve the greatest feat of mountaineering, for it is a mountain which combines in its defences not only severe handicaps of wind and weather and very high altitude, but technical climbing problems and objective dangers of an order higher than we found on Everest."

The Kanchenjunga expedition was a revelatory crucible in which the strengths and weaknesses of Crowley were drawn forth. The courage, skill, dauntless energy, and remarkable focus of will of the man are evident. The brilliance of conception is there as well, as demonstrated by Crowley's choice of a climbing route similar to that employed by the triumphant 1955 expedition. But his failings show equally plainly: blind arrogance, petty fits of bile, contempt for the abilities of his fellow men, and a corresponding inability to lead them. It is noteworthy that Crowley's prodigal climbing achievements, in the Alps and in Mexico, were either solo feats or collaborations with his trusted friend Eckenstein.

A further trait showed itself in the attempt on Kanchenjunga, one that was a strength and a weakness both—and a hallmark of the man. In the field of magic, Crowley claimed a status equal to the greatest magi. In the field of mountaineering, Crowley was, in his own words, "as keen as ever to capture the only world's record which he [Eckenstein] and I did not, severally or jointly, hold; that of having reached a higher point on mountains than any other climbers."

Eckenstein, the leader of the 1902 K2 expedition, declined Crowley's invitation to attempt Kanchenjunga. In the *Confessions,* Crowley was awkwardly vague: "Eckenstein had been approached, but for one reason or another had refused." Whatever he may have told Crowley, Eckenstein confided to their mutual friend, Gerald Kelly, that he felt the risks too great with Crowley as leader. Remarkably, Crowley also extended an invitation to Guy Knowles, another K2 expedition member, whom Crowley had threatened with a pistol during their extended encampment on the Baltoro Glacier. Knowles also declined. The offer indicates how little importance Crowley placed on the personal makeup of a Himalayan climbing team, which would necessarily endure extreme hardship in close, isolated quarters. Crowley's own inquiries having failed, he left it to Guillarmod, whom Crowley regarded as a mediocre climber, to select the team members. This delegation to Guillarmod may have been less a matter of indifference than of sheer necessity, given that Crowley was persona non grata in British Alpine Club circles. In either event, it would prove folly.

The speed with which Crowley commenced the expedition was equally unusual; typical Himalayan timetables called for months and even years of preliminary planning. It was in April 1905 that Guillarmod proposed Kanchenjunga; by May 12, Crowley had embarked on the S.S. *Marmora* for Calcutta. Some sense of the risks involved must have seized hold of him, for Crowley wrote out a will—magical, rather than practical—before departing. In it, he requested that, in the event of his death, his friend George Cecil Jones should arrange for Crowley's body to be embalmed, dressed in Golden Dawn and Abra-Melin robes and raiment, and then sealed—along with vellum-bound editions of all of Crowley's works—in a Christian Rosenkreutz-style pastos and vault in a hidden place. On the pastos was to be inscribed only his Golden Dawn Neophyte magical name: "Perdurabo."

Crowley landed at Bombay on June 9, and by June 12 arrived at Darjeeling, a British hill station from which—forty-five miles to the northwest—could be seen the towering peaks of Kanchenjunga. The western face of the mountain lies in Nepal, the eastern in Sikkim. Although Kanchenjunga is surrounded by glaciers on all sides, only those to the southeast (the Talung glacier, eight miles long) and to the southwest (the Yalung glacier, eleven miles long) would have been visible from Darjeeling. Even from a distance, the outsized scale of Kanchenjunga has been praised as one of the great vistas of the world.

Crowley had acquainted himself with the findings of previous British expeditions to the region, and concurred with the opinion of William Douglas Freshfield (formed during an 1899 reconnaissance) that the rock wall at the head of the Yalung glacier seemed the most promising breach in the great mountain's defenses. As previously mentioned, Crowley felt that he possessed clairvoyant ability with respect to mountains—that he could accurately describe conditions for ascent which he had not personally viewed in advance. This sense of clairvoyance filled in whatever gaps remained: The Yalung glacier would serve as the route to Kanchenjunga. Crowley spent the remainder of July arranging for supplies and porters; that same month, he wrote two articles for the *Pioneer*, an English-language newspaper based in Allahabad; one article included a fierce attack on the Alpine Club "that has crushed every spark of mountain ability from the youth of England." The Alpine Club would soon have the opportunity for revenge.

Much of the bundobust preparation had been delegated to the manager of the Drum Druid Hotel, where Crowley lodged in Darjeeling. This manager, an Italian named A. C. R. de Righi, volunteered, by Crowley's account, to come along and serve as transport manager for the climb. According to de Righi, however, Crowley demanded from him a participation payment of £100, as well as certain jewelry and Tibetan religious banners in de Righi's possession. Relations between the two men would be strained for virtually the entirety of the expedition. Crowley later lashed out racially at de Righi—"his character was mean and suspicious and his sense of inferiority to white men manifested itself as a mixture of servility and insolence to them and of swaggering and bullying to the natives. These traits did not seem so important in Darjeeling, but I must blame myself for not foreseeing that his pin brain would entirely give way as soon as he got out of the world of waiters."

The team that Guillarmod had assembled in haste prior to joining Crowley in Darjeeling on July 31 included two fellow Swiss, Alexis Pache and Charles Reymond. Pache was a Swiss army officer with little climbing experience; Crowley, however, formed an immediate liking for Pache—"a simple, unaffected, unassuming gentleman. He was perfectly aware of his own inexperience on mountains, and therefore in a state to acquire information by the use of his eyes rather than his ears." Reymond had often climbed solo in the Alps—a point in his favor; otherwise, Crowley found him "a quiet if rather dour man, who seemed to have a steady mind and common sense." Guillarmod appeared to Crowley, at this point, "a shade irritable and fussy," suffering from various minor health ailments and from what Crowley perceived as a wound to his ego at not being the expedition leader. Relations between the two would further decline as the altitude increased.

Such, then, were the unlikely dramatis personae for the disaster to come. While in Darjeeling, the five men—Crowley, Guillarmod, Pache, Reymond, and de Righi—entered into a written agreement. Guillarmod was to be the "sole and supreme" judge as to all matters of health and hygiene. Crowley was acknowledged as the "sole and supreme" judge as to all mountaineering questions. No one would be obliged to risk their lives for any reason. All disagreements would be subject to arbitration; no resort to the courts was allowed. The agreement was admirably comprehensive; in practice, however, it was ignored as events took their course.

The expedition set forth at last from Darjeeling on August 8. In addition to the five Europeans and their six personal servants, there were three Kashmiri guides (veterans of the K2 expedition) sent for by Crowley and seventy-nine porters plus their leader or *sirdar*—a total of ninety-four persons. As opposed to K2, the route to the outskirts of Kanchenjunga—roughly fifty miles—was relatively easy, consisting largely of government-tended carriage roads and mountain trails. The two major difficulties were the penetrating rains and the tenacious leeches. The first key destination was Chabanjong, eighteen miles northwest of Darjeeling, where the major food supplies had been stockpiled. En route, six porters deserted so as, Crowley surmised, to make off with their small advance wages.

As with the porters on the K2 expedition, Crowley claimed that his goal now was to establish both ease of relations and unblinking obedience: "I gave a prize to the first three men to come into camp every day and those who had come in first three times had their pay permanently raised. I made friends with them, too, by sitting with them round the camp fire and exchanging songs and stories." At the same time, the "Bara Sahib," as Crowley was called, utilized firmness of will to instill a lurking fear: "A moment's hesitation in complying with any order of mine and they saw a look in my eyes which removed the inhibition. They knew that I would not scold or wheedle, but had a strong suspicion that I might strike a man dead without warning; at the same time they knew that I would never give an unreasonable order and that my active sympathy with the slightest discomfort of any one of them was as quick as my insight to detect and deal with malingering or any other attempt to pull my leg." Even allowing for cultural differences, it is difficult to believe that Crowley won their trust in this manner.

Once the expedition reached the Yalung glacier, the tension between Crowley and the other Europeans—in particular, Guillarmod—began to mount significantly. There survive two primary versions of the events that ensued. The first is by Guillarmod who, nearly a decade later, in 1914, would publish a lengthy two-part article, "Au Kanchenjunga," in the mountaineering journal *Echo des Alpes*. The second, of course, is that of Crowley in the *Confessions*—and in an unpublished critique of the Guillarmod article that Crowley intended as an appendix to the *Confessions*. Both men were anxious to establish the propriety of their actions; both accounts will be utilized in reconstructing the events that follow.

Crowley left Tseram (designated as Camp 1) with a small contingent on August 21, proceeding northeast along the Yalung glacier to the base of Kanchenjunga. His mood was one of buoyant optimism. The altitude was over 14,000 feet, but none of the men was feeling its ill-effects, and the weather was favorable. Crowley established Camp 2 on the glacier, two miles from the Kanchenjunga summit. From here he made a reconnaissance to confirm the feasibility of the southwest-face route. The following day, August 22, Crowley pushed ahead to establish Camp 3 farther along the glacier, at a height of roughly 18,000 feet. From Camp 3, Crowley sent back one of his porters to inform Guillarmod and Reymond that it was safe to push on and join him. But Guillarmod, who led the march, found it difficult to trace Crowley's steps. Guillarmod described the glacier terrain as "crumbling moraine, crevasses, and torrents, often uncrossable, whose banks one has to ascend for a great distance before finding a ford." Crowley, in his later response, engaged in imperious punning: "In matter of fact, with a little effort, one might almost have gone in a Ford! There was never the slightest difficulty about the route."

Guillarmod led the porters in a circuitous route and ultimately encamped, at day's end, on an open patch of ice below the slopes that ascended—in Crowley's view, easily so—to Camp 3. Crowley viewed this decision as "inexplicable imbecility." The next day, Guillarmod and his men did ascend to Camp 3, which Crowley described as "extremely pleasant"—"I took pains to fix up an excellent shelter for the men by means of large tarpaulins, and saw to their comfort in every way." Whether Crowley was providing adequate comfort, or even essential equipment, was by this time a bone of contention between himself and Guillarmod. The latter, observing the porters climbing the icy mountain in their bare feet, grew convinced that Crowley had not spent the funds allocated to supply boots to them. Crowley claimed, instead, that the porters had packed away their boots so as to preserve them: "The economical natives of India always carry their shoes unless there is some serious reason for putting them on." Could the ascent of Kanchenjunga have failed to constitute a "serious reason," even for experienced porters? No subsequent expeditions to Kanchenjunga recorded such "economical" behavior. And why did not Crowley get his money's worth, so to speak, by ordering that the boots be worn? If they were unnecessary, why provide them at all?

Crowley was eager, on August 27, to push on to the proposed Camp 4 by way of an early morning march, to avoid the later sunlight and the potential dangers it could cause on certain stretches of snow. During the march, Crowley tried to buck up the porters—whom he felt had been demoralized by the complaints of Guillarmod and Reymond—by putting on a daredevil exhibition of glissading. Crowley later made use of this episode in his novel *The Diary of a Drug Fiend* (1922), wherein the feat is ascribed to King Lamus, a character based on Crowley: "I was in command of a Himalayan expedition some years ago; and the porters were afraid to traverse a snow slope which overhung a terrific cliff. I called on them to watch me, flung myself on the snow head first, swept down like a sack of oats, and sprang to my feet on the very edge of the precipice. There was a great gasp of awed amazement while I walked up to the men." The entire contingent arrived safely at the new Camp 4, a narrow site with only limited natural shelter afforded by rocks.

If Crowley's intent was to improve morale, he failed. The next day, several more porters deserted the expedition. One of them slipped and fell to his death because—according to Guillarmod—Crowley had carved inadequate steps in the ice. Crowley rejected the accusation: "I cannot think where he could have fallen. No-one ever showed me the place." On August 29, Guillarmod descended with a party of porters and found the mutilated body on a spur of rock some 1500 feet below. The porters performed a Tibetan Buddhist burial and, according to Guillarmod, saw the death as a sacrifice demanded by the god of Kanchenjunga.

Guillarmod was now convinced that an ascent up the southwest face was impossible and, as a practical matter, a dangerous folly. More immediately, he viewed Camp 4 as inadequate. The drawbacks of its location were highlighted when, that same August 29, Pache arrived there with men and supplies. This was contrary to Crowley's express order, conveyed by courier, that Pache settle in at Camp 3. This lack of coordinated movement—and respect for Crowley's judgment—was typical of the expedition. As Crowley would later acknowledge: "The root of the problem, apart from any ill-feeling, was that none of my companions (except Pache) understood that I expected them to keep their word. I had arranged a plan, taking into consideration all sorts of circumstances, the importance of which they did not understand and others of which they did not even know, and they did not realize that to deviate from my instructions in any way might be disasterous." Given Pache's untimely arrival at Camp 4, the question arises as to why Crowley so pointedly exempted him in the above quote. One possible answer: Crowley wished to stress his good relations with Pache in light of what was to come. For in three days, while attempting to descend the mountain, Pache would die.

During the next two days, August 30 and 31, Crowley further explored ascent routes, accompanied by Reymond and Pache. Guillarmod was sent down to Camp 3 with orders to take control over supply transport, as Pache had reported that de Righi was withholding food from the advance party. On August 30, the highest fixed site attained by the expedition was established at Camp 5, which Crowley estimated at 20,000–21,000 feet, or roughly 2,000–3,000 feet higher than Camp 3. The next day, August 31, in the course of an exploratory climb with six of the men, there arose the one instance of physical beating that Crowley himself acknowledged. During the ascent of a couloir, some snow dislodged (Crowley termed it "a little avalanche") and one of the men lost his nerve and began to untie himself from the rope linking him to Crowley and the other climbers—a taboo in terms of safety and technique. As Crowley explained, "There was only one thing to do to save him from the consequences of his suicidal actions, and that was to make him more afraid of me than he was of the mountain; so I reached out and caught him a whack with my axe. It pulled him together immediately and prevented his panic communicating itself to the other men. Things went on all right." Even Crowley could not fail to note, as they returned to Camp 5 at day's end, that the morale of the men had suffered: "Their imaginations got out of hand. They began to talk nonsense about the demons of Kanchenjunga and magnified the toy avalanche and Gali's [the beaten porter] slip and wallop to the wildest fantasies.

During the night some of them slipped away." Guillarmod recounted that he met with some of these porters in Camp 4 on August 31. They charged that Crowley had beaten them and declared their intent to leave the expedition. But in Camp 3—again according to Guillarmod—de Righi quelled the mutiny by promising that Crowley would beat them no more and that they would spend no further nights in the same camp with him. De Righi subsequently ascended to Camp 4, where he and Guillarmod resolved to depose Crowley as leader and to terminate the expedition, which now seemed to them a fatal folly.

On the morning of September 1, Guillarmod and de Righi commenced their ascent to Camp 5 and a confrontation with Crowley. That same morning, Crowley, Pache, and Reymond made a further exploratory climb, achieving the greatest height of the entire expedition— estimated by Crowley as "easily" 21,000 feet. Pache and Reymond were highly optimistic as to further ascent, according to Crowley. Upon their return to Camp 5, they found Guillarmod and de Righi, accompanied by twenty porters. Guillarmod demanded to be named leader. Crowley cited their written agreement, to no avail. According to Crowley, "There was no suggestion that I had acted improperly in any way. From first to last it was merely the feeling of foreigners against being bossed by an Englishman.[. . .] I did my best to reason with them and quiet them, like the naughty children they were." The divisive issues seem to have been three in number—the choice of an ascent route; the treatment of the men; and, as an intangible emotional factor, the festering ill will that had arisen between Crowley, on the one hand, and Guillarmod and de Righi, on the other.

In trying to assess these factors, there is little that need be said of the third. The ill will was a fact, and stemmed from the careless formation of the expedition team—an error that must be laid at Crowley's feet, as leader. The treatment of the men has been presented from the dual perspectives of Crowley and Guillarmod; both confirm that Crowley was feared by the porters, and that this fear flared on August 31. As for the ascent route, while it is impossible to determine retrospectively what success the expedition might have enjoyed, the evidence suggests that Crowley chose a feasible route. Testimony on this score comes from British mountaineer John Tucker, a member of a 1954 surveillance expedition to Kanchenjunga, the findings of which were instrumental to the success of the 1955 Evans expedition. Tucker was no admirer of the "notorious" Aleister Crowley. But he made an honest assessment that ended five decades of pointed silence in British climbing circles: "The disrepute attaching to this man has caused the high endeavor and achievement of this [1905] expedition to fall into undeserved obscurity." Specifically, Tucker vouched for Crowley's planned route:

> After our 1954 reconnaissance which, it is true, took the climbers nearer to the face itself—Guillarmod's pessimism appears excessive. Nor is it possible in the light of our reconnaissance to dismiss Crowley's excessive optimism as springing from a lack of technical knowledge. Guillarmod's defeatist attitude may well have contributed to the long-standing neglect of Kanchenjunga's West Ridge and South-West Face. It also must be conceded that Crowley's route up the steep slopes toward the Kangbachen Peak (one of the lower summits of the Kanchenjunga West Ridge), was not ill-chosen.

Tucker did, however, note that a traverse from the West Ridge to the summit of Kanchenjunga, as Crowley ultimately intended, might have proved impossible.

Satisfying as it may be to apportion merit and blame in retrospect, there was no such resolution on September 1. When Crowley would not be moved, Guillarmod seized leadership, supported by de Righi and Pache. Reymond alone decided to remain with Crowley, though he maintained good relations with the mutineers. Guillarmod led the men back down to Camp 4, departing at the relatively late hour of 5 P.M. Crowley had already ordered seventeen of the porters to descend to Camp 4, as supplies were inadequate in Camp 5 and the selected porters were capable of handling the treacherous descent late in the day. All of them reached Camp 4 safely. But Crowley felt no such confidence in the climbing capabilities of Guillarmod. In the *Confessions*, Crowley claimed to have prophesied Pache's death:

> To my horror, I found that Pache wanted to go down with them.[. . .] I explained the situation, but I suppose that he could not believe I was telling the literal truth when I said that Guillarmod was at the best of times a dangerous imbecile on mountains, and that now he had developed into a dangerous maniac. I shook hands with him with a breaking heart, for I had got very fond of the man, and my last words were, 'Don't go: I shall never see you again. You'll be a dead man in ten minutes.' I had miscalculated once more; a quarter of an hour later he was still alive.

Whatever may or may not have been said prior to the descent, the result was the death not only of Pache but of three of the porters (whose names are recorded by neither Crowley nor Guillarmod). According to Guillarmod, all six of the party were roped together. Proper safety technique demands that the rope be fully stretched at all times; Crowley claimed afterwards that Guillarmod failed to see to this, and there are ambiguities in Guillarmod's narrative that bear Crowley out here. Following Guillarmod on the rope was de Righi, then two of the porters, then Pache, and then a final porter. As Guillarmod tells it, the third porter slipped, dragging with him first his fellow porter, then Pache, and then the final porter. Their fall created an avalanche. Neither Guillarmod nor de Righi were seriously injured, but the other four were buried under the snow. The two survivors, still roped to the four others, cried out to Camp 5 (still within earshot) for help, then fell to digging. Reymond, hearing the cries, collected some of the scattered ice-axes as he made his descent, and with these as tools the three men continued to dig. It would take three days finally to uncover the victims, buried under ten feet of snow. ("Pache's Grave" has since become a site name on maps of Kanchenjunga.)

What of Crowley in all this? Simply put, when he heard the cries he chose not to respond. It was this behavior, amply publicized by Crowley himself in letters published shortly thereafter in the *Pioneer* of India and the London *Daily Mail*, which earned him a lasting ignominy in mountaineering circles. In one of these letters, written in his tent on that very night, Crowley described how he had remained in his sleeping gear drinking tea, then offered an explanation that dripped with contempt: "As it was I could do nothing more than send out Reymond on the forlorn hope. Not that I was overanxious in the circumstances to render help. A mountain 'accident' of this sort is one of the things for which I have no sympathy whatsoever. . . . To-morrow I hope to go down and find out how things stand." Crowley was fond of invoking the standards of honor of the English gentleman. His behavior on this night flaunted those standards. One can well speculate that, had Crowley been the one in danger, and had Guillarmod and de Righi failed to respond, he would have excoriated them for their perfidy and cowardice.

The next day, September 2, Crowley did descend to Camp 4. Guillarmod provided a terse account: "The following day one sees Crowley coming down from the upper camp without even knowing if our comrades will be found. He deserts the expedition in a cowardly manner [. . .]" Crowley offered his own version in one of his letters dashed off to the newspapers: "In consequence of this loss of life, I declined to assume further responsibility and returned with the remainder of the expedition. I am not altogether displeased with the present results. I know enough to make certain of success another year with a properly equipped and disciplined expedition." Crowley's claim to have returned from Kanchenjunga with the "remainder" of the expedition is misleading; a minority of the remaining porters transported Crowley's belongings. Only later would he allow that his emotions had been at high pitch in Camp 4: "I have very much minimized what I felt. If ever I am summoned before Almighty God to give an account of my deeds, my one great shame will be that I did not shoot down these mutinous dogs who murdered Pache and my porters." On no other occasion, in his mature writings, did Crowley ever imagine himself—even for rhetorical purposes—confessing before the paternal Christian God.

Crowley remained convinced that Kanchenjunga was his to conquer; indeed, shortly after his return, he proposed to Eckenstein that they mount an expedition the following year. There is no record of Eckenstein's reply, which was surely in the negative. Crowley would toy with the idea of an expedition in the years to come. But his descent from Kanchenjunga was, in fact, his farewell to the Himalayas.

He made his way back to Darjeeling well in advance of Guillarmod and the others, and utilized his lead time to arrange for the publication of some five letters in the *Pioneer* and the London *Daily Mail*, seeking to vindicate his conduct. Guillarmod and de Righi, who arrived in Darjeeling on September 20, launched counterattacks by way of letters to the press that vehemently attacked Crowley's character. The verdict of the mountaineering world (led by the British Alpine Club) and of the press went decisively against Crowley. On September 28, he left for Calcutta. A week later, he was somehow ensconced as a guest on the estate of the Maharajah of Moharbhanj, an eastern province along the Bay of Bengal, with an invitation to hunt big game. The Kanchenjunga expedition was at an end.

Crowley soon shifted from hunting to isolated camping in the wilds of Moharbhanj. He was practicing magic in the form of astral communications with his former love, Elaine Simpson, still married and living in Hong Kong. The importance of these astral sessions between Crowley and Simpson would intensify in the months to come. Crowley further enjoyed, in this month of October 1905, a renewal of poetic creativity, composing a number of lyrics (most of which were collected in *Gargoyles* (1906)) as well as the homoerotic mystical poems—a veiled homage to his Cambridge-era love, Pollitt—that make up *The Scented Garden of Abdullah,* or (in Persian) the *Bagh-i-Muattar* (issued privately and pseudonymously in 1910). It is striking that Pollitt should have remained so much in Crowley's mind over six years later. Perhaps Crowley was shaken by Kanchenjunga and felt the need to take stock of his life—including the fact that his marriage was, at root, discontented.

Crowley had, during October 1905, studied Persian with an Indian *munshi,* which provided him with knowledge sufficient to craft a plausible fifteenth-century poet, Abdullah el Haji, as the putative author of *The Scented Garden,* a pseudonymous volume of lyrics and prose poems in praise of earthly—and divine—love. Pollitt—to whom the book was intended by Crowley as a "great monument"—is identified through a concealed acrostic of his name in the vertical first letters of each verse of the erotic poem "The Riddle." The very next poem, "Bagh-i-Muattar" (Persian for "scented garden"), spells out Crowley's name in similar style, but from bottom to top, a sly reference to Crowley's preferred passive role in homosexual lovemaking; indeed, the title image of the book (rephrased as "the Garden of Perfume") is applied, in the conclusion of this poem, to the male buttocks. The veiled ribaldry is extended to the name of the fictitious Anglo-Indian major, Alain Luity, whom Crowley posed as the translator of Abdullah's Persian poems. In Persian, "luity" has, among other meanings, that of "sodomite"; "alain" means "eye," in this context an allusion to the hind eye or anus. To pile mask upon mask for this potentially criminal work, Crowley invented a bisexual English clergyman, P. D. Carey, to serve as editor of the volume. Carey's introductory essay is an homage to paganism and to homoerotic love: "I tell thee, man, that the first kiss of man to man is more than the most elaborately manipulated orgasm that the most accomplished and most passionate courtesan can devise. That is, it is not a physical, but a spiritual pleasure." Carey, like Crowley a husband and father, further observed: "With sodomy, too, no children come, to cloud one's love with cares material and profane. I love my own children deeply, intensely; but they are rivals to my wife."

The Scented Garden is, without question, the most frank and impassioned exploration of his own sexuality that Crowley ever achieved. Given the milieu in which he lived, it may be seen as an act—albeit veiled in pseudonyms—of literary heroism. Crowley's unsavory reputation, coupled with the scarcity of the book itself, must explain the otherwise unaccountable failure of critics to recognize *The Scented Garden* as a classic of gay literature.

After this fruitful literary period of writing in Moharbhanj, Crowley journeyed to Calcutta, where he looked up the Englishman Edward Thornton, whom he had befriended some three years earlier. One day, in conversation, Crowley brought up the argument, raised by Hume in his *An Enquiry Concerning Human Understanding*, that events could be said to be consecutive in time yet not proven to be linked by causality. Thornton replied to Crowley, "Quite so, but there is equally no continuity in yourself." This response had a sudden and unexpectedly shattering emotional effect. Crowley became quite literally sickened at the limitations of human thought. In a diary entry some weeks later, on November 18, he noted the continuing impact: "I realize in myself the perfect impossibility of reason; suffering great misery. I am as one who should have plumed himself for years upon the speed and strength of a favourite horse, only to find not only that its speed and strength were illusory, but that it was not a real horse at all, but a clothes-horse."

Crowley's interest in Buddhism—which held the impermanence (or voidness) of phenomena as a basic truth—had reached a crossroads. In a letter to Kelly, Crowley sensed himself at a dead end, emptied of convictions, hungry for experiences that would—if not enlighten—then enflame and transform him:

> After five years of folly and weakness, miscalled politeness, tact, discretion, care for the feeling of others, I am weary of it. I say today: to hell with Christianity, Rationalism, Buddhism, all the lumber of the centuries. I bring you a positive and primaeval fact, Magic by name; and with this I will build me a new Heaven and a New Earth. I want none of your faint approval or faint dispraise; I want blasphemy, murder, rape, revolution, anything, bad or good, but strong.

Given all this, it was a remarkable coincidence that led him, during his stay in Calcutta, to take an evening walk that would give him his fill of violence.

Perhaps Crowley was rueing the last of his days of unencumbered freedom in India. Rose and daughter Nuit were due to arrive in Calcutta on October 29. Husband and wife had been apart for six months. A few days before this date, Crowley set forth, one evening, to try to find a district of the city he had previously visited in 1901—"a street of infamy called 'Culinga Bazar.'" The festival of Durga-Puja—the worship of Durga, the goddess of *sakti* or female force—was underway. There were occasional fireworks in the sky, but the streets that Crowley walked were deep in shadow. At some point he felt himself being followed and ducked into a cul-de-sac: "And then I saw, faint glimpses in the gloom, the waving white of native robes. Men were approaching me and I was aware—though hardly by sight—that they moved in a semi-military order, in single file."

Crowley pressed against a wall. Three of the men passed by, but then the group surrounded him. Some grabbed his arms while others searched for his possessions. Crowley spoke in the commanding tones of a white sahib—to no avail. He thought he saw the flicker of a knife blade. Since first spotting the white robes in the alley, Crowley had been gripping the Webley pistol which he kept in his pocket. Now, feeling himself in mortal danger, he raised the pistol just over the edge of his pocket and pulled the trigger. As he later explained: "I had fired without aim, in pitch blackness; I could not even see the white robes of the men who held me. In the lightning moment of the flash I saw only that whitenesses were falling backwards away from me, as if I had upset a screen by accident."

In the aftermath of the shooting, Crowley made his way directly to the house of his friend Thornton. Of course, the sound of the gunshot had caused an alarm and, in addition, Crowley would have attracted attention due to his race. Yet Crowley averred that he left the scene of the crime without being noticed due to the magical technique of "invisibility" which he had practiced with limited success in Mexico in 1900 (achieving a "flickering" condition), but which—by dint of his unconscious acting in a survival mode—he achieved fully in the moments after the shooting. In the *Confessions*, Crowley concedes the reader's disbelief: "I am aware that this sounds like a fish story." His explanation hinges—as is often the case in his magical analyses—upon the conjoined impact of will, concentration, and intense emotion: "There is a peculiar type of self-absorption which makes it impossible for people to be aware of one.[. . .] My theory is that the mental state in question distracts people's attention from one automatically, as a conjuror does deliberately."

Thornton accompanied Crowley, the next day, to a Scottish barrister who advised that Crowley report nothing to the police, since to risk a trial would—given the tensions of colonialism—invite treatment as a racial scapegoat. The *Calcutta Standard* soon featured an offer of a reward, by the Commissioner of Police, of 100 rupees for information leading to the arrest of the unidentified European. Crowley chose silence. This was, from a practical standpoint, a most advisable retreat, given the likelihood of testimony as to recent events on Kanchenjunga.

When Rose arrived on October 29, Crowley greeted her with the words: "You've got here just in time to see me hanged!" Their original plans had called for some time spent together in India, before departing for Burma to visit Allan Bennett, or Ananda Metteyya, who was still living the life of a Buddhist monk. But now, with a manhunt under way, a hasty departure was essential. Burma would still be the first port of call but, for some reason, Crowley now wavered between Persia and China and left the choice to Rose, who selected China. They engaged the services of a nanny and of Crowley's favorite mountaineering servant, Salama Tantra, and promptly embarked to Rangoon. Whether as a matter of fate or of lingering fear, Crowley never again set foot in India.

It had been four years since Crowley and his mentor Bennett, now Metteyya, had met face-to-face. The recent events in India—from metaphysical despair to point-blank gunfire—had left him shaken. But there is a revelatory passage in the *Confessions* on his mood of the time, which reveals that the plea in his recent letter to Kelly—"I want blasphemy, murder, rape, revolution, anything bad or good, but strong"—had, in essence, been answered.

> I embrace hardship and privation with ecstatic delight; I want everything that the world holds; I would go to prison or to the scaffold for the sake of the experience. I have never grown out of the infantile belief that the universe was made for me to suck. I grow delirious to contemplate the delicious horrors that are certain to happen to me. This is the keynote of my life, the untrammeled delight in every possibility of existence, potential or actual.

Upon arrival in Rangoon, Crowley installed his family in a hotel and went off for a three-day visit to Metteyya's monastery two miles outside the city. Metteyya had advanced, within the monastery structure, to the position of a *sayadaw* who guided fellow monks. Despite his quiescent life, Metteyya had roused some suspicion not only amongst the local population (some of whom suspected him of acting as a surreptitious British agent), but also within the British colonial regime in Burma, which viewed askance any embrace by British citizens of native beliefs. In Crowley's view, Metteyya had adapted to monastic life, but at a cost—he seemed physically worn. When the two had parted in 1902, they had been in essential agreement as to the truth of Buddhist teachings. Now, however, Crowley was skeptical not only of the moral strictures of Buddhism, but also of its deterministic approach to the question of enlightenment. As Metteyya explained it, karma determined one's capability for higher development such as *Samadhi;* the metaphor Bennett employed was the turning wheel of life—one's ability to touch a certain stone on the road would depend upon one's position on the wheel. Concentrated effort could reveal one's true position on the wheel, but nothing could change the timing of its turning—upon which contact with the stone must ultimately depend. Crowley conceded that this was sound philosophy, but denied that it was good life sense; self-enervation alone could result once belief in the power of individual will had waned.

Though he fought off Bennett's karmic determinism, he took up with alacrity Bennett's suggestion that Crowley delve deeply, through concentrated meditation, on the question of what his own karma had laid in store for himself. In *The Temple of Solomon the King*, this portion of their dialogue is laid out in a solemn spiritual style: "It was from him [Bennett/Metteyya] that he received the instructions which were to help him to reach the great and terrible pinnacle of the mind whence the Adept must plunge into the Abyss, to emerge naked, a babe—the Babe of the Abyss." To cross the Abyss is to proceed, on the kabbalistic Tree of Life as taught by the Golden Dawn, past the limits of rational thought to a recognition of the true dimensions of the universe—in which truth ceases to be seen as binary, true or false, but rather as multifold, a comprehension of the pattern of being.

This exploration of the Abyss involved the training of the Magical Memory—a training that Crowley later explicated in *Liber Thisharb* (1911). "Thisharb" derives from a backward phonetic spelling of *Berashith* (Hebrew for "in the beginning"), the first word of the Bible. The primary technique, first utilized by Crowley during this period, involved conscious reversal of the order of time (hence the backward spelling of *Berashith*) by remembering events in reverse sequence, as a film might be run backwards. (Crowley allowed, in the *Confessions*, that he had never himself mastered this technique.) Ultimately, this method was to be employed to push ever further into one's own past life—and past lives.

After three days spent in such meditation—with no decided results—as Metteyya's guest at the monastery, Crowley rejoined his family in Rangoon and made arrangements to pursue an extensive trek along a route that fired his imagination. In the border region of Burma and southern China, three great rivers ran roughly parallel to each other—the Salween, the Mekong and the Jinsha Jiang—though they later diverged to empty out of Asia at markedly different points. The entirety of this region—highly difficult of access—was sparsely settled wilderness. Crowley resolved to explore it.

A number of British colonials advised him that it might be unwise to take his wife and child along on a journey that could involve unpleasant encounters with Burmese and Chinese natives, who would be especially curious (Crowley was told) to view firsthand a white woman and child. This advice Crowley held in contempt. "I knew," he wrote in the *Confessions*, "as I know that two and two make four, that it is only necessary to behave like a gentleman in order to calm the apprehensions of the aborigines and to appeal to the fundamental fact that all men are brothers. By this I do not mean anything stupid, sodden and sentimental; I mean that all men equally require food, clothing and shelter, in the first place; and in the second, security from aggression in respect of life and property." For the sake of daughter Nuit, barely two years old, a nanny was hired to accompany them.

Crowley was, in any event, convinced that the trek was essential to his spiritual progress. By applying his skill at designing and practicing magical ritual in difficult physical conditions, he would use the journey to explore the two fundamental questions set forth in *Liber Thisharb:* "Who am I?" and "What is my relation with nature?" In the *Confessions*, he confirmed that this time—from November 1905 through February 1906—was "the most important period of my life so far as my personal attitude to myself and the universe was concerned."

Nagging delays in approval by the British colonial regime delayed departure until November 15, when they boarded the steamship *Java* to journey north along the Irrawaddy River. The spiritual task before him now was to proceed along the kabbalistic Tree of Life from 7°=4□ (the grade of Adeptus Exemptus, which he formally granted himself in this period) to 8°=3□ (the grade of Magister Templi, and the entrance to the Great White Brotherhood, the City of the Pyramids, and the realm of the Secret Chiefs themselves). To progress would necessitate the crossing of the Abyss, becoming a Babe within it, emerging newborn, wholly other, the traditional boundaries of self, reason, and reality shattered and reformed. The magical name he chose for his new Adeptus Exemptus grade—the Greek OY MH—means "certainly not."

Crowley experienced a singular adventure on the physical plane in December 1905, just after he and family had crossed into China. His pony stumbled, and rider and animal tumbled—rolling over each other twice in the process—off a cliff of some forty feet. It was a fall that could have killed him, and yet Crowley had emerged unharmed. The jolt of the fall, and his remarkable survival, experientially affirmed his sense of a special purpose to his life (as later described, in the third person, in *The Temple of Solomon the King*):

> He had repeatedly escaped from death in manners almost miraculous. "Then I am some use after all!" was his conclusion. "I am indeed SENT to do something." For whom? For the Universe; no partial good could possibly satisfy his equation. "I am, then, the 'chosen Priest and Apostle of Infinite Space.' Very good: and what is the message? What shall I teach men?" And like the lightning from heaven fell upon him these words: "THE KNOWLEDGE AND CONVERSATION OF THE HOLY GUARDIAN ANGEL."

The attainment of the "Holy Guardian Angel" is, of course, the magico-mystical end of the Abra-Melin Operation. Again, Crowley was turning his spirit to this uncompleted—and, to his own mind, essential—aspect of his development. He would devote, not only the coming months in China, but nearly the entirety of the year 1906 to its attainment. As one might expect, Crowley began to experiment radically with the ritual methods put forth in *Abra-Melin*, until, he believed, he had fashioned the essence of its Operation as his daily magical task.

This experimentation proceeded in stages. As the trek progressed, Crowley continued with his *Sammasati* meditation, exploring the causal roots of his karma even as he acknowledged that "cause" was itself an illusory concept. It was in this period that the word "Augoeides" arose in Crowley's thoughts as the name of the central god-form of his transformed Abra-Melin Operation. "Augoeides" signifies one's Higher Genius in Golden Dawn teachings. The classical Greek meaning is "glittering" or "self-glittering one" and was employed by the third-century Neoplatonist Iamblichus in his *De Mysteriis*. "Augoeides" now became the new name of Crowley's Holy Guardian Angel in daily invocations.

Their first major stop on Chinese soil, in early January 1906, was Tengyueh (modern-day Tengchong), where the British consul, one Litton, earned Crowley's admiration. Litton advised him that one could not fraternize with the lower-class Chinese, as they did not (in Crowley's words) "respect any man who acts as their own mandarins act; with absolute lack of sympathy, justice or any other human feelings. They treat the traveller well in proportion as he is overbearing, haughty and avaricious." As we shall see, Crowley embraced this advice to the hilt.

Crowley and family pushed farther north, and relations between Crowley and his porters took a turn for the worse. As Crowley told it, one of the porters, Johnny White, was given a pony to ride due to his status as Crowley's translator:

> [N]aturally he had to be content with a somewhat sorry screw, while my own pony was a fairly decent animal. He thought the time ripe to attempt to force me to 'lose face'; that is, to become an object of ridicule to the porters. If he had succeeded, I need hardly point out, there would have been an end of all discipline and we should probably have been robbed and murdered in short order. His idea was to start out ahead of us on my pony. I did not find out what had happened for some time.
>
> When I did, I set out on foot at top speed after him. In two or three hours I came up with the culprit. As luck would have it, he was crossing a steep hillside; below the path were gigantic thorn bushes. I came up quietly and unperceived, put my left hand under his right foot and with one deft jerk flung him from the saddle into a thorn bush. It was quite impossible for him to extricate himself, the bush being very large and elastic, the thorns long and persuasive. So I waited, peacefully smoking, until the porters began to arrive, when I got up and gave him a whack with my whalebone whip as each man passed. When all had gone by, I mounted my pony and followed.[. . .] It was not I who had 'lost face' with the porters! And I had no more trouble of any kind for the rest of the journey to Yunnanfu.

As with the ice ax used against the porter on Kanchenjunga, Crowley's justification for his violence in this case was necessity—the need to maintain his own absolute authority in a time of crisis. But Crowley acknowledged, on other occasions, an element of sadism within himself. One may doubt, then, whether he could consistently refrain from unneeded violence, particularly when inflicted upon persons of a racial and social rank—as ruled colonials—well below his own.

How, it might be wondered, could such conduct occur simultaneously with the spiritual meditations conduced by the Adeptus Exemptus Frater OY MH? Crowley felt that he was proceeding through China on two distinct planes at once—of ordinary and magical consciousness. The isolation of the trek was crucial here. As Crowley explained it, all the prior life forces which had "impinged on my normal direction" had been removed:

> For the first time in my life I was really free. I had no personality left. To take a concrete case: I found myself in the middle of China with a wife and child. I was no longer influenced by love

for them, no longer interested in protecting them as I had been; but there was a man, Aleister Crowley, husband and father, of a certain caste, of certain experience, of travel in remote parts of the world; and it was his business to give them his undivided love, care and protection. He could do this very much more efficiently than before when I was aware of what he was doing, and consequently inclined to play the part.

There is a strange juxtaposition in chronology at this point, one that bears out Crowley's sense of a divided self. On February 11, two days after the thornbush episode, Crowley decided that he could perform the Abra-Melin Operation while trekking through the wilds of China—a decided contrast from the secluded temple setting called for by the text itself. His diary entry for that day is brief yet exalted: "Made many resolutions of a G[reat] R[etirement]. In dream flew to me an Angel, bearing an ankh [*crux ansata* or cross of life], to encourage me." As Crowley saw it, the dream ended a phase of intellectual insanity—the death of ordinary reason—that had endured since the previous November. The Operation of Abra-Melin would now reintegrate his consciousness on a higher plane.

As the text for his daily invocations, Crowley employed the "Bornless Ritual" first taught to him by Allan Bennett in 1899. The "Bornless Ritual" was an elaborate stylistic expansion (most likely by Bennett himself) of a surviving fragment of a Graeco-Egyptian ritual. Crowley now used this ritual "to work up a current, to acquire concentration, to invoke often." Its opening lines confirm the primal status of the god (in this case, Augoeides) being summoned:

> Thee I invoke, the Bornless one.
> Thee, that didst create the Earth and the Heavens:
> Thee, that didst create the Night and the Day.
> [...]
> Thou didst make the Female and the Male.
> Thou didst produce the Seed and the Fruit.
> Thou didst form Men to love one another, and to hate
> one another.

The seeming boundary between the human and the divine falls away at last, consumed by the magical enflaming of the aspirant:

> I am He! the Bornless Spirit! having sight in the Feet:
> Strong, and the Immortal Fire!
> I am He! the Truth!

I am He! Who hate that evil should be wrought in the
World!
[. . .]
I am He; the Grace of the World:

"The Heart Girt with a Serpent" is My Name!

Some sense of the physical technique Crowley utilized for this invocation is given in *Liber Samekh* (an expanded version of the ritual, written in 1921):

> Let the muscles take grip on themselves as if one were
> wrestling. Let the jaw and mouth, in particular, be tightened to
> the utmost. Breathe deeply, slowly, yet strongly. Keep mastery
> over the mind by muttering forcibly and audibly. But lest such
> muttering tend to disturb communion with the Angel, speak
> only His Name.

In his diary he noted the varying impact upon these invocations of
road conditions, the difficulties of horseback travel, and his own health
and moods. To create a suitable "temple"—on the order of the physical
temple he had constructed in Boleskine in 1900—he employed his
Golden Dawn training in astral travel:

> My plan was to transport the astral form of my temple at
> Boleskine to where I was, so as to perform the invocation in it. It
> was not necessary for me to stay in one place during the cere-
> mony; I frequently carried it out while riding or walking.[. . .]
> I had no difficulty in visualizing the astral temple by an effort of
> will, and of course I was perfectly able to watch the results of the
> invocations with my astral eyes.

Shortly after departing from Yunnanfu on March 2, Crowley decided
to call a halt to further explorations into China, and instead to turn
south toward Tonkin (in modern-day Vietnam). The China trek had
come to be more wearing; relations with his Chinese porters had
reached a nadir. On March 14, while Crowley was marching on ahead,
one of the porters allegedly got into a squabble with Rose and struck the
baby. Crowley was furious; when the party reached Manhao, on the Red
River, two days later, he saw his chance for a strategically secure revenge. Crowley hired a dugout to transport his family, baggage, and his
trusted servant Salama downriver south to Hokow:

Having got everything aboard, I proceeded to pay the head man the exact sum due to him—less certain fines. Then the band played. They [the porters] started to threaten the crew and prevented them from casting off the ropes. They incited the bystanders to take their part; and presently we had thirty or forty yelling maniacs prepared to stone us. I got out my .400 Cordite Express and told Salama to wade ashore and untie the ropes. But like all Kashmiris, thoughtlessly brave in the face of elemental dangers, he was an absolute coward when opposed to men. I told him that unless he obeyed at once I would begin by shooting him. He saw I meant it and did his duty; while I covered the crowd with my rifle. Not a stone was thrown; three minutes later the fierce current had swept us away from the rioters.

On March 18, they reached Hokow and "all got gloriously drunk celebrating the success of a journey which in the opinion of all reasonable people was a crazy escapade, doomed from the first to disaster."

They went on to Hanoi, the capital of Indochina, and took ship for Hong Kong on March 22. It was there that husband and wife parted company again. Crowley would return to England by the Pacific route to Japan, then to Canada and then, after a crossing of the entire North American continent, at last to sail for England from New York. Rose was to proceed by way of India (to pick up their remaining luggage) and then through the Suez Canal and the Mediterranean. The rationale later offered by Crowley for this decision was his intention to drum up support in New York for a new Kanchenjunga expedition (which he would attempt, vainly, to accomplish). But it is doubtful if this was his primary reason. For Elaine Simpson (Soror Fidelis of the Golden Dawn), with whom he had been in astral contact in the autumn of 1905—prior to Rose's arrival in India—now resided in Shanghai. And Shanghai was Crowley's first port of call after shipping out from Hong Kong, on April 3, 1906, on the *Nippon Maru*.

Crowley had long been deeply attracted to Simpson, despite their awkward encounter in 1902. He was also uncomfortable with the intensity of his feelings. In the *Confessions,* he stressed that Rose had been "an ideally perfect companion" during the China trek and that "I was absolutely in love with Rose in the ordinary sense of the term. My love for Fidelis excluded the material almost entirely. I was very proud of my love for Rose and very happy in it." But in his diary of the time, Crowley chided himself for accepting the physical limitations of their present relationship—"it is the puritan A. C. who is wrong in not frankly wooing Elaine." This intense sexual ambivalence was, however, integral to the magical workings they conducted in Shanghai during their two weeks together in April 1906. The basic goal was for the two of them to comb through the spiritual developments in Crowley's life since the reception of *The Book of the Law* two years before.

On April 18, they studied the *Book* together and Simpson told Crowley that she regarded it as a genuine revelation. Two days later, Crowley and Simpson together invoked Aiwass, the bestower of the *Book*. Aiwass now spoke out strongly against the chaste relations between Simpson and Crowley: "Yet I would wish you to love physically, to make perfect the circle of your union. [Simpson] will not do so, therefore she is useless. If she did, she would become useful." Aiwass further warned that Crowley had made a mistake by making Simpson a full magical collaborator: "She is spiritually stronger than you. You should have dominated her by your superior strength on other planes." Here, Aiwass seems to utter that which Crowley had concealed—that he wanted sex with Simpson, and that he feared her because he so respected her spiritual attainments—a respect unique in Crowley's life as regarded female lovers. As for Rose (the "S.W." or Scarlet Woman), Aiwass urged Crowley to return with Rose to Egypt: "Go with the S. W., this is essential: thus you shall get real power, that of God, the only one worth having."

The next day, April 21, Crowley left Shanghai to continue his voyage by way of Japan. His diary entry for April 22, on shipboard, dismissed the Shanghai invocations as a "morbid dream" and charged that Elaine's magical powers, while considerable, had been "rotted up" because of her "clinging" to Crowley. "Having won me, let her now lose me! As for me I will go on as if I had never landed." The challenge posed to Crowley's relations—marital and magical—with wife Rose had been fended off. While Crowley and Simpson would conduct an intermittent correspondence for two decades more, their relationship was essentially at an end.

Two days later, on April 24, at Kobe, Japan, Crowley wrote to Rose "with some reserve, of course utterly concealing" mention of either Simpson or the Shanghai invocations. This same day, he conducted an Augoeides Invocation and traveled astrally in his Body of Light. The results of the latter experiment were startling. Crowley found himself in a room in which a naked man was being nailed to a cruciform table. "Many venerable men sat around, feasting on his living flesh and quaffing his hot blood. These (I was told) were the adepts, whom I might one day join." Crowley was asked by them what he would be willing to sacrifice on an altar which now appeared in a great hall. He was resolute—but also stubborn:

I offered all save my will to know A[ugoeides] which I would only change for its own realization. I now became conscious of vast God-forms of Egypt sitting, so vast I could only see their knees. "Would not knowledge of the Gods suffice?" "No," said I. It was then pointed out that I was being critical i.e. rationalistic and made to see that A[ugoeides] was not fashioned in my image. Necessarily, that is. I apologized, and knelt at altar, placing my hands on it, right over left. Then One human, white, self-shining (my idea after all) came forth and put his hands over mine, saying "I receive thee into the Order of the Silver Star." Then, with advice to return, I sank back to earth in a cradle of flame.

This astral encounter represented, for Crowley, his acceptance into the exalted Third Order—the realm, symbolically, of the highest kabbalistic sephiroth, the supernals (Binah, Chokmah, Kether); the realm, ontologically, of the Secret Chiefs themselves, the governing spirits of life on the planet Earth. But Crowley declined formally to grant himself, at this point, the grade of 8°=3□. Eight months later, in December 1906, the Secret Chiefs would again extend to Crowley—this time through Jones—a Third Order invitation. Again he would decline. It was 1909 before he would accept, "after having passed ceremonially through the Abyss in the fullest possible measure." By the evidence of his writings in those intervening years, as well as his actions as the head of the A∴A∴, it is plain that—in essence, if not in title—Crowley felt himself one to whom the secrets of the Third Order had been revealed.

During May, Crowley continued his daily practice of Augoeides Invocations while he crossed the North American continent from Vancouver to New York. He also toiled at a "Comment" upon the Book, as required of him by the Book. This "Comment," which did not satisfy him, was ultimately published in 1912 in The Equinox. The North American journey proved no distraction, at any rate, leaving Crowley with nothing more vivid than an admiration for Niagara Falls. From New York, Crowley arrived in Liverpool on June 2, 1906.

There, through waiting letters, he learned that his daughter Nuit, not yet two years of age, had died of typhoid in a hospital in Rangoon, en route to India with her mother. The cause, according to Crowley, was an improperly sanitized bottle nipple; for this neglect, Crowley blamed Rose, who, he suspected, had failed to boil the nipple due to her drunkenness. A letter from Allan Bennett, who had learned of the baby's death, described Rose's desperate retreat into alcohol, in her hotel room, while the baby died in the hospital. Bennett suggested—out of concern for Rose's capacities as a mother—that Crowley refrain from further sexual relations with her. This advice was, in any event, too late, for Rose was already pregnant again.

The death of his daughter grieved Crowley. But it was a tendency of the man to make light of that which pained him most deeply, and so his account, in the *Confessions*, began with a joke made by his friend L. C. R. Duncombe Jewell, that Nuit Ma Ahathoor Hecate Sappho Jezebel Lilith Crowley had died of "acute nomenclature." "Cad," was Crowley's deadpan response, only then continuing: "In my ears rang that terrible cry of Macduff, 'He has no children.'" Beyond this sense of personal loss, Crowley sought to place the death within the spiritual pattern of his life. He arrived at two major conclusions. The first was that the death had resulted from "the malice of the Abra-Melin demons," which could have been warded off had he properly grasped the will of the Secret Chiefs. The second was that Rose, as Scarlet Woman, had failed in her function. In *The Book of the Law*, there was a warning verse: "Let the Scarlet Woman beware! If pity and compassion and tenderness visit her heart; if she leave my work to toy with old sweetnesses; then shall my vengeance be known. I will slay me her child [. . .]" [III, 43] In his 1912 commentary on this verse, Crowley averred that it had been "most terribly fulfilled, to the letter."

But Crowley's sense of Rose's failure as a Scarlet Woman was not immediate; when husband and wife reunited later in June, Crowley tried to persuade her to do magical work with him, even to pursue a Great Retirement together. Nothing came of this; perhaps her pregnancy posed a practical limitation. But both Rose and Crowley were shaken—to the point of illness—by lingering grief; a series of ailments (including an ulcerated throat) would plague Crowley through the remainder of 1906. He continued, with some lapses, his Augoeides Invocations. He also renewed a magical collaboration with George Cecil Jones, his old Golden Dawn mentor, who now again emerged as a needed ally. Crowley regarded Jones as an Adeptus Exemptus—equal to Crowley's own highest acknowledged grade. In July 29, the two discussed the formation of a new magical order, as to which Jones readily ceded organizational leadership to Crowley himself. This order would become the A∴A∴.

In late summer, Rose gave birth to a daughter, Lola Zaza. Rose had been drinking during her pregnancy, which surely contributed to the frail health of the new baby. According to Crowley, "it lay almost lifeless for more than three days and at three weeks old nearly died of bronchitis." Even before the arrival of a physician, Crowley had provided for oxygen to be on hand, and believed that this precaution saved the baby's life. He was fiercely proud of his paternal efforts during this crisis, although, in the *Confessions*, little tenderness shows through: "I fought like a fiend against death.[. . .] So Lola Zaza lives today. May her life prove worth the pains I took to preserve it." As in the case of the death of Nuit, his deeper emotions were concealed from his public autobiography. But in his private Augoeides practice, Crowley devised a special ritual of thanksgiving for the birth of Lola Zaza.

In September, Crowley and Jones reconstructed the Golden Dawn Neophyte Ritual with the aim, as Crowley viewed it, of "eliminating all unnecessary features and quintessentializing the magical formulae." There was a distinct continuity between the teachings of the Golden Dawn and the rituals crafted by Crowley for his A∴A∴, as Crowley himself recognized—albeit giving his own order (termed here the "Silver Star") the place of honor in his mystical poem "Aha!" (written in 1909):

> Master, how subtly hast thou drawn
> The daylight from the Golden Dawn,
> Bidden the Cavernous Mount unfold
> Its Ruby Rose, its Cross of Gold;
> Until I saw, flashed from afar,
> The Hawk's Eye in the Silver Star!

On his own, Crowley kept up his Augoeides Invocations, in which he frequently made use of hashish as a stimulating ingredient. While his diary reflects this, Crowley made no mention of hashish in his later accounts of this period in the *Temple of Solomon the King* and in the *Confessions*. It would seem that he saw it as a distracting or unworthy element. But another essay, "The Psychology of Hashish" (1909) provided—albeit in an oblique manner—an account of the role of hashish on the night of October 9, 1906, when Crowley felt himself at last (after some thirty-four weeks) to have completed the Abra-Melin Operation and to have attained the Knowledge of the Augoeides, his Holy Guardian Angel. All of Crowley's written accounts have been consulted for the discussion that follows.

In the Sanskrit language of Hindu yoga, Crowley termed his experience that night an *"Atmadarshana"* or "Vision of the Universal Peacock" in which there is "a consciousness of the entire Universe as One, and as All, in Its necessary relation to Itself in and out of Time and

Space." This *Atmadarshana* was soon supplanted by a *"Shivadar-shana,"* or "Vision of the Destruction of the Universe, the Opening of the Eye of Shiva" which destroys the split consciousness of self and other. In Hindu mythology, the opening of the eye of Shiva leads to the fiery conflagration of the universe, a metaphor Crowley used to describe his October 9 attainment in "Aha!":

> [. . .] The great sight
> Of the intolerable light
> Of the whole universe that wove
> The labyrinth of light and love,
> Blazed in me. Then some giant will,
> Mine or another's, thrust a thrill
> Through the great vision. All the light
> Went out in an immortal night,
> The world annihilated by
> The opening of the Master's Eye.
> How can I tell it?

On that night, Crowley had conducted a new ritual of his own devising, the purpose of which was to thank the gods and offer sacrifice for the benefit of his daughter, Lola Zaza. At 8 P.M., Crowley ingested some hashish, which by 10 P.M. was having an active effect. The next day, his diary entry was triumphant: "I am still drunk with Samadhi all day." But a degree of hesitancy showed itself, even as he strove to banish his own doubt:

> Remember how close to Samadhi the ritual brought me: perhaps even the control of the drug that arose and forced me to bed, plus my fear of the shock of R[ose]'s anticipated coming up to bed, operated to stop me. For in the "Thanksgiving and sacrifice for S.D. [Lola Zaza]" I *did* get rid of everything but the Holy Exalted One, and must have held him for a minute or two. I did. I am sure that I did. I expected Rose to see a halo round my head.
> But the hashish enthusiasm surged up against the ritual-enthusiasm; so I hardly know which phenomena to attribute to which.

The question of the interplay between hashish and Samadhi continued to occupy Crowley. He discussed the matter with Jones, who opined that the hashish had nothing to do with it, though it was perhaps useful as a "starter." On October 31, Crowley again conducted an Augoeides Invocation after smoking hashish cigarettes, though a smaller dosage than previously. It was past 10 P.M. when he commenced the ritual, invoking "nearly twice" and suffering "terrible agony." "Once again I nearly got there—all went brilliance—but not quite. I had too much drug and too little invocation. I completely forgot L[ola] thanksgiving altogether."

In December, Crowley continued his work on the esoteric compendium *777*, as well as his intensive communications with Jones. Crowley had, by this point—given his difficulties with Rose, and his lack of desire to participate in the day-to-day realities of raising a child—no settled residence, spending time alternately in London, Eastborne, and Bournemouth. But experimentation continued with hashish and the Augoeides Invocations. On December 27, Crowley ingested some two grams of hashish and subsequently stayed up through the night, transcribing, in his diary, rough notes of an *Atmadarshana* experience:

> The 'millions of worlds' game—the peacock multiform with each 'eye' of its fan a mirror of glory wherein also another peacock—everything thus. (Here consciousness has no longer any knowledge of normal impression. Each thought is itself visualized as a World-Peacock—such seems to me the interpretation of above.) 1.20 A.M. Head still buzzing: wrote above. Samadhi *is* Hashish, an ye will; but Hashish is not Samadhi (It's a low form this Atmadarshana.) (I don't, and didn't, quite understand this. I think it means that only an Adept can use Hashish to excite Samadhi; or else that Hashish is the evil and averse S.) ["S." likely signifies *Samadhi* in its negative aspect as base delusion.]

In "The Psychology of Hashish," written some two years later, Crowley sought to resolve this inner debate as to the relationship between drug intoxication and mystical states. The outcome was necessarily influenced by the express approval, in *The Book of the Law*, of drug use for ecstatic worship of its gods. Significantly, however, in "The Psychology of Hashish" Crowley makes no reference whatsoever to the *Book*. His goal was to examine the mental effects of the drug and its potential use to the interested scientist or mystic—whose linked quest was here termed "Scientific Illuminism." To skeptics who dismissed mysticism as inherently subjective, Crowley posed the analogy of bacteria, the existence of which was not credited until the invention of the microscope.

Hashish, he argued, could serve in like manner as a perceptual entrance to mysticism, the reality of which could be established empirically: "Hashish at least gives proof of a new order of consciousness, and (it seems to me) it is this prima facie case that mystics have always needed to make out, and never have made out." (A similar argument was put forward by Aldous Huxley in his famous study, *The Doors of Perception* (1954).)

As we have seen, Crowley—for all his training in yoga—found it difficult to separate the experience of Samadhi from the influence of hashish. He did assert, in "The Psychology of Hashish," that his travels in India had taught him that "many of the lesser Yogis employed hashish (whether vainly or no we shall discuss later) to obtain Samadhi." But what, at last, was the verdict of this essay as to the role of the drug in his October 9 experience? Ironically, Crowley adopted the fatalistic teaching of his old friend Ananda Metteyya: One's attainment is predestined by karma—the turning wheel of existence. Crowley, who believed his own place to have been most fortunate, thus relegated hashish to a tangential role in his attainment of Samadhi: "One may doubt whether the drug alone ever does this. It is perhaps only the destined adept who, momentarily freed by the dissolving action of the drug from the chain of the four lower Skandhas [Buddhist term for the chains of phenomenal existence—name, form, sensation, and perception], obtains this knowledge which is his by right, totally inept as he may be to do so by any ordinary methods."

Even so, the fact of hashish having been a part of his October 1906 experience seems to have displeased Crowley, or at least to have embarrassed him. "The Psychology of Hashish" makes no explicit reference to the October 1906 *Samadhi* (though the reader familiar with the facts of Crowley's life is invited to see the connection). In the *Confessions*, Crowley was again cautious and oblique, referring to experiments with hashish after his return from China which had been "unexpectedly successful" and pointed to "a striking analogy between this toxic excitement and the more legitimate methods of mental development." The reference to "more legitimate methods" is telling.

Crowley's discomfort here is further evidenced by *John St. John* (1909), a published diary account of a Magical Retirement in Paris in October 1908 that will be discussed in greater detail later in this chapter. Therein, Crowley argued that he could spur attainment of Adonai (a designation for his Holy Guardian Angel) through hashish "and the truth of it would have been 5 per cent. drug and 95 per cent. magic; but nobody would have believed me. Remember that this record is for the

British Public, 'who may like me yet.'" Crowley went on to reject any real hope of acceptance by his countrymen, but the relevant point was made: He feared public reaction to his use of hashish in this context. But then, Crowley shared the very ambivalence he attributed to the British public. Consider this subsequent *John St. John* entry, pointedly sarcastic in tone: "There are only two more idiocies to perform—one, to take a big dose of Hashish and record the ravings as if they were Samadhi; and two, to go to church. I may as well give up." Still later, while drinking in a Parisian cafe, Crowley rebuked himself for taking mere intoxication seriously: "He has drunk only about one third of his half-bottle of light white wine; yet he's like a hashish-drunkard, only more so. The loss of the time-sense which occurs with hashish he got during his experiments with that drug in 1906, but in an unimportant way. (Damn him! he is so glad. He calls this a Result. A result! Damn him!)"

Through all the exaltation and confusion of October 1906, Jones had served as a needed touchstone. But another friendship emerged during this same period that would ultimately prove more influential in fueling Crowley's sense of himself as a worthy public teacher. This new friend was Captain John Frederick Charles Fuller, who would ultimately rise to the rank of major general in the British Army. Fuller is widely acknowledged as one of the premier military theorists of all time. One of his few peers in this field, Captain Sir Basil H. Liddell Hart, pronounced that Fuller was "a true example of genius, a term often misapplied." Among Fuller's major achievements was the first modern conception—fully substantiated by the horrors of World War Two—of the potential and use of highly mobile armored tanks. Fuller also emerged as an early champion of the then controversial viewpoint—today regarded as a truism—that a flourishing peacetime industrial capacity was a prime requisite of success in protracted warfare; as one of Fuller's favorite maxims went, "The tools of peace are the weapons of war." Fuller, an arrogant man with a waspish wit who was disliked or ignored by the majority of the British high command, earned the nickname "Boney" for his persistent adulation of Napoleon Bonaparte, who had declared that he would "master the world by will alone." Fuller retired from the army in frustration in 1933, shortly thereafter joining the British Union of Fascists. He was one of only two Englishmen invited by Adolf Hitler—an admirer of Fuller's tactical writings—to the Führer's 50th birthday party in April 1939. Fuller died in 1966, having devoted his later years to the writing of history. This preamble on his life achievements enables one to appreciate the signal fact that, in a formative stage of his development, Fuller came to regard Aleister Crowley as a poetic and magical genius of the highest order. Fuller devoted himself for some four years—before breaking with Crowley irrevocably—to the New Aeon.

Fuller, three years Crowley's junior, had followed a somewhat parallel path in his childhood. Fuller's father was an Anglican cleric who had imposed a thoroughly Christian education on his son which did not take. Fuller graduated from Sandhurst, the Royal Military College, and then served in the Boer War before being stationed in India. There, as had Crowley, Fuller studied under a native tutor, or *munshi*, and met with numerous yogis and religious teachers. By 1905, Fuller—by then an ardent Social Darwinist—had published essays in the *Agnostic Journal*, a most unusual sideline pursuit for a British officer. In that same year, Fuller came on a copy of Crowley's privately issued verse satire *Why Jesus Wept*. Inserted in the book was a tongue-in-cheek leaflet written by Crowley to promote the sale of his forthcoming *Collected Works:*

> The Chance of the Year!
> The Chance of the Century!!
> The Chance of the Geologic Period!!!

The chance offered was an essay competition on—what else?—the *Collected Works*. The cash prize offered to the winner was £100. Fuller proved to be the only entrant. The two men ultimately met in August 1906, and Fuller quickly befriended both Crowley and Jones. Fuller's essay was published in book form as *The Star in the West* (1907). The £100 prize was never paid, but Fuller never objected.

Fuller accepted the phallocentric aspect of Crowley's teachings, but he was not comfortable with homosexuality. In 1906, Fuller had married Margarethe Karnatz, a beautiful woman who left intellectual matters to her husband while fiercely guarding his privacy. In *Star*, Fuller insisted that "if it be necessary for the initiate to gaze on the back parts of Jahveh, it is, however, most certainly not necessary for him to kiss the hind quarters of the goat of Mendes [a homoerotic magical ritual attributed to the medieval Knights Templar] or to revel in the secret orgies of the Agapae [a Gnostic sect]; for the tempting of man is but the tempering of the metal." But Fuller steadfastly defended free choice: "Yet the virtue of one man may be the vice of another." As to his own code of conduct, however, Fuller would have regarded an allegation of homosexuality as an insult to his honor. Here lay the seed of the quarrel that would—four years later—end his friendship with Crowley.

But for the remaining years of the decade, their alliance was unshakeable. By 1907, Fuller had joined the A∴A∴ with the magical name *Per Ardua Ad Astra* (Through Effort to the Stars) and was practicing astral travel and other rituals under Crowley's tutelage. Crowley was, by this time, living essentially a "single" life in London, having taken a flat of his own so as to get away from Rose, whose excessive drinking had palled his joy in marriage. In effect, Crowley now left the care of Lola Zaza to a woman whom he regarded as an unfit mother. He took female lovers during this period, two of whom, Ada Leverson and Vera Snepp, he celebrated in poems included in *Clouds Without Water,* a volume of erotomystical verse he would issue privately in 1909. As with *White Stains* and *The Scented Garden of Abdullah,* Crowley devised a pseudonymous editor for the volume—in this case, the Reverend C. Verey, who, in his pious preface, warned readers against the blasphemies contained therein: "Unblushing, the old Serpent rears its crest to the sky; unashamed, the Beast and the Scarlet Woman chant the blasphemous litanies of their fornication." For Crowley, the fires of the spirit were banked by surrender to erotic impulse. Such was the role of the women Crowley celebrated in *Clouds,* which forms, in this respect, a heterosexual counterpart to *The Scented Garden.*

The central female character in *Clouds,* with whom the poet experiences the heights and depths of eros and spirit, is named Lola (the nickname of Vera Snepp). There is, amid considerable stretches of straining and mediocre verse, some startlingly original imagery in *Clouds,* as in this paean to Lola:

> Our love is like a glittering sabre bloodied
> > With lives of men; upsoared the sudden sun;
> > The choral heaven woke; the aethyr flooded
> All space with joy that you and I were one.

From the evidence of *Clouds,* Crowley had, by 1907, utterly abandoned the trappings of a monogamous marriage. As a regular stop in his new London life, Crowley frequented a chemist's shop on Stafford Street run by one E. P. Whineray, a man of broad knowledge of the properties of chemical agents (he would later contribute an essay on hashish to *The Equinox*) and of the secret doings of London life. Whineray managed the task of filling Crowley's various needs for drugs (recall that hashish and like intoxicants were still legal in England) and for ingredients for incense admixtures, such as the rare onycha required for the incense sacred to Tetragrammaton (the four-lettered name of the Hebrew god). It was Whineray who introduced Crowley to the Earl of

Tankerville, thus setting into play a remarkable case study of an ill-fitted pupil driven to distraction by an ill-suited teacher.

Crowley frequently acknowledged his indebtedness to classical Sufi teachings. A fundamental tenet therein is that students may receive instruction only if they are in fact suited to do so, and then only at the right time, in the right place, and with the right conjunction of persons. But Crowley was not one to turn away a potential disciple. The Earl of Tankerville, by Crowley's own account, suffered from crippling paranoia, excessive brandy consumption, and cocaine addiction. Crowley at once undertook to remake him through rigorous magical training.

The story of their work together survives only through Crowley's version in the *Confessions*. Tankerville, a wealthy man in his early fifties, came to Crowley in the spring of 1907 convinced that his mother, in league with others, was out to kill him by magical means. He further felt that his wife and son might also be in danger. For all his nervousness and vices, Tankerville was devoted to his family—a trait Crowley viewed as a sentimental encumbrance from which his student required extraction. Their training began in April 1907; Crowley took Tankerville's tales of magical peril at face value so as "not to undeceive the patient" but rather conquer the obsession head-on. Surprisingly, Crowley suggested, as a means of defence, the precept to love one's enemy. According to Crowley, Christianity had misinterpreted this precept by imposing upon it a moral meaning. In truth, it was a paradox illustrating the energies of the mind: By emitting a calm, impersonal love, evil currents directed at one would necessarily recoil and destroy one's foe.

But Crowley concluded that their magical practice in England was insufficient to bring about a healing transformation. The Earl's wife remained a persistent distraction, as were the children. It was essential that they make a Great Retirement together. Crowley decided upon Morocco, by way of Paris, Marseilles, and Gibraltar. "I was of course in paradise," Crowley wrote, "to be once more among Mohammedans, with their manliness, straightforwardness, subtlety and self-respect!" The trip was, plainly, a fulfillment of Crowley's own desires, with the further hope that Tankerville, once forced into unfamiliar and rigorous conditions, would cast aside his Anglo-Saxon fears and prejudices. This was Crowley's standard prescription for spiritual transformation; it had served Crowley well, by his own lights. That it was not a suitable course of learning—or treatment—for all who came to him served to perplex him time and again. Tankerville proved immune to the charms of Morocco and soon insisted on a return to England.

There was a further element that contributed to the end of the relationship. Crowley was a great believer in pushing his students to the limit through means including intensive verbal abuse: The more difficult the training, the more a student would gain—if he was worthy; and if he was not, a kindlier manner would not, in any event, have sufficed. But Tankerville grew restive. We know this from Crowley's Preface to his satiric play, *The World's Tragedy*, in which he allowed that: "My readers, too, may be weary. They may say to me, as Lord Tankerville said to me at eleven A.M. on the 7th of July 1907, 'I'm sick of your teaching—teaching—teaching—as if you were God Almighty and I were a poor bloody shit in the street!'—

"I could not blame them."

Teaching efforts aside, Crowley proudly viewed 1907 as his *"annus mirabilis* in poetry." Prolific he certainly was, with *Clouds Without Water* and numerous lyrics that would be included in the mixed essay and verse volume *Knox Om Pax* (1907). But his most exceptional work may be found in two "Holy Books"—in A∴A∴ parlance, Class "A" reading materials that "represent the utterance of an Adept entirely beyond the criticism of even the Visible Head of the Organization," that is, Crowley himself. Their creation somewhat paralleled that of *The Book of the Law*, though Crowley always set the latter work unto itself as a primary revelation.

Crowley had been working with Fuller and Jones on the ritual design of the new A∴A∴. And then, without warning, the Holy Books—rhapsodic, jagged, epigrammatic utterances in a poetic prose style closely akin to that of the *Book*—"begin to be received at will," as Crowley later expressed it. These were, in his view, neither of his own composition nor instances of automatic writing. "I can only say that I was not wholly conscious at the time of what I was writing, and I felt that I had no right to 'change' so much as the style of a letter. They were written with the utmost rapidity without pausing for thought for a single moment, and I have not presumed to revise them. Perhaps 'plenary inspiration' is the only adequate phrase, and this has become so discredited that people are loath to admit the possibility of such a thing." There were a total of thirteen such Holy Books. Of these, eight were transcribed during the last three months of 1907. Crowley regarded as primary the first two received by him: *Liber Liberi Vel Lapidis Lazuli (The Book of Lapis Lazuli)*—which he put to paper in a three-hour span on the night of October 29—and *Liber Cordis Cincti Serpente (The Book of the Heart Girt with a Serpent)*—transcribed in four subsequent sessions from October 30 to November 3.

As to the former work, the precious stone lapis lazuli, an ornament of victory and attainment, is blue violet with specks of gold; these specks, by Crowley's kabbalistic interpretation, represent "that dust which is all that remains of the Exempt Adept after he has crossed the Abyss, is gradually surrounded by sphere after sphere of shining splendour, so that he becomes a fitting ornament for the bosom of the Great Mother." The dust becomes a pearl, and the joining with the Great Mother is the attainment of the sphere *Binah* (Understanding)—the first sphere of the Supernal Triad of the kabbalistic Tree of Life. *Lapis Lazuli* sets forth Crowley's new magical name as a Master of the Temple; V.V.V.V.V., for *Vi Veri Vniversum Vivus Vici*—"By the force of Truth I have conquered the Universe while living."

The Book of the Heart Girt with a Serpent is a still more striking achievement. The kabbalistic number assigned to this book by Crowley, sixty-five, signifies both Adonai (one of the Hebrew names of God) and also Augoeides, Crowley's Holy Guardian Angel. The five chapters which make up *Heart* explore the five spiritual elements of Western esotericism—earth, air, water, fire, and spirit. The opening lines blend Western symbolism (the heart as center of the human soul) and Eastern symbolism (the serpent as the rising Kundalini energy and the flowers as the highest *chakra* of enlightenment, the thousand-petalled lotus *Sahasrara*):

> I am the Heart; and the Snake is entwined
> About the invisible core of the mind.
> Rise, O my snake! It is now the hour
> Of the hooded and holy ineffable flower.
> Rise, O my snake, into brilliance of bloom
> On the corpse of Osiris afloat in the tomb!

The Holy Books reflect the best of Crowley the poet, though he would not have categorized them as "literature." He himself regarded, as his finest verse of this period, the satiric drama *The World's Tragedy,* composed in February 1908 with a Preface added later in the summer. *The World's Tragedy* is an impassioned assault upon Christianity as a death knell of the human spirit. The incarnation comes in for especial ridicule, as when the Holy Ghost—cast as a lusting fiend—impregnates an outraged yet impassioned Miriam (Mary), who is thus awakened to her true nature as a Scarlet Woman: "I am the Empress of the City of Sin,/ Wrapped in its purple robe/ Stained with mine own maid's blood." In the final act, there is prophesied—by Alexander, the pagan king of

Babylonia—the coming of a new prophet and saviour who (as Crowley specifies in his Preface) is Crowley himself.

It is this autobiographical Preface, and not the play itself, which forms the most remarkable portion of *The World's Tragedy*. Crowley later noted (without offering a reason therefor) that two pages of the Preface had been mutilated in all copies of the book except those given to close friends. Those two pages contained his *first* frank declaration of the homosexual aspect of his bisexuality. That Crowley himself had a hand in the mutilation cannot be confirmed, but it seems most likely, especially given his statement in the Preface that he had, for a time, considered publishing the book under a pseudonym. Given that mutilation, and the book's issuance in a private edition of 100 copies in 1910, his declaration can hardly be regarded as a public event. Nonetheless, it was an act of some courage in the climate of Edwardian England; one need only consider, by way of contrast, the lifelong cautious discretions of the Bloomsbury circle. The deleted pages of his Preface devoted to this subject were boldly subtitled "Sodomy" and argued that "in truth there seems no better way to avoid the contamination of woman and the morose pleasures of solitary vice. (Not that women themselves are unclean. It is the worship of them as ideals that rots the soul.)" Crowley had stressed earlier in this Preface that he was in love with his own wife. But his defiance was such that he vowed to "fight openly for that which no living Englishman dare defend, even in secret—sodomy!" In fact, Crowley did not fight openly for this cause; as previously discussed, even the *Confessions* are circumspect on this subject.

This Preface is also noteworthy for Crowley's careful distinction between his hatred for the slave morality of the Christian establishment as opposed to the teachings of Jesus (whom he held to be a "legendary" composite rather than a strictly historical figure). Indeed, Crowley strained here toward a moderation that seldom showed itself in his attacks: "I do not wish to argue that the doctrines of Jesus, they and they alone, have degraded the world to its present position. I take it that Christianity is not only the cause but the symptom of slavery." At this point, Crowley was not consciously arguing for *The Book of the Law*; he had, in fact, lost track of the whereabouts of the manuscript. But he nonetheless proclaimed himself a prophet in dire need of followers to overthrow the Christian yoke:

> One thing I must ask; let this book be assiduously circulated among the young. Let me seduce the boys of England, and the

oldsters may totter unconverted to their graves. Then these boys, becoming men, may bring about the new heaven and the new earth. You are not a Crowleian till you can say "Yes, thank God, I am an atheist." For the 'transvaluation of all values' must yet again take place, when those are all dead and damned who have forced us into the painful position we now occupy.[. . .]

Young men! there is the enemy. I am no coward, I hope; and believe that I may make a fairly good general—at least no traitor. But without an army I am useless; a Napoleon at St. Helena.

The hope of seducing "boys," conjoined with the defense of sodomy, would, of course, have particularly appalled right-minded readers—then and now (though it should be made clear that Crowley was referring to college students willing to be seduced, as opposed to child abuse or pedophilia). The military campaign metaphor showed the influence of Fuller. And it was with Fuller's assistance that Crowley now undertook to enlist young men to his cause by paying visits, in 1908 and 1909, to Oxford and, more frequently, to his old haunts at Cambridge.

There were few students at either institution who paid serious heed to Crowley. But he did leave a lasting mark on a small group of young admirers who believed in his role as teacher of a new esotericism, one both spiritually exalted and in accord with science. Victor Neuburg was one of these; he gave himself fully to Crowley, embracing the teachings of the Master and falling in love with the man.

The two men first met in the spring of 1908. Neuburg was twenty-five, seven years Crowley's junior. He had been raised in an upper middle-class Jewish family in London. After having proven himself unfit for commerce, Neuburg entered Trinity College, Cambridge—Crowley's alma mater—as a relatively old undergraduate in 1906. By this time, Neuburg had published poems in freethinking periodicals including *The Agnostic Journal,* to which Fuller had also contributed. It was through that journal that Fuller and Neuburg became acquainted in 1906; Fuller later recommended the young poet to Crowley as a suitable prospect for the A∴A∴. When Crowley, some two years later, paid an unannounced visit to Neuburg in his Trinity rooms, the impact of the meeting upon both men was profound. Neuburg had thick curly brown hair, intense blue eyes, languid features, and a head that seemed altogether too large for his body, which was wracked by curvature of the spine. Crowley declared that "from the first moment I saw him [. . .] I read an altogether extraordinary capacity for Magick." Neuburg had already rejected the Judeo-Christian concept of a personal God, but clung to the idea of an immanent Spirit. His first volume of poetry, *The Green Garland* (published in 1908), reflected these metaphysical concerns even prior to his meeting with Crowley. But Crowley the teacher seemed to offer a path to far more meaningful insights, by offering to guide the younger man through magical ordeals of the Beast's own design.

Neuburg's entrance into Crowley's life coincided with the further distancing of relations between Crowley and Rose, whose drinking continued to distress him. In January 1908, Crowley had moved out of their London home at 21 Warwick Road and took lodgings at 50 rue Vavin in Paris. The hotel and its tolerant owners—an amiable Parisian bourgeois family who understood and enjoyed Crowley's ways—suited the Beast, who would use the address as a pied-à-terre for years to come. Crowley remained in Paris through April 1908, when he returned to England and found no change in Rose's condition. In a letter from this period, Crowley detailed the behavior that had driven him from his wife: "Life with Rose is intolerable while she locks me out of the house, insults her own guests at my table, uses foul language to servants, reels up Bond St. [in London] charging into passers-by, goes from crisis to crisis of hysteria, tells people wild & impossible lies about me etc etc etc ad nauseam." To Fuller, in another letter, Crowley confided: "I don't think we should shut our eyes to the fact that I am now a batchelor [sic] to all intents and purposes; and what's better one in the glorious and unassailable position of not being able to marry if I want to! There's a stance!"

Crowley now employed a London physician, W. Murray Leslie, to treat his wife. In June 1908, Leslie at last prevailed upon Rose—who had rejected similar pleas by Crowley—to hire responsible live-in caretakers to watch over Lola Zaza and herself. Crowley returned to Paris in July, free to relish a bohemian life devoted to magic, literature, and pleasure. He also supervised Fuller in the writing of *The Temple of Solomon the King*. But Crowley's energies could not be fully occupied by writing alone. Neuburg came to join him once the Cambridge spring term ended, and Crowley now turned his primary attention to this young man.

Neuburg was almost assuredly a virgin when he arrived in Paris. Crowley promptly resolved to address this sheltered ignorance. Crowley's own erotic attentions were now being occupied by a new love, Euphemia Lamb, the wife of the artist Henry Lamb. She was, by all accounts, remarkable not only for her beauty—with her pale oval face, classical features, and honey brown hair, she sat as a frequent model for Augustus John and other painters—but also for her intelligence and fearless wit. It was with Euphemia's assistance that Crowley devised a means to shock Neuburg into consciousness of the sexual ways of the world.

The plan was for Crowley to encourage Neuburg, who was also attracted to Euphemia, to woo and then—as was proper—propose to her. Euphemia acted the innocent, smitten damsel to the hilt. Feigning ignorance of their chaste engagement, Crowley convinced Neuburg that he had to experience sexual initiation by visiting a prostitute—a woman named Marcelle, whom Crowley had himself frequented. Once this was accomplished, Crowley "discovered" the engagement and, with pretended horror, convinced Neuburg to reveal the truth of his infidelity to the wronged Euphemia. Neuburg, with great self-loathing, did so; Euphemia refused to forgive him. After three days of intense remorse, Neuburg was led to Crowley's hotel room, where Euphemia sat "unadorned, smoking a cigarette on my bed. The boy was absolutely stunned. Even with the evidence in front of his eyes, he was loth [sic] to admit the truth. His ideal woman was shattered thoroughly and forever." In this early teaching, Crowley declared himself—by displaying the nude Euphemia on his own bed—Neuburg's sexual master.

After roughly a month together in Paris, with Neuburg pursuing a course of vigils and fasts, Crowley adjudged that changed—and more rigorous—conditions were necessary. As with the Earl of Tankerville, Crowley proposed a walk through Spain and Morocco. For the bookish Neuburg, the experience was a physical and psychological terra incognita. They departed from Paris on July 31 and reached Morocco in September. Crowley was enraptured: "My spiritual self is at home in China, but my heart and my hand are pledged to the Arab."

During this walking trip, Crowley took the opportunity—in good military fashion (again reflecting the influence of Fuller)—to formulate five basic principles that could guide him in becoming a world teacher. In occult terms, it was essential to avoid the naïveté of "mixing the planes"—that is, of insisting that the heights of mystical insight enabled one to overlook the practicalities of daily life. First, social status was crucial, particularly given the foul reputation of magic: "I decided first of all, that the most important point was never to forget that I was a gentleman and keep my honour the more spotless [in] that I was assuming a position whose professors were rarely well born [. . .]" After this came four further standards of conduct: Not to receive money for the teaching of magic; not to commit himself to "any statement that I could not prove in the same sense as a chemist can prove the law of combining weights"; to uphold the dignity of magic through the application of science and philosophy and noble literary style; and finally, as "a point of honesty not to pretend to be better than I was. I would avoid concealing my faults and foibles. I would have no one accept me on false pretenses."

This latter point was particularly vital as Crowley was "anxious to prove that spiritual progress did not depend on religious or moral codes, but was like any other science. Magick would yield its secrets to the infidel and the libertine, just as one does not have to be a churchwarden in order to discover a new kind of orchid."

In his account of this summer walking trip in the *Confessions,* Crowley never alluded to his personal relations with Neuburg. It is in the latter's poetry that evidence is to be found of their passion. Neuburg's second volume of poems, *The Triumph of Pan* (1910), was published under the aegis of Crowley's *Equinox.* This volume, which remains Neuburg's major work, alludes to Crowley under the pseudonym "Olivia Vane"—a reflection both of Crowley's passive 'female' role in their lovemaking, and of Neuburg's caution on the subject of his own bisexuality. In one poem, Crowley is addressed as "Sweet Wizard, in whose footsteps I have trod/Unto the shrine of the most obscene god"— the latter a reference to Pan, the horned god whose all-encompassing life force (which included all forms of sexual union) was regarded as obscene by society at large. A later poem includes a deliberate gender fluctuation to express the bisexual psychological roles played by the two men in their magical practice and lovemaking:

> O thou who hast sucked my soul, lord of my nights and days,
> My body, pure and whole is merged within the ways
> That lead to thee, my queen [. . .]

In late September, Neuburg went off to visit relatives, while Crowley returned to Paris. They would reunite in London the following year. Prior to their parting, Neuburg took a Vow of Holy Obedience to study as a *chela* (student) under the direction of Crowley. This would constitute—in the years to come—a most painful and arduous course.

For now, however, Crowley had a more solitary project in mind. As with his practice in China in 1905–1906, Crowley resolved to experiment with the very concept of a Magical Retirement. In particular, he sought to establish that a trained adept could pursue such a Retirement in conditions exactly opposite to the cloistered quiet specified by *Abra-Melin.* His choice of locale was Paris; the timeframe was that of a typical two-week vacation. He would stay in a fine hotel and live the life of a gentleman—and invoke his Angel all the while. He would eat fine foods, drink wine, even take a lover—and devote himself throughout to that Angel. He would, further, keep a diary which would record his every action and serve as a model to others—a proof to them that they did not have to go off to the Himalayas or like fastnesses to gain enlightenment. This diary he entitled *John St. John* (his name for his human—as opposed to enlightened—self during the Retirement, with a play on St. John, the traditionally ascribed author of *Revelation*); it was published the following year in *The Equinox*.

For Crowley, the practice of magic was revelatory of the nature of mind itself. To disbelieve the possibilities of magical ritual was to place unjustified limits upon the powers of concentration and imagination—and to place too great a trust in so-called objective reality. As Crowley put it tersely in his Preface, "The Universe of Magic is in the mind of a man: the setting is but Illusion even to the thinker." If magic is no more and no less than mind, then the notion of higher divine intelligences becomes either unnecessary or merely subjective. Thus, on the eleventh day, Crowley declared his "Atheism":

> I believe that all these [magical] phenomena are as explicable as the formation of hoar-frost or of glacier tables.
>
> I believe "Attainment" to be a simple supreme sane state of the human brain. I do not believe in miracles; I do not think that God could cause a monkey, clergyman, or rationalist to attain.[. . .]
>
> I believe in the Law of Cause and Effect—and I loathe the cant alike of the Superstitionist and the Rationalist.

Similarly, in his essay "The Soldier and the Hunchback" (written in December 1908) Crowley posed, as a metaphor for the dialectical progress of human consciousness, the interplay between doubt ("?"—the hunchback) and realization ("!"—the upright soldier). Doubt always follows on the heels of insight, which in turn supersedes doubt—*!?!?!?!?!?*—and so forth ad infinitum.

The Magical Retirement recorded in *John St. John* began on October 1, 1908. The interplay of sex and spirituality—theoretically familiar to Crowley both through Indian Tantric writings and his studies in alchemy—was still largely foreign to him in practice. Thus sexuality is treated either as a distraction or as a perplexing unknown in *John St. John*. On the first day of the Retirement, Crowley recorded a late-night lovemaking with a young woman introduced to him by an obliging Nina Olivier. He gave her the name "Maryt"; she was a Polish Jew studying in Paris. But on the third day, Crowley noted that he had fallen "shockingly under the power of Tamas, the dark sphere." *Tamas* is the

Hindu term for a state dominated by animal desires. Crowley recorded the erotomystical fantasy that enveloped him in his *Tamas* state, even as he was reciting his mantra:

> I am so far from the Path that I have a real good mind to get Maryt to let me perform the Black Mass on her at midnight. I would just love to bring up Typhon, and curse Osiris and burn his bones and his blood! [. . .] I want trouble. I want to say Indra's mantram till his throne gets red-hot and burns his lotus-buttocks; I want to pinch little Harpocrates till he fairly yells . . . and I will too! Somehow!

The attainment of Adonai, the Holy Guardian Angel, took place on the twelfth day—October 12, Crowley's thirty-third birthday, the age of the crucified Christ. (Christ is, under Christian kabbalistic tradition, an archetype of the adept as he encounters Adonai.) Intense invocation, coupled with the recital of one of Crowley's own Holy Books, *Liber Ararita,* served as the prelude to the attainment. "Ararita" is a kabbalistic name for God; its letters stand, in the original Hebrew, for the sentence "One is His beginning, One is his Individuality, His Permutation One." The aim of *Liber Ararita* is to express the identification of all human conceptions with their opposites, so as to point to an ultimate unity. It was the attainment of this unity which Crowley sought to express in his diary:

> Then subtly, easily, imperceptibly gliding, I passed away into nothing. And I was wrapped in the black brilliance of my Lord, that interpenetrated me in every part, fusing its light with my darkness, and leaving there no darkness, but pure light.
>
> Also I beheld my Lord in a figure and I felt the interior trembling kindle itself into a Kiss—and I perceived the true Sacraments—and I beheld in one moment all the mystic visions in one; and the Holy Graal appeared unto me, and many other inexpressible things were known of me.
>
> Also I was given to enjoy the subtle Presence of my Lord interiorly during the whole of this twelfth day.
>
> Then I besought the Lord that He would take me into His presence eternally even now.
>
> But He withdrew Himself, for that I must do that which I was sent hither to do; namely, to rule the earth.

The thirteenth and final day of the Retirement was but briefly noted; such heights required a relative silence. As for its lasting impact, Crowley declared: "I not only achieved my stated object, but obtained access to a reserve of energy which carried me on for years, performing Herculean labors without conscious effort."

One matter required Crowley's prompt attention after the *John St. John* Retirement, as it challenged his status as a gentleman, that "most important point" resolved upon during the trek to Morocco with Neuburg. In late 1908, Crowley read the just-published Somerset Maugham novel *The Magician*. The portrayal therein of the villainous Oliver Haddo—inspired by Crowley—was discussed in Chapter Three, in connection with the encounter between Crowley and Maugham in Paris in 1903. Crowley bristled at the mélange of fact, rumor and fiction in the novel:

> Maugham had taken some of the most private and personal incidents of my life [. . .] He had added a number of the many absurd legends of which I was a central figure.[. . .] I was not in the least offended by the attempts of the book to represent me as, in many ways, the most atrocious scoundrel, for he had done more than justice to the qualities of which I was proud; and despite himself he had been compelled, like Balaam, to prophesy concerning me. He attributed to me certain characteristics which he meant to represent as abominable, but which were actually absurd.[. . .] *The Magician* was, in fact, an appreciation of my genius such as I had never dreamed of inspiring.

These "characteristics" included, first and foremost, Crowley's single-minded will to spiritual knowledge. The vividness of this trait appealed to Crowley sufficiently to place *The Magician* on his list of recommended reading for A∴A∴ members.

But Crowley could not leave *The Magician* unavenged. In truth, Maugham had plagiarized in the novel; sources from which he transcribed or paraphrased at length included *The Kabbalah Unveiled* by Mathers and other occult texts. This was documented by Crowley (under the pseudonym "Oliver Haddo") in the journal *Vanity Fair* on December 30, 1908; its editor, Frank Harris (later to gain fame for his sexually frank *My Life and Loves*), admired Crowley and provided the first broad outlet for his writing. According to Crowley, Maugham acknowledged the plagiarisms with good grace at their next encounter— "he merely remarked that there were many thefts besides those which I had pointed out." At that point, Maugham was not yet established in his fame; decades later, in its glow, he conceded discreetly that *The Magician* "was all moonshine. I did not believe a word of it. It was a game I was playing. A book written under these conditions can have no life in it."

As 1908 came to a close, Crowley felt that his path had grown clear. He would declare his new teachings and new Order through his founding of *The Equinox*. He would assemble the army of supporters envisioned in his Preface to *The World's Tragedy*. And he would seek, for the first time, to influence his homeland and the world.

It would be a campaign filled with brilliant triumphs and bitter defeats.

CHAPTER SIX

The Creation of *The Equinox*, the Rites of Eleusis, and a Confrontation in the Sahara with the God of Chaos (1909–14)

In conception, form, and scope, the ten book-sized "numbers" that comprise the first "volume" of *The Equinox* constitute Crowley's grandest publishing achievement—and that in a lifetime of exorbitant publishing projects. It was published biannually at the spring and fall equinoxes from 1909 to 1913—a total in excess of 4000 pages that aimed to present the essence of Western esotericism.

Consider the physical product itself: There were 1050 copies printed for each number, 50 subscription copies bound in cloth, the remaining 1000 in white-and-gold boards featuring the astrological sigils of the Sun, Aries and Virgo—with reference to the solar focus of Crowley's teachings and the signs of the spring and fall equinoxes. Crowley spent his inheritance unstintingly on *The Equinox* during these years. Sales could not possibly cover costs, as copies were priced below cost for the sake of affordability. In addition, the odd format of *The Equinox*—a periodical in the form of an outsized bound volume—made booksellers reluctant to distribute it. "In this way," Crowley later wrote, "I satisfied myself that no one could reproach me with trying to make money out of Magick." As Fuller would later observe, "like so many of his [Crowley's] projects, the aim was protean and the method erratic [. . .] It sold like hot cakes, and, in spite of its expensive production, had he not been so prodigal, it might have provided him with a modest income."

The two central purposes of *The Equinox* are reflected in its two subtitles: *The Official Organ of the A∴A∴* and *The Review of Scientific Illuminism.* *The Equinox* was to promote public awareness of the new magical order and its methodology: Mysticism pursued through methodical experimentation (documented through ongoing written records) with the powers of the mind. The motto of *The Equinox* was emblazoned on its title page: "The Method of Science—The Aim of Religion." Quite naturally, much of *The Equinox* was devoted to magic, yoga, and other mystical disciplines. Most of this material was written by Crowley in the forms of "holy books" and other instructional texts. There were also nine installments of *The Temple of Solomon the King,* a spiritual biography of Crowley, written largely by Fuller under Crowley's close supervision. *Temple* included texts of the central Golden Dawn rituals written by Mathers, for the New Aeon proclaimed in *The Equinox*—number VII of which included *The Book of the Law*—abrogated prior vows of secrecy by Crowley with respect to Old Aeon rituals. In 1900, the London revolt had wrenched practical control of the Golden Dawn from Mathers; ten years later, Crowley finished the job by wresting his teachings away.

But *The Equinox* was not solely devoted to esotericism. Crowley's view of magic held that artistic expression was one measure—a fitting one—of true attainment. As a result, *The Equinox* was a literary journal as well, featuring short stories, poems, plays—again, mostly written by Crowley (other contributors included Lord Dunsany and Frank Harris). Crowley had long chafed at the public indifference to his creative works; *The Equinox* allowed him a free venue in which to display his talents. There was one outside contributor to *The Equinox* who falls in a class by himself. This was Crowley's old friend Ananda Metteyya (Allan Bennett), who had briefly returned to England in 1908 to continue, in his homeland, work on behalf of the International Buddhist Society. Crowley published in *The Equinox* Bennett's essay on Buddhism, "The Training of the Mind," an act of admirable editorial objectivity, given the treatment that Crowley's esoteric compendium, *777*, received in Bennett's journal, *The Buddhist Review. 777*, which derived in part from tables of symbolic correspondences taught to Crowley by Bennett during their Golden Dawn days, was now treated with disdain: "No Buddhist would consider it worth while to pass from the crystalline clearness of his own religion to this involved obscurity. Some of the language is extremely undignified." Crowley tried to rekindle the bond that had been so vital between 1899 and 1905. What had changed is unclear, but the reluctant party was clearly Bennett. In a 1908 letter to Fuller, Crowley exhorted: "I hope you're sitting down to the siege of Allan & picking his brains." The use of "siege" is telling; the friendship was now at an end.

If Crowley had lost one longstanding ally, he was also gaining new ones for the A∴A∴, launched publicly in England in 1909. Fuller, with his esteemed military status, was primary amongst them; he now regarded *The Book of the Law* as "the utterance of a Master." Fuller's organizing intellect, floridly elegant literary style, and gifts as an illustrator for *The Equinox* afforded Crowley a trustworthy second-in-command.

As discussed in the previous chapter, one of the recruiting sites on which Crowley pinned his hopes was his alma mater—Trinity College, Cambridge. Neuburg was a member of a newly formed club, the Pan Society, devoted to free discussion of spiritual topics. To this society, Crowley had read papers on "mysticism and kindred subjects" three times in the latter part of 1908. But disturbing rumors were afoot in Trinity administrative circles as to the thoroughly non-Christian ideas that Crowley had put forward, as well as his success in winning disciples. Aside from Neuburg, these included Kenneth Ward, who would later be initiated into the A∴A∴, and Norman Mudd, a gifted mathematics student form a lower-class family attending Trinity on scholarship. This financial dependence would render Mudd a weak link in the battle to come.

The Senior Dean of Trinity, the Reverend R. St. J. Parry, was convinced that magic was, in itself, an objectionable teaching. Still more dire was an anonymous letter sent to the deans of Trinity in 1908, which alleged that Crowley had been shadowed by police in various European nations, on suspicion of commissioning sexual acts with boys. The truth of this charge cannot, at this point, be confirmed or denied. But its impact upon the deans was plain enough; they pressured Neuburg and his fellows to break off all ties with Crowley and to cancel his invitation to speak to another undergraduate club, the Cambridge University Freethought Association (CUFA). The deans confronted Mudd with the anonymous letter in late January 1909, and threatened him with expulsion if he did not move to cancel that invitation. After further pressure from his father, Mudd acquiesced. The other students, after issuing a protest, tacitly gave way as well. By the end of February, both Crowley and Fuller were officially excluded from the Trinity grounds, and the porters were so notified. As for Mudd (who, unlike Neuburg, was never erotically involved with Crowley), shame over his surrender would endure for over a decade, until he overcame it and contacted Crowley once more.

A year later, in January 1910, Crowley was still attempting, by way of a polished and indignant letter to Parry, to reinstate himself. The opening paragraphs of the letter—addressed to Trinity College itself—constitute, in miniature, a remarkable apologia as to Crowley's magical vocation:

> For three years you stood to me *in loco parentis,* and that I was a worthy child is evidenced by the fact that I never suffered rebuke or punishment from any of the College Authorities.
>
> To that paternity I now appeal for justice in the following circumstances.
>
> Since leaving Cambridge in 1898, I have travelled all over the world on one single business, the search for Truth.
>
> This truth [sic] I believe that I have found: it may be stated in the thesis following:
>
> By development of will-power, by rigorous self-control, by solitude, meditation and prayer, a man may be granted the Knowledge and Conversation of his Holy Guardian Angel; this being attained, the man may safely confide himself to that Guardianship: and that this attainment is the most sublime privilege of man.

Crowley concluded by requesting a formal hearing, public or private, before an unspecified tribunal, with legal representation and rules of evidence to apply. There is no record of a response by Parry or other Trinity officials. As for the New Aeon announced by *The Book of the Law,* it is left unmentioned in the letter. Its absence is striking, as a most signal event had taken place in Crowley's life in June 1909, a good six months before this letter was written. This was his full and final acceptance of his vocation as prophet of the New Aeon and of its ruling god, Horus, the Crowned and Conquering Child.

The event triggering this acceptance was mundane enough—an accident of the kind most persons have experienced—and yet it took on tremendous significance for Crowley. It will be recalled that, while still in Cairo in 1904, Crowley had several typescripts made of the *Book,* which he sent to fifteen friends and colleagues. Shortly thereafter, he lost track of the original manuscript.

The setting was Boleskine House in Scotland, to which Crowley had returned in the summer of 1909. He was joined there in June by two still-loyal Cambridge men, Neuburg and Kenneth Ward. Neuburg devoted his full attention to training with Crowley, whom he regarded as his "holy Guru." Ward, enjoying a less rigorous summer, wished to ski, and Crowley tried to oblige him by hunting up one of his spare pairs. This led Crowley to explore the attic where, beneath the skis, lay the long lost manuscript. The sight was a stunning *coup de foudre* to his psyche. His diary entry for June 28 begins with an ecstatic paean to the divine triumvirate of the *Book:* "Glory be to Nuit, Hadit, Ra-Hoor-Khuit in the Highest!"

The questions which had for so long vexed Crowley were now, with sudden certainty, resolved. Aiwass was his Holy Guardian Angel. Thelema was the teaching to which he would devote himself. As he later wrote, "For the first time since the spring of 1904 I felt myself free to do my will.[. . .] My aspiration to be the means of emancipating humanity was perfectly fulfilled. I had merely to establish in the world the Law which had been given me to proclaim: 'Thou hast no right but to do thy will.'" Crowley expressed here a vital distinction which has frequently been overlooked by commentators on his life and work. The rediscovery of the manuscript did *not* serve to confirm his vocation as a prophet to humankind—of that vocation he had been convinced since his 1905–06 Augoeides Invocations in China, which were guided by the postulate that he was the "Chosen One."

The June 28, 1909, manuscript rediscovery came directly on the heels of another magical working in Boleskine House. On the previous day, June 27, Victor Neuburg—or rather *Omnia Vincam* (I shall conquer all), a Probationer of the A∴A∴—had completed a ten-day magical retirement under the direction of his Holy Guru. The magical record kept by Neuburg, and annotated by Crowley, represents the earliest detailed account of Crowley's teaching methods with a magical disciple. This record follows Crowley's insistence—in line with the empirical approach of Scientific Illuminism—on precise accounts of mental states and practices entered virtually every waking hour. It reveals dark valleys of pitched emotion and jagged peaks of tentative insight. The completion of his retirement—a successful one, as Crowley adjudged it—entitled Neuburg to become a Neophyte in the A∴A∴. As Neuburg wrote at the end of his record: "I had always the sense of being God; also, I was waiting, it seemed, for something to happen—some event such as death. But nothing beyond the ecstasy ever occurred. My Holy Guru broke up this Vision entirely, giving me a purer but a far rarer one, which occurs very seldom indeed."

The basic course set for Neuburg was seclusion within his room with meals—sometimes hearty, sometimes meager—provided by Crowley.

(Meat was a frequent menu item; Crowley resolved to break down Neuburg's exclusionary belief system of vegetarianism.) Neuburg practiced basic yogic techniques, magical ritual (including the "Bornless One" invocation), astral travel, recitation of mantras and study of texts including the *Book* and other of Crowley's holy books. The seclusion was not a rigid one; Crowley, in his role of teacher, would pay frequent visits to Neuburg's room, and Neuburg was allowed to come to Crowley's bedroom at night to talk, ask questions, and even feed on biscuits to supplement his dietary regimen. Wife Rose was living at Boleskine during this period; Neuburg witnessed her, on at least one occasion, drunk and in a seemingly sunken condition. Her presence seems to have made Neuburg uncomfortable, and his late-night visits to Crowley's chambers were almost certainly premised on Rose sleeping in separate quarters.

Whether or not Crowley and Neuburg had sexual relations during this magical retirement is unclear; it is possible that Neuburg's final "Ordeal" as a Probationer included a sacred sexual act with his Guru. But there is certainly an erotic tension that shows through frequently in Neuburg's written record. Crowley saw Neuburg as a masochist and indulged to the hilt his own sadistic tendencies toward Neuburg—this was, indeed, a constant not only during this retirement, but throughout the whole of their relationship. During these ten days, Crowley leveled numerous brutal verbal attacks on Neuburg's family and Jewish ancestry (or "race," as Crowley posed it erroneously—an egregious lapse for one who had seen firsthand the Jews of Morocco). At times, Neuburg bore up and saw the abuse as a tactic on his Guru's part to shatter the limiting defenses of the personal ego. At other times, pain and anger prevailed, as in this entry:

> My worthy Guru is quite unnecessarily rude and brutal, I know not why. Probably he does not know himself. He is apparently brutal merely to amuse himself and to pass the time away. Anyhow I won't stick it any more.
>
> It seems to me unnecessary and brutal rudeness is the prerogative of a cad of the lowest type.[. . .] It is ungenerous also to abuse one's position as a Guru: it is like striking an inferior who will be ruined if he dares to retaliate.

Recall that Neuburg had taken, at the end of their walk through Spain and North Africa in 1908, a Vow of Holy Obedience to Crowley. For Neuburg even to consider breaking off the retirement was a sign of genuine desperation.

There were other occasions, however, when the sadomasochistic interplay between them was treated with mutual understanding—and banter. On occasion, the discipline, or abuse, took on physical form, as when Crowley scourged Neuburg on his naked back and buttocks with a gorse switch or a bundle of nettles. In an entry from the fifth day, Neuburg lamented that his Guru had upbraided him severely and was "apparently a homosexual Sadist." In notes appended to this entry a week later, Crowley wryly warned: "Slandering one's Guru is punished in the thirty-second and last Hell." To which Neuburg replied: "A small price to pay for the invention of a new vice."

After Neuburg had completed the prescribed ten-day retirement and had devoted three days more to inscribing a polished copy of his record in a beautiful bound volume, Crowley surprised Neuburg by insisting on a still further ten days of physical discipline—sleeping naked on the cold floor of his room on a litter of gorse that Neuburg was sent off to cut for himself. Neuburg remembered the chill of these nights for the rest of his life; his biographer, Jean Overton Fuller, has speculated that it caused lasting damage to Neuburg's health.

The intense relationship between Crowley and Neuburg, coupled with Crowley's frequent heterosexual affairs, must have been difficult for Rose to bear. Her drinking was, in turn, a source of embarrassment and sorrow for Crowley. At last, they reached the decision to divorce—a decision that Crowley later insisted was based on Rose's refusal to "sign away her liberty" for the two years of controlled treatment her physician deemed necessary for her alcoholism. The divorce was filed in Scotland, a jurisdiction which allowed, as England then did not, adultery as grounds. Out of a chivalric impulse to protect his wife, Crowley consented to have necessary evidence of his adultery introduced and to allow her to be the plaintiff; the testimony included mention of a fictitious mistress, "Miss Zwee," a working-class milliner. There would have been sufficient real mistresses to cite, but the goal was to avoid unnecessary embarrassment for living persons, as well as to protect Rose.

In the months preceding the November 24, 1909, hearing, Crowley and Rose continued to share the same 21 Warwick Road address and, according to Crowley, they "went on living together, more or less" for a year or more after the divorce. The ultimate decree was clearly favorable to Rose, who was awarded guardianship of Lola Zaza and £52 annually in child support. There was also a discretionary trust fund created by Crowley earlier in this year, at Rose's insistence, to shelter an anticipated £4000 that Crowley would inherit from his mother, Emily—as occurred when Emily died in 1917. The appointed trustees were Jones and

Oscar Eckenstein, and they would, in later years, frequently annoy the Beast by apportioning the discretionary funds in greater amounts to Lola Zaza than to Crowley himself. In the autumn of 1911, Rose was committed to an asylum with a diagnosis of alcoholic dementia; she ultimately recovered and remarried and passed completely out of Crowley's life, as did—but for very occasional correspondence—their daughter.

In November 1909, following the publication of the second number of *The Equinox*, Crowley and Neuburg went off together to Algeria. Crowley had packed along—by happenstance, he would later claim— one of his early magical notebooks that contained transcriptions of the Nineteen Calls of Enochian Magic. Through the Nineteenth of these Calls may be invoked the Thirty "Aethyrs" or "Aires"—realms of spiritual being which Crowley saw as progressive in purity and wisdom and related to the kabbalistic Tree of Life. Crowley had conjured the first two of these Aethyrs in Mexico in November 1900, but found himself, at that time, unable to continue. Nine years later, on November 21, 1909, in the Algerian town of Aumale, Crowley commenced anew the sequence of the Enochian Calls.

A letter by Crowley to Fuller dated October 30, 1909—just prior to his departure with Neuburg to Algeria—indicates that his choice of the notebook was anything but happenstance. On the contrary, he had just completed some days of intensive study at Oxford, copying manuscripts by and related to John Dee and Edward Kelly, the sixteenth-century creators (or recipients, if you will) of Enochian magic. Dee (1527–1608) was one of the archetypal figures of the Renaissance, a polymath scholar, court astrologer to Queen Elizabeth, and a likely model for Prospero in Shakespeare's *The Tempest*. Kelly, a disreputable rogue by virtually all accounts, possessed the mediumistic gift of "scrying" (from "descry") into a crystal (one provided him by Dee, who claimed that it had been given to him by an angel) and viewing therein visions from angelic realms. Kelly would speak aloud what was revealed while Dee acted as scribe. The resultant transcriptions filled several volumes. The sheer complexity of the contents weakens the rationalist theory that Kelly was somehow duping Dee, as that theory must hinge on an ironic assessment of Kelly as a literary and philological forger of genius. For the reciting angels taught a new language (with an alphabet, as well as a rudimentary grammar and syntax all its own) which Dee named "Enochian" after the Enoch of the Bible who was said to have walked with God. As Crowley explained to Fuller: "I am full of Kelly just now. I am perfectly miserable at having to stay away from the Bodder [Bodleian Library] all Sunday, and every word I read seems to bring me to the edge of a Great Revelation." The letter is signed "Edward Kelly," whom Crowley later dubbed "Sir Edward Kelly" and came to see as one of his prior incarnations.

Crowley landed in Algiers on November 18, accompanied, as he wrote in his diary, by "but a single chela [Neuburg] and only five legions of angels." These, it would seem, were the angels of the Enochian realms. The first invocation, of the Twenty-eighth Aethyr, took place in Aumale on November 23. During the following month, Crowley and Neuburg undertook a lengthy desert trek, interrupted by an extended stay in the garden oasis of Bou Saada, and concluding with the invocation of the First Aethyr in another luxurious oasis town, Biskra. For this trek, Crowley donned a turban, grew a beard, and acquired a ring with a large star sapphire—a precious stone that, according to Richard Burton, was revered by Moslems. As for Neuburg, Crowley shaved the younger man's thick curly hair, leaving only two twisted tufts to resemble the horns of a djinn or genie. As Crowley later explained, "This greatly enhanced my eminence. The more eccentric and horrible Neuburg appeared, the more insanely and grotesquely he behaved, the more he inspired the inhabitants with respect for the Magician who had mastered so fantastic and fearful a genie." To complete the effect, Crowley at times led Neuburg about on a chain leash.

Crowley composed a record of his exploration of the Aethyrs, entitled *The Vision and the Voice*, wherein he argued for the value of his researches:

> I admit that my visions can never mean to other men as much as they do to me. I do not regret this. All I ask is that my results should convince seekers after truth that there is beyond doubt something worth seeking, attainable by methods more or less like mine. I do not want to father a flock, to be the fetish of fools and fanatics, or the founder of a faith whose followers are content to echo my opinions. I want each man to cut his own way through the jungle.

This is a surprising statement, because it applies—Crowley's protestations notwithstanding—with equal force to *The Book of the Law*. As to the latter, he was never content with merely indicating that it offered "something worth seeking."

The Vision and The Voice, published in the fifth number of *The Equinox* (1911), emerged from transcriptions made by Neuburg of the exalted descriptions, visions, and ravings that issued from Crowley during the intensive series of twenty-eight invocations, conducted on a near daily basis, that were completed from November 23 to December 19, 1909. The text, highly polished for publication, is the most vivid and dramatic magical record Crowley ever produced. Crowley took care, in the *Confessions,* to delineate precisely the sense in which he had journeyed through the Aethyrs. Astral travel, such as he had utilized in Mexico, no longer seemed necessary nine years later:

> I realized that space was not a thing in itself, merely a convenient category (one of many such) by reference to which we distinguish objects from each other. When I say I was in any Aethyr, I simply mean in the state characteristic of, and peculiar to, its nature. My senses would thus receive the subtle impressions which I had trained them to record, so becoming cognizant of the phenomena of those worlds as ordinary men are of this.

The method by which Crowley explored the Enochian Aethyrs roughly paralleled that of Dee and Kelly, with Crowley taking the part of the scrying Kelly and Neuburg serving in the scribe role of Dee. Crowley had brought along a shewstone to Algeria—"a great golden topaz (set in a Calvary cross of six squares, made of wood, painted vermilion), engraved with a Greek cross of five squares charged with the Rose of forty-nine petals. I held this as a rule in my hand. After choosing a spot where I was not likely to be disturbed, I would take this stone and recite the Enochian Key [Call], and, after satisfying myself that the invoked forces were actually present, made the topaz play a part not unlike that of the looking-glass in the case of *Alice [in Wonderland]*."

The progression through the Aethyrs served as a psychological testing ground for Crowley in his role—ever more consciously assumed—as prophet of the New Aeon. In the Fifteen Aethyr, Crowley was found worthy, by the Secret Chiefs of the Third Order, of the grade of Master of the Temple. This was the formal confirmation for which Crowley had readied himself since his Augoeides Invocations of 1906. But the Enochian angels revealed that further ordeals would be necessary for Crowley to perfect himself in the knowledge of this grade. The Aethyrs which followed provided the framework for these ordeals. On the afternoon of December 3, on Da'leh Addin, a desert mountain outside of Bou Saada, Crowley attempted to invoke the Fourteenth Aethyr but failed. The angel dwelling therein commanded: "Depart! For thou must invoke me only in the darkness." Crowley began his descent from the mountain when, without warning or conscious effort, he received a command to return to the summit, construct a large magical circle out of rocks, with words of divine power inscribed in the sand and an altar erected in the center, and therein perform a ritual. This ritual, which is not set forth in *Vision*, is described only circumspectly in the *Confessions*:

> The first of the all-seeing sun smote down upon the altar, consuming utterly every particle of my personality. I am obliged to write in hieroglyph of this matter, because it concerns things of which it is unlawful to speak openly under penalty of the most deadly punishment; but I may say that the essence of the matter was that I had hitherto clung to certain conceptions of conduct which, while perfectly proper from the standpoint of my human nature, were impertinent to initiation. I could not cross the Abyss till I had torn them out of my heart.

What occurred was a magical sexual act—Crowley would later term it a rite of Pan—in which Neuburg took the active role. The "conceptions of conduct" alluded to here—conceptions which required shattering—likely refer to Crowley's lingering sense of humiliation in playing the passive role sexually with Neuburg, with whom Crowley otherwise kept the sadistic upper hand. That evening, Crowley and Neuburg returned to the mountain, and Crowley now gained entrance to the Fourteenth Aethyr, wherein a whispering male figure ("Chaos is my name, and thick darkness.") warned him of what was to come. The cost of becoming a Master of the Temple would be the excruciating death of his individual self: "Verily is the Pyramid a Temple of Initiation. Verily also is it a tomb."

In the Tenth Aethyr, Crowley would confront the Dispersion of the Abyss. A special precautionary vow was taken by Neuburg the Scribe in advance of the ritual. He would remain strictly within the magical circle, furnished with a consecrated dagger with which he was to "strike fearlessly at anything that may seek to break through the circle, were it the appearance of the Seer [Crowley] itself." The sense of danger expressed here raises the question of what role Crowley intended to play in this ritual. It has been stated as fact by virtually all of his previous biographers that Crowley chose to remain in the magical triangle—that consecrated area into which are bidden the spiritual beings summoned by the magician. As Crowley would be confronting Choronzon, the fearful and formless demonic abomination of Dispersion, a decision to remain within the triangle—if he did so decide—would have invited psychic possession by the most wrenching forces of the Enochian realms.

But whether or not Crowley stayed within the triangle must be viewed as an open question. The *Vision* text specifies that the Seer was to "retire to a secret place, where is neither sight nor hearing." Israel Regardie, among others, has argued that the phrase "secret place" was a cypher for the triangle itself. Then again, the setting of the Tenth Aethyr was a hollow in the dunes outside Bou Saada. Crowley could easily have concealed himself in an alternate "secret place." The Beast, who was fond of touting his magical achievements, never boasted of having remained in the triangle. Perhaps the effect upon him was too searing. Or perhaps he never did so.

Regardless of his physical location, Crowley's immersion into the demon Choronzon during the Call was total. As he later wrote, "I had astrally identified myself with Choronzon, so that I experienced each anguish, each rage, each despair, each insane outburst." The *Vision* record of the Tenth Aethyr is perhaps the most dramatically gripping narrative (taken as metaphysical fantasy, or as a demonic record, as the reader prefers) that Crowley ever produced. The first words which issue from Choronzon are both definition and warning of what is to come: "There is no being in the outermost Abyss, but constant forms come forth from the nothingness of it." Choronzon is thus a shape-shifter, who in his attempts to breach the magical circle of Neuburg took the forms of a "beautiful courtesan" (most likely Euphemia Lamb) with whom Neuburg had been in love in Paris, as well as of a snake, a holy man, and a serpent. In these forms, Choronzon sought to appeal to Neuburg's lust and pride. Against these temptations, Neuburg prevailed, at one point invoking Aiwass, the messenger of *The Book of the Law*. Choronzon replied by charging that the dealings of Crowley and Neuburg with Aiwass "are but a cloak for thy filthy sorceries." Indeed, Choronzon was lacerating in his invective, particularly when it came to Crowley himself.

The defence of Crowley was left to Neuburg, the magician in the circle. As to Neuburg's valor on this occasion, Crowley was always glowing in his praise. For Choronzon employed a most nefarious tactic, having noticed that Neuburg was furiously writing down everything it said. The demon began to spout nonsense and, while Neuburg was distracted, to throw sand upon the drawn magic circle. When the circle had thus been breached, Choronzon "leaped upon the Scribe, throwing him to the earth. The conflict took place within the circle. The Scribe called upon Tetragrammaton [the four-letter Hebrew name for God], and succeeded in compelling Choronzon to return into his triangle. By dint of anger and of threatening him with the Magick Staff did he accomplish this. He then repaired the circle." Such is the record in *The Vision and the Voice*. But in Crowley's later account in the *Confessions*, the deadly dagger comes into play: "Choronzon, in the form of a naked savage, dashed through and attacked O. V. [Neuburg] He flung him to the earth and tried to tear out his throat with froth-covered fangs. O.V. invoked the names of God and struck at Choronzon with the Magical Dagger. The demon was cowed by this courageous conduct and writhed back into the Triangle."

Who was the "naked savage" who lunged at Neuburg? The most reasonable explanation is that it was Crowley possessed. But the realm of magical theory allows for the possibility that a materialization—that is, a visible manifestation created through the exercise of their joint wills—had been achieved by Crowley and Neuburg. Neuburg was, Crowley later avowed, "a materializing medium in the strictest sense; that is, he could condense ideas into sensible forms.[. . .] In his presence I found it quite easy to produce phenomenal phantasms of almost any idea, from gods to demons, which I happened to need at the moment." With respect to the Tenth Aethyr attack by Choronzon, Crowley explained it as one of the "successive phantoms" formed by "the energy latent in the blood of the pigeons" that had been sacrificed when the triangle was first consecrated. For his part, Neuburg remained convinced for the rest of his life that he had wrestled with a demon in the desert.

"BABALON"—the wife of Chaos the All-Father, who is the conqueror of Choronzon—was the holy name Crowley wrote in the sand to bring the Call of the Tenth Aethyr to an end. Afterwards, he and Neuburg destroyed the circle and the triangle and built a large fire to purify the site.

The final nine Aethyrs were, as a whole, a peaceful denouement. On the final day of the year 1909, he and Neuburg boarded ship for home. The feeling Crowley had for their time together in Algeria is best summarized in a December letter to Fuller—"we have the Apocalypse beaten to a frazzle.[. . .] This is the holiday-holyday of my whole life."

The events of the year 1910 would seem, in retrospect, somewhat strange and disordered even to Crowley. Over a decade later, in the *Confessions*, Crowley offered an explanation in light of his Enochian visions:

> Part of the effect of crossing the Abyss is that it takes a long time
> to connect the Master with what is left below the Abyss.[. . .]

In the year 1910 Aleister Crowley was as a sheep not having a shepherd; the motives and controlling element had been removed and he was more or less cut off from the past. One thing seemed as good as another.[. . .] The attainment of the Grade of Magister Templi had to be paid for, and I might congratulate myself that the cashier accepted such worthless paper money as the mistakes and misfortunes of a man.

Crowley did not detail what these "mistakes" were. But there was one failing he stressed—his failure to maintain his own rule of privacy of A∴A∴ membership (maintained through anonymous ritual participation). Instead, his new London flat at 124 Victoria Street served as both the editorial offices of *The Equinox* and as a frequent site of gatherings in which talk, drink, drug experimentation, and magical ritual lasted literally through the night. Neuburg was not the only member with whom Crowley was erotically involved. Betty Bickers, a married Neophyte, had an affair with Crowley; there would be others.

Crowley was floundering in the aftermath of his divorce—seeking to fill his life with people and social occasions in a manner atypical for a self-described Shelleyan wanderer of the wastes. For example, in a May 16, 1910, letter to Fuller, written from Venice, where Crowley had gone on vacation, he confided his engagement to a woman whose initials he gave as "M. C." Her identity is uncertain; possible candidates are Maisie Clarke or Margot Cripps, but these are mere names from a list of lovers made by Crowley late in life. The key point is that Crowley, just out of an unhappy marriage, would so quickly consider marrying again.

It is just possible that part of the allure of marriage for Crowley may have been the heterosexual respectability it conferred. For Crowley would find himself, during this year, confronting a journalistic interest in himself and his works. This was, of course, gratifying. But the journalists were not always flattering, and behind the worst of the jibes was the tacit accusation that had barred him the previous year from Trinity College—Crowley's homosexuality.

Early on, however, Crowley enjoyed a substantial public triumph by way of the law courts. On March 11, 1910, just prior to the scheduled appearance of the third number of *The Equinox*, Mathers sought an injunction barring further publication of his Golden Dawn rituals. Mathers still had a small number of supporters in England who recognized him as a magical Chief. Indeed, when it came to sheer numbers, Crowley was just barely ahead of Mathers—in September 1910, his A∴A∴ would number only forty members. But *The Equinox* had drawn respectable reviews, and the scheduled third number would contain portions of the vital 5°=6° Portal and Adeptus Minor rituals. The March 1910 injunction suit was necessarily an act of desperation, for Mathers could ill afford legal fees.

Mathers prevailed in the initial hearing. But on appeal, argued before four Lord Justices on March 22, Crowley prevailed; *The Equinox* was promptly released the next day. Overall, the press coverage was favorable to Crowley and the A∴A∴; The London *Evening News* carried a front-page story with the enticing headline "Secrets of the 'Golden Dawn'" and concluded the piece by noting that "The revelations of Mr. Crowley have created utter consternation in the ranks of the Rosicrucians." As Crowley later commented, "The argument [in court] had been farcically funny and all the dailies had anything up to three columns on the case. On the very day of publication, for the first time, I found myself famous and my work in demand." If there was humor in the hearing, it is fair to note that it was directed at both Mathers and Crowley—and not only by the Lord Justices, but also by their own paid counsel. At one point, according to the transcript, Crowley's attorney was asked whether *The Temple of Solomon the King* was a "romance." His answer: "I do not know, my lord, I cannot describe it. (Laughter.)" Magic, to which both men had devoted their lives, was held up to the greatest ridicule of all.

But the immediate aftermath was pleasant enough. There began to arrive, through the mails, diplomas from all manner of obscure societies claiming Crowley as a member. He received occasional personal visits from emissaries of these societies, the most noteworthy of which, in March 1910, was from a learned and traveled occultist named Theodor Reuss, one of whose titles was Grand Master of Germany of the combined Scottish, Memphis and Mizraim Rites of Freemasonry. Reuss would return into Crowley's life as a major occult influence—a story that will be told later in this chapter. Another Masonic writer with whom Crowley corresponded during this time was John Yarker, Reuss's superior as the Master of the Memphis and Mizraim Rites.

His central focus remained, however, the development of the A∴A∴. While he did not draw great numbers, Crowley certainly attracted some vivid personalities. Not the least of these was Leila Waddell, a young Australian musician of part-Maori ancestry and striking beauty. In the short story "The Violinist," subsequently published in *The Equinox*, Waddell was cast as a vampiric femme fatale:

> The girl was tall and finely built, huntress-lithe. Her dress, close-fitted, was of a gold-brown silk that matched, but could

not rival, the coils that bound her brow—glittering and hissing like snakes.

Her face was Greek in delicacy; but what meant such a mouth in it? The mouth of a satyr or a devil. It was full and strong, curved twice, the edges upwards, an angry purple, the lips flat. Her smile was like the snarl of a wild beast.

Waddell and Crowley became lovers at once, and Crowley soon enrolled her as a Probationer on April 1, 1910 (her magical name: Sister Agatha). Crowley's familiar name for her, taken from her role in his rituals, was "Mother of Heaven," or "Mother" for short. With her Australian accent, Waddell pronounced Crowley's initials as "I. C." To Gwendolyn Otter, a prominent London socialite who took a liking to Crowley and showed him at her parties, Waddell once complained, "I. C. wants me to devote my life to magic, but I don't think I want to."

But Waddell did become a fixture of the expanding A∴A∴ magical scene, which had come to include the poet and critic Meredith Starr (Herbert Close), naval commander G. M. Marston, psychic researcher Everard Feilding and, most importantly, the esoteric thinker and artist Austin Osman Spare, whose brilliant draftsmanship and disturbing sexuality make him one of the most unique creative figures of the century. Spare joined in July 1910, though his tenure in the A∴A∴ was brief; he was not, by nature, suited to be a disciple. Crowley admired Spare highly, both as a writer on magic and as an artist, and solicited illustrations from Spare for *The Equinox;* there was, however, some fractious haggling (conducted through Fuller) over Spare's fee. For whatever reasons, Spare ultimately spurned Crowley both as a teacher and as a prospective friend. Nonetheless, one of Spare's drawings, presumably paid for, hung prominently in Crowley's *Equinox* offices.

Along with *The Equinox*, Crowley published at his own expense, during 1910, three volumes of his poetry—*Ambergris, The Winged Beetle*, and the pseudonymous *Scented Garden*. Such was the creative ferment in A∴A∴ circles that Crowley issued, under *The Equinox* imprint, volumes by literati from within its ranks. These included two works—a novel, *The History of a Soul*, and a story collection, *The Deuce and All*—by a Russian emigré, George Raffalovich, whom Crowley had befriended. But the most significant of these publications was *The Triumph of Pan* (1910), Neuburg's second book (quoted in Chapter Five in connection with Neuburg and Crowley's walk through Spain in 1908). Crowley and his magical teachings are all but omnipresent in the lyric poems, which move from mystic fervor to erotic rapture. The reviews of the British press were generally flattering, due in part to the careful veiling of the homoerotic element. Crowley, in great good humor (as indicated by his pseudonym, "Percy Flage"), offered a verse review of *Triumph* in *The Equinox* that let the secret out for those who could see through the satire:

> This is a most regrettable collection
> Of songs; they deal with unrestrained affection
> Unlicensed by the Church and State; what's worse
> There's no denying they are first-rate verse.
> It surely cannot be that Pan's in clover
> And England's days of Sunday-school are over!

The timing of this playful review—March 1911—took on a strange irony, given public allegations as to Crowley's own homosexuality, as we shall see later in this chapter.

Another book of poems issued under *The Equinox* imprint is worthy of mention principally because its author, a young Englishwoman named Ethel Archer, left so valuable a record of Crowley and the A∴A∴ circle of this time. Her debut volume of verse, *The Whirlpool* (1911), appeared with a flattering introduction by Crowley. Archer and her husband, Eugene (Bunco) Wieland, attended numerous A∴A∴ sessions at 124 Victoria Street. Some twenty years later, Archer published a novel, *The Hieroglyph* (1932) (the title being a pseudonym for *The Equinox*), in which Crowley ("Vladimir Svaroff"), Neuburg ("Newton") and other members of the A∴A∴ ("Silver Star") were portrayed.

Archer was devoted to her husband, and there was no flirtation between Crowley and herself. But in her novel Archer ("Iris") testified to the charisma of the enrobed Svaroff as he led a ritual: "His powerful neck bared to the base, gleaming above this priest-like garment, gave to the onlooker the impression of an almost superhuman strength. It suggested a granite column. Iris thought of Egyptian gods [. . .]" The relationship between Svaroff and Newton is marked by Svaroff's acerbic humor, on the one hand, and Newton's loving devotion, on the other. Newton is under a Vow of Holy Obedience to Svaroff, his Holy Guru, which will endure for some months—a course of practice which Svaroff suggests would benefit Iris as well, by liberating her poetic genius. "Genius," as Svaroff explains, "is another name for Divinity. Divinity another name for genius. Provided they proceed along the lines laid down for them, that I shall lay down, the most mediocre talent can develop into genius, and the genius becomes a god."

The setting in which Svaroff taught and practiced—modeled on Crowley's flat at 124 Victoria Street—was conducive to magical practice. The range of the artwork on display was most impressive. Alongside the drawing by Spare was a drawing by Aubrey Beardsley. Above the mantelpiece was a large early Byzantine crucifix of ivory and ebony; below were figures of the Buddha and of various Egyptian and Chinese gods, the latter in jade. On top of the bookshelves—which contained first editions of Baudelaire, Swinburne, and Wilde—rested busts by Rodin. Another wall featured a silken, embroidered Tibetan scroll. The flat itself was immaculately decorated, with bare floors painted black, walls of a "sugar-paper blue" with white woodwork, and scarlet curtains. The total effect must have been intoxicating to first-time visitors investigating the A∴A∴. Small wonder that Crowley conceived the idea to use so grand a setting for group magical rituals, and that these ultimately evolved into his most ambitious theatrical project, *The Rites of Eleusis*.

The *Rites* began as an admirable attempt to merge poetry, music, dance, theatrical staging, and magical ritual into a performance designed to heighten the consciousness of performers and audience alike. They became, for Crowley, a first and lasting defeat in terms of his standing with the British public in his lifetime.

The seven magical rituals of *The Rites of Eleusis* were intended to unite the performers and the audience in an ecstasy that would, as had the mysteries of ancient Eleusis, reveal the divine capacities of the awakened human soul. There is—beyond a common initiatory purpose—relatively little common ground between Crowley's *Rites* and the fragmentary knowledge we have of the content of the ancient Eleusinean Mysteries. These latter constitute a sacred drama celebrating the drama of the grain and fertility goddess Demeter seeking out her daughter Kore, who has been abducted by Hades, the god of the underworld, to his nether realm. The Eleusinian Mysteries included, as part of their portrayal of the rites of divine marriage, elements of extreme sexual frankness the precise nature of which is no longer known. The Greek goddesses and gods were celebrated as the spiritual guides through whom human souls might seek initiation.

By contrast, the structure of Crowley's seven rites derives from the seven traditional planetary influences of Western esotericism, which are, in turn, loosely linked by Crowley to Shakespeare's seven ages of man. The fundamental theme is the failure of the old gods to provide the necessary guidance for the New Aeon. The aged god Saturn can only counsel despair; Jupiter is impotent; Mars is beset by lust and lacking in wisdom; Apollo the Sun is slain because he cannot harmonize the good and evil natures that battle within him; Venus lovingly mourns Apollo but her sorrow lacks redemptive force; Mercury possesses the seeds of magical wisdom, but he can no longer serve as psychopomp to humankind. In the final ritual, the youngest of the planetary figures, the Virginal Moon, is granted a vision of the redemptive Aeon to come, when "the spirit of the Infinite All, great Pan, tears asunder the veil and displays the hope of humanity, the Crowned Child of the Future." This "Crowned Child" is Horus in his aspect of Ra-Hoor-Khuit. By such careful cross-symbolism in his Rites, Crowley conveyed the teachings of Thelema without expressly announcing the *Book* or his vocation as its prophet. In this sense, Crowley was most cautious in his approach to his intended public.

In other ways, however, Crowley threw caution to the winds. He made available to the small audience in his Victoria Street flat, during the July debut of the first of his scripted rites—*The Rite of Artemis* (later revised into *The Rite of Luna*)—a potent liquid mixture consisting of alcohol, fruit juices, possibly some type of opium derivative, and most certainly an infusion of a most potent drug of which Crowley had learned during his time in Mexico: *Anhalonium lewinii*, or peyote. Crowley claimed that he was the first to introduce peyote usage to Europe. This may perhaps have been true in terms of personal experimentation, as opposed to scholarly research, which had been conducted by physicians and anthropologists in the late nineteenth century. There is no evidence that Crowley provided peyote for audiences to the later public performances of the *Rites*. Those present in July seem to have been either A∴A∴ members or otherwise of Crowley's circle. For these persons, Crowley prepared a Cup of Libation. The beverage, according to Ethel Archer, was pleasant smelling and had the taste of "rotten apples." If Archer is any indication, neither the precise contents of the Cup of Libation, nor the nature of its effects, were uniformly explained to its partakers, though Crowley had taken care to have a physician friend on hand in case of serious adverse reaction, which does not seem to have occurred. There is a rapturous account of this night left by one of Crowley's friends, Raymond Radclyffe, a journalist and an admirer of Crowley's poetry. Radclyffe published a review in a respected London weekly, *The Sketch*, on August 24. In this passage, the three principals—Crowley, Waddell, and Neuburg—are described in the aftermath of the third Libation:

[T]hen the brothers led into the room a draped figure, masked in that curious blue tint we mentally associate with Hecate. The lady [Waddell], for it was a lady, was enthroned high on a seat above Crowley himself. By this time the ceremony had grown weird and impressive, and its influence was increased when the poet [Crowley] recited in solemn and reverent voice Swinburne's glorious first chorus from "Atalanta," that begins, "When the hounds of spring." Again a Libation, again an invocation to Artemis. After further ceremonies, Frater Omnia Vincam [Neuburg] was commanded to dance "the dance of Syrinx and Pan in honour of our lady Artemis." A young poet, whose verse is often read, astonished me by a graceful and beautiful dance, which he continued until he fell exhausted in the middle of the room where, by the way, he lay until the end. Crowley then made supplication to the goddess in a beautiful and unpublished poem. A dead silence ensued. After a long pause the figure enthroned took a violin and played—played with passion and feeling, like a master. We were thrilled to our very bones.

Neuburg, in turn, was assigned the draining task—an act of magical equilibration—of hurling himself into physical movement such as to "dance down" the gods. There was, tragically, a lasting cost to pay, which one may attribute to the magical efficacy of the *Rites*, or to the strength of Neuburg's belief in them, as one likes. According to Neuburg, during one performance of the *Rite of Luna*, Crowley forgetfully failed to pronounce the words to release Neuburg from his possession by the lunar planetary spirit. Neuburg tried to remedy the damage by later pronouncing the words himself—but to no avail. According to biographer Jean Overton Fuller, Neuburg believed, some two decades later, that "for a considerable period of years he had suffered from a greater than usual possession by the moon."

The full design of the *Rites of Eleusis* was fleshed out in August and September. The financially naive Crowley saw their public performance—on seven Wednesday nights in October and November 1910—as a means of raising funds to replenish his own rapidly draining inheritance. He also hoped that, by drawing the attention of an interested public, A∴A∴ membership might be expanded. The locale Crowley chose—or could afford—for the performances, Caxton Hall, was anything but a prestigious venue. One of the London tabloids described it as a "most respectable haunt of whist drives, subscription dances and Suffragette meetings." The Cup of Libation was passed exclusively amongst the participating A∴A∴ members on stage; it is possible, but not certain, that it contained peyote. The audience was invited to participate in creating the appropriate atmosphere for each rite by wearing the color corresponding to the particular planet—black for Saturn, violet for Jupiter, red for Mars, and so forth. The printed program insisted on decorum: "The etiquette to be observed is that of the most solemn religious ceremonies."

Before turning to the public reviews, it is worth considering Crowley's own view of the performances—an exceedingly harsh one: "I throw myself no bouquets about these Rites of Eleusis. I should have given more weeks to their preparation than I did minutes. I diminished the importance of the dramatic elements; the dialogue and action were little more than a setting for the soloists." As for the verdict of the British press, it ranged from skeptical to outraged. The more highbrow weeklies reported the proceedings in a perplexed but respectful tone. The headline run by *The Sketch* summed it up nicely: "The Elusive Rites of Eleusis." But the popular tabloids tore into the *Rites* with vehemence. *The Looking Glass*, a racing tabloid, led the assault; its editor, West De Wend Fenton, published a series of four attacks that betrayed a virtually feral hatred of Crowley. According to Crowley, Fenton had, after the first of these publications, tried to arrange a meeting for the purpose of blackmail; Crowley alleged that he sent Fenton packing. Three years after his attacks on Crowley, Fenton was fined for the indecency of the writings in another of his publications, the *Sporting Times*. But Fenton's *Looking Glass* pieces in October and November adopted the high ground of protecting British morals. The ringing conclusion was that blasphemy was afoot: "Remember the doctrine which we have endeavoured faintly to outline—remember the long periods of complete darkness—remember the dances and the heavily scented atmosphere, the avowed object of which is to produce what Crowley terms an 'ecstasy'— and then say if it is fitting and right that young girls and married women should be allowed to attend such performances under the guise of the cult of a new religion."

It is safe to say that there was nothing whatsoever salacious about the performances of the *Rites*. There are numerous testimonies from attendees to this effect, the most significant of which comes from Fuller, who was both sexually conservative and adamantly opposed to the *Rites* being presented to the public. He may be trusted when he avowed, decades later: "In every sense the performances were most proper, though dim, because the stage was candle lit. So innocent were they that I took my mother to one of them. Innocence, however, is no shield to the vomitings of the gutter press." Indeed, following the lead of *The Looking*

Glass, a number of other tabloids tore into Crowley, most notably *John Bull,* a weekly edited by the flamboyant Horatio Bottomley.

Of all these attacks, the most fateful would appear in the November 26 *Looking Glass.* In part three of its continuing expose of Crowley's life, there appeared information—almost certainly obtained from Mathers—about Crowley's early days in the Golden Dawn. Allan Bennett was maligned as a "rascally sham Buddhist monk" who had, while living with Crowley in 1899, engaged in "unmentionable immoralities." The implication was that Crowley and Bennett were homosexuals. George Cecil Jones, mentioned in the same paragraph, was thus included in that implication. For Jones, a father of four who made his living in respectable society as an analytical chemist, this was an appalling smear. Seconded vigorously by Fuller, Jones urged Crowley to take legal action against *The Looking Glass.* By vindicating himself, Crowley could, in turn, vindicate his friend.

Other A∴A∴ members, including Neuburg, concurred. As these men were aware of Crowley's bisexuality, their hope must have been that Crowley could disprove other attacks upon him, such as the slurs upon his sincerity as a spiritual teacher. Crowley briefly considered suing, then resolved not to do so, leaving Jones to file his own action. In early December, the *Rites* having concluded, Crowley and Neuburg departed for their third Sahara trek together. In the December 17 *Looking Glass* appeared this somewhat misguided note: "We understand that Mr. Aleister Crowley has left for Russia. This should do much to mitigate the rigour of the St. Petersburg winter. We have to congratulate ourselves on having temporarily extinguished one of the most blasphemous and cold-blooded villains of modern times. But what were Scotland Yard about to let him depart in peace?" Fenton got Crowley's destination wrong, but his sense of triumph was galling to Jones, Fuller, and other A∴A∴ members who now felt their Order under siege.

After the homophobic atmosphere of England, the more accepting social mores of Algeria, not to mention the seclusion of the Sahara itself, served as a release for both men. Crowley experienced, in these desert treks, a sharpening of consciousness that delighted him—"every incident acquires an intense and absolute value of its own. One can, for example, love as it is utterly impossible to do in any other conditions." This latter remark would seem to be a veiled reference to his passion for Neuburg. Yet the trip was magically barren; their plan to obtain Enochian "visions of the sixteen Sub-Elements, as a sort of pendant to the Aethyrs" failed for lack of will and energy. Further, there was a bad parting between the two at Biskra. Crowley claimed that he left Neuburg there to recuperate after the hardships of the journey. Neuburg, for his part, felt abandoned. The upshot was that, for the remainder of this year, they kept apart; in an October 1911 letter, Crowley charged that Neuburg had received "quite a lot of money for deserting me." If so, the logical source of the funds would have been Neuburg's family, which was distressed by his bond with the disreputable Crowley. Neuburg had, in past years, willingly placed his family funds at the disposal of Crowley and *The Equinox*. As Crowley was now beset by financial worries, the cutoff of funds could not have been pleasant. There is a startling story alleging the extent to which Crowley had gone to wring money from Neuburg's family. According to one family friend, during one of their trips to the Sahara, Crowley had sent Neuburg's mother a telegram reading "Send £500 or you will never see your son again." Neuburg's desertion would not be permanent, however; the two men renewed their erotic, magical and financial alliance the following year.

As for the April 1911 *Jones v. The Looking Glass* trial, suffice it to say that Jones was routed. The jury found that *The Looking Glass* had indeed defamed Jones by implication, but that the defamation was substantially true. Although Jones, not Crowley, was the aggrieved party, the bulk of the evidence pertained to Crowley. The two chief witnesses for *The Looking Glass* were Mathers and his staunch magical ally, Dr. Edward Berridge. The magical warfare was continuing apace, and this time it was Crowley who would take his lumps.

   Though Crowley sat in the courtroom during both days of the trial, he was never called as a witness. *The Looking Glass* would, of course, have violated accepted strategy by willingly summoning a hostile witness. Jones refrained from doing so on the grounds that honor forbade the use of a subpoena to coerce the aid of a friend. Crowley, in an instance of pure bluff in the *Confessions*, claimed that Jones had not called him "because he was afraid that my contempt for conventions [. . .] would lead me to make some damaging admission. He was ill advised. The intensity of my enthusiasm, my candour and my sheer personality would have dominated the court." More realistically, Crowley would have been mercilessly grilled and forced, at last, either to perjure himself or to disable Jones's case by speaking the truth—that Jones was the friend of a practicing bisexual.

Crowley could not bring himself to admit this, and Fuller would not allow it as a sufficient reason to betray a friend. A subsequent Crowley letter dated May 4 began with conciliatory words of praise for Fuller's courage in testifying at the trial: "If my friendship ever cooled it was completely revived by your conduct in the box." These words cast doubt on a later accusation, raised by Crowley in the *Confessions,* that after the negative verdict Fuller had "hinted that he could not afford to be openly associated with *The Equinox.*" Fuller's testimony on behalf of Jones had, given the press coverage, constituted as public an association with Crowley and *The Equinox* as could be imagined. Fuller was not without the courage of his convictions. But there was genuine hesitance on Fuller's part in continuing his friendship with Crowley, above and beyond the latter's failure to testify. In one letter to Fuller from North Africa (perhaps during early 1911), Crowley had enclosed a number of sexually explicit postcards. As Fuller later explained, "At night, when drunk, it may seem funny to put obscene postcards in an envelope, but when one opens it, in the morning, and has them fall out on the break-fast table, it is merely disgusting. It could have been opened in transit and it could have been wondered why I should be the recipient of such stuff. I decided I could no longer be associated with him."

The upshot was that the *Looking Glass* trial was the last time Fuller and Crowley saw each other. For all his subsequent efforts to retrieve him, Crowley had lost the greatest ally he would ever have.

The May 1911 break by Fuller paralleled a mounting disaffection with Crowley amongst A∴A∴ members generally. Crowley chastised the deserters in an *Equinox* piece entitled "X-Rays on Ex-Probationers": "Rats leave sinking ships; but you cannot be sure that a ship will sink because you see a rat running away from it." The disarray of 1911 spelled the practical end of Crowley's efforts to actively promote the A∴A∴. While Crowley affirmed its ongoing existence in a mystical sense (and would further, from time to time, enter new members into its ranks), he never again utilized it as the primary outward vehicle of the New Aeon. This left an organizational vacuum that would be filled dramatically in the following year.

For now, Crowley managed to take some pleasure in being released from the bulk of his public-oriented leadership duties. He spent the summer of 1911 at his favorite Paris pied-à-terre, 50 rue Vavin, and enjoyed there a frenzied and fruitful stint of writing which included both literary works (plays, poems, and short stories) and no fewer than nine-teen essays—each designated as a "book" or *liber* by Crowley—devoted to mystical and magical practices. All these were published in subsequent numbers of *The Equinox* as official instructions of the A∴A∴, as were the bulk of the literary works. They are highly heterogeneous in subject matter, ranging from philosophical exhortations to the Great Work; ritual enactments of the teachings of *The Book of the Law;* and practical instructions on breathing techniques, Tarot divination, and cultivation of the magical memory.

One such book, in particular, foreshadowed the focus of Crowley's subsequent magical career. In the *Confessions,* Crowley stressed that the secret of sexual magic—which he described in veiled terms as "the art of producing phenomena at will"—had been known to him since the summer of 1911, which he spent in Fontainebleau with Leila Waddell. This would seem to be an allusion to *Liber Stellae Rubeae (The Book of the Ruby Star),* written during that summer and designated as a Holy Book. In Crowley's system of symbolism, the star ruby represented the "Lingam, the Inner Robe of Glory." *Liber Stellae Rubeae* was Crowley's first formal ritual expression of the dynamics of sexual magic. His primary influence was not Indian Tantra, but rather that strand of the Western esoteric tradition that interpreted alchemical symbols in sexual terms and believed in the possibility of a *summum bonum* or philosopher's stone being created, on the physical level, by the esoteric preparation and admixture of sexual fluids. That Crowley believed literally in material transmutations through the use of sexual magic is made plain in one of the more startling passages of the *Confessions:*

> I personally believe that if this secret [of sexual magic], which is a scientific secret, were perfectly understood, as it is not even by me after more than twelve years' almost constant study and experiment, there would be nothing which the human imagination can conceive that could not be realized in practice.
>
> By which I mean such things as this: that if it were desired to have an element of atomic weight six times that of uranium that element could be produced. If it were desired to devise an instrument by which the furthest stars or the electrons could be brought within the range of every one of our senses, that instrument could be invented.[. . .] I make these remarks with absolute confidence, for even the insignificant approaches that I have been able to make towards the sanctuaries of the secret have shown me that the relations between phenomena are infinitely more complex than the wildest philosophers have ever

imagined, and the old proverb 'Where there's a will there's a way' needs no caveat.

Crowley did not undertake the task of conscious experimentation in this realm until January 1914, when his working partner would be Victor Neuburg. That adventure will close this chapter.

On a personal level, Crowley was living in apparent loving harmony with Leila Waddell throughout the summer of 1911. There was, however, another woman with whom Crowley had an affair during this time—Jane Chéron. She would later marry Walter Duranty, the then-famous foreign correspondent for *The New York Times*, who during this period was a close friend of Crowley and his occasional homosexual partner. Waddell, however, remained central to Crowley's life through these and other affairs. She fascinated him, even as she frustrated his hope that she would dedicate herself to magic; Crowley never came to regard her as a successor to Rose who, as Ouarda the Seer, had served as the first Scarlet Woman.

But on October 11, Crowley at last encountered a worthy successor. This was Mary Desti, an incandescent woman of medium height and abundant curly black hair. Desti possessed a remarkable range of talents. She had been a friend and confidante to the world-renowned dancer Isadora Duncan (Desti's memoir, *The Untold Story, The Life of Isadora Duncan* (1929) stands as a fundamental text on Duncan) and had founded a successful Parisian *parfumerie*, the Maison Desti. The origin of the name "Desti" reveals much about the woman. She was born Mary Dempsey into an Irish American family in 1871. At age five, she renounced the family Catholic faith. As she grew older, she grew convinced that the pronunciation of "Dempsey" was a slurring, over many generations, of the noble Italian name of "d'Este." She became Mary d'Este Dempsey, then dropped the last name altogether. Only after being sued by the d'Este family in 1911 for commercial infringement did she bend—barely—by changing the spelling to "Desti." She thus shared Crowley's fondness for nobilities bestowed upon oneself as one deserved them.

The two shared the same astrological sign of Libra, for it was at a fortieth birthday party for Desti at the Savoy Hotel in London on October 11 (the day before Crowley's thirty-sixth birthday) that they first met. Desti was married to an American stockbroker, Solomon Sturges, who did not accompany his wife on her European travels. There was an immediate mutual fascination between Desti and Crowley. As he later recalled, with gallant acceptance of her claims to nobility, "This lady, a magnificent specimen of mingled Irish and Italian blood, possessed a most powerful personality and a terrific magnetism which instantly attracted my own. I forgot everything. I sat on the floor like a Chinese god, exchanging electricity with her." By mid-November, they commenced a passionate affair—and magical collaboration.

Crowley had not been idle during the interim. The sculptor Jacob Epstein, with whom Crowley was acquainted, had just completed a controversial statue for the Parisian grave of Oscar Wilde which featured a bare penis. Crowley cared neither for Wilde nor for this particular work by Epstein. But the puritanical placement of a tarpaulin over the offending organ sparked his interest. He issued a press notice declaring that, on November 5, he would defiantly remove the tarpaulin. Crowley expected resistance from the authorities, but when he and two supporters arrived at the gravesite on the appointed morning, there was no one to oppose them. As he later wrote: "I made my speech and unveiled Epstein's effort to the dull drizzling weather. It was a disheartening success." But due to his prior notice, there was press coverage both in Paris and London. Epstein, however, took umbrage at these efforts on his behalf. In an indignant letter to the *London Times,* he stressed that "I do not consider any unofficial unveiling a compliment to me, though no doubt a jolly occasion for Mr. Crowley and his companions." The Parisian authorities commissioned a bronze butterfly to be attached, in fig-leaf manner. Crowley, undaunted, paid a second, unpublicized visit to the grave:

> I detached the butterfly and put it under my waistcoat. The gatekeeper did not notice how portly I had become. When I reached London, I put on evening dress and affixed the butterfly to my own person in the same way as previously to the statue, in the interests of modesty, and then marched into the Café Royal, to the delight of the assembled multitude. Epstein himself happened to be there and it was a glorious evening. By this time he had understood my motives, that I was honestly indignant at the outrage to him and determined to uphold the privileges of the artist.

This was Crowley's first public foray since the *Looking Glass* trial, and it earned him a degree of respect in the London artistic circles which he alternately reviled and longed to enter.

After Crowley rejoined Desti on November 14, they traveled together to Zurich, en route to a winter vacation at St. Moritz. On the night of November 21, strange communications began that signaled a great magical working by the Beast and his new Scarlet Woman. We have only Crowley's testimony as to what occurred, though Desti plainly manifested, by her devotion to the cause in the coming months, a conviction equal to if not greater than Crowley's own. On that first night, she and Crowley had gotten drunk and made passionate love. Around midnight, Crowley fell asleep, but was soon awakened by Desti—or Soror Virakam, as she may be called from this point, as Desti would shortly thereafter take Virakam (an amalgam of the Sanskrit for *vir*, man or strength, and *kama*, lust) as her magical name when Crowley initiated her as a Probationer in the A∴A∴. That night, Desti was, according to Crowley, "apparently seized with a violent attack of hysteria, in which she poured forth a frantic torrent of senseless hallucination." Crowley was at first skeptical, but soon recognized his own "language of symbols" in Desti's hurried words and sensed the onset of something akin to Cairo in April 1904—a contact from a higher, or at least other, intelligence.

There was an entity wishing to speak to Crowley—Desti envisioned him now (as she had, in a sleeping state, in a premonitory dream the night before) as "an old man with a long white beard" whose appurtenances included a magical wand. His name, as given to Desti, was "Abuldiz." This Abuldiz, communicating through Desti's voice, instructed Crowley—by his Golden Dawn Neophyte name of Frater Perdurabo—as follows: "Here is a book to be given to Fra. P. The name of the book is *Aba*, and its number IV." *Aba* is Hebrew for "father"; it is also sometimes used as an epithet for God; the kabbalistic numerical value of its letters is four. The book *Aba* would ultimately be renamed by Crowley as *Book Four*.

What Crowley would come to call the Abuldiz Working was a series of seven extended dialogues between Perdurabo and Abuldiz, with Virakam as the speaking and envisioning medium or "Seer." These dialogues occurred in an irregular sequence of evenings beginning on November 21 and concluding on December 19, 1911. Crowley made a transcript of the proceedings. It is an unrewarding document to quote at any length, as the bulk of its text consists of muddled and inconsequential attempts by Abuldiz and Crowley to communicate. Abuldiz did not care for Crowley's tone of cross-examination, while Crowley was frustrated by the vagueness of the communications issued by this unbidden disincarnate intelligence. All sessions were conducted in the late evening and typically extended well past midnight. Virakam, as Seer, began at least some sessions in an altered state—postcoitally satiated, or drunk from alcohol, a drug which Abuldiz had assured Crowley would be suitable. At times Virakam felt exalted by the proceedings; at other times she would panic, even come close to tears.

But Crowley was not spared certain psychological ordeals of his own. For Abuldiz was tantalizingly elusive, neither confirming nor denying—in response to a direct question by Crowley—Crowley's status as Logos of the Aeon. The diffidence of Abuldiz could drive Crowley to distraction, as in this December 4 exchange:

> P[erdurabo]: How shall I get this Book IV?
> A[b-ul-diz]: Waiting in London.
> P[erdurabo]: I don't want the rational answer I want the absurd.

At last it became sufficiently clear that Crowley and Desti were to go off to Italy and find a suitable villa to rent, so that the dictation of Book Four—a basic guide to the practices of yoga and magic—could proceed undisturbed. Just where in Italy had been left vague by Abuldiz, but Rome was chosen as a suitable starting point. There remained, however, a delicate matter to resolve. Desti's thirteen-year-old son, enrolled in a boarding school in Normandy, was due to join them during his Christmas vacation. The arrival of young Preston did not please Crowley, who found the boy "a most god-forsaken lout." That boy—who would grow up to be Preston Sturges, one of the most gifted comedic directors (The Great McGinty, Sullivan's Travels, Miracle at Morgan's Creek) in the history of Hollywood—liked Crowley even less. In his autobiography, Sturges inveighed against his mother's lover with inspired, though not strictly factual, venom:

> The practitioner and staunch defender of every form of vice historically known to man, generally accepted as one of the most depraved, vicious, and revolting humbugs who ever escaped from a nightmare or a lunatic asylum, universally despised and enthusiastically expelled from every country he ever tried to live in, Mr. Crowley nevertheless was considered by my mother to be not only the epitome of charm and good manners, but also the possessor of one of the very few genius-bathed brains she had been privileged to observe at work during her entire lifetime. Ask me not why!

It was January 1912 when the magical lovers and the disgruntled son settled into their temporary home—the Villa Caldarazzo, in Posilippo, on the southern outskirts of Naples. This locale had been discovered one day on a driving tour, by a sudden burst of inspiration by Desti, who directed their driver to take an overgrown side road off the main highway which led to an old villa under repair. Crowley was impressed by the fact that, by kabbalistic gematria, Villa Caldarazzo added to 418, the number of the Great Work and of Abrahadabra, the Magical Word of the new Aeon. Young Preston, unsurprisingly, was of a different opinion— "apart from its supernatural features, it had little to recommend it. It was cold and damp, few of its windows closed properly, it was completely inaccessible and the plumbing leaked."

The procedure—agreed upon by Crowley and Desti, rather than expressly ordered by Abuldiz—called for Crowley to dictate to Desti, who acted as amanuensis. Preston, an onlooker, was repulsed by the Beast's new hairstyle: "Mr. Crowley had his entire skull shaved except for one small tufted square in the exact middle of this cranium. On this lawn, or village green, he promenaded his fingers as if they were dogs one had taken out to water." Still more rankling for him was to observe Crowley in his role of spiritual teacher to his mother. Crowley was at this time employing techniques set down in *Liber Jugorum* (discussed in Chapter Three) designed to reduce the conditioned states of the mind. One such technique was to cut one's own arm each time one violated certain conditions of mental discipline. Crowley dryly remarked, in *Book Four*, that *Liber Jugorum* was "one of the most hilariously exciting parlour games for the family circle ever invented." It is thus safe to assume that Crowley was aware of the impression he was creating in the mind of young Preston, who would recall:

> [Crowley's] repugnant reaction each time my poor mother had so far forgotten his teachings as to utter in his hearing a singular personal pronoun like "I" or "me" or "mine." The instant his ears were so assaulted, he solemnly withdrew an open penknife from his robe, raised his arm so the loose sleeve of his robe fell back to expose his bare forearm, and then with the penknife slashed a small fresh slice under the ladder of slices he had already incised into his forearm [. . .]
>
> Reading about some of his subsequent exploits, I realize that my mother and I were lucky to escape with our lives. If I had been a little older, he might not have escaped with his.

Only after he had returned to his boarding school did Preston learn that, during this very January, his mother had filed for a divorce from his adoptive father, Solomon Sturges, who had given the boy his name.

As the winter of 1912 proceeded, Desti and Crowley fell to quarreling. Desti returned to Paris where—after a brief rapprochement with a pursuing Crowley, she married Veli Bey, a Turkish man whom Crowley believed to be a fortune hunter. This marriage endured; but surprisingly, Crowley and Desti managed to remain friends, with Desti serving as an editor for the final numbers of *The Equinox* through 1913. Crowley was always gracious to her in his later writings, blaming his own skepticism for driving her away from her role as Scarlet Woman.

As for their finished collaborative effort, *Book Four* stands as one of the most significant works ever issued by Crowley. It was published by Crowley in late 1912 or early 1913 in the physical form of a square (four equal sides) at a price of four groats (one shilling). Part I is dedicated to meditation, which Crowley equated with the practice of yoga. In essence, this Part I is a fleshed-out version of the notebooks kept by Crowley during his yogic studies under Allan Bennett in Ceylon in 1902. Part II is devoted to the fundamentals of ceremonial magic. Here, Crowley emerges as an esoteric modernist, exhorting the reader to magical endeavor in brisk prose on the grounds of common sense and practical psychology—a radical break from the veiled, sanctimonious tone that had dominated writings on magic since the Romantic period. Crowley followed the basic approach set forth in his 1903 essay "An Initiated Interpretation of Ceremonial Magic" (discussed in Chapter Three). That is, he argued for magic as a structured, empirical means for developing unrecognized capacities of the mind. The implements and rituals of magic were extensions or projections of mind, which—however apparently irrational—constituted a course of self-confirming initiation to the open-minded and dedicated practitioner. Most fundamental of all was the training of the Magical Will, through which yogic meditation became possible. Magic was thus linked to yoga as an advisable preliminary discipline; but Crowley also stressed that magic was a full equivalent to yoga and other forms of mysticism, itself sufficient to attain the Great Work, which is clinically defined as "an occurrence in the brain characterized essentially by the unity of subject and object."

In *Book Four*, for the first time, Crowley switched from "magic" to the older spelling of "magick" so as "to distinguish the Science of the Magi from all its counterfeits." The teachings of *The Book of the Law* are interspersed lightly, most often in footnotes. This is due in part to the status of this work as a beginner's text; but it also reflected a tension between Crowley's ambitions as a Prophet and his heterodox approach to spiritual practice (as expressed in an opening note by Desti, who was accorded coauthor status by Crowley):

> Frater Perdurabo is the most honest of all the great religious teachers. Others have said, "Believe me!" He says: "*Don't believe me!*" He does not ask for followers; would despise and refuse them. He wants an independent and self-reliant body of students to follow out their own methods of research.[. . .]
>
> The whole life of Frater Perdurabo is now devoted to seeing that you obtain this living experience of Truth for, by, and in yourselves!

Crowley never came to "despise and refuse" disciples—he tried to put all comers to use in some manner. But his belief in the value of independent practice by students was sincere, and he adhered to it to the end of his life.

Book Four is not without serious and even gratuitous flaws. It was of the essence of Crowley's narrative method to defy moral expectations, even as he courted the reader's admiration for his gentlemanly honor. As previously discussed (in Chapter Three), Crowley's analysis of two of the "limbs" of yogic practice—*yama* (moral restraint) and *niyama* (right action)—displays a naive, if not hubristic, faith in the power of inexperienced students to adequately assess and control their multifold earthly desires. In his Preliminary Remarks, Crowley inserted a vile repetition—gratuitously out of context—of the fraudulent "blood libel" charges of ritual murder made against the Jews of Eastern Europe. Blatant bigotry is a persistent minor element in Crowley's writings. He was aware of this, but regarded his bigotry as a kind of secondary excrescence that readers could take or leave as they liked, without undue concern; as he put it in the *Confessions*, "my spiritual apprehension of truth represents my real self, while my intellectual perceptions are necessarily coloured by my nationality, caste, education and personal predilection." This, of course, corresponded to his analysis of the moral content of the "limbs" of yoga: Crowley refused to allow that his personal views or behavior, however indefensible even by his own gentlemanly code of honor, could affect the value of his higher spiritual insights—which were, kabbalistically speaking, on different planes. This will be most unconvincing to readers who would hold, as a criterion of the attainments Crowley claimed, a more harmonious interweaving of all planes. *Book Four* is flawed by these failings, as are, in a similar manner, certain poems of Pound and Eliot. Nevertheless, it deserves to be recognized as a text of value both for scholars and practitioners in the fields of yoga and magic.

Crowley did not himself make the claim, but it could be argued that, in the opening months of 1912, he enjoyed the finest sustained stint of writing of his life. In addition to *Book Four*, Crowley also wrote a singular essay, "Energized Enthusiasm" (his first plainspoken effort to link—on a theoretical basis—sexuality and spirituality) and completed a volume of compressed brilliance, *The Book of Lies* (1913)—his greatest success in merging his talents as poet, scholar, and magus. *The Book of Lies* stands as a unique literary and philosophical delight for readers with the patience and wit to puzzle out its tiered paradoxes. There are 93 chapters in *Lies*, as 93 is the number of Thelema (Will) and Agape (Love), two key terms of *The Book of the Law*. The first two chapters are facing pages displaying only "?" and "!", the symbols explicated in his essay "The Soldier and the Hunchback" as representing the oscillating processes of doubt and insight. The remaining chapters, numbered 1 through 91, reflect to some degree the kabbalistic significance of each such number; in 1921, Crowley wrote a Commentary to *Lies*, included in all subsequent editions, which provided hints (and sometimes deliberate blinds) to aid and abet multiple and even contradictory interpretations.

The dominant style employed in *Lies* is that of the ironic prose poem. Crowley was deeply influenced, during this period, by the prose poems of Baudelaire, which he translated in 1913 (these translations were ultimately privately published in 1928). The Baudelarian stance of sensuous immersion and spiritual defiance—blended with Crowley's theurgic mysticism—shows itself in Chapter 34 of *Lies*, entitled "The Smoking Dog":

> Each act of man is the twist and double of an hare.
> Love and Death are the greyhounds that course him.
> God bred the hounds and taketh His pleasure in the sport.
> This is the Comedy of Pan, that man should think he
>   hunteth, while those hounds hunt him.
> This is the Tragedy of Man when facing Love and Death
>   he turns to bay. He is no more hare, but boar.
> There are no other comedies or tragedies.
> Cease then to be the mockery of God; in savagery of love
>   and death live thou and die!
> Thus shall His laughter be thrilled through with Ecstasy.

"The Smoking Dog" is a reference to a then popular item of bric-a-brac, a figurine dog with tiny surrogate cigarettes that could be fitted into its mouth and then lit to produce the appearance of a canine smoking. It is a symbol of an animal both unnatural and ridiculous in its actions—as humans appear to the gods when they deny their essential natures. The number 34 can refer kabbalistically to the laugher of Pan, the god form of earthly ecstasy and delight.

Several of the chapters in *Lies* were written in a pedagogical style. Despite the public buckling of the A∴A∴, Crowley was still eager for new students. In the summer of 1912, he immersed himself in an altogether different magical organization, the Ordo Templi Orientis (Ancient Order of Oriental Templars), or O.T.O. Crowley being Crowley, his governing aim was to remake the O.T.O. in the image of Thelema. In this aim, he was assisted by an exceedingly strange, if not impossible, series of events.

It was in May 1912 that Crowley, living again in London at the new address of 33 Avenue Studios, Fulham, received an unexpected visit from Theodor Reuss. Reuss now made the startling accusation that Crowley had violated the honor of the O.T.O. by openly publishing its greatest secret in *The Book of Lies.* Crowley protested both his innocence and his ignorance as to what this great secret was. Reuss then pulled from Crowley's bookshelf a copy of *Lies* and showed the offending passage to its author, who was at once transformed: "It instantly flashed upon me. The entire symbolism not only of free masonry but of many other traditions, blazed upon my spiritual vision. From that moment the O.T.O. assumed its proper importance in my mind. I understood that I held in my hands the key to the future progress of humanity."

The secret, of course, concerned sexual magic, as to which, as we have seen, Crowley had already drawn his own preliminary conclusions. But two key mysteries arise from Crowley's account of his meeting with Reuss. The first is insoluble, unless one posits a failure of Crowley's memory. For *Lies* was not published until 1913—a year *after* Reuss pulled it from the bookshelf. Crowley was aware of this discrepancy. As he later wrote, "My entire life was changed in its most important respect, by an incident which could not possibly have occurred." The second mystery is more tantalizing: Which chapter did Reuss point to? Crowley did not name it. The most likely candidate is Chapter 36, "The Star Sapphire, a Ritual of the Hexagram"—the symbolic interpenetration of upward and downward triangles, or spiritual polarities. In its opening sentence the ritual instructs: "Let the Adept be armed with his Magick Rood (and provided with his Mystic Rose)." The Rood or Cross may be read (as Crowley himself later instructed) as a symbol of the phallus or *lingam*, while the Rose is a symbol of the vagina or *yoni*.

Crowley never wrote down the details of his talk with Reuss that day. His close friend Gerald Yorke, who first met Crowley some fifteen years later, has provided an account based, presumably, on Crowley's private recollections:

> He explained to Crowley the theory behind that school of Alchemy which uses sexual fluids and the Elixir of Life. He enlarged on the Baphomet tradition of the Knights Templars and traced its alleged survival through the Hermetic Brotherhood of Light [a nineteenth-century esoteric society]. He then showed the connection with those Tantrics who follow the left hand path [utilizing ritual sexual intercourse as a means of spiritual union with the godhead], and the Hathayogins who practice sexual mudras [sacred postures]. What however was more to the point[,] he offered Crowley leadership in the O.T.O.[. . .]

Reuss initiated both Crowley and Waddell into the highest magical rank of the O.T.O.—the IX°, which was accorded only to those who had already attained, by their own efforts, knowledge of the great secret. Then, on June 1, Reuss—who was the supreme Outer Head of the Order (O.H.O.)—made Crowley the X° Supreme Rex and Sovereign Grand Master General of Ireland, Iona, and all the Britains. Crowley had become, in one stroke, the undisputed leader of the O.T.O. in Great Britain; just how many O.T.O. members there were at the time is unclear, but the number was certainly limited. Crowley gave the British chapter a new name—Mysteria Mystica Maxima (M.M.M.). He also promptly obtained permission from the A∴A∴—that is, from himself as a Master of the Temple—to reconstitute the O.T.O. on lines suited to the New Aeon. *The Book of the Law* became a part of O.T.O. ritual—each British lodge was to possess a copy and, by Crowley's express instruction, "no initiations upon any other document will be recognized by the Grand Lodge," that is, by Crowley. As a sign of his authority as national Supreme Rex, Crowley took a new magical name—Baphomet. As indicated above, Baphomet lore was regarded by Reuss as crucial to the great secret of the O.T.O. This name was already familiar to Crowley—indeed, Chapter 33 of *Lies* was entitled "Baphomet." But to understand the full significance of this name, and of Crowley's new identification with it, one must briefly consider the esoteric lineage of the O.T.O., which drew both from Indian Tantrism and from a host of past Western secret societies, including (as the name O.T.O. confirms), the Knights Templar. This latter society has taken on extreme legendary importance in Western esoteric circles, even as scholars continue to debate whether magic played any significant role in the historical Knights Templar military religious order founded in 1119, during the Crusades, for the purpose of defending Christian holy places against the Moslems. For some two hundred years, the Templars enjoyed great political and financial influence throughout both Palestine and Western Europe. But in the early fourteenth century, a persecution was instigated by Philip IV of France and approved by Pope Clement V. The motivation of the ruling persecutors was more financial (the Templars possessed great wealth) than theological. But charges of heresy were prominent in the trial of its members, who were routinely tortured to elicit their testimony, and faced the very real threat of burning at the stake. The principal heresies raised against the Templars included the denial of Christ, idol worship, and obscene initiation rites including the use of the "forbidden kiss" upon the male back and buttocks. The chief idol alleged to have been worshiped was Baphomet, a name the meaning of which has inspired considerable controversy in both esoteric and scholarly circles. The accusers at the Templar trial (which concluded in 1314) insisted that Baphomet was a cypher for Mohammed (Mahomet)—and thus was proof that the Templars had strayed, during their stay in the Holy Land, into heresy. A more persuasive recent interpretation, offered by Idries Shah, is that Baphomet is a corruption of the Arabic *abufihamat* ("faith of understanding"). Baphomet would thus be a cypher for the completed or enlightened human being.

Whatever the truth as to the historical practices of the Templars, their influence—or, more precisely, the influence of their legend—upon Crowley was enormous. The most familiar image of Baphomet for Crowley was that drawn by Eliphas Levi and included in his *Dogme et Rituel de la Haute Magie* (1854, 1856)—as the "Sabbatic Goat" with a pair of horns, a pair of wings, the goatish face of a bearded old man, an androgynous sexual physiognomy, and a pentagram emblazoned on his brow. Crowley, in taking the name Baphomet, was linking himself not only to the Templar tradition, but also to the blasphemous, even Satanic, connotations of Baphomet. He was well aware of the challenge thus posed to Christian believers. In *Magick in Theory and Practice*, Crowley dismissed them as a bloated majority that had perverted the Gnostic teachings of spiritual awakening:

This serpent, Satan, is not the enemy of Man, but He who made Gods of our race, knowing Good and Evil; He bade "Know Thyself!" and taught Initiation. He is "the Devil of the Book of Thoth [the Tarot deck], and his emblem is Baphomet, the Androgyne who is the hieroglyph of arcane perfection.[. . .] He is therefore Life, and Love. But moreover his letter is Ayin [the Hebrew letter assigned to trump called "The Devil" in the Tarot deck], the Eye; he is Light, and his Zodiacal image is Capricornus, that leaping goat whose attribute is Liberty.

Crowley made a special trip to Berlin in the summer of 1912 to be formally installed by Reuss as Baphomet and Supreme Rex of the Britains. During this summer, Reuss gave Crowley the task of rewriting the O.T.O. rituals, then closely based on Freemasonry. Crowley was thus assigned the role which, in the Golden Dawn, had been entrusted to Mathers. As had Mathers, Crowley took to the task with alacrity. By 1914, he had crafted O.T.O. rituals to reflect his own erotomagical discoveries. A series of nine rituals for each of the nine degrees, culminating in the heterosexual recognition of the great secret. The paradox of IX° is that it cannot be "conferred" but is instead "confirmed"—the candidate must experience it on his or her own. Crowley also added a new degree of his own devising—an XI° magical working utilizing anal sex which was, in practice, primarily homosexual.

In all of these rituals, the teachings of *The Book of the Law* receive prominent place. Reuss found this acceptable, but there were heated protests from O.T.O. members in Germany and elsewhere in Europe. Reuss was forced, on at least one occasion—in Denmark—to return to the original Masonic rituals so as to quell insurrection. The rift between Crowley and the continental O.T.O. would endure. In his own native England, Crowley used the O.T.O. as a means of spreading the word of Thelema. Given his haste, it is unsurprising that Crowley was soon disappointed by the quality of his recruits. One example was Vittoria Cremers, whom Crowley designated, in 1912, to manage the property of the M.M.M.

It was from Cremers that Crowley heard the tale of one Robert Donston, who had, in the late 1880s, competed with Cremers for the attentions of the bisexual Mabel Collins, the author of a then-popular occult novel, *The Blossom and the Fruit*. Cremers claimed that she had discovered, in a trunk under Donston's bed, five blood-soaked ties—corresponding to the five murders committed by Jack the Ripper in the Whitechapel district of London in 1888. Cremers believed that Donston was the Ripper, and Crowley took up her tale, viewing Donston as a gifted black magician and later claiming—to a member of the press—that he met Donston prior to the latter's death in 1912, and that Donston had given him the five bloody ties. It is far more likely that Crowley was merely embellishing Cremers's account—with which Crowley was sufficiently fascinated to write up (in versions which factually contradict each other) both in the *Confessions* and in a subsequent 1943 essay. One result—which would likely have delighted Crowley—is that the legend of Jack the Ripper is now frequently intertwined with that of the Beast in popular culture.

As for Cremers, Crowley soon grew disenchanted. By October 1913, he removed her from her M.M.M. post on grounds of embezzlement. It is by no means certain that these charges were true. Crowley was all too prone to raise charges of theft against others, and would later accuse George M. Cowie, Cremers' successor and M.M.M. treasurer, of insanity. For her part, Cremers would, years later, level her own charges against Crowley: "It was sex that rotted him. It was sex, sex, sex, sex, all the way with Crowley. He was a sex-maniac."

In fairness, Crowley was quite as much interested in cultivating disciples and influence. His methods in this sphere were, of course, unorthodox. For example, he met the brilliant New Zealand–born short story writer Katherine Mansfield at a party hosted by Gwendolyn Otter, a mutual friend. Accounts vary as to what precisely occurred, but it is clear that Crowley offered Mansfield a dosage of a drug—either anhalonium (peyote) or hashish—and that Mansfield ingested it and underwent highly vivid experiences. One friend of Mansfield offered this description of it—"up, up rose the spirit into a pink and paradisiacal contentment, whence she viewed space with rosy rapture; the effect beginning to wear off, or reaching terra firma, she became aware of hundreds of parcels or shelves, identically marked 'Jesus Wept.'" In another account, Crowley, Waddell, and Mansfield left the party together, with Crowley returning to entrust Mansfield to Otter's care:

> 'The stuff is beginning to work,' he [Crowley] said. 'She's not going to be interesting; she's only going to sleep.'
>
> Katherine lay on the sofa and lit a cigarette. She threw the match on the floor and it lay crookedly on the carpet. This caused her such acute distress that Gwen put it straight. 'That's much better,' said K.M. 'Pity that stuff had no effect.'
>
> Then she began to talk, about a princess who lived at the edge of the sea and when she wanted to bathe she just called to the

waves . . . It was as wonderful, in its creation of atmosphere, thought Gwen, as one of her short stories.[. . .]

Despite Crowley's gentle handling of Mansfield during her drug experience, the overall impression left upon her by Crowley was not a favorable one—"a pretentious and very dirty fellow" was her final verdict.

Such was the frequent impact of Crowley in proper circles. His reputation preceded him, and Crowley, in person, rarely disappointed. The tenth and final number of the first volume of *The Equinox*, published in the autumn of 1913, featured a frontispiece photo which was to become the most famous (and fearsome) image of Crowley—with shaven head and dark staring eyes that hinted of menace and resolve. Whatever Crowley may have intended by this photo (taken by his friend Hector Murchison), its effect upon the public has been a lasting one. The British tabloids have reprinted it countless times. It appeared amongst the throng on the cover of the Beatles's *Sgt. Pepper* album (1967). The most famous of modern-day Satanists, Anton Sandor LaVey, adopted the look to great effect, as have a host of lesser occultists and defiant artists. The shaved-head look might be said to be Crowley's lasting contribution to twentieth-century style.

It was during this prewar period that Crowley himself began to refer, in an ironic vein, to a persona he called "the demon Crowley"—the fearful aspect that so often affrighted students and even casual acquaintances. He played up to the part, allowing his sense of the dramatic—and the erotic—full rein, as in the case of "The Serpent's Kiss," employed with Mary Desti and other women. This was described in his novel *Moonchild* (1929): "He came over to her, caught her throat in both his hands, bent back her head, and taking her lips with his teeth, bit them—bit them almost through. It was a single deliberate act [. . .]" Crowley further took to stylizing his handwritten signature to suggest the O.T.O. great secret—the "A" of Aleister became a thick penis with dangling loops (testicles) at the base of the letter, while the "C" of Crowley was given a top loop to suggest a sperm.

Small wonder that the legends grew in scabrous horror. Rumor had it, during this time, that Crowley had squatted and shat on a fine carpet in an upper-class London home in which he was a guest, and then coolly explained that his excrement was sacred. This is almost certainly untrue; while Crowley was willing to shock the wealthy with his ideas, he was loyal to the codes of upper-class politesse. Experimentation with drugs and the occult was rather faddish, and hence Crowley could practice these openly. Homosexuality was a pervasive but private practice, and Crowley accepted this restraint.

There was an ominous and tragic episode in August 1912 which indicates why Crowley had so unsettling an effect upon so many of his contemporaries. Back in the autumn of 1910, Crowley had placed an ad in *Stage* seeking a young female to dance various parts, including Luna, in the *Rites of Eleusis*. The woman who won the role was Joan Hayes, whose stage name was Ione de Forest. Hayes had neither an interest in magic nor exceptional gifts as an actress or dancer, but she was possessed of a suitably unearthly beauty, with a small, slight body and long black hair. Neuburg, who danced with her on stage, was fascinated; they went on to have an affair. While she and Crowley did not become lovers, they were for a time flirtatious familiars; Ethel Archer recalled one occasion when Hayes ran her fingers through his hair and called him "Aleister"—a familiarity which no one else, not even Neuburg (who used "A.C." or "Holy Guru"), dared take. Crowley did not approve of Neuburg's involvement with Hayes, believing that it vampirically interfered with Neuburg's A∴A∴ work. But Neuburg continued the affair even after Hayes's marriage to a friend of Neuburg, Wilfrid Merton, in December 1911. Six months later, Hayes left Merton, who filed for divorce; it is possible that Neuburg would have been named as a corespondent on grounds of adultery. But in August 1912, Hayes killed herself by a pistol shot to the heart. Neuburg later expressed the conviction that Crowley had murdered her through psychological bullying or magical means. Crowley himself corroborated this charge in his *Magick in Theory and Practice*, in which he classified, as one type of magical operation:

> Works of destruction, which may be done in many different ways. One may fascinate or bend to one's will a person who has of his own right the power to destroy.[. . .]
>
> In private matters these works are very easy, if they be necessary. An adept known to The Master Therion [Crowley—referring obliquely to himself] once found it necessary to slay a Circe [Hayes] who was bewitching brethren [Neuburg]. He merely walked to the door of her room, and drew an Astral T ("traditore" [traitor], and the symbol of Saturn) with an astral dagger. Within 48 hours she shot herself.

This passage shows Crowley at his most vile and vainglorious. He went on to insist that "it is absolute Black Magic to use any of these powers if the object can possibly be otherwise obtained." For Crowley, the charge of Black Magic was a serious one, akin to Catholic Mortal Sin. But (as discussed in the "Introduction" to this biography) Crowley insisted that moral judgment by persons on lower spiritual planes was irrelevant; only Crowley (and those rare persons who could claim to be his equal) could judge Crowley:

> **Until the Great Work has been performed, it is presumptuous for the magician to pretend to understand the universe, and dictate its policy. Only the Master of the Temple can say whether any given act is a crime....** "Slay the ignorant child?" (I hear the ignorant say) "What a horror!" "Ah!" replies the Knower, with foresight of history, "but the child will become Nero. Hasten to strangle him!"

This will sound, to most readers, like the purest sophistry, and as applied to the case of Joan Hayes that seems a just verdict. Crowley was here invoking the rarest powers of clairvoyance and wisdom, such as are frequently claimed but seldom possessed by human teachers, and the results do nothing to bear him out. Neuburg went on to fail miserably—even after Hayes's death—to achieve signal progress in the A∴A∴. Crowley, as a teacher who justified provoking suicide in the name of such progress, must bear some responsibility here. This he refused to do.

Crowley never again resorted (or, at least, never claimed to resort) to this manner of magical destruction again. It is difficult to avoid the conclusion that, in the case of his beloved Neuburg, Crowley, motivated by a jealousy he could not confess (as unworthy of a Master of the Temple), employed what measures he could to psychically undermine the vulnerable Hayes during the crisis of her divorce. It should be added that, in her suicide note, Hayes placed the blame for her death squarely upon her husband. A contributing factor to the end of that marriage, noted by Neuburg biographer Jean Overton Fuller, was that Hayes was too slight to bear full penetration in intercourse. There were sufficient unhappy aspects surrounding the suicide to cast doubt on the notion that Crowley was solely or even primarily responsible. That he relished—and justified—her death seems plain, however.

There is little evidence of communication of any sort between Neuburg and Crowley in the months following her death. Crowley turned his primary personal attentions to Waddell, whose stage career he sought to promote. In March 1913, with Crowley acting as producer, *The Ragged Ragtime Girls*, a light follies review featuring Waddell's musical talents, enjoyed a brief run at the Old Tivoli in London. Crowley then managed to book a six-week run in Moscow, commencing in July 1913. It was common, in this prewar era, for touring British music hall companies to try their luck in Russia; sex appeal overcame the language barrier.

Once arrived in Moscow, Crowley was entranced by the beauty of the city and afire with the urge to write poetry and ritual. A key factor here was his discovery, within a few days, of an erotic muse of formidable power. Crowley's affair with Waddell had either diminished to low ebb, or was swept into the background with the onset of this new love, as rapturously described in the *Confessions*:

> In a cafe, I met a young Hungarian girl named Anny Ringler; tall, tense, lean as a starving leopardess with wild insatiable eyes and a long straight thin mouth, a scarlet scar which seemed to ache with the anguish of hunger for some satisfaction beyond earth's power to supply. We came together with irresistible magnetism. We could not converse in human language. I had forgotten nearly all my Russian; and her German was confined to a few broken cries. But we had no need of speech. The love between us was ineffably intense. It still inflames my inmost spirit. She had passed beyond the region where pleasure had meaning for her. She could only feel through pain, and my own means of making her happy was to inflict physical cruelties as she directed. The kind of relation was altogether new to me; and it was because of this, intensified as it was by the environment of the self-torturing soul of Russia, that I became inspired to create by the next six weeks.

Ringler fit a powerful erotic type for Crowley, with her lean frame, intense eyes, and broad, thin lips. (Recall the whore with "insatiable intensity of passion that blazed from her evil inscrutable eyes" in Mexico City in 1900, who inspired *Tannhäuser*.) In defense of the sexual dynamics of this affair, Crowley argued along libertarian lines that many modern readers will acknowledge: "Terms such as 'sadism' and 'masochism' have no valid application in a loving sexual encounter in which pain is a voluntarily given and received medium of genuine pleasure: The proof of the pudding is in the eating; my relations with Anny must be judged by their fruits; happiness, inspiration, spirituality, and romantic idealism."

The pattern of Crowley's days in Moscow was to see Anny for an hour or so, and then to wander about and find a suitable place to write. He produced two long poems, "The Fun of the Fair," which described Crowley's visit to the rural fair (made famous by Gogol) at Nijni Novgorod, and "The City of God," a rhapsodic lyric to Moscow which Crowley published in the *English Review*. (These poems were later issued by the O.T.O., as separate volumes, in 1942 and 1943, respectively.) But the two most memorable works of this summer were the "Hymn to Pan" and the *"Ecclesiae Gnosticae Catholicae Canon Missae,"* commonly termed the Gnostic Mass.

"Hymn to Pan," which was read at Crowley's funeral thirty-four years later, is perhaps his most rhetorically riveting, and emotionally unsettling, magical lyric. The "Hymn" was not intended by Crowley as a call to sexual violence, but it does utilize images of such violence to convey—in its final lines—the union of humankind and the fertility god. The refrain "Io Pan" is borrowed from the Greek classical tradition:

> And I rave; and I rape and I rip and I rend
> Everlasting, world without end,
> Mannikin, maiden, maenad, man,
> In the might of Pan.
> Io Pan! Io Pan Pan! Pan! Io Pan!

The Gnostic Mass, a formal, choreographed ritual with multiple speaking roles, was composed by Crowley with the express purpose—as indicated by its full Latin title—of providing for the O.T.O. a ceremony that paralleled the Eastern Orthodox or Roman Catholic Mass. In the Gnostic Mass, semen and menses—which may be transformed into physico-spiritual essences (the Great Work or *Summum Bonum*) by those in possession of the secret—are symbolized by the Priest (who bears the "Sacred Lance") and the Priestess (who should be "actually Virgo Intacta, or specially dedicated to the Service of the Great Order"). These two partake of the sacred Cake of Light and Cup of Wine. During the ritual, the Priest parts a sacred veil with his Lance and embraces the knees of the Priestess, who has removed her robes to embody the sacred nakedness of the goddess Nuit in *The Book of the Law*. Crowley conceded, in the instructions, that by the time of the embrace the Priestess could again have dressed herself "if necessary, as in savage countries"—an allusion to puritan England. But Crowley himself exercised voluntary restraint in this regard. As his friend Gerald Yorke later explained, "Crowley was a complete hedonist in that he used wine, drugs and sex in all its forms. But he did so in privacy. There is no recorded instance of more than two others being present when he worked or worshipped in this way. When he celebrated the Gnostic Mass in company he always used a stage property lance and both the Priestess and her two child acolytes were decorously clad." The Gnostic Mass continues, to this day, to be performed on a weekly basis by O.T.O. groups around the world. It has also earned a place in literature by virtue of its having been drawn from by James Branch Cabell in his classic fantasy novel *Jurgen* (1919). Crowley subsequently sought, through correspondence, to win over Cabell to Thelema. This effort was futile. Cabell later dismissed Crowley as amongst the "hordes of idiots and prurient fools" who dabbled in black magic.

Crowley and his Ragged Ragtime Girls returned to London in the autumn of 1913. The Beast now oversaw—in his fifth year of editorship—the tenth and final number of volume one of *The Equinox*. Completing the volume had been a formidable task, and a financially draining one. Crowley duly announced, in this final number, that the second volume of *The Equinox*—spanning the five years to come—would be a volume of "silence."

By late December, in Paris, Crowley decided upon his immediate future course: He would concentrate on his own spiritual progress (held in abeyance by his public efforts as teacher) through active experimentation in sexual magic. To understand Crowley, one must be willing to grant his sincerity here. To regard his magic as merely an elaborate disguise for lust is unjust; if Crowley had wanted sex and sex alone, he could have had it.

The partner chosen by Crowley for his first major experiment—which he named the Paris Working—was Neuburg. They would devote some seven weeks to the task—a total of twenty-four ritual workings, which varied widely in intensity and effect. Not even Crowley could term the Paris Working a complete success. But one result, at least, emerged clearly: he would henceforth devote himself primarily to sexual, as opposed to ceremonial, magic.

One might wonder, given Crowley's own professed lack of detailed knowledge, how the great experiment was to proceed. According to Jean Overton Fuller, Neuburg later recalled that "they made up a ritual along the lines of those they imagined to have been practiced in antiquity, and that the chief clues they had came through Roman texts though they believed the traditions they glimpsed went back to an antiquity far more remote, and to a culture which seemed to have been more general to the countries round the Mediterranean basin." The sense of such a tradition was evident in the Paris Working—on two occasions, Crowley and Neuburg experienced reincarnative visions in ancient Mediterranean settings.

The first of the Paris Working rituals took place on New Year's Eve, 1914. The initial magical act, which took place in the late afternoon, had Crowley "confess" himself and receive "the Sacrament from a certain priest A.B." A.B. was Walter Duranty, the *New York Times* foreign correspondent who, as earlier mentioned, had been Crowley's lover and also shared with Crowley the attentions of Jane Chéron, whom Duranty later married. The "Sacrament" received from Duranty was semen; the means of reception was not specified in the record. Semen and blood were the two primary essences—at once physical and symbolic—of the Paris Working; both served as quintessential fluids of life energy.

The banishing ritual of the pentagram, employed to purify the room, was now performed by Neuburg in the form of a dance that merged into an invocation—written by Crowley—of the two Roman gods central to the Paris Working, Mercury and Jupiter. Mercury, as the god of wisdom and the messenger who bridged the divine and human realms, could guide the quest for the secrets of sexual magic. Jupiter, as the spirit of wise, prosperous, and generous rule, could aid Crowley both in establishing Thelema and in replenishing his finances. While dancing, Neuburg was ritually scourged on the buttocks by Crowley, who further employed a dagger to cut a cross (almost certainly a light tracing on the skin) on Neuburg's chest; a chain was also bound over Neuburg's forehead.

At midnight of the New Year, the second stage commenced. Crowley and Neuburg engaged in ritual sex, reciting, as they did so, a Latin verse composed by Duranty and Crowley to focus the consciousness of the two participants:

> *Jungitur in vati votes: rex inclyte rhabdon*
> *Hermes tu venias, verba nefanda ferens.*
> [Magician is with magician joined: Hermes,
> King of the Wand, appear, bringing the ineffable word]

Crowley played the passive, and Neuburg the active, role. There were striking results. Mercury manifested in Neuburg, whom Crowley saw surrounded by a dazzling astral array—"the temple grew full of flashing caducei [the magical wand with intertwined serpents sacred to Mercury] of gold and yellow, the serpents alive and moving, Hermes bearing them. But so young and so mischievous was He that the sacrifice was impossible." This last sentence was a veiled reference to Neuburg's failure, on that opening night, to attain the steady erection necessary for the full manifestation of a Mercury.

The Third Working, on the night of January 3, included further instructions from the manifested Mercury on semen and shame. Semen, the life-giving principle, possesses an ambiguous power, for it creates the multitudes of worlds in which ignorance reigns. The key to enlightenment is—in a teaching akin to that of certain Gnostic sects—immersion in Chaos itself, that is, in the cosmic wisdom that transcends the illusory order of the earthly realm:

> Every drop of semen which Hermes sheds is a world. The technical term for this semen is KPATOS [Greek, *Kratos*, force or strength]. Those worlds are held in chains, but invisibly. People upon the worlds are like maggots upon an apple—all forms of life bred by the worlds are in the nature of parasites. Pure worlds are flaming globes, each a conscious being.[. . .]
>
> The name of this Phallus is Thoth, Hermes or Mà. Mà is the god who seduced the Phallus away from the Yoni; hence the physical Universe. All worlds are excreta; they represent wasted semen. Therefore all is blasphemy. This explains why man made god in his own image.
>
> The feminine side of Mà is Pan, which explains why Pan is a devil. The only way to be really born is by an annihilation—to be born into Chaos, where Pan is the Saviour.

The creation of the physical universe is thus portrayed as the side effect of a *coitus interruptus*. That much is paralleled in a number of world myths. But there is a cosmogonic innovation unique to the Paris Working. The seduction which leads to this is homoerotic in essence: The male god Mà seducing the Phallus away from the Yoni or vagina. Mercury goes on to affirm that sex, the unshaped primal energy, may be coveted and embraced without sin or shame. As Mercury exclaimed at one point (with commentary by Crowley):

> 'What fools to bother about the room, you don't think I am in the room, do you?' He wants us to overcome shame generally, and says 'There is no shame about me, is there?'
>
> He suggests an obvious method which I blush to repeat.

In a note to the record, Crowley described the "obvious method" as: "An holy act before the world. (This was done at the house of the Lay

Sister J.C. [Jane Chéron] The Art-Bachelor W. D. [Walter Duranty] was the victim." In plain terms, Crowley and Duranty engaged in the "holy act" of homosexual union with Cheron as witness. Whether others were present is unknown; but to display his homosexuality before a woman must have been sufficiently difficult to satisfy, in essence, the condition of performing the act "before the world." Mercury had prescribed for Crowley the same cure which Crowley invariably tendered to his disciples—acting out the shameful deed to the hilt. The Paris Working did not, however, suffice to eradicate this shame within Crowley.

In subsequent evenings, the Paris Working rituals continued to explore the themes of Jupiterian prosperity and of Hermetic exploration of the mysteries of sexual magic. The Ninth Working illustrated the former: Jupiter was manifested in the form of the Father—"with gold were his hands full." This promise of imminent riches was heartening to Crowley. In the Eleventh Working—and again in the Thirteenth—Crowley experienced intense visions of two prior incarnations, both pertaining to the erotomagical current between Crowley and Neuburg.

During the Eleventh Working, Crowley recalled his life as Astarte, a sacred prostitute in Agrigentum, a Greek city founded centuries before the time of Christ in southern Sicily. There is no historical basis to confirm or deny the existence of a sacred temple cult in that city; but then, Crowley was not pretending to historical accuracy. In *Magick in Theory and Practice*, Crowley would stress that the ultimate test of any "magical memory" of a past life was its usefulness to the adept himself: "Far be it from any apologist of Magick to insist upon the objective validity of these concoatenations![. . .] We may therefore say that any magical recollection is genuine if it gives the explanation of our external or internal conditions. Anything which throws light upon the Universe, anything which reveals to us ourselves, should be welcome in this world of riddles." In the Eleventh Working, it was further revealed to Crowley "that the essence of the Operation is the freeing of the elemental spirit of an animal soul. This may be done by death, or by complete exhaustion either through pleasure or through pain. In this death-like trance the spirit becomes free to wander, & is united to the invoked God." Crowley would, later this same year, encode these teachings into his *De Arte Magica* [*On the Magical Art*], one of his secret instructions (highly symbolic in style) as to the higher O.T.O. degrees devoted to sexual magic.

Sex and death were also intertwined in the Thirteenth Working. A second vision of a prior incarnation was set in the Minoan civilization of Crete. In this vision, however, both Crowley and Neuburg were explicitly present—and entangled in a tragic romance. In Crete, Crowley's name was Aia, after Gaia the earth goddess. Aia, like Astarte, serves in the sacred temple, but as a dancer as opposed to a prostitute. In function, however, there is little practical difference: arousal of sexual energy for sacred purposes is the vocation of Aia. Neuburg is Mardocles, a handsome merchant who falls in love with Aia—to his ruin. Indeed, Mardocles (according to the magical record) "hated" Aia "but was too chivalrous to leave her."

Mardocles and Aia come to a horrific end. As part of his initiation into the temple, Mardocles is compelled to watch Aia perform a seductive dance. There are two, and only two, possible responses allowed him by the priests: he can watch unmoved, or he can violently rape her. Failure to adhere to one of these carries a punishment of castration, followed by death. But Mardocles is incapable of either option, and instead arranges an escape from the temple with Aia. The two evade punishment, but are ritually disgraced. The esoteric idea embedded in this vision was that experimentation with sexual magic was rife in the ancient world:

> This is the great idea of magicians in all times—
> To obtain a Messiah by some adaptation of the sexual process.
> In Assyria they tried incest; also in Egypt; the Egyptians tried brothers and sisters, the Assyrians mothers and sons. Phoenicians tried fathers and daughters; Greeks and Syrians mostly bestiality. This idea came from India. The Jews sought to do this by invocation methods. (Also by *paedicatio feminarum* [buggery of women]). The Mohammedans tried homosexuality; mediaeval philosophers tried to produce homunculi by making chemical experiments with semen.
> But the root idea is that any form of procreation other than normal is likely to produce results of a magical character.

The principal difference between Crowley's sexual magic and traditional Tantric practices now becomes clear. For Crowley, the object of the ritual was not limited to mystical union with the goddess or god, but could further involve the creation of a new spiritual form—a "magical child," as Crowley would come to call it. This magical child could be, in essence, any form of concentrated inspiration, or it could manifest physically as a talisman or even within a human being—as in a newborn baby, or a newly spiritually transformed adult man or woman. Crowley would later devote considerable energies to the creation of these forms.

On a more personal level, the unhappiness of Mardocles and Aia prefigured what was to come between Neuburg and Crowley. In the vision, Aia–Crowley declares to Mardocles–Neuburg that she knows he has never truly loved her:

> I am always unlucky for you, you know; you always have to sacrifice everything for my love. You don't want to in the least; this is because we both have hold of the wrong end of the stick. If only I could leave you, and you could love me. It would be lucky. But that has apparently never happened. Mutual indifference and mutual passion, and so on.

The strain between them—foreshadowed by Aia's complaint to Mardocles—was growing.

The Paris Workings completed, Crowley turned again to the task of strengthening the O.T.O. A vital source of support here was George M. Cowie, whom Crowley first met in June 1914. Cowie had joined the O.T.O. in 1912—his magical name was Frater Fiat Pax ("Let there be peace")—and was a rapt devotee of Crowley's writings. Already in his fifties, Cowie suffered from deafness and was a model of decent propriety in his daily life. Crowley appointed him Grand Treasurer General of the British branch (M.M.M.) of the O.T.O. This was a crucial step, as Crowley had come to see the M.M.M. as the key to stabilizing his finances. The grand plan was for the M.M.M. to act as a kind of insurance fund for all members who made financial contributions. Its collective resources were to be apportioned to members as need arose. In practical operation, Crowley was both the principal contributor and the principal recipient. In late 1913, he had mortgaged Boleskine House. Now, in 1914, he put it up for lease, with rental proceeds to go to the M.M.M., which had been assigned title. Cowie was to manage Boleskine, to look after certain of Crowley's publishing ventures and, most importantly, to pay Crowley when—and in the amounts—Crowley demanded. But Crowley's books brought in nothing, and Boleskine very little; and so the dedicated Cowie took to supplementing his teacher's income out of his own pocket. He thus became a rare source of support for Crowley during the coming war years.

As for Neuburg, he would no longer serve as support or as lover. Something changed drastically between the two men shortly after the Paris Working. Crowley did not speak directly of their break in the *Confessions*. But according to a memoir penned decades later by Neuburg's son (born well after these events), the break was spurred by Neuburg's lingering remorse over the suicide of Joan Hayes in August 1912: "The association with Crowley ended in 1914, and the events of the previous two years pushed him into a nervous breakdown. The two following years of his life are almost a blank, but he probably spent some time with his mother, who was then living in Hove, Sussex."

Neuburg did not spend the remainder of his life in a shattered condition. By 1916, he had recovered sufficiently to enlist in the British Army as a private. He later married, raised a family, and founded a distinguished small publishing enterprise, the Vine Press. In 1933, while working as a literary editor for the *London Sunday Referee,* he "discovered" Dylan Thomas. But Neuburg's own poetic energies were clearly diminished after the break with Crowley. Until his death in 1940, Neuburg retained a lingering fear of his onetime magical master.

What caused the final break? At some point, in late September or early October of 1914, Crowley and Neuburg met in London. Neuburg informed Crowley that he would continue no longer as his disciple. By some accounts, Crowley responded by ritually cursing him. Neither the reasons offered by Neuburg nor the nature of the curse, if uttered, are known—for neither Neuburg nor Crowley left a record of this meeting. There is no question, however, as to its psychological impact on Neuburg. The "nervous breakdown" attested to by his son followed at once.

World War One commenced on July 28, 1914. Crowley later attested that, in late summer, he offered his services to various British governmental agencies on behalf of the war effort but was rejected on two primary grounds: his phlebitis (which flared up in September) and negative rumors as to his character. The fact that he was nearing forty could not have helped his chances. Still, there were private volunteer means by which Crowley could have served his country. Certainly the opportunities open to him in England exceeded, in real value to the war effort, those he would pursue in America.

To what extent the break with Neuburg, or the intrusions of war, played upon his mind at this time is unknown. There is no clear reason for the next dramatic step in Crowley's life.

On October 24, 1914, he embarked for America on the *Lusitania*—the U.S. passenger vessel the sinking of which, in 1916, by a German submarine, would precipitate America's entry into the war. Crowley was carrying some fifty pounds in cash and an eclectic baggage of magical texts and documents.

For the next five years, in America, Crowley would endure—for the first time in his life—the dark desperation of an impoverished exile.

CHAPTER SEVEN

In Exile in America, Crowley Endures Poverty and Accusations of Treason as Ordeals Necessary to Becoming a Magus (1914–19)

U pon arrival in New York in late October 1914, Crowley was already something of a celebrity, thanks to a lurid account of his London doings which preceded his arrival.

The account appeared in the August 2, 1914, *The World Magazine*, a publication of the *New York World* newspaper. The author was Harry Kemp, an American poet whose reputation has since gone into eclipse, but who was at the time a renowned bohemian. Kemp limned a portrait of forbidden practices at Crowley's Fulham Road studio in London:

> One by one the worshippers entered. They were mostly women of aristrocratic type. [. . .] It was whispered to me that not a few people of noble descent belonged to the Satanists. [. . .] Then came the slow, monotonous chant of the high priest: "There is no good. Evil is good. Blessed be the Principle of Evil. All hail, Prince of the World, to whom even God Himself has given dominion." A sound as of evil bleating filled the pauses of these blasphemous utterances.

Kemp privately acknowledged that the piece was "a turgid bit of sensational journalism." Crowley termed it "rubbish." *The World Magazine* ran a subsequent piece on Crowley (by a different reporter) in its December 13, 1914, issue. Crowley was now described—with admirable accuracy—as "a man about whom men quarrel. Intensely magnetic, he attracts people or repels them with equal violence. His personality seems to breed rumors. Everywhere they follow him." Crowley answered back at Kemp, declaring that he had made Kemp "dream a scene of black magic, and he thought it was actually happening and that I was participating. I don't practice black magic."

Shortly after his arrival, Crowley met with John Quinn, the wealthy lawyer and arts patron to whom Crowley hoped to sell some of his own limited editions. He further desired to win over Quinn as an ally, as Quinn was influential in intellectual circles both in America and in England, and in correspondence with the leading figures of literary modernism, including Pound, Yeats, and (a few years later) James Joyce. But by late February, Quinn resolved to sever relations. As he wrote to Yeats (who had crossed swords with Crowley in 1900): "Frankly, his 'magic' and astrology bored me beyond words. Whatever he may be, he has no personality. I am not interested in his morals or lack of morals. He may or may not be a good or profound or crooked student or practitioner of magic. To me, he is only a third- or fourth-rate poet."

This rejection by Quinn effectively ended Crowley's chances of forming sympathetic social ties with the modernist movement—for which Crowley, a poetic traditionalist, would always express a visceral contempt. In turn, Crowley was anathema to Pound, Yeats, and their circle. Thus in 1917, Pound, writing from London to the influential American quarterly *The Little Review*, objected strongly to the presence of a favorable footnote on Crowley in an essay by H. L. Mencken on "Puritanism as a Literary Force." The mention, Pound insisted, was an "awful slip [. . .] that would queer his [Mencken's] effect at once over here." Mencken and Crowley had been in friendly correspondence. But when they finally did meet, some years later in London, Mencken came over to Pound's camp, viewing Crowley as "surrounded by a group of idiots who regarded him as inspired and almost, indeed a god."

However wayward his quest for public recognition, Crowley continued privately to devote himself to experimentation with sexual magic. Crowley's written record of practice was entitled *"Rex de Arte Regia,"* or "The King on the Royal Art," a phrase that draws from alchemical imagery of the androgynous conjoining of the king and the queen (the male and the female) in the work of spiritual transformation. The record included physical details of the sexual acts in Latin, thus to convey a sense of dignity. Many entries addressed the preparation and use of "elixir," the commingled male and female fluids that Crowley regarded as quintessential to the O.T.O. IX° ritual. This was by no means a universal approach to sexual magic; numerous writings of Hindu and Buddhist Tantrism and of the Chinese Taoist tradition call for retention of semen by the male, even in the heights of mystical sexual union. Crowley followed that alchemical tradition which regarded the fluidic commingling as an "elixir" which, when imbibed, could heighten both one's physical and spiritual state.

His belief in the practical efficacy of sexual magic was, necessarily, put to a severe test during the war years in America, when for the first time he would endure poverty. Revile English society as Crowley often did, he was a product of that society and had relished his status as a gentleman. In America he had no such status, and no funds to obtain it. Small wonder, then, that many of his sexual magic operations during these years—as documented by his diary—were devoted to the obtaining of money, or the gift of oratory, or a wealthy marriage, or other means of obtaining a practical success.

Crowley was aware that practices of this sort could be viewed as sordid, ego-ridden deviations from the path of attainment. But in an essay from this period—"The Revival of Magick," a condensed autobiography written in a popular style—Crowley boasted of the efficacy of his "Magick" (its sexual nature was not disclosed here) in obtaining wealth or anything else that the magician might desire. The final "secret of high Magick" was within his reach:

> For example, one performs an operation "to have $20,000." A few days later a prospect of obtaining that exact sum suddenly arises, then fades slowly away. Exactly what to do in such a case is a problem of which I have not yet found the perfect answer. Fortunately, it rarely happens that this trouble supervenes. In five out of six times the desired event comes naturally to pass without further disturbance. But I confess that I should like to make that sixth time safe, and I believe that in another few months [he was writing in 1917] I shall have done so.

At the time Crowley penned those words, he was living on a tenuous and minimal income, incapable of even once—much less five times out of six—summoning up $20,000. Crowley was never able to conjure money—or any other desired practical benefits—at will.

However, as to access to the mystical Knowledge and Conversation of his Holy Guardian Angel, Crowley felt himself frequently successful. Especially during the first year of his stay in America, he experimented with an array of partners—female and male—in the respective IX° and XI° rituals. These included prostitutes from the streets of New York and men who he met in Turkish baths. But also included were women for whom Crowley felt a serious friendship or a deep romantic attachment. One of the strongest myths surrounding the persona of Aleister Crowley was that he was prodigious in his sexuality, with appetites and energies beyond the norm. But as the diaries from this American period confirm, Crowley was, at least at this stage (he turned forty in 1915) quite ordinary in the frequency of his sexual acts, if not in their method and intent. His friend Gerald Yorke made some tabulations based on the sexual operations meticulously recorded by Crowley. For example, from September 1, 1914, to June 16, 1915, there were sixty-eight operations, eleven of which were VIII° solitary masturbations. From February 26, 1917, to March 4, 1918, there were a mere eighty-seven operations. Yorke observed that, "It is rare for there to be more than one emission in a numbered working." The tabulations go on, but the point is made—Crowley's appetite and endurance were disappointingly normal.

A number of his operations—including some of the VIII° autoerotic variety—had as their explicit object the obtaining of a new Scarlet Woman. As for his desire for men, it was a source of discomfort within and social vulnerability without. Shortly after his arrival in New York, Crowley recorded in his diary his hope of attracting to himself a man like Jerome Pollitt, the love of his Cambridge youth. In his picaresque novel *Not the Life and Adventures of Sir Roger Bloxam*—written in the period 1916–17 and described by Crowley as a "Novelissim" (innovative curiosity)—Crowley offered a disguised paean to Pollitt that echoed his love poems in the pseudonymous *Scented Garden* (1910). Crowley never sought to publish *Bloxam* in his lifetime; had his fortune held out, it is likely that he would have pursued the same course (a private and limited printing) as with *The Scented Garden.* The main characters of the novel—bawdy in content, archaic in tone, with brief episodic chapters in the manner of Sterne's *Tristram Shandy*—are Sir Roger Bloxam (Crowley), Porphyrria Poppoea (Crowley's anus), Cardinal Mentula (Crowley's penis), Signor Coglio the Florentine and brave Don Cojone of Legrono (Crowley's balls), and Hippolytus (Pollitt). Porphyrria Poppoea—a feminine persona, in keeping with Crowley's preferred role with Pollitt and other male lovers—offers up this testimony of enduring love: "Many a lover has possessed her since Hippolytus; but she has scorned them even while she abandons herself to their caresses. She loves Hippolytus. Hippolytus!" Not even the break with Neuberg had eclipsed the loss of Pollitt. Publicly, however, Crowley continued to play the part of the strict heterosexual.

In January 1915, Crowley had his first meetings with George Sylvester

Viereck, a writer and editor who would play a pivotal role in Crowley's life during these war years. Viereck is remembered as the most influential propagandist for the German cause in America during both World War One and World War Two. Born in 1884 in Munich, Viereick moved with his family to America in 1896. A poet and memoirist, Viereck enjoyed a triumph with *Confessions of a Barbarian* (1909), which Crowley admired. In this memoir, Viereck praised German culture while affirming his attachment to his adopted American homeland. This would serve as Vierck's consistent strategy in addressing German-American issues in the prewar years. Viereck founded two influential journals—*The International* in 1912 and *The Fatherland* in 1914. Crowley's wartime livelihood came primarily from these two journals, to which he contributed literally dozens of pieces in the years from 1915 to 1917.

Viereck and Crowley first met in the London offices of Austin Harrison, editor of *The English Review*, prior to the war. Once in New York, Crowley renewed the acquaintance. With the war under way, Viereck and *The Fatherland* had a twofold political propaganda agenda: to argue the German cause in pro-British America, and to keep neutral America out of the war that Britain wished her to enter. In pursuit of these aims, Viereck was badly in need of credible British and American voices. The opportunity to wield genuine influence was there for Viereck. The circulation of *The Fatherland* went as high as 100,000 in its first year of publication. But a *New York World* exposé in August 1915 had damaged Viereck's alleged independent standing as an editor by reporting substantial funding by the German government for his propaganda efforts.

Viereck was understandably intrigued, then, by the willingness of Aleister Crowley, an "Irish" man of letters, to write for *The Fatherland*. Crowley's first appearance, on January 13, 1915, was entitled "Honesty is the Best Policy" and excoriated British hypocrisy in claiming justice as the motive for its mercenary wartime aims. Crowley had an undoubted talent for vituperating his native land:

> We are in for one of our periodical orgies of Cant. Right (and God, of course, thank God!) struggles gallantly in its tiny way against Armed Might, Tyranny, Barbarism; the Allies pit their puny force against the hordes of Huns. [. . .]
>
> My own view is simpler. We have waited for a long while to smash Germany and steal her goods. We have taken a first-class opportunity, and we shall never regret it.

The question, of course, is why Crowley should have taken on such a public role. Was he a traitor to the British cause? A good many persons have believed so. Sir Edward Grey, the British foreign secretary during the war, was one of these. Crowley claimed, however, that he deliberately cultivated the trust of Viereck to gain a prominent voice in *The Fatherland* that would—paradoxically—frustrate German aims by carrying the style of its propaganda to ludicrous extremes. In sum, he alleged to have played the role of a double agent, albeit one without official sanction from British intelligence, so as to poison the German propaganda apparatus by methods that today would be called "disinformation."

To gain the confidence of Viereck, Crowley argued, it was necessary for him to play the role of anti-British activist to the hilt, even to the point of claiming a fictitious Irish ancestry and making a public declaration of Sinn Fein sentiments. Thus it was that *The New York Times* reported, in its July 13, 1915, issue, under the headline "Irish Republic Born in New York Harbor," the pronouncements of "Aleister Crowley, Irishman—poet, philosopher, explorer, a man of mystic mind—the leader of an Irish hope." Crowley, the *Times* reported, had torn up his British passport in a ceremony held in a hired motorboat just off Bedloe's Island, the site of the Statue of Liberty. Crowley then called not merely for Irish independence but for full-scale war against England. In the *Confessions,* he explained that his fiery speech was a parody of the Declaration of Independence, and that the shredded passport was merely an old envelope. "The *New York Times* gave us three columns and Viereck was distinctly friendly."

Extravagant flattery was another means of gaining Viereck's trust. As a fellow poet ten years Viereck's senior, Crowley encouraged Viereck to become the great voice of America. His private views on Viereck, in the *Confessions,* were quite different. Crowley was frequently cruel in his assessments, but seldom as hypocritical as in his portrayal of Viereck, whom he pilloried as being "homosexual at heart—though I believe not so in practice—and conscious of this inferiority, which makes him timid." This alleged homosexuality became the pretext for a sermon by Crowley on the pitfalls of living with so dire a burden:

> The homosexual is comically innocent, and cannot understand the loathing with which the average man regards what to him is a natural impulse. [. . .] But Viereck had learned his lesson. He had learned to deny everything. Even to me, knowing my repu-

tation, totally undeserved as it happens to be, for similar abnormalities, he would admit nothing. This is a most remarkable cir-
cumstance, for the persecution attached to this passion has
created a freemasonry among its devotees which makes them
frank to the point of indiscretion when they think they recognize sympathy in an acquaintance. Bitter must have been
Viereck's initiation that it should have taught him to be so ex-
travagantly cautious; but it fitted him to handle the German
propaganda.

This passage, while addressed to Viereck, reveals the bitterness that underlay Crowley's own concealments. Rather than risk disclosure, he
adopted the persona of a pitying heterosexual to describe the humiliation of being classified amongst the "abnormalities" of society.

While suspecting Viereck of canny concealments, Crowley trusted in
Viereck's naïveté as an editor. He later asserted, as a key refutation of
the charge of treason, that his political writings of this time were so obviously ludicrous as to leave no doubt of his insincerity. This claim has
some merit—but only some. There were a few essays which were blatantly "over the top." These include "The New Parsifal" and "The
Crime of Edith Cavell." In the former piece, Crowley bathetically compared the German Kaiser to Jesus Christ; in the latter, he defended the
brutal murder by the Germans of Cavell, a private British citizen. But
the majority of his essays were not outlandish. In truth, they merged
nicely with the overall tone of *The Fatherland*. Crowley himself acknowledged that "(on the whole) I took few chances of letting the Germans perceive the tongue in my cheek." He also averred that
"Americans do not understand irony at all." But one might forgive them
this incapacity, given subtleties such as this endorsement of *The Fatherland* by Crowley, the "Great Irish Poet," in the August 11, 1915, issue:

> I refuse to take sides in any controversy. I observe dispassion-
> ately, sit in judgment. My own Fatherland is the Sun, and while
> I am traveling on this planet I never forget it. [. . .] I am not
> pro-German. I am pro-human. I have tried to save England from
> her fate by pointing out the elements of rottenness in her, so
> that she may set her house in order [. . .]

This passage—with its veiled reference to the solar creed of Thelema—
matched Crowley's later beliefs as expressed in the *Confessions*: "I am
English, and this in a very special sense, as being the prophet and poet

appointed by the gods to serve her. We do not accuse Isaiah of being unpatriotic because he thunders against Israel. Isaiah's motive is mine."

But the question of his treason or innocence is not decided by the fact that his views included sympathy for Germany. Whether Crowley was sincere in his alleged aim of working as an agent for the British and Americans remains the crux of the matter. Here the evidence weighs more strongly in Crowley's favor.

It must be conceded that Crowley's plan was an absurd one, carried out in isolation by a man with romantic fantasies of espionage and no established contacts with the British and American intelligence communities. When, in 1916, he wrote to Commodore Guy Gaunt, head of British Naval Intelligence in the United States, Gaunt offered Crowley no encouragement to continue with his self-styled espionage plans. Commodore Gaunt—who became Admiral Sir Guy Gaunt—would concur with biographer John Symonds's assessment of Crowley as a "small-time traitor." But then, public disavowal of suspected agents is standard intelligence procedure.

There is, however, firm evidence of at least one link between Crowley and Allied intelligence. This comes in the form of a 1929 letter by Everard Feilding, a prewar admirer of Crowley and a member of British Intelligence who held the rank of lieutenant during World War One. Crowley had contracted Feilding during the war about his plan to spy for the British. By 1929, Crowley and Feilding were no longer in regular communication, but Feilding was willing—at the request of Gerald Yorke—to offer his view of Crowley's actions. As this letter has not been discussed in past biographies of Crowley, it is worth quoting:

> During the time I was a naval censor in the London Press Bureau & afterwards employed on Intelligence work in Egypt, Crowley wrote me from time to time that he was anxious to do work for the British Intelligence & that meanwhile he was doing his best, by various preposterous performances, to represent himself as disaffected & to get in with German connections. [...] I sent his letters to the Intelligence authorities with whom I was personally acquainted, but as this branch of work was in no way my job, I did nothing more beyond forwarding to Crowley a test question, which they suggested, regarding the identity of a certain personage [involved with the pro-German movement in America]. Whether it was to test his knowledge against their own, or because they really wished to know who the personage was, I did not enquire. Anyway, his answer did not, I under-

stand, prove helpful, and, whether for that or other reasons I know not, they declined any direct communication with him.

I can only add that my own personal very strong belief was & is that, whatever other vagaries Crowley may have indulged in, which have caused him to be expelled from two countries as widely different as Italy & France [in 1923 and 1929, respectively], treachery to his country was not one of them.

It would seem that British Intelligence neither completely trusted Crowley nor—more to the point—found him particularly useful. Listen to his account, in the *Confessions,* as to why he failed the test posed him: "I was not going to risk my precarious position asking questions. The official English idea of a secret agent seemed to be that he should act like a newspaper reporter. The result was that the negotiations came to very little, though I turned in reports from time to time." The discipline required of intelligence agents was anathema to Crowley. Small wonder the British chose to do without his services. Crowley did meet with William Jackson, assistant to the Attorney General for the State of New York, on two occasions—in July and October 1918—and was interrogated on the subject of his propaganda efforts. According to a later U.S. Department of Justice summary of those meetings, Crowley "admitted that though he had tried to obtain connection with the British Secret Service, he had been unable to do so." The Department of Justice also stated (whether truthfully or not) that Crowley had never provided it with information during the war. But the fact that he did at least offer his services to the British may explain why, when Crowley did at last return to England in late 1919, he was not prosecuted for treason.

There is one final point to be made concerning Crowley's political stance during the war. While he was most certainly an Englishman at heart, it is reasonable to assume that—had the Germans emerged as victors—Crowley would not have hesitated to use whatever advantages came his way thereby. By the time World War One ended, Crowley and Viereck had parted company, their professional relations over. But in 1936, the two men would again correspond, and Crowley asked Viereck—still the pro-German spokesman in America—to mention *The Book of the Law* to the new German leader, Adolf Hitler, as it could serve as a suitable "philosophical basis for Nazi principles." In the pursuit of political influence for himself and for Thelema—they became one for him—Crowley never hesitated to explore all avenues. Nothing came of this overture, and by the outset of World War Two Crowley was a staunch British patriot—and a close friend of many members of British Intelligence. That story will be told in due course.

In June 1915, Crowley fell deeply in love with Jeanne Robert Foster, a striking beauty who had already made a name for herself on the New York scene as a fashion model (the archetypal "Harrison Fisher girl"), as well as a journalist, editor and poet.

Foster was thirty-six when they met. The fact of her marriage to Matlock Foster, a wealthy insurance agent twenty-five years her senior, seems never to have been a serious barrier. Indeed, it was Foster who early on—so great was her infatuation—was jealous of Crowley's previous marriage. Nor was Crowley's reputation a drawback, for Foster herself had already delved enthusiastically into occultism and theosophy and was eager to learn more.

Upon their first meeting, Foster was in the company of Helen Hollis, a friend and fellow New York journalist. Crowley would have affairs with both women, dubbing them with the theriomorphic names of The Cat and The Snake, drawn from the Egyptian gods Pasht and Apophis. Crowley saw himself, in this period, as passing through the initiation process—rooted in the experiences of daily life—of becoming a Magus. As he later explained, "In the ancient ceremonies of the Egyptians the candidate was confronted or guided on his journey by priests wearing the masks of various animals, the traditional character of each serving to indicate the function of its wearer. Quaint as it sounds, I found myself discovering an almost stupefying physical resemblance to divers symbolic animals in those individuals whose influence on me, during their appointed period, was paramount." These individuals were, by this stage in his life, always women—those who played the Scarlet Woman to his Beast. The Cat and The Snake were the first of these in America.

It was Foster, not Hollis, whom Crowley adored, but the three became entwined in a triangle due to what Crowley viewed as coy erotic hesitancies on Foster's part. When Foster left New York for a time, Crowley arranged an assignation with Hollis, The Snake. A touch of sadism sparked what he described as a twelve-hour "orgy":

> I had unusually pointed canine teeth. I fix a fold of flesh between the two points; and then, beating time with one hand, suddenly snap, thus leaving two neat indentations on the flesh concerned. I have often done this as a demonstration; often as a jest or a psychological experiment, sometimes as an intimation of affec-

tion, but never till then as a callous and cruel insult. Probably I misjudged my own motives. Somehow or other the genuineness and integrity of this lost soul [Hollis] began to appeal to me. I began to contrast her hard bitter cynical disbelief with the soft honied superficial assurance of her rival: before I knew what I was doing, our duel had developed into a death struggle in which my hate and hopelessness strove to swamp themselves in a surge of amorous frenzy.

The spasm swept me away. I no longer remember how we went out and dined, or how we got down to her house. Every nerve in my soul was screaming with implacable pain. Through it all I stuck to my guns; I never forgot that I loved the other woman and all that she stood for.

Crowley fell into an exhausted sleep. When he awoke, he felt himself *"innocent* in a sense more sublime than my imagination can conceive." He proceeded to experience a mystical vision. From an account he set down that same day: "Mentally, I woke into *Pure Love.* This was symbolized by a cube of blue-white light like a diamond of the best quality. [. . .] I cannot describe the quality of the emancipation given by this most wonderful experience. Aum."

As Crowley viewed it, the Magus is "to make his every act an expression of his magical formula." Hollis and Foster, The Snake and The Cat, were, on the magical plane, ordeals designed to test his "magical formula" of Thelema, or Will. With regard to these two, his will was to evade the blandishments of Hollis and to retain his ideal love for Foster, even if she was unworthy of it. Thus he would fulfill the essential paradox of the Magus—to make a lie become truth: "The word of a Magus is always a falsehood. For it is a creative word; there would be no object in uttering it if it merely stated an existing fact in nature. The task of a Magus is to make his word, the expression of his will, come true. It is the most formidable labour that the mind can conceive."

The practical challenges to the romance between Crowley and Foster were formidable in themselves. In early October 1915, Crowley resolved to make a trip to the West Coast, primarily to determine the state of affairs in the North American chapter of the O.T.O., headquartered in Vancouver. Foster was traveling with her husband, who was in poor health and apparently ignorant of the affair even as it was conducted under his nose.

En route, Crowley made a brief stop in Detroit and paid a visit to the Parke Davis chemical plant. The cooperation Crowley received there was, by his account, complete; Parke Davis was "kind enough to interest themselves in my researches in Anhalonium Lewinii [peyote] and made me some special preparations on the lines indicated by my experience which proved greatly superior to previous preparations."

As for the nature of these "researches," an amusing story was told by Louis Wilkinson, a British man of letters who befriended Crowley during these wartime years and would remain a friend and sympathizer—though never a disciple—for the rest of Crowley's life. Crowley, while in New York, hosted anhalonium parties just as he had in London during the heyday of *The Equinox*. In London, Crowley had initiated Katherine Mansfield in the ways of the drug; in New York, the chief literary lion drawn into the experimentation was the famed novelist Theodore Dreiser. As Wilkinson recalled:

> I persuaded Dreiser to come to one [of the anhalonium parties]. He did so with some misgiving. "It will take treble the usual dose to move Dreiser," said Crowley, as he prepared it for him. Dreiser, none the less, drank his glass of "the mixture" at one gulp, with determined bravado. Then he felt a little uneasy. He asked Crowley if there was a good doctor in the neighbourhood, "just in case anything goes wrong." "I don't know about a doctor," said Crowley, "but," he added in a tone of genial reassurance, "there's a first-class undertaker on the corner of Thirty-third Street and Sixth Avenue." Dreiser said nothing for a few moments, then he said, "I don't like that kind of joke, Crowley."

As it happened, Dreiser fared well under the influence of the drug, reciting aloud in prolix detail the visions he witnessed.

Having left Detroit and Parke Davis behind him, Crowley was on board a train on October 12, 1915, his fortieth birthday. As had become his habit on birthdays, Crowley engaged in Sammasati meditation—the technique of analysis of backward-flowing memory learned from Allan Bennett. During this meditation, Crowley felt suddenly compelled to rip the platinum lid off the engraved ring that symbolized his grade of Master of the Temple. The conjunction of these events produced an impact such that Crowley felt he could at last acknowledge himself as a Magus—completely identified with his word of Thelema.

One of his immediate goals was to make the word flesh in a literal sense by begetting a male child. His magical name as Magus was *To Mega Therion* (Greek for "The Great Beast"). Foster was to serve as his Scarlet Woman and produce the son that had been denied him in the past. The undertaking would be magic of the highest order, the mystical union of the sexes. Crowley composed, in the summer and autumn of 1915, a lengthy sequence of poems (as yet unpublished) entitled *The Golden Rose*, which contained his most passionate love poetry since his first years with his wife Rose. In these poems, he addressed her as "Hilarion," the magical name she had chosen for herself (that of a mahatma she had encountered in her Theosophical studies).

But relations worsened between them during the trip out west. Despite a series of Magical Operations, Foster did not become pregnant, although at the time Crowley was convinced that she had. Later, in the *Confessions*, Crowley would remark that "I did not know that I was attempting a physical impossibility." This was a bitter gibe at Foster, who had given birth during the first year of her marriage; the baby was stillborn. More to the point here is Crowley's attitude toward women and childbearing. In an essay of this period, "The Whole Duty of Woman," Crowley was adamant as to the nature of that duty in wartime: *"And let every woman capable of bearing a child consider herself shamed unless she bears one in her womb or at her breast!"* Crowley was not being intentionally humorous here; in his 1917 "Memorandum" written in defense of his propaganda efforts, he cited this essay as stating a serious and patriotic thesis. It surely was not Crowley's intent that his son be borne by Foster to support the war effort. But he believed that childbearing was the essential function of woman, and he was bitter over the failure of Foster to do so.

Together, Crowley and Foster paid a visit to the Vancouver O.T.O. Lodge. Its leader, Charles Robert Stansfeld Jones, was then twenty-nine and already an ardent disciple of Crowley for some years. An Englishman who earned his living as an accountant, Jones had joined the A∴A∴ in London as a Probationer in 1909; he met Crowley briefly during this period, but his primary instructor was J. F. C. Fuller. In 1910, Jones moved to British Columbia while maintaining contact with the London A∴A∴ headquarters. In 1913, he was promoted to the grade of Neophyte, for which he took the magical motto Achad (Hebrew for "one," with the esoteric meaning of cosmic unity). It was under the name of Frater Achad that Jones would ultimately produce writings that marked him as Crowley's most intellectually gifted disciple since Fuller. Jones had also become an O.T.O. VII°, and would ultimately be named, by Reuss, X° Grand Master for North America in 1921. Crowley inspected with approval the Lodge temple that Jones and his fellow members had constructed.

But his central concern was with Foster. At some point during their

West Coast journey, the two lovers quarreled fiercely. Foster returned to New York without him; when Crowley attempted to rejoin her some weeks later, Foster made it clear that the affair was over. The Beast was anguished by her loss, and did not acquiesce without a vicious struggle. The evidence here comes from letters written by the painter John Butler Yeats, the father of the poet, a confidant of Foster, and no admirer of Crowley. Yeats claimed that Foster had broken with Crowley as a result of a disturbing rumor—"to wit, that he had been libelling three distinguished novelists charging them with 'unspeakable vices.'" The form of the alleged libels parallels Crowley's inuendos against Viereck in the *Confessions.* According to Yeats, after Foster left him, Crowley fell to "persecuting her" by:

> sending her husband anonymous letters in which he asserts that she has been living with a wealthy lawyer & that she intends to poison her husband. Once he met her in the street by chance & then & there produced a curious looking knife & said that he would kill her. A crowd gathered & she escaped. He boasts that he is not afraid because John Quinn [to whom this letter by Yeats was addressed] will always find bail for him and protect him. She thinks he is a cocaine fiend. At the very start I had warned her, so that she has never let him get so much as a letter from her. He has some girl with him, and he sent this girl to her with a message to say that she must help him or he would destroy her. The girl wept all the time while giving the message. Mrs. Foster told her politely to go to the devil. *The Government here* and the *English government* are both busy watching him with detectives. The English authorities say he is a spy and that he has been to Canada.

No mention of any of this occurs in the *Confessions.* As for Foster, Crowley could not forget her. Some five years later, in May 1920, he wrote in his diary: "I have not been in love since 1915 [. . .] Did she really 'break my heart'?"

If his heart had been broken, his spirit had not. The next major love affair—or "ordeal," as Crowley termed it—commenced in the spring of 1916. Again the beloved was married, and again she was paired—in Crowley's mind—with a single but less noble woman. And again both women received theriomorphic names: The Monkey and The Owl.

The Monkey was Alice Richardson, an Englishwoman from Yorkshire and the wife of the famous art critic and historian of religion

Ananda K. Coomaraswamy. Under the stage name Ratan Devi, Richardson had made a name for herself as a gifted mezzo-soprano interpreter of traditional East Indian vocal music. Crowley and Devi together performed—beginning in April 1916—a series of sex magic operations at least one of which, on April 15, Crowley found extraordinary. From his diary: "This Operation is the most magnificent in all ways since I can remember. The orgasm was such as to have completely drowned the memory of the [magical] Object [which was to be retained in mind throughout], but after, I found myself saying, *"Namo Shivaya namaha Aum'* [mantra to the Hindu god Shiva, which would indicate that Crowley had identified himself with Shiva and Devi with his divine consort, Shakti]."

Just prior to commencing his affair with Devi, Crowley had also begun sexual operations with The Owl, otherwise known as Gerda Maria von Kothek. Little is known of The Owl beyond Crowley's brief allusions to her as a "German prostitute" and as a "regular Broadway type." The distinction Crowley drew between The Owl and The Monkey was the same as with The Snake and The Cat—that of the base, lustful woman (whom he cannot love) as opposed to the creative female (whom he adores but cannot trust).

As for Coomaraswamy, he too was given a theriomorphic name by Crowley—the only male acquaintance of this time to receive such a distinction. "The Worm," Crowley called him, and went on to accuse him of black magic. Crowley's portrait of Coomaraswamy is laced with malice and racism, and does not conform in the slightest with what is otherwise known of Coomaraswamy. In brief, Crowley alleged that The Worm consented to his wife going off with Crowley as he found her too expensive to care for; that he asked Crowley, during the affair, to procure substitute sex partners for him; and that he crassly decided to take Devi back when she began to enjoy financial success from her performances.

There was one further complicating factor. Crowley and The Monkey had succeeded in accomplishing that which had eluded Crowley and The Cat. Ratan Devi became pregnant by the end of their first month together. In late May, they performed sexual magic for the purpose of assuring a safe pregnancy. But here, Crowley charged, they were frustrated by Coomaraswamy, who in the summer of 1916 persuaded his wife to sail to England, where her other children lived, for the remainder of her confinement. According to Crowley, Coomaraswamy was aware that his wife was subject to extreme sea sickness and intended, by this plan, to cause the premature deaths of his unfaithful wife and the bastard child. In the *Confessions*, Crowley explained that while he suspected the worst, he refused to put pressure on Devi to stay in America. The worst occurred. As Crowley wrote: "The Eurasian's calculations were not far wrong. The voyage caused a miscarriage and she lay between life and death for over six weeks."

As with the death of his first child, which occurred after he left Rose to return to England on her own from India in 1905—Crowley responded to the tragedy by blaming others. The plan for Rose to travel separately was conceived by Crowley. The plan to have Devi sail while pregnant was passively allowed by him. In the first case, he reviled the stupidity of Rose. In the second, the "half-breed" Coomaraswamy was criminally at fault. The racism of Crowley's attacks was blatant and shameless. Coomaraswamy, whose South Asian father was knighted, was born in Ceylon of an English mother and taken to England to live at the age of eight months. He was already, when Crowley met him, one of the most influential art historians of his era. Early on, the two men had fruitful discussions on Buddhist philosophy. But to Crowley he remained "the Eurasian."

In June 1916, Crowley decided that the time had come for a Great Magical Retirement. The person to whom he turned for a suitably secluded location was Evangeline Adams, who would become the most famous writer on astrology in America. The previous year, Adams engaged Crowley to serve as a ghostwriter to produce the bulk of two books that would be published under Adams's name—*Astrology: Your Place in the Sun* (1928) and *Astrology—Your Place Among the Stars* (1930). Crowley's interest in astrology had been growing steadily, and he no doubt welcomed the opportunity to express himself at length on its workings while receiving needed funds from Adams, whose name would sell far more copies of the book than would Crowley's. Later, in the *Confessions*, he charged, with some justice, that Adams was ignorant of her field and had defrauded him of his promised share of the profits. But they were close enough friends in 1916 that Adams allowed Crowley the private use of her cottage on Lake Pasquaney near Bristol, New Hampshire. Crowley stayed on here for four months—from mid-June through mid-October—during which he would perform one of the most singular magical rituals of his career.

Uninhibited drug use was one of the delights of this magical retirement. Heroin was an adjunct stimulus in a number of solitary sex operations. Cocaine and opium were also on hand. But his primary delight came from a relatively recent discovery, ether or ethyl oxide, a pungent anesthetic liquid, the vapors from which he inhaled from a bottle with a long, thin neck. During this summer, Crowley commenced a series of experiments with this drug; the results were ultimately recorded in an essay, "Ethyl Oxide," written in 1923. There, Crowley argued that meditations conducted under the influence of the drug were helpful in ascertaining one's "True Will." Further, he drew the analogy between the ether experiences and sexual orgasm:

> The [ethyl oxide] experimenter will learn to recognize instinctively when he has reached the desired result. It comes as a climax with the force of a revelation. [...] The point is that a genuine 'revelation' exhausts the species of Energy involved for the time being. The parallel case is the occurrence of orgasm in sexual intercourse. A *perfect* orgasm should leave no lust: if one wants to go on, it simply shows that one has failed to collect every element of the personality, and discharge it utterly in a single explosion!

The equivalent of the perfect etheric orgasm was granted to Crowley that summer. The date was August 23. Crowley described it in his diary—just after it happened—as "the Ultimate Samadhi." His later name for it would be the "Star-Sponge Vision," and it remained a joyous touchstone of his spiritual quest:

> I lost consciousness of everything but a universal space in which were innumerable bright points, and I realized this as a physical representation of the universe, in what I may call its essential structure. I exclaimed, 'Nothingness but twinkles!' I concentrated upon this vision, with the result that the void space which had been the principal element of it diminished in importance; space appeared to be ablaze, yet the radiant points were not confused, and I thereupon completed my sentence with the exclamation, 'but what twinkles!'

This later account (in a commentary on *The Book of the Law*), which far exceeded the contemporaneous diary in detail, made no mention of his having taken ether. In his essay "Ethyl Oxide," Crowley referred to the 'revelation' afforded by the drug in single quotes. What ambiguity was thus implied? There is a telling passage in another writing of that summer—a lengthy study entitled *The Gospel According to St. Bernard Shaw*—that establishes the depth of Crowley's hesitancies on this matter.

A mention of the context in which *Gospel* was written is in order.

Crowley had long been fascinated by the career of George Bernard Shaw, who had achieved a status Crowley must have envied: that of a *respected* gadfly of British society. In his preface to his play *Androcles and the Lion* (1913), Shaw argued on behalf of Jesus not as a revealed god but as a wise social philosopher. Crowley was filled with a passion to refute this premise on the grounds that Jesus was not a genuine historical figure.

There is, in *Gospel*, a passage in which Crowley dismissed the claim of drugs to approach the heights of traditional mystical practice:

> But why should we talk of drugs? They are only counterfeit notes, or at best the Fiat notes of a discredited government, and we are seeking gold.
> This pure gold is ours for the asking; its name is mysticism.
> We may begin by reassuring ourselves. The gold is really in the vaults of the Treasury. [. . .] and the chief reason why we should not burglariously use such skeleton keys as morphia is that by so doing we are likely to hamper the lock.

Crowley drew heavily, in his attacks on the historicity of Jesus in *Gospel*, on the findings of what was then the supreme scholarly work in comparative religion, the multi-volume *Golden Bough* of Sir J. G. Frazer. Indeed, the influence of Frazer, whom Crowley was reading during this summer, was so strong that in August–September 1916 he dashed off a series of eight stories—six of which would be published in *The International*—entitled *Golden Twigs*, to underscore his debt.

But the influence of Frazer went still further. The structure of the central ritual conducted by Crowley during this Retirement came from Frazer, whom Crowley paraphrased in *Gospel* as to the spiritual framework of the Crucifixion: "The entire symbolism of the Jesus who died and rose again is astrological and mystic in its minutest points. [. . .] not at all the record of what happened to any one man, but of what happens to all men."

Crowley borrowed from this Crucifixion sequence for his "ceremony of the assumption of the curse of the Grade of Magus." The purpose of this ceremony stemmed from a psychological crisis now reaching desperate proportions within Crowley—his sense that he did not, in his daily self, resemble that which he understood to be the nature of the attained Magus. From his diary entry for July 12, 1916:

> There is nothing in me that corresponds at all to the grade. There is utter impotence on all planes. [. . .] I do not in the least

fail to understand the grade; I am simply unable to act. It is no good making up my mind to do anything material; for I have no means. But this would vanish if I could make up my mind. I am as it were inhibited from everything. I am tempted for example to crucify a toad, or copulate with a duck, sheep, or goat, or set a house on fire or murder someone with the idea—a perfectly good magical idea, of course—that some supreme violation of all the laws of my being would break down my Karma or dissolve the spell that seems to bind me. And I cannot do it, because (chiefly) I have no faith that it would actually do so.

That a Magus must break the bonds of karma—burn away his egoistic consciousness in the "urn" of initiation—was basic to Crowley's conception of the grade. Amongst these bonds was the Christian childhood that he would try—once again—to put to rest.

On July 17, Crowley commenced his ceremony, later recorded by him as *Liber LXX* (a number kabbalistically linked to the Devil trump of the Tarot deck). It consisted of seven stages performed in sequence from 2 A.M. to 9:45 P.M. First, in the dead of night, came the capture of the frog, who embodied both Mercury the Snake of wisdom and the "mystery of conception" as formulated in silence as an affirmation of one's will. Then followed the ritual birth, baptism, worship, trial, crucifixion, resurrection, and ascension of the frog. The trial was the most dramatic portion of the rite, as it portrayed the remembered pain of Crowley's childhood:

> Night being fallen, thou shalt arrest the frog, and accuse him of blasphemy, and so forth in these words:
>
> Do what thou wilt shall be the whole of the Law. Lo, Jesus of Nazareth, how thou art taken in my snare. All my life long thou hast plagued me and affronted me. In thy name—with all other free souls in Christendom—I have been tortured in my boyhood; all delights have been forbidden unto me, and that which is owed to me they pay not—in thy name. Now at last I have thee; the Slave-God is in the power of the Lord of Freedom. [. . .] Give thou place to me, O Jesus; thine aeon is passed; the Age of Horus is arisen by the Master the Great Beast that is a man; and his number is Six hundred and threescore and six. Love is the law, love under will.
>
> I *To Mega Therion* therefore condemn thee Jesus the Slave-God to be mocked and spat upon and scourged and then crucified.

The sentence was then executed, with the legs of the animal eaten to confirm the magical link between Magus and frog—which, invested with the spirit of Jesus, now served as a willing familiar. The rest of the body was burned to signify the end of the Old Aeon. This was one of the rare magical occasions when Crowley sacrificed a living creature. As his July 12 diary entry indicated, this went strongly against his conscious convictions.

Shortly after this ritual, Crowley received a telegram from Jones in Vancouver, who claimed that on June 21 he had passed beyond the stage of a Babe of the Abyss and emerged as an 8°=3□ Master of the Temple. His motto for this grade embodied his new mystical perspective: *Unus in Omnia, Omnia in Unum* (One in All, All in One). Crowley was delighted, albeit for two reasons having more to do with himself than with Jones. First, it proved the remarkable efficacy of the A∴A∴—how else could Jones have attained so much since becoming a Neophyte a mere seven years earlier? Second, it confirmed that operations with Jeanne Foster the previous autumn—nine months earlier—had indeed borne him a son. More precisely, Jones was a "Magical Son," one who had absorbed, by way of etheric or astral influence, the spiritual intent of those operations. Crowley wrote to Jones to confirm him in his new grade.

In October, the Beast returned to New York. He was still contributing to *The Fatherland*, but otherwise had few practical prospects. In December, he traveled to New Orleans, one of the few American cities for which he held a fondness. A more practical reason for heading south was to renew contact again with Keasbey, a history professor at the University of Texas. Keasbey had paid Crowley a visit at Lake Pasquaney in September; the reason, according to Crowley, was that Keasbey admired Crowley's writings and wanted to meet the man. Whether Crowley went to Austin to visit Keasbey is unclear; what is plain is that relations between them broke down. As we shall see, the bad blood between them would cost Crowley dearly before his time in America was over.

Crowley remained in New Orleans through the winter of 1917. It was a time marked by prolific writing strangely coupled with extreme doubt over his magical vocation. With the aim (which proved futile) of achieving a commercial success, Crowley created a detective, Simon Iff, whose exploits he chronicled in six stories under the title *The Scrutinies of Simon Iff;* these were published serially in *The International* from September 1917 through February 1918. (Over the next year, Crowley wrote over a dozen more Iff stories, none of which found an immediate publisher.)

Crowley carried the figure of Iff into a novel written during this same New Orleans winter, in which Iff shed his status as a detective and emerged as a mystic outright. The novel, *Moonchild*, would eventually be published in 1929. The original title of the novel, *The Butterfly Net*, refers to the capture of the soul (the butterfly) by the means of ritual magic (the net). In one sense, *Moonchild* is a literary response to Somerset Maugham, who had attempted the same basic theme in *The Magician* some ten years earlier. But the novel is also very much a product of Crowley's World War One years insofar as its central theme—the production of a homunculus or magical child—had become an obsession at this time. Its account of the war includes episodes of masterful spying for the Allied cause by one Cyril Grey, a dapper and brilliant magician who is a younger fantasy projection of Crowley. Grey is ultimately made an Officer of the Legion of Honour by a grateful British army—in stark contrast to Crowley's real status as an outsider suspected of treason. The evil counterpart to Grey, one Douglas, is based on Crowley's old Chief, Mathers. Douglas is portrayed not only as a black magician (whom Grey bests in magical warfare) but also as a traitor to England. What gives the portrait an especially uneasy twist is that Mathers served the British cause during the war, establishing a center to train volunteers in first-aid skills. Crowley's fictional projection of treason onto Mathers stands as a willed effort to wish upon one's enemy that which is tormenting oneself.

Back in September 1914, Crowley had composed—as his secret instruction for the IX° of the O.T.O., an essay-length instruction entitled "On the Homunculus." Here is set forth the essential theory around which the events of *Moonchild* are constructed. Crowley adopted the traditional esoteric view that the fetus is without a soul during its first three months in the womb. During this period, he deemed it magically possible to induce the incarnation of a nonhuman being—an elemental or planetary spirit—that embodied a quality such as eloquence or martial courage. The ritual couple would have to engage in sexual magic at astrologically favorable times until impregnation was achieved. If successful, the birth would produce a human form with formidable power and knowledge that would be dependent upon and subservient to the magician, as a human is to God. As Crowley later stressed, to achieve such a feat once in a lifetime would be remarkable, and to achieve it twice would mark one as a man who came along once in 100,000 years. Crowley longed to be such a man.

In *Moonchild*, Cyril Grey was hindered both by the magical opposition of Douglas and the flitting inconstancy of his magical consort, Lisa la Giuffria, based on Crowley's prewar lover, Mary d'Este Sturges. In a similar manner, Jeanne Foster had served to block Crowley's ambition in America. But the emergence of Jones as a magical son offered reassurance. *Moonchild* was written to affirm Crowley's hope that still greater feats could be achieved by way of the Royal Art of sexual magic.

His outlook on his prophetic vocation continued to fluctuate, however. Early on in his stay in New Orleans, Crowley felt himself granted the "Beautific Vision" of mystical tradition—"the archetypal idea of beauty and harmony." But the effect did not linger. As Crowley later wrote of his mood at this time: "Hope died in my heart. There was not one glimmer of light on the horizon anywhere. It seemed to me an obscene mockery to be called a Magus. I must have been afflicted by 'lust of result'; at least it came to this, that I felt that I could not go on with my work." Indeed, for a brief time Crowley committed what he termed "spiritual suicide"—a renunciation of his role as Magus. What drove Crowley back to this task was no sudden miracle, but rather a painful realization that he was fit for nothing else: "I found myself, like Othello, with my occupation gone. I might not be able to perform the task of a Magus, but there was certainly nothing else for me to do."

Late in March, while in Florida, Crowley received troubling news from George Cowie, his O.T.O. treasurer in London. Concerns raised over Crowley's articles in *The Fatherland* had led to a police raid on the London headquarters; the membership, never a large one, was dispersed by the threat of being publicly associated with a treasonous leader. Crowley's career in counterespionage was, in any event, about to end. On April 6, the United States declared war on Germany—an act which, Crowley felt, crowned his propaganda efforts with success. But he continued to write for Viereck for two reasons: the money and the outlet for his work.

In New York, Crowley received a second dose of troubling news from England—his mother, Emily, had died. His diary entry reveals a tone that is surprising for its sheer normality—that of a son grieved by the loss: "Had news of my mother's death. Two nights before news had dream that she was dead, with a feeling of extreme distress. The same happened two nights before I had news of my father's death. I had often dreamed that my mother had died, but never with that helpless lonely feeling." The estate of Emily Crowley was placed into a settlement trust; the majority of the funds went to his former wife Rose and their daughter, Lola Zaza. But Crowley received an annual sum of roughly £300, doled out in weekly installments. It was not enough for Crowley to live on, but it did serve as a financial buffer. As Gerald Yorke later observed of Crowley, "There is much exaggeration about his complete lack of money and about his extravagance." Crowley could make do when he had to, and the trust was his means of so doing.

A further buttress to Crowley's finances came in July when Viereck named Crowley the acting editor of *The International*. Unlike *The Fatherland*, this sister publication was primarily an arts journal with vaguely avant-garde sympathies. Viereck—beset by the declining circulation of *The Fatherland*—turned *The International* over to Crowley largely out of expediency. Crowley was willing to work for a mere twenty dollars per week; and he could, by himself, virtually fill the pages of *The International* on a monthly basis, minimizing the need to pay outside contributors. Crowley now had—for the first time since *The Equinox*—an unimpeded outlet for his works. To mask his omnipresence, he employed an array of pseudonyms for his contributions, which ranged from fiction to poems to reviews to ornate essays on magic and the New Aeon. Meanwhile, Viereck was shopping the magazine around to potential buyers.

Crowley would have been delighted to buy, but it was out of the question. Cowie, in London, had informed Crowley in a series of letters that the O.T.O. treasury was tapped (there was no more cash to be wrung from the mortgaged Boleskine House) and that Crowley had been selfish in his demands for support and should instead devise an income of his own. Relations between them soon came to an end; Cowie had lost a master, and Crowley had lost a loyal friend. The last vestige of a formal O.T.O. organization in England had come to an end.

But there were compensations. After a relative dry spell that had lasted since his break with Ratan Devi, Crowley enjoyed a series of romantic attachments in the late summer of 1917 and on into the following year. In August, he met a young woman, Anna Catherine Miller, whom he named The Dog, based on her physical and magical correspondence to Anubis, the dog-headed Egyptian god of the dead. One might speculate that Miller seemed, to Crowley, a guide through the perils of dying to oneself that accompanied the Magus grade. But Crowley was prosaic in his account of her: "She was a Pennsylvania Dutch girl, the only member of her family not actually insane. We joined forces and took a furnished apartment in a corner house on Central Park West near its northern limit at 110th Street." Early in October, Crowley moved to a studio on West 9th Street and—as was his romantic *modus operandi*—took up with a friend of Miller who would prove to be a far more serious love.

Her name was Roddie Minor. Crowley dubbed her alternately Eve,

Soror Ahitha and, most prominently, The Camel, because, in magical terms, "such a journey as I was now about to undertake required an animal of greater strength and size than the dog. To take me to the next oasis I required a camel [. . .]" Minor was married but living apart from her husband, and was employed as a chemist. Crowley described her ambiguously as "a near artist of German extraction. She was physically a magnificent animal, with a man's brain well stocked with general knowledge and a special comprehension of chemistry and pharmacy." This comprehension included a fondness for drug intake that suited Crowley well. As for her "man's brain," this also was to his liking—" for some months everything went as smoothly as if she had been really a man." A diary entry of January 7, 1918, illustrates Crowley's tendency to measure his spiritual progress by his ability to overcome shame and to exult in the power of sexuality:

> I now do all those things which voluptuaries do, with equal or greater enthusiasm and power; but always for an Ulterior End. In this matter I am reproached by that whore of niggers and dogs [Roddie Minor], with whom I am now living in much worse than adultery; for she exhorts me to the Way of the Tao. But is not this for me perhaps That Way, that I should always follow Art and the Salvation of the World? Am not I Saint Edward, the Warden, and Alexander, Helper of Men?

The phrase "whore of niggers and dogs" was less an attack upon Minor than a deliberate heightening of the foul—and hence, in Crowley's view, spiritually efficacious—nature of the desires he now indulged. That Minor was a "whore" was part and parcel of her ascension to the role of Scarlet Woman, a role which she cherished while she was with Crowley. The "dog" was Miller, who still engaged in sexual magic with Crowley early in 1918. As for the "nigger," this was Walter Gray, an African-American musician and a friend of Minor who became, during this time, a frequent partner of Crowley in XI° homosexual operations.

During this period, Crowley experienced his longest continuous communication with a denizen of an astral or unearthly realm. As always in such cases, Crowley required a psychic medium of some kind to sustain contact. Now, through the winter and spring of 1918, there was Roddie Minor and her visions of the spirit-being Amalantrah. As the months went on, there were a number of other women who took part in the invocations of Amalantrah; so too did Walter Gray. But Minor remained the primary seer.

It was Minor who first revealed this startling new spirit-being, whom she named, at first, "The Wizard." On the night of January 14, 1918, while smoking opium and lying on a mattress on the floor of their apartment, she began to experience visions. Crowley professed to be annoyed. But a mention by Minor of "an egg under a palm tree" roused him to attention, as it had been Abuldiz, some six years earlier, who had instructed Crowley to go to the desert to find just such a sight. Crowley took up the scent, and the Amalantrah Working, as he called it, was underway.

Minor kept a magical record for several months. The typical means of invocation was through sexual magic, often performed under the influence of drugs. The description of the Wizard Amalantrah recorded by Minor resembles Crowley's mystic detective Simon Iff; both are elderly and wise, and both take recourse in the wisdom of the East. On the astral plane, Minor approached the Wizard: "I asked who I was and he said 'Part of the Tao.'"

Minor was the primary Scarlet Woman during the first three months. But by March her role as consort to the Beast was threatened by new passions on Crowley's part, most notably for Eva Tanguay, then the preeminent female star of the vaudeville circuit. Tanguay was known as "The 'I Don't Care' Girl" after one of her trademark songs. She was a fearlessly sensuous and outlandish stage performer, employing elaborate costume changes and performing numbers such as Salomé's dance of the seven veils. Amongst her many reputed lovers was the African-American heavyweight champion Jack Johnson. And for a very brief time, she and Crowley were lovers, and Crowley—overtaken with passion—yearned to marry her.

The ends of the affairs with Tanguay and the others are all equally veiled in mystery. One of the goals of the Amalantrah Working was to determine the proper course of relations with these women. But this proved beyond Crowley's powers: "I doubt whether I trusted the Wizard as I should have done."

The reason for the end of Crowley's relationship with *The International* is far easier to determine. In the spring of 1918, Viereck sold that magazine to Crowley's former admirer, Professor Keasbey. Thereafter, Crowley was *persona non grata*. *The International* did not survive long under Keasbey's management, but the sudden expulsion from its offices stung Crowley to the quick. He weathered the loss of salary through a combination of family trust payments and sporadic assistance from Minor and the other women passing through his life.

During the same period as the Amalantrah Working, Crowley was at work on a volume that stands as one of his most striking literary and magical achievements: *Liber Aleph, the Book of Wisdom or Folly* (first published posthumously in 1962). *Liber Aleph* was written primarily as a text of instruction to his "magical son," Jones. The Hebrew letter *aleph* is a Tarot attribution of the Fool, and *Liber Aleph*, like *The Book of Lies* before it, is a series of compressed and paradoxical observations on the elusive nature of Wisdom that seem as mere Folly to the uninitiated. The book certainly has its weaknesses, first and foremost of which is its blatant and repetitive misogyny. But there are also, within it, singular examples of clarity and elegant concision, such as the second chapter— *"De Arte Kabbalistica"* ("On the Art of the Qabalah"). Nowhere did he express more aptly the nature and purpose of kabbalah from the perspective of the magical tradition—as a means of framing correspondences of thought and tendencies of mind:

> Do thou study most constantly, my Son, in the Art of the Holy Qabalah. Know that herein the Relations between Numbers, though they be mighty in Power and prodigal of Knowledge, are but lesser Things. For the Work is to reduce all other Conceptions to these of Number, because thus thou wilt lay bare the very Structure of thy Mind, whose rule is Necessity rather than Prejudice. Not until the Universe is thus laid naked before thee canst thou truly anatomize it.

Crowley's passionate affair with Roddie Minor came to a friendly end by the summer of 1918, though they continued now and then to be lovers. In its aftermath, Crowley deemed himself ready for another Great Magical Retirement. Crowley's budget-conscious selection of a retirement site was Esopus Island, a small uninhabited isle far up the Hudson River in Dutchess County. Crowley resolved to make his way there by the strenuous means of paddling upstream in a canoe fitted with a sail. His own ready funds were limited, but a number of friends came to the rescue. One of these was William Seabrook, a then-famous journalist. Seabrook, fascinated both by the occult and by Crowley the man, described the latter's flamboyant departure up the Hudson (the first part of the journey by a ferry that would transport Crowley and his canoe out of the city):

> The 'provisions' looked suspicious, and since we'd paid for them, we decided to inspect them. They consisted of fifty gallons of red paint, three big house-painter's brushes, and a heavy coil of

rope. [. . .] He'd blown every cent for the red paint. He had nothing in his pockets except the ticket for the trip up the river.

"What are you going to eat, for crying out loud?" we asked, and he replied, in his heaviest pontifical manner,

"My children, I am going to Esopus Island, and I will be fed as Elijah was fed by the ravens."

For his first weekend on the island, Minor came to visit, bringing along needed food supplies.

What became of the red paint and how did Crowley feed himself? The answers are intertwined. Shortly after arrival, Crowley decided upon a project to proclaim the word of Thelema, which might today be viewed as a controversial work of "environmental art." As Crowley described it, "On both the east and west shores of the island are wide steep cliffs of smooth rock, obviously provided by Providence for my convenience in proclaiming the Law. I devoted a couple of days of painting 'Do what thou wilt' on both banks for the benefit of passing steamers." According to Seabrook, this caught the attention of the farmer residents of the area. Curiosity aroused, they visited the island to meet its new resident and to bring gifts of eggs, milk and corn.

Jones also came to see his master for a time, though the nature of the magical work they performed together remains a mystery. Jones—some thirty years later—destroyed the bulk of Crowley's magical diary of that time, which had fallen into Jones's possession. Shortly after leaving the island, Jones sent Crowley a letter announcing his decision (for what would prove to be a brief period) to resign from the O.T.O. According to Jones, Crowley subsequently waged magical warfare against Jones's wife, whom Crowley blamed for inducing the resignation. Jones must have come to know of this warfare only at a later date, else it is difficult to conceive how the two men resumed a close magical alliance after Crowley's return to New York in mid-September, as was the case.

There were two primary magical accomplishments during this retirement. The first was a prolonged meditation, during August, by means of the Sammasati backward memory technique. The result was a recall, by Crowley, of a chain of past lives that had progressed karmically to his present status as Magus and prophet. This was not the first occasion on which Crowley had pondered his prior lives. As we have seen, he had already decided upon certain prior incarnations: the ancient Egyptian priest Ankh-af-na-Khonsu, the Grecian sacred prostitute Astarte (relived during the 1914 Paris Working), the Elizabethan scryer Edward Kelly, and the nineteenth-century magus Eliphas Levi. But on Esopus

Island, Crowley experienced intense meditative visions—from his "Magical Memory" —that revealed a course of highly wayward dramatic existences from over two millennia. Whether he employed drugs during these meditations is not known, but it seems likely.

Crowley never argued for the truth of these visions, nor did he reject the possibility of their truth. As he later wrote, "I refuse to assert any theory of what this really means. All memory is a re-awakening of ancient impressions. What I was really doing was penetrating to the deeper layers of my unconscious self."

As Crowley was remembering *backwards*, the lives he saw will be recounted in that order. Just prior to his own birth he was Levi. Before Levi, he was Count Cagliostro, born Giuseppe Balsamo, a Sicilian peasant who rose to become one of the most controversial figures of the eighteenth century, a self-proclaimed master of magic with rumored ties to radical French Freemasonry, who died in Rome, a prisoner of the Inquisition. Prior to his time as Cagliostro, Crowley passed through a rather squalid series of four incarnations. The first of these is described in his diary entry for August 24, 1918:

> The incarnation before Cagliostro is very obscure. It seems to have been the result of some serious magical error connected to the grade of Adeptus Major. I remember myself as a dark, pallid pimply youth with hollow eyes purple-ringed, a sparse beardlet, a head too big for the body, fleshless, without strength, nervous almost to insanity, a haunted look.
> I hanged myself at the age of 26–28. [. . .]

Before this, he was Heinrich von Dorn, an incarnation which Crowley regarded as "very black-magical, in an entirely futile way. It is a tale of grimoires and vain evil rites, of pacts at which Satan mocked, and crimes unworthy even of witches." Prior to this he was Father Ivan, a soldier in religious wars before joining a militant order of monks somewhere in southeastern Europe. Father Ivan served nominally as the librarian for these monks; his knowledge of Greek was immense and he wrote books on historical subjects. But his real interests lay elsewhere—in the furthering of unnamed political intrigues and the practice of fearsome magical rites: "My vices were sinister, not to be described, though I remember many details. I delighted in cruelty, especially towards women. I repeatedly, even habitually, invoked 'The Devil'." Prior to this, Crowley lived under a name he could not recall. But his character traits remained vivid:

I was really more girl than boy, an hermaphrodite dreadfully malformed. I was rich and well-born; I remember my dark blue velvet breeches and lace cape and feathered hat. My hair was a shock of fawn. I was thin, small, tuberculous, with some spinal curvature, very slight. I had a fierce temper, and was a hater of mankind. I died of syphilis contracted from a German Ritter, who raped me. [. . .] All these messes seem to have been expiations of [Edward] Kelly's blunder in not accepting the Law which was shadowed forth to him.

Crowley ultimately plotted out the course of existences that preceded Kelly. During the high Renaissance he was Alexander Borgia, who in 1492 became Pope Alexander VI and thereafter reigned as a supremely decadent pontiff—accusations of murder and incest swirling about him—until his death in 1503. Crowley's own assessment of his reign as Alexander VI was dismissive. His task had been "to bring oriental wisdom to Europe and to restore paganism in a purer form." But he deemed himself to have "failed in my task of crowning the Renaissance, through not being wholly purified in my personal character."

There is a sizable gap between the Borgia pope and a nameless but momentous incarnation just before the birth of Mohammed. In this life, Crowley recalled being "present at a Council of Masters. The critical question was the policy to be adopted in order to help humanity. A small minority, including myself, was hot for positive action; definite movements were to be made; in particular, the mysteries were to be revealed. The majority, especially the Asiatic Masters, refused even to discuss the proposal. They contemptuously refrained from voting, as if to say, 'Let the youngsters learn their lesson.'" The result was a series of incarnations in which the activist wing, as it were, was given its chance—with mixed results. Crowley himself was somehow involved in the tragic downfall of the Templars.

There is one more distant incarnation to tell. In the time of Lao Tzu—roughly the sixth century B.C.—Crowley lived as Ko Hsuen, a disciple of the great Chinese Taoist master. The *Khing Kang King*, known as the Classic of Purity, was the work of Ko Hsuen; fittingly, then, Crowley chose to cast it, from an extant translation, into English verse. The Wizard Amalantrah, associated with the Way of the Tao, proved a useful collaborator for a second translation—of the *Tao Te Ching*—that Crowley completed on Esopus Island. Just how Amalantrah was summoned "in almost daily communion" is unclear. Crowley's translation, in prose, was based on the well-known version by scholar James Legge; but

Crowley possessed the unique advantage of having Amalantrah exhibit to him "a codex of the original, which conveyed to me with absolute certitude the exact significance of the text."

In Crowley's view, all these past lives formed a sequence that had climaxed with his own birth. Certainly he cannot be accused of having overlooked unflattering prior incarnations. Nor can it be denied that there is a certain affinity between the personages Crowley cites—in particular, Borgia, Kelly, Cagliostro, and Levi—and himself.

In a June 1948 letter, Jones, who may have been present on Esopus Island during Crowley's past-life visions, offered his own commentary on them. Jones was by then a disgruntled ex-disciple. Nonetheless, his views are likely to echo the suspicions of many:

> Now I ask you this: If reincarnation be a true theory and these "memories" [be] of actual past lives or if these "memories" be but the outcropping of suppressed subconscious conditions acquired during his present life up till 1918—in either case, or any other supposition—does a man with this "background" (once the camouflage is off) appear worthy to be considered as a genuine Logos or Buddha, the true Leader of Humanity and representative on earth of The Sun. Or have we a genius duped and let down by dark forces?

It is noteworthy that Jones himself—in the aftermath of Crowley's death—sought to be considered a Logos, and thus opened himself to the same objections as he had raised against Crowley.

There was, however, one final magical attainment in store for Crowley prior to his departure from Esopus Island. On September 5, Crowley recorded in his diary, and later transcribed in the *Confessions* (leaving open the possibility of later editing), the "climax" of the retirement—a "Samadhi" realization he termed a "Vision of Jupiter" that occurred during his afternoon Sammasati meditation: "In a single instant I had the Key to the whole of the Chinese wisdom. In the light—momentary glimpse though it was—of this truth, all systems of religion and philosophy became absolutely puerile. Even the Law appears no more than a curious incident. I remain absolutely bewildered, blinded, knowing what blasting image lies in this shrine. It baffles me to understand how my brother Magi, knowing this, ever went on." Crowley offered this tentative summation—"I obtained a reconciliation of two contraries of which 'There is a discrimination between good and evil' is one." The second contrary, of course, would have denied the existence of any such discrimination. Crowley had come to see the ultimate limitation of all conceptions, including his own Law of Thelema. For a brief moment, not even his role as prophet of the New Aeon mattered. Small wonder that he was so shaken.

Crowley righted himself by the time he returned to New York. His friend Seabrook recalled Crowley's offer to prove that he had gained in magical power from his Retirement. They took a walk through midtown Manhattan on a course set by Seabrook. This led them to Fifth Avenue and the New York Public Library. Here Crowley bade Seabrook be silent and watch. As Seabrook described it:

> Ahead of us was strolling a tall, prosperous-looking gentleman of leisure, and Crowley, silent as a cat, fell into step immediately behind him. Their footfalls began to synchronize, and then I observed that Crowley, who generally held himself pompously erect and had a tendency to strut, had dropped his shoulders, thrust his head forward a little, like the man's in front, [and] had begun to swing his arms in perfect synchronization—now so perfect that he was like a moving shadow or astral ghost of the other.
>
> As we neared the end of the block, A.C., in taking a step forward, let both his knees buckle suddenly under him, so that he dropped, caught himself on his haunches, and was immediately erect again, strolling.
>
> The man in front of us fell as if his legs had been shot out from under him . . . and was sprawling. We helped him up, as a crowd gathered. He was unhurt. He thanked us, and looked for a banana peel.

Seabrook considered three explanations: (1) a prearranged confederate to take the pratfall; (2) unconscious identification, by way of the sound of footsteps, between the walking rhythms of Crowley and the man which, when suddenly broken, caused the fall; and (3) that Crowley possessed "supernormal powers." Seabrook declared himself dissatisfied with all three, and here we also must leave the matter.

Jones now rejoined Crowley, who had relocated, in the last months of 1918, to an apartment at 1 University Place on Washington Square. During the ensuing winter, they traveled together to Detroit with two primary goals. The first was to forge an alliance with a group of Masons who resided there; that effort was a failure. But the journey did result in one tangible success. After five years of silence (the silence constituting an unwritten second volume), the first number of volume three of *The Equinox* was published on March 21, 1919, the time of the spring equinox. (This third volume is often called the *Blue Equinox* due to its blue cover binding.) Its limited publication was made possible by the owner of a Detroit printing company, Albert Ryerson, who volunteered the costs.

But the bulk of the *Blue Equinox* was devoted to acquainting unfamiliar readers with the teachings of Thelema. There was also a presentation, written by Crowley, of the life and attainments of Jones (under his magical name *Frater Unus in Omnibus*), entitled *Liber CLXV: A Master of the Temple*. As Hymenaeus Beta has observed, "Crowley was sparing no effort to secure his son's future as a spiritual teacher."

But Jones had a sizable surprise in store for his father. During his time with Crowley in autumn 1918, Jones had begun to sense within himself a major kabbalistic insight that might cast light upon the mysteries of *The Book of the Law*. This insight he did not communicate to Crowley, even though, in November 1918, he set it down in an essay entitled (in the manner of the master) *Liber 31*. After the troubled times in Detroit, Jones moved to Chicago for a time and then returned to his wife in Vancouver. From here, in early September 1919, Jones at last sent the text of *Liber 31* to Crowley. The key discovery may be summarized briefly as follows: The Hebrew words for "God" [AL, the transliteration of the Hebrew letters *aleph* and *lamed*] and for "not" or "negation" [LA, the same two Hebrew letters reversed] both add up, by gematria, to thirty-one. This mutual identity reveals an ultimate mystery—that God, or any conception of life, is *and* is not. Surmounting the paradoxes of reason is essential to final attainment.

Upon reading *Liber 31*, Crowley became convinced that Jones was more than the "magical son" produced by his sexual operations with Jeanne Foster in October 1915. He now recognized Jones as the "child" prophesied by the *Book* itself (in III: 47)—a child who would unlock "mysteries that no Beast shall divine." The verse stressed that "It shall be his child & that strangely." Jones seemed perfectly to fulfill this. Crowley was elated and communicated this in a September 9 postcard to Jones. But Jones, in turn, was beginning to suspect (as he explained in a September 26, 1919, letter to Crowley) that his realization had to do with Kether, the Crown of the kabbalistic Tree of Life; this would make Jones an Ipsissimus, of the A∴A∴ grade of 10°=1□—the only possible higher grade from that of Crowley the Magus. Crowley would ignore hints in this direction from Jones, whom he never again saw in person. With the increasing assumption of magical authority by the "child," the seeds of dissension between the two men were sown. Within a few years, they would fully blossom.

Parallel in time to these developments with Jones was the emergence, in New York, of a new Scarlet Woman. Her name was Leah Hirsig. She was thirty-five when she and Crowley met, a teacher at Public School No. 40 in the Bronx, and the mother of an infant son named Hansi (Crowley's pet name for him would be "Dionysus") who had been born out of wedlock; the father had disappeared abruptly from her life. Hirsig was trying to better her lot by attending a series of lectures on law at New York University. To say the least, her plans were changed when she linked herself with Aleister Crowley. For over seven years, she would remain with him—as lover, magical consort, confidante, and aide de camp in the battles to establish the Law of Thelema in the world. Never before Hirsig—and never after her—would a Scarlet Woman play as deeply fundamental a role in the life of the Beast.

They were first introduced through Leah's sister, Alma Hirsig. Alma was intensely interested in the occult, and would go on—in the 1920s—to become a disciple of a master named Pierre Bernard, who called himself "Oom the Omnipotent" and taught the members of his "Secret Order of Tantricks" a form of sexual magic. Alma served for a time as the "High Priestess of Oom" but later recanted and wrote, under the pseudonym Marion Dockerill, *My Life in a Love Cult: A Warning to All Young Girls* (1928). There are, of course, obvious parallels in the paths of Alma as High Priestess and Leah as Scarlet Woman. There may have been a contributory cause in the shared pattern of their upbringing, which included a physically abusive alcoholic father. The mother alone cared for nine children (six sisters, three brothers), ultimately fleeing with them to America to escape her husband's tyranny. They settled in the Bronx, where both Alma and Leah came of age.

In the spring of 1918, Alma called on Crowley at his one-room studio at 1 University Place, bringing along her younger sister, Leah. On display for their viewing was a large triptych screen painted by Crowley himself—"my first attempt at painting in oil. The design was symbolic of the three principles, Sun, Moon and Agni (fire), of the Hindus." These principles may also be viewed as depicting the formula and result of Crowley's sexual magic. Crowley had begun, in the later years of the war, to devote himself seriously to painting, a discipline in which he had no formal training. He may have been encouraged here by a friend and disciple, Leon Kennedy, a painter in whose New York studio Crowley had lived for a time (after returning from New Orleans) in 1917. The frontispiece to the *Blue Equinox* is a painting by Kennedy—an idealized portrait of Crowley the Master in meditation. In furtherance of his new artistic career, Crowley placed an advertisement in a New York newspaper seeking highly particular types of models (thus showing the influence of British occult artist Austin Osman Spare, who often portrayed grotesques): "WANTED—DWARFS, Hunchbacks, Tattoed Women, Harrison Fisher Girls [of whom his former lover Jeanne Foster was the archetype], Freaks of All Sorts, Coloured Women, only if exceptionally ugly or deformed, to pose for artist."

The ostensible purpose of this first visit by the Hirsig sisters to Crowley's studio was for Alma to receive his advice on the proper choice of occult studies. But the meeting soon took a different turn. Here is Crowley's account:

> The 'little sister' reminded me of Solomon's friend, for she had no breasts. She was tall and strangely thin, with luminous eyes, a wedge-like face, a poignant sadness and a sublime simplicity. She radiated an indefinable sweetness. Without wasting time on words, I began to kiss her. It was sheer instinct. She shared it and equalled my ardour. We continued with occasional interruptions, such as politeness required, to answer her sister in the rare intervals when she got out of breath.

Despite this erotically auspicious first encounter, some nine months would pass before Crowley and Leah Hirsig met again. In early January 1919, the Hirsig sisters paid a return call on Crowley. Again, he was distracted from the subject at hand: "While we talked, I took off her [Leah's] clothes and asked her to come and pose for me when she felt inclined."

On January 11, Leah Hirsig returned to Crowley's studio—this time on her own. Crowley's explanation for her visit in the *Confessions*, brief as it is, reveals the complex interweaving of passion, dependence, shame, and contempt that would mark his feelings for Hirsig throughout their years together: "(She swears I telephoned to ask her and perhaps I did. I have my moments of imbecile impulse. I undressed her again, but this time not with impunity.) To appease conscience I proceeded to make a sketch, a rough rude scrawl. I had never drawn from the nude before." Crowley, the self-proclaimed shameless pagan, had never before—despite his previously quoted advertisement—brought himself to use an unclothed model in his painting.

Perhaps the sheer emotional difficulty of taking this step fueled what was to come—Crowley's breakthrough as a painter of frightening passion, with the help of Hirsig, his new muse.

I was seized with a spasm of creative energy and all night long I splashed the central canvas with paint. When she took the pose I had asked her, "What shall I call the picture; what shall I paint you as?" She had said, "Paint me as a dead soul." My screen is called *Dead Souls*.

She stood central, her head the keystone of the arch of monsters. Her face is ghastly green. Her fleshless body lustreless, white with grey-blue shadows beneath the ribs. [. . .]

Upon finishing the painting, he immediately consecrated Hirsig as his Scarlet Woman, painting the Mark of the Beast (the sun and moon conjoined) between her breasts. She took on the magical name Alostrael—the womb or grail of God (the Scarlet Woman in Revelation carries a grail filled with the blood of saints). Crowley also termed her the "Ape of Thoth" because, as the last of his female theriomorphic initiators into the grade of Magus, she translated "into action his thought or, in other words, is the instrument through which his idea assumes sensible form."

Not long after this, Crowley and Hirsig moved into new lodgings together—an apartment at 63 Washington Square South, "a long and lofty room with three wide windows, looking out across the tree tops to the opening of Fifth Avenue." It was here that, in February 1919, Crowley entertained a reporter from *The New York Evening World*—the same newspaper that had profiled him twice in 1914. The reporter described a lavish *chez Crowley:* "It is luxuriously fitted with cavernous easy chairs, mahogany davenports, expensive tapestries, a fine rug or two, an expensive and many-pillowed divan, with here and there a rare rosewood antique." Where did the funds for all this come from? That remains a mystery. In interview, Crowley the painter distinguished himself sharply from the prevailing avant-garde outlooks, though his method showed obvious parallels with the then emerging Surrealist movement: "But please, whatever you do, don't call me a cubist or a futurist or anything queer like that. I guess you might call me a subconscious impressionist or something on that order. My art is really subconscious and automatic."

Hirsig's lack of prudishness was one of her primary appeals for Crowley. According to Seabrook, who visited this lavish apartment, the living model for his dead souls was fond of going about naked within its confines, unembarrassed in the presence of visitors. Just where her son Hansi fit into this new and daring domestic arrangement is not clear. But the close presence of a baby boy may have spurred Crowley's decision, in the summer of 1919, to carry out a new Great Magical Retirement. The camping site he chose was at the end of Long Island, in the vicinity of Montauk.

Little is known of this Retirement; Crowley's diaries of this time have not survived. What is plain is that it was of short duration and that he regarded it as a failure—a confirmation that his magical current had run its course in America. Later that summer he paid a visit to Seabrook and his wife, Kate, at their home near Atlanta. Kate Seabrook became, briefly, a partner in sexual magic with Crowley. Seabrook himself seems not to have minded.

Crowley returned to London in late December, suffering from one of his recurrent bouts of asthma. Shortly after his arrival, a Harley Street physician prescribed heroin as a palliative both for the asthma and for Crowley's increasingly severe bronchitis. Crowley had taken heroin intermittently in the past, but from this point onwards his use became an addiction—a humiliation for one who had long boasted that only weaklings fell victim to a drug.

But as the year came to a close, Crowley felt like anything but an addict. Rather, he was resolved to carry the campaign of Thelema back to Europe. Hirsig, who had become pregnant by Crowley in the spring, had voyaged to France with Hansi and was waiting for Crowley there. As for his own spiritual progress, there were still greater heights in sight. The grade of Ipsissimus, the exalted $10°=1^{\square}$ vantage of Kether, the Crown, at the apex of the Tree of Life—this was Crowley's aim. It would entail the transcendence of all categories of morality and reason. As he noted in his diary on December 26, 1919: "Attainment is Insanity. The whole point is to make it perfect in balance. Then it radiates light in every direction, while the Ipsissimus is utterly indifferent to it."

CHAPTER EIGHT

The Founding and the Ruin of the Abbey of Thelema (1920–23)

For the brief time that Crowley remained in London—just long enough to see in the New Year of 1920—he was not pursued by the British authorities for his alleged treason during the war. His diaries of this time betray no anxiety that this was likely to occur. But just after his departure for Paris on January 2, *John Bull*—the same tabloid that had, ten years earlier, excoriated Crowley and his Rites of Eleusis, lashed out again: "the war which brought out the best in human nature, also forced the scum to the top, and Aleister Crowley is of the scum." The article concluded with a plea that the government take action against Crowley. In the *Confessions*, Crowley postured that the *John Bull* piece was too absurd to require a response. Privately, he felt it as an extreme humiliation that he lacked funds to wage legal battle.

Leah Hirsig joined him in Paris. She was now in the eighth month of her pregnancy, with her two-year-old son, Hansi, already under her care. But Hirsig had arrived at a practical solution. On board ship from America to Europe, she befriended a recently widowed woman, Ninette Shumway, herself the mother of a three-year-old boy, Howard. Shumway was twenty-five, twelve years younger than Hirsig, and had previously worked as a governess in America. Hirsig suggested that she take up the same work for Crowley and herself. Shumway accepted. By late February, Shumway had taken on the role of a second magical lover to Crowley (her magical name was "Sister Cypris," after Aphrodite; her nickname was "Beauty"). Hirsig, however, remained the chief Scarlet Woman.

Crowley was suddenly the *paterfamilias* and chief means of support for two women, their two sons, and the baby on the way. He had obtained some funds while in London (roughly £3000 in inheritances from various deceased aunts), and so had means for the time being. Deciding that a rural setting would best suit the needs of all, Crowley leased a house at 11 bis rue de Neuville in Fontainebleau, where they remained through early March. It was a time of seclusion and happiness. Crowley gave Hansi and Howard—whom he nicknamed "Dionysus" and "Hermes"—their first lessons in rock climbing. As they were mere toddlers, the ascents he chose must have been mercifully short. But the attitude Crowley displayed here was typical. Under his Thelemic creed, children were to be raised with full freedom to explore their talents and interests. Parents—especially mothers—were to refrain from fussing and over-protecting. The absence of hovering care, Crowley believed, could reduce the impact of the Freudian Oedipal complex, the remnants of which Crowley abhorred in himself.

On February 20, Leah gave birth to a daughter whom they named Anne Léa (the initials AL signifying "God" and adding to thirty-one, the key number of *The Book of the Law*); her less daunting nickname was Poupée. Crowley thought it best to send Hirsig and the baby to London for some weeks, perhaps to obtain medical care for the frail newborn. As for Crowley, Shumway, and the two boys, they began looking for a more affordable haven than Fontainebleau. On March 1, Crowley consulted the *I Ching;* the oracle gave a favorable reading for Cefalù, a small town on the northern coast of Sicily.

By April 1 they arrived in Cefalù—a town of fishermen and cobbled streets which had retained much of its medieval architecture, including a magnificent Norman cathedral. They spent a ghastly first night in a seedy hotel. But the very next day they found the perfect house to lease. The Villa Santa Barbara was located on the southeastern outskirts of the town—an unprepossessing but solidly built one-story house, with thick plaster walls and a tiled roof. From its front door there was a view of the great Rock that overlooks Cefalù and the Mediterranean, on the heights of which are the remains of ancient Roman temples.

All of this was most pleasing to Crowley. The day they moved in, he made his first ascent of the Rock—an arduous hike which offered the reward of a breathtaking vista of his new realm. As he exulted in his diary: "Traversed Rock of Cefalù, visiting Temples of Jupiter and Diana. At supper, I ate much thigh of kid, and may Priapus [the Roman phallic god] prosper!" The continued investigation of sexual magic was one of the central purposes that Crowley had in mind for his stay in the villa, which he would soon come to regard as the New Aeon realization of the Abbey of Thelema first imagined by Rabelais.

Shortly after the arrival of Hirsig and Poupée on April 14, Crowley entered into a formal lease with the Italian owner of the villa, which Crowley signed as "Sir Alastor de Kerval." Hirsig followed suit with "Contessa Lea Harcourt." In like manner, Crowley devised a more dignified name for the Abbey itself. He had cards and stationery printed on which his address included the designation *Collegium ad Spiritum Sanctum.*" This referred to a training ground—a "College of the Holy Spirit"—for disciples who demonstrated their resolve by making their way to Cefalù. Through them he would found the New Aeon; they would aid the Magus as the apostles had aided Jesus. Among the regular residents of the Abbey, there emerges a more homely nickname for the villa—the "horsel," a contracted form of "Whore's Cell," with reference to the magical practices that occurred within.

In the months that followed, Crowley undertook a substantial redecoration of the villa's interior. The basic layout featured five rooms radiating off a central chamber. This allowed for adequate bedroom and kitchen space, with the central chamber converted into a temple. In its center stood a six-sided altar, in which were kept the traditional implements and weapons of magic—the sword, dagger, cup, lamen, bell, and so forth. On top of the altar, surrounded by six candles, was *The Book of the Law.*

The Temple was the first of the interior rooms of the villa to be converted. But in the spring of 1921—a year after their arrival—the other rooms of the Abbey were also transformed pursuant to Crowley's vision. He was inspired by the example of Paul Gauguin, an exile from his native France (in Tahiti as opposed to Cefalù) who had created works of art glorifying his vision. Crowley now viewed Gauguin as a precursor-saint of Thelema (inserting his name into the Gnostic Mass) and followed Gauguin's example by filling the Abbey with his canvases and then painting—with the help of his disciples—extensive murals on the walls, the doors, and even the shutters.

The bedroom that Crowley shared with Hirsig (Shumway was a frequent guest nonetheless) he named "Le Chambre des Cauchemars"—The Room of Nightmares. It was on the walls of this room that Crowley the artist created his masterpiece—an astonishing montage (as revealed by photographs taken in the 1950s by Kenneth Anger) of unbridled sex-

The young poet in a Shelleyesque pose.
Courtesy Ordo Templi Orientis.

Crowley on pony-back during the approach to
Kanchenjunga (1905).
Courtesy Ordo Templi Orientis.

The adept, donned in robe and crown, with the consecrated implements of magic—cup, sword, pantacle, bell, sacred book, and holy oil (ca. 1910). *Courtesy Ordo Templi Orientis.*

Jan: 10th 1910

A family portrait of Rose, Lola Zaza and Aleister Crowley, January 10, 1910.
Courtesy Ordo Templi Orientis.

Imitating Winston Churchill, for whom Crowley claimed to have created the "V for Victory" hand sign (ca. 1942).
Courtesy Ordo Templi Orientis.

Crowley during his final years at Netherwood, Hastings.
Courtesy Lucas Mellinger.

uality, blasphemy, poetry, and magical prophecy. Crowley went so far as to write up a descriptive brochure in the hopes of drumming up a tourist trade—which never materialized—to pay to see the Chambre. (Ironically, a recent Cefalù tourist brochure featured the Abbey and a sample of Crowley's art.)

On the main wall of the Chambre was a tableau entitled "HELL—La Nature Malade" which included, as a centerpiece, a leering portrait of a red-lipped Hirsig and a quotation from the poem "Leah Sublime," an homage to the Scarlet Woman composed by Crowley in June 1920: "Stab your demoniac smile to my brain,/ Soak me in cognac, cunt, and cocaine." In his brochure, Crowley urbanely explained the theme of this painting: "The general idea is to present a variety of natural objects in such form and colour as is most antipathetic to their qualities. All we see depends on our senses: suppose they lie to us? Remember that as soon as you perceive the actual conditions of consciousness, there is no such thing as TRUTH.[. . .] What we call 'God' may be only our diseased delirium-phantom, and His reality the one-eyed rotten-toothed petrifaction of Malice shewn in the picture."

A selection from the titles chosen by Crowley give a sense of the impact of the Chambre, which in its various paintings depicted the three realms of Heaven, Hell, and Earth: *Four degenerates between Christian and Jew at prayer.* (Crowley's comment: "Men worship only their own weaknesses personified. 'Hell' is based upon false intellectual and moral consciousness.") *Japanese Devil-boy Insulting Visitors.* ("Each soul has its own Special Means of Grace.") *The Sea-Coast of Tibet; Egyptian Aztecs arriving from Norway.* ("You never know in how strange a world you live and what strange things may come to you.") *The Devil our Lord.* ("The Sacred Symbols—the Horns of Power, the Egg of Purity, Safety and Life, etc.—exist in the most terrifying appearances. Everything that is, is holy.") Other titles: *The Long-Legged Lesbians; Tahitian Girl and her Eurasian Lover; Pregnant Swiss Artist Holding Young Crocodile; Morbid Hermaphrodite from Basutoland.*

The brochure raptly assured potential visitors—from whom Crowley hoped to draw new disciples—that the purpose of the Chambre "is to pass students of the Sacred Wisdom through the ordeal of contemplating every possible phantom which can assail the soul. Candidates for this initiation are prepared by a certain secret process before spending the night in this room; the effect is that the figures on the walls seem actually to become alive, to bewilder and obsess the spirit that has dared to confront their malignity." This "secret process" may have included one or more drugs. Opium, ether, cocaine, heroin, laudanum, hashish, and anhalonium were in constant supply at the Abbey, and Crowley administered them to himself in the Chambre on an almost nightly basis. The brochure described, in the third person, the self-purgation that Crowley pursued in the Abbey:

> Those who have come successfully through the trial say that they have become immunized from all possible infection by those ideas of evil which interfere between the soul and its divine Self. Having been forced to fathom the Abysses of Horror, to confront the most ghastly possibilities of Hell, they have attained permanent mastery of their minds. The process is similar to that of "Psycho-analysis"; it releases the subject from fear of Reality and the phantasms and neuroses thereby caused, by externalizing and thus disarming the spectres that lie in ambush for the Soul of Man.

It was to this end—the creation of a "divine Self" fully released from the fears and inhibitions of the all-too-human soul—that Crowley created the images of the Chambre des Cauchemars, as well as the self-prescribed magical ordeals that were his chief focus in the summer of 1920. As he noted time and again in his diary, Crowley felt himself deeply flawed by his lingering puritanism and sense of sin—discriminations that went against the essence of *The Book of the Law*. To liberate himself, Crowley turned to Hirsig in her role as Alostrael, the Scarlet Woman, the shameless Whore to his Beast. Never before had Crowley mated with a Scarlet Woman who could so challenge him. Hirsig became, in this summer marked by incessant drug use (predominantly cocaine and heroin), the psychopomp who would compel Crowley to pass through the worst of his fears. Hirsig was, Crowley realized, the quintessential embodiment of his own teaching and guidance:

> When first I found Her, She was a woman, one that held godhead [. . .] She had ripe womanhood, wrapping her in Motherhood's blouse, in Intellect's shawl, in Passion's slattern skirt, and Human Loving-kindness perched on Her head, a dove's wing with an eagle's feather trimming the toque's soft straw.
> Now I, the God, have choked Her god in dung and bred the Basilisk, reared the fiend, Satan-Alostrael, to burn in hell with me—to burn, to writhe, to exult, to spend, to be, to will, to go, to change, to lust, to create life, to kindle love, to unveil light, to unleash liberty, my Word and Law Thelema to proclaim, to 'sta-

blish and to execute for ever. To build that Law into Man's Soul, as Nature builds a man from the fifth primate, is Her Satan-secret Asp-brew in Her Cup's Blood (Filth, Madness, Poison, In-chantment, Putrefaction): it aids Intoxication and its One Mystery of Mysteries, Initiation.

His arduous initiation—erotic and magical—through the summer of 1920 was the first time in Crowley's life that the ritual ordeals of an ex-alted magical grade were presided over not by himself but by a resolute other. On July 22 the Beast swore an oath of obedience to his Scarlet Woman: "She is to direct all action, taking the initiative throughout." That very day the first ordeal was administered. Crowley, taking the feminine persona of "Alys" (a name he also used when acting out his homosexual nature), made love in the role of Hirsig's lesbian slave. He described this coupling as "a frightful ordeal of cruelty and defilement" which "revolted even my own body, and made me free forever of my preference for matter, made me Pure Spirit."

Under the guidance of the Scarlet Woman, every fear to which Crow-ley had clung became, in this realm, fiercely exposed. To be sure, this process often dovetailed nicely with the sadomasochism that was, by Crowley's own admission, a strong component of his nature. It seems to have been so with Hirsig as well. Consider this diary entry of July 26, which tells of how the Scarlet Woman and the Beast administered pain:

> She discovered the physical cowardice and dread of pain which I had sunk so deep by means of daring death-mountains, wild beasts, poison, and disease. She held a lighted cigarette against my breast. I shrank and moaned. She spat her scorn, and puffed at it and put it back. I shrank and moaned. She made me fold my arms, sucked at the paper till the tobacco crackled with the fierceness of its burning; she put it back for the third time. I braced myself; I tightened lip and thrust my breast against it.

That very same day, Leah pressed on to a still more wrenching ordeal. This time the weakness in Crowley to be excoriated was his tendency toward "Bluff"—more bluntly, his frequent and elaborate lying. In his diary, Crowley offered telling examples of this. There was his pretence to multilingual scholarship, when, by his own account, he possessed lit-tle knowledge of any foreign tongue but French—in which he was barely passable. There was his tendency to boast of his wickedness and of the number of his mistresses. As for the legend of his sexual stamina,

Crowley confessed that "my secret is not vigor; I've the cheap cunning of the prostitute who saves herself [withholds orgasm], and loves her nightly score or so with no more effort than if she had cracked so many nuts."

Worst of all, however, was his boasting over his magical prowess. It had been Crowley's claim to Hirsig that his magic was capable of transcending all material distinctions, to the point that he could consume human excrement as an ingredient of the "cakes of light" prescribed by *The Book of the Law.* On the same July 26 as he endured the cigarette on his breast, he consumed the shit of the Scarlet Woman as the Thelemic Host:

> Then I obeyed. My mouth burned; my throat choked; my belly retched; my blood fled wither who knows, and my skin sweated. She stood above me hideous in contempt; she fixed snake's eyes on mine, and with most patient discipline, as with most eager passion, as with sublime delight, was face to face with me, epiphany of my duty's archetype. Hierophantia stood She, Her eyes uttering Light, Her mouth radiant Silence. She ate the Body of God, and with Her soul's compulsion made me eat. [. . .]My teeth grew rotten, my tongue ulcered; raw was my throat, spasm-torn my belly, and all my Doubt of that which to Her teeth was moonlight, and to her tongue ambrosia; to her throat nectar, in Her Belly the One God of whose Pure Body She should fresh Her Blood.

Hirsig, as described in these diary passages, seems a primordial earth goddess without shame or fear. But human she was, as fully human as Crowley himself. The weaknesses that would torment her during this year had to do, first, with jealousy over the primacy of her role as Scarlet Woman. This jealousy does not seem to have been extreme; Hirsig tolerated, for example, Crowley's intermittent homosexual liaisons with male prostitutes in Palermo, the Sicilian city to which he would journey by train now and then, as a way of breaking up the Abbey routine. But the presence of Shumway was far more threatening; strains mounted between the two women. These were exacerbated by Hirsig's terrible misfortunes as a mother. Shortly after the birth of Poupée in February 1920, Hirsig became pregnant again. So did Shumway. Crowley was awaiting two babies from two different mothers. Meanwhile Poupée, "first bastard" of the Beast and the Scarlet Woman, remained in poor health through the summer and early fall. Crowley felt his helplessness, as in this April 1920 diary entry:

> I have been howling like a mad creature nearly all day. I want my epitaph to be 'Half a woman made with half a god'. It is not My Will to save my baby's life. What is 'mine'? Not to save all the babies in the world, as I should do if I started to save one. My Will is to be the Logos of the Aeon; I am Thelema. Do what thou wilt shall be the whole of the Law. Beyond that, I am more helpless than the veriest quack magician.

On October 14, 1920, Poupée died in a hospital in Palermo. Crowley may never have grieved so deeply as he did for her; his *Confessions* are replete with that pain. Hirsig was devastated as well; six days later, Hirsig miscarried. The loss of two children in the face of Shumway's healthy pregnancy proved unbearable. Hirsig became convinced that Shumway had worked a black magical current that caused the deaths of the two children. She persuaded Crowley to review Shumway's magical diaries for the period. (All members of the Abbey kept such accounts to chart their spiritual progress.) Upon doing so, Crowley was "utterly appalled at the horrors of the human heart. I never dreamed such things were possible. I am physically sick—it is the greatest shock of my life. I had this mess in my own circle. It poisoned my work; it murdered my children." On November 5, he ordered Shumway banished. In Cefalù, Shumway gave birth to a daughter, Astarte Lulu Panthea; by November 26—whether out of forgiveness or practical need—she and her baby returned to the Abbey, where she resumed her role as nanny. Soon afterwards, Crowley leased a hut downhill from the Abbey to serve as a nursery, naming it, alternately, "The Umbilicus" and "Under the Hill" (after the erotic novel by Aubrey Beardsley).

One might imagine that, given the intensity of the passions within the Abbey, the added burden of housing and training new disciples would have been unthinkable. But Crowley intended the Abbey to serve as a beacon to those who would live the true life of Thelema, and none who came to live and study there were turned away. This proved, most often, to be an economic burden for Crowley. The guests would sometimes offer funds (the formal fee requested was fifty guineas in advance, for an expected stay of three months), but in certain cases Crowley himself paid for their food and housing costs. The results he attained as a teacher were uneven, but the sincerity he brought to the task cannot be questioned. Crowley yearned to train new souls in the ways of Thelema, just as his father Edward had yearned to bring new believers into the Brethren sect.

Early on, Crowley created a basic daily ritual framework that was to be followed by all Abbey residents. In the morning came the recitation of the brief "Adoration of the Sun" from Crowley's *Liber Resh:* "Hail unto Thee, who art Ra in Thy Rising." Other gods of the Egyptian solar pantheon were employed when this prayer was repeated at noon (Hathoor), eveningtime (Tum), and midnight (Khephra). There were also frequent services in the Abbey temple, in which Crowley's Gnostic Mass and other of his rites were performed. In the temple, the men wore blue robes with hoods lined with red, the women blue robes with hoods lined with gold.

The pattern of Abbey life for students, aside from the ritual practices outlined above, was to be (in Crowley's ideal scheme of things, though never carried out precisely in practice with any student) as follows: The training time frame would be just over three months. There would be an initial three days during which one was treated graciously as a guest, with an orientation on Abbey life. After this, one was either to leave or set to work. If the latter choice was made, there would be a day of silence, followed by three days of instruction, and then the taking of a solemn Magical Oath to pursue the Great Work pursuant to the teachings of Crowley's A∴A∴. The remaining weeks were devoted principally to the study of Crowley's writings, as well as careful yogic and magical practice (all to be carefully recorded in a diary, which was to be left available for others in the Abbey to read, so that all could learn from each other's work) and manual labor essential to Abbey functions—everything from cooking and shopping to the typing out of Crowley's manuscripts. As for recreation, the Thelemites frequently shocked the Cefalù natives by their preference for nude bathing. Crowley also trained Abbey members in the basics of climbing on the great Rock.

There were a number of individuals who passed through training of one sort or another at the Abbey—with markedly different impressions and results. One notable success story, from the perspective both of Crowley and of herself, was Jane Wolfe, who was forty-five at the time of her arrival in July 1920. Wolfe was an American who had carved out for herself a career as a character actress in Hollywood silent films. Having encountered Crowley's writings, she began writing to him in 1919. When at last she journeyed to the Abbey in July 1920, Wolfe found it deplorably filthy and nearly despaired; but having come so far, she resolved to continue with her plan to study with Crowley. Continue she did, remaining at the Abbey for some three years and maintaining a life-long relationship with Crowley as disciple and friend. As for the stench of the Abbey, she learned to bear it and at last to understand it. Thelemic historian Phyllis Seckler writes that, some years later, Wolfe broached the subject to another Crowley disciple, Norman Mudd (of whom more later), who explained that Crowley was exploring the "mystery of filth" along the lines expressed in one of his prewar holy books, *The Book of the Heart Girt with a Serpent:* "Thou strivest ever; even in thy yielding thou strivest to yield—and lo! thou yieldest not. Go thou unto the outermost places and subdue all things, Subdue thy fear and thy disgust. Then—yield!"

A more problematic disciple was Cecil Frederick Russell, a young American who had first been drawn to Crowley by his reading, back in 1917, of "The Revival of Magick" in *The International*. In June 1918 he paid a brief visit to Crowley at the latter's West 9th Street apartment in New York. As Russell described the occasion in his autobiography, *Znuz is Znees*, "He [Crowley] answered my knock with a hypnotic stare & made an appointment for lunch. I remained most of the day; we took an astral journey together[. . .]" That evening, a group including Crowley and Hirsig initiated Russell as a III° in the O.T.O. Russell again met with Crowley in autumn 1918, and the two men stayed in intermittent correspondence, with Russell proving an ardent student of *The Book of the Law*.

Russell arrived at the Abbey on November 21, 1920, intent on personal study with the Master. But relations between the two were anything but smooth. Russell was bright, brash, vigorous, and the first male to join Crowley at the Abbey. Crowley sought to employ Russell as an aide in the exploration of the kabbalistic mysteries of the *Book*. Crowley was also attracted to Russell, while revulsed by the hold that this crude younger man had upon him. In addition to all this, there was Crowley's desire to maintain authority as a teacher and Russell's difficulty in accepting this authority as a matter of daily routine.

Shortly after Russell's arrival, on November 27, Crowley commenced the Cephaloedium Working, Cephaloedium being the ancient Roman name for Cefalù. The central purpose of this working, which was carried out through intermittent sexual magic operations into January 1921, was "to establish the *Book of the Law*; in particular to finish the *Comment* [begun in 1919] & to publish the *Book* as therein commanded." As for this *Comment*, while Crowley devoted much time in the coming year to a "New Version," he remained dissatisfied with it. In this aim, the Working was a failure.

The tension between its three central participants—Crowley, Hirsig, and Russell—did not bode well for successful sexual magic. Russell's principal magical name was Frater Genesthai (The flowers that come into being); but in his record of the Cephaloedium Working Crowley frequently inscribed Russell's name as "Iacchaion" after the Greek Iacchus or Dionysius. As Crowley viewed the situation, Russell was to afford a Dionysian sexual ecstasy to the workings. In his diary entry for December 12, Crowley set forth both his diagnosis of Russell's shallow innocence and the corresponding sexual plan of action:

> He [Russell] want Pure Love, 17-years-old with real gold hair and the Ideal Ideal, and expects to pay Three Dollars for it, that being the recognized price all over the United States. The Passion of a Prostitute, the Vice of a Vampire, seem to him funny: how much more then the coprophilic and bestial joys of those who know—know all and delight in all, having achieved and experienced all [. . .]
>
> This truth learn thou, Genesthai, brother of mine! Learn this, thou Bull in my Pasiphae-pasture! Learn thou that I, worn out with wallowing though I be, or seem to be to thee, can breed thee Minotaur, while those meek calves that tempt thee with soft comeliness will but give birth to their base kind, to kine potential of no more than milk, veal, beef, and leather. Come, brother, come, my Bull! Desire me thou, delight me! Defile me and destroy me; I swear to thee my Magick shall repay thy pains.

His resolution to seduce Russell survived even the premature end of the Cephaloedium Working on January 20, 1921—which Crowley blamed on the failure of Russell to maintain sufficient sexual energy. Some four months later, on May 10, he wrote:

> Now I'll shave and make up my face like the lowest kind of whore and rub on perfume and go after Genesthai like a drunken two-bit prick-pit in old New Orleans. He disgusts me sexually, and I him, as I suspect (bitcheroo, switcheroo!); the dirtier my deed, the dearer my darling will hold me; the grosser the act the greedier my arse to engulph him! It maddens me that I have always been so bashful and sheepish (or by reaction) absurdly overbold. But unless there is magnetism, it is impossible for me to unite with either woman or man.

Crowley was correct in suspecting that he disgusted Russell sexually. Russell left this account (utilizing Crowley's personal homosexual pseudonym, Alys Cusack) of Crowley's method of expressing his bisexuality in the Chambre des Cauchemars: "On the wall above the wide bed on the floor of the Cauchemars was a small plaque engraved with six words, the initial letter of the fourth was variable, it could be an N or an H: 'ALYS CUSACK IS _OT AT HOME!' Unfortunately for her, she was not my type [. . .]"

Russell departed the Abbey in the fall of 1921. His ultimate assessment of Crowley was a harsh one—hardly surprising, as Russell's memoirs were written, in part, to counter the unflattering portrait of himself in Crowley's *Confessions*. But Russell did strike at a central contradiction in Crowley—the conflict between the ambitious man of letters and the aspiring egoless Magus: "You see, Crowley was first, last and always an Author, a Litterateur; with this always in his mind is it any wonder his Magick sometimes did not achieve his anticipated results! Ever hunting the happy phrase, modeling the merriest metaphor—even while fucking he was recording the Opus in his mind rather than endeavoring to establish Ekagrata [focused energy] to effect Samadhi! Like a professional magician deceiving Destiny with misdirection not realising Fate was his own Higher Self."

There was, in early 1921, a hiatus (February 1–April 6) during which Crowley left Russell, Hirsig, Wolfe, Shumway, and the children to tend to the Abbey while he paid an extended visit to Paris. A change of scene, pure and simple, was what he wanted most. Soon after his arrival, he became entangled in a love triangle with the added stakes of obtaining disciples for Thelema.

The married couple with whom Crowley became involved were the writer John William Navin Sullivan and his wife, Sylvia. Sullivan was a gifted polymath—a mathematician and music critic whose study *Beethoven: His Spiritual Development* (1927) remains a classic in its field. Sullivan was impressed by Crowley and went so far as to sign an Oath, witnessed by the Beast, to devote himself to the Great Work of discovering his own True Will. As for Sylvia Sullivan, she became Crowley's lover—according to Crowley—in the same manner as had Ratan Devi, the wife of Ananda Coomaraswamy: Sullivan, as the bored husband, passed her on to the waiting Crowley, who desired her but would remain dispassionate in any possessive quarrels that ensued. Sullivan did soon succumb to a fit of jealousy, but relations between the two men were ultimately patched, though Sullivan abandoned any formal discipleship. The plans for the couple to come to Cefalù were abandoned.

Crowley was rueful, not as to Sylvia, but as to the loss of her husband's talents: "I could have made him the evangelist of Thelema; with his abilities he might have been more important in history than St. Paul." Crowley blamed Sullivan's sexual insecurities for the failure; that his own sexual proclivities may have played an equal role did not occur to him.

Crowley returned to the Abbey in April and turned his energies to the artistic transformation of its walls and ceilings, previously described. This same spring, Crowley came to a resolution for which he had been bracing himself for some six years, since his assumption of the grade of Magus. His destiny was to evolve to the highest grade conceivable by human consciousness—that of Ipsissimus, $10°=1°$, on the plane of Kether, the kabbalistic Crown of the Tree of Life, where the first emanation of pure Godhead is made manifest. Crowley's diary entry on this new and final grade was as much terrified as exultant. The "deed" referred to is unknown:

> I am by insight and initiation an Ipsissimus; I'll face the phantasm of myself, and tell it so to its teeth. I will invoke Insanity itself; but having thought the Truth, I will not flinch from fixing it in word and deed, whatever come of it.
>
> 9:34 p.m. As a God goes, I go.
>
> 10:05 I am back at my desk, having done the deed, before the Scarlet Woman as my witness. I swore to keep silence, so long as I live, about the fact of my attainment. (The Scarlet Woman is not thus bound, of course.)

As to this vow of silence, Crowley seems to have been as good as his word. He never made direct mention of the Ipsissimus attainment in his writings. But in the private sanctity of the Abbey, Crowley had at last jumped the gap between God and himself.

He was well aware that it was only an aspect of himself—an accessible but extremely intermittent state of consciousness, one might say—that warranted the status of Ipsissimus. His relentless private analyses of the weakness of his human nature continued apace; the confines of the Abbey, and the influence of Hirsig, seemed to compel such introspection. There was a further stimulus as well. Crowley was beginning to utilize heroin with alarming regularity and in alarming quantities. He blamed any number of factors for this—the cold and gray of Paris and Cefalù, the bouts of asthma and dyspnoea from which he suffered, and from which heroin provided a respite. He tried to will himself free from physical dependence—this effort would occupy much of his energy in the year to come. He tried further to will himself to believe that this effort was succeeding even as his steady intake continued. Increasingly often, despite himself, he battled the bouts of despair of an addict.

In the spring and summer of 1921, the Abbey received a number of new visitors, straining its physical and economic resources to the limit. There was a brief visit paid, in April, by a Captain M. E. Townshend of the British Army. Townshend was a friend of Crowley's old ally, J. F. C. Fuller, who had by this time been promoted to colonel and was serving in the War Office in London. Crowley yearned to impress Townshend, as Townshend had the ear of Fuller. Crowley himself had written to Fuller earlier this same year, declaring, with as much humility as Crowley would ever muster: "Your friendship stands out as the best thing in my life of that kind. We were mules to let envious monkeys manoeuvre us into dissension. I know it was mostly the fault of my silly pride. The Crowned Child needs a Warrior to command the armies of Liberty: thou art the man!" The letter was personally delivered to Fuller at the War Office, in an envelope that had become filthy in transit, by an emissary of Crowley who remains unknown. Fuller made no reply.

Nonetheless, Crowley made his best efforts to win over Captain Townshend, and to a certain extent he succeeded—a tribute to his charisma in a tawdry physical environment that could hardly have been impressive to a British officer, especially one familiar with Crowley's propaganda efforts during the late war. In an April 17 letter to Fuller, Townshend transcribed an impassioned sermon delivered to him by Crowley:

> "Do what you like," he said, "not the haphazard wishes and desires of the conscious mind but the unchangeable idea of your inner self. You must dig down into that and find out what it is— drag it out into the daylight. You, like Fuller, are not living in accordance with your real will. You soldier to make a living, your real self remains unexpressed. Why do I have these erotic pictures? There, in the corner, are lesbians as large as life. Why do you feel shocked and turn away: or perhaps overtly turn to look again? Because, though you may have thought of such things, you have been afraid to face them. Drag all such thoughts into the light. If you stayed here for a little you would be like the others and notice nothing wrong.

Townshend declared to Fuller that he was deeply interested in getting to know Crowley better. But a prompt cabled reply by Fuller, which has not survived, quashed that notion. As Townshend declared in a responsive letter of April 28: "You have quite convinced me of the utter undesirability of visiting Cefalù."

The first long-term guests at the Abbey, arriving at the end of June, were Mary Butts and Cecil Maitland, a romantic couple, both of whom were minor figures in the British literary world. Crowley met them during his winter stay in Paris and had invited them to come to the Abbey for instruction in magic, a subject in which both Butts and Maitland had already dabbled. They made the trip to Cefalù some months later and stayed the course of a trying three months of instruction at the Abbey.

It fascinated Crowley that Maitland was the son of an Anglican clergyman father who had converted to Catholicism. This set in motion a ritual specially devised by Crowley, three days after their arrival, to make use of Maitland's background. This ritual featured the Cakes of Light specified by the warlike god Ra-Hoor-Khuit in *The Book of the Law* (III, 24–5): "The best blood is of the moon, monthly: then the fresh blood of a child, or dropping from the host of heaven: then of enemies; then of the priest or of the worshippers: last of some beast, no matter what. This burn: of this make cakes and eat unto me." There is no evidence that Crowley ever used the fresh blood of a child or of an enemy in preparing the cakes. Indeed, in his comment on this verse, written during this period, Crowley was careful to specify that the "child" was "Babalon and the Beast conjoined"—that is, the elixir of sexual magic. Here is Crowley's diary account of the ritual, which resembles in structure the frog crucifixion at Lake Pasquaney in 1916:

> The ceremony of preparing the Cakes of Light. A young cock [. . .] is to be baptized *Peter Paul* into the Catholic Church by C.J.A. Maitland, the son of an apostate Romish Priest & therefore the ideal "Black" Hierophant. Mary [Butts] and I are its sponsors. Peter Paul as the founders of the Christian Church, & we want its blood to found our own church. Alostrael then dances against the will of Mary, on my swearing to give her the half of my Kingdom. She demands P.P.'s head on the Disk. I behead him, & the blood is caught in the silver 'charger' on the Disk. In this charger is the meal etc for the Cakes of Light, ready except for the blood. I conjure the spirit of P.P. to serve these cakes to found our Church with, as we may use them. The cock

is slain in honour of Ra Hoor Khuit who is invoked before the killing.

Crowley biographer John Symonds records that Butts refused to partake, and that she remarked (after her return to London) that Crowley had offered her "a goat's turd on a plate." But her sarcasm came later. Butts's diary confirms that, for much of their stay at the Abbey, she and Maitland were convinced of the value of its methods and worked intensively at their magical studies.

In late July, Crowley devised a "Seth ceremony" which called for the sacrifice of a virgin goat, the horns of which were to represent Aiwaz, and the blood of which would be employed for the Cakes of Light. Prior to the sacrifice, the goat was to be induced to have intercourse with Hirsig the Scarlet Woman, so that the drinking of its blood could be a true "drinking thereof from the Cup of our Lady of Whoredom." The goat, however, refused to comply; somewhat later, the Beast himself engaged in sexual magic with the Scarlet Woman to remedy the omission. But the ritual proceeded on course, with the sacrifice carried out. According to a later account of this ritual by Butts, Hirsig—her bare back covered with goat's blood after the Beast had slit its throat—had asked Butts, "'What shall I do now?' And Mary had replied, 'I'd have a bath if I were you.'"

Butts and Maitland returned to London in mid-September, their three-month course completed. They would later claim that their time at the Abbey had injured their health and instilled a drug habit in them both. For his part, Crowley would acknowledge the editorial help Butts gave him, during her stay, with his work-in-progress manuscript of *Magick in Theory and Practice.* In November 1922, Butts would offer highly caustic comments on Crowley to the London *Sunday Express*— thus contributing to a new wave of press attacks.

There were still further visitors to the Abbey that summer. Frank Bennett, a fifty-three-year-old Australian bricklayer, arrived on July 17 and remained for some four months, thriving under Crowley's teachings. Bennett had first learned of Crowley's teachings back in 1909, while living in London, through his readings in *The Equinox.* Thereafter, Bennett—not yet having met Crowley personally—joined the A∴A∴ and took the magical name Frater Progradior ("I Progress"); he later joined the O.T.O., then emigrated to Australia. Crowley ultimately summoned him to the Abbey. Bennett, determined to conquer the blockage to his spiritual progress, made the lengthy voyage.

By the time Bennett left Cefalù he had attained to the 6°=5□ Adeptus Major grade in the A∴A∴ and an exalted IX° in the O.T.O. The latter degree, which signified an intimate knowledge of the transcendental powers of sexuality, addressed precisely the issue that had puzzled Bennett most upon arrival. For Bennett had long suffered from head pains and auditory inner voices—symptoms which indicated, he believed, an inner complex that required healing. During this summer with Crowley, the healing occurred. Crowley told of the day when he and Bennett walked toward the beach "and just as we reached the edge of the cliff above the bay I made some casual remark which proved a winning shot." In essence, Crowley explained that the discovery of one's true will was based largely on freeing the desires of the subconscious mind from the strictures of the conscious mind. In particular, the strictures placed upon sexual expression were destructive because the phallus was, both symbolically and functionally, the microcosmic human manifestation of the power of divine creation. For Bennett, these insights confirmed the emphatic insistence of Thelema on true will being "the whole of the Law." This epiphany brought a consequent sense of increased physical well-being. After completing a solitary magical retirement on the Rock, Bennett returned to Australia in late 1921.

As winter came on at Cefalù, Crowley traveled once more to Paris. This time Hirsig accompanied him. They arrived in February 1922 and stayed at Crowley's favorite Parisian lodgings at 50 rue Vavin, just off the Boulevard Montparnasse. But Hirsig went on to London, and Crowley did not remain long in Paris. In the *Confessions* he offers mere evasions as to the motives behind his departure: "For the first time in my life, Paris disappointed me. All the old enchantments had somehow vanished."

The harsher truth was that Crowley felt himself near the breaking point with respect to his dependence upon cocaine and heroin. The other drugs he had employed in his life—hashish, ether, anhalonium, and the rest—had never taken hold of him as these two had. In the light of modern knowledge of addiction, this is unsurprising. But Crowley held a view of drugs that was governed (or mirrored) by the voice of Hadit in *The Book of the Law* (from II, 22): "I am the Snake that giveth Knowledge & Delight and bright glory, and stir the hearts of men with drunkenness. To worship me take wine and strange drugs whereof I will tell my prophet, & be drunk thereof! They shall not harm ye at all." As that selfsame prophet, it was inconceivable that he could not make himself master of any drug he wished. Yet, since January 1921, his average intake of heroin alone had been three grains per day. On February 14, he went to Fontainebleau, booked a room at an inn, Au Cadran Bleu, and began a diary that he entitled *Liber Tzaba vel Nike*—*Tzaba* being the Hebrew verb root for waging war, *Nike* the Greek for victory. Crowley thus utilized—some sixty years ahead of Ronald Reagan—the metaphor of a war on drugs.

Here is the opening inscription of *Liber Tzaba vel Nike*, or *The Fountain of Hyacinth*. The "Storm-fiend" referred to was Crowley's personal metaphor (inspired by legends of guardian storm spirits for the Himalayan peak Kanchenjunga) for his asthma and bronchitis symptoms:

> I, The Beast 666 wishing to prove the strength of my Will and the degree of my courage, have poisoned myself for the last two years and have succeeded finally in reaching a degree of intoxication such that withdrawal of the drugs (heroin & cocaine) produce a terrible attack by the "Storm-fiend." The acute symptoms arise suddenly, usually on awaking from a nap. They remind me of the "For God sake turn it off" feeling of having an electric current passing through one, and of the "Sugar-starvation" of the Baltoro Glacier. The psychology is very complex and curious: I think a detailed record of my attempt at breaking the habit will be interesting and useful.

Crowley, in his expeditions both to Chogo-Ri and to Kanchenjunga, had firmly insisted that high altitudes posed inherent physiological limitations to which climbers could not "acclimate" themselves. But he was unwilling to draw an analogous conclusion with respect to the physiological impacts of heroin and cocaine. He believed, rather, that he had poisoned himself so as to test the truth of his will and courage. These qualities would serve—must serve—to "acclimate" him to the force of the drugs.

In *Liber Tzaba*, Crowley detailed the degradations stemming from his drug usage in the period just prior to his arrival at Fontainebleau:

> [M]y memory is quite clear that I have been taking heroin continuously for many weeks: three or four doses to help me get up, & others practically all day at short intervals. As to Cocaine, I must have had at least two or three prolonged bouts of it every week, plus a few "hairs of the dog" on most of the 'off-days'. Most of my mental & moral powers were seriously affected in various ways, while I was almost wholly dependent on them for physical energy, in particular for sexual force, which only ap-

peared after unusual excesses, complicated by abnormal indulgence in alcohol. My creative life had become spasmodic & factitious.[. . .]I avoided washing, dressing, shaving, as much as possible. I was unable to count money properly, to inspect bills, & so on; everything bored me. I could not even feel alarm at obviously serious symptoms.

In his first week at Fontainebleau, Crowley struggled to reduce gradually his intake by the method of allowing himself dosages during certain portions of the day—the "Open Season"—but not others—the "Close Season." He felt acutely the need for drugs when the "Stormfiend" symptoms arose, though he tried—with very intermittent success—to employ substitute palliatives such as alcohol and strychnine. Struggles with his Thelemic vocation are frequent in *Liber Tzaba*, as in this February 20, 1922, entry:

Mine inmost Identity says: "To worship me take wine and strange drugs whereof I will tell my prophet, and be drunk thereon": it is lawful to do this, for to worship Him is to make him manifest, & so to fill the world with Truth & Beauty. But I have erred in going too far; the worship has become forced, & fallen into fanatical frenzy which blasphemes Him. [. . .] I must justify Him (& myself) by making myself unchallengably master of these "means of grace". I must be as capable of using them, & as confident in my capacity, as an engineer is of handling high explosives; & every piece of work undertaken with the aid of these tools, must prove by its perfection that His precepts & His promises are wrought of Righteousness & tested by Truth.

Here was a decisive interpretation of—and limitation upon—*The Book of the Law*, one which Crowley never incorporated into his formal commentaries. Drug use required subtlety and care if harm was to be evaded; the principle of moderation in all things withstood even the ecstatic verses of the *Book*. But moderation was difficult to achieve, particularly for the prophet of that *Book*. The hold of the drugs would not yield to mere written analyses. Thus it was that Crowley, after returning to Paris, contacted a Dr. Edmund Gros in early March to seek advice as to a suitable sanitorium. But, as he noted in *Liber Tzaba*, the facility would have to be one "where I can direct my own treatment. To submit to medical treatment would be to destroy my whole theory, & blaspheme the Gods whose chosen minister I am." Dr. Gros prescribed luminal for Crowley and recommended the open air of Geneva, but unsurprisingly, could recommend no facility along the lines insisted upon by Crowley.

Hirsig the Scarlet Woman had, at this same time, come to Paris to rejoin the Beast. It was an emotionally difficult reunion for Crowley, who back on February 12—in anticipation of his difficult self-treatment at Fontainebleau—had inscribed a "last Will and Testament" in his *Liber Tzaba* diary volume which left the whole of his property (nil, but for his books, magical implements, and the unprofitable rights to his writings) to Hirsig, whom he made his executrix. This, in essence, left the care and nurture of Thelema in her hands. But when they were face-to-face once more, Crowley sensed the mounting difficulties between them: "Lea[h] is a violent spiritual poison to me. We love deeply & truly; we sympathize; we do all we can to help each other; but we act on each other like Cancer. It is the formula of the independent growth in the One Flesh." The "independent growth," Crowley believed, was taking place in himself—he was, for the moment, confident of overcoming his drug dependence. Their bond continued, but by the end of March, the Beast recorded that he had escaped the delusion "that women exist in reality."

With little money in their pockets, the two journeyed to London in May 1922. Upon arrival, Crowley was without an adequate wardrobe, and so went to retrieve some traditional Highland garments—kilts and tunics—kept in storage by a friend since 1914. In these, Crowley made his way about 1920s London, renewing old contacts and seeking out new prospects, after having found an apartment for Hirsig and himself that overlooked Russell Square.

There was, early on, a particularly awkward encounter. Crowley paid a call at Wellington Square, Chelsea, where his former brother-in-law, the now-eminent painter Gerald Kelly, resided. Kelly was bearing a considerable responsibility for the upbringing of Lola Zaza, Crowley's daughter by Rose Kelly. Lola Zaza, now fourteen, was on hand for this visit; it may have been the first time she had seen her father since the divorce in 1910. Neither she nor her uncle bore any great love for Crowley. One may surmise the particulars of the visit from the brief diary account by a proud papa Crowley: "I have just seen Gerald Kelly, annoyed & bewildered because Lion's Daughters do not grow wool! Lola Zaza is unmanageable. She despises everybody, thinks she is a genius, is stupid, inaccurate, plain, ill-tempered, etc. etc. God! but it's good to be a Lion! For the first time in my life I taste the true pleasures of immortality. But the sheep are many, & their pressure may suffocate Lion cubs[. . .]" The sense of identification with his daughter is manifest, but after this all contact between them ceased. Gerald Yorke recalled that Lola Zaza "became a nursery governess, disowned her father, and when I tried to arrange for them to meet, she refused. She has married, and when last I met her she seemed a normal, happy wife."

Undaunted by his meeting with Kelly and Lola Zaza, Crowley attempted to pay a personal call on Fuller at the War Office on May 13. Fuller refused to see him, transmitting to his former master a terse note of two words: "Nothing Doing." But Crowley would continue to send letters to Fuller—letters that received no answer—for years to come.

Matters fared somewhat better with Austin Harrison, the editor of *The English Review*, with whom Crowley now renewed a friendship. Harrison took on Crowley as a regular—and prolific—contributor through the summer of 1922. Harrison paid Crowley little but allowed him considerable creative freedom. Crowley thus contributed essays under a variety of pseudonyms. Two such essays, "The Great Drug Delusion" and "The Drug Panic," appeared in the June and July 1922 issues under the authorial guise, respectively, of "A New York Specialist" and "A London Physician." These were written in opposition to the Dangerous Drugs Act of 1920, the first major instance in which Parliament sought to establish criminal penalties for possession of designated narcotic drugs. The Act included criminal penalties for heroin obtained through nonprescription channels. As Berridge and Edwards have observed in their study, *Opium and the People*, the 1920 Act "was not part of a smooth historical evolution, but a sharp and imposed change." Certainly it was a change felt sharply by Crowley, who was anxious, on behalf of Thelema, to defend the value of drugs and the freedom of choice to use them. It is remarkable, however, that Harrison saw fit to accede to Crowley's idea to give his arguments the coloration of official medical expertise. Crowley had long regarded himself as a gifted amateur diagnostician, and while at the Abbey he had, as Martin P. Starr has noted, "stationery printed up, listing his various imaginary medical degrees, including 'M.D. Damc.'—Damcar being the mythical home of the Arab wise men included in the *Fama Fraternitatis*." The *Fama* was a seventeenth-century Rosicrucian work, and it was in the esoteric tradition of the Rosicrucians, who regarded the work of the spiritually enlightened physician as a paramount human task, that Crowley viewed his own expertise.

But these pieces offer alleged medical advice that, based upon Crowley's own bitter experience, he must have known to be lies. For example, in "The Great Drug Delusion," the pseudonymous Crowley emphasized his extensive personal knowledge of drugs, then added cavalierly that "I attempted to produce a 'drug-habit' in myself. In vain. My wife literally nagged me about it; 'Don't go out without your cocaine, sweetheart!' or 'Did you remember to take your heroin before lunch, big boy?'" At the end of this article, a note was appended recommending the "private clinic" of the "New York Specialist," located in Cefalù, for readers interested in having their drug use treated not as a physiological habit but rather as a matter of human weakness to be cured by principles of "moral reconstruction."

The dilemma of his own personal addiction—as to which he alternated between lucidity and denial—now fused with his sense of mission on behalf of Thelema. Public expression on the drug question became a major priority for Crowley. As it happened, J. W. N. Sullivan had suggested that Crowley approach publisher Grant Richards with a view to selling his memoirs. When Richards was cool to this idea, Crowley offered an alternative project: "I would write a shocker on the subject which was catering to the hysteria and prurience of the sex-crazed public: the drug traffic insanity.[. . .] I proposed as a title *The Diary of a Drug Fiend* and sketched out a synopsis of its contents on a sheet of notepaper. This was mostly bluff. I had not really any clear idea of my story." Richards rejected *Drug Fiend*, but it was thereafter accepted at Collins, which offered a £60 advance—a godsend to the financially strapped Crowley. Further, both Crowley and Hirsig saw the contract as a vital confirmation, on the spiritual plane, of their work on behalf of the New Aeon. According to Crowley, the contract called for delivery of the manuscript within a month of signing. This would have been most unusual, but in any event Crowley had his own reason for wishing to write in haste—he hoped that *Drug Fiend* could be rushed to release before the end of summer, as it would be "suitable for holiday reading."

Crowley and Hirsig took a new lodging at 31 Wellington Street, Chelsea, and there the Beast and the Scarlet Woman worked in a feverish flurry. From June 4 to July 1, a course which Crowley calculated at 27 days, 12¾ hours, he dictated to Hirsig (who wrote in longhand) a novel some 121,000 words in length. Moreover, it was a readable and even, at times, a stylish and charming novel, particularly in its opening chapters, which chronicled the mad and giddy exploits of two perfectly cast Lost Generation romantic types, the former World War One flying ace Sir Peter Pendragon (knighted for his courage in the skies) and his true lady love with whom he eloped to Paris, nicknamed Unlimited Lou. The novel is written in three "books" or sections titled in the paradoxical sequence "Paradiso," "Inferno," and "Purgatorio," turning the Christian narrative structure of Dante inside out. "Paradiso" is the realm of first unbridled indulgence by the two lovers in heroin and cocaine. "Inferno" is the cost of that indulgence—physical degeneration and psychological despair. "Purgatorio" is the ironic title for their cure and salvation by means of submitting themselves to the wisdom of King Lamus (his name, and not a literal royal title), who serves as the leader of the Abbey of Thelema located in the far-off town of "Telepylus." The novel makes expressly clear—on the introductory page to "Purgatorio"—that the Abbey was a "real place" and that interested readers could communicate with the author.

Drug Fiend is a roman à clef in which a number of figures from Crowley's life appear. We know from notes made by Crowley in his own copy of the book that the dislikable aspects of Pendragon's character were based on Cecil Maitland. As for Lou, she was "partly a wish-phantasm of my daughter, Lola Zaza Crowley." The settled residents of the Abbey—Hirsig, Wolfe, Shumway, and the children—all were given secondary character roles. But the figure of King Lamus—based on Crowley himself—grows ever more dominant as the novel progresses. King Lamus is brilliant, gracious, and sufficiently impassive to stand up to the foul rumors and press libels that beset him during his visits to London. But in Telepylus there are no such distractions. Utopian peace and harmony reign. There Pendragon and Lou discover the truth of Thelema and the natural guidance their own True Wills could provide. As for the drugs that had enchained them, they could still be used in magical training—a vocation which suited Pendragon, but as for which Lou, a woman, had no affinity.

Treatment through the exercise of True Will will justly be regarded as naive in the extreme by modern-day readers, but it fit nicely with the views of many of Crowley's English contemporaries, who viewed drug abuse strictly as a moral weakness. *Drug Fiend* was accepted immediately upon completion by Collins; there seem to have been no editorial requests for changes. Indeed, so pleased was Collins with the work that it promptly advanced Crowley £120 for a second book, a full-scale autobiography which would ultimately be published—though not for seven years, and not by Collins—as the *Confessions*.

Initial reviews of *Drug Fiend* upon its publication in November 1922 were mixed. *The Times Literary Supplement* offered an acute assessment: "Mr. Crowley has not the literary fascination of a DeQuincey or the power and stark realism of a Zola. His most conspicuous gift is an effervescent imagination, an exuberant direction[. . .] It is impossible to

say that at any moment in the career of Peter and his wife do we seem
to be in touch with reality."

Whatever weaknesses *Drug Fiend* possessed, it hardly deserved the
fate it was about to receive—a public thrashing at the hands of James
Douglas, the book reviewer for the tabloid *Sunday Express*, who earlier
that year had castigated James Joyce's *Ulysses* as "the pinnacle and apex
of lubricity and obscenity." The headline for his review of *Drug Fiend*
ran: "A Book for Burning." Douglas reviled both Crowley's methods of
drug treatment and his Thelemic creed: "Although there is an attempt to
pretend that the book is merely a study of the deprivation caused by cocaine, in reality it is an ecstatic eulogy of the drug and of its effects upon
the body and the mind." He urged that Collins withdraw the book from
circulation. The *Sunday Express* followed up this review with a November 26, 1922, front-page story featuring a photo of a shaven-headed
Crowley. Tiers of lurid headlines above it proclaimed "Orgies in Sicily"
and the "Black Record of Aleister Crowley" and his "Preying on the De-
based." Collins was again urged to withdraw *Drug Fiend*. The publisher
all but capitulated. *Drug Fiend* was not immediately withdrawn, but
Collins ended marketing support and printed no further copies. The
contract for the *Confessions* was abruptly canceled.

Crowley was, at this time, already back in Cefalù. He had no funds for
a libel action; he lacked the desire for a pitched court battle; and, ironically, he somewhat relished the publicity afforded by the *Sunday Express*, as he believed that it would ultimately bring attention to what he
viewed as the true meaning of his life and writings. In the long term—
that is, posthumously—he has been borne out in this. But in the short
term, the impact was devastating in terms of establishing himself as a
mainstream author. His failure with Collins ended his last serious hopes
in that direction. As for his complementary hope of attracting disciples
to Cefalù, *Drug Fiend* was a disappointment here as well. There were a
small number of written inquiries, but none of its readers journeyed to
the Abbey.

There was, however, a new disciple upon whom Crowley found himself, in late 1922, placing the greatest hopes.

His birth name was Frederick Charles Loveday. As a young man he
took on the name "Raoul," and it is as Raoul Loveday that he is remembered. His parents were lower middle class, but Loveday managed not
only to win a scholarship to Oxford, but also to graduate with a First in
History from St. John's College. Loveday's range of interests included
Egyptology and the occult. He possessed fair hair which he wore rather

long for the period. His eyes were deepset and his face lean with prominent cheekbones.

Loveday was twenty-three, and just recently married, when he and Crowley first met in London in the late summer of 1922. His wife, an artist's model named Betty May, was several years Loveday's senior and had been twice previously married. May had earned a considerable reputation in bohemian circles by sitting for the sculptor Jacob Epstein (whose "Balzac" Crowley had championed back in 1911) for the creation of his bust "The Savage," which featured May's dramatically angular face and flared nostrils. May and Crowley had met briefly back in 1914, but neither left a lasting impression on the other. They would now engage quite literally in a battle of wills for the soul of Raoul Loveday.

At this time, Loveday and May were living together—primarily on May's earnings as a model—in a tawdry third-floor flat just off Regent Street. Loveday had already delved into Crowley's published works, and when their mutual acquaintance Betty Bickers offered the younger man an introduction to the famed and notorious Crowley, Loveday accepted with alacrity. According to May—who in 1929 would publish an autobiography of her own, entitled *Tiger-Woman*, after her nickname within bohemia—Loveday did not return for two days. When Loveday did at last come home, he was "covered with dust and soot, and his breath reeked of ether. I put him to bed, where he lay in a doped sleep until the middle of the following day. When he awoke I found out that he had spent the whole time he had been away with the great mystic, and that he had taken the drug to excite the mystical activities of his soul."

May was herself no stranger to drugs, acknowledging in *Tiger-Woman* that, for several years during her twenties, she had been a cocaine addict. She now took a dim view of Loveday's entrancement both with drugs and with Crowley and sought to make her husband give up both. For Crowley, the stakes were equally high. His efforts at developing disciples had come to a standstill. Now there was Loveday: "This was the man I had needed for the past ten years, a man with every gift that a Magus might need, and already prepared for initiation by practically complete knowledge, not only of the elements but of the essence of Magick." The time frame of ten years indicates that, in Loveday, Crowley sought a successor to Victor Neuburg. But unlike with Neuburg, there is no evidence that Crowley desired Loveday as a lover. Betty May, for all her accusations against Crowley, alleged nothing of the sort.

In October 1922, Crowley departed for Cefalù. En route, he posted a letter to Loveday urging him to follow with May in tow. May threatened to stay behind—only to have her bluff called by Loveday, who declared himself willing to go on alone. She then reluctantly agreed to accompany him, in the hope of thereby saving the marriage. The two found themselves without funds by the time they reached the Sicilian port city of Palermo. To pay for their train fares to Cefalù, Loveday sold the wedding ring he had given May. Enraged, she ran off and considered throwing herself at the mercy of the British consul for fare money back to London. But after some hours, she rejoined her husband.

They arrived at Cefalù on November 26, 1922. Their knock upon the Abbey door was answered by Crowley, who admitted Loveday after a proper exchange of the Thelemic greeting lines, "Do what thou wilt shall be the whole of the Law" and "Love is the law, love under will." But when May offered only "Good evening" in response, Crowley— "absolutely quivering with rage" according to May—demanded that she follow form or be denied entrance. It was the first of many assertions of Thelemic jurisdiction that May would face. In this case, she complied.

The responses of husband and wife to Abbey life were fundamentally opposed. For Loveday, it was an opportunity to pursue the path of wisdom under a living master. For May, it was forced confinement in a remote and eccentric household. Crowley saw Loveday as achieving in mere weeks what would have required long years under the Old Aeon Golden Dawn framework. Loveday's new magical name of Frater Aud was a Hebrew reference to astral or magical light and, through kabbalistic gematria, to the number eleven ascribed to magic.

By late December, the couple moved into their own separate room in the Umbilicus. There is no evidence that either husband or wife participated in sexual magic during their stay. But they were both made subject to Crowley's strict magical discipline—though with rather differing results. Both May and Loveday were given razors, to be self-administered upon their arms should they lapse into the use of "I"—a pronoun permitted to Crowley alone amongst the Abbey residents. May would have none of it. "I spoke exactly as I should wherever I was. I believe I threw the razor away. But poor Raoul, who took the whole thing with deadly seriousness, could not prevent himself from constantly saying 'I,' and he was so conscientious that he always wounded himself as a punishment, until his body was covered with cuts."

The enmity between May and Crowley flared all the more as a result of the illness that befell Loveday in January 1923. May conceded that, initially, she mistakenly attributed it to two causes—drug use (Loveday had, at Crowley's urging, been experimenting with large quantities of hashish) and the toxic effect of the consumption of cat's blood as part of a ritual sacrifice in which Loveday presided. Crowley did not speak of this ceremony in the *Confessions;* May's account, which may be exaggerated, is nonetheless fascinating in its depiction of Crowley's "hypnotic powers."

According to May, a cat that frequented the Abbey for food scraps was perceived by Crowley to be an evil spirit. Crowley grabbed the cat, which in turn severely scratched his arm. Crowley then resolved that it would be sacrificed in three days time by Loveday. As he announced this decree, "The Mystic held up his wand and made the sign of the Pentagram. 'You will not move till the hour of sacrifice,' he said to the cat. The animal stiffened and became as if petrified." Beyond question, if this occurred, it was most unusual feline behavior. The next morning, May carried the cat from the Abbey, but it returned on its own.

Alas, Crowley's powers were insufficient to render the cat immobile during the ceremony itself. Loveday had been supplied by Crowley with a Gurkha *kukkri*—a weapon with a boomerang-shaped blade. Loveday wielded it awkwardly and his first slash at the cat's neck failed to end its life. Despite having been quieted by a dab of ether, the wounded cat now escaped from Loveday's grasp and ran about before being all but decapitated by Loveday's second slash. A bowl captured a quantity of the flowing blood, which was then consecrated by Crowley. Dipping his finger in the blood, Crowley traced a pentagram on Loveday's forehead, then scooped some of the blood into a silver cup and gave it to Loveday who, May wrote, "drained it to the dregs."

All of this made for high drama, but the actual cause of Loveday's illness—diagnosed by the attending physician, a Dr. Maggio, as enteric fever—was an infection contracted by drinking from a mountain spring in the countryside outside Cefalù. Loveday and May had gone off on a hiking expedition; the diversion had been suggested by Crowley, who also warned the couple about drinking from the local springs. May heeded him, but Loveday, who had grown very thirsty, could not resist.

By the second week in February, Loveday had weakened to the point that any physical movement was difficult for him. He and May had been writing a series of letters to Loveday's mother in England, reassuring her—despite the ongoing tabloid attacks—that Crowley and his Abbey were respectable and that they were safe there. But in a letter of February 11—dictated by Loveday from his bed and transcribed by May—a tone of desperation emerged. Loveday confessed that he had been suffering from fever and diarrhea for some ten days and that "it has left me as weak as water." He also stated his intention to return with May to England as soon as he felt well enough to do so.

Unbeknownst to her husband, May added a note to the back of Loveday's letter which conveyed—for the first time, after two months of reassurance—an urgent warning to his mother. Her son was too weak to be moved, and Crowley had become a manipulative tyrant:

> He is laying down all sorts of rules, rules that could not possibly
> be kept. I have never worked so hard in my life as I have here. I
> am very ill, myself, but I am looking after Raoul as best I can. He
> wants a good warm bed and nourishment which we cannot get
> here. If Raoul gets better Crowley thinks of parting us and what
> can we do. We have got no money and are dependent upon him
> for our food.

On this very day, May explained, Crowley had ordered her out of the Abbey, but she had refused to leave Loveday in his hands.

As to the events of this day—February 11, 1923—differing versions survive in writings by May, Hirsig, and Crowley. The initial cause of the uproar was May's insistence on reading—while on the Abbey premises, and hence in violation of the Abbey rules, to which both May and Loveday had sworn adherence in writing upon their arrival—English newspapers sent by Loveday's mother on a fortnightly basis at Loveday's request. On February 11, Loveday was too weak to read them. May retired to her own room to do so. Here is her account of what ensued:

> I had not been reading long when the Mystic strode in, his face
> twitching with rage. He ordered me to go. There was a terrific
> scene. I should have said before that there were several loaded
> revolvers which used to lie about the abbey. They were very
> necessary, for we never knew whether brigands might not attack
> it. The Mystic used to shoot any dogs that came anywhere near
> the abbey with his revolver. He was an extremely good shot. It
> so happened that I had found one of these revolvers lying about
> the day before, and it suddenly occurred to me that it would be
> a wise precaution to hide it under my pillow. I now seized it and
> fired it wildly at the Mystic. It went wide of the mark. He
> laughed heartily. Then I rushed at him, but could not get a grip
> on his shaved head. He picked me up in his arms and flung me
> bodily outside, through the front door.

Crowley, in the *Confessions,* described the fight in a sangfroid tone and made no mention of a pistol. May did fling a glass at his head, he allowed, but at no time did his own emotions rise to rage. "I tried to soothe her and abate her violence. Poor Raoul, weak as he was, got up and held her and begged her to be quiet. At last she calmed down, but the room was a wreck." Loveday was moved to Crowley's room. And then, according to Crowley, May made her departure into Cefalù—not by his order, but by her resolve. "Both Raoul and Alostrael begged her to be sensible, but off she went to the hotel where she was at once consoled by a series of admirers."

The sneering implication here is sexual, but the more real concern for Crowley was the sympathy May might win from the authorities, both Sicilian and British. Wolfe was sent down to the hotel early the next morning—February 12—to visit with May and learn her intentions. May informed her that she planned to send an urgent telegraph to Loveday's father and to speak with both the Commissario of Cefalù and the British Consul in Palermo. Wolfe promptly returned to the Abbey, where she transcribed a letter dictated by Loveday which pleaded with May to return. May did so, whereupon she was given an affidavit drawn up by Hirsig and told to sign it as a condition of her reentry. That affidavit concurs with Crowley's version in essential details. No mention is made of a gun.

The next morning Loveday's condition worsened. The following day, February 14, Dr. Maggio was summoned from town and made the diagnosis of acute enteritis. As to this turn of events, Crowley felt intense grief but no real surprise. On February 13 he had recorded in his diary: "I feel a current of Magical force—heavy, black and silent—threatening the Abbey." According to May, Crowley had, during this period, cast the horoscope of Loveday and concluded that there had fallen, upon the latter, "A very gloomy depression. It looks as though you might die on the sixteenth of February at four o'clock." Crowley never himself claimed to have performed this act of prescience. Loveday—in Crowley's view the most brilliant disciple to have come to Cefalù—died on February 16 at approximately 4 P.M.

Neither Crowley nor May were present at the moment of his passing. In the *Confessions*, Crowley offered what must have been his wish for Loveday's final moments: "Raoul developed paralysis of the heart and died at once without fear or pain. It was as if a man, tired of staying indoors, had gone out for a walk."

May remained peacefully at the Abbey for three more days, when money for her return fare arrived from the British consulate—this in response to a subdued letter (drafted by Hirsig and signed by May) sent on February 12. There had, in short, been a détente achieved between

May and Crowley—bitter adversaries for over two months—during the final week of Loveday's life.

As for Crowley, he fell seriously ill immediately after the conclusion of the funeral and was bedridden, with bouts of high fever, for several weeks. Hirsig and Wolfe served as his nurses; but toward the end of February Wolfe was sent to London to raise funds for the Abbey. For the first time in roughly two years, the original residents of the Abbey were alone.

But not for long. May, upon returning to London, was interviewed by the *Sunday Express*—the same tabloid that led the attack on *Drug Fiend*. A front-page article ran on February 25, 1923 with the tiered headline:

NEW SINISTER RELATIONS OF ALEISTER CROWLEY.
VARSITY LAD'S DEATH.
Enticed To "Abbey".
Dreadful Ordeal of a Young Wife.
Crowley's Plans.

The article itself was an admixture of bare fact and troweled-on innuendo. While Loveday's death is correctly ascribed to enteritis, he is also referred to as one of Crowley's "latest victims"—along with May herself. The melodramatic plotline was pursued throughout the piece. For example: "Once they were in Sicily, however, they found they had been trapped in an inferno, a maelstrom of filth and obscenity. Crowley's purpose was to corrupt them both to his own ends."

The *Sunday Express* followed up—on March 4—with a further account of the horrors of the Beast and his Abbey: "This man Crowley is one of the most sinister figures of modern times. He is a drug fiend, an author of vile books, the spreader of obscene practices." *John Bull*, which had nipped at Crowley's heels since the Rites of Eleusis in 1910, now took over as the lead attacker. In a series of six pieces published in April and May 1923, Crowley was headlined as "The King of Depravity," "The Wickedest Man in the World," and "A Cannibal at Large." The latter title was not intended metaphorically; *John Bull* averred that Crowley had, during a Himalayan expedition, killed and eaten two of his native porters. The legend of Crowley had reached its exfoliating apex.

In the *Confessions*, Crowley insisted that he was above it all—as indeed, in certain of his moods, he was. When he learned that his friend William Seabrook was doing a similar series of lurid features on Crowley in

America, tailored to the tastes of the Hearst Sunday tabloid chain—with headlines such as "SECRETS BEHIND THE SCENES AMONG THE DEVIL-WORSHIPPERS"—Crowley concluded that Seabrook "was as fair as his circumstances permitted" and that the result would be "to familiarize the American public with my name and interest them in my career sufficiently to induce the few intelligent individuals who have read it to inquire independently into the facts of my case." The lurid publicity did attract intelligent interest amongst a few. But it also served to fascinate a large number of fools drawn to imitate the worst of the gothic legend. These fools are with us to this day. There was, however, a more immediate result of the 1923 attacks which Crowley never acknowledged. In his native England, for the remainder of his life, his reputation had at last been damaged beyond repair.

Back in Cefalù, Crowley was preparing for the arrival of a disciple named Norman Mudd—the same Mudd who had been a compatriot of Victor Neuburg in the Cambridge student–club efforts on Crowley's behalf back in 1910. Mudd arrived at the Abbey on April 22, 1923. His timing could not have been less fortunate. An order of expulsion was read to Crowley, in the Office of the Commissario in Cefalù, on the morning of April 23.

At first, by Crowley's account, the police insisted that all Abbey members were to leave. But Crowley prevailed on his point that the order, as issued, applied to himself alone. Crowley then asked for a week to prepare for his departure; this was granted. Mudd and Shumway would stay behind to care for the Abbey; Hirsig would accompany Crowley in his exile. With the departure of the Beast and the Scarlet Woman, however, the energies that fueled the Abbey were gone. There would be various residents over the next two years, with Shumway the most consistent presence. But the vital existence of the Abbey was at an end.

Why did the Fascist regime of Benito Mussolini (named Premier six months before, in October 1922) take action? Crowley would later insist, in a piece written for the London *Sunday Express* in 1933, that "The explanation of why I left is quite simple and unsensational. . . . Several people who were my guests at the 'abbey' made imaginative copy out of their visits. Then the Fascists came into power and some foreign newspaper correspondents were asked to leave. And so was I." This is inaccurate as to basic chronology—the interviews given by Mary Butts and Betty May to the *Sunday Express* appeared after Mussolini came into power. But it may have been the case that the negative publicity was viewed by the Fascists as reflecting poorly upon their regime.

Just what feelings Crowley would have held toward Mussolini, had the expulsion not occurred, is open to question. In the *Confessions*—completed in the months just after Crowley left Cefalù—Crowley allows that his first glimpse of Fascism—in Rome in October 1922, on his way back to the Abbey from London—was a favorable one: "Rome was wild with enthusiasm. The Fascisti swarmed all over the city. I thought their behaviour admirable. They policed the towns and suppressed any attempted breach of the peace with the utmost efficiency [. . .]" By April, however—prior to the expulsion—Crowley claimed to have concluded that Mussolini was a failure by virtue of having compromised his principles to obtain papal support. But Mussolini had been making overtures to the Church as early as the spring of 1921. Either Crowley was uninformed, or his politics were influenced by his exile—for it was only after May 1923 that Crowley spoke out against Mussolini.

Crowley consulted the *I Ching*, plotting potential relocations. At last, he decided upon Tunisia, then under French rule. And so the Beast and the Scarlet Woman departed the Abbey over which they had ruled in a manner befitting their belief in the New Aeon. On May 1, they sailed from Palermo. The following day, they arrived in the port of Tunis. North Africa had served Crowley before as a place in which to test and cleanse his soul. It would do so now again.

CHAPTER NINE

Years of Exile and Wandering—and the Publication of a Masterwork (1923–30)

C rowley and Hirsig landed in Tunisia as the Beast and Scarlet Woman in exile. By May 11, 1923, they found a cheap room in a hotel, Au Souffle du Zephir, in La Marsa Plage, a tourist beach town northeast of Tunis. Once ensconced here, Crowley tried, in his diary, to cheer himself by wishfully imagining that those who dared oppose him were futilely opposing the forces of destiny. In this case, the victim would be Mussolini: "It is the beginning of the end for this upstart renegade with his gang of lawless ruffians, and his crazy attempt to restore the tyranny of the Dark Ages. Only twenty-eight days since he signed the order for my expulsion from Italy, and already he totters."

Crowley was still struggling with his dependence on drugs—primarily heroin, but also cocaine, which he would attempt to employ (along with luminal and ethyl oxide) as a palliative for the heroin craving. His average heroin usage since October 1922 had reached three grains per day. Insomnia, dyspnoea, diarrhea, and days lost in lassitude were his most prominent symptoms.

Yet Crowley was productive during this time, composing two incisive essays, "Ethyl Oxide" and "What is Qabalah?", on consecutive days. But his primary labor during this summer, fostered by isolation, was to complete the dictation to Hirsig of the *Confessions*. Hirsig was a tireless amanuensis who also returned to the Abbey, this same summer, to look in on Shumway and the children. These now included a new arrival, born to Shumway on May 19—a baby girl whose father was Baron La

Calce, the landlord of the Abbey. Baron La Calce took no responsibility for the child, nor did Shumway press him to. Crowley, in absentia, named the girl, in his typical exhaustive manner, Isabella Isis Selene Hecate Artemis Diana Hera Jane.

Shumway would continue on at the Abbey until evicted by the Baron in late 1924 for failure to pay rent. It was Shumway, and Shumway alone, who cared for her daughter by Crowley, Astarte Lulu Panthea, whom Crowley would see but once more—late in 1928, when the girl paid her itinerant father a brief visit in Paris.

For Crowley, in Tunisia, the psychological task of concluding his "Autohagiography," as he termed it (half-seriously, half in jest), must have been severe. He had lost both his Abbey and his reputation, and no longer had a publisher for the massive work on which he labored. The tone of the *Confessions* reveals none of this—throughout, it is all but unremitting in its braggadocio. His diaries of the time reveal a more anguished self-analysis. On May 19, during an ethyl oxide session, Crowley considered, in studied hypothetical terms, what suicide would mean in the case of a man, such as himself, who might have been damaged by his drug "experiments" and might further be left "a mere shadow of my former self" should he subject himself to a "regular cure"—one administered by physicians, and not self-prescribed in a kingly manner as befitted the prophet of Thelema. "Why drag out a useless life, dishonouring my reputation, discrediting my methods, etc?" Crowley perceived a magical virtue in the capacity to embrace death as a needed means of change—in contrast to the self-absorption that marks the practitioner of black magic: "Here is another argument against the Black Brothers, against the idea of resistance to change in general, against the static conception of the Ego etc." He further argued that suicide would represent, not the demise of his prophetic vocation, but rather a shifting of tactics—incarnations—for the sake of Thelema: "Suicide should not be taken as an indication of failure (in such a case) but of the (proper) determination to be done with a worn-out tool, or to make way for new ones, or (perhaps) to get a new one oneself."

Two subsequent entries, on June 4 and June 10, confirm how deeply shaken he was by his exile. In the first, Crowley revisited the Christian childhood that still lived within him, despite three years of arduous self-transformation in the Chambre des Cauchemars. The insistent critics of his character, to whom Crowley refers below, remain unknown:

> I got the intimation that I should be exceedingly welcome in the ranks of the enemy [Christianity, should Crowley convert to it]

on account of my importance as the Incarnation of Evil.[. . .] Such at least are the imbecile arguments advanced by the people who are at present engaged in attacking me. They tell me too that this is my last chance to put myself right with God. They recall to me all sorts of psychological facts about my past. It is all part of a plan for making my excuses to an offended Deity. [. . .] They point out to me that I am a perfectly eligible candidate as King of the Puritans. They show me how easy it would be to interpret every incident of my career in this light. It is perfectly true, moreover, that I am legitimately the King of the Puritans, that the Law of Thelema is in fact the most perfect statement of Puritanism that has ever been promulgated.

They also prove to me with the greatest wealth of detail (I am really rather ashamed that I have already forgotten it) that the *Book of the Law* is after all the perfect expression of my subconscious self & therefore much more truly my work than anything else I have ever written.[. . .] Of course they do not throw any doubt upon my sincerity; their idea seems to be that I am self-deluded through a lack of the sense of proportion; this being my most sensitive point. The attack is venomous.

For Crowley to so much as consider the response of Christendom to a penitent Beast returning to the fold shows how deeply the attack struck.

In a June 10 entry, Crowley tried to rally himself by reflecting upon his role as keeper of the age-old esoteric wisdom. If the risks he ran in obtaining and transmitting this wisdom had led him astray—even *fundamentally* astray—history would nonetheless absolve him. As Stephen Skinner has noted, the "Universal knowledge, wisdom" and other qualities referred to by Crowley below represent the sephiroth of the kabbalistic Tree of Life, which are coiled about by the serpent of wisdom. Crowley wrote:

Nobody before Aleister Crowley had the means of tracing to their inmost recesses the secrets of the Magi[. . .]because I have got the secrets of Universal knowledge, wisdom & power & understanding & of the beauty & victory & splendour that proceed from Him that is coiled within its coils. I may be a Black Magician but I'm a bloody great one. The world may have to pass through a period of error through me, but even the error will tend toward the truth.

To resort to greatness as a Black Magician as a justification for his life was a low point to which Crowley did not—in his surviving writings—return.

As for disciples such as Norman Mudd, they came to Crowley in dead earnest seeking no less than truth. And if Mudd pestered the life out of Crowley, Crowley gave as good as he got. The story of Mudd's long devotion to Crowley is as remarkable and cautionary a tale of esoteric discipleship as one could wish.

Mudd, it will be recalled, had been a student supporter of Crowley during the latter's failed attempt to lecture to the young men of Cambridge in 1910. While fellow undergraduate Victor Neuburg went on to an eventful partnership with the Beast, Mudd had faded away.

But Mudd remained obsessed by a sense of shame at having abandoned Crowley. Over the next decade, Mudd desultorily pursued an academic career and emigrated to South Africa to become head of the Department of Applied Mathematics at Grey University College, Bloemfontein. A bachelor, he lost sight in one eye in 1915 due to gonorrheal complication. But in 1920, Mudd took advantage of a sabbatical leave to come to London and find the Master he still revered. Crowley, of course, was by this time in Cefalù. Poor Mudd abandoned his London search and—deceived by the address given in the *Blue Equinox*—crossed the Atlantic to Detroit.

Crowley was nowhere to be found, but Charles Robert Stansfeld Jones (Frater Achad) was. Jones accepted Mudd as his student in early 1921, with unsatisfactory results from the perspective of both men. As a newly admitted Probationer of the A∴A∴, Mudd took the name *Omnia Pro Veritate* ("All for Truth"). He may fairly be said to have lived up to this name—in the years that followed, Mudd would indeed sacrifice all that he had in the name of Truth as he saw it or, ultimately, failed to see it.

While studying under Jones, Mudd at last made contact through the mails with Crowley, who encouraged Mudd both to send money and to come to Cefalù. Paradoxically, this contact heightened Mudd's doubts as to his magical vocation. On April 12, 1921, Mudd set aside his Oath as a Probationer, left Detroit with no explanation to Jones, and returned to South Africa. But on Christmas Day 1922, Mudd reversed himself once more. In a despairing frame of mind, Mudd read en masse the letters that Crowley had sent him since 1921—letters which Mudd had left unopened and unanswered, in a final futile effort to forget his teacher.

These letters now confirmed his new course. Mudd, balding and entering middle age, would vindicate—at last—the cowardly Cambridge boy.

He resigned his teaching post, liquidated his possessions, and set sail for Cefalù where, as previously described, he arrived on April 22, 1923, the day before Crowley's expulsion. Mudd was now ordered by his long-sought Master to remain with Shumway at the Abbey while the Beast and Scarlet Woman went into exile.

But Mudd did his best, bequeathing his funds to Crowley and his labor—for two months—to the dying Abbey. Mudd also became Crowley's personal secretary, composing letters to potentially sympathetic persons who might intervene on the Beast's behalf with the Italian government. But to proceed effectively, Mudd felt in need of an explanation as to why Crowley's reputation was quite so black. Crowley composed a remarkably frank letter to Mudd on June 13, just prior to the latter's arrival in Tunisia to join the Beast and the Scarlet Woman. The opening sentence may seem suspect to the reader, but it may be taken as sincere, in light of the extreme disclosures that follow:

> I have always been temperate and cautious until recently. I now find myself thrown into a spiritual state unfamiliar and terrible by the simple process of stopping Heroin for a short time. I get dissociation both of personality and ideas such as I never had even in the Abyss [the kabbalistic passage between the Second and the Third Orders of the A∴A∴]. Several fundamental ideas peculiar to A.C. have been ruthlessly annihilated in the last week. My point of view has been revolutionized. Also, I have ceased to struggle against death or insanity.[. . .]
>
> I quite agree that my career for all these 19 years [since 1904] has been a brilliant failure; a classic example of the results of a magical blunder.[. . .] I refused to act by CCXX [the *Book of the Law*]. I took all the reasonable measures I could to secure the success of my works. That is what has smashed my career. Might it then not be the final disastrous mistake to get myself back to normality as every reasonable element in my mind urges. At no time have I feared to risk insanity or death for the sake of the Work but there is still this feeling that part of my proof is to be a fine healthy old boy so as to escape the reproach of the ungodly.
>
> Here is a point where your 'love' is wanted. I can trust you because you once wrote that it doesn't matter a fart whether I lived or died.

In what context Mudd made this latter remark is unknown, but Mudd's actions, at least, bespeak that it mattered very greatly. Once arrived in Tunisia, Mudd served as secretary and de facto worldly liaison. A letter by Mudd in praise of Crowley was published in the November 14, 1923, issue of the Oxford University magazine *Isis*. This was followed, in 1924, by the pamphlet *An Open Letter to Lord Beaverbrook*, privately printed and mailed to all manner of British literary and political figures. In it, Mudd cited the lies printed by Beaverbrook's *Sunday Express*, confessed the Beast's inability to bear litigation costs, and demanded fair play by the wealthy lord. The pamphlet had no impact whatsoever.

For his part, Crowley struggled throughout the year to raise his flagging magical energies. He took a room in the Tunisia Palace, a swank hotel in the capital, while Hirsig remained in La Marsa. Crowley's companion was a young black male, Mohammed ben Brahim, whom Crowley had hired as a servant and with whom he performed sexual magic. Life in the Tunisia Palace was well beyond Crowley's means, but he managed it for a time.

In September, a perturbation arose. As a result of working closely with her, Mudd had fallen in love with Hirsig, the gaunt Scarlet Woman. He had even gone so far to broach the suggestion to Crowley that he, Mudd, could legally marry the Scarlet Woman, a step that the Beast had never taken. One might imagine this a friction-free matter in the realm of Thelema, in which love was identified with will and restriction with sin. But Crowley found nothing to admire in Mudd's emotional state, which Hirsig seems to have reciprocated with affection, as opposed to passion. When Mudd, in his magical diary, accused Crowley of an "attitude of possession," Crowley penned his denial: "No: unity with her. She is 'mine' just as my liver is." Crowley also probed at Mudd's sexual fear of "an ordeal of utter shame before Alostrael." Wrote Crowley, perhaps remembering his own abasements in the Chambre des Cauchemars: "If you only knew! It was touch and go my saying, first time you came into the room, 'There's a choice of orifices, go to it' and filling a fresh pipe. But I couldn't inflict it on you: I'm getting tender-hearted in my old age!"

Crowley depended upon Hirsig, and though he would not admit it to Mudd, he must have felt challenged by Mudd's aspirations to his Scarlet Woman. After all, he had recently confided to his diary that "the enemy"—respectable Christendom—could best undermine him by undermining his Scarlet Woman: "If they could get me to distrust her, even in thought, the rest would be easy." In a more intimate vein, there is this all-too-human confession on June 29: "I am always thinking of Alostrael, loving her.[. . .] The truth is (I fear) that the beauty of human love—as she & I know it—does really give a new meaning to the old foolish fear of death." Small wonder that Mudd's proposal of marriage rankled.

To combat his lapse of love, Mudd was sent to the nearby village of Hamman-Lif for a Magical Retirement, from September 28 to October 8, during which he was to meditate upon the danger of abandoning the Great Work for the sake of a woman. The more Mudd pondered in isolation, the more he felt able to subjugate his desire. By October 1, he could write that his longing for Hirsig had been merely an example of a "false Will."

Crowley was no doubt pleased to have gotten Mudd back on tow, but he had greater tasks at hand. One such was to fire a poetic volley at Mussolini. He composed a pamphlet of verse, *Songs for Italy*, in the summer of 1923; copies were sent in October 1923 to members of the press. There was a conscious linkage to Byron and Shelley (who found inspiration in Italy) in the poem "Resurgam et Libertas," in which Crowley proclaimed himself "the first English poet ever thrust/From Italy." But there was little notice paid to *Songs* in England or anywhere else.

On a quite different endeavor, Crowley remained determined to complete the *Comment* prophesied by the *Book*. He had failed at this twice before—neither the "Old Comment," published in *The Equinox* in 1912, nor the "New Comment," completed in Cefalù, satisfied the Beast. In November 1923, while conducting a Magical Retirement in Nefta in the company of Hirsig and Mohammed ben Brahim, Crowley girded himself once more and produced the "Djeridensis Comment," a reference to the nearby lake Chott Djerid, which, as Hymenaeus Beta has pointed out, was the mythological birthplace of the Greek goddess of wisdom, Athena. Crowley was ultimately displeased with this Comment as well. But stylistically, it was by far the finest effort of the three. The complementary roles of the Beast and the Scarlet Woman were set forth in terms that aptly blended Christian, Taoist, and Thelemic symbolism: "I am a Sun, giving out Light and Life; but She their guide in darkness, making them pure, single of heart, awake to the Highest."

During their stay at Nefta, both the Beast and the Scarlet Woman were bed-ridden by illness. Their moods suffered as well, leading to quarrels and a premature abandonment of the proposed month-long Retirement. They returned to Tunis. Then, in late December, Crowley set sail for France, leaving behind an emotionally and financially bereft

Hirsig. The funds for his journey were provided by his old friend—and fellow *Fatherland* contributor—Frank Harris, himself in severe straits. Despite their mutual poverty, the two men corresponded avidly in the first months of 1924 as to an utterly futile scheme of raising some 800,000 francs for the purchase of the Paris *Evening Telegram*. Once in Paris, in January 1924, Crowley lodged again with Monsieur Bourcier at the Hotel de Blois at 50 rue Vavin in Montparnasse. Crowley still owed money from prior stays, and it is a tribute to Bourcier's feeling for the Beast that he allowed him again to run up debt. Mudd was dispatched to London, joining Jane Wolfe, who worked a night shift in a nursing home and sent money when she could. There Mudd attempted to raise funds and public support for Crowley, failing on both counts.

During February 1924, while in the throes of his heroin addiction and asthma attacks, Crowley visited his old haunt of Fontainebleau. Here he paid a visit to the Institute for the Harmonious Development of Man that had been established by the spiritual teacher G. I. Gurdjieff. Gurdjieff is as influential a figure in twentieth-century esotericism as Crowley himself, and their careers are markedly similar in certain respects—not only their shaven heads and penetrating gazes, but also their mutual fondness for outlandish behavior and hyperbole. A detailed comparison between the two men is not possible here, but in fundamental terms, it may be said that Crowley sought to establish a religion while Gurdjieff employed disparate teaching methods with individual students.

Just what relations existed between Crowley and Gurdjieff must remain in some doubt, although varying accounts of an alleged meeting between them have become the stuff of legend. Let us begin with the less melodramatic version offered by Crowley. On February 10, he called upon Gurdjieff's Institute, the main château of which was known as the Prieure des Basses Loges. Gurdjieff was not in, but a disciple named Major Pindar received Crowley graciously. In his diary, Crowley's remarks on Gurdjieff were respectful:

> Gurdjieff, their prophet, seems a tip-top man. Heard more sense and insight than I've done for years.[. . .] Gurdjieff clearly a very advanced adept. My chief quarrels are over sex (I doubt whether Pindar understands G's true position) & their [the Institute's] punishments—e.g. depriving the offender of a meal or making him stand half an hour with his arms out. Childish & morally valueless.

There was no mention by Crowley himself of a later visit to Fontainebleau. And yet, in circles sympathetic to Gurdjieff, the story passes of a face-to-face meeting with a combative denouement, as in this account by occult historian James Webb:

> Crowley arrived for a whole weekend and spent the time like any other visitor to the Prieure; being shown the grounds and the activities in progress, listening to Gurdjieff's music and his oracular conversation. Apart from some circumspection, Gurdjieff treated him like any other guest until the evening of his departure. After dinner on Sunday night, Gurdjieff led the way out of the dining room with Crowley, followed by the body of pupils who had also been at the meal. Crowley made his way toward the door and turned to take his leave of Gurdjieff, who by this time was some way up the stairs to the second floor. "Mister, you go?" Gurdjieff inquired. Crowley assented. "You have been guest?"—a fact which the visitor could hardly deny. "Now you go, you are no longer guest?" Crowley—no doubt wondering whether his host has lost his grip on reality and was wandering in a semantic wilderness—humored his mood by indicating that he was on his way back to Paris. But Gurdjieff, having made the point that he was not violating the canons of hospitality, changed on the instant into the embodiment of righteous anger. "You filthy," he stormed, "you dirty inside! Never again you set foot in my house!" [. . .] White-faced and shaking, the Great Beast crept back to Paris with his tail between his legs.

Webb portrayed Gurdjieff's triumph—and Crowley's putative inner thoughts—with a heavy-handed novelistic touch. If this brutal banishment did occur, then it is remarkable that Crowley, who harbored animus toward so many rival teachers, never did so toward Gurdjieff.

Hirsig joined Crowley in Paris toward the end of March 1924, having completed yet another mission of assistance to the failing Abbey in Cefalù. She was a solace to him now, as his health broke down decisively. Crowley underwent two painful surgeries during the winter of 1924, in hopes of alleviating his asthma symptoms. Hirsig wrote to Frank Bennett on April 14: "Beast lay ill in Paris for months—no care, and damn little food.[. . .] Since I've been here—two weeks—he has picked up remarkably but we still wonder where our next near-meal is to come from. Only the greatest tact has kept a roof over our heads & heaven knows what is happening in Cefalù!" By the end of the month, even tact had failed them—Bourcier at last evicted them. It was a dire time for Crowley; his physician, Dr. Jarvis, recommended a nursing home. Given his Thelemic convictions, Crowley could not have been pleased.

The two returned that May to a former haunt, the inn Au Cadrau Bleu at Chelles-sur-Marne. With Crowley in a listless state, Hirsig tried to maintain herself as the fearless Scarlet Woman. In her magical diaries of this period, commenced in autumn 1923 and entitled *Alostrael's Visions*, she vowed to cultivate a wisdom worthy of her exalted role. She repeatedly invoked Aiwass and, on December 12, felt herself "sliding into a vision." It should be remembered that, while Hirsig had proven herself the most loyal and durable of Crowley's Scarlet Women, she had never served as a medium for a revelation—as had Rose Kelly, Mary Desti, and Roddie Minor before her. The *Vision* diaries, which she kept through the end of 1924, were an attempt to remedy this.

But the Scarlet Woman found herself challenged both by Crowley's frailties and by her own lack of magical resolve. One night in June, she watched as Crowley spoke with Alexander Xul Solar, a moneyed Argentinian artist whom the Beast hoped to win as a disciple. Later she wrote that Crowley's "rasping voice so jarred me that I wanted to scream." On other occasions, she found the stink of his ether unbearable. As for the Beast, there is the sense, in his diary entries, of a low ebb between them. It was not a state of being for which he had a great appreciation.

In late August he met Dorothy Olsen, who would, within weeks, formally supplant Hirsig as the primary Scarlet Woman. It is worth reflecting on the magnitude of this change. Crowley was sundering an intimate magical relationship that had endured since 1919. Hirsig was the last woman with whom Crowley would form so deep an alliance— or, in Rosicrucian terms, an alchymical marriage. The change was no less fundamental for Hirsig. She tried to retain an independent role as a Scarlet Woman capable of her own visions—and initiations of new sexual partners. But she would anoint no new Beast to replace Crowley. And in his absence, Thelema waned for her. Still, she persevered for nearly three years more, despite Crowley's mounting indifference to her.

The arrival of Dorothy Olsen transformed all. Olsen, of Norwegian extraction and raised in Wisconsin, was the product of a stable American middle-class background; she turned thirty-three just as her affair with Crowley began. Judging from her letters that survive (these are from the late 1920s, after the affair had ended), Olsen was warm and direct, with an enthusiasm rather than a passion for magic and a solicitous fondness for Crowley that stopped short of a devotion to Thelema itself. Olsen could not spiritually challenge the Beast as had the prior Scarlet

Woman. But Hirsig had grown haggard, and Olsen was striking, with wavy blond hair and a Garboesque profile. Crowley tersely described the scene upon bringing Olsen to the Paris hotel room that he had been sharing with Hirsig: "Invaded 207. Leah collapsed." The next day, September 23, Crowley and Olsen were off by train to Marseilles, en route to North Africa where Crowley had hopes of inspired magical workings with the new Scarlet Woman, who was also now "Soror Astrid"—her new magical name subsequent to her A∴A∴ initiation.

On board a ship to Tunis, Crowley was moved by the Secret Chiefs to write a brief proclamation, "To Man," later called "The Mediterranean Manifesto." Crowley incorporated this into *The Heart of the Master*, a brief compendium of spiritual autobiography and esoteric arcana written the following year. The fundamental purpose of both "To Man" and *The Heart of the Master* was to proclaim Crowley as the World Teacher of the New Aeon. The former writing was specially directed to the Theosophical Society, then under the leadership of Annie Besant and Charles W. Leadbeater, who would soon announce the ascension of their protégé, the young Jiddu Krishnamurti, as the World Teacher. It was Crowley's futile hope to dissuade the Society from this plan. Ironically, Krishnamurti soon renounced that role voluntarily, though he went on to become one of the most widely read of twentieth-century writers on mysticism.

"To Man" concluded with an adjuration to prospective seekers to contact, not Crowley, but Dorothy Olsen, in Sidi bou Said, Tunisia—where Crowley had the manifesto printed shortly after their arrival. In honor of Olsen, Crowley found a jeweler in Tunis who transformed his $9°=2^\square$ Magus ring (pawned and then retrieved by Crowley just before their departure from Paris) "into a Jewel for the Brows of Astrid." They spent the autumn of 1924 in wanderings along the Tunisian coast. In late November they returned to Tunis. En route, Crowley penned this blithe poem:

> I have got the girl I wanted
> (In my heart are dagger-thrusts)
> Her wicked little bats' eyes slanted
> Gleaming with unfathomable lusts
> Glittering slits through which the soul
> Burns in hell like a live coal.

The theme of torment at the hands of a woman governed by "unfathomable lusts" persisted through the years.

As for Hirsig—the one amongst Crowley's Scarlet Women who could be said to have possessed lusts which Crowley truly found "unfathomable"—she spent the last months of 1924 in spiritual and physical misery in Paris. Having endured the agony of losing Crowley, she learned shortly thereafter, by way of a telegram from Shumway, that her sister Alma, who had long detested Crowley, had come to Cefalù and—with no opposition from the local authorities—had taken Hirsig's son, Hansi, back with her to America on the grounds that the Abbey was unfit for the boy. It could not have been made more plain that the standing of the Abbey—of Thelema itself—was a nullity in the eyes of the world.

In her magical diary entry for September 26, 1924, Hirsig tried to see the destiny of Thelema whole; Olsen would play her necessary part, while Hirsig herself would fade away:

> A word to Dorothy. She is the Scarlet Woman & she will show her failure or her success quite differently to previous Scarlet Women, for she is the mother of a *race* of a new Dynasty. How I would love to write up my ideas of succession and breeding and all that. But it isn't my job. That will be done by my Beloved Beast all in good time.
>
> He will arrange everything for the New Civilization—
>
> And I shall live in that Civilization I suppose. I don't know and don't care.

Hirsig went on to cite—in a starkly stoic and unnerving passage—the brave example of Poupée, the infant daughter she had borne for the Beast, who had died in 1921: "A Thelemite doesn't need to die with a doctor poking at him. He finishes up what he has to do and then dies. That's what Poupée did. She didn't pay attention to anything or anybody. Her eyes grew filmy & she died with a grin on her face. Such a wise grin."

Death was much on Hirsig's mind now. She suffered often from cold and hunger. Unable to pay the rent, she was evicted from the hotel room she had once shared with the Beast. On September 28 she confessed to her diary: "I should have liked, as a human creature, to have died in the arms of the Beast 666 who, it will be noted in my very first diary, (commencing Mar. 21, 1919), was and is my lover, my mate, my Father, my child and everything else that Woman needs in Man. But I have never interfered with his Work; which was my Work, the Great Work, except in ignorance."

On September 30, Mudd left London, where he had failed in his efforts to vindicate the Beast, and joined Hirsig in Paris—but with no funds to help her in her plight. The meeting between the two Thelemic devotees—once primary in Crowley's circle, and now left behind to type the *Confessions* (this was Hirsig's task) and to promote potential lawsuits and literary deals (this to Mudd)—must have been a grim one. But then Hirsig saw the possibilities. As Scarlet Woman she was the magical Mother of Mudd the Son—whom Hirsig now termed a perfect esoteric Fool, a Parsifal. Her pet German nickname for him was *"Dummling,"* Little Fool. But Parsifal could be initiated—trained to utilize his lance by virtue of the Mother transforming into the Whore. The frustrated sexual energy in Mudd could become a magical boon both to his own progress and to the well-being of the Scarlet Woman. As she explained it plainly to him: "That was my only way in which to gain health quickly." Mudd, who had for so long fretted over his adequacy, performed honorably for his Scarlet Woman. As Hirsig recorded, "Parsifal used his lance in my defence and being my champion will do so whenever his lady needs protection." For his part, Mudd felt himself renewed. Five days later, after the completion of another opus, Hirsig described her partner as "a man who does not know who he is, but is commonly called Norman Mudd."

It was the hope of the Mother that the Son would at last discover who he was, but there was no signal breakthrough on that score. By early December, Mudd returned to London to renew his lonely efforts on that front. Neither he nor Hirsig had received any financial or moral support from the Beast in his desultory and sometimes surly correspondence. Hirsig passed a terrible early winter in Paris, briefly holding a job in a grubby little restaurant in Montparnasse. She waited tables, peeled vegetables, performed all manner of scullery work and wore herself to a frazzle. There is no evidence, despite the assertions of prior biographers, that Hirsig ever sold herself as a prostitute on the streets of Paris. But she was now pointedly snubbed in the Montparnasse cafés in which, with Crowley, she had been a habitué.

Then came a summons from Crowley, in late January 1925, to come to Tunis. Olsen was pregnant and Hirsig's assistance was required while the Beast continued with his magical work. Once Hirsig arrived, she resumed her duties as secretary for the Beast. She also became pregnant; the father was not Crowley but a new disciple, William George Barron, whom Crowley had met in Paris. Barron played no lasting role in the life of the mother or child.

In the spring, Crowley attained a higher pitch of inspiration than during his magical pilgrimage the previous autumn. *The Heart of the Master* was composed in Sidi Bou Said. His diary entry on the rapt occasion, in which Barron (Brother Bar-On) was in attendance: "At night went into Trance, & beheld the Vision called *The Heart of the Master*. At one moment I nearly fainted: & just then Brother Bar-On saw physically in the courtyard an inverted cone of blue light." *Heart* was written under the pseudonym "Khaled Khan," a seeker who receives great wisdom from an unnamed Teacher (tacitly identified as Christian Rosenkreutz) who gives the good tidings that a new Prophet (tacitly, the Beast) has come.

Crowley was not alone in seeking out visions in the desert. Dorothy Olsen, the Scarlet Woman, was conscious of her own role in the *Book*, and—like Hirsig before her—she sought vainly to induce in herself a worthy magical revelation. In a certain sense, her path was more difficult than Hirsig's, for Olsen lacked the magical vocation that Hirsig possessed strongly, and she further lacked the ability to hold her own, psychologically or physically, with the Beast. There is no evidence that Crowley ever physically abused Hirsig. But in the early months of 1925, he most surely did abuse Olsen—a cruel blow to her eye that shattered the surrounding bone and left her in need of medical care through the spring. In a March 1925 letter to Mudd, Olsen displayed the complaisant attitude to domestic beatings that was part and parcel of her upbringing—and affirmed her devotion to her sadistic lover and teacher: "I am still alive in Tunis, with many of the bones of my head removed. This is a good thing; it gives more room for my brain, such as it is, to expand."

A month later, Crowley detailed a scene of ongoing domestic horror: "A single drink of rum (on top of a good deal of mental worry during the day) was enough to induce in D.O. an attack of acute mania. Lying in bed, close cuddled, I nearly asleep, she suddenly started to scratch my face without the least warning, with a spate of the filthiest incoherent abuse of me and everybody connected with me." It is doubtful that a single drink of rum was the effective cause; since Rose Kelly, Crowley viewed women who drank with extreme suspicion. And the history of abuse between them surely played its part in Olsen's "mania," if such it was.

Matters in North Africa were clearly at a crisis point. All the more reason, then, for a new leadership prospect—and a new setting—to appeal so strongly to Crowley. What came to be called the "Hohenleuben Conference" promised both an expansion of Thelema and a means of resolving his financial woes. Unlike his overtures to the Theosophical Society, there now stood a real chance for Crowley to gain unified control over the O.T.O., which had lacked a recognized worldwide Outer Head of the Order (O.H.O.) since the death of Theodor Reuss in October 1923.

A brief background to the Hohenleuben Conference is in order. In the final two years of Reuss's life, relations between him and Crowley had grown unpleasant. The tensions began after Reuss suffered an impairing stroke in 1920. Crowley wrote to Frank Bennett, head of the O.T.O. in Australia (appointed by Crowley), as to the possibility of himself replacing Reuss as worldwide O.H.O. According to O.T.O. historians Tau Apiryon and Soror Helena, "Reuss discovered the correspondence and wrote Crowley an angry, defensive response on November 9, 1921, in which he appeared to distance himself from Thelema. Crowley replied to Reuss's letter on November 23, 1921, and stated in his letter, 'It is my will to be O.H.O. and Frater Superior of the Order and avail myself of your abdication—to proclaim myself as such.'" But Crowley never claimed that Reuss abdicated. Rather, he asserted that Reuss designated him—in his last letter to the Beast—as the successor O.H.O. Just how the rift had been healed Crowley did not explain.

The Hohenleuben Conference—at which Crowley was to emerge publicly as O.H.O.—would prove to be a tangled tale indeed. That tale begins in late 1924, when Crowley was contacted by one Heinrich Tranker (Frater Recnartus), who lived in the village of Hohenleuben in the region of Thuringia in eastern Germany. Tranker has been appointed by Reuss, prior to the latter's death, as the X° Grand Master for Germany. But Tranker's loyalty to Reuss was limited. His true ambition was to found an esoteric order of his own, which he did in 1924—the *Collegium Pansophicum,* or in more extended form, "The Pansophic Lodge of the Light Seeking Brethren of the Orient." Tranker now wished to ascertain the whereabouts of Crowley, as to whom Tranker had received a vision indicating that he was the true World Teacher.

According to Crowley, Tranker led him to believe that there would be available, in Hohenleuben, written evidence of the legitimacy of both Tranker and his order. This evidence was not produced. Alas, Crowley failed the same standard with respect to his claim to Tranker that Reuss had "definitely designated me to succeed him." For Crowley no longer had possession of the substantiating letter. Was it indeed sent? It is possible, but two countervailing points stand out: (1) There is no evidence, in Crowley's own prior diaries or letters, that he had received such a designation. It would have been a signal enough event to merit notice. (2) Had Crowley received express designation, why not assert his O.H.O. status as a fait accompli? Instead, Crowley expressed to Tranker his humble acceptance of the Latter's "nomination" of Crowley as the new

O.H.O., when that position was a matter of appointment rather than election.

In early 1925, Tranker extended an invitation to Crowley and Olsen to come stay as his guests at the time of the summer solstice. In mid-June they arrived in Hohenleuben where, early on, prospects seemed bright to the Beast. That outlook would not survive the summer, as relations with Tranker steadily—and then precipitously—worsened.

But in the neighboring village of Weida there lived another high-ranking member of the *Collegium Pansophicum*, one who would prove as stable an ally as Tranker was fleeting. Karl Johannes Germer, born in 1885, was ten years Crowley's junior. But, as a matter both of strict upbringing (albeit in a secular rather than a Christian household) and of pronounced sexual unease, Germer was very much a member of Crowley's own generation—the generation chronicled by Freud. Ironically, given the centrality to Thelema of sexual magic, Germer would later acknowledge to Crowley (in an English that was Germer's second language) that he had never experienced "physical satisfaction" with any woman and rued the fact that he had "heard many people express themselves most exultedly [sic] about the pleasures derived from the coition, an act which—try as I would—never was more to me than the act like dumping ashes or garbage." Germer's erotic fantasies stressed invisibility and escape: "Up to about 20 or 25 I got most enthusiasm out of imagining myself or actually seeing myself in the mirror with the sexual organs hidden. I saw myself as a girl then." He allowed that "the idea of hermaphroditism has always appealed to me," but there is no evidence that he ever acted upon it beyond the contemplation of alchemical symbolism; there were no sexual overtures whatsoever between Germer and Crowley.

Germer had long struggled to transform what he regarded as a neurotic and sterile middle-class existence, which included a troubled marriage to his wife, Maria. But his ardent esoteric yearnings were in paradoxical contrast with Germer's own frank and humble assessment of his actual abilities. As he later declared in a letter to Crowley (written in an English that was a second language):

> For me everything has been dark all the time since I have been in touch with occultists. The fact is, I never understood their language.[. . .]The same is with your books, though I have read in the *Equinox, Magick* etc. time and again. I guess I have no organ for the understanding of such things You might ask that cannot be so for why should I have kept on interesting myself then. The

answer is, I think, that I vaguely felt there was something back of it and that some day miraculously the understanding of the expressions will spring up in my mind. That then I could start where others have started at an earlier age.

Germer was already a member of the *Collegium Pansophicum*, with the magical name Frater Saturnus, perhaps with reference to his brooding, saturnine nature. With Tranker and Otto Wilhelm Barth, Germer founded the Pansophia publishing house, for which Germer served as chief translator and funding source. By 1925, Pansophia had issued seven titles, three of which were by Crowley. Germer also paid the travel costs of Crowley and Olsen out of his own pocket. But Germer was not yet, prior to Crowley's arrival, a committed Thelemite. It was not until Germer's personal encounter with Crowley during this summer that he would cast his allegiance utterly to the Master Therion.

Crowley would gain two other key allies while in Thuringia. Martha Küntzel, Soror *Ich Will Es* ("I Will It"), had a history of occult involvement that stretched back to the nineteenth century, when she had joined the Theosophical Society and made the acquaintance of Madame Blavatsky. Küntzel now became an ardent Thelemite. And while Germer would be imprisoned by the Nazis and then forced to leave Germany, Küntzel—who embraced Hitler and the Nazi ideology—remained the standard-bearer of Thelema during the Third Reich until her death during the war. She formed, shortly after meeting Crowley, the Thelema Verlag press in Leipzig, aided by Otto Gebhardi, the only other attendee at Hohenleuben who accepted the Beast as Prophet.

It was Tranker, of course, whom Crowley wished most to win over—and with whom he encountered the most bitter difficulties. Crowley went to considerable effort to document these troubles in two formal written accounts as well as a pseudonymous account (under the name of Gerard Aumont, a Frenchman with whom Crowley had struck a friendship in Tunis). The briefest of these, "Statement Re Tranker," encapsulates the Beast's indignation: "I found this man completely ignorant even of the language of the classics of Magic and Mysticism. He was even unacquainted with elementary Latin. I found further that in his dealings with other people he was mean, unscrupulous and dishonest. I tested him magically and found his pretensions worthless and ridiculous." As the summer wore on, Crowley spent ever more time at Germer's residence in Weida, and finally moved there in the autumn.

In addition to reviling Tranker, Crowley waged character attacks on a second front during this same period. In July and August 1925, he launched an angry correspondence with his Magical Son Jones (Frater Achad) in Chicago, accusing him both of "megalomania" and of the theft of a valuable collection of books and manuscripts which Crowley had left in Jones's possession when he returned from the United States to England in 1919. As to the former charge, it centered upon a series of three kabbalistic volumes authored under the name Frater Achad— Q.B.L., or The Bride's Reception (1922); The Egyptian Revival (1923) and The Anatomy of the Body of God (1925)—in which, Crowley charged, "One who ought to have known better tried to improve the Tree of Life by turning the Serpent of Wisdom [a traditional kabbalistic symbolic figure of gnostic ascent] upside down!" In fairness to Jones, it must be said that these works continue to be read with interest by students of magical kabbalah. Jones would, some two decades later, teach kabbalah to the British novelist Malcolm Lowry, when both men lived in British Columbia; the influence of kabbalah shows itself in Lowry's masterpiece, Under the Volcano (1947).

It was the second charge—the alleged theft of Crowley's books and manuscripts from a Detroit warehouse—that proved the breaking point between the two men. As Hymenaeus Beta has confirmed, "Jones was in fact innocent, as the books were found by the warehouse after both men were long dead." Although the two reached a legal settlement in 1926, Jones soon thereafter ceased to be a Thelemite. His subsequent magical career included, on Christmas Day 1928, the taking of communion in the Roman Catholic Church and, in the 1930s, the dawning conviction that a New Aeon governed by Maat, the Egyptian goddess of Truth and Justice, would imminently supersede the Aeon of Horus declared by Crowley. Small wonder that Crowley (who agreed that the Aeon of Maat would come—some millennia hence) would, after an attempted rapprochement in 1936, expel Jones from the O.T.O. Thus ended relations between Crowley and the most gifted theorist of all his magical students.

But in Hohenleuben, just before relations with Tranker began their fatal decline, Crowley did achieve a brief paper victory during this summer of 1925. The remarkable document entitled Ein Zeugnis der Suchenden—"A Testament of the Seekers"—which purported to confirm Crowley as Prophet of the New Aeon included as its signatories Tranker and his wife Helene as well as Collegium Pansophicum members Germer, Küntzel, and Otto Gebhardi. Hirsig and Mudd, who had joined Crowley in Hohenleuben that summer, also signed the Zeugnis, which was to be used as a persuasive document with other German occultists. It declared that "We, the undersigned, have seen with our own eyes and heard with our own ears, and we know, 'certain beyond lies,' that He is in truth the Bearer of the Word which the soul of mankind thirsted for." However, only three of the signatories, Gebhardi, Germer, and Küntzel, would keep to the sworn testimony of the *Zeugnis* for the rest of their lives. Tranker and his wife renounced it within roughly one month, Mudd in under one year, Hirsig within two years. Olsen would disappear from Crowley's life, albeit gradually and with affection. Crowley, in one of his early letters to Tranker, had described a kind of "glamour" (a baffling and seductive quality; the term is used, in British folklore, to describe denizens of the Faerie realm) that distracted persons from a clear perception of Crowley's character and teachings. A species of this glamour, working to Crowley's benefit (at least, during August 1925), must have accompanied the signing of the *Zeugnis*.

By autumn, when Crowley and Olsen moved to Weida to stay with Germer, the German occult scene resembled a busy game board. Tranker retained leadership both of the German O.T.O. and of the *Collegium Pansophicum* (which would prove short-lived). As for the tiny German faction that valued Thelema but did not accept Crowley as a World Teacher, they founded a new order, the *Fraternitas Saturni*, led by Eugen Grosche, who would head its operations for some thirty years. For his part, Crowley had gained the valuable allegiance of Germer and Küntzel (Gebhardi was already very elderly and hence could play but a secondary role). Germer would henceforth serve as his aide-de-camp, with special emphasis on raising funds, while Küntzel became his trusted German contact. Her letters to Crowley in the years to come combined the ardor of a disciple and the chidings of a devoted mother.

By November 1925, Crowley and Olsen returned to Tunisia, taking up residence in a villa, the Seniat el Kitou, in La Marsa. Shortly thereafter, he penned what he regarded as the definitive "Comment" on the *Book*, at last fulfilling the dictate of III, 40: "But the work of the comment? That is easy; and Hadit burning in thy heart shall make swift and secure thy pen." The reason for his prior failures, Crowley later explained, was that "I mistook 'Comment' for 'Commentary'—a word-by-word exposition of every verse (and much of it I loathed with all my heart!) including the Qabalistic interpretation, a task obviously endless." Succinct as it is, the "Comment" is suitably perplexing. Signed by "The priest of the princess, Ankh-f-n-khonsu," it reads in full:

Do what thou wilt shall be the whole of the Law.
    The study of this Book is forbidden. It is wise to destroy this copy after the first reading.

Whosoever disregards this does so at his own risk and peril. These are most dire.

Those who discuss the contents of this Book are to be shunned by all, as centers of pestilence.

All questions of the Law are to be decided only by appeal to my writings, each for himself.

There is no law beyond Do what thou wilt.

Love is the law, love under will.

This "Comment" was first published in 1926 by Crowley in a private limited edition of the *Book*. Plainly, a literal reading will not unlock its meaning. The "Comment" is written in esoteric, symbolic language. It may be interpreted as calling for swift and rapt absorption as opposed to repeated analytical study, and for the shunning of discussion in favor of private labor and insight. Crowley later noted, in his *Eight Lectures on Yoga* (1939), that matters of ultimate experiential insight are necessarily beyond words: "It is no use discussing the results of Yoga, whether that Yoga be the type recommended by Lao-Tzu, or Patanjali, or St. Ignatius Loyola, because for our first postulate we have: that these subjects are incapable of discussion. To argue about them only causes us to fall into the pit of Because, and there to perish with the dogs of Reason." As to the 1925 "Comment," Crowley added: "I myself did not understand that injunction; I do so now."

During the same period as the "Comment" was written, Crowley received a singular piece of correspondence from Mudd, who had been, for all that Crowley excoriated him, as devoted a disciple as a true-willed master could wish. Mudd had long felt entitled to goad Crowley to live up to his role as Prophet. Now, however, Mudd's goadings reached an unparalleled intensity. In one letter, Mudd detailed Crowley's errors since receiving the *Book* in 1904. Amongst these was that Crowley had "proceeded to exploit the divulged Script exactly like an infallible Pope." The Beast's tendency to judge others harshly—including Mudd—was explained by Mudd as stemming from Crowley's own bitter psychological projections. In a subsequent February 1926 letter, Mudd broke with Crowley outright.

Hirsig, for her part, tried to assuage the enraged Beast—who now regarded Mudd as a traitor to Thelema. But she was facing difficulties of her own. Her son (by Crowley's onetime disciple Barron) was born in Leipzig in December 1925. She named him Alexander Barron-Hirsig, though Barron had long since departed. "Alexander" was a cipher for

"AL," the key term of the *Book* discovered by Frater Achad. Hirsig now established a residence for herself and her infant son in Switzerland.

Then, in July and August 1927, came a series of letters in which Hirsig, like Mudd, renounced the *Zeugnis*. Again like Mudd, her reasons for so doing lay not with the *Book* but with Crowley's failure to heed its teachings. She now argued that the *Book* did not substantiate his claim to be its rightful Prophet: "The script alone cannot prove this: for no matter what its terms and qualities may be it is a mere piece of writing in your hand [. . .] it is not an executed instrument conveying authority." Crowley's response was to dismiss Hirsig's "imbecile letter" and to declare her "cut off from all communication unless and until you write to me pledging your word of honour not to repeat this offense, & reaffirming your obligations to me personally." Hirsig's prompt reply formally revoked "all my recognitions [of Crowley] heretofore as Beast, or Priest of the Princes, or as having any authority whatsoever in respect of the Law of Thelema." She forwarded copies of her renunciation to the other *Zeugnis* signatories, as had Mudd.

There is a final chapter—four years later—to these communications between Crowley and his two disciples. On September 6, 1930, a letter from Hirsig to "E. A. Crowley, Esq."—a pointed absence here of any magical title—was written in the hand of Mudd as amanuensis. Hirsig and Mudd were together in Escorial, Spain; the nature of their relations at this point is not known. But Hirsig plainly felt that matters between Crowley and herself required final resolution. The letter consisted of four handwritten pages, with key points carefully outlined in the style of a mathematical proof, in support of Hirsig's proposition that "I now Notify you that all promises which I have ever made to personally— whether called or describable as *oaths, vows, obligations, pledges* or what not [. . .] are now defunct in my sight." In a handwritten note, written at the top of Hirsig's letter after he had received it, Crowley denounced it as having been "composed by Norman Mudd—lunatic and thief." What is most striking—and poignant—is that Hirsig and Mudd, in their isolation in Spain, should have bothered to compose it at all.

Their subsequent fates may be briefly told. Hirsig ultimately returned to the United States and, according to John Symonds, was rumored to have converted to Roman Catholicism. She resumed her work as a schoolteacher and died in 1951. As for Mudd, he returned to England and committed suicide on May 6, 1934, drowning himself in Portelet Bay on the Island of Guernsey. Crowley would later claim to have prophesied this death.

At the time of Mudd's break from Crowley in 1926, Crowley was busy cultivating a new potential disciple, Thomas Driberg, then twenty years old and an undergraduate at Christ Church College at Oxford. Driberg had, in November 1925, written in response to the Beast's invitation to readers (included in *Drug Fiend*) to correspond with the author. A well-heeled product of the upper middle class, Driberg was precisely the sort of disciple Crowley most desired. Driberg would not have had occasion to meet Mudd—who was on the way out as Driberg was on the way in, as it were. But in his memoir, *Ruling Passions* (1977), Driberg, by then Baron Bramwell, took occasion to repeat a joke that Crowley must have told him, about "a dim, grey little man called Norman Mudd, who used to come up to one at parties and say 'You won't remember me—my name is Mudd.'" Given the pitiful sums on which Mudd lived while serving the Beast, as well as the duties assigned him, one might wonder when he would have had occasion to attend a party. One might also wonder how Crowley, as Mudd's teacher, could have failed to see that the joke was ultimately on himself.

Driberg was one of Crowley's key hopes in 1926, a year in which the Beast's financial fortunes ebbed and flowed—his trust fund checks intermittently supplemented by gifts from scattered disciples. But though Driberg professed, in his letters from Oxford, great ardor for Crowley's teachings, he was far too canny to emulate Mudd and give up all (or even a substantial portion) of his money to the World Teacher. Driberg never seriously pursued magic, nor did he deem it wise to make public the extent of his admiration—now at its peak—for the Beast. The social and political consequences would have been devastating, and Driberg was an ambitious man. He became, in the 1930s, a prominent political columnist, writing under the name "William Hickey" for the *London Daily Express*. Ultimately he was elected to Parliament and became a member of the Labour Party's National Executive. Driberg was, typically for his time, an active but closet homosexual, though there is no evidence of erotic relations with Crowley. In his memoirs, Driberg was unwilling to admit that he had ever been drawn to Crowley. Rather, he described their relationship as a series of casual meetings during which Driberg could observe a fascinating eccentric.

Driberg did offer one interesting bit of anecdotal testimony as to Crowley's personal charms in the 1920s and after: "[H]e claimed to have learned wisdom from the 'secret masters' in Tibet. This wisdom may have included certain formulae for sexual potency; for, though he was bisexual, I was to observe over the years that, ugly as he was, he could exercise a compelling fascination over women, particularly elderly women with a fair amount of money." Driberg's feigned surprise that Crowley's bisexuality did not repel women is explained by the social sanctions of the time.

As for Crowley, he remained active on both sexual fronts. Jane Wolfe, who visited chez Crowley in La Marsa in early 1926, recorded in her diary that Olsen showed manic-depressive patterns and often drank to excess. Wolfe further noted: "On practically every occasion that I find myself alone with her [. . .] she raved about A.C.; that in Paris he had tried to blackmail a former lover; what she had endured there etc. etc.; that in Sidi-bou-Said he had run around with Arab boys [. . .]" Olsen told Wolfe that Crowley had once almost killed her while they were out in the desert, and that an Arab boy had once come to Olsen "weeping, saying, 'I don't want him! I want him to leave me alone!'" Wolfe added loyally, in her diary, "But what really annoyed me was the fact that she [Olsen] would rave thus to me, pass through a door, go straight to Beast, & lovingly caress 'my Big Lion'."

The jealousy Olsen felt toward Crowley's male lovers was well founded. There was, in particular, one man with whom Crowley conducted a passionate affair, as well as magical workings, during his time in Tunis. Nothing is known of him aside from a handful of Crowley diary entries; this one, in Paris on September 11, 1926, is the most telling: "Letter from Dridi Salah ben Mohammed. Replied. As Shakespeare might have asked: 'Could you on this fair mountain have to feed, And batten on the Moon?'"

Despite such erotic distractions, Olsen joined the Beast in Paris some weeks later. But their intimate relationship was coming to an end. Her abrupt departure is chronicled in a series of startlingly brief Crowley diary entries. The first, for October 8, 1926: "Astrid blew in from the South." For October 9 there is the symbol for a sexual opus and the comment: "Big Lion night! Astrid." On October 10 the opus symbol reappears. Then, on October 12, Crowley's 51st birthday: "Astrid blew out to the West"—that is, she returned to America. Crowley then consulted the I Ching. The "Omen" he received was terse—"get a lover."

Olsen would remain, through the 1920s, a long-distance correspondent and moral support. For example, she made efforts, through family contacts, to forward to Henry Ford a letter (written in spring 1926) in which Crowley argued—to win the industrialist's support—that Ford's enmity toward organized labor was in perfect keeping with Thelema. It is not known if Ford received the letter; in any event, there was no response.

Crowley harbored an array of hopes for financial support. Still fascinated with the possibility of a libel action, Crowley was aroused by the news—which reached him during this summer—that a film version of Somerset Maugham's novel, *The Magician*, was being shot in Nice. The evil Oliver Haddo, Maugham's roman à clef protagonist, had been based on Crowley. The Beast now annotated his copy of the novel, writing on the flyleaf that his notes would "demonstrate the defamation alleged in my lawsuit against Metro Goldwyn in France." But the lawsuit was never brought; Crowley seems not to have entertained the notion for long. It is a pity that the Beast never visited the set or made the acquaintance of the film's director, Rex Ingram. The two might have been friends. Ingram, an English R.A.F. hero during World War One, had established himself in Hollywood as a singularly bizarre filmmaker. One of his earlier silent films, *Trifling Women*, with a lusting vampiress as its protagonist, "contained enough poisoning, satanism, and necrophilia to make it one of the commercial disasters of 1922," according to one critic. But Ingram had enjoyed successes with films such as *The Four Horsemen of the Apocalypse* and *Scaramouche*, and so could pursue a lavish Jazz Age lifestyle that included the hiring of a dwarf as his personal valet. Ingram and his wife, actress Alice Terry, had now settled in the south of France. *The Magician*, with Terry in the lead female role, was one of the last big-budget silent productions—a melodramatic horror film charged with eros. The lurid plot was very freely adapted from Maugham. Haddo (played by German actor Paul Wegener) has become a Frankenstein-type, seeking the heart blood of a virgin (Terry) in order to give life to an inanimate body of Haddo's creation. In a dream sequence, the virgin finds herself "in the midst of an orgiastic rite presided over by Pan himself, a prancing, naked satyr played by Stowitts, the American dancer at the Folies Bergère." Released in America in September 1927, *The Magician* was lambasted by critics and died a quick box office death; it scarcely impacted Crowley's image.

But the Beast's primary concern in Paris was the obtaining of lovers. His diaries of the period are filled with musings on erotic possibilities, including remarriage—for which, intermittently, he longed. But a poem with a contrary sentiment, "Gigolomastix," was written in Paris on December 7, 1926:

> If I was just a Pekinese,
>   I'd have some fat old greasy sow
> To pet me, comb me, catch my fleas
>   See to my comfort and my chow. . . .

> Thank God, although I starve and freeze,
> That I am not a Pekinese.

Crowley tallied his current women, in a January 1927 entry, at nine—six white and three black. But relations were far more amicable, on all planes, with men such as Louis Eugène de Cayenne, with whom Crowley had enjoyed a prewar affair that was now rekindled. Crowley pronounced a November sexual opus with Eugène "a huge success. I have more pep than I have had for months." But by the New Year of 1927 he noted that "Eugene and all his tribe disappeared." It was growing clearer to Crowley, in his middle age, that it was men for whom he had the strongest feelings. As he wrote in a letter to his American friend Montgomery Evans, "There have been about four men in my life that I could say I have loved . . . Call me a bugger if you like, but I don't feel the same way about women. One can always replace a woman in a few days.[. . .] But with men it is altogether different. What attracts one is the positive individuality."

Crowley had never fared well without the fuel of passion, and for the first months of 1927 he floundered somewhat, urging disciples to carry out long-distance schemes on behalf of Thelema—and to supply him with needed funds. Karl Germer, who now lived in New York City and worked at an office job, was far and away the most faithful. From his own meager salary of $180 per month, Germer sent Crowley $100. But it was another American disciple, Wilfred T. Smith, who provided the Beast with what appeared—at the time—to be the most welcome news of the year. Crowley had met Smith briefly in Vancouver in 1915 (the only time the two would come face-to-face, despite Smith's long years of discipleship). Now living in southern California, Smith had, in the summer of 1927, given Crowley's Paris address to a seemingly well-to-do Polish woman, Kasimira Bass, who resided in California but was undertaking a trip to her homeland. En route, Bass looked Crowley up and found herself enraptured by this magician who lived in apparent luxury. (Crowley's unpaid debts, of which Bass was unaware, were substantial.) In a letter to Smith, Bass reported:

> He has a nice place on the outskirts of Paris, a Jap butler and a female housekeeper. He received me with great attention at the door and served me a new cocktail called 'Maya', strong as himself. We chatted and smoked fine cigarettes and after an hour he took me to some funny people in a studio for dinner. He loves, as you know, adventures, and he likes to observe the lives of un-

balanced human beings—so we stayed there for some time and then came back to his home. He gave me some answers to the questions I had been asking, and we talked till 3 A.M. It was all very charming and he is very interested and enthusiastic about me. He wants me to work with him. Now, Wilfred, I am going to tell you something more. Don't faint! He proposed 4 times to me and wants me to marry him! He wanted me to marry him next week in Paris; it is not so easy.[. . .] I was frank with him and asked him about his finances. He replied that he has plenty of money to make a nice home for me and to make me happy as I will be 'the Queen of Sheba'.

For his part, Crowley wrote to thank Smith "for the galleon of Treasure which came under full sail into port here last week.[. . .] This may be for the Great Work a most important move."

Bass went on to Poland, but rejoined Crowley in Fontainebleau for the winter of 1928. In the spring, they returned to Paris. Crowley made plans for them to travel to Egypt—where Bass, as the Scarlet Woman, would play a catalytic role in the advent of the New Aeon. But the trip to Egypt never came to pass, and by autumn their relationship was coming to an end. In December, Bass disappeared. Crowley beseeched Smith to find her new whereabouts, as he believed himself to have been swindled by her.

Strangely, Crowley engaged—at this same time—in a second financial wrangle with a woman. This was Cora Eaton, a middle-class, middle-aged American woman with modest savings who was deeply in love with Germer. Germer felt fondly toward Eaton, but—given his sexual outlook—harbored nothing like passion. Crowley bluntly demanded that Germer marry Eaton—but only on the condition that she fund Crowley's publication efforts with a $10,000 investment. Crowley did not obtain quite that sum. But in subsequent months Eaton did contribute $6,500 to the cause, though she harbored severe doubts about Crowley. In June 1929, Eaton and Germer were married. Judging by Germer's subsequent letters, they were as happy as could have been expected.

Two new disciples now emerged to aid the Beast. The first of these was Gerald Yorke, a young Englishman of distinguished background and attainments. His family, to which Yorke was intensely loyal, lived in the distinguished medieval house of Forthampton Court. Yorke himself had attended Eton and Cambridge, and a lucrative business career was his for the asking, should he have cared to ask. But Yorke had become an enthusiast of Crowley's writings, and in late 1927 he traveled to Paris to meet with their author. The relationship between the Beast and Yorke—who dubbed Crowley "the old sinner"—would evolve into an enduring friendship. Yorke never quite embraced Thelema, nor did he remain a loyal disciple. But the younger man felt a lifelong debt for what Crowley taught him during their first years as master and student.

Yorke possessed both spiritual ardor and business sense—a combination Crowley dearly valued. But while Yorke paid the Beast frequent visits in Paris, he maintained his residence in London. The disciple who came into closest contact with Crowley during this period was a young American, age twenty, who had studied Crowley's writings and now had journeyed to Paris to study with (and serve as secretary for) the man.

Israel Regudy was born to a family of orthodox Jewish immigrants who lived in a slum in London's East End. The family changed its name to "Regardie" during World War One and emigrated to America in 1921. Israel Regardie, as a teenager, attended an art school in Philadelphia and had dreams of becoming a painter. But an encounter with the works of H. P. Blavatsky at age fifteen sparked instead a consuming passion for esoteric thought, which led Regardie to write to Crowley, who ultimately arranged for Regardie to join him in Paris. Regardie, wary of the Beast's horrific reputation, told his parents that he was going off to France to study art. But he took one of his sisters into his confidence, which would lead to distressing consequences.

Regardie arrived in Paris on October 12, 1928—Crowley's fifty-third birthday. Crowley met him at the Gare St. Lazare, dressed in blue-grey tweeds with plus fours and a matching cap, and intoned the Thelemic greeting to his new secretary and pupil. His very first night at Crowley's apartment, Regardie—then a virgin deeply embarrassed by sexual frankness of any sort—had dinner with Crowley and his soon-to-be-departed mistress, Kasimira Bass. After coffee and cognac, Crowley and Bass made love passionately. As Regardie later recalled, "they fell down on the floor and started fucking like a pair of animals right there in front of me. Today [decades later] that wouldn't bother me one jot, but then . . . I was so amazed, I think I just staggered out of the room."

This exhibition reflected the Beast's desire to initiate a prudish pupil into the ways of Thelemic learning. Crowley would soon insist that Regardie frequent Parisian prostitutes to gain experience and overcome all visceral disgust. Indeed, Regardie wrote that it was Crowley's "considered opinion that I should for the time being relinquish all my interests in mysticism, to walk and work my way around the world to familiarize myself with every conceivable vice." This had been Crowley's course of action—futile at root—with respect to his own puritanism; direct confrontation with psychic bêtes noires was a hallmark of his teaching. Regardie did not take Crowley's advice in this regard.

He did, however, on his first day in Paris, tender some $1200—his entire savings—to the Beast. As Regardie later described the scene:

> Well, suddenly Crowley said: "Got any money on you, Regardie?" and like the young fool I was, I handed it over and he went and spent it on champagne and brandy—always the best for him—and I never saw it again. Except in another sense. Later, when I was stuck in Brussels for months because I couldn't get entry back into England, it was the old man who supported me financially throughout that time, so it all worked out even. Then when I finally arrived in England, he had a few quid so he sent me to his tailor in Jermyn Street, as I recall. "One needs a good suit in England, Regardie," he said. "Have one made and tell them to send me the bill."

Whether Crowley paid the bill upon it being sent is most unlikely. Nonetheless, the incident establishes the importance he placed upon proper appearances, which, after all, could be seen as a means of exerting one's magical will; Crowley's various titles of nobility were another such means.

The sad irony, however, was that Crowley often seemed, to his contemporaries, unsettlingly "over the top." His appearance and wardrobe only served to confirm that impression. An example is found in the memoirs of Lance Sieveking, a British R.A.F. hero during the war and the author of *The Psychology of Flying*, a book to which Crowley briefly alluded in *Drug Fiend*. In 1928, while in Cassis, the two men had a chance encounter. Sieveking recalled:

> As he talked I was surprised to see that his tongue was strangely fat and swollen, and of a particular dark purple in colour, quite different from the dull red of his lips. The round dome of his head was completely bald but for three long black hairs of unusual thickness which stood up like ferns from the top of the dome. His eyes were very large and, except that they did not hang downwards, reminded me of elephants' ears. His face, though it was deeply sunburnt, was actually more green than

brown. Under his eyes were deep saucers of black. His skin, which, though the face was fat, was loose in a fat sort of way, moved as he talked as an elephant's skin moves. The texture, too, reminded me of an elephant's skin.

Later, while Crowley was swimming, Sieveking observed "that his body was like his face, sunburned all over, but green." Sieveking ascribed this coloring—and the swollen tongue—to some unknown drug that Crowley might be taking.

Discomfited as he was by Crowley's appearance, Sieveking was unaware that, at times, in their conversations, Crowley was blatantly pulling his leg. For example, Sieveking inquired of Crowley if he had ever met Montague Summers. The question was natural enough, as Crowley and Summers were the two greatest figures in the British occult world at that time. Summers, an enormously learned and eccentric man who claimed to have been ordained a Catholic priest, had recently published his influential study, *The History of Witchcraft and Demonology*. Summers believed in the literal truth both of the Devil and of the accusations made against witches by the Inquisition.

It would also have been natural for Sieveking to assume the two men to be mortal enemies. It was this assumption to which Crowley played. As Sieveking described it:

> "I haven't seen Monty Summers for years," answered Crow-
> ley, knocking the end off his cigar with an air of an executioner.
> "He takes care of that. He knows what would happen."
> "What would happen?"
> "I should change him into a toad."

In fact, Crowley met amicably with Summers in London just a year after this threat. His diary entry for July 5, 1929: "Dinner with Montague Summers—the most amusing evening I have spent in decades!" Crowley's friend and biographer Charles R. Cammell reported that, in the 1930s, Crowley and Summers again enjoyed a pleasant evening of talk in Cammell's flat. Clearly, there was respect and good feeling between the two men. But the precise nature of their relations remains mysterious. Publicly, Summers was guarded. In his posthumously published autobiography, *The Galanty Show* (1980), Crowley is briefly dismissed as a sinister charlatan, albeit with "flashes of genius." Privately, Summers was far more accepting. As Cammell recalled, "In Crowley he took a remarkable interest. He had amassed an astonishing dossier of press-cuttings and magazine articles concerning him, which he kept in a large portfolio in his desk. To my enquiry about this collection, he replied that everything concerning Crowley should be preserved, because he was 'one of the few original and really interesting men of our age.'"

According to Sieveking, who met both men, "Montague Summers said quite a lot about Aleister Crowley, who it appeared, he knew quite well, and in whose company he had attended many a sabbat. It seemed that they were both honorary members of several of the best covens of witches." Crowley made no mention of any of this in his writings. But there is corroborating testimony offered by Yorke. In later years, Yorke met with a woman named Aemeth, the Maiden of a Cumberland coven. Aemeth, whom Yorke respected, told him "that A.C. was in the St. Albans coven as a young man, but left because he refused to be ordered about by a bunch of old hags." Yorke merely noted: Could be true. The matter must remain speculative.

Sieveking agreed, during his meeting with Crowley in Cassis, to make efforts on the Beast's behalf in British publishing circles. To this end, Sieveking paid a visit—after his return to London—to Yorke, in whose residence certain Crowley manuscripts were in storage. (Yorke may, of necessity, have brought these manuscripts into England surreptitiously. For, back in November 1924, Crowley had shipped two large cases filled with his books, manuscripts, and paintings to London. Those cases were destroyed by British Customs on the grounds of obscenity.) Neither Yorke nor Sieveking were successful in finding a willing British publisher.

In the alternative, Yorke was willing to partially fund a private printing of *Magick in Theory and Practice*. It was this option that Crowley resolved upon—out of desperation—by the end of 1928, with the Lecram Press in Paris chosen as the printer as it would be unhindered by the legal restrictions of England. Yorke put up an initial £300 for a print run of 3,000—an optimistic number, based on Crowley's assurances that there would be eager subscribers. (In fact, the Lecram Press received payment for a mere seven subscriptions by May 1929.) But in late 1928, Crowley was buoyant enough—not only as to *Magick*, but also as to his unpublished novel *Moonchild* and the *Confessions*—to hire a publicity agent. This was a British journalist based in Paris, C. de Vidal Hunt, whom Crowley had met some years earlier.

Hunt was initially optimistic, convinced that Crowley was a gifted writer unfairly pilloried by the press. But the Beast simply could not conduct himself properly. In a November letter to Yorke, Hunt complained:

> The unfortunate part of all this is his utter inability to 'act' pretty over a cup of tea. As an impresario I am very discouraged. He can't be taught new tricks. When in company he appears to be plunged into a mental torpor from which it is difficult to arouse him. And this is not exactly the way to make himself popular with the ladies. However, we'll carry on and present the lion as a surly old beast whose gnarls should frighten no one.

The "torpor" and reticence were likely the symptoms of ongoing heroin use. Relations between Crowley and Hunt soon came to an unpleasant end. Crowley claimed that Hunt threatened blackmail and then went to the French police with dire stories of the doings of the Beast. Whether Hunt played the part of informer remains unclear, but Crowley's troubles with the authorities did ensue shortly after Hunt's departure.

Crowley had every reason to wish to remain peacefully in France. It was there that *Magick* would appear. He was being kept in a comfortable apartment by the funding of Germer and other disciples. Regardie was on hand as a promising student and a willing worker. And, as 1928 came to an end, Crowley found an admirable successor to Kasimira Bass to serve as Scarlet Woman.

Her maiden name was Ferrari, but it was as Maria Teresa de Miramar that Crowley encountered her in Paris. She was born in Granada, Nicaragua, in 1894, of an Italian father and a French mother. Aged thirty-four when she and Crowley met, her appearance was sufficiently exotic that Crowley was—for the first time—paired with a woman who produced as great a startle on sight as he did. Jack Lindsay, a literary editor who became acquainted with Crowley during this time, recalled that she drank "heavily" and was formidable. Here is his portrait of the couple:

> She was a fairly well-blown woman, oozing a helpless sexuality from every seam of her smartly cut suit, with shapely legs crossed and uncrossed, and keeping all the while a sharp glittering gaze on her swarthy and unsavory husband with his bow-tie, his staring uneasy pop-eyes, his prim lax rosebud mouth, his sallow skin and brown shaven egg-shaped head, which at the time I mistook as naturally bald. There was a mustiness about

him that perhaps came from his scent of mingled civet, musk and ambergris, which was said to have a compelling effect on women and to make horses neigh after him in the street. Maria spoke in various languages, including English, which I could not understand, and he listened attentively like a well-behaved poodle, giving an impression of uxorious dependence. However I gathered that in private she made many scenes, accusing him and his friends of attempting to poison her.

There is no evidence—and no likelihood—that Crowley had any intention of poisoning de Miramar. That she was capable of scenes and accusations, there can be no doubt. The romance—and ultimate marriage—between de Miramar and Crowley was as turbulent as any in Crowley's lifetime. De Miramar showed her nerve when she stayed by Crowley's side even after a troubling encounter with her predecessor. In February, while riding on a bus in Paris, she was accosted and threatened by Kasimira Bass—whether out of jealousy on Bass's part, or for other motives, remains unknown.

Unsettling as this must have been, it paled beside what had already befallen the couple. On January 17, an inspector from the Préfecture of Police paid a visit to Crowley's flat, based on negative information provided by the Sûreté Générale. The source of this information could have been Hunt; Regardie, however, believed that his American sister had been the primary accuser by way of concerned letters from America as to the sinister man with whom her brother had fallen in. On March 8, the inspector returned with a *refus de séjour*—a revocation of the residency permits of Crowley, de Miramar, and Regardie. They were given twenty-four hours to leave France. The reason for the expulsion remains unclear. According to the *Paris Midi*—one of the many newspapers in France, England, and America to cover this latest furor surrounding the Beast—Crowley was regarded as a German spy, based both on his World War One activities and his leadership role in the German-origin O.T.O. One may speculate that allegations of black magic and immorality also played a key role.

But Crowley would not leave tamely—not with the printing of *Magick* under way. Regardie and de Miramar were placed on a boat to England on March 9, with assurances by Crowley that he would join them as soon as he could. But the two were refused permission to land in England. According to Regardie, they were viewed, by virtue of their association with the Beast, as "undesirable aliens"—this despite the fact that England was the birthplace of Regardie. The British authorities put them on a Channel steamer to Brussels, where they subsisted on funds provided by Crowley.

Prior to his forced departure from Paris, Regardie had lost his virginity—at Crowley's urging—by paying a visit to a brothel. Now, in Brussels, Regardie experienced sex with the Scarlet Woman herself. De Miramar seduced the young man. It may have been a respite of a sort for de Miramar, who had grown weary of Crowley's proclivities. As Regardie recalled: "That pair used to have the most godawful rows, though. The trouble was that Crowley loved giving it to her up the arse and she used to get sick of it. When she was annoyed, she suddenly used to turn on him and hiss, 'Pederast!' And he'd be going, 'Oh, *mon cherie*, how can you say this to me!' as he tried to kiss her and she'd still be hissing 'Pederast!' until finally he grabbed her and they'd start fucking again." Crowley, in a diary entry made the day that de Miramar and Regardie left for England, responded to de Miramar's objections: "The real inferiority of women to men is shown by their hate of paederasty, which they regard as unfair competition. Men on the other hand rather approve of Sapphism, as saving them trouble & expense." For his part, Regardie found de Miramar "a magnificent animal of a woman." Crowley was nonplussed by the affair when Regardie confessed it to him some weeks later; perhaps, as with Sapphism, he appreciated the trouble it had saved him in keeping de Miramar content during a time of chaos.

Crowley tenaciously delayed his own *refus de séjour* by obtaining a certificate from a cooperative French doctor declaring him unfit for travel due to poor health. This gambit bought the time he needed. Eight days later, on April 12, came the fruition: "Advance copy *Magick* arrived 5:55 p.m. Victory!" Delay tactics were no longer necessary. Over the next four days—as the story of the expulsion of the Great Beast from France went public—Crowley gave out numerous interviews and posed in dignified mien for photographs. On April 17, he went by train to Brussels, where he and de Miramar enjoyed a passionate reunion. It has been held that Crowley decided, later in this year, to marry de Miramar strictly as a legal expedient to obtain her entry into England. On the contrary, on the very night he arrived in Brussels, the two engaged in sexual magic for the dual purposes of "success to our campaign [of revoking the *refus de séjour* and returning to France] & happiness in marriage." Sexual workings with the latter aim in mind continued over the next two months. Crowley's desire to marry de Miramar was no mere stratagem.

In late May, Crowley went over to England to assess legal and publishing options. His fare was paid for by Colonel Carter, a Scotland Yard investigator who had met with Yorke and received the latter's assurances that Crowley was, for all his traitorous reputation, a loyal British subject. Crowley and Carter met for a four-hour dinner on June 11—a meeting that Crowley summarized with the diary entry "all clean." Such, indeed, was the case. Despite the flamboyant press coverage in Britain of his ejection from France, and the fear of Yorke and others that Crowley would be prosecuted or harrassed by authorities in England, nothing of the sort occurred at this point—nor for the remaining years of Crowley's life, most of which were spent in England.

Crowley and Carter continued to meet sporadically on into early 1930. The inspector seemed to view the Beast as a useful contact on various secret societies of some concern to His Majesty's government; the O.T.O. was not one of these. Crowley was happy to oblige with information, relishing his role as a mysterious "insider" and hoping to parley Carter's interest into a source of income—and power within the British establishment.

Despite the rapprochement with Carter and Scotland Yard, Crowley's reputation, in the eyes of most British publishers, could not have been more repugnant. Graphic testimony of this is offered in the memoirs of publisher Rupert Grayson, to whose office Crowley came during this time, in hopes of placing the *Confessions:*

> Alastair [sic] Crowley, the Black Magician, had propelled his drug-charged body to see us; looking into his yellow eyes, set in a brown-pocked yellow face, across the two-foot-wide Georgian table that divided us, I was truly revolted.[. . .] When he left the room I opened the door and windows to rid the room of the atmosphere of aromatic evil he had left on his brief visit.[. . .]
>
> The manuscript Crowley brought us was as strange and sinister a work [. . .] as one would expect; it was the only book I remember turning down for no better reason than our instant dislike for its author.

The irony was that Crowley considered, at this very time, creating a perfume for public sale. With Montague Summers, he discussed the prospects of a perfume that Crowley named, simply, "It." The ingredients, if it ever was concocted, are not known. It is safe to say that Crowley, from decades of magical practice that included the use of incenses of all kinds, had developed a range of olfactory tolerance beyond the norm of his contemporaries—hence the oft unfortunate impact of his scent experiments upon them.

But the primary task on Crowley's mind was neither to build relations with Scotland Yard nor to market elixirs, but rather to find a publisher for *Magick*. The printed pages were still with the Lecram Press —along with an unpaid bill for printing costs. Crowley's luck with publishers did, however, take a sharp turn for the better when he called upon P. R. Stephensen, the editorial director of the newly founded Mandrake Press, in June 1929.

Stephensen, a young Australian who had gone to Oxford on a Rhodes Scholarship, had a taste for writing that was sexually frank, morally nonconformist, and polemically spiced. He was, in short, the ideal editor for Aleister Crowley. The Mandrake Press, owned by rare book dealer Edward Goldston, cut its teeth on controversy with its very first title, *The Paintings of D. H. Lawrence,* issued in the very month that Crowley paid his call. Lawrence was then at the height of his notoriety as the author of *Lady Chatterley's Lover.* The *Paintings* volume created a *succès de scandale.* The *Observer* and the *Daily Express* led the media cry of outrage against the sensuous paintings of Lawrence, and a London exhibition of Lawrence's works (held in conjunction with publication) was raided by the police in July.

The heated reception for Lawrence's work underscores the gamble Stephensen took in signing on Crowley. Their contract in late June, which provided a badly needed £50 advance for Crowley, resulted first in the September 1929 publication of *The Stratagem and Other Stories,* a slim collection of three unexceptional stories that attracted little attention. Stephensen further issued Crowley's novel, *Moonchild* (also in September 1929), and the massive *Confessions* (the first two volumes of which, exquisitely printed and bound, appeared that autumn).

In so doing, Stephensen incurred the skepticism not only of owner Goldston but also of his chief author, D. H. Lawrence. In a letter to Stephensen, Lawrence offered this counsel: "I'm a bit sorry you've got Aleister Crowley at such heavy tonnage, I feel his day is rather over." Lawrence—who died the following year—was correct to doubt the market draw of Crowley. The public notoriety that had plagued the Beast for two decades now failed to manifest, just when it might have drawn the interest of young Bloomsbury rebels and fashionable book collectors. The Mandrake titles of Crowley were altogether ignored.

The association with the Mandrake Press intensified, for Crowley, the appeal of once more establishing roots in England. But there remained the problem of de Miramar, which was still being denied entry to the country. Marriage, which they both already desired, was now the obvious answer to the problem of British residence. But Belgium, where de

Miramar resided, posed legal restrictions to marriage by foreigners on its soil. So in late July 1929, Crowley went to Germany to meet there with de Miramar. In Leipzig, on August 16, the Beast and the Scarlet Woman were wed, and shortly thereafter returned to London.

De Miramar, in poor health and under a nurse's care, was now buffeted by emotions the causes of which are not known; the results, however, were anguish for them both. Crowley wrote of one anguished night: "M. [Miramar] had a quite bad attack of insane temper, & wrote to G.Y. [Yorke]—I don't know what. She makes imbecile accusations about Nurse Walsh—that I am making love to her &—sometimes—that we are trying to poison her—She 'has witnesses'." An October 1929 move to Ivy Cottage in Knockholt, Kent brought no change in de Miramar's condition. Crowley could be a fearful misogynist, but his perceptions of de Miramar at this time were shared by Yorke, a trustworthy observer. For Crowley, these scenes must have inspired memories of his first wife, Rose. As with Rose, Crowley would minister aid to de Miramar for a time—and then move on. But with de Miramar, the time cycle of despair and departure would be severely foreshortened.

Through the winter of 1930, the couple resided in relative isolation, with hopes of making their marriage work. But the publication of the remaining volumes of the *Confessions* (now canceled by the failing Mandrake Press) and of *Magick* (still held captive by the Lecram Press) still required Crowley's attention. To bolster his literary reputation, Stephensen—Crowley's neighbor in Kent—was persuaded to embark on a work entitled *The Legend of Aleister Crowley*, which would document and decisively refute the long-time press campaign of vilification against the Beast. Crowley had an ample scrapbook of press clippings on hand, and Regardie—who had at last been cleared for entry into England—could serve Stephensen as amanuensis and guide to Crowley's thought. In fact, Regardie emerged as a full collaborator; when *Legend* was republished in 1970, he was credited as a coauthor.

Stephensen was a believer in Crowley's literary talent, not in his occult mission. But the two men were united in their desire to keep the Mandrake Press afloat. They took desperate financing measures which amounted to a temporary infusion of life. A new company, the Mandrake Press Ltd., was founded in March 1930. There were four new directors: Yorke, Stephensen, Major Robert Thynne (whose reasons for interest in the venture remain unclear), and an associate of Thynne's, Major J. C. S. Mac Allen. It was anything but a stable alliance. Crowley soon accused Thynne of misappropriating funds, a charge Yorke rejected. According to Yorke, it was Crowley who blatantly diverted the

£500 invested by Cora Germer. Stephensen, in retrospect, saw both Crowley and Thynne as overly free with the working funds of the press, indulging themselves in fine dining at posh London establishments.

It is clear that Crowley continued to insist on his luxuries, even with the publication of his major works in the balance. The assertion of his "kingly nature" was fundamental to Crowley's Thelemic outlook. Those who were exasperated earned Crowley's contempt for lacking the courage to live by a like standard. Dining at the famous Café Royal in Piccadilly was one of his favorite extravagances. There is one strange account—set in this café—which, if true, testifies both to the Beast's outlandish public image and to his own sanguine acceptance of it:

> He [Crowley] believed that he possessed a magic cloak which rendered him invisible. One day he appeared in it, a magestic figure in star-encrusted conical hat and a black cloak decorated with the symbols of mysticism, and walked slowly through the Café from Regent Street to Glasshouse Street in an awestruck silence.
>
> No one could convince him that the flabbergasted patrons had seen him. "If they saw me," he would ask unanswerably, "why did nobody speak to me?"

The Café Royal was a stage upon which Crowley could create remarkable effects. And perhaps there was no real extravagance to his patronage; one patron testified that on the last occasion Crowley dined there, he left "an unpaid bill for over £100."

The irony is that the one small publishing success Crowley and Stephensen did enjoy came in February 1930, when the old Mandrake was in abeyance and the new had yet to be formed. Crowley had been invited by the student committee of the Oxford University Poetry Society to give a lecture. The subject he chose—the infamous fifteenth-century Frenchman Gilles de Rais, a feudal nobleman, a military warlord, alleged black magician, and putative murderer of some 800 children, who was ultimately hanged—had nothing whatsoever to do with poetry. One of the members of this committee was Arthur Calder-Marshall, who went on to enjoy minor success as a man of letters. Calder-Marshall and his peers were fascinated with Crowley's aura and erudition, just as had been (twenty years earlier) Victor Neuburg and his fellow students in the Cambridge University Freethought Association. And just as the Cambridge authorities had objected to Crowley's presence in 1910, so too did the Oxford authorities in 1930, led by the eminent theologian Father Ronald Knox, the Catholic chaplain. While no formal action was ever taken, Knox made it plain that severe sanctions would result if the Crowley lecture went on as scheduled on February 3.

As scholar Keith Richmond has observed, "Stephensen and Crowley were no fools when it came to financial matters, and it must have occurred to them that any publicity arising from the incident would be helpful in selling Crowley's books." Stephensen had 1,000 copies of the lecture text printed up posthaste as a sixteen-page pamphlet titled *The Banned Lecture. Gilles de Rais.* Thanks to prominent coverage of the controversy by the Oxford newspapers, and the deployment of Calder-Marshall and other students wearing sandwich-signs to hawk the pamphlet in the streets, sales were brisk—and Crowley attracted far more attention than he would have had the lecture been held without opposition.

As for the text of *The Banned Lecture*, it is rather disappointing—in essence, a polemic against Christianity that repeats arguments made more artfully in the works of his youth. Clearly, Crowley perceived certain parallels between the blackened public reputations of Gilles and himself. But Crowley downplayed the likelihood that Gilles had committed murder on the grand scale: "The one thing of which I feel certain is that 800 children is a lot. I don't know over how many years these practices were supposed to have spread. As I think you must all feel sure by now, I know nothing whatever of my subject." Crowley was admirably forthright here. The French cultural theorist Georges Bataille, who cannot be accused of Catholic bias, reviewed both secular and ecclesiastical trial records and concluded that Gilles was indeed a mass murderer of children. But in *Magick*—which would at last be published in this same year, 1930—Crowley again courted comparison with Gilles, this time by an esoteric joke fashioned so as to entice credulous readers to believe that Crowley himself was a murderer of children.

The passage in question occurs in Chapter 12, "Of the Bloody Sacrifice and Matters Cognate," which analyzes the significance of human and animal blood—and other bodily fluids and substances (the "Matters Cognate")—in magical ritual. Drawing a direct parallel to teachings of Catholicism, Judaism, Hinduism, and other world religions, he argued that blood and other bodily substances were traditionally—and rightly—viewed as primal, divine sources of energy. With respect to magical ritual, Crowley concluded: "For the highest spiritual working one must accordingly choose that victim which contains the greatest and purest force. A male child of perfect innocence and high intelligence is the most satisfactory and suitable victim." Then, in an accompanying footnote, Crowley added, "It appears from the Magical Records of Frater Perdurabo that He made this particular sacrifice on an average about 150 times per year between 1912 E.V. and 1928 E.V."

At the outset of this chapter, Crowley had pointedly observed that his concluding remarks on sacrifice alluded to a mystery that might be misunderstood. But a goodly percentage of readers could have been counted on to take his remarks literally, as proved to be the case. Hymenaeus Beta has observed that "There is no passage in Crowley's writings with as many warnings against misinterpretation, yet no passage has been used against Crowley as frequently, in life or posthumously.[. . .] it is sexual sacrifice, the 'sacrifice of oneself spiritually,' that is the thinly veiled subject of the chapter." This veil was also a venting of rage against Christendom. Why else exceed, by one's own estimates, the murder total of Gilles himself?

The British occult writer Violet Firth—better known as Dion Fortune—who gained a broad readership during this period, openly acknowledged her indebtedness to Crowley's writings, most notably in her "Foreword" to *The Mystical Qabalah* (1935). In a contemporaneous essay "The Occult Field Today," Fortune stressed both the value and the danger of Crowley's *Magick:* "[O]nly the advanced student could use it with profit. It is very uneven in its literary quality; contains much grossness and ribaldry, like all Crowley's writings, and much of it is deliberately obscure and allusive."

Fortune's criticisms illustrate the difficulties Crowley faced in winning over the "respectable" wing of British and American occultism, for whom Fortune spoke then and now. They contain just points: *Magick* is undoubtedly a text for advanced students, and much of it is "deliberately obscure and allusive." But the "deliberately" deserves emphasis, for Crowley also made it clear to the reader that his subject matter required a subtle presentation. As for the "literary quality" of the book, it is anything but uneven; *Magick* is a modernist masterwork. The "grossness and ribaldry" Fortune refers to would include the matter of male sacrifices discussed above. Fortune, like Crowley, mirrored the prudishness of the time—Fortune by her tact (sexual magic is the subject of several of her fictional and nonfictional works, but no sexual act is ever explicitly described) and Crowley by his outlandish defiance.

Fortune's essay did include this qualified endorsement: "But while I entirely dissociate myself from Crowley's methods, I would not wish to minimize his contribution to occult literature, which is of the highest value. From his books the advanced student, who knows how to read between the lines and refine the gold from the dross, can learn an immense amount, and if our interest is limited to an author's writings, we need not concern ourselves with his personal character or private life."

Fortune is correct in her judgment of Crowley's "contribution to occult literature." *Magick* is a watershed in the history of that literature—the first work to strip the subject of its gothic trappings and bring it fully into the modern world. Its arguments are ruthlessly practical—assuming, of course, that the reader will allow that there is such a thing as the "Great Work" that is attainable by human consciousness. There is, indeed, a religious belief at the heart of the book: a conviction that the life of fulfillment of the inmost spirit—the Will—is the highest form of life. Scoff at this and you scoff not only at *Magick* but at religion itself. Grant it as a nondenominational goal and *Magick* may have something to teach you. After all, the definition of "Magick" offered in the Introduction is catholic enough: **"MAGICK is the Science and Art of Causing Change to occur in conformity with Will."**

Consider this brief sampling of metaphysical maxims from various chapters of *Magick;* the boldfacing (as with the definition above) is by Crowley himself:

> **All discussions upon philosophy are necessarily sterile, since truth is beyond language. They are, however, useful if carried far enough—if carried to the point when it becomes apparent that all arguments are arguments in a circle.** But discussions of the details of purely imaginary qualities are frivolous and may be deadly. For the great danger of this magical theory is that the student may mistake the alphabet for the things which the words represent.

> [T]here is no doubt that an assemblage of persons who really are in harmony can much more easily produce an effect than a magician working by himself. The psychology of "Revival meetings" will—alas! be familiar to almost everyone, and though such meetings are the foulest and most degraded rituals of black magic, the laws of Magick are not thereby suspended. **The laws of Magick are the laws of Nature.**

> The student must guard himself constantly against supposing that this art [of divination, by tarot, the *I Ching* or other like means] affords any absolute means of discovering "truth," or indeed, of using that word as if it meant more than the relation

of two ideas each of which is itself as subject to "change without notice" as a musical programme.

The issuance of *Magick* in the summer of 1930 had little public impact. But there was one remarkable response. Victor Neuburg, Crowley's magical disciple and great love of the prewar years, glowingly reviewed the book for *The Sunday Referee* in October 1930: "The writer's accomplishment is patent; he is a master, at any rate, of prose; his power of expression is as near perfect as that of any author I have read." This judgment by Neuburg, who bore a lasting unease toward his former master, may be seen both as an instance of intellectual courage and as a gesture of tacit reconciliation—at a distance. As to the latter, Neuburg succeeded; the Beast, in his diary, noted his pleasure at the review.

But few joined with Neuburg in offering praise. Meanwhile, the Mandrake Press, Ltd.—the anticipated vehicle for Crowley's work in England—sank into bankruptcy in November 1930. Later in the decade, the American comic strip "Mandrake the Magician" derived its name from the deceased press and its association with Crowley, though the Beast never knew of this.

As to *Magick*, Crowley was prepared to take the long view. As to his marriage, he was not. New upheavals of love were in the offing.

CHAPTER TEN   A Staged Suicide, an Unavenged Libel, and the Equinox of the Gods (1930–36)

C rowley and his Scarlet Woman were having a difficult time with marriage. As so little is known of de Miramar prior to her encounter with the Beast, the formative factors behind her alcoholism and her mental anguishes must remain a mystery. It is reasonable to assume that life with Crowley—life on the terms Crowley lived it—only exacerbated her condition.

The complaints he now raised against her will sound familiar. They resemble those he raised against his first wife, Rose Kelly, and other Scarlet Women who succeeded her, notably Dorothy Olsen. The demands upon the woman who held this office were extreme, and yet Crowley never seemed to observe the obvious parallelism in their fates. Adoring them at the height of their reigns, he moved on with a cutting disdain when those reigns came to an end. The oaths and consecrations of these Scarlet Women set no termination dates. These Crowley imposed when he saw fit—that is, whenever there arose a sufficiently powerful passion for another woman. This contingency now occurred.

In April 1930, Crowley and de Miramar paid a visit to Berlin, trying to raise interest in an exhibition there of his paintings. Two months later, *John Bull* (which caught wind of Crowley's ambitions) ran a scalding piece opposing any such exhibition in England. But the atmosphere in Germany, in the latter years of the Weimar Republic, was far more permissive; openly gay and bisexual nightclubs were accepted as a matter of course by the authorities. Some of the best and brightest of the young British literati, such as Christopher Isherwood and Stephen Spender, found Berlin an ideal locale for expatriate living.

The *Berliner Tageblatt* interviewed the Beast for a brief feature that appeared in early May. The tone of the piece was quizzical and bemused: "In England Crowley, the gentleman bohemian, is a much contested personality. One group considers him as a revolutionary philosopher, another as a foolish artist; that this mountaineer, chessplayer, poet-philosopher and painter is one of the most peculiar personalities is denied by nobody." There was skepticism enough in this account, but it nonetheless delighted Crowley, who was used to far worse. His hopes for a Berlin showing mounted.

Crowley had not devoted much time to his painting since the early 1920s. But his canvases did match remarkably well with the German Expressionist aesthetic of the time, in mood, coloration, and impassioned distortion, if not in technical skill. The Beast and Scarlet Woman paid a call, on April 24, on a German painter named Steiner—part of an effort to gain a footing in Berlin artistic circles. In Steiner's studio, Crowley, age fifty-four, met a nineteen-year-old artist named Hanni Larissa Jaeger. Physically, he found her gauntly beautiful. Emotionally, he was swept off his feet at once. "I am quite in love with this Hanni," he wrote in his diary that night. Crowley's passion for Jaeger signaled the end of his marriage. But he and Jaeger did not become lovers that spring, and Crowley and de Miramar returned to England in May.

The summer did not pass smoothly. In June, the two moved into a flat at 89 Park Mansions, Knightsbridge, where they remained through the end of July. According to Crowley, de Miramar was frequently drunk, carried out violent scenes, and flirted lasciviously with male visitors. He further complained that she made no effort to learn English—a failing that had not perturbed him prior to this time. It was a vile period for Crowley on all fronts; he was short both of money and of influence and felt his entrapment keenly. On June 1 he penned this sharply satiric self-portrait in verse:

> Bury me in a quicklime grave!
> Three parts a fool, & one part a knave.
> A Superman—bar two wee 'buts'
> I had no brains, & I had no guts.
> My soul is a lump of stinking shit,
> And I don't like it a little bit!

Small wonder that Crowley resolved to return to Germany. He set a departure date of August 1, with de Miramar to be left behind. Whether the Beast openly threatened divorce prior to leaving is unknown; but shortly after his arrival in Germany, he directed his London solicitors to plot a legal strategy to that end. De Miramar, still in love with her husband, was miserable when the time for their separation arrived. Crowley's terse entry for July 31: "Marie drunk & vomiting all day. The Farewell Cocktail Party. Decided to leave."

Crowley never saw de Miramar again. Once in Germany, he withdrew all financial support for her. Yorke stepped in to offer assistance in finding her a lodging in Hampstead. But the burden placed upon Yorke rankled, and he suffered misgivings as to Crowley's character, even as he continued to respect the brilliance of the Beast's magical teachings. By late 1930, as Crowley had, in Yorke's view, left "his wife penniless and without support in London, I kept back what little money I had of his and doled it out to her. At the same time I refused to have further dealings with him, i.e. refused to act again as his agent. The Mandrake Press went bankrupt."

Meanwhile, ensconced in Berlin, Crowley wasted no time in consummating, in early August 1930, a sexual opus with Hanni Jaeger, who reciprocated his passion in full measure. Their lovemaking took place on cushions embroidered by de Miramar. Crowley wrote of it: "I *must* have been too terribly in love. I didn't know at that time what fucking was with Her!" During this first month of their relationship, Crowley nicknamed Jaeger "the Monster"—perhaps in tribute to the ferocity of her lovemaking. Another nickname for her was "Anu," a play upon "anus" and thus a veiled reference to the sexual style Crowley preferred.

Many of their sexual rituals were conducted with the aim of "health" or "energy." As for health, both of them suffered from bouts of illness during their time together. But the energy—sexual and otherwise—they aroused in each other was intense. The Beast, in their early months together, could be quite tender. After one opus—which he deemed a success—Crowley wrote:

Hanni Larissa Jaeger—child of Earth! [. . .] She is the Pure Woman in difficult circumstances; must never accept her own limitations. Hence she does the only right thing in seeking the Magical Path. [. . .] My poor sweet baby had another melancholy fit. Brandy makes her worse. Toward 1 A.M. she came to herself, & explained quite a lot. I am nearly insane with loving her, & feeling my powerlessness to help her as I want to.

As was often the case when Crowley was in the throes of new love, his desire to travel intensified. He departed with Jaeger for Portugal in late August, having been invited there by a poet who had written to Crowley after reading the two volumes of the *Confessions* issued by the Mandrake Press. This was Fernando Pessoa, who, since his death at age forty-seven in 1935, has emerged as an acclaimed figure in the Modernist movement; the Novel laureate Octavio Paz was among Pessoa's prominent admirers. Of course, none of this future glory was known to Crowley—or to Pessoa—at the time. But the Beast did see the possibilities in cultivating Pessoa, who was translating Crowley's "Hymn to Pan" into Portuguese (the translation was ultimately published in November 1931). There were obvious affinities between the two men. Pessoa, like Crowley, employed pseudonymous names ("heteronyms," Pessoa termed them) for various of his works; the deliberate fragmentation of identity and the relentless exploration of mind were key themes in the writings of both. "I am a nomadic wanderer through my consciousness," Pessoa once wrote, in words that could have been Crowley's. Nothing came of their plans to promote Crowley with Portuguese publishers. But the trip was far from wasted, for a memorable publicity stunt was fashioned—and put over artfully—by the two men.

The basic idea—a feigned suicide—was conceived by Crowley. Pessoa would serve as accomplice, contacting the press after the staging was complete. This was not the first time that Crowley had considered the potential publicity that would ensue from his demise. In March 1929, while in Paris, he had asked Francis Dickie, a British journalist, to serve as press agent for just such a stunt, with the intention of promoting—and raising prices—for Crowley's previous works, of which Crowley still possessed a substantial inventory. Dickie had flatly declined the proposal. Pessoa was far more enthusiastic.

The events leading to the feigned suicide arose soon after the arrival of Crowley and Jaeger in Lisbon on September 2. They decided upon a tour of the picturesque locales of Portugal. Amongst these was the coastal town of Cascais; nearby was the Boca do Infierno (Mouth of Hell), a funnel-shaped cliff face battered by the wind and waves of the Atlantic. They found a hotel room nearby and conducted several sexual opera; but Jaeger was unsettled by one of these, on September 13, and fell into what Crowley described as "a very long fit of hysterical sobbing." Three days later, on September 16, Jaeger again wept after the completion of the opus. A violent quarrel ensued, and they were asked by the hotel manager to depart the next day. Jaeger fled to Lisbon. The Beast tracked her down there, and they engaged in sexual magic with the object of reconsecrating their love. But the rapprochement did not hold; Jaeger departed for Germany, leaving Crowley to recommence touring Portugal on his own. The Beast returned to the Boca do Infierno where, on September 21, as he recorded in his diary: "I decide to do a suicide stunt to annoy Hanni. Arrange details with Pessoa."

The "stunt," which received coverage in major newspapers in Lisbon, Paris, and London, consisted of Crowley's leaving a suicide note weighted by his monogrammed cigarette case (so as to assure ready personal identification) upon a rock ledge above the Boca do Infierno. According to *The Empire News* of London, it read: "I cannot live without thee. The other Mouth of Hell will catch me. It will not be as hot as thine. *Hisos*, Tu Li Yu." The pseudonymous Oriental signature was a punning play on a standard British expression of farewell. *The Empire News* regarded the note as inscrutable, though it did identify Crowley as its author and quoted the Portuguese police to the effect that a man identified as Crowley had departed from the country two days later, on September 23. This was indeed the case; Jaeger (identified in the newspapers as the romantic cause of Crowley's suicide) had sent him a conciliatory telegram upon her return to Berlin, and Crowley hastened to join her, leaving Pessoa to handle reporters. *The Empire News*, like most papers that carried the story, was skeptical: "Is the mystical letter a fake or a practical joke by someone who has borrowed Crowley's name for the occasion?" Nonetheless, the story played well in the press for a brief time. Crowley, of course, had hoped that this publicity would enable him to sell a novel based on the suicide stunt to a prominent English publisher. That was not to be.

Back in Germany, Crowley tried to keep up ties with members of the British literati who were tasting life in Berlin. In October 1930, he dined with his old friend J. W. N. Sullivan, who brought along Aldous Huxley to meet the Beast. "Huxley improves on acquaintance," was Crowley's terse note in his diary. One persisting legend has it that the Beast now fostered in Huxley an interest in mescaline that led, over twenty years later, to Huxley's famous essay, *The Doors of Perception* (1954). This is most dubious. In *Doors*, Huxley confirmed that he did not try mescaline until 1953, and made no mention of Crowley as an influence. Crowley did, however, think Huxley worthy of cultivation. He daubed a portrait of the younger man, later confiding, "I thought he had a lot of money and painted him like this to flatter him."

But Crowley's primary interest in the Berlin scene had to do with its untrammeled sexual possibilities. He remained there through early 1932, pursuing numerous affairs with both women and men; frequently, in his diary, he would extol the magical efficacy of his amorous workings in the German capital. It was a remarkable sexual run for Crowley; by the evidence of his subsequent diaries, his time in Berlin represented a final "peak" in his erotomagical explorations.

Through the autumn of 1930, the Monster, Hanni Jaeger, remained supreme amongst Crowley's passions. On October 16, Crowley noted that he had suffered through a series of "very bad nightmares" during the night. But he tenderly added: "One strangest thing is that in spite of the catastrophe, & of the daily worry, & imminence of disaster, I give myself wholly to love, & am serenely happy in it. This has never happened before in my life. Before, the least annoyance put me off entirely."

Serenity did not long prevail. One source of tension was the presence of Karl and Cora Germer, upon whom Crowley was largely dependent for his financial survival. They, in turn, rankled under his constant demands. The Depression had depleted Cora's savings, and she resented Crowley's spendthrift dispersal of funds that Germer had pleaded with her to bestow to the cause of Thelema. Germer was thus forced both to serve his master and to defend the honor of his wife—whom Crowley reviled for her accusations against him.

All this would have been tangled enough. But further disturbing factors were at work. In November 1930, Crowley wrote: "Anu showed me her drawing of Karl masturbating into a toilet W. C. He forced her to look on—date uncertain—under threat to withdraw support unless she complied. She was afraid that he would murder her unless she sat quiet: so she did. True? I'm not sure: but it sounds very much like him." Crowley ultimately decided it was true. By December, he was roundly cursing—in the privacy of his diary—his most loyal disciple: "Karl is a filthy asexual maniac. The masturbating swine! He is resolved to destroy Anu spiritually by wrecking her nerves. The Gods upon him—I mean—upon it!"

But Jaeger had her own unusual ways. The day after his curse against Germer, Crowley wrote of her: "Anu has been playing a very foolish sexual game all the week. This A.M. she insisted on my using her as a W.C. in spite of the repeated warnings I have given her as to the appalling results of such behaviour. She will soon be taught by punishment." Later, in recording a sexual opus between them, Crowley added plaintively: "She is always awakening my deepest & tenderest feelings, only to trample on them with the coarsest brutality." After another sexual working (the result of the Monster seducing the Beast after breakfast), Crowley offered this portrait of Jaeger's state of being:

She is violently excited all day—sexually & otherwise. Severe melancholic & erotic outbursts. There is absolutely no reason for any nervous upset of any kind; but she changes from mood to mood in the most sudden way. This attack is more prolonged & severe than any I have observed so far. And it is more than usually causeless. She ended by wanting to go out; when I objected, pretended to ring up the police—a too familiar trick. She then calmed down, & at last woke up into an infantile state. I undressed her, & put her to bed in my pajamas. In short, every possible phase—She has now called me in, to listen to hallucinations, real or no; e.g. "I don't want you to go away behind the tree".

As Crowley explained in a subsequent entry, Anu's melancholies could take on a survival function in terms of her fierce day-to-day interactions with the Beast: "She explains her psychological fears as deliberate psych. protection. E.g.: she pretends to herself that I am going to cut her throat, so she thinks she is getting off easy if I call her a bitch!"

The relationship began to decline in January 1931, when Jaeger left Crowley for a time; in typical fashion, he promptly accused her of having stolen his personal copy of *The Book of Lies*. They reconciled later in the month, but it was an unhappy time, as they both suffered from severe ailments that left them bedridden and diarrhetic. Their affair went on into the summer, and they tried to have a child together; Jaeger was briefly pregnant, but seems to have miscarried. But the primacy of place that the Monster had enjoyed was no more. According to Crowley, she may have taken to selling drugs to support herself, or to working in a cabaret, or to "walking the streets." The fact that he took no trouble to ascertain the truth of these rumors was evidence of his diminishing interest.

During this spring and summer, Crowley took on a number of lovers, female and male. Some of the names survive whole—Louise Aschaetzsch, Renate Gottsched and, most prominently, Hanni Richter. In other cases, only a first name or a nickname remains—Gertrude, Sonia, Pola, "Fanny" (a man). It was a time of rampant fulfillment. As he wrote to Gerald Yorke in June: "The idea of my coming to England unless someone will give me £1,000,000 per day to do it—in which case I will come for 10 days with a flock of Eagles—is the idea of someone who has never been in Berlin. *Pue* Pagan Thelema! *Nunc dimittis!!*"

The events of Wednesday, May 6, 1931, as described by Crowley in prose and verse (a poem to Jaeger), are representative of the intricate sexual and emotional dramas in which the Beast delighted during this period:

A marvellous day. Made Hanni Richter cry—by being ordinarily decent to her.

Made Hanni Jaeger cry—by proving to her that she loved me. She had to admit it. We want our baby.[. . .]

Made Louise Aschaetzsch cry by sincere sadistic work (for Hanni Jaeger's sake).

It doesn't matter, my Hanni
That you are a whore & a thief
You've got a miraculous cunnie
Not a mere chunk of beef.
And if I can't fix it to fuck you
I'd rather not fuck at all
But have Fanny puncture my podex
After the ball.

The "sadistic work" was likely a beating of Aeschaetzsch; he certainly beat her on other occasions. As he declared proudly in another May entry: "Louise to dinner. She cried some more. That was a snapper on the snoot I snitched her on Saturday!"

Crowley was, by his own standards, equally successful in dealing with the long-distance turmoil created by de Miramar, to whom he was still legally married, much to his displeasure. De Miramar was in terrible straits, financially and psychologically. In one brusque letter to her, in September 1930, Crowley declared: "I gave you a great chance in life, and you threw it away. *Tant pis!*" Crowley urged her to seek a divorce, providing adequate grounds by boasting of his infidelities with Jaeger. But he also warned his wife: "It will be no good asking for alimony because we are all in the soup together with the Rt. Honorable Lord Beaverbrook and the British Empire. Best of all to you!"

Despite this overt defiance, Crowley had two reasons to take the matter of divorce seriously. The first was his family trust income—administered by trustees George Cecil Jones and Yorke—to which, Crowley feared, de Miramar might have a claim. The second was that the powerful Colonel Carter of Scotland Yard had written what Crowley described as a "mysterious and sinister" letter in October 1930, with this advice: "I suggest to you that you had better cease knocking round the Continent and come back to your wife at once or you will be getting yourself into serious trouble perhaps." "The impudence of the lunatic," Crowley scrawled across the bottom of the letter.

But Carter was playing a bluff here; in a letter to Yorke in March 1931, the inspector—in describing how de Miramar sought the help of Scotland Yard (her quoted language reflects her imperfect English)—declared himself both powerless and indifferent:

> As regards Mrs. A.C. she wrote a letter to Scotland House omitting to put my name on it, dated 28th February as follows:—"Nobody is responsible of my suicide only Aleister Crowley—please don't inquire I will not noise in the newspaper. Marie Crowley"
>
> It is difficult to know whether this woman means it seriously or not. It is not a matter for the police; suicide only becomes an offence if you attempt it and do not succeed!! If you do see the lady and she has not done away with herself, you might pat her on the back and tell her that when life looks gloomiest it very often turns round the corner and looks bright again. Also, it is not the slightest good her getting in touch with me, I cannot do anything for her and, indeed, I do not feel that I have any moral obligation to do so. I expect she has got rather a Latin temperament.

De Miramar's condition only declined. In June 1931, she was incarcerated in a public workhouse due to her financial indigence. The following month, she was admitted to the Colney Hatch Mental Hospital in New Southgate, with Crowley providing a written past history of his wife for use in treatment. On August 1, the Medical Superintendent wrote back to Crowley and offered this diagnosis: "Unfortunately her earlier phantasy formation has resulted in definite delusions, and she now believes she is the daughter of the King and Queen and of pure English blood: also that she married the Prince of Wales twelve years ago, though he is ignorant of the blood relationship. At present her conduct is satisfactory but she is resentful that her claims are not acknowledged and is likely to become difficult."

Difficult she must have become, for de Miramar remained in Colney Hatch until her death over three decades later. Indeed, she outlived Crowley, who never obtained a divorce (as he feared that a formal action might result in her winning some right to support) and never remarried. But at least one of de Miramar's "delusions" was dispelled in Colney

Hatch, thanks to a visit from Yorke. In addition to the Prince of Wales, de Miramar had claimed the Great Beast, Aleister Crowley, as her husband. Yorke confirmed this—to the astonishment of her treating physicians.

Upon first hearing of de Miramar's commitment, the Beast had written in his diary, "It is very English to regard insanity as a joke." He also noted that the commitment of his first wife, Rose, had somehow prompted the passionate entry of Leila Waddell into his life. Would the same good fortune now recur? It did. On August 3, 1931, Crowley met Bertha Busch, whose nickname was "Billie," and who would eclipse all other loves in Berlin.

Busch was thirty-six, previously divorced, gaunt (as Crowley preferred), in poor physical health and prone (according to Crowley) to violent melancholic outbursts and excessive drinking. In an August 12 entry, Crowley showed uncharacteristic concern for what might befall a woman who entered his life: "I love Billie passionately & truly—& I must avoid her. She might return my love; & if Germer succeeds in dragging me down altogether [through lack of adequate financial support], what tragedy!"

He did not avoid her, of course. They became ardent magical lovers. Of one September opus, Crowley exclaimed: "Most wonderful fuck I've had in years. Nearly tore her bottom off." The opus the very next day was even better: "The best fuck within recorded memory of living man." On September 30, Crowley consecrated Busch as the new Scarlet Woman. By now, they were living together in a flat at Karlsruhestrassez 2 in Berlin. Germer had paid—through funds provided by a most reluctant Cora—the Beast's prior Berlin debts and the first month's rent on the new flat. It was, given the standards of instability in which Crowley lived, a blissful honeymoon stretch.

In October and November 1931, the Galerie Neumann-Nierendorf (also known as the "Porza") in Berlin put on an exhibition of seventy-three of Crowley's paintings—landscapes, dreamscapes, and portraits, some of which dated from the postwar years in New York and Cefalù, while others had been completed in Berlin. There was a catalog with a flattering text and a photograph of Crowley in an Indian-style turban on the cover. Portrait subjects included, in addition to Huxley, Leah Hirsig, Norman Mudd, J. W. N. Sullivan, de Miramar, and H. P. Blavatsky. But Crowley made no record of any painting having sold. As in the case of his limited-edition books (languishing in storage in London), Crowley would not live to see these paintings fetch their current high prices from collectors.

But the exhibition did heighten the Beast's reputation amongst his fellow British exiles. His flat became a frequent site of dinners and parties that included Christopher Isherwood and Stephen Spender. Isherwood later told of seeing Crowley—in the Cosy Corner, a Berlin bar—imperiously rake his fingernails against the chest of a tough-looking boy in an open shirt. The boy had to be paid a sizable sum (by whom is unclear) to refrain from pummeling Crowley on the spot. Isherwood used Crowley as the model for his title character in "A Visit to Anselm Oakes," a story published in Isherwood's *Exhumations*. Some three decades later, in his journal, Isherwood reflected upon his acquaintance with the Beast: "The truly awful thing about Crowley is that one suspects he didn't really believe in anything. Even his wickedness. Perhaps the only thing that wasn't fake was his addiction to heroin and cocaine."

More sympathetic to the Beast among the British exiles was Gerald Hamilton, a writer and raconteur with, at this time, Communist leanings. Hamilton was the model for "Mr. Norris" in Isherwood's novel (set in the Berlin of this period) *Mr. Norris Changes Trains*. It was a mark of Crowley's multifarious nature that he felt friendship for Hamilton (but no passion, though both men were carrying on homosexual affairs during this period) while, at the same time, garnering £50 from Colonel Carter of Scotland Yard for reporting on Hamilton's leftist activities. Hamilton, who displayed a similar ambivalence toward Crowley, later wrote: "What is piquant in this matter is that on one of my journeys to London, Gerald Yorke asked me to take some English money back to Berlin and to give it to Crowley. This I did. The amount entrusted to me was the very £50 in cash that my host had earned by writing a report upon my very harmless activities." Turnabout is fair play. Hamilton later confided that he had, in turn, received sums from British Intelligence for reporting on Crowley.

Hamilton, who ultimately moved into Crowley's flat in January–February 1932, both out of friendship and of their mutual need to save rent by sharing, was witness to a good many strange events there. According to a fellow British writer, Maurice Richardson, Hamilton was present at a party at Crowley's flat during which Busch "was showering the Magus with plates, knives and forks, one of which would have put Hamilton's lights out had it not been for some dexterous interposition by Stephen Spender." In December 1931, there was a dire scene in which Hamilton found the Beast suffering from a stab wound inflicted by Busch. And then there is Crowley's February 1932 account of what ensued after he and Busch inhaled some nitrous oxide: "Bill—whew! the best show yet. Started to fuck—she got sadistic—then savage—poor Hamilton!—(I had got her quiet when he came in & woke her) doctor—morphia—hell till 6:30 [A.M.]"

The Beast was often beastly, but now and then patience and kindness showed themselves. Take, for example, the knife wound observed by Hamilton. Here is Crowley's account:

> Then began a most furious fuck. Marie [a Berlin friend, not Crowley's wife] came in & found us on sofa! Bill went to kitchen, I to study. Suddenly Bill walked in on me & stabbed me with the carving-knife. She then became violent. I had to hold her down. So I bled till Marie got a doctor, about 2 hrs. later.

What Crowley does not mention is the severity of his wound, which was just below the shoulder blade. The Beast was sufficiently weakened to contemplate—cheerfully—his own mortality in a Christmas Eve letter to Yorke: "The wound was not dangerous, though I lost quarts of blood; but it just missed being fatal which is different. I am preparing to get on to the next inc.[arnation] simply because unless we get cash in significant quantity by say Jan 7 at latest I shall have nowhere to sleep, and the exposure would doubtless kill me at once . . ."

This letter was couched to stimulate increased financial support from Yorke in London. But Crowley was serious enough to have had a formal will drawn up, three days earlier, which named Yorke as his executor to distribute his estate (which did not exist, but for unsaleable books and manuscripts) for the joint benefit of Busch and his eleven-year-old daughter, Astarte Lulu Panthea. Crowley's requested terms for his burial are a grandiloquent testimony to the lasting impact upon him of the Rosicrucian teachings of the Golden Dawn, coupled with a sly wink at his own literary aspirations, which included the fantasy of burial in the "Poet's Corner" of England's most famous church:

> I direct my Executor to take the necessary steps to ensure that my body is embalmed in the ancient Egyptian fashion and then treated as nearly as possible like that of Christian Rosencreutz as described in my book *The Equinox Volume 1 Nr. 3* but if my body be disfigured, damaged or mutilated then I direct my Executor to have it cremated and the ashes preserved in an Urn and kept as stated in *The Equinox I.v. Supplement*. The place should be either (a) the broad ledge on the cliff behind Boleskine

House, Scotland (b) the top of the rock at Cefalù, Sicily, about the "Bath of Diana", (c) Westminster Abbey.

But Crowley did live on, and relations with Busch continued in their turbulent manner through the spring of 1932. The Beast suffered from bouts of asthma (for relief from which he turned to heroin) through the winter and underwent painful nasal surgery to improve his breathing. Busch traveled to London in May; Crowley hoped that she might succeed in raising funds from Yorke and others. Such was not the case. After she phoned from London, Crowley wrote of their talk: "Bill half insane with pain & worry." Shortly thereafter, Crowley was ejected from the latest in a series of Berlin flats for nonpayment of rent. He was compelled at last to return—on June 22—to England.

Crowley solicited enough funds from personal connections to lease a new flat at 27 Albemarle Street in July. During that month, he again tried to raise interest in British publishers for projects including his *Confessions* and a prospective book (never written) on his experiences in Berlin. He consulted on this score with Regardie, who had, ironically, excelled his teacher in his ability to place magical works with British publishing houses. Regardie had, by this point, moved on to independent studies in the Golden Dawn tradition, though he dedicated his first two books, *A Garden of Pomegranates* (1932) and *The Tree of Life* (1932), to Crowley, the latter in the form of a disciple's farewell addressed to one of the Beast's poetic pseudonyms: "Dedicated with poignant memory of what might have been to Marsyas." As Regardie freely admitted, both books drew heavily from Crowley's teachings.

According to Regardie, he and Crowley "merely drifted apart" during this period. But wounds had been left to fester. Five years later, in 1937, Regardie sent Crowley a copy of a recent work, accompanied by a friendly note. Crowley replied with a mocking letter including an anti-Semitic jibe over the new first name of "Francis" (after St. Francis) which Regardie had adopted. Angered, Regardie fired back a missive which began: "Darling Alice, You really are a contemptible bitch!" This derisive allusion to Crowley's homosexuality was, to the Beast, an unforgivable insult. In the fall of that year, Crowley circulated an anonymous, libelous letter laced with vitriol and evidencing special resentment over the borrowings made by Regardie for his books. Regardie, Crowley claimed, had "betrayed, robbed and insulted his benefactor." The letter anguished Regardie at the time; but he came to forgive his teacher. Some thirty years later, Regardie, by then a respected elder statesman of the occult world, would seek to defend the Beast's reputation in *The Eye in the Triangle* (1970). Near the end of his life (Regardie died in 1985), he said of Crowley, "Everything I am today, I owe to him."

In July 1932, Crowley visited the Colney Hatch asylum, in hopes of persuading de Miramar to execute a document that would grant him a divorce and waive any claims for support. But no meeting between husband and wife occurred. According to Crowley, one of her attending physicians "advised me to leave Marie severely alone. He agreed that the case is hopeless." For some reason, Busch had accompanied Crowley on this visit and "insisted on making rows" and "[s]creamed in street." Crowley's response was to take a horrified Busch on a guided tour through the Colney Hatch environs: "So showed her two other ladies doing it. One specialized in 'fucking old piss-hole' the other 'fucking old shit-bag.' Edifying." But the Beast was beginning to despair of his Scarlet Woman. "I'm sorry: but I can no longer stand her constant nagging & abuse & idiot jealousy," he avowed in a diary entry that summer. The relationship continued, albeit on a downward slope.

Crowley did achieve one small step toward public respectability during this time. Christina Foyle, proprietress of the famous Foyle's Bookshop in London, invited Crowley to be the guest-of-honor speaker at a "Foyle's Literary Luncheon" on September 15. A number of well-known British authors—and even clergymen—had addressed these occasions in the past. Crowley's invitation evoked no outrage from the tabloids; by all accounts, his talk on "The Philosophy of Magick" was well-attended and well-received by an audience of several hundred persons at Grosvenor House. The memoirist Viola Banks, who sat at Crowley's right hand during the luncheon, recalled: "At the end of the luncheon a queue of people, mostly women anxious to be presented to him, approached with autograph books to meet the poet whom *John Bull* described as 'The Worst Man in England.'"

Crowley also delivered, on October 5, 1932, a speech to the National Laboratory of Psychical Research, entitled "The Elixir of Life: Our Magical Medicine." Crowley was invited to speak by Harry Price, then the most famous researcher of paranormal phenomena in England. Crowley's speech on this occasion was more erudite than his Foyle's talk, though he stopped short—pursuant to his magical oath—of explicitly mentioning sexual magic or detailing its practices. (In an advertisement distributed by Crowley during this same year, there was the same approach—a guarded allusion to "a method of restoring youth and energy" that was "the principal secret of the O.T.O.") The irony is that

Crowley received far less publicity for these appearances than he did for being banned from speaking at Oxford two years earlier. As Crowley, in his advertisement, had set a rather lordly sum of 100 guineas per month for the "A.M.R.I.T.A." treatment, he could have used publicity of any sort to attract clients. The seriousness of his business intentions was underscored by his purchase of a pill-making machine to produce the elixir. But sales were minimal.

On the very day that Crowley spoke at Foyle's, Gerald Yorke departed for China and the Far East on an extended trip that would serve as an effective break from his "disciple" relationship with Crowley. Yorke had come to realize that "the Old Sinner" would find a way to survive with or without him. Yorke's departure was hastened by Crowley's decision, on September 6, to file a legal action against him. The grounds were mismanagement of Crowley's literary properties and financial assets. Yorke later summarized the suit with terse sarcasm: "He writted me for the £40,000 he would have made had I not been his trustee." But Crowley had no funds to pursue the action, and it was ultimately forgotten by both men in the interests of friendship.

Yorke's departure left Crowley without a single trusted disciple in England. As for Busch, Crowley had grown disgusted with her bouts of drunkenness; though one must remember that it is Crowley's voice, and not Busch's, that survives to tell of these times. In February 1933, Crowley took on a new lover—Marianne, from Bulgaria, whom he declared "the most marvellous fuckstress alive." By March, Busch's reign as Scarlet Woman was over.

Crowley took on a number of female lovers during the winter and spring of 1933, but designated none as the new Scarlet Woman. These women were passionate media for his magical workings, no more and no less. The most frequent object of these workings during this period was personal rejuvenation—to offset recurrent bouts of asthma and bronchitis and, of course, the onset of old age. Crowley was approaching sixty.

He continued to pay calls upon a variety of London acquaintances whom he hoped to transform into benefactors. One such was Nancy Cunard, the wealthy shipping-line heiress and patroness of the avant-garde. Cunard did not fund Crowley, but the two did become friends. Cunard invited Crowley, in April 1933, to contribute to a broadside she was publishing on behalf of the "Scottsboro Boys"—nine young black men falsely accused and convicted of raping two white women by an all-white jury in Alabama. His statement, signed "Aleister Crowley, Scientific Essayist," read: "This case is typical of the hysterical sadism of the American people—the result of Puritanism and the climate."

The heart of the matter—racism—was absent from Crowley's assessment. Perhaps this was because Crowley embodied the contradiction that writhed within many Western intellectuals of the time: deeply held racist viewpoints courtesy of their culture, coupled with a fascination with people of color. On April 10, Crowley attended a London demonstration on behalf of the Scottsboro Boys, but his delight in the occasion was not based upon politics: "Great Public Meeting to protest against the Scottsborough [sic] Outrage turned to African Rally 8 P.M. It would have been a perfect party if the lads had brought their razors! I danced with many whores—all colours."

In early August, the Beast met Pearl Brooksmith, a tall, thin middle-class English woman in her thirties with angular features that were—to judge from surviving photographs—reminiscent of Leah Hirsig. The Beast seems to have swept her off her feet. Certainly, his reputation had preceded him. "She was staggered when I told her my name," Crowley duly recorded. Six days later, they had their first sexual working together. By August 18, Crowley had penned his first bawdy "Epitaph" to her:

> Here lies a Pearl of women
> Who lived in open sin.
> One end collected semen,
> The other guzzled gin.

On September 1, Brooksmith was consecrated as the new Scarlet Woman. With the onset of autumn, however, discord arose. Crowley, who required Brooksmith's menstrual blood to create the type of Elixir to which he applied the alchemical term "Red Gold," now accused her of holding back—whether psychologically or physically is not clear: "Told her we must cut out [workings] unless she was prepared to play up to her body (& also to avoid confusion). She said yes: 'all great Saviours have been bastards.'" Matters were ironed out, and the workings continued with renewed intensity in November. The effects of the Elixirs they obtained varied considerably. On November 14, after a working performed with the aim of "Health," Crowley noted: "Remarkable success—woke up utterly fit. But El. only works for a short spasm on bodies not properly purified: hence some relapse later—after I had started long walk." But by December 5, Crowley's doubts had grown after their sixty-eighth working in some four months: "S.W. goes on prolonged wild visions, very uncontrolled, & is near the border-line. I don't like it too well."

The Beast concluded his diary for the year 1933 with a poem to the

Scarlet Woman (Brooksmith's initials—"P.E.B."—include her middle name of Evelyn) that well-reflected the bouts they had undergone together:

> Bitched buggered & bewildered P.E.B.
> Fucked frittered & frustrated
> Crashed cuntstruck & confuted
> Poxed petrified & putrid.

Alongside this poem, there is an epigram concerning another of Crowley's great concerns—making financial ends meet. "The Gods," he wrote, "have forbidden only one use for money: to count it." The Beast demanded a standard of living that was, if not luxurious, then capricious and indulgent—pleasures of the finest order to be obtained whenever possible, without regret. Though he did not "count" his funds, he was not impervious to greed. It was this weakness that led him to a legal debacle in April 1934—a libel trial against his old acquaintance Nina Hamnett. The costs of the suit would cast Crowley into bankruptcy, and the publicity surrounding it would add a taint of ridicule to his notoriety.

Hamnett and Crowley first met in prewar London, when she won renown as the model for the sculpture "Laughing Torso" by Henri Gaudier-Brzeska. Hamnett was also a talented painter—and Crowley employed her as a muralist for his prewar studio at 124 Victoria Street. Hamnett, in turn, admired Crowley's magical knowledge sufficiently to enroll as a member of the A∴A∴ in 1913, though she never seriously pursued its course of studies. It was Hamnett who first discovered, in 1912, the dead body of her friend Joan Hayes (a.k.a. Ione de Forest), the mistress of Victor Neuburg who had committed suicide—a suicide in which Crowley was frequently implicated by rumor. Further, while Hamnett and Crowley never had an affair (his own written list of female lovers confirms this), Crowley nonetheless "claimed to have been to bed with her, and was very rude about the experience," according to Constantine Fitzgibbon, a friend of Hamnett. Whether this indicated attraction—or merely braggadocio—on Crowley's part is unclear. In any event, the two maintained pleasant relations for over two decades, socializing in Paris during the 1920s.

When the British publisher Constable and Company issued her memoir, *Laughing Torso*, in 1932, Hamnett sent a letter to Crowley—who was mentioned in a number of its pages—to explain: "I have written quite a lot about you, very nice and appreciative. No libel, no rubbish, simply showing up the *sale bourgeois* attitude to all our behaviour." Crowley showed no acrimony to Hamnett in person; but in his diary, the Beast was bellicose. "Abominable libels," he wrote upon his first perusal of *Laughing Torso* in September 1932. Crowley was in a litigious mood at this point, having just filed the action against Yorke, previously discussed, for trustee mismanagement. He consulted with his solicitors about the libels in *Laughing Torso*; though they had their misgivings, given the vast potential for rebuttal evidence against the character of their client, their recommendation was to proceed.

The passage upon which the claim of libel would be based was innocuous enough, given the history of past press invective against the Beast, not to mention the accounts in Betty May's ghostwritten *Tiger-Woman* (1929). Hamnett briefly described the "dreadful stories of his wickedness" that had circulated in 1920s Paris: "Crowley had a temple in Cefalù in Sicily. He was supposed to practice Black Magic there, and one day a baby was said to have disappeared mysteriously. There was also a goat there. This all pointed to Black Magic, so people said, and the inhabitants of the village were frightened of him." The two libels Crowley would press were that he practiced black magic and that a baby had disappeared from the Abbey. The former, with its breadth of interpretive context, would prove his undoing.

Crowley commenced proceedings against Hamnett and her publisher in September 1932, demanding a restraining order against further publication of the book. No such order was granted, and the libel action proper came to trial in April 1934. In that interim, Crowley enjoyed a legal success that must have buoyed his confidence. In January 1933, he spied a placard in a bookshop window on Praed Street in London. The placard was attached to a copy of Crowley's novel *Moonchild* and declared—as a sales enticement—that "Aleister Crowley's first novel *The Diary of a Drug Fiend* was withdrawn from circulation after an attack in the sensational press." Crowley sued for libel, on the particular grounds that *Drug Fiend* had never been removed from circulation (though sales had certainly suffered) and on the general grounds that the placard implied that his works were indecent. The one-day trial took place on May 10, 1933; Crowley was awarded £50 plus costs. Mr. Justice Bennett, who presided, ruled that: "There was not the smallest ground for suggesting that any book Mr. Crowley had written was indecent or improper. Mr. Gray [the bookshop owner] wanted the public to believe that the book to which the label was attached was an indecent book."

Of course, Mr. Gray had not the means to hire counsel of the caliber available to Constable and Hamnett. Further, Mr. Gray had not introduced into evidence works by Crowley that could have substantiated that indecencies existed in his writings. Suddenly, libel actions seemed to the Beast a means to easy money. In June 1933, Crowley contemplated, in addition to his pending action against Hamnett, a suit against memoirist Ethel Mannin, who wrote in her *Confessions and Impressions* (1930) of asking Crowley's friend, society hostess Gwendolyn Otter, if "she could tell me the truth about him and the dark stories of drugs and black mass circulating about him [. . .]" Crowley's interest in this passage confirms his intended strategy of suing on the basis of vague allusions of black magic—just the opposite of the narrow claim that had brought him victory against the bookseller.

Still, Crowley must have known, in advance of the Hamnett trial, that he was facing stiff odds. In a pretrial memorandum, one of Crowley's solicitors warned that if the defendants obtained a copy of *White Stains*, "your chances of winning this action are negligible." (In fact, the defense did find a copy, which was produced in the courtroom but not read from.) A further difficulty Crowley faced was the lack of a noteworthy character witness. Appeals to Major General J. F. C. Fuller (who must have recalled, with grim satisfaction, Crowley's failure to testify on behalf of George Cecil Jones in the *Looking Glass* action of 1910) and to J. W. N. Sullivan were rebuffed. In the end, the only willing voice was Karl Germer, whose testimony on behalf of his Prophet displayed noble integrity. The impact on the jury of the accented words of an unknown German acolyte? Surely nil.

Crowley would later aver that he had hoped to settle out of court. Nonetheless, the four-day trial commenced on April 9, 1934, with J. P. Eddy (later a magistrate) as lead counsel for Crowley, while Malcolm Hilbery (later Mr. Justice Hilbery) represented Constable and Martin O'Connor, a luminary of the London bar, appeared on behalf of Hamnett. Eddy made an effective opening statement in which he emphasized the Beast's earnest lifelong search for spiritual truth and his avowed enmity, as a white magician, against the forces of "Black Magic" alluded to in Hamnett's book. Crowley's unconventional life could be attributed to the repressions he had endured as a young boy raised within the Plymouth Brethren creed. As for his Abbey in Cefalù, it was the site of white magical practices. No baby had disappeared.

Crowley was called as first witness on his own behalf. The impression he made upon judge and jury could not have been less effective. On the basis of the trial transcript alone, one might conclude that Crowley was a canny and even—at times—an eloquent witness. But tone and presence worked severely against him, as they so often did in public contexts. The British novelist Anthony Powell was at that time employed as an editor by Duckworth, the publisher of Betty May's *Tiger-Woman*. A victory by Crowley would have left Duckworth exposed to a subsequent legal salvo, and so Powell was sent to observe the Hamnett trial. Powell was sufficiently fascinated by Crowley to employ him as the model for the ominous Dr. Trelawney in Powell's novel series, *A Dance to the Music of Time* (1951–75). But as a witness, Crowley failed to impress Powell, who later observed that the Beast's performance "was altogether futile. He seemed unable to make up his mind whether to attempt a fusillade of witty sallies in the manner of Wilde (a method to which Crowley's musical-hall humour was not well adapted), or grovel before the judge, who had made plain from the start that he was not at all keen on magic or magicians. Crowley's combination of facetiousness and humility could hardly have made a worse impression."

Under examination by his own counsel, Crowley did make some initial headway, quoting the two key salutations of *The Book of the Law*: "Do what thou wilt shall be the whole of the Law," and "Love is the law, love under will." These, he cogently explained, meant devoting oneself earnestly to one's true work on earth, which could be discovered through honest self-examination guided by the advice of wise men. When Eddy asked if all this had to do with Black Magic, Crowley replied: "My principles would forbid it, because Black Magic is suicidal."

As Powell noted, there was a distinct echo of Oscar Wilde's 1895 libel action testimony in certain of Crowley's sallies with opposing counsel. Irony upon irony, Crowley had been—in his Cambridge days—one of those who had pilloried Wilde. On the first day of trial, Hilbery astutely addressed the risible—to the court and jury—subject of Crowley's magical names, one of which (the Greek *Therion*) the court reporter, as reflected below, had difficulty transcribing:

> Hilbery: Did you take to yourself the designation of "The Beast, 666"?
>
> Crowley: Yes.
>
> Hilbery: Did you call yourself the "Master Therium" [sic]?
>
> Crowley: Yes.
>
> Hilbery: What does "Therium" mean?
>
> Crowley: Great wild beast.
>
> Hilbery: Do these titles convey a fair expression of your practice and outlook on life?

Crowley: "The Beast, 666" only means "sunlight." You can call me "Little Sunshine." (Laughter.)

Was the laughter here in Crowley's favor? The aging Beast was bald, stout, toothy, sallow, and eccentrically dressed, wearing an outdated top hat on his way to and from the daily court proceedings. The moniker "Little Sunshine" must have induced astonishment on the part of the jury and public onlookers.

Further cross-examination by Hilbery established a vulnerable point—Crowley's failure to prosecute libel actions against prior attacks, such as those by *John Bull* and the *Sunday Express*, that were far more venomous than anything authored by Hamnett. Crowley argued that he had lacked the funds to bring those actions, but the sense of selective opportunism was likely established with the jury. This impression was heightened by Hilbery's quoting from an article Crowley had written for the London *Sunday Dispatch* in June 1933, in which he had boasted that "They have called me the worst man in the world." In that same article, Crowley told (as he did, at greater length, in the *Confessions*) of his early experiments, in his Golden Dawn years, with black magic. Crowley was now fairly caught at his own game, played throughout his life, of simultaneously reviling and exulting in his own infamy.

Day three of the trial went very badly. O'Connor took up the cross-examination of Crowley and challenged him to prove his powers by launching a magical attack against Hilbery then and there in the courtroom. Crowley declined with a statement that can be viewed as a shameless lie or, as Crowley would have conceived it, as the retrospective life vision of an Ipsissimus: "I have never done any harm to any human being." O'Connor, who spoke in a broad Irish brogue that radiated incredulous humor, then urged Crowley to render himself invisible—a power claimed in his own writings. Crowley declined. By the Beast's own definition of black magic in *Magick*—any use other than the Knowledge and Conversation of the Holy Guardian Angel—it could have been an instance of it to employ magic to evade a lawyer's insult. But then, Crowley had stated in his *Confessions* that he had made himself invisible to evade detection after shooting an assailant in India. What was the real difference here? A skeptic would say—the presence of witnesses to call his bluff. A practitioner of magic could argue the wisdom of Crowley's refusal by noting that the conditions upon which magic depends could not have been present in the courtroom. But Crowley did not so argue. If magic had its secrets, and Crowley had spent much of his life divulging them, this time he refused:

O'Connor: You say that on one occasion you rendered yourself invisible. Would you like to do so now, for if you do not I shall denounce you as an imposter?

Crowley: You can ask me to do anything you like, but it will not alter the truth.

When this grilling came to an end, Germer took the stand for his brief, inconsequential stint as Crowley's character witness. Hilbery then opened the case for the defense by calling to the stand Betty May—now Betty Sedgwick—who recounted her dire tales of Crowley's Abbey at Cefalù. Sedgwick's testimony continued on into the fourth and final day of the trial, when it emerged that Crowley had received letters stolen from Sedgwick by an intermediary in June 1933. Those letters were being used by Eddy in an ill-conceived effort to impeach Sedgwick as a "bought" witness out to extract money from Hamnett's counsel for alleged expenses in connection with her court appearance. This attempt at impeachment rebounded badly against Crowley, once the facts came out. In a subsequent criminal trial—some two months after the libel action, in July 1934—Crowley was found guilty of feloniously receiving the letters and was bound over for two years (the equivalent of probation) and compelled to pay a £50 fine.

As for the libel action, it was concluded on that fourth day. Mr. Justice Swift gave his own summing up to the jury:

I have been over forty years engaged in the administration of law in one capacity or another. I thought I knew of every conceivable form of wickedness. I thought that everything which was vicious and bad had been produced at some time or another before me. I have learnt in this case that we can always learn something more if we live long enough. I have never heard such dreadful and horrible, blasphemous and abominable stuff as that which has been produced by a man who describes himself to you as the greatest living poet.

It is doubtful if the jury needed Swift's impassioned words to reach its own unanimous decision in favor of Hamnett and Constable. Crowley's public demeanor in the face of this verdict was altogether remarkable. An anonymous journalist for the *Sunday Express* offered this brief portrait:

Friday the 13th was an unlucky day for magician ALEISTER CROWLEY.

At luncheon interval ambled off from Law Courts to his hotel, hatless but in orthodox black coat, made a hearty meal of *pilaf de langoustes* and a glass of milk.

After jury's verdict against him in his libel case seemed unperturbed, quoted to me Kipling's "If"—

> 'If you can meet with Triumph and Disaster
> 'And treat those two impostors just the same . . .'

Crowley will almost certainly appeal.

As part of the verdict, Crowley was judged liable for the defendants' costs; these he never paid, finding shelter in bankruptcy court the following year. He did indeed appeal; arguments were heard on November 7, 1934, but to no avail.

Crowley's diary entry for April 13, the day the trial ended, is suitably perplexing: "Case violated by collapse of Swift & Nina. General joy— the consternation of Constable & Co. & co." Was this denial? A joke? A perception of the verdict as adjudged on higher planes? That Crowley felt genuinely good-humored over his loss is doubtful in the extreme. A diary entry over three years later—on October 19, 1937, the day Crowley learned of the death of Mr. Justice Swift—makes clear that anger had lingered, and also provides a clue as to what had buoyed him on that day of defeat. "The drunken blackguard Swift is dead. N.B. the sot's swinish injustice gave me the best thing that ever happened: Deidre and Ataturk!"

The reference here is to what had happened as Crowley exited the courthouse on the day of his defeat. A nineteen-year-old woman, Patricia MacAlpine, whom Crowley came to call Deidre, approached him, expressed her outrage at the unjust verdict, and offered to bear Crowley's child. Deidre already had two illegitimate children; her willingness to have another with a man nearly forty years her senior who could not provide for her or the child is a wonder that Crowley himself never sought to explain. But some nine months later, a son, his first, was born to him—Aleister Ataturk, the Beast named him, though the filial nickname he employed in his diaries was "the Christ Child," a title both humorous and sincere in terms of the spiritual hopes he held for his son. Crowley left the boy's upbringing to Deidre, whom he saw only occasionally—an arrangement that suited them both. Deidre was never consecrated as a Scarlet Woman and maintained her own independence, going on to have a fourth child by another man.

One final aftermath of the trial is the stuff of legend rather than of fact: When Nina Hamnett died in 1956, it was rumored that she had committed suicide due to the lingering effect of a curse cast upon her by Crowley, himself nine years dead. There is evidence that, quite to the contrary, Hamnett had the good sense not to take Crowley's suit too seriously. There survives a copy of *Laughing Torso* in which Hamnett penned, on the flyleaf, a playful drawing of the Beast with this caption: "Aleister Crowley who started & finished the fun & games at the Law Courts in 1934."

At the insistence of forty-eight listed creditors—including assorted landlords and tradesmen who had lodged or done business with the Beast since his return to London in 1932—Crowley entered into involuntary bankruptcy proceedings in February 1935. His total debts came to some £4695, and his assets—aside from the ill-founded claim against Yorke, discussed earlier—were nil. Small trust payments, donations from disciples, sporadic gifts from Yorke and other friends, rare sums from the few souls who came to him seeking magical healing and the Elixir of Life—these were the tenuous means of maintaining a frayed gentility that befitted a Prophet awaiting his Aeon.

As for his Scarlet Woman, Brooksmith underwent a menopausal hysterectomy in January 1936. It was part of a general decline in her well-being that would, some years later, necessitate psychiatric treatment. In May 1936, Crowley recorded that Brooksmith was suffering from "almost constant hallucinations" and "showing serious symptoms of insanity." Crowley had, for months, borne up to the strain of nursing her; Brooksmith, of course, had done the same for him. But the Beast was restive. Loyalty alone in a Scarlet Woman was not enough; a sexual current capable of fueling the highest magical states was essential. Here, Brooksmith was falling far short. By the end of May, a caustic Crowley observation foreshadowed the end for this Scarlet Woman (the last of his lovers to be so designated): "Pearl's devotion to me like that of a penguin to her egg: so exclusive that she is too stupid to defend the position."

When Yorke returned to London in 1936, he resumed his duties as Crowley's trustee and, on his own, supplied the Beast with cash gifts now and then. But Yorke had drawn a definite line. As he later wrote, "for the rest of my life I refused to have any financial or other business connection with the old sinner." Henceforth, Crowley would pursue his publishing plans primarily through funding from his one loyal contingent—the O.T.O. Agapé Lodge in Los Angeles. Crowley corresponded prolifically with Wilfred T. Smith and a number of other Agapé Lodge members until the end of his life. In many respects, he was better suited to long-distance leadership, composing penetrating letters on magical practice and conduct, while facilitating—by his absence—the growth of a small but distinct American Thelemic offshoot, one that has continued to the present day.

These setbacks in his personal and financial affairs failed to diminish Crowley's zeal on behalf of Thelema. The evidence is clear that he attempted to capture the attention both of His Majesty's Government and of the Führer's Reich. Crowley's fascination with the latter had to do, in part, with epistolary urgings by his German-based supporter Martha Küntzel. In the late 1920s, Küntzel tried to place a copy of the German translation of the *Book* in the hands of Adolf Hitler, then a mere aspirant to power. Crowley later asserted (in annotations, made during the war years 1942–44, to his copy of the book *Hitler Speaks*, a compendium of the Führer's table talk of the 1930s by Hermann Rauschning) that Küntzel had succeeded in so doing: "She had been told in 1925 by the Master Therion [Crowley] that the nation which first accepted the *Book of the Law*, officially, would thereby become the leading nation in the world. She accordingly supplied Hitler with a copy of her translation of the *Book*, and other such parts of the extensive commentary on that *Book* by the Master Therion (which she was engaged in translating) as seemed to her of topical importance. His replies, at present inaccessible, and many passages in this volume *Hitler Speaks*, show clearly how far he profited by her teaching, and wherein his interpretations erred."

Crowley thus viewed Küntzel as having conveyed the truth of Thelema to Hitler, whom both Crowley and Germer regarded as her "magical son." But Küntzel had, in an earlier letter to Crowley, explicitly denied such a link to Hitler, and implicitly rejected any direct connection between Hitler and the *Book*, aside from the natural similarities of similar minds:

> You are perfectly right when you say I can't think politically. I never cared for politics except during the [First World] War and then since the time of Hitler's rising, though late enough, as it was when I began to see that Hindenburg was too old to give the

helm of the Reich the necessary turn. And then it began to dawn on me how much of Hitler's thoughts were as if they had been taken from the Law of Thelema. I became his fervent admirer and am so now, and will be to my end. I have ever so often owned to this firm conviction that the close identity of Hitler's ideas with what the *Book* teaches endowed me with the strength necessary for my work.[. . .] But Germer's letter amused me greatly. Isn't it a lark to hear him bring forth his 'theory' about Hitler's "magic birth"!

Note that Küntzel places the time of her first intense attachment to Hitler as the early 1930s; for it was on January 30, 1933 that the aging Paul von Hindenburg, President of the German Republic, named Hitler Chancellor. Crowley's indication of 1925 as the approximate time of her initial contacts with Hitler is therefore highly dubious. Küntzel's observation that it was "as if" Hitler had borrowed from Thelema would seem, in itself, to preclude the truth of any direct contact on her own part with the Führer.

Why, then, did Crowley persist—both privately, and in the manuscript of *Magick Without Tears*, written in 1944 and published posthumously—in the belief that he had influenced Hitler? Was it a case of vanity, or the deliberate construction of a mythos for future Thelemites? Or had Küntzel actually told him—in communications other than the letter above—of contacts with Hitler? The latter alternative seems most unlikely. There is still further reason for doubt that any such contact occurred. Yorke later recalled (presumably on the basis of Crowley's statements to him on this subject) that a copy of the *Book* had been given to Hitler "when in prison at Nuremburg." Hitler was imprisoned, as a result of his role in the Munich Beer Hall Putsch of 1923, for nine months spanning the years 1923–24; Germer's German translation of the *Book* was issued in 1925.

The 1924 publication of *Mein Kampf* establishes beyond question that Hitler had, early on, fashioned a rhetoric of hatred, violence and power as ultimate justification that owed nothing to Crowley. Nonetheless, Crowley was convinced to the contrary. His marginal notes to *Hitler Speaks* are replete with what he saw as unmistakable parallels to the *Book* (or *Liber AL*). One of Hitler's remarks particularly fascinated Crowley: "Our revolution is not merely a political and social revolution; we are at the outset of a tremendous revolution in moral ideas and in men's spiritual orientation." Crowley's glowing response: "*AL*, the whole book." But the Beast made no comments whatsoever aside Hitler's long harangue against the Jews, and showed, in his response to certain other passages, that he held serious reservations concerning the means Hitler was willing to employ. For example, Hitler described the primary duty of great historical personages (such as himself): "Their supreme, their only purpose in all they do must be to maintain their power." Crowley's judgment: "But this is dangerously near the Left Hand Path." As to the necessity for race-based politics, Hitler declared: "The 'nation' is a political expedient of democracy and liberalism. We have to get rid of this false conception and set in its place the conception of race, which has not yet been politically used up." Crowley replied: "This only means Race Wars. The master class is above all these distinctions." But Crowley had no difficulty with the concept of a dictatorial rule by this "master class." He penned a resounding "Yes!" next to this statement by Hitler: "After all these centuries of whining about the protection of the poor and lowly, it is about time we decided to protect the strong against the inferior." Crowley, however, denied that race was a valid criterion for "master class" membership. Only the Law of Thelema — implemented by a nation—could ensure proper selection.

In his marginal notes, Crowley made a further surprising assertion— that Hitler had "almost certainly gotten the idea to use the swastika as the Nazi symbol" from us. I personally had suggested it to Ludendorff in '25 or '26—when he started talking about reviving Nordic Theology—pointing out that the Swastika is the only universal magical symbol which had an ancient title peculiar to that system:—the 'Hammer of Thor.'" "Ludendorff" was General Erich Ludendorff, a nationalist cohort of Hitler in the abortive Putsch of 1923. If Crowley did speak to Ludendorff on this score, he was conveying no new information, as the swastika had already been used as a symbol by other postwar German nationalist groups; Hitler (the Führer's own claims notwithstanding) merely borrowed it for his Nazi Party. In any event, Crowley was plainly eager to link Thelema with a political force he felt would be significant in shaping the Aeon to come. His rejection of Nazi racial doctrines was of little comparative importance to him.

While Crowley's annotations were made some six years later, there is no reason to doubt that they represented his essential viewpoint as to Hitler in 1936, when the Beast made his only substantial effort to contact the Führer directly. In May, Crowley had a luncheon talk with an unnamed companion about "93 [Thelema] as base for Nazi New Order." Then, in July, Crowley received a visit from George Sylvester Viereck, Crowley's employer—through Viereck's pro-German journals, *The Fatherland* and *The International*—during World War One. Later that day, the Beast recorded with delight that "Viereck will sign affidavit that I had no trouble with authorities in U.S.A. He said also that after war he made friends with our N.I. [Naval Intelligence] chiefs, who told him that I had been working for them during the War."

Ironically, Crowley sought from Viereck both proof of his British patriotism and access to the Führer. Following their meeting, Crowley wrote to Viereck to explain anew the fundamentals of Thelema and to urge Viereck—who was planning to visit Germany—to contact Hitler on the Beast's behalf. Note that, in this letter, Crowley made no claim of prior familiarity on Hitler's part with the *Book*:

> Now let me come to brass tacks about your visit to Germany. One of my colleagues [Küntzel] informed me a couple of months ago that the Fuehrer [sic] was looking for a philosophical basis for Nazi principles.[. . .] Some of my adherents in Germany are apparently trying to approach the Fuehrer with a view to putting the *Book of the Law* in its proper position as the Bible of the New Aeon. I expect that you will be in close touch with the Chancellor and his immediate officers, and I should be very grateful if you would put the matter tentatively before them. . . . Incidentally, I should be very glad to clear up my own position with the Gestapa [sic], who apparently believe all the rubbish written about me in papers like the *'Judenkenner'* [Jew-knower], *'Detective'* [a French publication] and the Hearst papers in their less philosophical moments . . . Of course, anyone who is at the head of an International Secret Order is suspect, but my Order is not international in that sense at all . . . Hitler himself says emphatically in *Mein Kampf* that the world needs a new religion, that he himself is not a religious teacher, but that when the proper man appears he will be welcome.

There is no reason to believe that Viereck—no admirer of Thelema—made any effort on Crowley's behalf. It would have been foolhardy for Viereck to claim any occult connections whatsoever, much less one with Crowley, for the Third Reich had outlawed virtually all esoteric groups (alleged to be under covert Jewish control) in Germany—including the O.T.O. Numerous historians have pondered the dual questions of (1) the influence of occultism upon Hitler and other Nazi leaders, and (2) the reasons for Nazi suppression of occult groups. These issues are beyond the scope of this biography; but one might consider the caution offered

by Nicholas Goodrick-Clarke, in his *The Occult Roots of Nazism* (1985),
that "there is a persistent idea, widely canvassed in a sensational genre
of literature, that the Nazis were principally inspired and directed by occult agencies from 1920 to 1945.[. . .] This fascination is perhaps
evoked by the irrationality and macabre policies of Nazism and the
short-lived continental dominion of the Third Reich.[. . .] The total defeat of the Third Reich and the suicides and executions of its major figures have further mystified the image of Nazism."

But it is no exaggeration to state that the Nazi regime was inimical to
the O.T.O. Crowley knew this full well, and thus had couched his letter
to Viereck carefully. For the Nazis had already persecuted Karl Germer,
who was arrested in February 1935 on the charge of illegal Masonic connections (Germer was never a Mason, but certain O.T.O. rituals owed
much to Masonic symbolism, and hence Germer's connection to Crowley sufficed in this regard) and spent several months in Nazi prison
camps in Berlin and Esterwegen. By his own account, Germer was sustained, during this ordeal, by a vision of the Holy Guardian Angel—the
fulfillment of years of magical study under Crowley. In a November
1935 letter to Agapé Lodge member Max Schneider, written after his release, Germer set forth what he believed to have been the motives and
methods of the Nazis in suppressing occult groups:

> When the Gestapo were investigating secret societies in general
> [. . .] they discovered my personal relations with Crowley. And
> it was the secrets of the O.T.O. that they believed to be of
> supreme political importance. Ever since their ascent to power
> the Nazis suspected the existence of some secret organization
> which wields some sort of mysterious power and orders the af-
> fairs of the planet.[. . .] It was from me that they expected to
> obtain the requisite information. I was exposed to the severest
> cross-examination and to third-degree methods in order to
> force me to reveal the secrets. Finally I was sent to the terrible
> Esterwegen Camp with the instruction to break me and to treat
> me with particular brutality for 'obstinately refusing to reveal
> the truth.'

Germer shortly thereafter moved to Belgium, where he was arrested
and deported to France; he was then interned by French authorities for
several months before emigrating to America, where he spent the final
decades of his life. All of these legal problems were a direct consequence

of his links with Crowley. And Crowley, for all the criticisms he continued to level at Germer in their correspondence, retained a lasting respect for Germer's courage.

The fate of Germer places in proper perspective Crowley's chances for success in swaying Hitler. But with boundless optimism, Crowley also sought, in this same period, to influence the British government. In October 1936, he drafted "Propositions" for His Majesty's Government which he sent to Alfred Duff Cooper, the British Secretary of War. Here Crowley focused on the controversial issue of British military recruitment in the face of the German build-up. He argued that universal compulsory service for both sexes would create the disciplined force necessary for the impending crisis. However, to "preserve the noble principles of liberty on which the greatness of our country has been founded, and which may indeed be said to be dearer to us each one than life itself," the British public would have to be persuaded to accept this measure by "Science," as reflected in *The Book of the Law*: "[T]he Law of Thelema is an altogether new instrument of Government, infinitely elastic, in the proper hands, from the very fact of its scientific rigidity. I offer this Law to His Most Gracious Majesty in my duty as a loyal and devoted subject; and I suggest that it be adopted secretly by His Majesty's Government, so that I may be supported by the appropriate Services in my efforts to establish this Law as the basis of conduct, to the better security and more acceptable hence more natural government of the Commonwealth."

Crowley thus carefully tailored his respective overtures to Germany and England. For the Führer, Thelema was the new Religion that would justify the master class; for England, it was the unifying Science that would transcend democratic squabblings. Crowley worked, in both cases, from two intertwined premises: That Thelema was the ideal framework for the exercise of power, and that this truth could be established by an earthly ruler of might. It hardly mattered which ruler that would be. (He had, some years earlier, attempted to contact Stalin as well.) Crowley the Prophet would go where Thelema could flourish. His strategizing here casts retrospective light on his World War One activities as well: Crowley was perfectly capable of playing two political hands at once.

At the Autumn Equinox in September 1936, Crowley took a more constructive step in furthering Thelema—the issuance of the capstone *Book 4*, Part IV—*The Equinox of the Gods*, a volume discussed in Chapter Four in connection with Crowley's reception of *The Book of the Law*. The beautiful first edition, designed by Crowley, was limited to 1000 copies plus 250 copies for subscribers, one of whom was George Bernard Shaw. In a slip pocket was a sixty-five-page facsimile of the original handwritten manuscript of the *Book*—fulfilling, at last, a requirement for publication set forth in the *Book* itself. Crowley received the advance copies on September 18. Five days later, in the early dawn, Crowley noted in his diary: "had vision of four adepts, the Chinese, the Central Asian & two others."

This vision inspired a ceremony over one year later. A small second edition of *Equinox* was published, and in the early dawn of December 23, 1937, Crowley assembled representatives of what he took (along with himself) as all the "races" of the world—a Jew, a subcontinent Indian, a Malayan, and an African—to receive the Word of the New Aeon. The Indian was a Bengali Muslim and the African was a dancing girl. The setting was Cleopatra's Needle on the London Embankment, no doubt chosen for its Egyptian linkage, and journalists were invited. A press clipping inserted into Crowley's diary, which the Beast presumably enjoyed, offered this overview:

> Prospectus of book says it's [the *Book*] been published 3 times before; adds sinisterly, that first publication was 9 months before the outbreak of Balkan war, second 9 months before outbreak of world war, third 9 months before outbreak of Sino-Japanese war. No coincidence, it says: "the might of this Magick burst out & caused a catastrophe to civilization". Well, we'll see next September . . .
>
> "It's a bit hard of you to wish another war on us," I said to Crowley. "Oh, but if everyone will only do as I tell them to," he replied, "the catastrophe can be averted."
>
> Somehow I fear they won't.

If only everyone would heed him. Crowley would devote the last years of his life to the pursuit of that seemingly simple possibility. The passion to attain it never left him.

CHAPTER ELEVEN

The Final Years of a Magus in the Guise of a Disreputable Old Man (1937–47)

I f *The Equinox of the Gods* was a battle cry to the world—a declaration of the changing of Aeons—then Crowley seems to have been lightened by it. He now sought a popular audience to which he would convey the Word of Thelema with concision and brio.

Three works emerged from this effort. The first, *Eight Lectures on Yoga* (1939), was earlier discussed in Chapter Three in connection with Crowley's yoga practice in Ceylon in 1901. It contains transcriptions of two series of lectures delivered by Crowley at various London sites—various due to funding difficulties—during the winter of 1937. The satiric titles of the two series were "Yoga for Yahoos: and "Yoga for Yellowbellies," exemplifying Crowley's fondness for injecting humorous startles into spiritual discourse.

The second and briefest of the works of this period—a pamphlet rather than a book—was "The Scientific Solution of the Problem of Government," published in 1937 under the pseudonym of the "Comte de Fenix." The allusion to a great bird rising from the ashes suited Crowley, who was speaking for himself here, rather than seeking to please Hitler or Chamberlain. The pamphlet opens with axioms such as *"The average voter is a moron,"* and *"In brief, we govern by a mixture of lying and bullying."*

Remarkably, Crowley included his own claim to praeterhuman inspiration within the scope of his invective: *"The theories of Divine Right, aristocratic superiority, the moral order of Nature, are all to-day ex-*

ploded bluffs. Even those of us who believe in supernatural sanctions for our privileges to browbeat and rob the people delude ourselves with the thought that our victims share our superstitions." The Nazi racial theory was excoriated as well: "Hitler has invented a farrago of nonsense about Nordics and Aryans; nobody even pretends to believe either, except through the 'Will-to-believe.'"

The "Scientific Solution" to all this rampant chaos is the formula of Thelema: "Do what thou wilt shall be the whole of the Law." But how could a world be fashioned in which all were in accord as to their respective True Wills? To enforce the Law, the Beast proposed a Thelemic bureaucracy:

> *Let this formula be accepted by every government.* Experts will immediately be appointed to work out, when need arises, the details of the True Will of every individual, and even that of every corporate body whether social or commercial, while a judiciary will arise to determine the equity in the case of apparently conflicting claims. (Such cases will become progressively more rare as adjustment is attained). All appeal to precedent and authority, the deadwood of the Tree of Life, will be abolished, and strictly scientific standards will be the sole measure by which the executive power shall order the people. The absolute rule of the state shall be a function of the absolute liberty of each individual will.

In the aftermath of his libel trial, it is startling that Crowley could hold the capacities of any potential "judiciary" in so high a regard. As for strict "scientific standards," the Beast had not yet formulated them; Crowley himself allowed the difficulty of assessing even his closest students. And from whence did his global optimism spring, given his opening axiom as to the utter stupidity of the average citizen? From the conviction, it would seem, that the social practice of Thelema would be an Elixir for the body politic. While Crowley saw this as Science, most would regard it as Religion.

The third work of this period, *Little Essays in Truth,* completed and published in 1938, succeeded in lucidly presenting the intertwining principles of kabbalah, magic, and Thelema as they relate to the common and uncommon states of humankind. The titles of the sixteen essays range from "Sorrow" and "Wonder" to "Silence," "Love," and "Truth." Their style is limpid yet precise, even epigrammatic. The concision of the essays—each roughly four pages long—allows a reader without occult background to sense something of the meaning of the ascent of the Tree of Life. The satiric tone of *Eight Lectures* is replaced here by a new—for Crowley—patience and even graciousness toward the reader.

But Crowley no longer hoped that his books would bring him an income. The peripatetic changes of address continued. One of his landlords, Alan Burnett-Rae, a young Oxford man in whose house on Welbeck Street Crowley leased a flat in 1936–37, left "A Memoir of 666" that detailed the Beast's domestic ways—including the burning of immense quantities of incense, repeated rows with Brooksmith the Scarlet Woman, and a penchant for spicy home cooking. Burnett-Rae was made the victim when first invited to one of Crowley's dinners:

> At the first mouthful I thought I had burned my tongue with caustic acid and reached for the water and thereafter took water with every successive spoonful. Crowley, however, shovelled an enormous plateful away with record speed, fortifying it as he went with chillies and other spices, the sweat pouring down his face, as if he were in a Turkish bath.[. . .] He explained that he had learnt about real curry in India, Burma and Ceylon, that its object was to produce sweating, and hence a cooling process, also designed to stimulate the system generally in hot climates. He pointed out that this was only one of many cooling processes he was familiar with in these lands and that one of the great points of hospitality was to have one's *partes viriles* lifted up by a maiden attendant [. . .]He assured me that I would soon get to enjoy such things, as well as curry, once I got out there, to say nothing of the delights of opium, hashish and heroin.

One of Burnett-Rae's other tenants, who had imbibed Crowley's reputation, asked his landlord if he knew the risk he was running in lodging the Beast. Recalled Burnett-Rae, "I explained that the principal risk was in losing the use of a perfectly good flat without obtaining any rent for it." Ultimately, Burnett-Rae evicted Crowley—still an undischarged bankrupt—for nonpayment. But the two remained friends for years afterwards, though Burnett-Rae evaded requests to fund Crowley's publications.

Through the remainder of 1937, with its constant changes in lodgings, Crowley and Brooksmith continued, intermittently, together. The bonds between them were mutual care and affection. Crowley's diary for the year lists twenty-seven magical "operations"—and not one was with the Scarlet Woman, whose reign seems tacitly to have come to an end. For all his still-vigorous sexual activity, with its attendant Elixirs, Crowley still felt the pains of mounting old age. In a 1938 letter to Yorke, Crowley confessed to infirmities beyond his control: "I do wish you'd help out on the health job. The IX degree doesn't replace regular treatment; indeed ought not to be used when one is full of poison."

In the summer of that year, however, Crowley launched his own brief public practice as a health provider. His home office at 6 Hasker Street (a house owned by the son of a British military family, of whom more shortly) offered not only Elixir of Life pills but also osteopathic treatment, body vibrators, infrared lights and "Zotofoam" equipment. At least one defaulted creditor of this short-lived enterprise claimed that Crowley had represented himself as a doctor. The Beast resided at this Hasker Street address for eight months. His young landlord, just turned twenty, had dropped his studies at Cambridge to pursue an acting career. Crowley persuaded him to provide free lodgings and office space and to agree to a shared expenses arrangement (the young man bearing the brunt of it) in exchange for a proposed year of magical training. But by February 1939, arguments over money and the young man's growing mistrust of the Beast led to an end of this arrangement.

Crowley found new lodgings at Gordon Chambers, 20 Jermyn Street; shortly thereafter, he moved to 24 Chester Terrace. In the face of insistent creditors and inconsistent funds, the Beast still managed to enjoy a roisterous year, replete with magical operations, festive dinners, and intrigues. On May 2, he held a birthday party for the four-year-old Aleister Ataturk in which several of his female lovers were in attendance, as well as C. R. Cammell, Gerald Hamilton, and the British man-of-letters Louis Wilkinson, whose friendship with the Beast had commenced in America during the World War One years.

Two days after this celebration, the journalist Maurice Richardson came to lunch at Crowley's invitation. Richardson had included a faintly slighting reference to Crowley in a book review, and Crowley had written to suggest a meeting, using this banter as bait: "Perhaps in future before you pass animadversions on my character you will take the trouble to make my acquaintance." If it was Crowley's hope to win Richardson over, he failed. Richardson later produced a stinging essay, "Luncheon with Beast 666," in which he averred of Crowley "that when you got used to his eccentricities, and so long as you were not impressed by his mystical pretensions, he was apt to become a fearful bore. He had no capacity for selection, no notion of when to stop. How sinister was he? Obviously he would con a mug, pluck a pigeon." It is striking that Louis Wilkinson seconded Richardson's complaint as to the Beast's lack of a "capacity for selection." Wilkinson admired the best of Crowley's poetry but deplored its unevenness. The explanation offered by Wilkinson:

> Vanity was his handicap. He was too sure of his genius to criticize or revise adequately his own work. [. . .] His poetry could be very bad as well as very good. He could write mere imitative pieces, he could write superbly, with an exultant vigour entirely his own, but he never seemed to know whether he was doing the one or the other.

A measure of his vanity—or prophetic dedication, if you will—was that Crowley still yearned to play a role upon the world's stage. In certain of his dreams, his ambitions took on the form of gratifying fantasies. In February 1938, for example, he recorded an "Elaborate dream about Hitler & cigars & Magick & my horse Sultan. I was running Germany for him." In a diary entry later that month, Crowley consciously dismissed the Nazi ideology: "Fascism must always fail because it creates the discontent which it is designed to suppress." But a fascism purified by Thelema, a rule of the true rulers—that fantasy could not be banished. Over a year later, in June 1939, there was a similar dream: "I had several long talks with Hitler a very tall man. Forget subjects, but he was pleased and impressed: ordered all my books translated & made official in Germany. Later, a dusk night in a city. A man in gold-braid went round a corner, saw several horsemen, similarly gorgeous, one fired the first shot of the war."

The first shot of the war was fired some two months after this dream. Crowley, who had been predicting a world conflagration, noted simply in his diary for September 1, 1939: "Germany attacked Poland." By September 6, Crowley had composed a poem, "England, Stand Fast!" that was issued as a pamphlet on September 23. For all his dreams of serving Hitler, it was his patriot voice that spoke forth here:

> England, stand fast! Stand fast against the foe!
> They struck the first blow: we shall strike the last.
> Peace at the price of Freedom? We say No.
> England, stand fast!

Once the war began, the Beast was passionate in his support of the British cause. If imitation be the sincerest flattery, then Crowley paid great homage to Winston Churchill—named Prime Minister in 1940—

by posing for photographs in which, clad in bowler hat with scarf, cigar, and contemplative scowl, he struck a striking resemblance to Churchill himself. Crowley also claimed to have originated the popular 'V for victory' hand gesture employed by Churchill. According to Crowley, the letter 'V' was suited to the task of bringing victory due to its numerous esoteric correspondences. Crowley's claims have never been accepted; David Ritchie of the British Broadcasting Corporation is widely credited as having suggested it to Churchill.

Plainly, the Beast yearned to play a role of prominence in the war effort. A week after the German invasion of Poland, Crowley wrote the Naval Intelligence Department (N.I.D.) offering his services. The N.I.D. never offered a position. But Crowley was a figure of interest to certain members of the British intelligence community, including Maxwell Knight, the head of Department B5(b), the British counterespionage unit within M.I.5, during World War Two. Knight had been introduced to Crowley in the mid-1930s by Dennis Wheatley, the popular British horror novelist. According to Anthony Masters, the biographer of Maxwell Knight, both Knight and Wheatley attended rituals led by Crowley for the purpose of background research for Wheatley's books. Indeed, Crowley served as the principal model for at least one of Wheatley's black-magical villains, Mocata in *The Devil Rides Out* (1934). Knight's nephew, Harry Smith, stated that the two men had "jointly applied to Crowley as novices and he accepted them as pupils. But my uncle stressed that his interest—and also Wheatley's—was purely academic." Knight and Wheatley were apparently not the only members of British intelligence to study with Crowley. One scholar has noted "the fascinating accounts given of witchcraft soirees held by Mr. Aleister Crowley. M.I.5 agents who attended these festivities disguised as witches and wizards, wrote long memoranda about the corruption of goat's blood." Just where Crowley could have obtained goat's blood in London is not specified, nor are the alleged memoranda quoted.

Whatever Knight's views on magic, his respect for Crowley was genuine—a telling indication that, in British intelligence circles, Crowley was not regarded as a traitor for his World War One activities. Once World War Two began, Crowley continued to enjoy access to Knight. Masters recorded that "Crowley had put up some of his own mad-cap ideas about helping the war effort to Wheatley and Knight. These included a project that involved the dropping of occult literature on the Germans, but neither Wheatley nor Knight felt this would have any practical application."

But the Beast was *almost* utilized by the N.I.D. in connection with an occult disinformation plot targeted at Hitler's deputy, Rudolf Hess, who was both an ardent believer in astrology and highly skeptical of the long-term military prospects for the Reich. The plot was devised largely by Ian Fleming (later the creator of James Bond, then a Commander in the N.I.D.) and approved by Knight. In brief, it called for the infiltration of Hess's circle by means of an M.I.5 planted astrologer who would convey, through a faked horoscope, the falsehood that a pro-German circle existed in Britain that could, with the aid of Hess, topple the Churchill government and conduct peace negotiations with Germany.

At first, it was envisaged that Crowley could play a role in contacting Hess in Germany. Knight had Crowley "in mind for some time as a potential M.I.5 agent, but because of his eccentric personality he was considered just a little too much larger than life to be successful. Yet here was a top Nazi leader who believed in the occult and here was Crowley, the artful perpetrator of occult practices." But there was a serious snag—one that reveals a further twist in the tangled relations between Crowley and Gerald Hamilton. According to historian Richard Deacon, Crowley was a known intelligence suspect to the Germans as far back as the early 1930s. "The German Intelligence Service certainly knew all about Crowley's ventures in espionage for Crowley lived in Berlin with another notorious spy, Gerald Hamilton. Crowley was spying on Hamilton for M.I.5 and Hamilton was almost certainly spying on Crowley for the Germans." Recall that Hamilton had claimed that he was spying on Crowley for the British. Curioser and curioser.

It was decided that Crowley could assist, in England, in preparing the initial astrological "bait" for Hess. This plan was rendered moot, however, by one of the most bizarre incidents of the war—the secretive flight to Scotland by Hess in May 1941. Hess parachuted to British soil in hopes of commencing independent negotiations on Germany's behalf that would end the war. Fleming proposed that Crowley would be an ideal interrogator on the key question of the extent of the influence of astrology upon various Nazi leaders. Crowley assented eagerly, but was ultimately rebuffed. As Donald McCormick, an associate of Fleming during this period, later recalled, "it never came off and the very idea must have horrified the Admiralty! But there was an exchange of letters on the subject. Ian also had a theory that Enochian could be used as a code and was a perfect code for using when one wanted to 'plant' bogus evidence in the right place." As a constructor of codes in the angelic Enochian language, there could hardly have been a more qualified expert in Britain than Crowley; one wonders if the Beast had first suggested the idea to Fleming. It was never pursued, but Fleming did not forget the Beast. In his first James Bond novel, *Casino Royale* (1953), the villain, "Le Chiffre," is modeled in part on Crowley. Maxwell Knight, in turn, served as the principal inspiration for "M.," Bond's chief.

Crowley was once more disappointed in his hopes of serving British intelligence. But his patriotism remained intact. Shortly before the outbreak of war, Crowley had moved to 57 Petersham Road, Richmond, which served as his primary residence through the summer of 1940. German bombing raids were frequent in the vicinity, which strained the Beast's nerves and intensified his asthmatic difficulties. But he also found the raids exhilarating. Cammell recalled a night spent with Crowley during a German air attack. British antiaircraft guns had hit a German bomber that was plummeting to earth in flames. Cammell wrote:

> Here was a man who had been gasping his life away all through the night; and now at the crack of dawn he ran downstairs two steps at a time, and was shouting Hooray! And waving his arms skyward in a passion of boyish excitement and jubilation. No trace of asthma: it was gone to whence it came. Crowley was twenty-one again. [. . .]
>
> As dawn broke we drank our stirrup-cup—or "night-cap"— the toast, damnation to the Dictators! I went home for a few hours' sleep. Crowley, his asthma cured by that blazing bomber, slept like a child.

This summer of 1940 was the apex of the friendship between Cammell and Crowley; Montague Summers was a neighbor and occasional companion as well. Relations with Cammell ended the following year, when Crowley refused to pay Cammell's wife, Iona, for a large quantity of tweed cloth (handwoven by herself) he had agreed to purchase. Writing of this in a veiled manner (Cammell did not wish to name his wife as Crowley's victim), Cammell offered an epitaph for this—and many other—of the Beast's lost friendships:

> I did my best to arrange matters; to persuade him to act honourably or at least reasonably and courteously. It was useless. As was his wont when challenged, he became defiant. In some such

way he lost so many of his best friends: George Cecil Jones, Eck-enstein, Mathers, Allan Bennett, General Fuller, Sir Gerald Kelly, Victor Neuburg. They were, each in turn, compelled to break with Crowley, even as I was. I saw him only once again—in London, after the war. We did not speak.

Crowley's relationships with his female lovers during this period—chief of whom was one Alice Upham—were equally stormy. None of them held his heart, and none could alleviate—for all the sexual work-ings devoted to "Health" during this period—the mounting weakness caused by his asthma. Crowley had continued his heroin use through the 1930s. But in the war years, the dosages and dependence heightened still more to subdue the intensified asthma attacks. He also took luminal to combat recurrent insomnia.

In September 1940, Crowley resolved to leave Richmond and its bombing raids for the relative tranquility of Torquay. He found lodgings at The Gardens, Middle Warberry Road, where he stayed some six months. In the grip of age and illness, Crowley longed for companion-ship; he was no longer, at heart, Alastor the Wanderer of the Wastes. A letter to Yorke, both a friend and a failed disciple, reflected his present isolation and unease:

> I wish you had always understood me; I could have worked out the details with you. But there was a time when you distrusted me entirely: a lot of it my own fault. Is it too late to get together heart and soul? "Trust not a stranger; fail not of an heir." I feel so lonely, like a frightened child. So much to do and my physi-cal instrument untrusty!

However "untrusty" he may have felt, the Beast continued on the prowl—largely futile—for women during this autumn of 1940. The hunger was reflected in this entry for October 9: "Nerves on edge for lack of cunt." The number of workings dropped off rather sharply in the second half of this year. On December 22, a solitary Crowley ejaculated onto a rosebud which he sent to Alice Upham. If there was a magical goal in mind, Crowley did not record it. At the end of his diary for the year, Crowley penned, as was his fashion in his later years, an obscene ditty, this time concerning a boy named "Anthony." But the days of male lovers were over. This was purely a fantasy, one in which sexual and political power were blended in rousing lines:

> They gave me command of the Navy
> I sailed up the Shore of Berlin
> Stick it out! Was the signal I gave: I
> Hear Anthony say "Stick it in!"

Triumphant military power wielded as an open homosexual—it was Crowley's private vision of victory, one he dared not share with the British public as he had "England, Stand Fast!"

Though Crowley found no real wartime role, his presence was certainly noted by the enemy. William Joyce ("Lord Haw Haw"), a British traitor who broadcast gibing propaganda for the Nazis and was hanged after the war, suggested in one broadcast that, as a National Prayer Day held in March 1941 had not availed the British cause, why not have Aleister Crowley conduct a Black Mass in Westminster Abbey? Crowley drew no rancor from his Torquay neighbors as a result of Joyce's remarks. He created friction by mundane means: credit problems with the local grocer, insistent demands for back rent from his landlord. In March 1941, he moved to Barton Brow, a house just outside Torquay.

Two new amours emerged in this spring—Mildred Churt, and a woman whom Crowley referred to as "Charis" [Greek for "Grace"] and "X." Her full name was Grace M. Pennel, and she was the sole cosignatory, with Crowley, of an April 20 entry in his diary specifying them as "members of the Abbey of Thelema at Barton Brow." As for Alice Upham, she became, in the latter half of 1941, the last recorded lover of the Beast, who—surprisingly—was stoic as to his loss of the energy central to his Magick. On June 18, he was unable to achieve an erection after having birched Upham—a standard component of their foreplay; the planned opus could not be fulfilled. Four months later, on October 21— Crowley was by now back in London, in a service flat at 10 Hanover Square in the West End—a temporary solution had been found. Crowley noted dourly: "Alice here for Cunnilingus. The 'last infirmity of a noble mind'." There is no evidence of any sexual activity by Crowley after this.

But Crowley was fortunate to have one woman who would remain an emotional and economic support through his final years. Frieda Lady Harris was never romantically involved with the Beast, but she collaborated with him on the last great work of his life: the writing of *The Book of Thoth* and (Harris's task) the pictorial creation of a new Tarot deck design—one replete with lust and force, the couplings and breakings of the Thelemic universe, in which the One is always manifested in Duality.

The "Thoth deck" (or "Crowley deck") remains one of the most influential Tarot versions to be produced in this century. Harris was no mere passive collaborator. Crowley provided the initial written explanations and rough sketches. But she would then barrage him with further questions of her own. In some cases, at Crowley's urging, she painted eight different versions of a single card.

Crowley and Harris first met in 1937. She was sixty years old and married to Sir Percy Harris, a baronet and Parliamentary whip for the Liberal Party. Their marriage was not particularly happy, and Harris had taken on at least one lover. But she aspired to spiritual development and believed in Crowley as a teacher, receiving from him the name Soror Tzaba. Harris never became an unwavering Thelemite. But she was a sincere and forthright student, admirably frank in her letters to the Beast as to her views on Tarot design and proper publicity for the project. Their formal collaboration began in the summer of 1938 and would occupy much of their energies through early 1944. Harris also helped to support Crowley, giving him £2 weekly during this period. As for Sir Percy Harris, he tolerated his wife's devotion to the Beast but gave no credence to Thelema—a frustration to Crowley, who further disliked Sir Percy for being Jewish.

Frieda Harris became more than an artistic collaborator. In many respects, she filled the void left by the absence of a Scarlet Woman or even a stable lover, accompanying Crowley to social occasions and tending to his health. Cammell recalled that, while Crowley lived in Torquay, "she had come to his call, and found him stricken by pneumonia, only half-conscious. She met a man at his door, who was going out to order the coffin. By night she sought for doctor, nurse, and the necessities of existence. At that time she had saved Crowley's life."

Harris and Crowley endured frictions and frustrations, including the abrupt cancellation—in June 1941—of a proposed exhibition of Harris's Tarot paintings in an Oxford gallery. Opposition to Crowley, not to Harris, was the cause of the difficulty, and this made Harris publicly cautious, though her loyalty to Crowley remained intact. Still, Harris pleaded with Crowley to refrain from his plan to issue *Liber Oz* in late 1941 in the form of postcards and broadsides. ("Oz" is Crowley's transcription of the Hebrew word for goat.) *Liber Oz*, first composed by Crowley during World War One to serve as part of an O.T.O. ritual, is written almost entirely in monosyllabic words. Crowley blended, in its brief compass, quotations from the *Book* with pithy, cadenced declarations. The first and fifth of these show where Crowley stood and why Harris feared public outrage:

1. Man has the right to live by his own law—
   to live in the way that he wills to do:
   to work as he will:
   to play as he will:
   to rest as he will:
   to die when and how he will.

[. . .]

5. Man has the right to kill those who would
   thwart those rights.

"the slaves shall serve." AL II:58

"Love is the law, love under will."
                                AL I:57

Harris's objections made no impress upon the Beast, who received precious little response to *Liber Oz* in any event. The silence of his contemporaries did not diminish his ardor. In a missive to Yorke, Crowley explained that "the revival of true Aristocracy" had been "my deepest idea all my life. [. . .] We must first of all have a sound physical stock to pick out rulers from." Where did the right to kill fit in? A hint comes from a 1941 diary entry in which Crowley observed that, in a Thelemic society, "the problem is not how to boss the herd, which is automatic, or to thwart the unworthy, who are ejected into impotence; but how to prevent emulation developing into warfare." It was competition between rulers and aspirants that posed, for Crowley, the most likely cases of justified homicide. Should punishment be meted if a murderer acts in accord with his True Will? Crowley never clarified that scenario—the exact obverse of the "insanity defense," as it would rest on ultimate self-realization.

In May 1942, Crowley moved from his West End location to a more central and cosmopolitan flat in Hamilton House, 140 Piccadilly. It proved to be an auspicious summer for the Crowley-Harris collaboration, as they succeeded in staging two exhibitions for the Tarot paintings—at the Berkeley Galleries at 20 Davies Street in July, and at the Royal Society of Painters of Water Colours in August. Their key concern was to fund publication both of the Tarot deck and of *The Book of Thoth*. Robert Cecil, a writer and scholar who befriended Crowley during the war, held out the hope that T. S. Eliot, who served as an editor at Faber and Faber, might be approached with the manuscript. There is no evidence that this occurred. Eliot's response would have been a fascinating one. We do know, however, what Crowley thought of Eliot's "The Waste Land," which draws from "The Hanged Man" trump and other Tarot symbolism. After reading that poem in the spring of 1942, Crowley pronounced himself "nauseated and ineffably contemptuous [. . .] Note: modern 'school' of 'poetry' the much-beslavered 'observation' is all sniffing sexual privies. They never get away from it; and they see only the sordid dirty side of it." A similar criticism, equally reductive, could easily be raised against certain of Crowley's works. There was a blinding bitterness in the isolation he felt as a poet.

Yet he persisted. In the summer of 1942, Crowley issued, in pamphlet form, a poem written in French and entitled "La Gauloise, Song of the French." Its express purpose was to inspire the French resistance effort; Crowley sent out some 1000 copies, including one to the French government-in-exile headed by General Charles De Gaulle. An aide of De Gaulle responded, in late May, with a brief and formal letter expressing thanks; there was also a positive feature piece in July in the London *Star*. Crowley attempted to go further by having an Agapé Lodge member—Roy Leffingwell—compose music for the poem. The two subsequently worked on a new national anthem for America—an example of Crowley's astonishing naïveté. During these same war years, Crowley did not move to California—as he had been invited to do by devoted Agapé Lodge members—largely because of the potential for denial of entry by American authorities. How could a man so suspect have hoped to persuade a nation to change its anthem—an act charged with the utmost political symbolism? Anthems aside, Crowley was sufficiently fascinated with the possibilities of sound recording that he paid at least two visits to Levy's Sound Studios on New Bond Street to record on wax cylinders—in his reedy, plaintive voice—his "Hymn to Pan" and the Calls (in English and Enochian) of the First and Second Aethyrs; a handful of other recordings, presumably done at the same locale, also survive from this period.

Crowley pursued yet another artistic avenue at this time. Long a frustrated playwright, he was at last given a chance to consult on a theatrical project. The young Peter Brook, who would become one of the most eminent directors in postwar Britain, was staging an October 1942 production of Marlowe's *Doctor Faustus* at the Torch Theatre in Oxford. Brook, impressed with the eloquence of Crowley's writings on magic, wrote to the Beast for suggestions on staging the conjuring scenes. Crowley attended at least two rehearsals. On opening night, the Beast pronounced: "All considered, an A1 performance—it held the audience."

Brook's interest in Crowley reflected the status the Beast had achieved as the foremost occult expert—or bogeyman, depending on one's viewpoint—in England. There were those who fantasized as to the nature and extent of Crowley's powers, or feared him outright. Crowley, for his part, knew well how to create what might be called "stage effects." The poet Dylan Thomas was one of those who believed in the Beast's powers. Thomas had, during the period of Crowley's libel action, enjoyed an affair with one of its chief witnesses, Betty May. May almost certainly warned Thomas about Crowley, for the young poet harbored a fear that the Beast played upon to fine effect. Constantine Fitzgibbon, Thomas's friend and biographer, reported that, in the early 1940s in London, Thomas "was sitting with my former wife Theodora in the Swiss, doodling as he frequently did when in a bad mood. The cause of his bad mood that evening was the presence, at the far end of the pub, of Crowley. When Crowley walked across and placed in front of Dylan a duplicate of his doodle, Dylan was extremely frightened. He insisted that Theodora and he leave the pub immediately, without waiting for the man they were supposed to meet." Assuming this to be true, it can, of course, be explained as a mere conjurer's trick; a confederate could have stolen a glance at the doodle and reported its shape to Crowley. The more important point is that Crowley, conscious of appearances and fond of frightening susceptible souls—especially lauded modern poets—may well have pulled the prank to augment his legendary status.

During the winter of 1943, ensconced in his 93 Jermyn Street flat, Crowley enjoyed the rare comfort of being admired—early on—by his landlady, Miss Manning, who would later name a room on the premises after the Beast, in which she conducted séances. Their relations palled as her tolerance of his irregular rent payments declined. Miss Manning would later report an episode so atypical of Crowley that one must view it with great skepticism: during a German bombing raid, while the tenants and proprietess of 93 Jermyn Street were huddled in the kitchen, the Beast proceeded—at his own suggestion—to read in devout manner the Twenty-third Psalm of the Bible to the group. This was, according to Miss Manning, an evident reversion to the Christian faith of Crowley's childhood. Crowley never wrote of this experience, if it indeed occurred.

Shortly after moving in, Crowley did experience a striking realization as to the impact upon his psyche of sexual dotage: "I note that when I have been for any long time free from the sexual impulse a whole group of ideas becomes 'obscene', 'disgusting', 'revolting' & so on. This group includes contemplation of Yoni (not Lingam so much), disease, accident, the spectacle of meat, the ideas of war, pain of the physical order and so on. I conclude that humanitarianism, pacifism—all such feelings—are functions of sexual weakness, atrophy, or the like. This thesis can be developed very far." For Crowley, sexuality was the essential life energy, and its decline necessarily debilitated the kingly temperament required by the Thelemic life. This debilitation included, by his own argument, puritanical squeamishness—which Crowley had never succeeded in uprooting.

The Beast was posed with a different set of difficulties—stemming from what he viewed as a vile overabundance of sexuality—by the founding Master of Agapé Lodge, Wilfred Talbot Smith, Frater 132 (the gematria sum of his magical name, *Velle Omnia Velle Nihil*) and, as O.T.O. Grand Master of the United States, Ramaka X°. Crowley had maintained amicable relations with Smith—at a distance, through correspondence—for over a decade. But in early 1943, letters from a number of Agapé Lodge members seemed, to Crowley, to point to a crisis in leadership. A key disruption had occurred: Smith had seduced Helen Parsons, the wife of a fellow Lodge member, John Whiteside (Jack) Parsons, Frater 210. Parsons was a brilliant scientist without a college degree. He was part of the experimental rocket research group attached to the California Institute of Technology, and would later become a cofounder of Aerojet Corporation. Parsons's work in solid fuel research was deemed, by Professor Theodore von Karman of Caltech, to have "made possible such outstanding rockets as the Polaris and the Minuteman." In 1972, twenty years after his death, the International Astronomical Union named a lunar crater "Parsons" in his honor.

Parsons was plainly a most promising disciple for Crowley. Smith's behavior seemed to jeopardize that relationship, though Parsons had rebounded by commencing an affair with his wife's sister, Sarah Elizabeth (known as Betty). Crowley would not tolerate Smith's lustful interference. Further, there was a pattern of sexual aggression in Smith that Crowley believed to have tainted the reputation of the O.T.O. Indeed, scandalous rumors had led to an F.B.I. investigation of Agapé Lodge; no charges resulted, but Crowley was unsettled nonetheless. Many have condemned Crowley as a hypocrite for objecting to Smith's promiscuities when his own life was rife with them. But in a letter to Smith, Crowley pointed to a key difference—what today we would call sexual harassment, practiced by Smith through the threat of occult disfavor. Crowley, for all his brutal treatment of his lovers, never resorted to offering attainment in exchange for erotic compliance. His indignation here is genuine:

> Your attempts to seduce newly initiated women by telling them
> that you were now in a position to order them to sleep with you,

were acts of despicable blackguardism. What grosser violation of the Law of Thelema can one imagine? Not to mention that by English law you might, if successful, have been found guilty of rape, and I should have heartily approved a sentence of penal servitude.

In May 1943, the Beast composed a treatise, entitled *Liber Apotheosis*, that prescribed a corrective ritual. Smith was to commence a Great Magical Retirement on the isolated grounds of the then O.T.O. headquarters at Rancho Royal, outside Los Angeles. By the time Smith received *Liber Apotheosis* in October 1943, Crowley had already designated Parsons as the new Master of Agapé Lodge. Smith soon assented both to his loss of leadership and to the solitary retirement. Judging from his morosely repentant letters to Crowley, that retirement induced no apotheosis, but rather an overwhelming sense of failure. In any event, Crowley's interest in Smith was at an end.

Parsons, whom Crowley hoped would right the ship, now became the source of a new set of difficulties. In a September 1943 letter, Parsons tendered his resignation to Crowley, condemned the character of many of his fellow Lodge members, and accused Crowley of pomposity and blundering leadership, particularly in the choice of Karl Germer as his second in command. Germer had—after a host of travails in Europe (including the interment camp experience described in Chapter 10)—established himself in New York City and there served as O.T.O. Grand Treasurer General, with special responsibility for raising funds (primarily from Agapé Lodge members) and transmitting those funds promptly to Crowley. Crowley, in his October 1943 reply, answered the younger man's attacks (Parsons was then twenty-nine) with a salvo of patient rebukes:

> With regard to bungling, you are not in a position to judge; for one thing anything I do is done with an eye on centuries to come. The immediate results of any action are no test of it from my point of view. [. . .]
> I don't know what you mean by pompous; I suppose you get this from my writings, but if you mean my literary writings, I suspect you don't understand their inner meaning in many cases. If you read the suspected passage carefully, you will probably find that there is a little laugh somewhere. I wish therefore that you would realize that my universe is very much larger than yours. [. . .] Some time ago I thought of writing a book on

internationally famous people with whom I had been intimate. The number ran to over 80. Am I wrong to suppose that you never met such people?

Take another point: have you visited the monuments of antiquity; have you seen the majority of the great paintings and sculptures? Have you discussed all sorts of intimate matters with natives of every civilized quarter of the globe? Perhaps more than any of the above in importance, have you made your way alone in parts of the earth never before trodden by any human foot—perhaps in hostile and nearly always inhospitable country? You may think it pompous of me to mention these matters, but the fact is that they don't matter unless you think they don't matter.

The point that I am trying to get you to realize is that any statement or action of mine is enormously modified by my having had these experiences.

The letter succeeded in persuading Parsons to continue as Master of the Lodge through the war.

Meanwhile, a new personage from California was attracting Crowley's attention as a potential future leader for the O.T.O. Grady Louis McMurtry, age twenty-five, was a lieutenant in the United States Army. Some three years earlier, he had made contact with the Agapé Lodge, primarily through Parsons, with whom McMurtry shared an interest in science fiction. Stationed in England in the autumn of 1943, McMurtry paid a call upon Crowley at 93 Jermyn Street. The two men met frequently through the end of the war and remained in correspondence for the remaining years of Crowley's life. McMurtry and Crowley often played chess while sharing brandy and pipefuls of perique tobacco. Over one of these games, Crowley abruptly pronounced McMurtry as worthy of the IX° Degree of the O.T.O., which was thereupon bestowed.

McMurtry accepted Crowley both as a Prophet and as a remarkable eccentric. One striking episode is described by McMurtry's biographer, J. Edward Cornelius, who quotes from the former's memoirs:

Christmas 1943 was cold, one of those typically snowy English winter days which found Grady at Crowley's apartment at 93 Jermyn Street enjoying a nice dinner. Afterwards, as they were sitting talking and playing chess, there came "a raucous noise at the door." Crowley looked up saying "I wonder what in the world that is?" He slowly got up out of his chair and walked toward the door. As he opened it he found four young English boys engaging in the British festivity of caroling on Christmas Day. It is the custom to continue caroling until one is given money for their services. Crowley, not amused, did what most of us have probably always wanted to do. He slammed the door in their faces, screaming at the top of his lungs "To the lions with them! To the lions with them!" Not surprisingly, that day the kids went away without being paid. Grady said, "That's the Aleister Crowley I knew."

It is just possible that Crowley was playing the Dickensian role of Scrooge to the hilt for his young American visitor.

McMurtry contributed to the ongoing funding effort that led, at last, to the publication of *The Book of Thoth* on March 21, 1944, as the Sun moved into Aries. Its release in straitened wartime Britain was itself a remarkable achievement on Crowley's part. There were the typical billing disputes with the Chiswick Press, which printed the 200 signed and numbered copies of *Thoth*. But Crowley was determined that the book would serve as the capstone of his career. With justification, his prospectus boasted: "The Book has been *nobly* produced; no other consideration was allowed to weigh." Printed on prewar "mould-made paper" and bound "in genuine native-tanned and native-dyed Morocco from the Niger," *Thoth* featured eight color reproductions of Harris's paintings, ninety black-and-white illustrations and a text by "The Master Therion"—Crowley's magical name as a Magus. Yet *Thoth*, an elegant and probing work, is uninsistent as to Thelema. Those themes are present, but they do not intrude upon the larger framework of the text, which seeks to harmonize the esoteric wisdoms of the East and the West, as Crowley understood them. He subtly reconfigured the Tarot deck to reflect the Universe as viewed by the Magus—a Universe in which, for all the conflagrations foretold by the *Book,* an encompassing unity reigns.

Numerous occult thinkers before Crowley, most notably the eighteenth-century scholar Antoine Court de Gebelin, held that the Tarot deck was a pictorial text—the *Book of Thoth,* Court de Gebelin termed it—that preserved the wisdom of ancient Egypt. By retaining that title, Crowley paid due homage to Thoth, the Egyptian god of wisdom and magic; at the same time, Crowley dismissed the importance of supposed Tarot lineages, Egyptian or otherwise: "The origin of the Tarot is quite irrelevant, even if it were certain. It must stand or fall as a system on its own merits." By the Beast's ahistorical criteria, the proof of any interpretation of the Tarot deck lay in its practical use: "Each card is, in a sense, a living being; and its relations with its neighbours are what one might call diplomatic. It is for the student to build these living stones into his living Temple."

The depth of *Thoth* reveals itself in the precision of Crowley's prose. His account of the Crowley–Harris Devil trump design, for example, conveys a forcible impress upon the mind of a reader who recognizes that active imagination is essential to magical practice, and who further rejects identification of the pagan horned god with Evil:

> This card represents creative energy in its most material form; in the Zodiac, Capricornus occupies the Zenith. It is the most exalted of the signs; it is the goat leaping with lust upon the summits of earth. The sign is ruled by Saturn, who makes for selfhood and perpetuity. In this sign, Mars is exalted, showing in its best form the fiery, material energy of creation. The card represents Pan Pangenetor, the All-Begetter. It is the Tree of Life as seen against a background of the exquisitely tenuous, complex, and fantastic forms of madness, the divine madness of spring, already foreseen in the meditative madness of winter; for the Sun turns northward upon entering this sign. The roots of the Tree are made transparent, in order to show the innumerable leapings of the sap; before it stands the Himalayan goat, with an eye in the center of its forehead, representing the god Pan upon the highest and most secret mountains of the earth. His creative energy is veiled in the symbol of the Wand of the Chief Adept, crowned with the winged globe and the twin serpents of Horus and Osiris.

This passage illustrates the manner in which Crowley subtly integrated the secrets of sexual magic into his discourse. As Richard Cavendish has noted, Crowley connected "Ayin," the Hebrew letter attributed to the Devil trump, with "the 'secret eye' of the phallus." That secret eye—the "eye in the center of its forehead"—is conjoined with the "most secret mountains"—the vagina or *mons veneris*. The wand is a further veil for the phallus as creative life fount. The sap within the Tree of Life is the Amrita and Elixir.

The public reception of *Thoth* was all but nonexistent. In the final year of a brutal war, the niceties of Tarot were of interest to few, and the price of ten guineas was prohibitive to all but the most avid of these. Still, the limited edition of *Thoth* did find appreciative subscribers—and managed to put some money in Crowley's pockets. Louis Wilkinson recalled Crowley's boast of having made £1500 from *Thoth* in three months:

> "Now you see," he then said, "how idiotic it is to have a publisher." I pointed out that the very considerable cost of producing the book should be put to the debit account. Crowley looked surprised. "Oh, of course," he said, "if the author is fool enough to pay for the printing and binding—" I might have reminded him that that was what in the old days he had always been foolish enough to do.

Wilkinson also recounted Crowley's integrity in handling the publication funds supplied to him by the O.T.O. Frieda Harris told Wilkinson that Crowley had refrained, though his health was now in sharp decline, from touching some £500 pounds stored in a strongbox under his bed. Harris persuaded Crowley to use some of the money to hire a trained nurse, on the grounds that the health of the leader of the O.T.O. was a suitable purpose upon which to expend its funds.

Just how long Crowley enjoyed the services of a nurse is unclear. What is plain is that, beginning in the winter of 1943, his health slumped to the point that his heroin dependence deepened. Crowley averaged four to six grains of heroin per day in 1943 and 1944, and roughly ten grains per day for the first half of 1945. These levels might have killed a man less accustomed than Crowley to the drug. The Beast obtained prescriptions from sometimes-reluctant doctors and pharmacists—the drugs he used included not only heroin, but also veronal, ethyl oxide, and cocaine. This strained the tolerance of the British law-enforcement authorities, who on at least one occasion paid a call on Crowley to investigate his prescriptions. Legalities aside, Crowley was well aware that his drug use was both desperate and debilitating. In one 1943 diary entry, he noted the frustration of trying to hold to lower heroin dosages without being able to wean himself from the drug: "Much of this is just fighting through. This passive courage is all very well, but it's so aimless."

Crowley undertook one last major writing effort in the latter months of 1944 and on into 1945. This was a series of informal letters—in response to the queries of a female aspirant to the Great Work—on a potpourri of magical subjects. The name of the aspirant, not given in the published work, was Anne Macky (Soror *Fiat Yod*, "Let there be a Foundation"), an Englishwoman whom Crowley met in 1943. Macky had a strong interest, but little background, in magic. For Crowley, she exemplified the ordinary reader who might wish to approach the subject—but without intimidation. Most of his letters were actually sent to Macky, who seems not to have progressed far in her studies. Nonetheless, Crowley fashioned the idea for a book originally titled *Aleister Explains Everything,* but later changed by Crowley to *Magick Without Tears;* the letters were published posthumously, by the loyal Germer, in 1954. It is a disappointing work. Crowley was straining both to be gallant to the lady and pithily amusing; the results were garrulity, repetition, and overlong quotations from his own prior works.

In April 1944, as this last book project was under way, Crowley moved from 93 Jermyn Street to an outlying country residence, the venerable Bell Inn at Aston Clinton, Bucks. This transfer of residence stemmed from two primary factors—Crowley's unsatisfied back rent, and the frequency of the London bombing raids that had worn on the Beast's nerves. Daphne Harris, Crowley's landlady at the Bell Inn, where he lived until January 1945, recalled that the old man was decidedly unusual, albeit polite, and possessed a sense of humor that was as much self-mocking as wicked. An R.A.F. squadron was using the Bell Inn as a mess hall during the war, and several of the pilots took note of the now-gaunt Crowley, with his flamboyant red cloaks, plus-fours, knee buckles, filmy white hair, and elfin beard. "They would laugh at him and say he looked like the Devil," said Harris in an interview. "So one day he came to the bottom of the stairs having arranged his remaining side wisps of hair in a devilish fashion. He said to them, 'Dear boys, now you can see the horns.'" Crowley evoked a deeper fear in a nurse who was tending him during this period, and whom he asked one day to take a large hatchet to be sharpened, for reasons that remain unknown to Harris. The nurse was terrified by this request, fearing that Crowley would use the hatchet to sacrifice her son.

For her part, Harris regarded the fear and mystery surrounding Crowley as bunk. "I treated him as a joke. All the things people used to say about him—stupid nonsense. He wouldn't allow us to go in his room. Finally, one day when he went into London, we let ourselves in and opened all the windows to air it out, which it needed—the stink was awful." Crowley was receiving regular packets from his London pharmacist, and also had (by what means is unknown) a steady supply of partridge eggs, with which he repeatedly attempted to bribe Harris into providing him with other foodstuffs subject to wartime rationing. When the bribes failed, Crowley did not hesitate to filch from the kitchen. Said Harris, "He stole sugar, which he said he needed. He was wicked enough to steal and obviously a phony. If he was such a great

God, as he believed, he wouldn't have had to steal. Given the wartime situation, he was just a bore and a nuisance in a time of great stress, a worry to us all."

It was, perhaps, declining relations with Harris that led Crowley to seek out more hospitable lodgings. In late January 1945, Crowley relocated for the last time in his life—the wandering was at an end. His choice was the sedate guest house at Netherwoods, The Ridge, Hastings. The proprietors were Vernon Symonds, a playwright and actor of modest accomplishments, and his wife, Johnny. They were a buoyant middle-aged couple determined to create a unique atmosphere for their establishment. The brochure composed by Vernon Symonds declared that "this house will never be a guest house in the ordinary sense of the term. Those seeking a conventional establishment in this district will be able to find better accommodations elsewhere, for my friends care more for fine food than for the ritual of dressing for dinner, and more for culture and the arts than for bridge and poker."

The capacity of his new landlords to weather Crowley's eccentricities was tested on the very day of his arrival. Johnny Symonds recalled that no definite date of occupancy had been fixed. "Then out of the blue we got a telegram which read: EXPECT CONSIGNMENT OF FROZEN MEAT ON (date given). Well, we were somewhat perplexed by this because we hadn't ordered any meat and we were even more surprised when the day arrived and two food inspectors turned up in anticipation of the delivery. While we were talking to them an ambulance suddenly came down the drive and deposited, on our doorstep, Aleister Crowley and 40 brown paper parcels. The frozen meat had arrived."

Crowley's routine at Netherwood was a regular and largely private one. His housekeeper—whom he teased, to her lack of amusement, by claiming that she was a witch who had flown past his window on a broomstick—would bring him breakfast at nine. A brief garden stroll followed at ten. Crowley spent most of the day in his sitting room, No. 13, at the front of the house, which featured a wardrobe, writing table, bookshelf, single bed, and bathroom. He often entertained visiting guests, such as Louis Wilkinson, Robert Cecil, Frieda Harris, and Michael Houghton, the then owner of the Atlantis Bookshop in London, in which Crowley's limited editions fetched steep prices.

Crowley also became acquainted with his neighbors on The Ridge, many of whom found him a charming old gentleman with courtly manners and a winning appeal with their children. One of these children had a party at Netherwood and specially requested that Crowley attend. According to Mrs. Pitcairn-Knowles, the child's aunt, the Beast rose wonderfully to the occasion, arriving "dressed in a magnificent turquoise robe with a cummerbund, into which was pushed a large dagger, and with a turban on his head. And on his fingers he had enormous rings made from lumps of uncut turquoise. He just sat and beamed at the children, ate some food and then, later, went to bed. The children all seemed very much at home with him."

Crowley had been led initially to Netherwoods through the help of Louis Wilkinson, who had enlisted the aid of his son Oliver to find new lodgings for the Beast. Oliver Wilkinson had, as a young boy, encountered Crowley in New York during the final years of World War One. His mother, Frances Gregg, was still married to Louis Wilkinson at that time, and she strongly disapproved of her husband's friendship with Crowley. This angered Crowley, who mounted a strategy of playing upon Gregg's nerves by means including subtle threats of harming her children. Gregg's nerves were shaken to the point that she was in danger of being psychiatrically committed—through the dual complicity of Crowley and her husband. This was averted, and the couple moved away from New York (and Crowley) for a time; but Gregg's health was damaged and the marriage ended but a few years later. Small wonder that Oliver Wilkinson later declared: "I was eight when I determined to hunt Crowley down and kill him for the fear he caused my mother, and the evil he brought into the world."

In later years, Oliver Wilkinson took a more moderate view of the aged Beast, whom he helped install at Netherwood. "Aleister Crowley has earned himself a place a place among the remembered names of the world. He deserves more than the interest we might give to a two-headed sheep at the fair." The fundamental disagreement between Oliver Wilkinson and his father on the merits of Crowley's life outlook were aptly summarized by the son:

> Crowley's belief in the words with which he ended his letters, 'Do what thou wilt shall be the whole of the Law,' seems inexact for so intelligent a man; for there was always equal emphasis on 'The slave shall serve.' 'Is that the slave's will?' I asked my father. 'Yes,' he answered without hesitation, 'The slave wishes to serve—knows that is what he is fitted for.' Which is, of course, convenient for the slave-owner. Compare Christ washing the feet of the disciples.

This anecdote confirms the strong degree to which Crowley and Louis Wilkinson shared a philosophical, if not a religious, outlook; thus it was that, in 1946, Wilkinson agreed, at Crowley's request, to edit the Beast's prior commentaries on the *Book* and so produce an "Authorized Popular Commentary." Wilkinson completed this work in 1946; the text remained unpublished until 1996, well after the death of both men.

Wilkinson was a good friend rather than a loyal Thelemite (though Crowley did make him an honorary IX° O.T.O. in 1946). But there now arose a young candidate of exceptional promise whom Crowley undertook to train in Thelemic magick during the first months of 1945. This was Kenneth Grant, a precocious student of the occult who had first encountered Crowley's works at age fourteen. Grant was twenty when, having initiated a correspondence, he met with Crowley in December 1944. After the Beast's move to Netherwood, he suggested that Grant move there as well, a cottage on the grounds being available. In advance letters, Crowley held forth alluring promises of contacts with London literati and, ultimately, a good salary from the O.T.O. The more modest but, to Grant, quite satisfactory reality was, as he later recalled, that "in return for magical instruction, I would act as his secretary, nurse, factotum, everything. In other words, do service to the guru, *gurusev.*"

Grant has, in the past decades, become one of the most prominent interpreters of Crowley's magick. In his memoir, *Remembering Aleister Crowley* (1991), Grant left an invaluable portrait of life as a student of the Beast. By now, Crowley was a mere wisp of the forbidding figure he had once cut before disciples such as Neuburg, Mudd, Yorke, and Regardie. Grant observed: "The paunchy, seedy, bohemian appearance of a decade ago had given way to a refinement that suggested the fragile ivory figure of a mandarin, of which the hands were, perhaps, the most singular feature; slightly yellow, beautifully articulated and curiously small. Approaching the house, he threw up his arms and muttered the lines from *Liber Resh* [*Liber Resh vel Helios*, containing Crowley's four daily prayers to the Sun]: 'Hail unto thee who art Ahathor in thy beauty'—the midday adoration."

The two studied together, page by page, Crowley's *Magick*. The Beast assigned written examinations for Grant on subjects including Buddhism, the creation of magical rituals, and the astrological interpretation of nativities. There was also practical training in astral visions. Crowley employed, as a talisman for his own astral work, a gold disk or coin which he would slip into his mouth. He tested Grant's ability in the astral realm by a procedure that included the use of unknown symbols (to determine if the student would explore the spiritual realm indicated without conscious foreknowledge) and the taking of ether. Grant described this latter procedure in another of his works, *The Magical Revival* (1972):

He would draw a glyph or symbol that was quite unknown to me, and I proceeded as follows: With eyes closed I imagined the dark surface of a door, closed and set in a blank wall. When this mental image did not waver, but not before, I superimposed the symbol upon it so that it glowed vividly in white light. Still holding the image steady, I inhaled the ether. As I inhaled, the symbol appeared to grow immensely bright, increasing or diminishing in size despite my attempts to keep it steady. This defect in concentration took me some time to overcome. When the image remained invariable, I proceeded to the next stage of the experiment which was to visualize the gradual opening of the door in the wall. The vista beyond was wrapped in a hazy mist. I transferred the symbol to the mist and then projected my consciousness through the door by willing myself through it. I found myself, suddenly, bereft of my body [. . .] It seemed as real, if not more so, as a mundane landscape. It conformed in one way or another with a region of the astral plane consonant with the nature of the symbol visualized.

Crowley was initially reluctant, in their discussions, to so much as hint at the sexual magic doctrines that were at the heart of his work. "Crowley told me," Grant wrote, "that the procedure was, that if I could tell him the secret of the Ninth Degree O.T.O., it would be his duty to confirm it, but only then." Gradually, during his studies at Netherwood, Grant achieved an understanding of that secret which he conveyed, at Crowley's request, in essay form. The essay satisfied Crowley and the IX° was bestowed without formality. Grant offered a valuable hint, in *The Magical Revival*, as to the nature of sexual magic; contrary to the usual understanding, Grant argued, the texts and rituals of sexual magic were "exoteric"; the actual physiological phenomena, which had to be experienced to be understood, constituted the true "esoteric" secret.

Grant's duties as Crowley's student included procurement of drugs and whiskey and management of the Beast's mundane affairs. The young man was, by his own admission, ill-suited for such tasks. As Grant later admitted, "I was beginning to realize that Crowley's demands were unending. As Austin Spare frequently observed: 'Enough is too much!'" Grant's stay ended in June 1945 when, at the urging of his father, who yearned for more practical prospects for his son, Grant returned to London—with, however, his interest in Crowley's magick very much intact. For his part, Crowley regarded Grant as a potential future leader of the British O.T.O.

During his first months at Netherwood, Crowley received visits from Dion Fortune, the prominent occultist whose essay on Crowley's *Magick* was discussed in Chapter Nine. Fortune and Crowley first met in person in March 1939; the site was a London lecture hall named The Belfry and, according to some sources, the two eminences merely bowed without exchanging words. In his caustic diary entry noting the occasion, however, Crowley confirmed that they did speak: "Dion Fortune—Public Bat No. 1 at The Belfry. Like a hippo with false teeth. Talk—bubbling of tinned tomato soup."

It was hardly to be expected that Crowley would be gracious to a rival, particularly one who had achieved a respectability that eluded him. For her part, Fortune seems, prior to the time of their meeting, to have adopted the viewpoint of Crowley the person (as opposed to the author, to whose works she paid homage) promulgated by the tabloid press. In her 1935 novel *The Winged Bull*, the character of the villanous black magician, "Hugo Astley," is modeled on this "public" Crowley.

But the mutual respect which underlay their suspicions resulted not only in Fortune paying visits to Netherwood, but also in a correspondence that endured until Fortune's death from leukemia in January 1946. Nearly all of that correspondence has been lost. Those few letters which survive—one by Crowley, one and a portion of a second by Fortune—indicate a comfortable tone between two persons who shared an absolute dedication to magic. In his missive, Crowley adopted a ready air of superiority. In hers, Fortune played the submissive role; she chided the Beast, in January 1942, for overestimating her intelligence and averred that "My mentality always has hampered my work, and, I am afraid, always will." Jeanne Chapman, in her biography of Fortune, argued plausibly that "Crowley was sixteen years her senior, which tended to create a sort of father-daughter or male-teacher-female-pupil relationship. The self-derogatory statement can be ascribed to this relationship dynamic, but also, I hate to admit, to the nauseating way many intelligent women used to deprecate themselves and minimize their accomplishments and abilities when in the presence of the 'all-powerful male.'" But this explanation seems patronizing to Fortune, an accomplished author and occult leader. It is just possible that Fortune was expressing what she believed to be the truth—that her intellect was not the greatest of her gifts, and that Crowley was her superior as a theorist and scholar. Certainly, Fortune was every bit Crowley's equal as a novelist, and arguably his superior as an expositor—in numerous lucid volumes—of basic magical practice. There is no reason to believe that she was in doubt as to these latter points.

Fortune and Crowley undoubtedly shared an enthusiasm for the revival of pagan ritual and practice. But there remains the question as to the extent to which Fortune, by the end of her life, assented to the truth of Thelema. Crowley, in effect, created this question by his claim, in letters written after Fortune's death in January 1946, that Fortune had sworn him a kind of allegiance. To Agapé Lodge member Frederic Mellinger, he explained that "With her I had an arrangement by which she acknowledged my authority, but she was wisely, or rather prudently, most anxious to keep this fact secret from her own followers on account of the old nonsense which was knocked to pieces in *Crowley v. Constable*, and others. A great deal of difficult negotiation is necessary in order to pick up her following." It is typical of Crowley to claim his 1934 legal defeat as a triumph on behalf of his name. As for the proposed negotiations with Fortune's followers, Crowley never undertook them, and they remain unaccomplished to the present day. It is fair to say that most of those followers regarded him with distaste. This is exemplified by the viewpoint of Fielding and Collins, authors of a biography on Fortune: "Probably the best way to sum it up is to say that Crowley did not seem to know the difference between a whore and a priestess; and undoubtedly, Dion Fortune did." Crowley's claim that Fortune acknowledged his authority is rejected by virtually all of her present disciples.

But Crowley had reason to assert what he did. A letter from Fortune to the Beast, dated March 14, 1945 (the period of her two Netherwood visits), confirms this. Fortune begins by describing the public cost to her of admiring Crowley's writings:

> The acknowledgement I made in the introduction of *The Mystical Qabalah* [1935 book by Fortune] of my indebtedness to your work, which seemed to me to be no more than common literary honesty, has been used as a rod for my back by people who look on you as Antichrist. I am prepared to dig in my toes and stand up to trouble if I have got to, but I don't take on a fight if I can help it nowadays because it wastes too much time. I am fully aware that there *will* come a time when I shall have to come out in the open and say: this is the law of the New Aeon, but I want to pick my time for that, because I propose to be in a strong strategic position when I do so, and if you give Mrs. Grundy (a stock figure of puritanical disapproval) advance information, I may not be properly entrenched when the inevitable blitz starts. Therefore I ask you not to mention my name at present.

Fortune died less than a year later. She never took a public stance on behalf of Thelema, and her words to Crowley can be interpreted as agreement on basic principles—such as the primacy of individual will unfettered by Christian puritanism—rather than an acknowledgment of Crowley as Prophet. But those who would extol Fortune as the exemplar of white magic, and Crowley as the converse, are asserting a false opposition.

The degree to which Crowley could influence other occult movements, while not converting them to a Thelemite focus, is exemplified in the case of Crowley's relations with Gerald Gardner, widely regarded as the founder of the modern-day Witchcraft or Wicca movement. The dispute over the extent to which Gardner's writings and rituals reflect a genuinely ancient historical tradition does not concern us here. It is enough to understand that Gardner, a widely traveled man who had served as a British customs officer in colonial Malaya, claimed to have been initiated into a British coven in 1939, and (after the repeal of the old Witchcraft Act in 1951, which had posed a threat to open practitioners) owned and operated a Museum of Witchcraft and Magic on the Isle of Man. In 1954, he published *Witchcraft Today*, a work that would ultimately spur widespread interest in both England and America.

In the late 1940s, Gardner put forth a set of witchcraft rites known as the *Book of Shadows*. A controversy has raged over whether Crowley composed those rites for Gardner. (Ironically, Gardner himself fueled this controversy by declaring ambiguously, in his *Witchcraft Today*, that "The only man I can think of who could have invented the rites was the late Aleister Crowley.") Certain facts stand out, however. Gardner paid at least one visit to Crowley at Netherwood; but the time of the first visit was not 1946, as some commentators have maintained, but rather May 1947, according to Crowley's diary, which offers no details as to what was discussed between the two men. This was roughly six months before Crowley's death, and for most of that time, Crowley was in a state of severe decline. The notion that he could have engaged in significant drafting of rituals for Gardner's witchcraft movement is farfetched in the extreme. The further notion that Crowley was paid by Gardner to draft such rituals stems from confusion over the fact that Gardner did pay Crowley roughly £300 for O.T.O. dues and fees. There was issued an O.T.O. charter (in Gardner's handwriting, but signed by Crowley) that entitled Gardner to establish an O.T.O. chapter, though Gardner never did so.

Plainly, Crowley's influence upon Gardner's *Book of Shadows* was substantial, for the simple reason that Gardner himself drew liberally from Crowley's writings (in particular, *Magick*) to flesh out those rituals, which Gardner publicly claimed to have received from the coven that had initiated him. Wiccan historian Aidan Kelly has confirmed that Gardner "borrowed wholesale from Crowley." Doreen Valiente, who became a High Priestess in Gardner's rituals, later suggested to Gardner, in the aftermath of his success with *Witchcraft Today*, that the revival of the Old Religion of Witchcraft would be hampered by any seeming connection with Crowley. Gardner agreed and authorized Valiente to rewrite the *Book of Shadows*: "I accepted the challenge [. . .] cutting out the Crowleyanity as much as I could."

Gardner, however, raised a further mystery concerning Crowley's connection with witchcraft. We have previously examined, in connection with Crowley's relations with Montague Summers, the possibility that Crowley was somehow involved with a British coven in his earlier years. Gardner reported that, during his visits with Crowley, the Beast had confided to him that "he had been inside when he was very young." Later, to author J. L. Bracelin, Gardner recalled Crowley saying that he had declined to pursue witchcraft seriously because he "refused to be bossed around by any damn woman." To add to the welter of possibilities here, Valiente has recorded the testimony of an anonymous male source who claimed knowledge of Crowley's brief membership in a coven circa 1899–1900; his Golden Dawn mentor Allan Bennett was also, according to this source, a member. Allegedly, while Bennett voluntarily broke off, Crowley was expelled by the priestess of the coven, who regarded him (in the words of this source) as "a dirty-minded, evilly-disposed, vicious little monster!" If such was the case—and it seems most doubtful—small wonder that Crowley bore a lasting resentment.

To this day, the issue of Crowley's relationship to Wicca can raise hackles amongst its adherents. There is, however, beyond question, a remarkable similarity between Crowley's Thelema and the Wiccan Creed: "An ye harm none, do what ye will."

To arrive at a just appreciation of Crowley remains difficult; it was all the more so in the final span of Crowley's life. This is borne out by the memoir testimony of E. M. Butler, a Cambridge professor then conducting research for her book, *The Myth of the Magus*. Butler thought it appropriate to arrange an interview with the man who claimed to be a living exemplar of that myth. She had read several of Crowley's works and realized that his was a formidable intellect. But the reputation of the Beast had preceded him, and Butler was full of trepidation en route to Hastings on January 1, 1946: "I tried to steady my mind in the train by reading a *Report on the Duties and Stipends of Cambridge University Teaching Officers*, but it was a bad choice; for I could not help feeling as the engine gathered speed that it was no part of such duties to spend a day with Old Crow, and that my stipend might well be in jeopardy."

The meeting lived up to, or down to, her expectations. Crowley greeted her in the front hall of Netherwood. He seemed, to her, older than his seventy-two years, not so much wrinkled as decomposing. He wore thick spectacles, his face was yellow, "and his voice was the ugliest thing about him: thin, fretful, scratchy—a pedantic voice and a pretentious manner." He excused himself shortly thereafter to administer, privately, an injection for his asthma. The interview took place in Crowley's bed-sitting room. Butler avowed that "it would need a Kafka to describe it. There was a battered writing-table, some half-empty bookshelves, a frowsy-looking, tumbled bed, a cracked wash-basin; and all of them hanging crookedly from the discoloured walls, some very disturbing pictures: violently clashing colours, leering faces, one of the otherwise lovely woman with a diabolical squint, and various designs indicative of delirium tremens. 'All my own work,' said the magician rather proudly, motioning me to a seat facing one of the worst of them."

Butler was correct in surmising that the Beast was hoping for a favorable mention in *The Myth of the Magus*, which was published in 1948, just months after his death. It would have been a welcome coup to receive, at long last, recognition from a member of the faculty of his alma mater. But that was not to be; he was barely mentioned in that work, and witheringly dismissed as a failed Satanist in her subsequent book, *Ritual Magic* (1949). In interview, Butler found Crowley forthcoming and intelligent; but she was also helplessly revulsed by him. "Yet there he sat, a wreck among ruins, living or rather dying in penury on the charity of friends, speaking of himself in all seriousness as an 'instrument of Higher Beings who control human destiny.' In order to prove this, he offered to make himself invisible on the spot; and nothing would have been a greater relief; but I felt that I must keep him under my eye whilst questioning him [. . .]" At one point, Crowley read to Butler from one of his works (unnamed by her, but describing one of his past visions), then broke into tears: "'It was a revelation of love,' he whispered, wiping his eyes; and then, almost ecstatically: 'Magic is not *a* way of life, it is *the* way of life.' Poor old Crow. It was a way of life that had led to drug addiction."

Crowley's encounters with Fortune, Gardner, and Butler were all, in their varied ways, efforts to extend the outward influence of Thelema. But he faced an equally difficult challenge within, minding the magical affairs of the Agapé Lodge in far-flung California. Jack Parsons, the Master of the Lodge, had entered into a new phase of magical exploration, the roots of which lay in the events of the summer of 1945, when Parsons met and befriended L. Ron Hubbard, who would go on, some years later, to found the Church of Scientology. In August 1945, however, Hubbard was a lieutenant in the U.S. Navy, from which he would be mustered out in December. Parsons and Hubbard shared interests in science fiction and magic, and Parsons was so taken with his new acquaintance that he invited Hubbard to move into the mansion owned by Parsons—and converted by him into a rooming house—on South Orange Grove Avenue in Pasadena. In that mansion, Parsons reserved two rooms for the conduct of the Gnostic Mass and other O.T.O. rituals. Parsons was convinced that Hubbard had remarkable magical potential, and he soon divulged to Hubbard the knowledge of certain O.T.O. rituals which should have, by the vows Parsons had taken, remained secret. The intimacies increased when Hubbard and Parsons's wife Betty commenced a passionate affair. The couple had been practicing an open marriage at Parsons's insistence, as a matter of Thelemic liberty. In fact, while Parsons was wracked with jealousy by this affair, he stood up rather nobly to the strain, which ended in Hubbard supplanting Parsons altogether as Betty's lover. For his part, Hubbard later denied that he had any sincere interest in the magic practiced by Parsons. In a statement issued by the Church of Scientology and printed in the London *Sunday Times* in December 1969, it was asserted that "Hubbard broke up black magic in America" by bringing a halt to a dangerous situation:

> Dr. Jack Parsons of Pasadena, California, was America's number one solid fuel rocket expert. He was involved with the infamous English black magician Aleister Crowley . . . [whose organization] . . . had savage and bestial rites. Dr. Parsons was head of the American branch . . . which had paying guests who were the U.S.A. nuclear physicists working at Cal Tech. Certain agencies objected to nuclear physicists being housed under the same roof.
>
> L. Ron Hubbard was . . . sent in to handle the situation. He went to live at the house and investigated the black magic rites and the general situation and found them very bad.
>
> Parsons wrote to Crowley in England about Hubbard. Crowley, "The Beast 666," evidently detected an enemy and warned

Parsons. This is all proven by the correspondence unearthed by the Sunday *Times*. Hubbard's mission was successful far beyond anyone's expectations. The house was torn down. Hubbard rescued a girl they were using. The black magic group was dispersed and destroyed and has never recovered.

The correspondence alluded to between Parsons and Crowley does include warnings by the Beast about Hubbard. Events at the Agapé Lodge seemed generally troubling, based on the correspondence Crowley had received from Parsons and other members. In January 1946, Parsons commenced what he termed the "Babalon Working"—a series of rituals conducted by Parsons with the aim of obtaining for himself the "magical partner" he needed. His textual inspiration was the O.T.O. VIII° ritual instructions by Crowley, entitled *De Nuptiis Secretis Deorum cum Hominibus* (On the Secret Marriages of Gods with Men). This ritual is described by Kenneth Grant as containing "methods of evoking an Elemental, or familiar spirit.[. . .] On being appropriated by a human organism, the elemental finally becomes absorbed in the immortal principle in man." Specifically, Parsons sought an air elemental and so employed the Call for the Enochian Air Tablet. He also consecrated a talisman with his own semen.

On February 23, 1946, after a long and often discouraging series of ritual workings, Parsons wrote triumphantly to Crowley: "I have my elemental! She turned up one night after the conclusion of the Operation, and has been with me since, although she goes back to New York next week. She has red hair and slant green eyes as specified. If she returns she will be dedicated as I am dedicated! All or nothing—I have no other terms. She is an artist, strong minded and determined, with strong masculine characteristics and a fanatical independence . . ." The elemental was named Marjorie Cameron, and she was indeed a remarkable woman, who would make her own mark as a student of magic, performance artist, and actress in films by Kenneth Anger. She became Parsons's magical partner in a series of further workings, recorded by Parsons in his *Book of Babalon*, designed to produce the physical birth of a moonchild who would incarnate, in human form, the spirit of the goddess Babalon—the feminine aspect of the New Aeon. (This process of magical incarnation was, it will be recalled, the focus of Crowley's novel, *Moonchild*.) In these workings, Parsons served as a scribe and astral seer through which the invoked Babalon issued her instructions.

Crowley, in a March 27, 1946, letter to Parsons, warned the younger man of the potential dangers of the work he was pursuing:

I am particularly interested in what you have written to me about the Elemental, because for some little while past I have been endeavouring to intervene *personally* in this matter on your behalf. I would however have you recall (Eliphas) Levi's aphorism "the love of the Magus for such beings is insensate and may destroy him."

It seems to me that there is a danger of your sensitiveness upsetting your balance. Any experience that comes your way you have a tendency to over-estimate.[. . .]

At the same time, your being as sensitive as you are, it behooves you to be more on your guard than would be the case with the majority of people.

But it was too late. Parsons had, in early March, already achieved, through an IX° sexual working with Cameron, "direct touch with One who is most Holy and Beautiful as mentioned in The Book of the Law. I cannot write the name at present. First instructions were received direct through Ron [Hubbard], the seer. I have followed them to the letter. There was a desire for incarnation. I do not yet know the vehicle, but it will come to me bringing a secret sign. I am to act as instructor guardian for nine months; then it will be loosed on the world. That is all I can say now . . ." Parsons believed that the birth of this child (whose physical mother he did not yet know) could lead to the fulfillment of *The Book of the Law*—the arising of the leader who would bring Thelemic freedom to the world. In the messages he was receiving from Babalon, Parsons now perceived material that could become an as-yet-unwritten fourth chapter of the *Book*.

All of this was too much for Crowley, who was not prone to accept competing prophecies. To Parsons, in April 1946, he wrote in a patronizing tone: "You have got me completely puzzled by your remarks about the elemental [. . .] I thought I had a most morbid imagination, as good as any man's, but it seems I have not. I cannot form the slightest idea what you can possibly mean." That same day, Crowley wrote to Germer to complain that "Apparently Parsons or Hubbard or somebody is producing a Moonchild. I get fairly frantic when I contemplate the idiocy of these goats."

There is no evidence that Parsons ever believed that he had located his moonchild. But in the summer of 1946, matters came to a head on a distinctly human plane. Parsons, Hubbard, and Betty formed a partnership called "Allied Enterprises"; the plan was that they would jointly purchase yachts on the East Coast, then sail them to California and sell them there for a profit. Parsons put up nearly the entirety of his savings, but the partnership soon declined into acrimonious chaos. In July, Parsons filed a suit against Hubbard and Betty, which led to a settlement later that month. The couple then passed out of Parsons's life.

Parsons would break with Crowley as well, as the younger man would not accept the Beast's view of the Babalon Workings as a failure. By 1949, two years after Crowley's death, Parsons's magical operations with Babalon had culminated in *The Book of Antichrist*, a brief treatise divided into two sections—"The Black Pilgrimage" and "The Manifesto of the Antichrist." In the former, Parsons cataloged his sufferings in the cause of Magick and cataloged the prior incarnations he could recall, including that of Cagliostro, the eighteenth-century magus whom Crowley also claimed as a past life. The concluding "Manifesto" declared that Parsons—now Belarion the Antichrist—would overturn "the Black Brotherhood called Christianity" and would "bring all men to the law of the Beast 666, and in His law I shall conquer the world." In an analogy to Christian history (that Parsons did not make), Parsons would become Paul to Crowley's Christ. As for the awaited incarnation of Babalon, the "Manifesto" declared that she would manifest herself within seven years.

Parsons did not live to see the prophecy fulfilled. On June 20, 1952, while working alone in a laboratory he had created in a garage, Parsons died in an apparently accidental explosion caused by a dropped vial of fulminate of mercury. Upon learning of his death, Parsons's elderly mother committed suicide as well.

Parsons and his workings, the Agapé Lodge and its struggles, these were the birthpangs of Thelema a continent away. Crowley fretted over these doings in his letters to America. But in the isolation of Netherwood, they were plainly beyond his control. There was, however, a task that Crowley could complete—the creation of a self-chosen legacy from the poems he had written throughout his life. Crowley had first conceived of this volume in 1942; he entitled it *Olla* (having considered, as an alternate title, *The Book of Tears*). The subtitle, *An Anthology of Sixty Years of Song*, reflected a pride which Crowley expressed privately in a March 1946 letter to Yorke: "I doubt whether anyone else can boast (if it is a boast) of 60 years of Song.[. . .] I have picked out 54 poems, all as different as possible and all written in as many different parts of the Northern Hemisphere as possible."

Olla was published by the O.T.O. in December 1946 in a limited edition of 500 copies, with a special edition of 20 copies on prewar mould-made paper. Within was a frontispiece sketch by Augustus John which the latter had completed during a visit to Crowley in July 1946. As opposed to Harris, John captured the face of the old man at a moment of perplexity—as if, at the end of his days, Crowley had startled even himself. *Olla* was issued to little response in the British press, and none whatsoever in literary circles. As to this, Crowley could hardly have been surprised.

The small but steady stream of visitors continued. In 1946, Crowley befriended John Symonds, a man of letters whom Crowley sought to interest in the establishment of a new Abbey of Thelema. It is remarkable, given the Beast's tenuous health, that he still harbored this dream so deeply. Another visitor was James Laver, the author of a biography of Nostradamus which Crowley admired, and the Keeper of Prints and Drawings at the Victoria and Albert Museum. Laver aptly portrayed the Beast's sangfroid charm in the face of addiction and approaching death: "Hardly pausing in his conversation he took up the syringe, dissolved a little scarlet pellet in the glass chamber, rolled back his sleeve and gave himself a *piqure*. The heroin injection seemed to give him new life. The muddy look in his face vanished, and the wonderful brown eyes glowed. From time to time he turned them upon me, and I began to understand the hypnotic fascination he must once have possessed." To Laver, Crowley insisted upon magic as "something we do to ourselves," a rational use of one's mental capacities: "It is *more convenient* to assume the objective existence of an Angel who gives us new knowledge than to allege that our invocation has awakened a supernatural power in ourselves."

In May 1947, Crowley wrote his first and only letter to his son, Aleister Ataturk, then age twelve. The letter was a conscious paternal summation and bequest. In its opening paragraph, Crowley informed the boy that this letter would be "very important and you should keep it and lay it to heart." Crowley then offered advice on the subjects of handwriting ("you must write in such a way that it will impress your personality on the reader"), the proud family lineage, allegedly descended from the fifteenth-century French Duke of La Querouaille ("the Dukedom is no longer in existence legally, but morally it is so, and I want you to learn to behave as a Duke would behave"), the proper curriculum of studies (an admonition to learn Latin and Greek), and suitable recreation (chess was recommended as a lifelong pursuit and pleasure). Crowley concluded with a plea that the boy one day master the English language:

The best models of English writing are Shakespeare and the Old Testament, especially the Book of Job, the Psalms, the Proverbs,

Ecclesiastes, and the Song of Solomon. It will be a very good thing for you to commit as much as you can, both of these books and of the best plays of Shakespeare to memory, so that they form the foundation of your style: and in writing English, the most important quality that you can acquire is style. It makes all the difference to anyone who reads what you write, whether you use the best phrases in the best way.

The letter reads, in most respects, like that of a proper Victorian gentleman to his son, down to the admonition to study the Bible, albeit on stylistic grounds (did Crowley not wonder how its contents might impact his son?). Overall, the Beast seemed more concerned with laying a foundation for eminence than with directing his son to Thelema. Crowley did not live to influence further the future course of the boy, who chose to take his mother's last name.

The months that remained to him after this letter were a time of steady, and then precipitous, decline. "This is a good world to leave," he told Wilkinson near the end. This sea change in Crowley's life outlook was one that Wilkinson found telling: "I had always felt that there was something of pathos about him but in his last years this element seemed to me much stronger and he was in consequence lovable as I had not known him to be before. He knew then that he had not done what he wanted to do, that he had done only a part of it: he knew that, during his lifetime at least, he would have infamy rather than fame. When he had been again dangerously ill a year or two before his death he inscribed a book to the man who had devotedly tended him: 'To _____, who saved my worthless life,' and it is likely that in some moods he did think of his life as worthless." Wilkinson, in a touching delicacy, did not wish to disclose, in this memoir, that the man who tended Crowley was himself.

Crowley died on December 1, 1947, from myocardial degeneration coupled with severe bronchitis. As one might expect, there are different accounts of Crowley's last words and moments. John Symonds recorded that "Frieda Harris told me that Crowley died unhappily and fearfully. She held his twitching hands while the tears flowed down his cheeks. 'I'm perplexed,' he said. She was not with him at the very end. A Mr. Rowe was there; he was in the room with a nurse, and according to him, Crowley's last words were: 'Sometimes I hate myself.'" Biographer Gerald Suster offers further variants. In one of these, which reached Suster secondhand, "Crowley is alleged to have passed from Samadhi to Super-Samadhi to Nirvana to Super Nirvana, expiring in the boundless bliss of the Infinite." From another secondhand source, Suster learned of a Hastings bookseller who had espied, on the exterior brickwork of Netherwood, a magical sign apparently drawn by Crowley; in alarm, the bookseller wiped it away, and consequently Crowley expired the next day. Suster adjudged the accurate version of events to be that supplied him by a "Mr. W.H.," an employee at Netherwood, according to whom "Crowley used to pace up and down his living-room. One day the Beast was pacing and Mr. W.H. was on the floor below, polishing furniture. Suddenly there was a crash. Mr. W.H. went upstairs and entered Crowley's rooms to find him dead on the floor."

There is, however, credible testimony which contradicts all of the above accounts. Patricia MacAlpine, whom Crowley called "Deidre," was the mother of his son, Aleister Ataturk. For some years, by her own volition, she had stayed out of the Beast's life. But in the summer of 1947, she came to Netherwood with her four children, including Aleister Ataturk, spent most of the final months with Crowley, and was there beside him during his last days. According to MacAlpine, Frieda Harris had not come to visit at the end, and there had been no scenes of weeping. On the contrary, the Beast remained in good spirits, enjoying the comings and goings of Aleister Ataturk and the other children, who adored him in turn. Crowley did, however, remain in bed. The day before he died, he talked calmly and at length with MacAlpine. The following day was a still one, but at the moment of Crowley's death, which came quietly, the curtains of his room were caught by a gust of wind, and a peal of thunder was heard. "It was the gods greeting him," said MacAlpine.

A legend has arisen from the circumstances of Crowley's passing. His treating physician, Dr. William Brown Thomson, age sixty-eight, was found dead in his bath within twenty-four hours of the demise of his patient. Rumors immediately circulated that Crowley had murdered his doctor by means of a ritual curse, in revenge for the latter's refusal to supply adequate amounts of heroin. According to one London press account, a year before their near-simultaneous deaths, "Crowley tried to get more morphia than was prescribed. After that, Dr. Thomson always went to the chemist with him. Three months ago Crowley's morphia was stopped. He put a curse on the doctor." There was no source offered to support the allegation of a curse. But the story possesses the virtue of allowing the Beast to exit amidst fumes of brimstone.

In his final Obsequies, executed in the summer of 1947, Crowley asked that Wilkinson read, at his funeral, the "Hymn to Pan," *The Book of the Law* (Wilkinson chose to read extracts only), and the "Collects" and "Anthem" from the "Gnostic Mass." This was done in a nondenominational chapel of the funeral home where Crowley, at his request, was cremated. The audience that day included both fervent mourners and discomfited members of the press. The ensuing headlines, in England and America, trumpeted the demise of the "World's Worst Man" and his "'Black Magic' Farewell." When the Brighton Council learned of the blasphemous service within its precincts, it formally resolved that there would be no recurrence.

The urn containing Crowley's ashes was sent to Germer in New York. In a June 1947 letter to the most loyal of his disciples, Crowley specified that Germer should succeed him in the leadership of the O.T.O. And now Crowley's mortal remains were in Germer's possession. In a letter to Crowley's disciple Jane Wolfe, Germer specified that he buried the urn beside the largest pine tree on his property in Hampton, New Jersey—a tree he now named "Aleister." But later, to Grady McMurtry, Germer claimed that his third wife, Sascha, had, of a sudden, smashed the urn against a tree to set the ashes free. Clear it is, at least, that no grave marking stands for the Wanderer of the Wastes.

Crowley had, some three years before his death, written his own "Elegy" in the Maytime setting of a country farmyard. In the lineage in which Crowley placed himself, it is difficult to imagine that Lao Tzu, Christ, Mohammed, or the Buddha could have written such lines. They are, distinctly, the words of a man who sought to be a Prophet for a time that would have none:

> Here rests beneath this hospitable spot
> A youth to flats and flatties not unknown,
> The Plymouth Brethren gave it to him hot;
> Trinity, Cambridge, claimed him for her own.
>
> At chess a minor master, Hoylake set
> His handicap at 2. Love drove him crazy;
> Three thousand women used to call him "pet,"
> In other gardens daffodil or daisy?
>
> He climbed a lot of mountains in his time,
> He stalked the tiger, bear and elephant.
> He wrote a stack of poems, some sublime.
> Some not. Plays, essays, pictures, tales—my aunt!
>
> He had the gift of laughing at himself.
> Most affably he talked and walked with God.
> And now the silly bastard's on the shelf,
> We've buried him beneath another sod.

EPILOGUE An Assortment of Posthumous
Assessments and Developments

1955: Experimental filmmaker Kenneth Anger makes a pilgrimage to Cefalù to restore and photograph the paintings and ritual decor of the Abbey of Thelema. Later, Anger would choose, as the epigraph for his underground classic on celebrity decadence, *Hollywood Babylon* (1975), the dictum of *The Book of the Law* that "Every man and every woman is a star." Anger's book is dedicated "To the Scarlet Woman," to whom tacit reverence is paid in the title.

1967: Crowley's shaven head appears amongst the elite psychedelic throng on the cover of the Beatles' *Sgt. Pepper's Lonely Hearts Club Band.*

1969: The *London Times* cites Crowley as one of the "1000 Makers of the Twentieth Century."

1970: The words "Do What Thou Wilt" are subtly engraved in the center vinyl of the *Led Zeppelin III* album. This same year, Jimmy Page, guitarist of Led Zeppelin, who had already amassed a major collection of Crowley books, manuscripts, and artifacts, purchases Boleskine House in Scotland, where Crowley began the Abra-Melin ritual working in 1900. From this time onward, Crowley becomes a recurrent presence in the Heavy Metal music scene.

1970: In the *New York Review of Books,* Nigel Dennis reviews Crowley's reissued *Confessions* and addresses the vexing issue of the

Beast's self-declared spiritual attainments: "The strong prose, the hilarious stories, the superb self-confidence—these are just as apparent after Crowley became God as they were when he was only a Saint. Criticism, in my opinion, is never just when it shows signs of envy."

1972: Gerald Yorke, in his "Foreword" to *The Magicians of the Golden Dawn* by Ellic Howe, warns that "the majority of those who attempt to tread the occult path of power become the victims of their creative imagination, inflate their egos and fall." Crowley, Yorke's teacher in his youth, is termed a "pseudo-Messiah."

1974: *The Beast,* by British playwright Snoo Wilson, is staged in London. Wilson, in interview, observes that "The point about Crowley is that he seems to contain all these sorts of ideas and identities—indeed most of the vices of the 20th century—and he was dead at the end of 1947."

1979: Timothy Leary, who regarded Crowley as his neurogenetic predecessor, offers this judgment, in *The Game of Life,* on the Beast's life and influence: "The evolutionary process moves or freezes. Aleister Crowley represents human intelligence at its transition point. The rapturous body, floating detached from terrestrial-life lines, all wired up and nowhere to go. As he got older, he increasingly amused himself with childish jokes, playing on the 'Black Magick' and 'Satanist' image given to him by vulgar tabloids. Funny, frivolous, futile. Crowley understood the interstellar goal of human evolution and was bitterly aware of his imprisonment on the planet. Gravity and the inability of current technology to reach *escape velocity* kept him from breaking out."

1984: Tom Whitmore, a Berkeley bookseller, discovers the original manuscript of *The Book of the Law,* lost since the death of Karl Germer in 1962. Whitmore graciously donates the manuscript to the O.T.O.; it was received by Grady McMurtry and presently resides in a safety deposit box in Texas.

1990: Blanche Barton publishes *The Secret Life of a Satanist,* the authorized biography of the late Anton Sandor LaVey, founder of the Church of Satan, author of *The Satanic Bible,* and the most famous public Satanist in postwar America. Crowley is frequently cited as a guiding influence upon him. Barton offers this account: In 1951, LaVey "visited a chapter of the Order of Thelema in Berkeley, followers of Aleister Crowley, who prided himself on being 'The Wickedest Man in the World' [. . .] Anton was disappointed to find the Berkeley bunch mystically-minded card readers who emphasized the study of Eastern philosophy, Oriental languages, stars and contemplation to reach the spiritual Nirvana of Oneness.[. . .] Anton concluded that the Thelemites' founder was a druggy poseur whose greatest achievements were as a poet and mountain climber."

1993: The name of Aleister Crowley is added to *The Dictionary of National Biography,* the grand register of British achievement published by the Oxford University Press.

At the dawn of the new millennium: The formal membership of Thelemite organizations worldwide numbers is in the low thousands. Websites devoted to Crowley and Thelema proliferate. Crowley's major works remain in print. His first editions, paintings, and magical artifacts are regarded as investments. He continues to fascinate and terrify, far more so through his photographs and sobriquets than by way of his writings. The unremitting bloodshed of the world confirms the descriptive power, if not the prophetic truth, of his *Book.*

Endnotes

Unpublished documentary material drawn upon for this biography comes from several different institutional sources, notably the Yorke Collection established by Crowley's friend Gerald Yorke at the Warburg Institute, University of London; the Harry Ransom Humanities Research Center, University of Texas at Austin; the Library of King's College, London; and the George Arents Research Library, Syracuse University. However, as copies of all such materials are held within the Ordo Templi Orientis (O.T.O.) Archives, I shall, for simplicity's sake, cite the source of all of these documents as O.T.O. Archives. Quotations the sources of which are evident from the main text have not been cited herein. Full citations for materials are provided with the first reference thereto.

INTRODUCTION

"There is no sense . . ." Robert Anton Wilson, "Introduction" to Israel Regardie, *The Eye in the Triangle: An Interpretation of Aleister Crowley*, (Phoenix: Falcon Press, 1986) p. xiii.

"I myself was first consciously . . ." Aleister Crowley (with Mary Desti and Leila Waddell), *Magick (Liber Aba) Book Four: Parts I–IV*, second revised edition, ed. Hymenaeus Beta (York Beach: Samuel Weiser, 1997) (hereinafter *Magick*), p. 125.

"Let me explain . . ." Ibid., pp. 125–6.

"The Microcosm . . ." Ibid., p. 139.

"High magic . . ." Richard Cavendish, *A History of Magic* (London: Sphere Books, 1978), p. 20.

"because Christians as they read . . ." Elaine Pagels, *The Origin of Satan* (New York: Random House, 1995), p. xxiii.

"The union of . . ." Mircea Eliade, *A History of Religious Ideas*, vol. 2 (Chicago: University of Chicago Press, 1984), p. 375.

"But you [Peter] will . . ." Quoted in Kurt Rudolph, *Gnosis: The Nature & History of Gnosticism* (New York: Harper & Row, 1987), p. 297.

"All of these systems . . ." Mircea Eliade, "Spirit, Light, and Seed," in his collection *Occultism, Witchcraft, and Cultural Fashions: Essays in Comparative Religions* (Chicago: University of Chicago Press, 1976), p. 112.

"Magic is worked . . ." Idries Shah, *The Sufis* (New York: Doubleday Anchor, 1971), pp. 379–80.

Magick, pp. 275–6.

CHAPTER ONE

"He bore on his body . . ." Aleister Crowley, *the Confessions of Aleister Crowley,* ed. John Symonds and Kenneth Grant (New York: Hill and Wang, 1970), c. 1. The edition cited here is slightly abridged. A small portion of Crowley's voluminous memoir has yet to appear in print; those unpublished pages have been consulted by the present author. Volumes one and two of the *Confessions* were first published by the Mandrake Press in London in 1929. Given the tangled publishing history and multiple editions of the *Confessions*—as this work shall hereinafter be cited—the reference given will be to chapter rather than page number.

Ibid., c. 1.

Ibid., Prelude.

"I am born for supreme . . ." Quoted in Lucien Stryk, ed., *World of the Buddha* (New York: Doubleday Anchor, 1978), p. 15.

"In the 1870s . . ." E. J. Hobsbawm, *Industry and Empire* (Harmondsworth: Penguin Books, 1982), p. 164.

"Fed upon privilege . . ." Barbara Tuchman, *The Proud Tower: A Portrait of the World Before the War (1890–1914)* (New York: Bantam, 1972), p. 33.

"preparations for a distant future . . ." *Confessions*, c. 1.

"psychic phenomena" and "regrettable incident" Ibid., c. 10.

"My intellectual activity . . ." Ibid., c. 7.

"her powerful natural instincts . . ." Ibid., c. 1.

"And I had had her . . ." Ibid., c. 7.

"To hear Vladimir being chided . . ." Ethel Archer, *The Hieroglyph* (London: Denis Archer, 1932), p. 181. In a February 10, 1961 letter (a copy of which is preserved in the Yorke Collection, Warburg Institute, University of London), Archer confirmed that her protagonist was based on Crowley.

"I very much wish . . ." A copy of this December 12, 1912, letter by Emily was kindly provided to me by Geraldine Beskin.

"In a way, my mother . . ." *Confessions*, c. 48.

"The Elders . . ." Ibid., c. 2.

"His father was his hero . . ." Ibid., c. 3.

"Indeed, his name does not appear . . ." See F. Roy Coad, F.C.A., *A History of the Brethren Movement: Its Origins, its Worldwide Development and its Significance for the Present Day* (Grand Rapids, MI: Eerdmans, 1968); Peter L. Embley, "The Early Development of the Plymouth Brethren," in Bryan R. Wilson, ed. *Patterns of Sectarianism: Organisation and Ideology in Social and Religious Movements* (London: Heinemann, 1967); Napoleon Noel, *The History of the Brethren* (Two Volumes), ed. William F. Knapp (Denver: W.P. Knapp, 1936).

"swayed thousands . . ." *Confessions*, c. 3.

"The boy seems . . ." Ibid.

"there can be no remissions . . ." Edward Crowley, *The Plymouth Brethren (So Called)/ Who They Are—Their Creed—Mode of Worship, &c./ Explained in A Letter to his Friends and Relatives* (London: George Morrish, 1865), p. 5. Other tracts by Edward included *Why, Sir, It's Better and Better/ With A Word To/ The Striving One, The Doubting One, The Happy One* (London: George Morrish, 1868); and *Cease to Do Evil: Learn to Do Well/ A Word To Christians* (London: George Morrish, 1861).

"waxing bolder . . ." Ibid., p. 11.

"He said that abstainers . . ." *Confessions*, c. 3.

"In the case of the sinner . . ." Ibid., c. 4.

"It is as if . . ." Ibid., c. 3.

"The incident made . . ." Ibid., c. 2.

"This attitude continued . . ." Ibid.

"Accordingly, he aimed . . ." Ibid., c. 3.

"It is impossible to suppose . . ." Ibid., c. 5.

"The apparent discrepancy . . ." Ibid.

"It seems as if I possessed . . ." Ibid., c. 6.

"Previous to the death . . ." Ibid., c. 3.

"a ruthless, petty tyrant . . ." Ibid., c. 4.

"May God bite into . . ." Crowley, *The World's Tragedy* (Phoenix: Falcon Press, 1985), pp. xv–xvi.

"In a state of health . . ." Quoted in Steven Marcus, *The Other Victorians: A Study of Sexuality and Pornography in Mid-Nineteenth-Century England* (New York: Basic Books, 1966), p. 13.

"[A] boy named Glascott . . ." Crowley, *The World's Tragedy*, pp. xvi–xvii.

"Victorian prep schools . . ." J. R. de S. Honey, *Tom Brown's Universe: The Development of the Victorian Public School* (London: Millington Books, 1977), pp. 201–3.

"I had been told . . ." *Confessions*, c. 6.

"The battle between . . ." Ibid., c. 5.

"Here was certainly . . ." Ibid., c. 6.

"Strangely enough . . ." Ibid., c. 8.

"I did not allow him . . ." Ibid., c. 6.

"Though Douglas called . . ." Ibid., c. 7.

"it was too late . . ." Ibid.

"By the time I reached . . ." Ibid., c. 8.

"The problem of life . . ." Ibid.

"Chalk is probably . . ." and "One does not climb . . ." and "It was my first experience . . ." Ibid., c. 10.

"a fine climber . . ." Tom Longstaff, *This My Voyage* (London: John Murray, 1950), p. 24. Long after he met Crowley, Longstaff served from 1947 to 1949 as president of the English Alpine Club.

"I had no intention . . ." *Confessions*, c. 19.

"I spent the whole . . ." Ibid., c. 12.

"It seemed to me absurd . . ." Ibid.

"the weekly records disclose . . ." these records are contained in Volume "Rec.8.6." of the collection of the Wren Library, Trinity College, Cambridge.

"I hardly entered . . ." *Confessions*, c. 16.

"the greatest opportunities . . ." Ibid., c. 13.

"There was no fear . . ." Ibid., c. 14.

"I was awakened . . ." Ibid.

"Then came the great . . ." "The Temple of Solomon the King" in *Equinox I(2)* (London: 1909), reprinted (York Beach, ME: Weiser, 1992), pp. 233–4.

"In invocation . . ." *Magick*, p. 147.

"special attention . . ." Ibid.

"The forces of good . . ." *Confessions*, c. 14.

"It was a windy night . . ." Prefatory note to "Aceldama, A Place to Bury Strangers In. A Philosophical Poem," in Crowley, *The Collected Works of Aleister Crowley*, vol. 1 (Foyers, Scotland: Society for the Propagation of Religious Truth, 1905), p. 1.

"The incarnation was . . ." *Confessions*, c. 17.

"androgyne troublant . . ." Quoted in Robert Hewison, *Footlights! A Hundred Years of Cambridge Comedy* (London: Methuen, 1983), p. 16.

"in a manner which . . ." Ibid.

"Pollitt was rather plain . . ." *Confessions*, c. 17.

"To the re-seeing . . ." See letter, Crowley to Gerald Kelly, n.d. [c. 1903], O.T.O. Archives.

"The relation between us . . ." *Confessions*, c. 17.

"The stupidity of . . ." Ibid., c. 12.

"They had no true . . ." Ibid., c. 17.

Crowley, "The Sage," unpublished (and apparently unfinished) short story by Crowley, the first eighteen pages of which were preserved by Gerald Yorke, O.T.O. Archives.

"The intense refinement . . ." *Confessions*, c. 17.

"My scheme . . ." Crowley, letter to Gerald Yorke, quoted in Timothy d'Arch Smith, *The Books of the Beast: Essays on Aleister Crowley, Montague Summers, Francis Barrett and Others* (London: Aquarian Press, 1987), p. 28. The title essay is a stylish and invaluable study of Crowley's aims and methods as book designer and publisher.

"Of man's delight . . ." Crowley, *White Stains*, second edition, ed. John Symonds (London: Duckworth, 1973), p. 67.

"I felt in my subconscious . . ." *Confessions*, c. 17.

"I told him frankly . . ." Ibid.

"I was taught . . ." Ibid., c. 11.

CHAPTER TWO

"I liked him . . ." Quoted in David Dean, T. S. Blakeney and D. F. O. Dangar, "Oscar Eckenstein, 1859–1921," in *Alpine Journal* (Vol. 65, 1960), p. 66.

"Eckenstein recognized . . ." *Confessions,* c. 18.

"O.E. often spoke . . ." *Alpine Journal* (Vol. 65, 1960), p. 73.

"Sir Richard Burton . . ." *Confessions,* c. 19.

"the greatest pace . . ." Crowley, *The Equinox of the Gods* (London: O.T.O., 1936), comprising part IV of *Book Four* or *Magick,* p. 394. Citations to *The Equinox of the Gods* will hereafter be given by page number in *Magick.*

"the greatest number . . ." Ibid.

"Eckenstein, provided he . . ." Crowley, letter to Harry Doughty (1924), quoted in John Symonds, *The Beast 666* (London: The Pindar Press, 1997), p. 40.

"a rough diamond . . ." *Alpine Journal* (Vol. 65, 1960), p. 74.

"Eckenstein, though a . . ." Ibid.

"ultimately to revolutionize . . ." Ibid., p. 64.

The scholar R. A. Gilbert has argued, by way of documentary evidence, that November 18, 1898, was the date Crowley signed his Golden Dawn application, rather than the date of his Neophyte initiation. But as Crowley held to the latter view all his life, the date the man himself believed to be accurate shall be retained here.

"I had no idea . . ." *Confessions,* c. 20.

"If I had not made . . ." Quoted in George Mills Harper, *Yeats's Golden Dawn* (Wellingborough, UK: Aquarian Press, 1987), p. 2.

"that has perhaps . . ." William Butler Yeats, *Memoirs,* ed. Denis Donoghue (London: Macmillan, 1972), pp. 27–8.

"I allowed my mind . . ." Ibid., p. 28.

"He was in delirium . . ." Ibid., p. 75.

"You will readily . . ." "The Temple of Solomon the King" in *Equinox I(2)* (London: 1909), p. 239.

"I believe that his mind . . ." Yeats, *The Autobiography of William Butler Yeats* (New York: Doubleday Anchor, 1958), p. 124.

"It was through him . . ." Ibid.

"the eighteenth century . . ." Ibid., pp. 224–5.

"One that boxed . . ." Ibid., p. 124.

"Mathers had much . . ." Ibid., pp. 126–7, 227.

"But unless the Chiefs . . ." Quoted in Ellic Howe, *The Magicians of the Golden Dawn: A Documentary History of a Magical Order* (York Beach: Weiser, 1984), p. 131.

"I said, 'How . . ." Yeats, *Memoirs*, p. 106.

"A true vision . . ." "The Temple of Solomon the King" in *Equinox I(2)* (London: 1909), p. 300.

"sexual peculiarities"; "impending homosexual scandal" The former is alleged in R. A. Gilbert, *Golden Dawn: Twilight of the Magicians* (Wellingborough: Aquarian Press, 1983), p. 41. The latter speculation may be found in Howe, p. 206.

"fed from time to time . . ." *Confessions*, c. 21.

"I reverence more . . ." Bennett, letter to Frederick Leigh Gardner, n.d. [c. 1897], O.T.O. Archives.

"His cycle of life . . ." *Confessions*, c. 21.

"went on to experiment . . ." The friend, Paul Brunton, who became an influential writer on yoga, is quoted in Joscelyn Godwin, *The Theosophical Enlightenment* (Albany: State University of New York Press, 1994), p. 369.

"To my amazement . . ." *Confessions*, c. 20.

"Iehi Aour never had . . ." Ibid., c. 21.

"Allan Bennett was . . ." Ibid.

"One day, a party . . ." Ibid.

"Like Huckleberry Finn's . . ." Crowley (under the pseudonym "Oliver Haddo"), "The Herb Dangerous, Part II, The Psychology of Hashish" in *Equinox I(2)* (London: 1909), p. 36.

"Yeats and Crowley . . ." Kathleen Raine, *Yeats the Initiate: Essays on Certain Themes in the Work of W. B. Yeats* (London: George Allen & Unwin, 1986), p. 218.

"I had never thought . . ." *Confessions*, c. 19.

"What hurt him . . ." Ibid.

"At the Fork of the Roads" *Equinox I(1)* (London: 1909), p. 101.

"a characteristic move . . ." Ethel Archer, *The Hieroglyph* (previously cited), p. 181. The quotes here come from Archer's roman à clef treatment of Crowley and his mother.

"Susan Strong" I am indebted to Scott Hanson, an impeccable librarian, for tracking down the identity of Susan Strong based on the veiled clues offered by Crowley in the *Confessions*.

"She begged me . . ." *Confessions*, c. 21.

"He seems nearly . . ." Quoted in Howe, *Magicians of the Golden Dawn*, p. 219.

"This is concerned . . ." Ibid., p. 206.

"sex intemperance" Ibid., p. 223.

"a person of unspeakable life" Quoted in Harper, *Yeats's Golden Dawn* p. 29.

"[W]e did not think . . ." Ibid., p. 182, n. 19.

"aspirant on the threshold . . ." Quoted in Israel Regardie, *What You Should Know About the Golden Dawn* (Phoenix: Falcon Press, 1985), p. 77.

"a man without principles" Howe, *Magicians of the Golden Dawn*, p. 227.

"Ponder the matter . . ." Abraham the Jew (pseudonym), *The Book of the Sacred Magic of Abra-Melin the Mage*, S. L. MacGregor-Mathers, trans. and ed. (New York: Causeway Books, 1974), p. 54.

"Buried with that LIGHT . . ." This quotation, along with an abridgement of the Adeptus Minor ritual, is contained in "The Temple of Solomon the King" in *Equinox I(3)* (London: 1910).

"embalmed in the ancient . . ." Crowley set forth this request in a will executed by him on December 2, 1931. I would like to thank Keith Richmond for graciously providing me with a copy of this will, as well as copies of other relevant documents.

"I again reiterate . . ." Quoted in Howe, p. 210.

"bona fide posted letters" Ibid., p. 215.

the power of changing . . ." Ibid., p. 204.

"His face was fixed . . ." Crowley Abra-Melin diary, O.T.O. Archives.

"as in the case . . ." "The Temple of Solomon the King" in *Equinox I(3)* (London: 1910).

Ibid., p. 267.

"Trades Protection Association" See Howe, *Magicians of the Golden Dawn*, p. 226.

"Even the fact . . ." Quoted in Harper, *Yeats's Golden Dawn*, p. 31.

"He described the doings . . ." Arthur Machen, *Things Near and Far* (London: Martin Secker, 1923), p. 148.

CHAPTER THREE

"Indoors and out . . ." *Confessions,* c. 23.

"I see all nature . . ." "The Ghost of God" is contained in *The Temple of the Holy Ghost,* Crowley, *Collected Works* (previously cited), vol. 1, p. 178.

"One afternoon, in Mexico . . ." *Confessions,* c. 23.

"Mine was, by weakness . . ." Crowley, *Tannhäuser,* in *Collected Works,* vol. 1, p. 256.

"a descendant of . . ." *Confessions,* c. 23.

"I reached a point . . ." Ibid.

"the real secret . . ." Ibid.

"cut thyself sharply . . ." *Liber Jugorum,* included in *Magick,* pp. 658–60. Hymenaeus Beta notes that the cuts need not leave scars and that some modern-day Thelemites use rubber bands instead.

"My results were . . ." *Confessions,* c. 23.

"Now, the year being . . ." Crowley, Diary, January–May 1901, typescript, O.T.O. Archives.

"the greatest pace uphill . . ." Crowley, *Magick,* p. 394.

"On the boat . . ." Crowley, letter to Gerald Kelly, n.d. [1901], O.T.O. Archives.

"I had intoxicated . . ." *Confessions,* c. 26.

"So the last kiss . . ." *Alice: An Adultery* in Crowley, *Collected Works,* vol. 2, pp. 84–5.

"the poets of Mr. Crowley's school . . ." G. K. Chesterton, book review, *London Daily News,* June 18, 1901.

"I had got to learn . . ." *Confessions,* c. 27.

"The Inmost knew . . ." Ibid., c. 26.

"Their aristocracy . . ." Ibid.

"not only contrite . . ." and "I exist not . . ." "The Temple of Solomon the King" in *Equinox I(4)* (London: 1910), p. 123.

Ibid., p. 150.

"According to tantra . . ." Ajit Mookerjee and Madhu Khanna, *The Tantric Way: Art, Science, Ritual* (Boston: New York Graphic Society, 1977), p. 29. An analogous approach to spiritual sexuality, as practiced by certain Gnostic sects, is discussed in the "Introduction" of this biography.

"One of my principal . . ." *Confessions,* c. 28.

"let the student decide . . ." Crowley, *Magick,* p. 23.

"[O]ne's real country . . ." Crowley [pseud. Mahatma Guru Sri Parama-hansa Sivaji], *Eight Lectures on Yoga* (London: O.T.O. 1939), rev. 2nd edition, ed. Hymenaeus Beta (New York: 93 Publishing, 1992), pp. 45–6. All citations to this work are to this latter edition. As Hymenaeus Beta observed therein, the "abortion" referred to in the quoted passage was Gerald Yorke (1902–83), a student and friend of Crowley in the 1920s and after who figures in the latter chapters of this biography.

"Dharana is . . ." *Magick*, p. 30.

"After some eight hours . . ." *The Writings of Truth*, Crowley diary, typescript, O.T.O. Archives. Crowley polished and slightly revised the original diary entries for publication in *The Temple of Solomon the King* in *Equinox I(4)* (London: 1910), pp. 166–7.

"But why revile . . ." "Ascension Day," *The Sword of Song*, in Crowley, *Collected Works*, vol. 2, p. 147.

"An enormous head . . ." *Confessions*, c. 31.

"It was a woman . . ." Ibid., c. 32.

"and so making . . ." Crowley, 1902 Diary, typescript, O.T.O. Archives.

"a magnificent gymnasium . . ." *Berashith—An Essay in Ontology*, in Crowley, *Collected Works*, vol. 2., p. 242.

"waylaying one great man . . ." *Alpine Journal*, (Vol. 65, 1960), pp. 68, 73.

"Had I failed . . ." *Confessions*, c. 34.

"England is losing . . ." Ibid.

"The result was . . ." Ibid.

"having red hot . . ." Ibid., c. 39.

"the expedition had . . ." Ibid., c. 40.

"Many climbers died . . ." Galen Rowell, *In the Throne Room of the Mountain Gods* (San Francisco: Sierra Club Books, 1986), p. 90. Rowell provides an excellent historical overview on the various K2 expeditions.

"The only thing . . ." *Confessions*, c. 39.

"I hope I may . . ." Ibid., c. 40.

"Never anywhere . . ." Oscar Eckenstein, July 27, 1902, letter to D. W. Freshfield, subsequently printed in *Alpine Journal*.

"There we found . . ." *Confessions*, c. 40.

"I have business also . . ." Crowley, letter to Gerald Kelly, October 25, 1902, O.T.O. Archives.

"middle-aged woman . . ." "The Temple of Solomon the King" in *Equinox I(4)* (London: 1910), p. 175. Crowley's handwritten annotations to his personal copies of the *Equinox* often identify the real names of persons alluded to in the published works.

"who would later dismiss . . ." See Symonds, *The Beast 666*, p. 56.

"Crowley was widely . . ." *Alpine Journal,* (Vol. 65, 1960), p. 68.

"It had already . . ." *Confessions*, c. 42.

"I took an immediate . . ." W. Somerset Maugham, *The Magician* (London: Heinemann, 1908), reprinted with "A Fragment of Autobiography" (Harmondsworth, UK: Penguin, 1986), p. 7.

"more striking . . ." Ibid. p. 9.

"The hero's witty . . ." *Confessions*, c. 63.

"He was clearly . . ." Maugham, *The Magician*, p. 33.

"D . . .'s cold acumen . . ." Crowley, *Snowdrops from a Curate's Garden* (1904), revised and enlarged edition, ed. with a "Prolegomenon" by Martin P. Starr (Chicago: Teitan Press, 1986). Starr posits the respective identities of "D . . ." (Crowley) and "L . . ." (Kelly). Ibid., p. 191, n. 10.

"its unexpected flower . . ." Quoted in Frederic V. Grunfeld, *Rodin: A Biography* (New York: Henry Holt, 1987), pp. 455–6.

"from the fatal mischief . . ." "New Year, 1903," Crowley, *Collected Works*, vol. 2, p. 127.

"If Science is never . . ." Crowley, "Science and Buddhism," ibid., p. 261.

"It is strange . . ." *Confessions*, c. 45.

"I cannot deny . . ." "The Temple of Solomon the King" in *Equinox I(4)* (London: 1910), p. 177.

"For me these . . ." *The Goetia: The Lesser Key of Solomon the King,* trans. S. L. MacGregor Mathers, ed. with introductory essay ("The Initiate Interpretation of Ceremonial Magic") by Aleister Crowley, illus. second edition ed. Hymenaeus Beta (York Beach: Weiser, 1995), p. 18.

"ye Wise . . ." Ibid., p. 95.

"The spirits of . . ." Ibid., p. 17.

"My interpretation . . ." *Confessions*, c. 45.

"I never thought . . ." Ibid., c. 46.

"I am ashamed . . ." Ibid.

"I may have . . ." Crowley, August 12, 1903, letter to Gerald Kelly, O.T.O. Archives.

"From her mother . . ." Crowley, *Magick*, pp. 432–3.

"Rose on the breast . . ." This poem (numbered "XIX.") appears in *Rosa Mundi and Other Love Songs* (1905), in Crowley, *Collected Works*, vol. 3, p. 64.

"The error here . . ." and "Hats off . . ." Crowley's annotated copy of Shelley's poetical works forms part of the Yorks Collection, Warburg Institute, University of London.

"Physically and morally . . ." *Confessions*, c. 47.

"Once, in the . . ." Ibid., c. 46.

"Bornless Ritual" The ritual text employed by Crowley appears, with useful editorial annotations, in *The Goetia*, pp. 5–12.

"The King's Chamber . . ." *Confessions*, c. 46.

"Rose of the World!" "Rosa Mundi," Crowley, *Collected Works*, vol. III,. p. 51.

Chapter Four

"at the outset . . ." Crowley, *Magick*, p. 443.

"with a Being . . ." Ibid, p. 427.

"I, Aleister Crowley . . ." Ibid.

"I was not for . . ." *Confessions*, c. 48.

"many of the secrets . . ." Ibid.

"They're waiting . . ." Crowley, *Magick*, p. 410.

"all about the child" Ibid.

"I am to formulate . . ." Ibid., p. 414.

"the Secret Chiefs . . ." *Confessions*, c. 49.

"G.D. to be . . ." Crowley diary entry quoted in Crowley, *Magick*, p. xxxviii (footnote).

"A glass case . . ." Ibid., p. 412.

"quite obscure . . ." *Confessions*, c. 49.

"Any questions . . ." Crowley, *Magick*, p. 434.

"to enter the 'temple' . . ." Ibid.

"a rich tenor . . ." Ibid., p. 435.

"a body of 'fine . . ." Ibid.

"a man as I am . . ." Ibid.

"a Being whose nature . . ." Ibid., p. 291.

"pushed hard . . ." Ibid., p. 435.

"I remember clearly . . ." Crowley, *The Law is for All*, ed. Israel Regardie, (Phoenix: Falcon Press, 1986), p. 170.

"As is well known . . ." Ibid.

"I lay claim . . ." *Magick*, p. 440.

"The first period . . ." Ibid., p. 444.

"The Antecedents of Thelema" This essay, written in 1926, was first published in Crowley, *The Revival of Magick and Other Essays (Oriflamme 2)* ed. Hymenaeus Beta and Richard Kaczynski, Ph.D. (Tempe: New Falcon, 1998), pp. 162–9.

"St. Augustine's . . ." Ibid., p. 162.

"Everyone should . . ." Crowley, *The Law is for All*, p. 111.

"Why can't they . . ." Ibid., p. 112.

"Nature's way . . ." Ibid., p. 177.

"could never bring himself" Gerald Yorke, "Notes from G. Y. Regarding Book of the Law," O.T.O. Archives.

"inhuman cruelty . . ." Crowley, *Magick*, p. 422.

"I, the Beast . . ." Crowley, *Magical and Philosophical Commentaries on the Book of the Law*, ed. John Symonds and Kenneth Grant (Montreal: 93 Publishing, 1974), p. 307.

"I and my woman . . ." Ibid.

"the attraction should . . ." Crowley, *The Law is for All*, pp. 126, 132.

"women are nearly . . ." Ibid., p. 133.

"The best women . . ." Ibid., p. 311.

"Sexual disease . . ." Ibid.

"Prostitution (with its . . ." Ibid.

"It is we of Thelema . . ." Ibid., pp. 307–8.

"It really makes . . ." Israel Regardie, "Introduction" to *The Law is for All*, pp. 40–1. See also, Kenneth Grant, "Introduction" to *Magical and Philosophical Commentaries on the Book of the Law*, p. xvii, where Grant writes: "Should *The Book of the Law* prove to be wholly the brain child of a human being—Aleister Crowley—this would be no indictment of its truth. Rather would it prove that Crowley the man had somehow gained access to knowledge of a superhuman order, the very existence of which is only now beginning to be suspected by the most brilliant minds of our age."

"a reason for this . . ." Crowley, *Magick*, pp. 423–4.

"the law of Parsimony . . ." Ibid.

"a sin of his youth . . ." and "for the sake . . ." C. G. Jung, *Memories, Dreams, Reflections*, ed. Aniela Jaffe (New York: Vintage, 1965), p. 378.

"Archetypes speak . . ." Ibid., p. 178.

"I called him . . ." Ibid., p. 182.

"the crucial insight . . ." Ibid., p. 183.

"Psychologically, Philemon . . ." Ibid.

"I was compelled . . ." Ibid., p. 190.

"attempting automatic . . ." William Butler Yeats, *A Vision*, reissue with the author's final revisions (New York: Collier Books, 1973), p. 8.

"gained in . . ." Ibid.

"But Muses resemble . . ." Ibid., p. 24.

"My teachers did not . . ." Ibid., p. 10.

"A *primary* dispensation . . ." Ibid., p. 263.

"Why should we . . ." Quoted in Helen Vendler, *Yeats's Vision and the Later Plays* (Cambridge: Harvard University Press, 1963), p. 102.

"The reader must . . ." Crowley, *Magick*, p. 443.

"my own 'conversion' . . ." Ibid., p. 423.

"My sincerity . . ." Ibid., p. 428.

"powers of clairvoyance" *Confessions*, c. 50.

"A large red . . ." Crowley [pseud. as given in title], *The Scented Garden of Abdullah the Satirist of Shiraz (Bagh-i-Muattar)*, facsimile of 1910 privately printed (in London) first edition with "Introduction" by Martin P. Starr (Chicago: Teitan Press, 1991), p. 39.

"But for private . . ." Gerald Yorke, "Notes from G. Y. Regarding Book of the Law," O.T.O. Archives.

"the printing bill . . ." d'Arch Smith, *The Books of the Beast*, p. 36.

"a deliberate mimicry . . ." Ibid., p. 37.

"Nuit was given . . ." *Confessions*, c. 50.

"arouse every instinct . . ." Ibid.

"to clean all . . ." Crowley, letter to Norman Mudd [c. 1925], quoted in Symonds, *The Beast 666*, p. 78.

"I used to experiment . . ." *Confessions*, c. 50.

"There was a young lady . . ." Crowley, *Snowdrops from a Curate's Garden*, p. 150.

"Rose, that you . . ." Ibid., p. 160.

"I see below . . ." "Rosa Inferni" is included in Crowley, *Selected Poems*, ed. Martin Booth (Great Britain: Aquarian Press, 1986), pp. 139–44.

"My marriage taught . . ." *Confessions,* c. 50.

CHAPTER FIVE

"as keen as ever . . ." *Confessions,* c. 50.

"Perdurabo" Quoted in Symonds, *The Beast 666,* p. 81.

"his character was mean . . ." *Confessions,* c. 51.

On Pache, Reymond, Guillarmod Ibid.

"sole and supreme" Ibid.

"I gave a prize . . ." Ibid., c. 52.

"A moment's hesitation . . ." Ibid.

"crumbling moraine . . ." Crowley, written response to Dr. J. Jacot Guillarmod, "Au Kanchenjunga: Voyage et explorations dans l'Himalaya du Sikkim et du Nepal," (serialized in *Echo des Alpes,* (Nos. 8–9, 1914)), typescript, O.T.O. Archives.

"In matter of fact . . ." Ibid.

"I took pains . . ." *Confessions,* c. 52.

"The economical . . ." Crowley, written response to Guillarmod, O.T.O. Archives.

"I cannot think . . ." Ibid.

"The root of the . . ." *Confessions,* c. 52.

"There was only one . . ." Ibid.

"Their imaginations . . ." Ibid.

"There was no suggestion . . ." Ibid.

"After our 1954 . . ." John Tucker, *Kanchenjunga* (London: Panther, 1957), p. 42.

"To my horror . . ." *Confessions,* c. 52.

"As it was . . ." Crowley, letter to *Pioneer* of India, September 11, 1905.

"The following day . . ." Crowley, written response to Guillarmod, O.T.O. Archives.

"In consequence . . ." Crowley, letter to London *Daily Mail,* September 11, 1905.

"I have very much . . ." Crowley, written response to Guillarmod, O.T.O. Archives.

"I tell thee, man . . ." Crowley, *Scented Garden,* p. 27.

"With sodomy . . ." Ibid., pp. 27–8.

"I realize in myself . . ." "The Temple of Solomon the King" in *Equinox I(8)* (London: 1912), p. 11.

"After five years . . ." Crowley, letter to Gerald Kelly, n.d. [c. October, 1905], O.T.O. Archives.

"And then I saw . . ." *Confessions,* c. 53.

"I had fired . . ." Ibid.

"There is a peculiar . . ." Ibid.

"I embrace hardship . . ." Ibid., c. 54.

"It was from him . . ." "The Temple of Solomon the King" in *Equinox I(8)* (London: 1912), p. 10.

"I knew as I know . . ." *Confessions, ,* 54.

"He had repeatedly . . ." "The Temple of Solomon the King" in *Equinox I(8)* (London: 1912), p. 13.

"[N]aturally he had . . ." *Confessions,* c. 55.

"For the first time . . ." Ibid., c. 58.

"Made many resolutions . . ." Crowley, 1906 Diary, typescript, O.T.O. Archives.

"Thee I invoke . . ." The ritual text employed by Crowley appears, with useful editorial annotations, in *The Goetia,* pp. 5–12.

"Let the muscles . . ." Crowley, *Magick,* p. 538.

"My plan was . . ." *Confessions,* c. 58.

"Having got everything . . ." Ibid., c. 56.

"it is the puritan A.C. . . ." Crowley, 1906 Diary, O.T.O. Archives.

"Go with the S.W. . . ." Ibid.

"Having won me . . ." Ibid.

"I offered all . . ." Ibid. The diary entry quoted here differs from the polished and edited version offered by Crowley in his *Confessions,* c. 59.

"Master, how subtly . . ." Crowley, *Aha!* (Phoenix: Falcon Press, 1987), p. 80.

"The great sight . . ." Ibid., p. 59.

"Remember how close . . ." Crowley, 1906 Diary.

"Once again I . . ." Ibid.

"The 'millions of worlds' . . ." Ibid.

"Hashish at least . . ." Crowley, "The Psychology of Hashish," in *Equinox I(2)* (London: 1909), p. 53.

"One may doubt . . ." Ibid., p. 80.

"and the truth of it . . ." Crowley, "John St. John," in *Equinox I(1)* (London: 1909), p. 45.

"There are only two . . ." Ibid., p. 85.

"He has drunk . . ." Ibid., p. 107.

"a true example . . ." Quoted in Brian Holden Reid, *J.F.C. Fuller: Military Thinker* (New York: St. Martin's Press, 1987), p. 2.

"if it be necessary . . ." Fuller, *The Star in the West: A Critical Essay Upon the Works of Aleister Crowley* (London: Walter Scott, 1907), p. 172.

"Unblushing, the old . . ." Crowley, *Clouds Without Water* (Des Plaines, IL: Yogi Publication Society, n.d.), p. x.

"Our love is like . . ." Ibid., p. 6.

"My readers, too . . ." Crowley, *The World's Tragedy*, p. xxxiv.

"I can only say . . ." Crowley, *Confessions*, c. 62.

"that dust which . . ." Crowley, *777 and Other Qabalistic Writings*, ed. Israel Regardie (New York: Weiser, 1977), p. 102.

"I am the heart . . ." Crowley, *The Holy Books of Thelema*, ed. Hymenaeus Alpha and Hymenaeus Beta (Yorke Beach: Weiser, 1983), p. 53.

"in truth there seems . . ." Crowley, *The World's Tragedy*, p. xxvii.

"I do not wish . . ." Ibid., p. xxiv.

"One thing I must . . ." Ibid., p. xxv.

"Life with Rose . . ." Crowley, letter to Fuller, June 8, 1908, O.T.O. Archives.

"I don't think we . . ." Crowley, letter to Fuller, May 23, 1908, O.T.O. Archives.

"unadorned, smoking . . ." *Confessions*, c. 63.

"My spiritual self . . ." Ibid., c. 64.

"a point of honesty . . ." Ibid.

"O thou who hast . . ." Quoted in Jean Overton Fuller, *The Magical Dilemma of Victor Neuburg*, rev. ed. (Oxford: Mandrake, 1990), p. 126.

"I believe that all . . ." Crowley, "John St. John," pp. 128–9.

"I am so far . . ." Ibid., pp. 29–30.

"Then subtly . . ." Ibid., pp. 133–4.

"I not only achieved . . ." *Confessions*, c. 65.

"Maugham had taken . . ." Ibid., c. 63.

"he merely remarked . . ." Ibid.

"was all moonshine . . ." Quoted in Robert Calder, *Willie: The Life of W. Somerset Maugham* (London: Heinemann, 1989), p. 99.

CHAPTER SIX

"In this way . . ." *Confessions,* c. 65.

"like so many . . ." J. F. C. Fuller, "Introductory Essay" to Keith Hogg, *666-Bibliotheca Crowleyana* (catalog of Fuller's collection of Crowley writings and manuscripts) (Kent, UK: 1966), p. 5.

"No Buddhist . . ." Quoted in P. R. Stephensen and Israel Regardie, *The Legend of Aleister Crowley* (Saint Paul: Llewellyn, 1970), p. 70.

"I hope you're sitting . . ." Crowley, letter to Fuller, May 23, 1908, O.T.O. Archives.

"For three years . . ." Crowley, letter to Parry, January 28, 1910, O.T.O. Archives.

"Glory be . . ." This diary entry is quoted in *Confessions,* c. 65.

"For the first time . . ." Ibid.

"I had always . . ." Neuburg (Omnia Vincam), 1909 Diary, typescript, O.T.O. Archives.

"My worthy Guru . . ." Ibid.

"apparently a homosexual . . ." Ibid.

"I admit that . . ." Crowley (with Victor B. Neuburg & Mary Desti), *The Vision and the Voice with Commentary and Other Papers* (York Beach: Weiser, 1998), p. 18.

"I realized that space . . ." *Confessions,* c. 66.

"a great golden topaz . . ." Ibid.

"Depart! For thou . . ." Crowley, *The Vision and the Voice,* p. 139.

"The first of the . . ." *Confessions,* c. 66.

"Verily is the Pyramid . . ." Crowley, *The Vision and the Voice,* p. 141. Crowley's own note to this passage reads: "It is also a Phallus, which dies itself to communicate Life to Others." Ibid.

"I had astrally . . ." *Confessions,* c. 66.

"There is no being . . ." Crowley, *The Vision and the Voice,* p. 163.

"leaped upon the Scribe . . ." Ibid., pp. 168–9.

"Choronzon, in the form . . ." *Confessions,* c. 66.

"a materializing medium . . ." Ibid., c. 64.

"successive phantoms . . ." Ibid., c. 66.

"we have the Apocalypse . . ." Crowley, letter to Fuller, December 5, 1909, O.T.O. Archives.

"Part of the effect . . ." *Confessions,* c. 67.

"The revelations of Mr. Crowley . . ." London *Evening News*, March 23, 1910.

"The argument . . ." *Confessions*, c. 67.

"I do not know . . ." *Special Law Reports* transcript of March 22, 1910, hearing.

"The girl was . . ." Crowley, "The Vixen," in *Equinox I(4)* London, 1910), p. 277.

"I.C. wants me . . ." Quoted in James Laver, *Museum Piece* (London: Andre Deutsch, 1963), p. 117.

"This is a most . . ." Crowley, book review, *Equinox I(5)* (London, 1911), p. 146.

"His powerful neck . . ." Archer, *The Hieroglyph*, p. 100.

"Genius is another . . ." Ibid., p. 131.

"[T]hen the brothers . . ." Quoted in Crowley, *The Rites of Eleusis* (Thame, UK: Mandrake Press, 1990), pp. 24–5. The "Introduction" to this volume by Keith Richmond provides a useful overview and assessment of the staging and impact of the Rites.

"I throw myself . . ." *Confessions*, c. 67.

"The Elusive Rites . . ." *The Sketch*, October 26, 1910.

"Remember the doctrine . . ." *The Looking Glass*, October 29, 1910.

"In every sense . . ." J. F. C. Fuller, "Introductory Essay" to *Bibliotheca Crowleyana*, p. 7.

"every incident . . ." *Confessions*, c. 68.

"quite a lot . . ." Letter, Crowley to Fuller, October 20, 1911, O.T.O. Archives.

"Send £500 . . ." Jean Overton Fuller, *The Magical Dilemma of Victor Neuburg*, p. 174.

"because he was afraid . . ." *Confessions*, c. 67.

"hinted that he . . ." Ibid.

"At night, when drunk . . ." Quoted in Jean Overton Fuller, *The Magical Dilemma of Victor Neuburg*, p. 176.

"Rats leave . . ." Crowley, "X-Rays on Ex-Probationers," in *Equinox I(5)* (London: 1911), p. 142.

"I personally believe . . ." *Confessions*, c. 72.

"This lady . . ." Ibid., c. 70.

"I made my speech . . ." Ibid., c. 67.

"I do not consider . . ." Jacob Epstein, letter to *London Times*, November 8, 1911.

"I detached the butterfly . . ." *Confessions*, c. 67.

"apparently seized . . ." Ibid., c. 70.

"Here is a book . . ." Crowley, *The Vision and the Voice*, p. 301.

"P[erdurabo]: How shall . . ." Ibid., p. 314.

"The practitioner . . ." *Preston Sturges by Preston Sturges*, ed. Sandy Sturges (New York: Simon and Schuster, 1990), p. 75.

"apart from its supernatural . . ." Ibid., p. 77.

"Mr. Crowley had . . ." Ibid.

"[Crowley's] repugnant . . ." Ibid., pp. 77–8.

"Frater Perdurabo is . . ." Crowley, *Magick*, p. 3.

"It instantly flashed . . ." *Confessions*, c. 72.

"My entire life . . ." Letter, Crowley to J. W. Dunne, n.d., O.T.O. Archives.

"Let the Adept . . ." Crowley, *The Book of Lies* (New York: Weiser, 1970), p. 82.

"He explained to Crowley . . ." Yorke, "666, Sex, and the O.T.O.," n.d., typescript, O.T.O. Archives.

"faith of understanding . . ." See Shah, *The Sufis*, pp. 254–6.

"This serpent, Satan . . ." Crowley, *Magick*, p. 277, note.

"subsequent 1943 essay" The assertion by John Symonds *(The Beast 666*, p. 18) that Crowley claimed that H. P. Blavastsky was Jack the Ripper stems from a basic misreading of Crowley's 1943 essay "Jack the Ripper." Crowley opens the essay with the humorously ironic remark that "It is hardly one's first, or even one's hundredth guess, that the Victorian worthy in the case of Jack the Ripper was no less a person than Helena Petrovna Blavatsky." But the remainder of the essay focuses on the case for Donston being the Ripper.

"It was sex . . ." Quoted in Jean Overton Fuller, *The Magical Dilemma of Victor Neuburg*, p. 46.

"up, up rose . . ." Anne Estelle Rice, "Memories of Katherine Mansfield," in *Adam 300*, ed. Miron Grindea (London: Curwen Press, 1966), p. 78.

"'The stuff is beginning . . ." Laver, *Museum Piece*, pp. 118–9.

"a pretentious and . . ." Jane Moore, *Gurdjieff and Mansfield* (London: Routledge Kegan Paul, 1980), p. 18 n. 2.

"*Sgt. Pepper* album . . ." According to Hymenaeus Beta, a more youthful photograph of Crowley was rejected by the album designers as it too closely resembled Paul McCartney.

"Works of destruction . . ." *Magick*, p. 279.

"Until the Great Work . . ." Ibid., p. 275.

"In a cafe . . ." *Confessions*, c. 73.

The proof of . . ." Ibid.

"And I rave . . ." Crowley, "Hymn to Pan," in Crowley, *Selected Poems*, pp. 61–62.

"Crowley was a complete . . ." Gerald Yorke, "666, Sex, and the O.T.O.," O.T.O. Archives.

"hordes of idiots . . ." Leslie A. Fiedler, "The Return of James Branch Cabell; or, The Cream of the Cream of the Jest," in M. T. Inge and E. E. Mac-Donald, eds. *James Branch Cabell: Centennial Essays* (Baton Rouge: Louisiana State University Press, 1983), p. 141.

"they made up a ritual . . ." Jean Overton Fuller, *The Magical Dilemma of Victor Neuburg*, p. 193.

"*Jungitur in vati* . . ." Crowley, *The Vision and the Voice*, p. 406.

"the Temple grew . . ." Ibid., p. 354.

"Every drop of semen . . ." Ibid., p. 362.

"'What fools to bother . . ." Ibid., pp. 364–5.

"An holy act . . ." Ibid., p. 365 n. 1.

"Far be it . . ." Crowley, *Magick*, pp. 179–80.

"that the essence . . ." Crowley, *The Vision and the Voice*, p. 380.

"This is the great idea . . ." Ibid., pp. 385–6.

"I am always unlucky . . ." Ibid., p. 388.

"The association with . . ." Victor E. Neuburg, *Vickybird: A Memoir of Victor B. Neuburg by his son* (London: The Polytechnic of North London, 1983), p. 5.

Chapter Seven

"a turgid bit . . ." William Brevda, *Harry Kemp: The Last Bohemian* (Lewisburg: Bucknell University Press, 1986), p. 94.

"rubbish" *Confessions*, c. 77.

"Frankly, his 'magic' . . ." Alan Himber, *The Letters of John Quinn to William Butler Yeats* (Ann Arbor: UMI Research Press, 1983), letter of February 25, 1915, p. 148.

"awful slip . . ." Ezra Pound, letter to Margaret Anderson, editor of *The Little Review*, November 17, 1917, in *The Little Review Correspondence*, ed. T. L. Scott, M. Friedman and J. R. Bryer (New York: New Directions, 1988), p. 154.

"surrounded by . . ." H. L. Mencken, *My Life as Author and Editor* (New York: Alfred A. Knopf, 1993), p. 119.

"For example, one . . ." Crowley, *The Revival of Magick*, pp. 36–7.

"It is rare . . ." Gerald Yorke, notes c. 1965 re: manuscript of Israel Regardie's study of Crowley, *The Eye of the Triangle* (1970), O.T.O. Archives.

"Many a lover . . ." Crowley, *Not the Life and Adventures of Sir Roger Bloxam*, in *The Magical Link* VII(2) (1993), p. 3. The work was part-serialized in *The Magical Link* IV(3)–VII(4), 1990–4.

"The homosexual is . . ." *Confessions*, c. 76.

"(on the whole) . . ." Ibid.

"I am English . . ." Ibid.

"small-time traitor" Symonds, *The Beast 666*, p. 210.

"During the time . . ." Everard Feilding, letter to Gerald Yorke, May 1, 1929, O.T.O. Archives.

"I was not . . ." *Confessions*, c. 76.

"admitted that . . ." "Memorandum for Mr. Hoover," Department of Justice, Bureau of Investigation, Washington, D.C., August 1, 1924, O.T.O. Archives. See also, letter, Acting Director to E. J. Brennan, August 1, 1924, in which it is stated that there was "nothing in the Bureau files indicating that any information was furnished to the [Justice] Department, by CROWLEY during the war, or at any time subsequent thereto [. . .]" Both documents were obtained through the Freedom of Information Act.

"philosophical basis . . ." Crowley, letter to George Sylvester Viereck, July 31, 1936, O.T.O. Archives.

"In the ancient . . ." *Confessions*, c. 81.

"I had unusually . . ." Ibid.

"Mentally, I woke . . ." Ibid.

"to make his every . . ." Ibid.

"kind enough . . ." Ibid., c. 77.

"I persuaded Dreiser . . ." Louis Marlow [pseud. Louis Wilkinson], *Seven Friends* (London: The Richards Press, 1953), pp. 57–8.

"*And let every woman . . .*" Crowley, "The Whole Duty of Woman," in *Magical Link* (Vol. 9, No. 3, 1996).

"sending her husband . . ." J. B. Yeats, letter to John Quinn, March 16, 1916, O.T.O. Archives.

"I have not been . . ." Crowley, *The Magical Record of the Beast 666* eds. John Symonds and Kenneth Grant (London: Duckworth, 1972), p. 137.

"This Operation is . . ." Ibid., p. 35.

"German prostitute" *Confessions*, c. 77.

"The [ethyl oxide] . . ." Crowley, "Ethyl Oxide," in *Magical Link*, (Vol. 1, No. 9, 1987/88).

"I lost consciousness . . ." *Confessions*, c. 82.

"But why should . . ." Crowley, *The Gospel According to St. Bernard Shaw* (Barstow, CA: Thelema Publishing Company, 1953), pp. 114–5.

"The entire symbolism . . ." Ibid., pp. 214–5.

"There is nothing . . ." Crowley, 1916 Diary, typescript, O.T.O. Archives.

"Night being fallen . . ." Ibid.

"Hope died in . . ." *Confessions*, c. 84.

"I found myself . . ." Ibid.

"Had news of . . ." Crowley, May 6, 1917, diary entry, 1917 Diary, typescript, O.T.O. Archives.

"There is much exaggeration . . ." Gerald Yorke, notes c. 1965 re: manuscript of Regardie, *The Eye of the Triangle*, O.T.O. Archives.

"She was a Pennsylvania Dutch . . ." *Confessions*, c. 78.

"such a journey . . ." Ibid., c. 84.

"a near artist . . ." Ibid., c. 78.

"I now do . . ." Crowley, 1918 Diary, typescript, O.T.O. Archives.

"I asked who . . ." Crowley, "The Amalantrah Working," typescript, O.T.O. Archives.

"I doubt whether . . ." *Confessions*, c. 85.

"Do thou study . . ." Crowley, *Liber Aleph vel CXI. The Book of Wisdom or Folly* rev. 2nd edition edited with "Prolegomenon" by Hymenaeus Beta (New York: 93 Publishing, 1991), p. 2.

"The 'provisions' looked . . ." William Seabrook, *Witchcraft* (London: Sphere Books, 1970), pp. 195–6.

"On both the east . . ." *Confessions*, c. 79.

"I refuse to assert . . ." Ibid., c. 86.

"The incarnation before . . ." Crowley, "The Hermit of Oesopus Island," title for a series of diary entries made in late August and early September 1918, 1918 Diary, typescript, O.T.O. Archives.

"very black-magical . . ." Ibid.

"My vices were . . ." Ibid.

"I was really more . . ." Ibid.

"to bring oriental wisdom . . ." *Confessions,* c. 86.

"present at a Council . . ." Ibid.

"a codex of . . ." Crowley, *Tao Teh King* ed. with "Introduction" by Stephen Skinner (London: Askin Publishers, 1976), p. 20.

"Now I ask you . . ." Charles Robert Stansfeld Jones, letter to Gerald Yorke, June 18, 1948, O.T.O. Archives.

"In a single instant . . ." *Confessions,* c. 86.

"Ahead of us . . ." Seabrook, *Witchcraft,* pp. 197–198.

"Crowley was sparing . . ." Crowley, *Liber Aleph,* p. xxii.

"The 'little sister' . . ." *Confessions,* c. 80.

"While we talked . . ." Ibid.

"(She swears I . . ." Ibid.

"I was seized with . . ." Ibid.

"It is luxuriously fitted . . ." *New York Evening World,* February 26, 1919.

"Attainment is Insanity." Crowley, *Magical Record,* p. 86.

Chapter Eight

"the war which . . ." *John Bull,* January 10, 1920.

"Traversed Rock . . ." Crowley, *Magical Record,* p. 105.

"The general idea . . ." Crowley, untitled brochure on Cefalù paintings, c. 1922, O.T.O. Archives.

"Four degenerates . . ." Ibid. The other titles and comments by Crowley are also from this brochure.

"is to pass students . . ." Ibid.

"Those who have come . . ." Ibid.

"When first I found . . ." Crowley, *Magical Record,* pp. 251–2.

"She is to direct . . ." Ibid., p. 230.

"a frightful ordeal . . ." Ibid.

"She discovered the . . ." Ibid., p. 234.

"my secret is not . . ." Ibid., p. 235.

"Then I obeyed . . ." Ibid.

"I have been howling . . ." Ibid., p. 110.

"utterly appalled at . . ." Ibid., p. 289.

"mystery of filth" Phyllis Seckler *In the Continuum*, O.T.O. Archives, pp. 35–36.

"Thou strivest ever . . ." Crowley, *The Holy Books of Thelema*, p. 56.

"He [Crowley] answered . . ." C. F. Russell, *Znuz is Znees: Memoirs of a Magician* vol. 1, 2nd edition (Privately printed: 1970), p. 29.

"to establish the *Book* . . ." "The Book of the Cephaloedium Working" in Crowley, *The Fish* ed. Anthony Naylor (Thame, UK: Mandrake Press, 1992), p. 118.

"He [Russell] wants . . ." Crowley, *Magical Record*, pp. 295–6.

"Now I'll shave . . ." Crowley, 1921 Diary, typescript, O.T.O. Archives.

"On the wall . . ." Russell, *Znuz is Znees*, p. 155.

"You see, Crowley . . ." Ibid., p. 131.

"I could have made . . ." *Confessions*, c. 90.

"I am by insight . . ." Crowley, 1921 Diary, typescript, O.T.O. Archives.

"Your friendship stands out . . ." Crowley, undated 1921 letter to Fuller, O.T.O. Archives.

"'Do what you like . . ." Capt. M. E. Townshend, letter to Fuller, April 17, 1921, O.T.O. Archives.

"You have quite . . ." Townshend, letter to Fuller, April 28, 1921, O.T.O. Archives.

"The ceremony of . . ." Crowley, June 30, 1921, diary entry, 1921 Diary, typescript, O.T.O. Archives.

"a goat's turd . . ." Symonds, *The Beast 666*, p. 287, n. 1.

"Butts's diary . . ." Consider, for example, the following entry by Butts, dated August 21, 1921, in *A Sacred Quest: The Life and Writings of Mary Butts* ed. Christopher Wagstaff (McPherson: Kingston, NY, 1995), p. 130: "Part of the trouble here is a complex about complexes, i.e., our artificial inhibitions are cleared up, certain things will remain good and bad, pleasant and unpleasant. This is not realised, yet the silly people imply it all to him [Aleister Crowley]—when it suits them. It is right to promulgate his law. It is wrong to criticise it—if you do, you have a complex. C[ecil]. M[aitland]. said last night: they are making a sacrifice of personality to personality. He said that it makes A[leister] C[rowley] tragic because he is a kind, wise, honorable man crucified by his belief in his own teaching."

"drinking thereof from . . ." Crowley, July 29, 1921 diary entry, 1921, Diary, typescript, O.T.O. Archives.

"'What shall I do . . ." Quoted in Symonds, *The Great Beast*, p. 299.

"and just as we . . ." *Confessions*, c. 90.

"I, The Beast 666 . . ." Crowley, *Liber Tzaba vel Nike (The Fountain of Hyacinth)*, in *The Magical Link* (Vol. 1, No. 8, 1987).

"[M]y memory is quite . . ." Ibid.

"Mine inmost identity . . ." Ibid.

"where I can direct . . ." Ibid.

"Lea[h] is a violent . . ." Ibid.

"became a nursery . . ." Yorke, letter to Barrucand, December 23, 1956, O.T.O. Archives.

"Nothing Doing." Fuller, note to Crowley, May 13, 1922, O.T.O. Archives.

"was not part . . ." Virginia Berridge and Griffith Edwards, *Opium and the People: Opiate Use in Nineteenth Century England* (New York: St. Martin's Press, 1981), p. 268.

"stationery printed up . . ." Martin P. Starr, "Introduction" to Crowley, *Amrita: Essays in Magical Rejuvenation* ed. Martin P. Starr (Kings Beach, CA: Thelema Publications, 1990), p. xiv.

"I attempted to produce . . ." Crowley [pseud. as given in title], "The Great Drug Delusion" ("By a New York Specialist"), in *The English Review*, June 1922.

"I would write . . ." *Confessions*, c. 92.

"partly a wish-phantasm . . ." This note by Crowley was transcribed by Gerald Yorke into a copy of *Drug Fiend* that forms part of the Yorke Collection, Warburg Institute, University of London. It is one of several notes by Crowley not included in the published annotated edition of *Drug Fiend* (London: Sphere Books, 1972).

"Mr. Crowley has not . . ." Book review, *The Times Literary Supplement*, November 16, 1922.

"Although there is . . ." James Douglas, "A Book for Burning," London *Sunday Express*, November 19, 1922.

"covered with dust . . ." Betty May, *Tiger-Woman* (London: Duckworth, 1929), p. 134.

"This was the man . . ." *Confessions*, c. 94.

"I spoke exactly . . ." Betty May, *Tiger-Woman*, pp. 169–70.

"The Mystic held up . . ." Ibid., p. 182.

"it has left me . . ." Loveday, letter to his mother, February 11, 1923, O.T.O. Archives.

"He is laying down . . ." May, note to Loveday letter of February 11, 1923, O.T.O. Archives.

"I had not been reading . . ." May, *Tiger-Woman*, pp. 186–187.

"I tried to soothe . . ." *Confessions*, c. 96.

"Both Raoul and Alostrael . . ." Ibid.

Raoul developed . . ." Ibid.

"was as fair as . . ." Ibid.

"Rome was wild . . ." Ibid., c. 95.

Chapter Nine

"It is the beginning . . ." Crowley, May 12, 1923, diary entry, in Crowley, *The Magical Diaries of Aleister Crowley* (Jersey, UK: Neville Spearman, 1979), p. 16.

"a mere shadow . . ." Ibid., p. 20.

"Here is another . . ." Ibid.

"Suicide should not . . ." Ibid.

"I got the intimation . . ." Ibid., pp. 45–6.

"Nobody before Aleister Crowley . . ." Ibid., pp. 56–7. Skinner's observation on this quote is contained in his editorial footnote thereto.

"I have always been . . ." Crowley, letter to Mudd, June 13, 1923, O.T.O. Archives.

"attitude of possession . . ." Norman Mudd, diary entry in "Retirement Diary of O.P.V.," September 23, 1923, with subsequent response by Crowley, typescript, O.T.O. Archives.

"an ordeal of utter . . ." Ibid. (The date of this diary entry by Mudd is not specified.)

"If they could get me . . ." Crowley, *Magical Diaries*, p. 46.

"I am always thinking . . ." Ibid., p. 78.

"I am a Sun . . ." Crowley, *Magical and Philosophical Commentaries*, p. 307.

"Gurdjieff, their prophet . . ." Crowley, February 10, 1924, diary entry, 1924 Diary, typescript, O.T.O. Archives.

"Crowley arrived for . . ." James Webb, *The Harmonious Circle: The Lives and Work of G.I. Gurdjieff, P.D. Ouspensky, and Their Followers* (Boston: Shambhala, 1987), p. 315.

"Beast lay ill . . ." Leah Hirsig, letter to Frank Bennett, April 14, 1924, O.T.O. Archives.

"rasping voice so . . ." Hirsig June 8, 1924, entry in diary entitled *Alostrael's Visions*, typescript, O.T.O. Archives.

"Invaded 207 . . ." Crowley, September 22, 1924, diary entry, 1924 Diary, typescript, O.T.O. Archives.

"I have got the girl . . ." Crowley. November 1924 diary entry (no specific date), 1924 Diary, typescript, O.T.O. Archives.

"A word to Dorothy . . ." Hirsig, September 26, 1924, entry in diary entitled *The Magical Diary of Babalon*, typescript, O.T.O. Archives.

"A Thelemite doesn't need . . ." Ibid.

"That was my only . . ." Ibid., October 5, 1924, entry.

"Parsifal used his lance . . ." Ibid.

"a man who does not . . ." Ibid., October 10, 1924, entry.

"At night went into . . ." Quoted in Hymenaeus Beta, "Editor's Introduction" to Crowley, *The Heart of the Master* (Scottsdale, AZ: New Falcon Publications, 1992), p. xiv.

"I am still alive . . ." Dorothy Olsen, March 1925 letter to Norman Mudd, O.T.O. Archives.

"A single drink . . ." Crowley, April 24, 1925, diary entry, 1925 Diary, typescript, O.T.O. Archives.

"Reuss discovered the . . ." Tau Apiryon and Soror Helena, *Mystery of Mystery: A Primer of Thelemic Ecclesiastical Gnosticism*, published as issue No. 2 of *Red Flame: A Thelemic Research Journal*, (Berkeley: Pangenetor Lodge O.T.O., 1995), p. 220.

"physical satisfaction . . ." Karl Germer, letter to Crowley, June 2, 1929, O.T.O. Archives. I am grateful to Keith Richmond, who first provided me with copies of the 1927–30 Germer letters to Crowley.

"Up to about 20 . . ." Karl Germer, letter to Crowley, December 28, 1928, O.T.O. Archives.

"For me everything . . ." Karl Germer, letter to Crowley, June 2, 1929, O.T.O. Archives.

"I found this man . . ." Crowley, "Statement Re: Tranker" (1925), O.T.O. Archives.

"One who ought . . ." Crowley, *Magick*, p. 131.

"Jones was in fact . . ." Hymenaeus Beta, "Prolegomenon" to Crowley, *Liber Aleph* (New York: 93 Publishing, 1991), p. xxvi.

"I mistook 'Comment' . . ." Crowley, *Magick Without Tears* ed. Israel Regardie (Saint Paul: Llewellyn, 1973), p. 316.

The 1925 Comment may be found in Crowley, *Magick*, p. 386.

"It is no use . . ." Crowley, *Eight Lectures on Yoga*, pp. 100–1.

"I myself . . ." Ibid., p. 101.

"proceeded to exploit . . ." Norman Mudd, letter to Crowley, October 30, 1925, O.T.O. Archives I am again grateful to Keith Richmond, who first provided me with a copy of this letter.

"The script alone . . ." Leah Hirsig, letter to Crowley, August 4, 1927, O.T.O. Archives. Again my thanks go to Keith Richmond, who first provided me with copies of the Hirsig–Crowley 1926–7 correspondence.

"imbecile letter . . ." Crowley, letter to Hirsig, August 8, 1927, O.T.O. Archives.

"all my recognitions . . ." Leah Hirsig, letter to Crowley, August 19, 1927, O.T.O. Archives.

"I now Notify you . . ." Leah Hirsig, letter to Crowley, September 6, 1930, with response noted on letter by Crowley, O.T.O. Archives.

"a dim, grey little . . ." Tom Driberg, *Ruling Passions* (London: Jonathan Cape, 1977), p. 85.

"[H]e claimed to have . . ." Ibid., p. 83.

"On practically every . . ." Jane Wolfe, 1926 Diary, O.T.O. Archives. There are no specific dates provided for the entries quoted here and below.

"weeping, saying . . ." Ibid.

"But what really . . ." Ibid.

"Letter from Dridi . . ." Crowley, September 11, 1926, diary entry, 1926 Diary, typescript, O.T.O. Archives.

"demonstrate the defamation . . ." Crowley's personally annotated copy of Maugham's *The Magician*, which contains this statement, forms part of the Yorke Collection of the Warburg Institute, University of London.

"contained enough poisoning . . ." Carlos Clarens, *An Illustrated History of the Horror Film* (New York: Putnam, 1974), p. 53.

"in the midst of . . ." Carlos Clarens, *Horror Movies* (London: Secker and Warburg, 1968), pp. 72–3.

"If I was just . . ." This poem is contained in Crowley, December 7, 1926, diary entry, 1926 Diary, typescript, O.T.O. Archives.

"a huge success . . ." Crowley, November 13, 1926, diary entry, 1926 Diary, typescript, O.T.O. Archives.

"Eugene and all . . ." Crowley, January 2, 1927, diary entry, 1927 Diary, typescript, O.T.O. Archives.

"There have been about . . ." Crowley, letter to Montgomery Evans, January 17, 1929, O.T.O. Archives. I thank Randall Bowyer for his assistance in obtaining a copy of this letter for me.

"He has a nice place . . ." Kasimira Bass, letter to Wilfred T. Smith, September 2, 1927, O.T.O. Archives.

"for the galleon . . ." Crowley, letter to Wilfred T. Smith, September 1927, O.T.O. Archives.

"they fell down . . ." Gerald Suster, *Crowley's Apprentice: The Life and Ideas of Israel Regardie, the Magical Psychologist* (London: Rider & Co., 1989), p. 38.

"considered opinion that . . ." Israel Regardie, *The Eye in the Triangle*, p. 17.

"Well, suddenly Crowley . . ." Suster, *Crowley's Apprentice*, p. 38.

"As he talked . . ." Lance Sieveking, *The Eye of the Beholder* (London: Hulton Press, 1957), p. 251.

"I haven't seen . . ." Ibid., p. 252.

"In Crowley he took . . ." Charles R. Cammell, *Aleister Crowley: The Black Magician* (original title: *Aleister Crowley: The Man, the Mage, the Poet*) (London: New English Library, 1969), p. 96.

"Montague Summers said . . ." Sieveking, *The Eye of the Beholder*, pp. 247–8.

"that A.C. was in . . ." Gerald Yorke, letter to Barracaud, November 7, 1955, O.T.O. Archives.

"The unfortunate part . . ." C. de Vidal Hunt, letter to Gerald Yorke, November 7, 1928, O.T.O. Archives.

"She was a fairly . . ." Jack Lindsay, *Fanfrolico and After* (London: The Bodley Head, 1962), p. 173.

"That pair used to . . ." Suster, *Crowley's Apprentice*, pp. 39–40.

"The real inferiority . . ." Crowley, March 9, 1929, diary entry, 1929 Diary, typescript, O.T.O. Archives.

"success to our campaign . . ." Crowley, April 17, 1929, diary entry, 1929 Diary, typescript, O.T.O. Archives.

"Alastair [sic] Crowley . . ." Rupert Grayson, *Stand Fast, the Holy Ghost* (London: Tom Stacey, 1973), pp. 142–3.

"I'm a bit sorry . . ." Quoted in Craig Munro, *Wild Man of Letters: The Story of P. R. Stephensen* (Melbourne: Melbourne University Press, 1984), p. 91.

"M. [Miramar] had . . ." Crowley, October 8, 1929, diary entry, 1929 Diary, typescript, O.T.O. Archives.

"He [Crowley] believed . . ." Leslie Frewin ed. *Parnassus Near Picadilly: The Cafe Royal Centenary Book* (London: Leslie Frewin, 1965), p. 33.

"an unpaid bill . . ." Ibid., p. 35.

"Stephensen and Crowley . . ." Keith Richmond, "Introduction" to Crowley, *The Forbidden Lecture: Gilles de Rais* (Thame, UK: Mandrake, 1990), p. 23.

"The one thing . . ." Ibid., p. 54.

"It appears from . . ." Crowley, *Magick*, p. 207.

"There is no passage . . ." Hymenaeus Beta, "Editor's Introduction" to Crowley, *Magick*, p. lxvii.

"[O]nly the advanced . . ." Dion Fortune, *Applied Magic* (essay collection) (Wellingborough, UK: Aquarian Press, 1983), p. 65.

"But while I . . ." Ibid., p. 66.

"All discussions upon . . ." Crowley, *Magick*, p. 141.

"[T]here is no doubt . . ." Ibid., p. 191.

"The student must guard . . ." Ibid., p. 261.

CHAPTER TEN

"Bury me in a . . ." Crowley, June 1, 1930, diary entry, 1930 Diary, type-script, O.T.O. Archives.

"his wife penniless . . ." Gerald Yorke, note [n.d.], O.T.O. Archives.

"I *must* have been . . ." Crowley, August 4, 1930, diary entry, 1930 Diary, typescript, O.T.O. Archives.

"Hanni Larissa Jaeger . . ." Ibid., October 18, 1930, diary entry, 1930 Diary, typescript, O.T.O. Archives.

"Huxley improves . . ." Ibid., October 4, 1930, diary entry, 1930 Diary, typescript, O.T.O. Archives.

"I thought he had . . ." Quoted in Symonds, *The Beast 666*, p. 463.

"very bad nightmares . . ." Crowley, October 16, 1930, diary entry, 1930 Diary, typescript, O.T.O. Archives.

"Anu showed me . . ." Ibid., November 16, 1930, diary entry, 1930 Diary, typescript, O.T.O. Archives.

"Karl is a filthy . . ." Ibid., December 13, 1930, diary entry. 1930 Diary, typescript, O.T.O. Archive.

"Anu has been playing . . ." Ibid., December 14, 1930, diary entry, 1930 Diary, typescript, O.T.O. Archives.

"She is always . . ." Ibid.

"She is violently . . ." Ibid., November 22, 1930, diary entry, 1930 Diary, typescript, O.T.O. Archive.

"She explains her . . ." Ibid., December 15, 1930, diary entry, 1930 Diary, typescript, O.T.O. Archive.

"The idea of my . . ." Crowley, letter to Gerald Yorke, June 2, 1931, O.T.O. Archives.

"A marvelous day ..." Crowley, May 6, 1931, diary entry, 1931 Diary, typescript, O.T.O. Archives.

"Louise to dinner ..." Ibid., May 7, 1931, diary entry, 1931 Diary, typescript, O.T.O. Archives.

"It will be no good ..." Crowley, letter to Maria Teresa de Miramar, September 1930, O.T.O. Archives.

"I suggest to you ..." Colonel Carter, letter to Crowley (with noted response on letter by Crowley), October 1930, O.T.O. Archives.

"As regards Mrs. A.C. ..." Colonel Carter, letter to Gerald Yorke, March 3, 1931, O.T.O. Archives.

"Unfortunately her earlier ..." Medical Superintendent of Colney Hatch Medical Hospital, letter to Crowley, August 1, 1931, O.T.O. Archives.

"It is very English ..." Crowley, July 18, 1931, diary entry, 1931 Diary, typescript, O.T.O. Archives.

"Most wonderful fuck ..." Ibid., September 5, 1931, diary entry, 1931 Diary, typescript, O.T.O. Archives.

"The best fuck ..." Ibid., September 6, 1931, diary entry, 1931 Diary, typescript, O.T.O. Archives.

"The truly awful thing ..." Christopher Isherwood, *Diaries, Volume One: 1939–1960* ed. Katherine Bucknell (New York: Harper Collins, 1997), p. 550.

"What is piquant ..." Gerald Hamilton, *The Way It Was With Me* (London: Leslie Frewin, 1969), p. 56.

"was showering the Magus ..." Maurice Richardson, "Epilogue" to Gerald Hamilton, *Mr. Norris and I: An Autobiographical Sketch* (London: Allan Wingate, 1956), p. 169.

"Bill—whew! ..." Crowley, February 25, 1932, diary entry, 1932 Diary, typescript, O.T.O. Archives.

"Then began a most ..." Crowley, December 6, 1931, diary entry, 1931 Diary, typescript, O.T.O. Archives.

"I direct my Executor ..." Crowley, "Will" dated December 22, 1931, O.T.O. Archives.

"Bill half insane ..." Crowley, May 31, 1932, diary entry, 1932 Diary, typescript, O.T.O. Archives.

"Everything I am ..." Gerald Suster, *Crowley's Apprentice*, p. 50.

"advised me to leave ..." Crowley, July 5, 1932, diary entry, 1932 Diary, typescript, O.T.O. Archives.

"insisted on making ..." Ibid.

"So showed her . . ." Ibid.

"I'm sorry: but . . ." Ibid., July 20, 1932, diary entry, 1932 Diary, typescript, O.T.O. Archives.

"At the end of . . ." Viola Banks, *Why Not* (London: Jarrolds, 1934), ch. 15.

"method of restoring . . ." Crowley, *Amrita*, p. 1.

"He writted me . . ." Gerald Yorke, note to Crowley 1932 Diary, typescript, O.T.O. Archives.

"This case is typical . . ." Crowley, 1933 statement copied by Gerald Yorke into Crowley 1933 Diary, typescript, O.T.O. Archives.

"Great Public Meeting . . ." Crowley, April 10, 1933, diary entry, 1933 Diary, typescript, O.T.O. Archives.

"Here lies a Pearl . . ." Crowley, August 18, 1933, diary entry, 1933 Diary, typescript, O.T.O. Archives.

"Told her we must . . ." Crowley, October 25, 1933, diary entry, 1933 Diary, typescript, O.T.O. Archives.

"Bitched buggered . . ." Crowley, final undated page of 1933 Diary, O.T.O. Archives.

"The Gods have forbidden . . ." Ibid.

"claimed to have been . . ." Constantine Fitzgibbon, *The Life of Dylan Thomas* (London: J.M. Dent, 1965), p. 172.

"I have written quite . . ." Denise Hooker, *Nina Hamnett: Queen of Bohemia* (London: Constable, 1986), p. 197.

"Abominable libels . . ." Crowley, September 7, 1932, diary entry, 1932 Diary, typescript, O.T.O. Archives.

"Crowley had a temple . . ." Nina Hamnett, *Laughing Torso* (London: Constable, 1932), pp. 173–4.

"There was not the . . ." "Law Report," London *Daily Telegraph*, May 11, 1933.

"she could tell me . . ." Ethel Mannin, *Confessions and Impressions* (Garden City, NY: Doubleday, 1930), p. 195.

"your chances of winning . . ." Quoted in Symonds, *The Beast 666*, p. 497.

"Dr. Trelawney" See Timothy d'Arch Smith "'Dr. Trelawney' and Aleister Crowley," *London Magazine*, March 1988.

"was altogether futile . . ." Anthony Powell, *To Keep the Ball Rolling: The Memoirs of Anthony Powell, Volume Two, Messengers of Day* (London: Quality Book Club, 1979), p. 84.

"Hilbery: Did you take . . ." "Law Report," London *Daily Telegraph*, April 11, 1934.

"O'Connor: You say that . . ." "Law Report," London *Daily Telegraph*, April 13, 1934.

"I have been over . . ." "Law Report," London *Daily Telegraph*, April 14, 1934.

"Friday the 13th . . ." London *Sunday Express*, April 15, 1934.

"Aleister Crowley who started . . ." This copy of *Laughing Torso* forms part of the Yorke Collection, Warburg Institute, University of London.

"almost constant . . ." Crowley, May 11, 1936, diary entry, 1936 Diary, O.T.O. Archives.

"showing serious signs . . ." Ibid., May 12, 1936, diary entry, 1936 Diary, O.T.O. Archives.

"Pearl's devotion . . ." Ibid., May 29, 1936, diary entry, 1936 Diary, O.T.O. Archives.

"for the rest of . . ." Gerald Yorke, note to Crowley memorandum re: 1932 writ against Yorke, O.T.O. Archives.

"She had been told . . ." Crowley's personally annotated copy of Hermann Rauschning, *Hitler Speaks* (London: Thornton Butterworth, 1939), is part of the O.T.O. Archives. Another copy, in which Gerald Yorke transcribed Crowley's marginal notes, forms part of the Yorke Collection, Warburg Institute, University of London.

"You are perfectly right . . ." Quoted in Francis King, *The Magical World of Aleister Crowley* (London: Arrow Books, 1987), p. 162.

"when in prison . . ." Gerald Yorke, handwritten annotation to a first-edition copy of Francis King, *The Magical World of Aleister Crowley* (London: Weidenfeld & Nicholson, 1977), that forms part of the Yorke Collection, Warburg Institute, University of London.

"Our revolution is . . ." Hermann Rauschning, *Hitler Speaks*, O.T.O. Archives, p. 220.

"Their supreme, their . . ." Ibid., p. 275.

"The 'nation' is . . ." Ibid., p. 229.

"After all these . . ." Ibid., pp. 140–1.

"almost certainly . . ." Ibid., p. 212.

"93 as base . . ." Crowley, May 5, 1936, diary entry, 1936 Diary, O.T.O. Archives.

"Viereck will sign . . ." Ibid., July 30, 1936, diary entry, 1936 Diary, O.T.O. Archives.

"Now let me come . . ." Crowley, letter to George Sylvester Viereck, July 31, 1936, O.T.O. Archives.

"there is a persistent . . ." Nicholas Goodrick-Clarke, *The Occult Roots of Nazism: The Racist and Nationalist Fantasies of Guido von List and Jorg Lanz von Liebenfels and Their Influence on Nazi Ideology* (Wellingborough, UK: Aquarian Press, 1985), p. 217.

"When the Gestapo were . . ." Karl Germer, letter to Max Schneider, November 8, 1935, O.T.O. Archives.

"preserve the noble . . ." Crowley, "Propositions for consideration of H.M. [His Majesty's] Government," written October 1936, sent January 27, 1937, O.T.O. Archives.

"Prospectus of book . . ." Press clipping appended to Crowley, December 23, 1937, 1937 Diary, typescript, O.T.O. Archives. The original source of the clipping is unclear.

Chapter 11

"*The average voter* . . ." Crowley [pseud. Comte de Fenix], *The Scientific Solution to the Problem of Government* (London: O.T.O., n.d.) [c. 1937].

"*The theories of* . . ." Ibid.

"Hitler has invented . . ." Ibid.

"*Let this formula* . . ." Ibid.

"At the first mouthful . . ." Alan Burnett-Rae, "A Memoir of 666," in Sandy Robertson, *The Aleister Crowley Scrapbook* (York Beach, ME: Weiser, 1988), p. 27.

"I explained that . . ." Ibid., p. 25.

"I do wish you'd . . ." Crowley, letter to Gerald Yorke, May 10, 1938, O.T.O. Archives.

"Perhaps in future . . ." Quoted in Maurice Richardson, "Luncheon with Beast 666," in *Fits and Starts: Collected Pieces* (London: Michael Joseph, 1979), p. 113.

"that when you got . . ." Ibid., p. 117.

"Vanity was his . . ." Louis Wilkinson [pseud. Louis Marlow], *Seven Friends*, pp. 43–4.

"Elaborate dream . . ." Crowley, February 4, 1938, diary entry, 1938 Diary, typescript, O.T.O. Archives.

"Fascism must always . . ." Ibid., February 21, 1938, diary entry, 1938 Diary, typescript, O.T.O. Archives.

"I had several long . . ." Crowley, June 2, 1939, diary entry, 1939 Diary, typescript, O.T.O. Archives.

"jointly applied to Crowley . . ." Quoted in Anthony Masters, *The Man Who Was M: The Life of Maxwell Knight* (Oxford: Basil Blackwell, 1984), p. 68.

"Crowley had put up . . ." Anthony Masters, *The Man Who Was M*, p. 128.

"in mind for some . . ." Ibid., p. 127.

"The German Intelligence . . ." Richard Deacon, *A History of the British Secret Service* (London: Frederick Muller, 1969), p. 311.

"it never came off . . ." Donald McCormick, letter to Gerald Yorke, May 10, 1967, O.T.O. Archives.

"Here was a man . . ." Charles R. Cammell, *Aleister Crowley*, p. 104.

"I did my best . . ." Ibid., p. 105.

I wish you had . . ." Crowley, letter to Gerald Yorke, September 6, 1941, O.T.O. Archives.

"They gave me command . . ." Crowley, poem written on last, undated page of 1940 Diary, typescript, O.T.O. Archives.

"she had come to . . ." Charles R. Cammell, *Aleister Crowley*, p. 106.

"the revival of true . . ." Crowley, letter to Gerald Yorke, September 11, 1944, O.T.O. Archives.

"the problem is not . . ." Crowley, April 3, 1941, diary entry, 1941 Diary, typescript, O.T.O. Archives.

"nauseated and ineffably . . ." Crowley, April 13, 1942, diary entry, 1942 Diary, typescript, O.T.O. Archives.

"All considered . . ." Ibid., October 1, 1942, diary entry, 1942 Diary, typescript, O.T.O. Archives.

"was sitting with my . . ." Constantine Fitzgibbon, *The Life of Dylan Thomas*, p. 174.

"I note that when . . ." Crowley, January 25, 1943, diary entry, 1943 Diary, typescript, O.T.O. Archives.

"made possible such . . ." Quoted in Harry Wulforst, *The Rocketmakers* (New York: Orion Books, 1989), p. 102.

"Your attempts to seduce . . ." Crowley, letter to Wilfred T. Smith, autumn 1943, O.T.O. Archives.

"With regard to bungling . . ." Crowley, letter to Jack Parsons, October 19, 1943, O.T.O. Archives.

"Christmas 1943 was . . ." J. Edward Cornelius (Frater Achad Osher), "The Warrior-Troubadour: The Life & Times of Grady Louis McMurtry," in

Red Flame: A Thelemic Research Journal, issue No. 1 (Berkeley: Pangenetor Lodge O.T.O., 1994), p. 14.

"The origin of the Tarot . . ." Crowley, *The Book of Thoth* (York Beach, ME: Weiser, 1986), p. 20.

"Each card is . . ." Ibid., pp. 47–8.

"This card represents . . ." Ibid., p. 105.

"the 'secret eye' . . ." Richard Cavendish, *The Tarot* (New York: Crescent Books, 1986), p. 120.

"'Now you see' . . ." Louis Wilkinson [pseud. Louis Marlow], *Seven Friends,* pp. 46–7.

"Much of this is . . ." Crowley, March 3, 1943, diary entry, 1943 Diary, typescript, O.T.O. Archives.

"They would laugh . . ." Lawrence Sutin, interview with Daphne Harris, March 1990.

"I treated him . . ." Ibid.

"He stole sugar . . ." Ibid.

"this house will . . ." Rod Davies, "Crowley in Hastings: Last Days of the Great Beast," Warburg Collection.

"Then out of the blue . . ." Ibid.

"dressed in a magnificent . . ." Ibid.

"I was eight . . ." Oliver Wilkinson, "Aleister Crowley Rest In?", in Colin Wilson, ed. *Men of Mystery: A Celebration of the Occult* (London: Star Books, 1977), p. 95.

"Aleister Crowley has . . ." Ibid., p. 94.

"Crowley's belief in . . ." Ibid., p. 99.

"in return for magical . . ." Quoted in Symonds, *The Beast 666,* p. 578.

"The paunchy, seedy . . ." Kenneth Grant, *Remembering Aleister Crowley* (London: Skoob Books, 1991), pp. 61–62.

"He would draw a . . ." Kenneth Grant, *The Magical Revival* (New York: Weiser, 1972), p. 93.

"Crowley told me . . ." Kenneth Grant, *Remembering Aleister Crowley,* p. 47.

"exoteric", "esoteric" Kenneth Grant, *The Magical Revival,* pp. 2–3.

"I was beginning . . ." Kenneth Grant, *Remembering Aleister Crowley,* p. 41.

"Dion Fortune—Public Bat . . ." Crowley, March 30, 1939, diary entry, 1939 Diary, O.T.O. Archives.

"My mentality always..." Dion Fortune, letter to Crowley, January 8, 1942, quoted in Janine Chapman, *Quest for Dion Fortune* (York Beach, ME: Weiser, 1993), p. 153.

"Crowley was sixteen..." Ibid., p. 156.

"With her I had..." Crowley, letter to Frederic Mellinger, n.d. [c. March 1946], O.T.O. Archives.

"Probably the best way..." *The Story of Dion Fortune* as told to Charles Fielding and Carr Collins (Star & Cross Publication, distributed by Weiser, 1985), p. 157.

"The acknowledgment..." Dion Fortune, letter to Crowley, March 14, 1945, quoted in Kenneth Grant, *Remembering Aleister Crowley*, pp. 33–4.

"The only man..." Gerald B. Gardner, *Witchcraft Today* (New York: Magical Childe, 1982), p. 47.

"I accepted the challenge..." Doreen Valiente, *The Rebirth of Witchcraft* (London: Robert Hale, 1989), p. 61.

"borrowed wholesale..." Aidan A. Kelly, *Crafting the Art of Magic, Book 1: A History of Modern Witchcraft, 1939–1964* (Saint Paul: Llewellyn, 1991), p. 174.

"he had been inside..." Gerald B. Gardner, *Witchcraft Today*, p. 47.

"refused to be bossed..." J. L. Bracelin, *Gerald Gardner: Witch* (London: Octagon Press, 1960), p. 174.

"a dirty-minded..." Quoted in Doreen Valiente, *Witchcraft for Tomorrow* (London: Robert Hale, 1983), p. 17.

"I tried to steady..." E. M. Butler, *Paper Boats: An Autobiography* (London: Collins, 1959), pp. 167–8.

"and his voice..." Ibid., p. 168.

"it would need a Kafka..." Ibid., p. 169.

"Yet there he sat..." Ibid., p. 171.

"It was a revelation..." Ibid., p. 173.

"Hubbard broke up black magic..." The Church of Scientology, letter to London *Sunday Times*, December 28, 1969.

"methods for evoking..." Kenneth Grant, *The Magical Revival*, p. 164.

"I have my elemental!" Jack Parsons, letter to Crowley, February 23, 1946, O.T.O. Archives.

"I am particularly..." Crowley, letter to Jack Parsons, March 27, 1946, O.T.O. Archives.

"direct touch with One . . ." Jack Parsons, letter to Crowley, March 6, 1946, O.T.O. Archives.

"You have got me . . ." Crowley, letter to Jack Parsons, April 19, 1946, O.T.O. Archives. Note that "the idiocy of these goats" is the correct transcription of Crowley's language here, rather than "the idiocy of these louts" as stated in Symonds, *The Beast 666*, p. 572.

"I doubt whether anyone . . ." Crowley, letter to Gerald Yorke, March 27, 1946, O.T.O. Archives.

"Hardly pausing in his . . ." James Laver, *Museum Piece*, p. 228.

"something we do . . ." Ibid.

"very important and you . . ." Crowley, letter to Aleister Ataturk, May 30, 1947.

"The best models . . ." Ibid.

"This is a good world . . ." Quoted in Clifford Bax, *Some I Knew Well* (London: Phoenix House, 1951), p. 54.

"I had always felt . . ." Louis Wilkinson [pseud. Louis Marlow], *Seven Friends*, p. 53.

"Freida Harris told me . . ." Symonds, *The Beast 666*, p. 585.

"Crowley is alleged . . ." Gerald Suster, *The Legacy of the Beast: The Life, Work and Influence of Aleister Crowley* (York Beach, ME: Weiser, 1989), p. 75.

"Crowley used to pace . . ." Ibid., p. 76.

"It was the gods . . ." Snoo Wilson, videotaped interview with Patricia MacAlpine, O.T.O. Archives.

"Crowley tried to get . . ." *London Sunday Express*, December 1947, O.T.O. Archives.

"Here rests beneath . . ." Crowley, May 1, 1944, diary entry, 1944 Diary, typescript, O.T.O. Archives.

SELECTED
BIBLIOGRAPHY

The reader interested in a broader listing of books and other publications by and about Aleister Crowley may consult the endnotes hereto, as well as the extensive bibliographical references in *Magick* (listed below). The purpose of the present bibliography is to provide a basic (and necessarily subjective) guide to further reading in the key texts of a most prolific author.

The fundamental works of Aleister Crowley include:

The Book of the Goetia of Solomon the King, trans. S. L. Mathers, ed. Aleister Crowley, Foyers, UK: Society for the Propagation of Religious Truth, 1904; illustrated second revised edition, ed. Hymenaeus Beta, York Beach, ME: Weiser, 1995, 1997. Contained herein is one of Crowley's finest essays, "The Initiated Interpretation of Ceremonial Magic."

The Book of the Law. (See *Magick* below.)

The Book of Lies which is also falsely called Breaks. Frater Perdurabo [pseud.]. London: Wieland, 1913, rpt. York Beach, ME: Weiser, 1993.

The Book of Thoth: A Short Essay on the Tarot of the Egyptians, The Master Therion [pseud.]. London: O.T.O., 1944, rpt. York Beach, ME: Weiser, 1993.

The Collected Works of Aleister Crowley, Foyers, UK: Society for the Propagation of Religious Truth, 3 vols., 1905–7, rpt. Des Plaines, IL: Yogi Publication Society [c. 1974]. Despite its grand title, readers should note that these volumes are principally devoted to Crowley's early poetical works (through 1907) and, even within that period, exclude his most erotically charged verse.

The Confessions of Aleister Crowley. London: Mandrake, 1929 (only two of the projected six volumes issued); one-volume edition, ed. John Symonds and Kenneth Grant, London: Jonathan Cape, 1969 and New York: Hill and Wang, 1970, rpt. London and New York: Arkana, 1989.

Diary of a Drug Fiend. London: Collins, 1922; rpt. York Beach, ME: Weiser, 1994.

Eight Lectures on Yoga, Mahatma Guru Sri Paramahansa Sivaji [pseud.]. London: O.T.O., 1939; rev. second edition ed. Hymenaeus Beta, Scottsdale, AZ: New Falcon, 1991.

Gems from the Equinox, ed. Israel Regardie, St. Paul: Llewellyn, 1974; rpt. Las Vegas: Falcon, 1989.

Liber Aleph vel CXI. The Book of Wisdom or Folly, ed. Karl Germer and Marcelo Motta, *The Equinox* III (6), Barstow, CA: Thelema Publishing Co., 1961; revised second edition, ed. Hymenaeus Beta, York Beach, ME: Weiser, 1991.

Little Essays Toward Truth. London: O.T.O., 1938; rev. second edition, ed. Hymenaeus Beta and A. W. Iannotti, Scottsdale, AZ: New Falcon, 1996.

Magick. Book 4, Parts I-IV (coauthors: Mary Desti and Leila Waddell), second revised edition, ed. Hymenaeus Beta, York Beach, ME: Weiser, 1997. This most useful volume contains *Book 4* (1912–3); *Magick in Theory and Practice* (1930); *The Equinox of the Gods* (1936) and *The Book of the Law*. A scholarly introduction and extensive notes and bibliography by Hymenaeus Beta are also included.

Moonchild. London: Mandrake, 1929; rpt. York Beach, ME: Weiser, 1992.

The Scented Garden of Abdullah the Satirist of Shiraz (Bagh-i-muattar). London: privately printed, 1910; facsimile reprint with introduction by Martin Starr, Chicago: Teitan Press, 1991.

The Secret Rituals of the O.T.O., ed. with introduction by Francis King. New York: Weiser, 1973.

777 and Other Qabalistic Writings, ed. Israel Regardie. York Beach, ME: Weiser: 1993.

Thelema: The Holy Books of Thelema, ed. Hymenaeus Alpha and Hymenaeus Beta, corrected second printing, York Beach, ME: Weiser, 1990, 1997.

White Stains, London, 1898; second edition, ed. John Symonds, London: Duckworth, 1973, 1993.

INDEX